Bayard Taylor (January 11, 1825 – December 19, 1878) was an American poet, literary critic, translator, travel author, and diplomat. Taylor was born on January 11, 1825, in Kennett Square in Chester County, Pennsylvania. He was the fourth son, the first to survive to maturity, of the Quaker couple, Joseph and Rebecca (née Way) Taylor. His father was a wealthy farmer. Bayard received his early instruction in an academy at West Chester, Pennsylvania, and later at nearby Unionville. At the age of seventeen, he was apprenticed to a printer in West Chester. The influential critic and editor Rufus Wilmot Griswold encouraged him to write poetry. The volume that resulted, Ximena, or the Battle of the Sierra Morena, and other Poems, was published in 1844 and dedicated to Griswold. Using the money from his poetry and an advance for travel articles, he visited parts of England, France, Germany and Italy, making largely pedestrian tours for almost two years. He sent accounts of his travels to the Tribune, The Saturday Evening Post, and The United States Gazette. (Source: Wikipedia)

Literary works:
Egypt And Iceland In The Year 1874
Boys of Other Countries:
Stories for American Boys (1876)
Echo Club and Other Literary Diversions (1876)
Picturesque Europe Part Thirty-Six (1877)
National Ode: The Memorial Freedom Poem, The
Bismarck: His Authentic Biography (1877)
"Assyrian Night-Song" (August 1877)
Prince Deukalion (1878)
Picturesque Europe (1878)
Studies in German Literature (1879)
Faust(1890)
Travels in Arabia (1892)
A school history of Germany (1882)

NORTHERN TRAVEL,
THE LANDS OF
THE SARACEN
&
WHO WAS SHE?
BAYARD TAYLOR

PRINCE CLASSICS

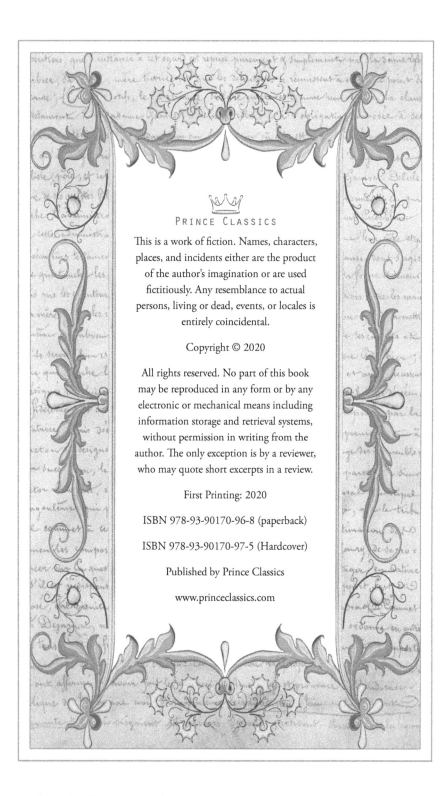

PRINCE CLASSICS

Copyright © 2020

All rights reserved. No part of this book may be reproduced in any form or by any electronic or mechanical means including information storage and retrieval systems, without permission in writing from the author. The only exception is by a reviewer, who may quote short excerpts in a review.

First Printing: 2020

ISBN 978-93-90170-96-8 (paperback)

ISBN 978-93-90170-97-5 (Hardcover)

Published by Prince Classics

www.princeclassics.com

Contents

NORTHERN TRAVEL,

THE LANDS OF

THE SARACEN
&
WHO WAS SHE?

NORTHERN TRAVEL

PREFACE.

This book requires no further words of introduction than those with which I have prefaced former volumes—that my object in travel is neither scientific, statistical, nor politico-economical; but simply artistic, pictorial,— if possible, panoramic. I have attempted to draw, with a hand which, I hope, has acquired a little steadiness from long practice, the people and the scenery of Northern Europe, to colour my sketches with the tints of the originals, and to invest each one with its native and characteristic atmosphere. In order to do this, I have adopted, as in other countries, a simple rule: to live, as near as possible, the life of the people among whom I travel. The history of Sweden and Norway, their forms of Government, commerce, productive industry, political condition, geology, botany, and agriculture, can be found in other works, and I have only touched upon such subjects where it was necessary to give completeness to my pictures. I have endeavoured to give photographs, instead of diagrams, or tables of figures; and desire only that the untravelled reader, who is interested in the countries I visit, may find that he is able to see them by the aid of my eyes.

BAYARD TAYLOR.

London: November, 1857.

CHAPTER I. A WINTER VOYAGE ON THE BALTIC.

We went on board the little iron Swedish propeller, Carl Johan, at Lübeck, on the morning of December 1, A.D. 1856, having previously taken our passage for Stockholm. What was our dismay, after climbing over hills of freight on deck, and creeping down a narrow companion-way, to find the cabin stowed full of bales of wool and barrels of butter. There was a little pantry adjoining it, with a friendly stewardess therein, who, in answer to my inquiries, assured us that we would probably be placed in a hut. After further search, I found the captain, who was superintending the loading of more freight, and who also stated that he would put us into a hut. "Let me see the hut, then," I demanded, and we were a little relieved when we found it to be a state-room, containing two of the narrowest of bunks. There was another hut opposite, occupied by two more passengers, all that the steamer could carry and all we had, except a short deck-passenger, who disappeared at the commencement of the voyage, and was not seen again until its close.

The day was clear and cold, the low hills around Lübeck were covered with snow, and the Trave was already frozen over. We left at noon, slowly breaking our way down the narrow and winding river, which gradually widened and became clearer of ice as we approached the Baltic. When we reached Travemünde it was snowing fast, and a murky chaos beyond the sandy bar concealed the Baltic. The town is a long row of houses fronting the water. There were few inhabitants to be seen, for the bathing guests had long since flown, and all watering places have a funereal air after the season is over. Our fellow-passenger, a jovial Pole, insisted on going ashore to drink a last glass of Bavarian beer before leaving Germany; but the beverage had been so rarely called for that it had grown sharp and sour, and we hurried back unsatisfied.

A space about six feet square had been cleared out among the butter-kegs in the cabin, and we sat down to dinner by candle-light, at three o'clock. Swedish customs already appeared, in a preliminary decanter of lemon-colored brandy, a thimbleful of which was taken with a piece of bread and sausage, before the soup appeared. The taste of the liquor was sweet, unctuous and not agreeable. Our party consisted of the captain, the chief officer, who was his brother-in-law, the Pole, who was a second-cousin of Kosciusko, and had a name consisting of eight consonants and two vowels, a grave young Swede with a fresh Norse complexion, and our two selves. The steward, Hildebrand, and the silent stewardess, Marie, were our attendants and purveyors. The ship's officers were rather slow and opaque, and the Swede sublimely self-possessed and indifferent; but the Pole, who had been condemned to death at Cracow, and afterwards invented cheap gas, was one of the jolliest fellows alive. His German was full of funny mistakes, but he rattled away with as much assurance as if it had been his native tongue. Before dinner was over, we were all perfectly well acquainted with each other.

Night had already set in on the Baltic; nothing was to be seen but snow; the deck was heaped with freight; the storm blew in our teeth; and the steamer, deeply laden, moved slowly and labouriously; so we stretched ourselves on the narrow bunks in our hut, and preserved a delicate regard for our equilibrium, even in sleep. In the morning the steep cliffs of Möen, a Danish island, were visible on our left. We looked for Rügen, the last stronghold of the worship of Odin in the Middle Ages, but a raw mist rolled down upon the sea, and left us advancing blindly as before. The wind was strong and cold, blowing the vapory water-smoke in long trails across the surface of the waves. It was not long, however, before some dim white gleams through the mist were pointed out as the shores of Sweden, and the Carl Johan slackened her speed to a snail's pace, snuffing at headland after headland, like a dog off the scent, in order to find her way into Ystad.

A lift of the fog favored us at last, and we ran into the little harbor. I walked the contracted hurricane deck at three o'clock, with the sunset already flushing the west, looked on the town and land, and thought of my friend Dr. Kane. The mercury had fallen to 16°, a foot of snow covered the house-roofs, the low, undulating hills all wore the same monotonous no-color, and the yellow-haired people on the pier were buttoned up close, mittened and fur-capped. The captain telegraphed to Calmar, our next port, and received an answer that the sound was full of ice and the harbor frozen up. A custom-house officer, who took supper with us on board, informed us of the loss of the steam-ship Umeå, which was cut through by the ice near Sundsvall, and sunk, drowning fifteen persons—a pleasant prospect for our further voyage—and the Pole would have willingly landed at Ystad if he could have found a conveyance to get beyond it. We had twelve tons of coal to take on board, and the work proceeded so slowly that we caught another snow-storm so thick and blinding that we dared not venture out of the harbor.

On the third morning, nevertheless, we were again at sea, having passed Bornholm, and were heading for the southern end of the Island of Oland. About noon, as we were sitting huddled around the cabin stove, the steamer suddenly stopped. There was a hurried movement of feet overhead—a cry—and we rushed on deck. One of the sailors was in the act of throwing overboard a life buoy. "It is the Pole!" was our first exclamation. "No, no," said Hildebrand, with a distressed face, "it is the cabin-boy"—a sprightly, handsome fellow of fourteen. There he was struggling in the icy water, looking toward the steamer, which was every moment more distant. Two men were in the little boat, which had just been run down from the davits, but it seemed an eternity until their oars were shipped, and they pulled away on their errand of life or death. We urged the mate to put the steamer about, but he passively refused. The boy still swam, but the boat was not yet half-way, and headed too much to the left. There was no tiller, and the men could only guess at their course. We guided them by signs, watching the boy's head, now a mere speck, seen at intervals under the lowering sky. He struggled gallantly; the boat drew nearer, and one of the men stood up and looked around. We watched with breathless suspense for the reappearance of the brave young swimmer, but we watched in vain. Poor boy! who can know what was the agony of those ten minutes, while the icy waves gradually benumbed and dragged down the young life that struggled with such desperate energy to keep its place in the world! The men sat down and rowed back, bringing only his cap, which they had found floating on the sea. "Ah!" said Hildebrand, with tears in his eyes, "I did not want to take him this voyage, but his mother begged me so hard that I could not refuse, and this is the end!"

19

We had a melancholy party in the cabin that afternoon. The painful impression made by this catastrophe was heightened by the knowledge that it might have been prevented. The steamer amidships was filled up to her rail with coal, and the boy was thrown overboard by a sudden lurch while walking upon it. Immediately afterwards, lines were rove along the stanchions, to prevent the same thing happening again. The few feet of deck upon which we could walk were slippery with ice, and we kept below, smoking gloomily and saying little. Another violent snow-storm came on from the north, but in the afternoon we caught sight of some rocks off Carlscrona, and made the light on Oland in the evening. The wind had been blowing so freshly that our captain suspected Calmar Sound might be clear, and determined to try the passage. We felt our way slowly through the intricate sandbanks, in the midst of fog and snow, until after midnight, when only six miles from Calmar, we were stopped by fields of drift ice, and had to put back again.

The fourth morning dawned cold and splendidly clear. When I went on deck we were rounding the southern point of Oland, through long belts of floating ice. The low chalk cliffs were covered with snow, and looked bleak and desolate enough. The wind now came out of the west, enabling us to carry the foresail, so that we made eight or nine knots, in spite of our overloaded condition. Braisted and I walked the deck all day, enjoying the keen wind and clear, faint sunshine of the North. In the afternoon, however, it blew half a gale, with flurries of mingled rain and snow. The sea rose, and the steamer, lumbered as she was, could not be steered on her course, but had to be "conned," to keep off the strain. The hatches were closed, and an occasional sea broke over the bows. We sat below in the dark huts; the Pole, leaning against the bulkhead, silently awaiting his fate, as he afterwards confessed. I had faith enough in the timidity of our captain, not to feel the least alarm—and, true enough, two hours had not elapsed before we lay-to under the lee of the northern end of Oland. The Pole then sat down, bathed from head to foot in a cold sweat, and would have landed immediately, had it been possible. The Swede was as inexpressive as ever, with the same half-smile on his fair, serious face.

I was glad to find that our captain did not intend to lose the wind, but would start again in an hour or two. We had a quieter night than could have been anticipated, followed by a brilliant morning. Such good progress had been made that at sunrise the lighthouse on the rocks of Landsort was visible, and the jagged masses of that archipelago of cloven isles which extends all the way to Torneå, began to stud the sea. The water became smoother as we ran into the sound between Landsort and the outer isles. A long line of bleak, black rocks, crusted with snow, stretched before us. Beside the lighthouse, at their southern extremity, there were two red frame-houses, and a telegraph station. A boat, manned by eight hardy sailors, came off with a pilot, who informed us that Stockholm was closed with ice, and that the other steamers had been obliged to stop at the little port of Dalarö, thirty miles distant. So for Dalarö we headed, threading the channels of the scattering islands, which gradually became higher and more picturesque, with clumps of dark fir crowning their snowy slopes. The midday sun hung low on the horizon, throwing a pale yellow light over the wild northern scenery; but there was life in the cold air, and I did not ask for summer.

We passed the deserted fortress of Dalarö, a square stone structure, which has long since outlived its purpose, on the summit of a rock in the sound. Behind it, opened a quiet bay, held in a projecting arm of the mainland, near the extremity of which appeared our port—a village of about fifty houses, scattered along the abrupt shore. The dark-red buildings stood out distinctly against the white background; two steamers and half a dozen sailing crafts were moored below them; about as many individuals were moving quietly about, and for all the life and animation we could see, we might have been in Kamtchatka.

As our voyage terminated here, our first business was to find means of getting to Stockholm by land. Our fellow-passengers proposed that we should join company, and engage five horses and three sleds for ourselves and luggage. The Swede willingly undertook to negotiate for us, and set about the work with his usual impassive semi-cheerfulness. The landlord of the only inn in the place promised to have everything ready by six o'clock the next morning, and our captain, who was to go on the same evening, took notices of our wants, to be served at the two intervening post-stations on the road. We then visited the custom-house, a cabin about ten feet square, and asked to have our luggage examined. "No," answered the official, "we have no authority to examine anything; you must wait until we send to Stockholm." This was at least a new experience. We were greatly vexed and annoyed, but at length, by dint of explanations and entreaties, prevailed upon the man to attempt an examination. Our trunks were brought ashore, and if ever a man did his duty conscientiously, it was this same Swedish official. Every article was taken out and separately inspected, with an honest patience which I could not but admire. Nothing was found contraband, however; we had the pleasure of repacking, and were then pulled back to the Carl Johan in a profuse sweat, despite the intense cold.

CHAPTER II. STOCKHOLM.—PREPARATIONS FOR THE NORTH.

On the following morning we arose at five, went ashore in the darkness, and after waiting an hour, succeeded in getting our teams together. The horses were small, but spirited, the sleds rudely put together, but strong, and not uncomfortable, and the drivers, peasants of the neighborhood, patient, and good-humoured. Climbing the steep bank, we were out of the village in two minutes, crossed an open common, and entered the forests of fir and pine. The sleighing was superb, and our little nags carried us merrily along, at the usual travelling rate of one Swedish mile (nearly seven English) per hour. Enveloped from head to foot in our fur robes, we did not feel the sharp air, and in comparing our sensations, decided that the temperature was about 20°. What was our surprise, on reaching the post-station, at learning that it was actually 2° below zero!

Slowly, almost imperceptibly, the darkness decreased, but the morning was cloudy, and there was little appearance of daybreak before nine o'clock. In the early twilight we were startled by the appearance of a ball of meteoric fire, nearly as large as the moon, and of a soft white lustre, which moved in a horizontal line from east to west, and disappeared without a sound. I was charmed by the forest scenery through which we passed. The pine, spruce, and fir trees, of the greatest variety of form, were completely coated with frozen snow, and stood as immovable as forests of bronze incrusted with silver. The delicate twigs of the weeping birch resembled sprays of crystal, of a thousand airy and exquisite patterns. There was no wind, except in the open glades between the woods, where the frozen lakes spread out like meadow intervals. As we approached the first station there were signs of cultivation—fields inclosed with stake fences, low red houses, low barns, and scanty patches of garden land. We occasionally met peasants with their sleds—hardy, red-faced fellows, and women solid enough to outweigh their bulk in pig-iron.

The post-station was a cottage in the little hamlet of Berga. We drove into the yard, and while sleds and horses were being changed, partook of some boiled milk and tough rye-bread, the only things to be had, but both good of their kind. The travellers' room was carpeted and comfortable, and the people seemed poor only because of their few wants. Our new sleds were worse than the former, and so were our horses, but we came to the second station in time, and found we must make still another arrangement. The luggage was sent ahead on a large sled, while each pair of us, seated in a one horse cutter, followed after it, driving ourselves. Swedish horses are stopped by a whistle, and encouraged by a smacking of the lips, which I found impossible to learn at once, and they considerately gave us no whips. We had now a broad, beaten road, and the many teams we met and passed gave evidence of our approach to Stockholm. The country, too, gently undulating all the way, was more thickly settled, and appeared to be under tolerable cultivation.

About one in the afternoon, we climbed a rising slope, and from its brow looked down upon Stockholm. The sky was dark-gray and lowering; the hills were covered with snow, and the roofs of the city resembled a multitude of tents, out of which rose half a dozen dark spires. On either side were arms of the Mälar Lake—white, frozen plains. Snow was already in the air, and presently we looked through a screen of heavy flakes on the dark, weird, wintry picture. The impression was perfect of its kind, and I shall not soon forget it.

We had passed through the southern suburb, and were descending to the lake, when one of our shafts snapped off. Resigning the cutter to the charge of a stout maiden, who acted as postillion, Braisted and I climbed upon the luggage, and in this wise, shaggy with snowy fur, passed through the city, before the House of Nobles and the King's Palace, and over the Northern Bridge, and around the northern suburb, and I know not where else, to the great astonishment of everybody we met, until our stupid driver found out where he was to go. Then we took leave of the Pole, who had engaged horses to Norrköping, and looked utterly disconsolate at parting; but the grave Swede showed his kind heart at last, for—neglecting his home, from which he had been absent seven years—he accompanied us to an hotel, engaged rooms, and saw us safely housed.

We remained in Stockholm a week, engaged in making preparations for our journey to the North. During this time we were very comfortably quartered in Kahn's Hotel, the only one in the capital where one can get both rooms and meals. The weather changed so entirely, as completely to destroy our first impressions, and make the North, which we were seeking, once more as distant as when we left Germany. The day after our arrival a thaw set in, which cleared away every particle of snow and ice, opened the harbor, freed the Mälar Lake, and gave the white hills around the city their autumnal colors of brown and dark-green. A dense fog obscured the brief daylight, the air was close, damp, and oppressive, everybody coughed and snuffled, and the air-tight rooms, so comfortable in cold weather, became insufferable. My blood stagnated, my spirits descended as the mercury rose, and I grew all impatience to have zero and a beaten snow-track again.

We had more difficulty in preparing for this journey than I anticipated—not so much in the way of procuring the necessary articles, as the necessary information on the subject. I was not able to find a man who had made the journey in winter, or who could tell me what to expect, and what to do. The mention of my plan excited very general surprise, but the people were too polished and courteous to say outright that I was a fool, though I don't doubt that many of them thought so. Even the maps are only minute enough for the traveller as far as Torneå, and the only special maps of Lapland I could get dated from 1803. The Government, it is true, has commenced the publication of a very admirable map of the kingdom, in provinces, but these do not as yet extend beyond Jemteland, about Lat. 63° north. Neither is there any work to be had, except some botanical and geological publications, which of course contain but little practical information. The English and German Handbooks for Sweden are next to useless, north of Stockholm. The principal assurances were, that we should suffer greatly from cold, that we should take along a supply of provisions, for nothing was to be had, and that we must expect to endure hardships and privations of all kinds. This prospect was not at all alarming, for I remembered that I had heard much worse accounts of Ethiopia while making similar preparations in Cairo, and have learned that all such bugbears cease to exist when they are boldly faced.

Our outfit, therefore, was restricted to some coffee, sugar, salt, gunpowder, lucifer-matches, lead, shot and slugs, four bottles of cognac for cases of extremity, a sword, a butcher-knife, hammer, screw-driver, nails, rope and twine, all contained in a box about eighteen inches square. A single valise held our stock of clothing, books, writing and drawing materials, and each of us carried, in addition, a double-barrelled musket. We made negotiations for the purchase of a handsome Norrland sleigh (numbers of which come to Stockholm, at this season, laden with wild-fowl), but the thaw prevented our making a bargain. The preparation of the requisite funds, however, was a work of some time. In this I was assisted by Mr. Moström, an excellent valet-de-place, whom I hereby recommend to all travellers. When, after three or four days' labour and diplomacy, he brought me the money, I thought I had suddenly come in possession of an immense fortune. There were hundreds of bank-notes, and thousands of silver pieces of all sizes—Swedish paper, silver and copper, Norwegian notes and dollars, Danish marks, and Russian gold, roubles and copecks. The value belied the quantity, and the vast pile melted away so fast that I was soon relieved of my pleasant delusion.

Our equipment should have been made in Germany, for, singularly enough, Stockholm is not half so well provided with furs and articles of winter clothing as Hamburg or Leipsic. Besides, everything is about fifty per cent dearer here. We were already provided with ample fur robes, I with one of gray bear-skin, and Braisted with yellow fox. To these we added caps of sea-otter, mittens of dog-skin, lined with the fur of the Arctic hare, knitted devil's caps, woollen sashes of great length for winding around the body, and, after long search, leather Russian boots lined with sheepskin and reaching half-way up the thigh. When rigged out in this costume, my diameter was about equal to half my height, and I found locomotion rather cumbrous; while Braisted, whose stature is some seven inches shorter, waddled along like an animated cotton-bale.

Everything being at last arranged, so far as our limited information made it possible, for a two months' journey, we engaged places in a diligence which runs as far as Gefle, 120 miles north of Stockholm. There we hoped to find snow and a colder climate. One of my first steps had been to engage a Swedish teacher, and by dint of taking double lessons every day, I flattered myself that I had made sufficient progress in the language to travel without an interpreter—the most inconvenient and expensive of persons. To be sure, a week is very little for a new language, but to one who speaks English and German, Swedish is already half acquired.

CHAPTER III. FIRST EXPERIENCES OF NORTHERN TRAVEL.

The diligence was a compact little vehicle, carrying four persons, but we two were so burdened with our guns, sword, money-bag, field-glass, over-boots and two-fathom-long sashes, that we found the space allotted to us small enough. We started at eight o'clock, and had not gone a hundred yards before we discovered that the most important part of our outfit—the maps—had been left behind. It was too late to return, and we were obliged to content ourselves with the hope of supplying them at Upsala or Gefle.

We rolled by twilight through the Northern suburb. The morning was sharp and cold, and the roads, which had been muddy and cut up the day before, were frozen terribly hard and rough. Our fellow-passengers were two Swedes, an unprepossessing young fellow who spoke a few words of English, and a silent old gentleman; we did not derive much advantage from their society, and I busied myself with observing the country through which we passed. A mile or two, past handsome country-seats and some cemeteries, brought us into the region of forests. The pines were tall and picturesque in their forms, and the grassy meadows between them, entirely clear of snow, were wonderfully green for the season. During the first stage we passed some inlets of the Baltic, highly picturesque with their irregular wooded shores. They had all been frozen over during the night. We were surprised to see, on a southern hill-side, four peasants at work ploughing. How they got their shares through the frozen sod, unless the soil was remarkably dry and sandy, was more than I could imagine. We noticed occasionally a large manor-house, with its dependent out-buildings, and its avenue of clipped beeches or lindens, looking grand and luxurious in the midst of the cold dark fields. Here and there were patches of wheat, which the early snow had kept green, and the grass in the damp hollows was still bright, yet it was the 15th of December, and we were almost in lat. 60° N.

The houses were mostly one-story wooden cottages, of a dull red color, with red roofs. In connection with the black-green of the pine and fir woods they gave the country a singularly sombre aspect. There was little variation in the scenery all the way to Upsala. In some places, the soil appeared to be rich and under good cultivation; here the red villages were more frequent, and squat church-towers showed themselves in the distance. In other places, we had but the rough hills, or rather knobs of gray gneiss, whose masses were covered with yellow moss, and the straggling fir forests. We met but few country teams on the road; nobody was to be seen about the houses, and the land seemed to be asleep or desolated. Even at noon, when the sun came out fairly, he was low on the horizon, and gave but an eclipsed light, which was more cheerless than complete darkness.

The sun set about three o'clock, but we had a long, splendid twilight, a flush of orange, rose and amber-green, worthy of a Mediterranean heaven. Two hours afterwards, the lights of Upsala appeared, and we drove under the imposing front of the old palace, through clean streets, over the Upsala River, and finally stopped at the door of a courtyard. Here we were instantly hailed by some young fellows, who inquired if we did not want rooms. The place did not appear to be an inn, but as the silent old gentleman got out and went in, I judged it best to follow his example, and the diligence drove off with our baggage. We were right, after all: a rosy, handsome, good-humored landlady appeared, promised to furnish us with beds and a supper, to wake us betimes, and give us coffee before leaving.

The old gentleman kindly put on his coat and accompanied us to a bookstore on the public square, where I found Akrell's map of Northern Sweden, and thus partially replaced our loss. He sat awhile in our room trying to converse, but I made little headway. On learning that we were bound for Torneå, he asked: "Are you going to buy lumber?" "No," I answered; "we are merely going to see the country." He laughed long and heartily at such an absurd idea, got up in a hurry, and went to bed without saying another word. We had a supper of various kinds of sausage, tough rye bread, and a bowl of milk, followed by excellent beds—a thing which you are sure to find everywhere in Sweden.

We drove off again at half-past six in the morning moon light, with a temperature of zero. Two or three miles from the town we passed the mounds

29

of old Upsala, the graves of Odin, Thor and Freja, rising boldly against the first glimmerings of daylight. The landscape was broad, dark and silent, the woods and fields confusedly blended together, and only the sepulchres of the ancient gods broke the level line of the horizon. I could readily have believed in them at that hour.

Passing over the broad rich plain of Upsala, we entered a gently undulating country, richer and better cultivated than the district we had traversed the previous day. It was splendidly wooded with thick fir forests, floored with bright green moss. Some of the views toward the north and west were really fine from their extent, though seen in the faded light and long shadows of the low northern sun. In the afternoon, we passed a large white church, with four little towers at the corners, standing in the midst of a village of low red stables, in which the country people shelter their horses while attending service. There must have been fifty or sixty of these buildings, arranged in regular streets. In most of the Swedish country churches, the belfry stands apart, a squat, square tower, painted red, with a black upper story, and is sometimes larger than the church itself. The houses of the peasants are veritable western shanties, except in color and compactness. No wind finds a cranny to enter, and the roofs of thick thatch, kept down by long, horizontal poles, have an air of warmth and comfort. The stables are banked with earth up to the hay-loft, and the cattle enter their subterranean stalls through sloping doorways like those of the Egyptian tombs.

Notwithstanding we made good progress through the day, it was dark long before we reached the bridge over the Dal Elv, and of the famous cascades we saw only a sloping white glimmer, between dark masses of forest, and heard the noise of the broken waters. At Elfkarleby we were allowed twenty minutes for dinner—boiled salmon and beefsteak, both bad. I slept after this, until aroused by the old Swede, as we entered Gefle. We drove across a broad bridge, looked over vessels frozen into the inlet of the Gulf, passed a large public square, and entered the yard of the diligence office. A boy in waiting conducted us to a private house, where furnished rooms were to be had, and here we obtained tea, comfortable beds, and the attendance of a rosy servant-girl, who spoke intelligible Swedish.

30

My first care the next morning, was to engage horses and send off my förbud papers. We were now to travel by "skjuts" (pronounced shoos), or post, taking new horses at each station on the road. The förbud tickets are simply orders for horses to be ready at an appointed time, and are sent in advance to all the stations on the road, either by mail or by a special messenger. Without this precaution, I was told, we might be subjected to considerable delay. This mode of travelling is peculiar to Sweden and Norway. It has been in existence for three or four centuries, and though gradually improved and systematized with the lapse of time, it is still sufficiently complex and inconvenient to a traveller coming from the railroad world.

Professor Retzius had referred me to the botanist Hartman, in case of need, but I determined to commence by helping myself. I had a little difficulty at first: the people are unused to speaking with foreigners, and if you ask them to talk slowly, they invariably rattle away twice as fast as before. I went into a variety shop on the public square, and asked where I could engage horses for Sundsvall. After making myself understood, as I supposed, the clerk handed me some new bridles. By dint of blundering, I gradually circumscribed the range of my inquiries, and finally came to a focus at the right place. Having ordered horses at six the next morning, and despatched the förbud tickets by the afternoon's mail, I felt that I had made a good beginning, and we set out to make the tour of Gefle.

This is a town of eight or ten thousand inhabitants, with a considerable shipping interest, and a naval school. It is a pretty place, well built, and with a neat, substantial air. The houses are mostly two stories high, white, and with spacious courts in the rear. The country around is low but rolling, and finely clothed with dark forests of fir and pine. It was a superb day—gloriously clear, with a south wind, bracing, and not too cold, and a soft, pale lustre from the cloudless sun. But such a day! Sunrise melting into sunset without a noon—a long morning twilight, a low, slant sun, shining on the housetops for an hour or so, and the evening twilight at three in the afternoon. Nothing seemed real in this strange, dying light—nothing but my ignorance of Swedish, whenever I tried to talk.

In the afternoon, we called on the Magister Hartman, whom we found

31

poring over his plants. He spoke English tolerably, and having made a journey through Lapland from Torneå to the Lyngen Fjord, was able to give us some information about the country. He encouraged us in the belief that we should find the journey more rapid and easy in winter than in summer. He said the Swedes feared the North and few of them ever made a winter journey thither, but nothing could stop the Americans and the English from going anywhere. He also comforted us with the assurance that we should find snow only six Swedish (forty English) miles further north. Lat. 60° 35' N., the 17th of December, and no snow yet! In the streets, we met an organ-grinder playing the Marseillaise. There was no mistaking the jet-black hair, the golden complexion and the brilliant eyes of the player, "Siete Italiano?" I asked. "Sicuro!" he answered, joyously: "e lei anche?" "Ah," he said, in answer to my questions, "io non amo questo paese; è freddo ed oscuro; non si gagna niente—ma in Italia si vive." My friend Ziegler had already assured me: "One should see the North, but not after the South." Well, we shall see; but I confess that twenty degrees below zero would have chilled me less than the sight of that Italian.

We were at the inn punctually at six in the morning, but our horses were not ready. The hållkarl, or ostler, after hearing my remonstrances, went on splitting wood, and, as I did not know enough of Swedish to scold with any profit, I was obliged to remain wrathful and silent. He insisted on my writing something (I could not understand what) in the post-book, so I copied the affidavit of a preceding traveller and signed my name to it, which seemed to answer the purpose. After more than half an hour, two rough two-wheeled carts were gotten ready, and the farmers to whom they belonged, packed themselves and our luggage into one, leaving us to drive the other. We mounted, rolled ourselves in our furs, thrust our feet into the hay, and rattled out of Gefle in the frosty moonlight. Such was our first experience of travelling by skjuts.

The road went northward, into dark forests, over the same undulating, yet monotonous country as before. The ground was rough and hard, and our progress slow, so that we did not reach the end of the first station (10 miles) until nine o'clock. As we drove into the post-house, three other travellers, who had the start of us, and consequently the first right to horses, drove away. I was dismayed to find that my förbud had not been received, but the ostler informed me that by paying twelve skillings extra I could have horses at once. While the new carts were getting ready, the postman, wrapped in wolf-skin, and with a face reddened by the wind, came up, and handed out my förbud ticket. Such was our first experience of förbud.

On the next station, the peasant who was ahead with our luggage left the main road and took a rough track through the woods. Presently we came to a large inlet of the Bothnian gulf, frozen solid from shore to shore, and upon this we boldly struck out. The ice was nearly a foot thick, and as solid as marble. So we drove for at least four miles, and finally came to land on the opposite side, near a sawmill. At the next post-house we found our predecessors just setting off again in sleds; the landlord informed us that he had only received my förbud an hour previous, and, according to law was allowed three hours to get ready his second instalment of horses, the first being exhausted. There was no help for it: we therefore comforted ourselves with breakfast. At one o'clock we set out again in low Norrland sleds, but there was little snow at first, and we were obliged to walk the first few miles. The station was a long one (twenty English miles), and our horses not the most promising. Coming upon solid snow at last, we travelled rather more swiftly, but with more risk. The sleds, although so low, rest upon narrow runners, and the shafts are attached by a hook, upon which they turn in all directions, so that the sled sways from side to side, entirely independent of them. In going off the main road to get a little more snow on a side track, I discovered this fact by overturning the sled, and pitching Braisted and myself out on our heads. There were lakes on either side, and we made many miles on the hard ice, which split with a dull sound under us. Long after dark, we reached the next station, Stråtjära, and found our horses in readiness. We started again, by the gleam of a flashing aurora, going through forests and fields in the uncertain light, blindly following our leader, Braisted and I driving by turns, and already much fatigued. After a long time, we descended a steep hill, to the Ljusne River. The water foamed and thundered under the bridge, and I could barely see that it fell in a series of rapids over the rocks.

At Mo Myskie, which we reached at eight o'clock, our horses had been ready four hours, which gave us a dollar banco väntapenningar (waiting money) to pay. The landlord, a sturdy, jolly fellow, with grizzly hair and a prosperous abdomen, asked if we were French, and I addressed him in that language. He answered in English on finding that we were Americans. On his saying that he had learned English in Tripoli, I addressed him in Arabic. His eyes flashed, he burst into a roaring laugh of the profoundest delight, and at once answered in the majestic gutturals of the Orient. "Allah akhbar!" he cried; "I have been waiting twenty years for some one to speak to me in Arabic, and you are the first!" He afterwards changed to Italian, which he spoke perfectly well, and preferred to any foreign language. We were detained half an hour by his delight, and went off forgetting to pay for a bottle of beer, the price of which I sent back by the skjutsbonde, or postillion.

This skjutsbonde was a stupid fellow, who took us a long, circuitous road, in order to save time. We hurried along in the darkness, constantly crying out "Kör på!" (Drive on!) and narrowly missing a hundred overturns. It was eleven at night before we reached the inn at Kungsgården, where, fortunately, the people were awake, and the pleasant old landlady soon had our horses ready. We had yet sixteen English miles to Bro, our lodging-place, where we should have arrived by eight o'clock. I hardly know how to describe the journey. We were half asleep, tired out, nearly frozen, (mercury below zero) and dashed along at haphazard, through vast dark forests, up hill and down, following the sleepy boy who drove ahead with our baggage. A dozen times the sled, swaying from side to side like a pendulum, tilted, hung in suspense a second, and then righted itself again. The boy fell back on the hay and slept, until Braisted, creeping up behind, startled him with terrific yells in his ears. Away then dashed the horse, down steep declivities, across open, cultivated valleys, and into the woods again. After midnight the moon rose, and the cold was intenser than ever. The boy having fallen asleep again, the horse took advantage of it to run off at full speed, we following at the same rate, sometimes losing sight of him and uncertain of our way, until, after a chase of a few miles, we found the boy getting his reins out from under the runners. Finally, after two in the morning, we reached Bro.

Here we had ordered a warm room, beds and supper, by förbud, but

34

found neither. A sleepy, stupid girl, who had just got up to wait on a captain who had arrived before us and was going on, told us there was nothing to be had. "We must eat, if we have to eat you," I said, savagely, for we were chilled through and fierce with hunger; but I might as well have tried to hurry the Venus de Medici. At last we got some cold sausage, a fire, and two couches, on which we lay down without undressing, and slept. I had scarcely closed my eyes, it seemed, when the girl, who was to call us at half-past five o'clock, came into the room. "Is it half-past five?" I asked. "Oh, yes," she coolly answered, "it's much more." We were obliged to hurry off at once to avoid paying so much waiting money.

At sunrise we passed Hudiksvall, a pretty town at the head of a deep bay, in which several vessels were frozen up for the winter. There were some handsome country houses in the vicinity, better cultivation, more taste in building, and a few apple and cherry orchards. The mercury was still at zero, but we suffered less from the cold than the day previous, and began to enjoy our mode of travel. The horses were ready at all the stations on our arrival, and we were not delayed in changing. There was now plenty of snow, and the roads were splendid—the country undulating, with beautiful, deep valleys, separated by high, wooded hills, and rising to bold ridges in the interior. The houses were larger and better than we had yet seen—so were the people—and there was a general air of progress and well-doing. In fact, both country and population improved in appearance as we went northward.

The night set in very dark and cold, threatening snow. We had an elephant of a horse, which kicked up his heels and frisked like an awkward bull-pup, dashed down the hills like an avalanche, and carried us forward at a rapid rate. We coiled ourselves up in the hay, kept warm, and trusted our safety to Providence, for it was impossible to see the road, and we could barely distinguish the other sled, a dark speck before us. The old horse soon exhausted his enthusiasm. Braisted lost the whip, and the zealous boy ahead stopped every now and then to hurry us on. The aurora gleamed but faintly through the clouds; we were nearly overcome with sleep and fatigue, but took turns in arousing and amusing each other. The sled vibrated continually from side to side, and finally went over, spilling ourselves and our guns into a snow-bank. The horse stopped and waited for us, and then went on until the shafts came off. Toward ten o'clock, the lights of Sundsvall appeared, and we soon afterwards drove into the yard of the inn, having made one hundred and fifty-five miles in two days. We were wretchedly tired, and hungry as bears, but found room in an adjoining house, and succeeded in getting a supper of reindeer steak. I fell asleep in my chair, before my pipe was half-finished, and awoke the next morning to a sense of real fatigue. I had had enough of travelling by förbud.

CHAPTER IV. A SLEIGH RIDE THROUGH NORRLAND.

Sundsvall is a pretty little town of two or three thousand inhabitants, situated at the head of a broad and magnificent bay. It is the eastern terminus of the only post-road across the mountains to Trondhjem (Drontheim) in Norway, which passes through the extensive province of Jemteland. It is, consequently, a lively and bustling place, and has a considerable coasting trade. The day after our arrival was market-day, and hundreds of the Norrlanders thronged the streets and public square. They were all fresh, strong, coarse, honest, healthy people—the men with long yellow hair, large noses and blue eyes, the women with the rosiest of cheeks and the fullest development of body and limb. Many of the latter wore basques or jackets of sheepskin with the wool inside, striped petticoats and bright red stockings. The men were dressed in shaggy sheepskin coats, or garments of reindeer skin, with the hair outward. There was a vast collection of low Norrland sleds, laden with butter, cheese, hay, and wild game, and drawn by the rough and tough little horses of the country. Here was still plenty of life and animation, although we were already so far north that the sun did not shine upon Sundsvall the whole day, being hidden by a low hill to the south. The snowy ridges on the north, however, wore a bright roseate blush from his rays, from ten until two.

We called upon a merchant of the place, to whom I had a letter of introduction. He was almost the only man I met before undertaking the journey, who encouraged me to push on. "The people in Stockholm," said he, "know nothing about Northern Sweden." He advised me to give up travelling by förbud, to purchase a couple of sleds, and take our chance of finding horses: we would have no trouble in making from forty to fifty English miles per day. On returning to the inn, I made the landlord understand what we wanted, but could not understand him in return. At this juncture came in a handsome fellow; with a cosmopolitan air, whom Braisted recognised, by certain invisible signs, as the mate of a ship, and who explained the matter in very good English. I purchased two plain but light and strongly made sleds for 50 rigs (about $14), which seemed very cheap, but I afterwards learned that I paid much more than the current price.

On repacking our effects, we found that everything liquid was frozen—even a camphorated mixture, which had been carefully wrapped in flannel. The cold, therefore, must have been much more severe than we supposed. Our supplies, also, were considerably damaged—the lantern broken, a powder-flask cracked, and the salt, shot, nails, wadding, &c., mixed together in beautiful confusion. Everything was stowed in one of the sleds, which was driven by the postilion; the other contained only our two selves. We were off the next morning, as the first streaks of dawn appeared in the sky. The roads about Sundsvall were very much cut up, and even before getting out of the town we were pitched over head and ears into a snow-bank.

We climbed slowly up and darted headlong down the ridges which descend from the west toward the Bothnian Gulf, dividing its tributary rivers; and toward sunrise, came to a broad bay, completely frozen over and turned into a snowy plain. With some difficulty the skjutsbonde made me understand that a shorter road led across the ice to the second post-station, Fjäl, avoiding one change of horses. The way was rough enough at first, over heaped blocks of ice, but became smoother where the wind had full sweep, and had cleared the water before it froze. Our road was marked out by a double row of young fir-trees, planted in the ice. The bay was completely land-locked, embraced by bold sweep of wooded hills, with rich, populous valleys between. Before us, three or four miles across, lay the little port of Wifsta-warf, where several vessels—among them a ship of three or four hundred tuns—were frozen in for the winter. We crossed, ascended a long hill, and drove on through fir woods to Fjäl, a little hamlet with a large inn. Here we got breakfast; and though it may be in bad taste to speak of what one eats, the breakfast was in such good taste that I cannot pass over it without lingering to enjoy, in memory, its wonderful aroma. Besides, if it be true, as some shockingly gross persons assert, that the belly is a more important district of the human economy than the brain, a good meal deserves chronicling no less than an exalted impression. Certain it is, that strong digestive are to be preferred to strong thinking powers—better live unknown than die of dyspepsia. This was our first country meal in Norrland, of whose fare the Stockholmers have a horror, yet that stately capital never furnished a better. We had beefsteak and onions, delicious blood-puddings, the tenderest of pancakes (no omelette soufflée could be more fragile), with ruby raspberry jam, and a bottle of genuine English porter. If you think the bill of fare too heavy and solid, take a drive of fifteen miles in the regions of Zero, and then let your delicate stomach decide.

In a picturesque dell near Fjäl we crossed the rapid Indal River, which comes down from the mountains of Norway. The country was wild and broken, with occasional superb views over frozen arms of the Gulf, and the deep rich valleys stretching inland. Leaving Hernösand, the capital of the province, a few miles to our right, we kept the main northern road, slowly advancing from station to station with old and tired horses. There was a snow-storm in the afternoon, after which the sky came out splendidly clear, and gorgeous with the long northern twilight. In the silence of the hour and the deepening shadows of the forest through which we drove, it was startling to hear, all at once the sound of voices singing a solemn hymn. My first idea was, that some of those fanatical Dissenters of Norrland who meet, as once the Scotch Covenanters, among the hills, were having a refreshing winter meeting in the woods; but on proceeding further we found that the choristers were a company of peasants returning from market with their empty sleds.

It was already dark at four o'clock, and our last horses were so slow that the postilion, a handsome, lively boy, whose pride was a little touched by my remonstrances, failed, in spite of all his efforts, to bring us to the station before seven. We stopped at Weda, on the Angermann River, the largest stream in Northern Sweden. Angermannland, the country which it drains, is said to be a very wild and beautiful region, where some traces of the old, original Asiatic type which peopled Scandinavia are yet to be traced in the features of its secluded population. At Weda, we found excellent quarters. A neat, quiet, old-fashioned little servant-girl, of twelve or fourteen, took charge of us, and attended to all our wants with the greatest assiduity. We had a good supper, a small but neat room, clean beds, and coffee in the morning, beside a plentiful provision for breakfast on the way, for a sum equal to seventy-five cents.

We left at half-past seven, the waning moon hanging on the horizon, and the first almost imperceptible signs of the morning twilight in the east.

The Angermann River which is here a mile broad, was frozen, and our road led directly across its surface. The wind blew down it, across the snow-covered ice, making our faces tingle with premonitory signs of freezing, as the mercury was a little below zero. My hands were chilled inside the fur mittens, and I was obliged to rub my nose frequently, to prevent it from being nipped. The day was raw and chilly, and the temperature rose very little, although the hills occasionally sheltered us from the wind. The scenery, also, grew darker and wilder as we advanced. The fir-trees were shorter and stunted, and of a dark greenish-brown, which at a little distance appeared completely black. Nothing could exceed the bleak, inhospitable character of these landscapes. The inlets of the Bothnian Gulf were hard, snow-covered plains, inclosed by bold, rugged headlands, covered with ink-black forests. The more distant ridges faded into a dull indigo hue, flecked with patches of ghastly white, under the lowering, sullen, short-lived daylight.

Our road was much rougher than hitherto. We climbed long ridges, only to descend by as steep declivities on the northern side, to cross the bed of an inland stream, and then ascend again. The valleys, however, were inhabited and apparently well cultivated, for the houses were large and comfortable, and the people had a thrifty, prosperous and satisfied air. Beside the farmhouses were immense racks, twenty feet high, for the purpose of drying flax and grain, and at the stations the people offered for sale very fine and beautiful linen of their own manufacture. This is the staple production of Norrland, where the short summers are frequently insufficient to mature the grain crops. The inns were all comfortable buildings, with very fair accommodations for travellers. We had bad luck with horses this day, however, two or three travellers having been in advance and had the pick. On one stage our baggage-sled was driven by a poike of not more than ten years old—a darling fellow, with a face as round, fresh and sweet as a damask rose, the bluest of eyes, and a cloud of silky golden hair. His successor was a tall, lazy lout, who stopped so frequently to talk with the drivers of sleds behind us, that we lost all patience, drove past and pushed ahead in the darkness, trusting our horse to find the way. His horse followed, leaving him in the lurch, and we gave him a long-winded chase astern before we allowed him to overtake us. This so exasperated him that we had no trouble the rest of the way. Mem.—If you wish to travel with

40

speed, make your postilion angry.

At Hörnäs they gave us a supper of ale and cold pig's feet, admirable beds, and were only deficient in the matter of water for washing. We awoke with headaches, on account of gas from the tight Russian stove. The temperature, at starting, was 22° below zero—colder than either of us had ever before known. We were a little curious, at first, to know how we should endure it, but, to our delight, found ourselves quite warm and comfortable. The air was still, dry, and delicious to inhale. My nose occasionally required friction, and my beard and moustache became a solid mass of ice, frozen together so that I could scarcely open my mouth, and firmly fastened to my fur collar. We travelled forty-nine miles, and were twelve hours on the way, yet felt no inconvenience from the temperature.

By this time it was almost wholly a journey by night, dawn and twilight, for full day there was none. The sun rose at ten and set at two. We skimmed along, over the black, fir-clothed hills, and across the pleasant little valleys, in the long, gray, slowly-gathering daybreak: then, heavy snow-clouds hid half the brief day, and the long, long, dusky evening glow settled into night. The sleighing was superb, the snow pure as ivory, hard as marble, and beautifully crisp and smooth. Our sleds glided over it without effort, the runners making music as they flew. With every day the country grew wilder, blacker and more rugged, with no change in the general character of the scenery. In the afternoon we passed the frontier of Norrland, and entered the province of West Bothnia. There are fewer horses at the stations, as we go north, but also fewer travellers, and we were not often detained. Thus far, we had no difficulty: my scanty stock of Swedish went a great way, and I began to understand with more facility, even the broad Norrland dialect.

The people of this region are noble specimens of the physical man—tall, broad-shouldered, large-limbed, ruddy and powerful; and they are mated with women who, I venture to say, do not even suspect the existence of a nervous system. The natural consequences of such health are: morality and honesty—to say nothing of the quantities of rosy and robust children which bless every household. If health and virtue cannot secure happiness, nothing can, and these Norrlanders appear to be a thoroughly happy and contented race. We had occasional reason to complain of their slowness; but, then, why should they be fast? It is rather we who should moderate our speed. Braisted, however, did not accept such a philosophy. "Charles XII. was the boy to manage the Swedes," said he to me one day; "he always kept them in a hurry."

We reached Lefwar, our resting-place for the night, in good condition, notwithstanding the 22° below, and felt much colder in the house, after stripping off our furs, than out of doors with them on. They gave us a supper consisting of smörgås ("butter-goose"—the Swedish prelude to a meal, consisting usually of bread, butter, pickled anchovies, and caviar flavored with garlic), sausages, potatoes, and milk, and made for us sumptuous beds of the snowiest and sweetest linen. When we rose next morning it was snowing. About an inch had fallen during the night, and the mercury had risen to 6° below zero. We drove along in the dusky half-twilight toward Angesjö, over low, broad hills, covered with forests of stunted birch and fir. The scenery continued the same, and there is no use in repeating the description, except to say that the land became more cold and barren, and there seemed to be few things cultivated except flax, barley and potatoes. Still the same ridges sweeping down to the Gulf, on one hand, the same frozen bays and inlets on the other, and villages at intervals of eight or ten miles, each with its great solid church, low red belfry and deserted encampment of red frame stables. Before reaching the second station, we looked from a wooded height over the open expanse of the Gulf,—a plain of snow-covered ice, stretching eastward as far as the eye could reach.

The day gradually became still and cold, until the temperature reached -22° again, and we became comfortable in the same proportion. The afternoon twilight, splendid with its hues of amber, rose and saffron, died away so gradually, that it seemed scarcely to fade at all, lighting our path for at least three hours after sunset. Our postilions were all boys—ruddy, hardy young fellows of fourteen or fifteen, who drove well and sang incessantly, in spite of the cold. They talked much with us, but to little purpose, as I found it very difficult to understand the humming dialect they spoke. Each, as he received his drickpenningar (drink-money, or gratuity), at the end of the station, expressed his thanks by shaking hands with us. This is a universal custom throughout the north of Sweden: it is a part of the simple, natural habits of the people; and though it seemed rather odd at first to be shaking hands with everybody, from the landlord down to the cook and the ostler, we soon came to take it as a matter of course. The frank, unaffected way in which the hand was offered, oftener made the custom a pleasant one.

At Stocksjö we decided to push on to a station beyond Umeå, called Innertafle, and took our horses accordingly. The direct road, however, was unused on account of the drifts, so we went around through Umeå, after all. We had nearly a Swedish mile, and it was just dark when we descended to the Umeå River, across whose solid surface we drove, and up a steep bank into the town. We stopped a few moments in the little public square, which was crowded with people, many of whom had already commenced their Christmas sprees. The shops were lighted, and the little town looked very gay and lively. Passing through, we kept down the left bank of the river for a little distance, and then struck into the woods. It was night by this time; all at once the boy stopped, mounted a snow-bank, whirled around three or four times, and said something to me which I could not understand. "What's the matter?" I asked; "is not this the road to Innertafle?" "I don't know—I think not," he said. "Don't you know the way, then?" I asked again. "No!" he yelled in reply, whirled around several times more, and then drove on. Presently we overtook a pedestrian, to whom he turned for advice, and who willingly acted as guide for the sake of a ride. Away we went again, but the snow was so spotless that it was impossible to see the track. Braisted and I ran upon a snow-bank, were overturned and dragged some little distance, but we righted ourselves again, and soon afterwards reached our destination.

In the little inn the guests' room lay behind the large family kitchen, through which we were obliged to pass. We were seized with a shivering fit on stripping off our furs, and it seemed scarcely possible to get warm again. This was followed by such intense drowsiness that we were obliged to lie down and sleep an hour before supper. After the cold weather set in, we were attacked with this drowsy fit every day, toward evening, and were obliged to take turns in arousing and stimulating each other. This we generally accomplished by singing "From Greenland's icy mountains," and other appropriate melodies.

At Innertafle we were attended by a tall landlady, a staid, quiet, almost grim person, who paid most deliberate heed to our wants. After a delay of more than two hours, she furnished us with a supper consisting of some kind of fresh fish, with a sauce composed of milk, sugar and onions, followed by gryngröt, a warm mush of mixed rice and barley, eaten with milk. Such was our fare on Christmas eve; but hunger is the best sauce, and our dishes were plentifully seasoned with it.

CHAPTER V. PROGRESS NORTHWARDS.—A STORM.

We arose betimes on Christmas morn, but the grim and deliberate landlady detained us an hour in preparing our coffee. I was in the yard about five minutes, wearing only my cloth overcoat and no gloves, and found the air truly sharp and nipping, but not painfully severe. Presently, Braisted came running in with the thermometer, exclaiming, with a yell of triumph, "Thirty, by Jupiter!" (30° of Reaumur, equal to 35-1/2° below zero of Fahrenheit.) We were delighted with this sign of our approach to the Arctic circle.

The horses were at last ready; we muffled up carefully, and set out. The dawn was just streaking the East, the sky was crystal-clear, and not a breath of air stirring. My beard was soon a solid mass of ice, from the moisture of my breath, and my nose required constant friction. The day previous, the ice which had gathered on my fur collar lay against my face so long that the flesh began to freeze over my cheek-bones, and thereafter I was obliged to be particularly cautious. As it grew lighter, we were surprised to find that our postilion was a girl. She had a heavy sheepskin over her knees, a muff for her hands, and a shawl around her head, leaving only the eyes visible. Thus accoutred, she drove on merrily, and, except that the red of her cheeks became scarlet and purple, showed no signs of the weather. As we approached Sörmjöle, the first station, we again had a broad view of the frozen Bothnian Gulf, over which hovered a low cloud of white ice-smoke. Looking down into the snowy valley of Sörmjöle, we saw the straight pillars of smoke rising from the houses high into the air, not spreading, but gradually breaking off into solid masses which sank again and filled the hollow, almost concealing the houses. Only the white, handsome church, with its tall spire, seated on a mound, rose above this pale blue film and shone softly in the growing flush of day.

We ordered horses at once, after drinking a bowl of hot milk, flavored with cinnamon. This is the favourite winter drink of the people, sometimes with the addition of brandy. But the finkel, or common brandy of Sweden, is a detestable beverage, resembling a mixture of turpentine, train oil, and bad molasses, and we took the milk unmixed, which admirably assisted in keeping up the animal heat. The mercury by this time had fallen to 38° below zero. We were surprised and delighted to find that we stood the cold so easily, and prided ourselves not a little on our powers of endurance. Our feet gradually became benumbed, but, by walking up the hills, we prevented the circulation from coming to a stand-still.

The cold, however, played some grotesque pranks with us. My beard, moustache, cap, and fur collar were soon one undivided lump of ice. Our eyelashes became snow-white and heavy with frost, and it required constant motion to keep them from freezing together. We saw everything through visors barred with ivory. Our eyebrows and hair were as hoary as those of an octogenarian, and our cheeks a mixture of crimson and orange, so that we were scarcely recognizable by each other. Every one we met had snow-white locks, no matter how youthful the face, and, whatever was the colour of our horses at starting, we always drove milk-white steeds at the close of the post. The irritation of our nostrils occasioned the greatest inconvenience, and as the handkerchiefs froze instantly, it soon became a matter of pain and difficulty to use them. You might as well attempt to blow your nose with a poplar chip. We could not bare our hands a minute, without feeling an iron grasp of cold which seemed to squeeze the flesh like a vice, and turn the very blood to ice. In other respects we were warm and jolly, and I have rarely been in higher spirits. The air was exquisitely sweet and pure, and I could open my mouth (as far as its icy grating permitted) and inhale full draughts into the lungs with a delicious sensation of refreshment and exhilaration. I had not expected to find such freedom of respiration in so low a temperature. Some descriptions of severe cold in Canada and Siberia, which I have read, state that at such times the air occasions a tingling, smarting sensation in the throat and lungs, but I experienced nothing of the kind.

This was arctic travel at last. By Odin, it was glorious! The smooth, firm road, crisp and pure as alabaster, over which our sleigh-runners talked with the rippling, musical murmur of summer brooks; the sparkling, breathless firmament; the gorgeous rosy flush of morning, slowly deepening until the orange disc of the sun cut the horizon; the golden blaze of the tops of the bronze firs; the glittering of the glassy birches; the long, dreary sweep of the landscape; the icy nectar of the perfect air; the tingling of the roused blood in every vein, all alert to guard the outposts of life against the besieging cold—it was superb! The natives themselves spoke of the cold as being unusually severe, and we congratulated ourselves all the more on our easy endurance of it. Had we judged only by our own sensations we should not have believed the temperature to be nearly so low.

The sun rose a little after ten, and I have never seen anything finer than the spectacle which we then saw for the first time, but which was afterwards almost daily repeated—the illumination of the forests and snow-fields in his level orange beams, for even at midday he was not more than eight degrees above the horizon. The tops of the trees, only, were touched: still and solid as iron, and covered with sparkling frost-crystals, their trunks were changed to blazing gold, and their foliage to a fiery orange-brown. The delicate purple sprays of the birch, coated with ice, glittered like wands of topaz and amethyst, and the slopes of virgin snow, stretching towards the sun, shone with the fairest saffron gleams. There is nothing equal to this in the South—nothing so transcendently rich, dazzling, and glorious. Italian dawns and twilights cannot surpass those we saw every day, not, like the former, fading rapidly into the ashen hues of dusk, but lingering for hour after hour with scarce a decrease of splendour. Strange that Nature should repeat these lovely aerial effects in such widely different zones and seasons. I thought to find in the winter landscapes of the far North a sublimity of death and desolation—a wild, dark, dreary, monotony of expression—but I had, in reality, the constant enjoyment of the rarest, the tenderest, the most enchanting beauty.

The people one meets along the road harmonise with these unexpected impressions. They are clear eyed and rosy as the morning, straight and strong as the fir saplings in their forests, and simple, honest, and unsophisticated beyond any class of men I have ever seen. They are no milksops either. Under the serenity of those blue eyes and smooth, fair faces, burns the old Berserker rage, not easily kindled, but terrible as the lightning when once loosed. "I would like to take all the young men north of Sundsvall," says Braisted, "put them into Kansas, tell them her history, and then let them act for themselves." "The cold in clime are cold in blood," sings Byron, but they are only cold through superior self-control and freedom from perverted passions. Better is the assertion of Tennyson:

> "That bright, and fierce, and fickle is the South,
>
> And dark, and true, and tender is the North."

There are tender hearts in the breasts of these northern men and women, albeit they are as undemonstrative as the English—or we Americans, for that matter. It is exhilarating to see such people—whose digestion is sound, whose nerves are tough as whipcord, whose blood runs in a strong full stream, whose impulses are perfectly natural, who are good without knowing it, and who are happy without trying to be so. Where shall we find such among our restless communities at home?

We made two Swedish miles by noon, and then took a breakfast of fried reindeer meat and pancakes, of which we ate enormously, to keep up a good supply of fuel. Braisted and I consumed about a pound of butter between us. Shriek not, young ladies, at our vulgar appetites—you who sip a spoonful of ice-cream, or trifle with a diminutive meringue, in company, but make amends on cold ham and pickles in the pantry, after you go home—I shall tell the truth, though it disgust you. This intense cold begets a necessity for fat, and with the necessity comes the taste—a wise provision of Nature! The consciousness now dawned upon me that I might be able to relish train-oil and tallow-candles before we had done with Lapland.

I had tough work at each station to get my head out of my wrappings, which were united with my beard and hair in one solid lump. The cold increased instead of diminishing, and by the time we reached Gumboda, at dusk, it was 40° below zero. Here we found a company of Finns travelling southward, who had engaged five horses, obliging us to wait a couple of hours. We had already made forty miles, and were satisfied with our performance, so we stopped for the night. When the thermometer was brought in, the mercury was frozen, and on unmuffling I found the end of my nose seared as if with a hot iron. The inn was capital; we had a warm carpeted room, beds of clean, lavendered linen, and all civilised appliances. In the evening we sat down to a Christmas dinner of sausages, potatoes, pancakes, raspberry jam, and a bottle of Barclay and Perkin's best porter, in which we drank the health of all dear relatives and friends in the two hemispheres. And this was in West Bothnia, where we had been told in Stockholm that we should starve! At bedtime, Braisted took out the thermometer again, and soon brought it in with the mercury frozen below all the numbers on the scale.

In the morning, the landlord came in and questioned us, in order to satisfy his curiosity. He took us for Norwegians, and was quite surprised to find out our real character. We had also been taken for Finns, Russians and Danes, since leaving Stockholm. "I suppose you intend to buy lumber?" said the landlord. "No," said I, "we travel merely for the pleasure of it." "Ja so-o-o!" he exclaimed, in a tone of the greatest surprise and incredulity. He asked if it was necessary that we should travel in such cold weather, and seemed reluctant to let us go. The mercury showed 25° below zero when we started, but the sky was cloudy, with a raw wind from the north-west. We did not feel the same hard, griping cold as the day previous, but a more penetrating chill. The same character of scenery continued, but with a more bleak and barren aspect, and the population became more scanty. The cloudy sky took away what little green there was in the fir-trees, and they gloomed as black as Styx on either side of our road. The air was terribly raw and biting as it blew across the hollows and open plains. I did not cover my face, but kept up such a lively friction on my nose, to prevent it from freezing, that in the evening I found the skin quite worn away.

At Daglösten, the third station, we stopped an hour for breakfast. It was a poverty-stricken place, and we could only get some fish-roes and salt meat. The people were all half-idiots, even to the postilion who drove us. We had some daylight for the fourth station, did the fifth by twilight, and the sixth in darkness. The cold (-30°) was so keen that our postilions made good time, and we reached Sunnanå on the Skellefteå River, 52 miles, soon after six o'clock. Here we were lodged in a large, barn-like room, so cold that we were obliged to put on our overcoats and sit against the stove. I began to be troubled with a pain in my jaw, from an unsound tooth—the commencement of a martyrdom from which I suffered for many days afterwards. The existence of nerves in one's teeth has always seemed to me a superfluous provision of Nature, and I should have been well satisfied if she had omitted them in my case.

The handmaiden called us soon after five o'clock, and brought us coffee while we were still in bed. This is the general custom here in the North, and is another point of contact with the South. The sky was overcast, with raw violent wind—mercury 18° below zero. We felt the cold very keenly; much more so than on Christmas day. The wind blew full in our teeth, and penetrated even beneath our furs. On setting out, we crossed the Skellefteå River by a wooden bridge, beyond which we saw, rising duskily in the uncertain twilight, a beautiful dome and lantern, crowning a white temple, built in the form of a Greek cross. It was the parish church of Skellefteå. Who could have expected to find such an edifice, here, on the borders of Lapland? The village about it contains many large and handsome houses. This is one of the principal points of trade and intercourse between the coast and the interior.

The weather became worse as we advanced, traversing the low, broad hills, through wastes of dark pine forests. The wind cut like a sharp sword in passing the hollows, and the drifting snow began to fill the tracks. We were full two hours in making the ten miles to Frostkage, and the day seemed scarcely nearer at hand. The leaden, lowering sky gave out no light, the forests were black and cold, the snow a dusky grey—such horribly dismal scenery I have rarely beheld. We warmed ourselves as well as we could, and started anew, having for postilions two rosy boys, who sang the whole way and played all sorts of mad antics with each other to keep from freezing. At the next station we drank large quantities of hot milk, flavored with butter, sugar and cinnamon, and then pushed on, with another chubby hop-o'-my-thumb as guide and driver. The storm grew worse and worse: the wind blew fiercely over the low hills, loaded with particles of snow, as fine as the point of a needle and as hard as crystal, which struck full on our eyeballs and stung them so that we could scarcely see. I had great difficulty in keeping my face from freezing, and my companion found his cheek touched.

By the time we reached Abyn, it blew a hurricane, and we were compelled to stop. It was already dusk, and our cosy little room was doubly pleasant by contrast with the wild weather outside. Our cheerful landlady, with her fresh complexion and splendid teeth, was very kind and attentive, and I got on very well in conversation, notwithstanding her broad dialect. She was much astonished at my asking for a bucket of cold water, for bathing. "Why," said she, "I always thought that if a person put his feet into cold water, in winter, he would die immediately." However, she supplied it, and was a little surprised to find me none the worse in the morning. I passed a terrible night from the pain in my face, and was little comforted, on rising, by the assurance that much snow had fallen. The mercury had risen to zero, and the wind still blew, although not so furiously as on the previous day. We therefore determined to set out, and try to reach Piteå. The landlady's son, a tall young Viking, with yellow locks hanging on his shoulders, acted as postilion, and took the lead. We started at nine, and found it heavy enough at first. It was barely light enough to see our way, and we floundered slowly along through deep drifts for a mile, when we met the snow-plows, after which our road became easier. These plows are wooden frames, shaped somewhat like the bow of a ship—in fact, I have seen very fair clipper models among them— about fifteen feet long by ten feet wide at the base, and so light that, if the snow is not too deep, one horse can manage them. The farmers along the road are obliged to turn out at six o'clock in the morning whenever the snow falls or drifts, and open a passage for travellers. Thus, in spite of the rigorous winter, communication is never interrupted, and the snow-road, at last, from frequent plowing, becomes the finest sleighing track in the world.

The wind blew so violently, however, that the furrows were soon filled up, and even the track of the baggage-sled, fifty yards in advance, was covered. There was one hollow where the drifts of loose snow were five or six feet deep, and here we were obliged to get out and struggle across, sinking to our loins at every step. It is astonishing how soon one becomes hardened to the cold. Although the mercury stood at zero, with a violent storm, we rode with our faces fully exposed, frost-bites and all, and even drove with bare hands, without the least discomfort. But of the scenery we saw this day, I can give no description. There was nothing but long drifts and waves of spotless snow, some dim, dark, spectral fir-trees on either hand, and beyond that a wild chaos of storm. The snow came fast and blinding, beating full in our teeth. It was impossible to see; the fine particles so stung our eyeballs, that we could not look ahead. My eyelashes were loaded with snow, which immediately turned to ice and froze the lids together, unless I kept them in constant motion. The storm hummed and buzzed through the black forests; we were all alone on the road, or even the pious Swedes would not turn out to church on such a day. It was terribly sublime and desolate, and I enjoyed it amazingly. We kept warm, although there was a crust of ice a quarter of an inch thick on our cheeks, and the ice in our beards prevented us from opening our mouths. At one o'clock, we reached the second station, Gefre, unrecognisable by our nearest friends. Our eyelashes were weighed down with heavy fringes of frozen snow, there were icicles an inch long hanging to the eaves of our moustaches, and the handkerchiefs which wrapped our faces were frozen fast to the flesh. The skin was rather improved by this treatment, but it took us a great while to thaw out.

At Gefre, we got some salt meat and hot milk, and then started on our long stage of fifteen miles to Piteå. The wind had moderated somewhat, but the snow still fell fast and thick. We were again blinded and frozen up more firmly than ever, cheeks and all, so that our eyes and lips were the only features to be seen. After plunging along for more than two hours through dreary woods, we came upon the estuary of the Piteå River, where our course was marked out by young fir-trees, planted in the ice. The world became a blank; there was snow around, above and below, and but for these marks a man might have driven at random until he froze. For three miles or more, we rode over the solid gulf, and then took the woods on the opposite shore. The way seemed almost endless. Our feet grew painfully cold, our eyes smarted from the beating of the fine snow, and my swollen jaw tortured me incessantly. Finally lights appeared ahead through the darkness, but another half hour elapsed before we saw houses on both sides of us. There was a street, at last, then a large mansion, and to our great joy the skjutsbonde turned into the courtyard of an inn.

CHAPTER VI. JOURNEY FROM PITEÅ TO HAPARANDA.

My jaw was so painful on reaching Piteå, that I tossed about in torment the whole night, utterly unable to sleep. The long northern night seemed as if it would never come to an end, and I arose in the morning much more fatigued and exhausted than when I lay down. It was 6° below zero, and the storm still blowing, but the cold seemed to relieve my face a little, and so we set out. The roads were heavy, but a little broken, and still led over hills and through interminable forests of mingled fir and pine, in the dark, imperfect day. I took but little note of the scenery, but was so drowsy and overcome, that Braisted at last filled the long baggage-sled with hay, and sat at the rear, so that I could lie stretched out, with my head upon his lap. Here, in spite of the cold and wind, I lay in a warm, stupid half-sleep.

It was dark when we reached Ersnäs, whence we had twelve miles to Old Luleå, with tired horses, heavy roads, and a lazy driver. I lay down again, dozed as usual, and tried to forget my torments. So passed three hours; the night had long set in, with a clear sky, 13° below zero, and a sharp wind blowing. All at once an exclamation from Braisted aroused me. I opened my eyes, as I lay in his lap, looked upward, and saw a narrow belt or scarf of silver fire stretching directly across the zenith, with its loose, frayed ends slowly swaying to and fro down the slopes of the sky. Presently it began to waver, bending back and forth, sometimes slowly, sometimes with a quick, springing motion, as if testing its elasticity. Now it took the shape of a bow, now undulated into Hogarth's line of beauty, brightening and fading in its sinuous motion, and finally formed a shepherd's crook, the end of which suddenly began to separate and fall off, as if driven by a strong wind, until the whole belt shot away in long, drifting lines of fiery snow. It then gathered again into a dozen dancing fragments, which alternately advanced and retreated, shot hither and thither, against and across each other, blazed out in yellow and rosy gleams or paled again, playing a thousand fantastic pranks, as if guided by some wild whim.

We lay silent, with upturned faces, watching this wonderful spectacle.

Suddenly, the scattered lights ran together, as by a common impulse, joined their bright ends, twisted them through each other, and fell in a broad, luminous curtain straight downward through the air until its fringed hem swung apparently but a few yards over our heads. This phenomenon was so unexpected and startling, that for a moment I thought our faces would be touched by the skirts of the glorious auroral drapery. It did not follow the spheric curve of the firmament, but hung plumb from the zenith, falling, apparently, millions of leagues through the air, its folds gathered together among the stars and its embroidery of flame sweeping the earth and shedding a pale, unearthly radiance over the wastes of snow. A moment afterwards and it was again drawn up, parted, waved its flambeaux and shot its lances hither and thither, advancing and retreating as before. Anything so strange, so capricious, so wonderful, so gloriously beautiful, I scarcely hope to see again.

By this time we came upon the broad Luleå River, and were half an hour traversing its frozen surface, still watching the snow above us, which gradually became fainter and less active. Finally we reached the opposite shore, drove up a long slope, through a large village of stables, and past the imposing church of Old Luleå to the inn. It was now nearly eight o'clock, very cold, and I was thoroughly exhausted. But the inn was already full of travellers, and there was no place to lay our heads. The landlord, a sublimely indifferent Swede, coolly advised us to go on to Persö, ten miles distant. I told him I had not slept for two nights, but he merely shrugged his shoulders, repeated his advice, and offered to furnish horses at once, to get us off. It was a long, cold, dreary ride, and I was in a state of semi-consciousness the whole time. We reached Persö about eleven, found the house full of travellers, but procured two small beds in a small room with another man in it, and went to sleep without supper. I was so thoroughly worn out that I got about three hours' rest, in spite of my pain.

We took coffee in bed at seven, and started for Rånbyn, on the Råneå River. The day was lowering, temperature 8-1/2° below zero. The country was low, slightly undulating with occasional wide views to the north, over the inlets of the gulf, and vast wide tracts of forest. The settlements were still as frequent as ever, but there was little apparent cultivation, except flax. Rånbyn is a large village, with a stately church. The people were putting up booths for a fair (a fair in the open air, in lat. 65° N., with the mercury freezing!), which explained the increased travel on the road. We kept on to Hvitå for breakfast, thus getting north of the latitude of Torneå; thence our road turned eastward at right angles around the head of the Bothnian Gulf. Much snow had fallen, but the road had been ploughed, and we had a tolerable track, except when passing sleds, which sometimes gave us an overturn.

We now had uninterrupted forest scenery between the stations—and such scenery! It is almost impossible to paint the glory of those winter forests. Every tree, laden with the purest snow, resembles a Gothic fountain of bronze, covered with frozen spray, through which only suggestive glimpses of its delicate tracery can be obtained. From every rise we looked over thousands of such mimic fountains, shooting, low or high, from their pavements of ivory and alabaster. It was an enchanted wilderness—white, silent, gleaming, and filled with inexhaustible forms of beauty. To what shall I liken those glimpses under the boughs, into the depths of the forest, where the snow destroyed all perspective, and brought the remotest fairy nooks and coverts, too lovely and fragile to seem cold, into the glittering foreground? "Wonderful! Glorious!" I could only exclaim, in breathless admiration. Once, by the roadside, we saw an Arctic ptarmigan, as white as the snow, with ruby eyes that sparkled like jewels as he moved slowly and silently along, not frightened in the least.

The sun set a little after one o'clock, and we pushed on to reach the Kalix River the same evening. At the last station we got a boy postilion and two lazy horses, and were three hours and a half on the road, with a temperature of 20° below zero. My feet became like ice, which increased the pain in my face, and I began to feel faint and sick with so much suffering and loss of rest. The boy aggravated us so much by his laziness, that Braisted ran ahead and cuffed his ears, after which he made better speed. After a drive through interminable woods, we came upon the banks of the Kalix, which were steep and fringed with splendid firs. Then came the village of Månsbyn, where, thank Heaven, we got something to eat, a warm room, and a bed.

While we were at supper, two travellers arrived, one of whom, a well-made, richly-dressed young fellow, was ushered into our room. He was a bruk-patron (iron-master), so the servant informed us, and from his superfine broad-cloth, rings, and the immense anchor-chain which attached him to his watch, appeared to be doing a thriving business. He had the Norse bloom on his face, a dignified nose, and English whiskers flanking his smoothly-shaven chin. His air was flushed and happy; he was not exactly drunk, but comfortably within that gay and cheerful vestibule beyond which lies the chamber of horrors. He listened to our conversation for some time, and finally addressed me in imperfect English. This led to mutual communications, and a declaration of our character, and object in travel—nothing of which would he believe. "Nobody can possibly come here for pleasure," said he; "I know better; you have a secret political mission." Our amusement at this only strengthened him in his suspicions. Nevertheless he called for a bottle of port wine, which, when it came, turned out to be bad Malaga, and insisted on drinking a welcome. "You are in latitude 66° north," said he; "on the Kalix, where no American has ever been before, and I shall call my friend to give a skål to your country. We have been to the church, where my friend is stationed."

With that he went out, and soon returned with a short, stout, broad faced, large-headed man of forty or thereabouts. His manner was perfectly well-bred and self-possessed, and I took him to be a clergyman, especially as the iron-master addressed him as "Brother Horton." "Now," said he, "welcome to 66° north, and prosperity to free America! Are you for Buchanan or Fremont?" Brother Horton kept a watchful eye upon his young friend, but cheerfully joined in the sentiment. I gave in return: "Skål to Sweden and the Swedish people," and hoped to get rid of our jolly acquaintance; but he was not to be shaken off. "You don't know me," he said; "and I don't know you—but you are something more than you seem to be: you are a political character." Just then Braisted came in with the thermometer, and announced 24° of cold (Reaumur). "Thousand devils!" exclaimed Brother Horton (and now I was convinced that he was not a clergyman), "what a thermometer! How cold it makes the weather! Would you part with it if I were to give you money in return?" I declined, stating that it was impossible for us to procure so cold a thermometer in the north, and we wanted to have as low a temperature as could be obtained.

56

This seemed to puzzle the iron-master, who studied awhile upon it, and then returned to the subject of my political mission. "I suppose you speak French," said he; "it is necessary in diplomacy. I can speak it also"—which he began to do, in a bungling way. I answered in the same language, but he soon gave up the attempt and tried German. I changed also, and, finding that he had exhausted his philology, of which he was rather proud, especially as Brother Horton knew nothing but Swedish, determined to have a little fun. "Of course you know Italian," said I; "it is more musical than German," and forthwith addressed him in that language. He reluctantly confessed his ignorance. "Oh, well," I continued, "Spanish is equally agreeable to me;" and took up that tongue before he could reply. His face grew more and more blank and bewildered. "The Oriental languages are doubtless familiar to you;" I persisted, "I have had no practice in Arabic for some time," and overwhelmed him with Egyptian salutations. I then tried him with Hindustanee, which exhausted my stock, but concluded by giving him the choice of Malay, Tartar, or Thibetan. "Come, come," said Brother Horton, taking his arm as he stood staring and perplexed—"the horses are ready." With some difficulty he was persuaded to leave, after shaking hands with us, and exclaiming, many times, "You are a very seldom man!"

When we awoke, the temperature had risen to 2° above zero, with a tremendous snow-storm blowing. As we were preparing to set out, a covered sled drove in from the north, with two Swedish naval officers, whose vessel had been frozen in at Cronstadt, and who had been obliged to return home through Finland, up the eastern coast of the Bothnian Gulf. The captain, who spoke excellent English, informed me that they were in about the same latitude as we, on Christmas day, on the opposite side of the gulf, and had experienced the same degree of cold. Both of them had their noses severely frozen. We were two hours and a half in travelling to the first station, seven miles, as the snow was falling in blinding quantities, and the road was not yet ploughed out. All the pedestrians we met were on runners, but even with their snow skates, five feet long, they sank deep enough to make their progress very slow and toilsome.

By the time we reached Näsby my face was very much swollen and inflamed, and as it was impossible to make the next stage by daylight, we wisely determined to stop there. The wind blew a hurricane, the hard snow-crystals lashed the windows and made a gray chaos of all out-of-doors, but we had a warm, cosy, carpeted room within, a capital dinner in the afternoon, and a bottle of genuine London porter with our evening pipe. So we passed the last day of A. D. 1856, grateful to God for all the blessings which the year had brought us, and for the comfort and shelter we enjoyed, in that Polar wilderness of storm and snow.

On New Year's morning it blew less, and the temperature was comparatively mild, so, although the road was very heavy, we started again. Näsby is the last Swedish station, the Finnish frontier, which is an abrupt separation of races and tongues, being at the north-western corner of the Bothnian Gulf. In spite of the constant intercourse which now exists between Norrland and the narrow strip of Finnish soil which remains to Sweden, there has been no perceptible assimilation of the two races. At Näsby, all is pure Swedish; at Sängis, twelve miles distant, everything is Finnish. The blue eyes and fair hair, the lengthened oval of the face, and slim, straight form disappear. You see, instead, square faces, dark eyes, low foreheads, and something of an Oriental fire and warmth in the movements. The language is totally dissimilar, and even the costume, though of the same general fashion, presents many noticeable points of difference. The women wear handkerchiefs of some bright color bound over the forehead and under the chin, very similar to those worn by the Armenian women in Asia Minor. On first coming among them, the Finns impressed me as a less frank and open hearted, but more original and picturesque, race than the Swedes. It is exceedingly curious and interesting to find such a flavour of the Orient on the borders of the Frigid Zone.

The roads were very bad, and our drivers and horses provokingly slow, but we determined to push on to Haparanda the same night. I needed rest and medical aid, my jaw by this time being so swollen that I had great difficulty in eating—a state of things which threatened to diminish my supply of fuel, and render me sensitive to the cold. We reached Nickala, the last station, at seven o'clock. Beyond this, the road was frightfully deep in places. We could scarcely make any headway, and were frequently overturned headlong into the drifts. The driver was a Finn, who did not understand a word of Swedish, and all our urging was of no avail. We went on and on, in the moonlight, over arms of the gulf, through forests, and then over ice again—a flat, monotonous country, with the same dull features repeated again and again. At half-past nine, a large white church announced our approach to Haparanda, and soon afterwards we drove up to the inn, which was full of New-Year carousers. The landlord gave us quarters in the same room with an old Norrlander, who was very drunk, and annoyed us not a little until we got into bed and pretended to sleep. It was pretence nearly the whole night, on my part, for my torture was still kept up. The next morning I called upon Dr. Wretholm, the physician of the place,—not without some misgivings,—but his prescription of a poultice of mallow leaves, a sudorific and an opiate, restored my confidence, and I cheerfully resigned myself to a rest of two or three days, before proceeding further northward.

CHAPTER VII. CROSSING THE ARCTIC CIRCLE.

I was obliged to remain three days in Haparanda, applying poultices, gargles, and liniments, according to the doctor's instructions. As my Swedish was scarcely sufficient for the comprehension of prescriptions, or medical technicalities in general, a written programme of my treatment was furnished to Fredrika, the servant-maid, who was properly impressed with the responsibility thereby devolving upon her. Fredrika, no doubt, thought that my life was in her hands, and nothing could exceed the energy with which she undertook its preservation. Punctually to the minute appeared the prescribed application, and, if she perceived or suspected any dereliction on my part, it was sure to be reported to the doctor at his next visit. I had the taste of camomile and mallows in my mouth from morning till night; the skin of my jaw blistered under the scorching of ammonia; but the final result was, that I was cured, as the doctor and Fredrika had determined.

This good-hearted girl was a genuine specimen of the Northern Swedish female. Of medium height, plump, but not stout, with a rather slender waist and expansive hips, and a foot which stepped firmly and nimbly at the same time, she was as cheerful a body as one could wish to see. Her hair was of that silky blonde so common in Sweden; her eyes a clear, pale blue, her nose straight and well formed, her cheeks of the delicate pink of a wild-rose leaf, and her teeth so white, regular and perfect that I am sure they would make her fortune in America. Always cheerful, kind and active, she had, nevertheless, a hard life of it: she was alike cook, chambermaid, and hostler, and had a cross mistress to boot. She made our fires in the morning darkness, and brought us our early coffee while we yet lay in bed, in accordance with the luxurious habits of the Arctic zone. Then, until the last drunken guest was silent, towards midnight, there was no respite from labour. Although suffering from a distressing cough, she had the out-door as well as the in-door duties to discharge, and we saw her in a sheepskin jacket harnessing horses, in a temperature 30° below zero. The reward of such a service was possibly about eight American dollars a year. When, on leaving, I gave her about as much as one of our hotel servants would expect for answering a question, the poor girl was overwhelmed with gratitude, and even the stern landlady was so impressed by my generosity that she insisted on lending us a sheepskin for our feet, saying we were "good men."

There is something exceedingly primitive and unsophisticated in the manners of these Northern people—a straight-forward honesty, which takes the honesty of others for granted—a latent kindness and good-will which may at first be overlooked, because it is not demonstrative, and a total unconsciousness of what is called, in highly civilised circles, "propriety." The very freedom of manners which, in some countries, might denote laxity of morals, is here the evident stamp of their purity. The thought has often recurred to me—which is the most truly pure and virginal nature, the fastidious American girl, who blushes at the sight of a pair of boots outside a gentleman's bedroom door, and who requires that certain unoffending parts of the body and articles of clothing should be designated by delicately circumlocutious terms, or the simple-minded Swedish women, who come into our bedrooms with coffee, and make our fires while we get up and dress, coming and going during all the various stages of the toilet, with the frankest unconsciousness of impropriety? This is modesty in its healthy and natural development, not in those morbid forms which suggest an imagination ever on the alert for prurient images. Nothing has confirmed my impression of the virtue of the Northern Swedes more than this fact, and I have rarely felt more respect for woman or more faith in the inherent purity of her nature.

We had snug quarters in Haparanda, and our detention was therefore by no means irksome. A large room, carpeted, protected from the outer cold by double windows, and heated by an immense Russian stove, was allotted to us. We had two beds, one of which became a broad sofa during the day, a backgammon table, the ordinary appliances for washing, and, besides a number of engravings on the walls, our window commanded a full view of Torneå, and the ice-track across the river, where hundreds of persons daily passed to and fro. The eastern window showed us the Arctic dawn, growing and brightening through its wonderful gradations of color, for four hours, when the pale orange sun appeared above the distant houses, to slide along their roofs for two hours, and then dip again. We had plentiful meals, consisting mostly of reindeer meat, with a sauce of Swedish cranberries, potatoes, which had been frozen, but were still palatable, salmon roes, soft bread in addition to the black shingles of fladbröd, English porter, and excellent Umeå beer. In fact, in no country inn of the United States could we have been more comfortable. For the best which the place afforded, during four days, with a small provision for the journey, we paid about seven dollars.

The day before our departure, I endeavored to obtain some information concerning the road to Lapland, but was disappointed. The landlord ascertained that there were skjuts, or relays of post-horses, as far as Muonioniska, 210 English miles, but beyond this I could only learn that the people were all Finnish, spoke no Swedish, were miserably poor, and could give us nothing to eat. I was told that a certain official personage at the apothecary's shop spoke German, and hastened thither; but the official, a dark-eyed, olive-faced Finn, could not understand my first question. The people even seemed entirely ignorant of the geography of the country beyond Upper Torneå, or Matarengi, forty miles off. The doctor's wife, a buxom, motherly lady, who seemed to feel quite an interest in our undertaking, and was as kind and obliging as such women always are, procured for us a supply of fladbröd made of rye, and delightfully crisp and hard—and this was the substance of our preparations. Reindeer mittens were not to be found, nor a reindeer skin to cover our feet, so we relied, as before, on plenty of hay and my Scotch plaid. We might, perhaps, have had better success in Torneå, but I knew no one there who would be likely to assist us, and we did not even visit the old place. We had taken the precaution of getting the Russian visé, together with a small stock of roubles, at Stockholm, but found that it was quite unnecessary. No passport is required for entering Torneå, or travelling on the Russian side of the frontier.

Trusting to luck, which is about the best plan after all, we started from Haparanda at noon, on the 5th of January. The day was magnificent, the sky cloudless, and resplendent as polished steel, and the mercury 31° below zero. The sun, scarcely more than the breadth of his disc above the horizon, shed a faint orange light over the broad, level snow-plains, and the bluish-white hemisphere of the Bothnian Gulf, visible beyond Torneå. The air was perfectly still, and exquisitely cold and bracing, despite the sharp grip it took upon my nose and ears. These Arctic days, short as they are, have a majesty of their own—a splendor, subdued though it be; a breadth and permanence of hue, imparted alike to the sky and to the snowy earth, as if tinted glass was held before your eyes. I find myself at a loss how to describe these effects, or the impression they produce upon the traveller's mood. Certainly, it is the very reverse of that depression which accompanies the Polar night, and which even the absence of any real daylight might be considered sufficient to produce.

Our road was well beaten, but narrow, and we had great difficulty in passing the many hay and wood teams which met us, on account of the depth of the loose snow on either side. We had several violent overturns at such times, one of which occasioned us the loss of our beloved pipe—a loss which rendered Braisted disconsolate for the rest of the day. We had but one between us, and the bereavement was not slight. Soon after leaving Haparanda, we passed a small white obelisk, with the words "Russian Frontier" upon it. The town of Torneå, across the frozen river, looked really imposing, with the sharp roof and tall spire of its old church rising above the line of low red buildings. Campbell, I remember, says,

"Cold as the rocks on Torneo's hoary brow,"

with the same disregard of geography which makes him grow palm trees along the Susquehanna River. There was Torneå; but I looked in vain for the "hoary brow." Not a hill within sight, nor a rock within a circuit of ten miles, but one unvarying level, like the western shore of the Adriatic, formed by the deposits of the rivers and the retrocession of the sea.

Our road led up the left bank of the river, both sides of which were studded with neat little villages. The country was well cleared and cultivated, and appeared so populous and flourishing that I could scarcely realise in what part of the world we were. The sun set at a quarter past one, but for two hours the whole southern heaven was superb in its hues of rose and orange. The sheepskin lent us by our landlady kept our feet warm, and we only felt the cold in our faces; my nose, especially, which, having lost a coat of skin, was very fresh and tender, requiring unusual care. At three o'clock, when we reached Kuckula, the first station, the northern sky was one broad flush of the purest violet, melting into lilac at the zenith, where it met the fiery skirts of sunset.

We refreshed ourselves with hot milk, and pushed ahead, with better horses. At four o'clock it was bright moonlight, with the stillest air. We got on bravely over the level, beaten road, and in two hours reached Korpikylä, a large new inn, where we found very tolerable accommodations. Our beds were heaps of reindeer skins; a frightfully ugly Finnish girl, who knew a few words of Swedish, prepared us a supper of tough meat, potatoes, and ale. Everything was now pure Finnish, and the first question of the girl, "Hvarifrån kommar du?" (Where dost thou come from?) showed an ignorance of the commonest Swedish form of address. She awoke us with a cup of coffee in the morning, and negotiated for us the purchase of a reindeer skin, which we procured for something less than a dollar. The hus-bonde (house-peasant, as the landlord is called here) made no charge for our entertainment, but said we might give what we pleased. I offered, at a venture, a sum equal to about fifty cents, whereupon he sent the girl to say that he thanked us most heartily.

The next day was a day to be remembered: such a glory of twilight splendors for six full hours was beyond all the charms of daylight in any zone. We started at seven, with a temperature of 20° below zero, still keeping up the left bank of the Torneå. The country now rose into bold hills, and the features of the scenery became broad and majestic. The northern sky was again pure violet, and a pale red tinge from the dawn rested on the tops of the snowy hills. The prevailing color of the sky slowly brightened into lilac, then into pink, then rose color, which again gave way to a flood of splendid orange when the sun appeared. Every change of color affected the tone of the landscape. The woods, so wrapped in snow that not a single green needle was to be seen, took by turns the hues of the sky, and seemed to give out, rather than to reflect, the opalescent lustre of the morning. The sunshine brightened instead of dispelling these effects. At noon the sun's disc was not more than 1° above the horizon, throwing a level golden light on the hills. The north, before us, was as blue as the Mediterranean, and the vault of heaven, overhead, canopied us with pink. Every object was glorified and transfigured in the magic glow.

At the first station we got some hot milk, with raw salmon, shingle bread and frozen butter. Our horses were good, and we drove merrily along, up the frozen Torneå. The roads were filled with people going to church, probably to celebrate some religious anniversary. Fresh ruddy faces had they, firm features, strong frames and resolute carriage, but the most of them were positively ugly, and, by contrast with the frank Swedes, their expression was furtive and sinister. Near Päckilä we passed a fine old church of red brick, with a very handsome belfry. At Niemis we changed horses in ten minutes, and hastened on up the bed of the Torneå to Matarengi, where we should reach the Arctic Circle. The hills rose higher, with fine sweeping outlines, and the river was still half a mile broad—a plain of solid snow, with the track marked out by bushes. We kept a sharp look-out for the mountain of Avasaxa, one of the stations of Celsius, Maupertius, and the French Academicians, who came here in 1736, to make observations determining the exact form of the earth. Through this mountain, it is said, the Arctic Circle passes, though our maps were neither sufficiently minute nor correct to determine the point. We took it for granted, however, as a mile one way or the other could make but little difference; and as Matarengi lies due west of Avasaxa, across the river, we decided to stop there and take dinner on the Arctic Circle.

The increase of villages on both banks, with the appearance of a large church, denoted our approach to Matarengi, and we saw at once that the tall, gently-rounded, isolated hill opposite, now blazing with golden snow, could be none other than Avasaxa. Here we were, at last, entering the Arctic Zone, in the dead of winter—the realization of a dream which had often flashed across my mind, when lounging under the tropical palms; so natural is it for one extreme to suggest the opposite. I took our bearings with a compass-ring, as we drove forward, and as the summit of Avasaxa bore due east we both gave a shout which startled our postilion and notably quickened the gait of our horses. It was impossible to toss our caps, for they were not only tied upon our heads, but frozen fast to our beards. So here we were at last, in the true dominions of Winter. A mild ruler he had been to us, thus far, but he proved a despot before we were done with him.

Soon afterwards, we drove into the inn at Matarengi, which was full of country people, who had come to attend church. The landlord, a sallow, watery-eyed Finn, who knew a few words of Swedish, gave us a room in an adjoining house, and furnished a dinner of boiled fish and barley mush, to which was added a bottle labelled "Dry Madeira," brought from Haparanda for the occasion. At a shop adjoining, Braisted found a serviceable pipe, so that nothing was wanting to complete our jubilee. We swallowed the memory of all who were dear to us, in the dubious beverage, inaugurated our Arctic pipe, which we proposed to take home as a souvenir of the place, and set forward in the most cheery mood.

Our road now crossed the river and kept up the Russian side to a place with the charming name of Torakankorwa. The afternoon twilight was even more wonderful than that of the forenoon. There were broad bands of purple, pure crimson, and intense yellow, all fusing together into fiery orange at the south, while the north became a semi-vault of pink, then lilac, and then the softest violet. The dazzling Arctic hills participated in this play of colors, which did not fade, as in the South, but stayed, and stayed, as if God wished to compensate by this twilight glory for the loss of the day. Nothing in Italy, nothing in the Tropics, equals the magnificence of the Polar skies. The twilight gave place to a moonlight scarcely less brilliant. Our road was hardly broken, leading through deep snow, sometimes on the river, sometimes through close little glens, hedged in with firs drooping with snow—fairy Arctic solitudes, white, silent and mysterious.

By seven o'clock we reached a station called Juoxengi. The place was wholly Finnish, and the landlord, who did not understand a word of Swedish, endeavoured to make us go on to the next station. We pointed to the beds and quietly carried in our baggage. I made the usual signs for eating, which speedily procured us a pail of sour milk, bread and butter, and two immense tin drinking horns of sweet milk. The people seemed a little afraid of us, and kept away. Our postilion was a silly fellow, who could not understand whether his money was correct. In the course of our stenographic conversation, I learned that "cax" signified two. When I gave him his drink-money he said "ketox!" and on going out the door, "hüweste!"—so that I at least discovered the Finnish for "Thank you!" and "Good-bye!" This, however, was not sufficient to order horses the next morning. We were likewise in a state of delightful uncertainty as to our future progress, but this very uncertainty gave a zest to our situation, and it would have been difficult to find two jollier men with frozen noses.

CHAPTER VIII. ADVENTURES AMONG THE FINNS.

We drank so much milk (for want of more solid food) at Juoxengi, that in spite of sound sleep under our sheepskin blankets, we both awoke with headaches in the morning. The Finnish landlord gave me to understand, by holding up his fore-finger, and pronouncing the word "üx," that I was to pay one rigsdaler (about 26 cents), for our entertainment, and was overcome with grateful surprise when I added a trifle more. We got underway by six o'clock, when the night was just at its darkest, and it was next to impossible to discern any track on the spotless snow. Trusting to good luck to escape overturning, we followed in the wake of the skjutsbonde, who had mounted our baggage sled upon one of the country sledges, and rode perched upon his lofty seat. Our horses were tolerable, but we had eighteen miles to Pello, the next station, which we reached about ten o'clock.

Our road was mostly upon the Torneå River, sometimes taking to the woods on either side, to cut off bends. The morn was hours in dawning, with the same splendid transitions of colour. The forests were indescribable in their silence, whiteness, and wonderful variety of snowy adornment. The weeping birches leaned over the road, and formed white fringed arches; the firs wore mantles of ermine, and ruffs and tippets of the softest swan's down. Snow, wind, and frost had worked the most marvellous transformations in the forms of the forest. Here were kneeling nuns, with their arms hanging listlessly by their sides, and the white cowls falling over their faces; there lay a warrior's helmet; lace curtains, torn and ragged, hung from the points of little Gothic spires; caverns, lined with sparry incrustations, silver palm-leaves, doors, loop-holes, arches and arcades were thrown together in a fantastic confusion and mingled with the more decided forms of the larger trees, which, even, were trees but in form, so completely were they wrapped in their dazzling disguise. It was an enchanted land, where you hardly dared to breathe, lest a breath might break the spell.

There was still little change in the features of the country, except that it became wilder and more rugged, and the settlements poorer and further apart. There were low hills on either side, wildernesses of birch and fir, and floors of level snow over the rivers and marshes. On approaching Pello, we saw our first reindeer, standing beside a hut. He was a large, handsome animal; his master, who wore a fur dress, we of course set down for a Lapp. At the inn a skinny old hag, who knew a dozen words of Swedish, got us some bread, milk, and raw frozen salmon, which, with the aid of a great deal of butter, sufficed us for a meal. Our next stage was to Kardis, sixteen miles, which we made in four hours. While in the midst of a forest on the Swedish side, we fell in with a herd of reindeer, attended by half-a-dozen Lapps. They came tramping along through the snow, about fifty in number, including a dozen which ran loose. The others were harnessed to pulks, the canoe-shaped reindeer sledges, many of which were filled with stores and baggage. The Lapps were rather good-looking young fellows, with a bright, coppery, orange complexion, and were by no means so ill-favoured, short, and stunted as I had imagined. One of them was, indeed, really handsome, with his laughing eyes, sparkling teeth, and a slender, black moustache.

We were obliged to wait a quarter-of-an-hour while the herd passed, and then took to the river again. The effect of sunset on the snow was marvellous—the spotless mounds and drifts, far and near, being stained with soft rose colour, until they resembled nothing so much as heaps of strawberry ice. At Kardis the people sent for an interpreter, who was a young man, entirely blind. He helped us to get our horses, although we were detained an hour, as only one horse is kept in readiness at these stations, and the neighbourhood must be scoured to procure another. I employed the time in learning a few Finnish words—the whole travelling-stock, in fact, on which I made the journey to Muonioniska. That the reader may see how few words of a strange language will enable him to travel, as well as to give a sample of Finnish, I herewith copy my whole vocabulary:

one	üx
two	cax
three	kolma

four	nelia
five	viis
six	oos
seven	settima
eight	kahexa
nine	öhexa
ten	kiumene
a half	puoli
horses	hevorste
immediately	varsin
ready	walmis
drive on!	ayò perli!
how much?	guinga palia
a mile	peligorma
bread	leba
meat	liha
milk	maito
butter	voy
fire	valkär
a bed	sängu (Swedish)
good	hüva
bad	páhá

We kept on our way up the river, in the brilliant afternoon moonlight. The horses were slow; so were the two skjutsbonder, to whom I cried in vain: "Ayò perli!" Braisted with difficulty restrained his inclination to cuff their ears. Hour after hour went by, and we grew more and more hungry, wrathful and impatient. About eight o'clock they stopped below a house on the Russian side, pitched some hay to the horses, climbed the bank, and summoned us to follow. We made our way with some difficulty through the snow, and entered the hut, which proved to be the abode of a cooper—at least the occupant, a rough, shaggy, dirty Orson of a fellow, was seated upon the floor, making a tub, by the light of the fire. The joists overhead were piled with seasoned wood, and long bundles of thin, dry fir, which is used for torches during the winter darkness. There was neither chair nor table in the hut; but a low bench ran around the walls, and a rough bedstead was built against one corner. Two buckets of sour milk, with a wooden ladle, stood beside the door. This beverage appears to be generally used by the Finns for quenching thirst, instead of water. Our postilions were sitting silently upon the bench, and we followed their example, lit our pipes, and puffed away, while the cooper, after the first glance, went on with his work; and the other members of his family, clustered together in the dusky corner behind the fireplace, were equally silent. Half an hour passed, and the spirit moved no one to open his mouth. I judged at last that the horses had been baited sufficiently, silently showed my watch to the postilions, who, with ourselves, got up and went away without a word having been said to mar the quaint drollery of the incident.

While at Haparanda, we had been recommended to stop at Kingis Bruk, at the junction of the Torneå and Muonio. "There," we were told, "you can get everything you want: there is a fine house, good beds, and plenty to eat and drink." Our blind interpreter at Kardis repeated this advice. "Don't go on to Kexisvara;" (the next station) said he, "stop at Kengis, where everything is good." Toward Kengis, then, this oasis in the arctic desolation, our souls yearned. We drove on until ten o'clock in the brilliant moonlight and mild, delicious air—for the temperature had actually risen to 25° above zero!—before a break in the hills announced the junction of the two rivers. There was a large house on the top of a hill on our left, and, to our great joy, the postilions drove directly up to it. "Is this Kengis?" I asked, but their answers I could not understand, and they had already unharnessed their horses.

There was a light in the house, and we caught a glimpse of a woman's face at the window, as we drove up. But the light was immediately extinguished, and everything became silent. I knocked at the door, which was partly open, but no one came. I then pushed: a heavy log of wood, which was leaning against it from the inside, fell with a noise which reverberated through the house. I waited awhile, and then, groping my way along a passage to the door of the room which had been lighted, knocked loudly. After a little delay, the door was opened by a young man, who ushered me into a warm, comfortable room, and then quietly stared at me, as if to ask what I wanted. "We are travellers and strangers," said I, "and wish to stop for the night." "This is not an inn," he answered; "it is the residence of the patron of the iron works." I may here remark that it is the general custom in Sweden, in remote districts, for travellers to call without ceremony upon the parson, magistrate, or any other prominent man in a village, and claim his hospitality. In spite of this doubtful reception, considering that our horses were already stabled and the station three or four miles further, I remarked again: "But perhaps we may be allowed to remain here until morning?" "I will ask," he replied, left the room, and soon returned with an affirmative answer.

We had a large, handsomely furnished room, with a sofa and curtained bed, into which we tumbled as soon as the servant-girl, in compliance with a hint of mine, had brought up some bread, milk, and cheese. We had a cup of coffee in the morning, and were preparing to leave when the patron appeared. He was a short, stout, intelligent Swede, who greeted us courteously, and after a little conversation, urged us to stay until after breakfast. We were too hungry to need much persuasion, and indeed the table set with tjäde, or capercailie (one of the finest game birds in the world), potatoes, cranberries, and whipped cream, accompanied with excellent Umeå ale, and concluded with coffee, surpassed anything we had sat down to for many a day. The patron gave me considerable information about the country, and quieted a little anxiety I was beginning to feel, by assuring me that we should find post-horses all the way to Muonioniska, still ninety-five miles distant. He informed me that we had already got beyond the daylight, as the sun had not yet risen at Kengis. This, however, was in consequence of a hill to the southward, as we afterwards found that the sun was again above the horizon.

We laid in fuel enough to last us through the day, and then took leave of our host, who invited us to visit him on our return. Crossing the Torneå, an hour's drive over the hills brought us to the village of Kexisvara, where we were obliged to wait some time for our horses. At the inn there was a well forty feet deep, with the longest sweep-pole I ever saw. The landlady and her two sisters were pleasant bodies, and sociably inclined, if we could have talked to them. They were all spinning tow, their wheels purring like pleased lionesses. The sun's disc came in sight at a quarter past eleven, and at noon his lower limb just touched the horizon. The sky was of a splendid saffron hue, which changed into a burning brassy yellow.

Our horses promised little for speed when we set out, and their harness being ill adapted to our sleds increased the difficulty. Instead of hames there were wide wooden yokes, the ends of which passed through mortices in the ends of the shafts, and were fastened with pins, while, as there was no belly-bands, the yokes rose on going down hill, bringing our sleds upon the horses' heels. The Finnish sleds have excessively long shafts, in order to prevent this. Our road all day was upon the Muonio River, the main branch of the Torneå, and the boundary between Sweden and Russia, above the junction. There had been a violent wind during the night, and the track was completely filled up. The Torneå and Muonio are both very swift rivers, abounding in dangerous rapids, but during the winter, rapids and all, they are solid as granite from their sources to the Bothnian Gulf. We plunged along slowly, hour after hour, more than half the time clinging to one side or the other, to prevent our sled from overturning—and yet it upset at least a dozen times during the day. The scenery was without change: low, black fir forests on either hand, with the decorative snow blown off them; no villages, or signs of life, except the deserted huts of the wood-cutters, nor did we meet but one sled during the whole day. Here and there, on the banks, were sharp, canoe-like boats, twenty or thirty feet long, turned bottom upward. The sky was overcast, shutting out the glorious coloring of the past days. The sun set before one o'clock, and the dull twilight deepened apace into night. Nothing could be more cheerless and dismal: we smoked and talked a little, with much silence between, and I began to think that one more such day would disgust me with the Arctic Zone.

It was four o'clock, and our horses were beginning to stagger, when we reached a little village called Jokijalka, on the Russian side. The postilion stopped at a house, or rather a quadrangle of huts, which he made me comprehend was an inn, adding that it was 4 polàn and 3 belikor (a fearfully unintelligible distance!) to the next one. We entered, and found promise

73

enough in the thin, sallow, sandy-haired, and most obsequious landlord, and a whole herd of rosy children, to decide us to stop. We were ushered into the milk-room, which was warm and carpeted, and had a single narrow bed. I employed my vocabulary with good effect, the quick-witted children helping me out, and in due time we got a supper of fried mutton, bread, butter, and hot milk. The children came in every few minutes to stare at our writing, an operation which they probably never saw before. They would stand in silent curiosity for half an hour at a time, then suddenly rush out, and enjoy a relief of shouts and laughter on the outside. Since leaving Matarengi we had been regarded at all the stations with much wonder, not always unmixed with mistrust. Whether this was simply a manifestation of the dislike which the Finns have for the Swedes, for whom they probably took us, or of other suspicions on their part, we could not decide.

After a time one of the neighbors, who had been sent for on account of his knowing a very few words of Swedish, was ushered into the room. Through him I ordered horses, and ascertained that the next station, Kihlangi, was three and a half Swedish miles distant, but there was a place on the Russian side, one mile off, where we could change horses. We had finished writing, and were sitting by the stove, consulting how we should arrange the bed so as to avoid contact with the dirty coverlet, when the man returned and told us we must go into another house. We crossed the yard to the opposite building, where, to our great surprise, we were ushered into a warm room, with two good beds, which had clean though coarse sheets, a table, looking-glass, and a bit of carpet on the floor. The whole male household congregated to see us take possession and ascertain whether our wants were supplied. I slept luxuriously until awakened by the sound of our landlord bringing in wood to light the fire. He no sooner saw that my eyes were open than he snatched off his cap and threw it upon the floor, moving about with as much awe and silence as if it were the Emperor's bedroom. His daughter brought us excellent coffee betimes. We washed our faces with our tumblers of drinking water, and got under way by half-past six.

The temperature had changed again in the night, being 28° below zero, but the sky was clear and the morning moonlight superb. By this time we were so far north that the moon did not set at all, but wheeled around the sky, sinking to within eight degrees of the horizon at noonday. Our road led across the river, past the church of Kolare, and through a stretch of the Swedish forests back to the river again. To our great surprise, the wind had not blown here, the snow still hung heavy on the trees, and the road was well beaten. At the Russian post-house we found only a woman with the usual troop of children, the eldest of whom, a boy of sixteen, was splitting fir to make torches. I called out "hevorste!" (horses), to which he made a deliberate answer, and went on with his work. After some consultation with the old woman, a younger boy was sent off somewhere, and we sat down to await the result. I called for meat, milk, bread, and butter, which procured us in course of time a pitcher of cold milk, some bread made of ground barley straw, horribly hard and tough, and a lump of sour frozen butter. There was some putrid fish in a wooden bowl, on which the family had breakfasted, while an immense pot of sour milk, butter, broken bread, and straw meal, hanging over the fire, contained their dinner. This was testimony enough to the accounts we had heard in Stockholm, of the year's famine in Finland; and we seemed likely to participate in it.

I chewed the straw bread vigorously for an hour, and succeeded in swallowing enough to fill my stomach, though not enough to satisfy my hunger. The younger children occupied themselves in peeling off the soft inner bark of the fir, which they ate ravenously. They were handsome, fair-skinned youngsters, but not so rosy and beautiful as those of the Norrland Swedes. We were obliged to wait more than two hours before the horses arrived, thus losing a large part of our daylight. The postilions fastened our sleds behind their own large sledges, with flat runners, which got through the snow more easily than ours. We lay down in the sledge, stretched ourselves at full length upon a bed of hay, covered our feet with the deerskin, and set off. We had gone about a Swedish mile when the postilions stopped to feed the horses before a house on the Russian side. There was nobody within, but some coals among the ashes on the hearth showed that it had been used, apparently, as a place of rest and shelter. A tall, powerful Finn, who was travelling alone, was there, smoking his pipe. We all sat down and did likewise, in the bare, dark hut. There were the three Finns, in complete dresses of reindeer skin, and ourselves, swaddled from head to foot, with only a small segment of scarlet face visible between our frosted furs and icy beards. It was a true Arctic picture, as seen by the pale dawn which glimmered on the wastes of snow outside.

We had a poor horse, which soon showed signs of breaking down, especially when we again entered a belt of country where the wind had blown, the trees were clear, and the track filled up. At half-past eleven we saw the light of the sun on the tops of the hills, and at noon about half his disc was visible. The cold was intense; my hands became so stiff and benumbed that I had great difficulty in preventing them from freezing, and my companion's feet almost lost all feeling. It was well for us that we were frequently obliged to walk, to aid the horse. The country was a wilderness of mournful and dismal scenery—low hills and woods, stripped bare of snow, the dark firs hung with black, crape-like moss, alternating with morasses. Our Finnish postilions were pleasant, cheerful fellows, who insisted on our riding when there was the least prospect of a road. Near a solitary hut (the only one on the road) we met a man driving a reindeer. After this we lost all signs of our way, except the almost obliterated track of his pulk. The snow was deeper than ever, and our horses were ready to drop at every step. We had been five hours on the road; the driver said Kihlangi was "üx verst" distant, and at three, finally, we arrived. We appreciated rather better what we had endured when we found that the temperature was 44° below zero.

I at once ordered horses, and a strapping young fellow was sent off in a bad humor to get them. We found it impossible, however, to procure milk or anything to eat, and as the cold was not to be borne else, we were obliged to resort to a bottle of cognac and our Haparanda bread. The old woman sat by the fire smoking, and gave not the least attention to our demands. I paid our postilions in Norwegian orts, which they laid upon a chair and counted, with the assistance of the whole family. After the reckoning was finished they asked me what the value of each piece was, which gave rise to a second general computation. There was, apparently, more than they had expected, for they both made me a formal address of thanks, and took my hand. Seeing that I had produced a good effect I repeated my demand for milk. The old woman refused, but the men interfered in my behalf; she went out and presently returned with a bowl full, which she heated for us. By this time our horses had arrived, and one of our new postilions prepared himself for the journey, by stripping to the loins and putting on a clean shirt. He was splendidly built, with clean, firm muscle, a white glossy skin, and no superfluity of flesh. He then donned a reindeer of pösk, leggings and boots, and we started again.

It was nearly five o'clock, and superb moonlight. This time they mounted our sleds upon their own sledges, so that we rode much higher than usual. Our way lay up the Muonio River: the track was entirely snowed up, and we had to break a new one, guided by the fir-trees stuck in the ice. The snow was full three feet deep, and whenever the sledge got a little off the old road, the runners cut in so that we could scarcely move. The milk and cognac had warmed us tolerably, and we did not suffer much from the intense cold. My nose, however, had been rubbed raw, and I was obliged to tie a handkerchief across my face to protect it.

While journeying along in this way, the sledge suddenly tilted over, and we were flung head foremost into the snow. Our drivers righted the sledge, we shook ourselves and got in again, but had not gone ten yards before the same thing happened again. This was no joke on such a night, but we took it good-humouredly, to the relief of the Finns, who seemed to expect a scolding. Very soon we went over a third time, and then a fourth, after which they kept near us and held on when there was any danger. I became very drowsy, and struggled with all my force to keep awake, for sleeping was too hazardous. Braisted kept his senses about him by singing, for our encouragement, the mariner's hymn:—

"Fear not, but trust in Providence,

Wherever thou may'st be."

Thus hour after hour passed away. Fortunately we had good, strong horses, which walked fast and steadily. The scenery was always the same— low, wooded hills on either side of the winding, snowy plain of the river. We had made up our minds not to reach Parkajoki before midnight, but at half-past ten our track left the river, mounted the Swedish bank, and very soon brought us to a quadrangle of low huts, having the appearance of an inn. I could scarcely believe my eyes when we stopped before the door. "Is this Parkajoki?" I asked. "Ja!" answered the postilion. Braisted and I sprang out instantly, hugged each other in delight, and rushed into the warm inn. The thermometer still showed -44°, and we prided ourselves a little on having travelled for seventeen hours in such a cold with so little food to keep up our animal heat. The landlord, a young man, with a bristly beard of three weeks' growth, showed us into the milk room, where there was a bed of reindeer skins. His wife brought us some fresh hay, a quilt and a sheepskin coverlet, and we soon forgot both our hunger and our frozen blood.

In the morning coffee was brought to us, and as nothing else was to be had, we drank four cups apiece. The landlord asked half a rigs (13 cents) for our entertainment, and was overcome with gratitude when I gave him double the sum. We had the same sledges as the previous night, but new postilions and excellent horses. The temperature had risen to 5° below zero, with a cloudy sky and a light snow falling. We got off at eight o'clock, found a track partly broken, and went on at a merry trot up the river. We took sometimes one bank and sometimes the other, until, after passing the rapid of Eyanpaika (which was frozen solid, although large masses of transparent ice lay piled like rocks on either side), we kept the Swedish bank. We were in excellent spirits, in the hope of reaching Muonioniska before dark, but the steady trot of our horses brought us out of the woods by noon, and we saw before us the long, scattering village, a mile or two distant, across the river. To our left, on a gentle slope, stood a red, two-story building, surrounded by out-houses, with a few humbler habitations in its vicinity. This was Muoniovara, on the Swedish side—the end of our Finnish journey.

CHAPTER IX. LIFE IN LAPLAND.

As we drove up to the red two-story house, a short man with dark whiskers and a commercial air came forward to meet us. I accosted him in Swedish, asking him whether the house was an inn. He replied in the negative, adding that the only inn was in Muonioniska, on the Russian side, a mile or more distant. I then asked for the residence of Mr. Wolley, the English naturalist, whose name had been mentioned to me by Prof. Retzius and the botanist Hartman. He thereupon called to some one across the court, and presently appeared a tall, slender man dressed in the universal gray suit which travelling Englishmen wear, from the Equator to the Poles. He came up with extended hand, on hearing his own language; a few words sufficed for explanation, and he devoted himself to our interests with the cordiality of an old acquaintance. He lived with the Swede, Herr Forström, who was the merchant of the place; but the wife of the latter had just been confined, and there was no room in his house. Mr. Wolley proposed at first to send to the inn in Muonioniska, and engage a room, but afterwards arranged with a Norsk carpenter, who lived on the hill above, to give us quarters in his house, so that we might be near enough to take our meals together. Nothing could have suited us better. We took possession at once, and then descended the hill to a dinner—I had ventured to hint at our famished condition—of capercailie, cranberries, soft bread, whipped cream, and a glass of genuine port.

Warmed and comforted by such luxurious fare, we climbed the hill to the carpenter's house, in the dreary Arctic twilight, in the most cheerful and contented frame of mind. Was this, indeed, Lapland? Did we, indeed, stand already in the dark heart of the polar Winter? Yes; there was no doubt of it. The imagination could scarcely conceive a more desolate picture than that upon which we gazed—the plain of sombre snow, beyond which the black huts of the village were faintly discernible, the stunted woods and bleak hills, which night and the raw snow clouds had half obscured, and yonder fur-clad figure gliding silently along beside his reindeer. Yet, even here, where Man seemed to have settled out of pure spite against Nature, were comfort and hospitality and kindness. We entered the carpenter's house, lit our candles and pipes, and sat down to enjoy at ease the unusual feeling of shelter and of home. The building was of squared fir-logs, with black moss stuffed in the crevices, making it very warm and substantial. Our room contained a loom, two tables, two beds with linen of voluptuous softness and cleanness, an iron stove (the first we had seen in Sweden), and the usual washing apparatus, besides a piece of carpet on the floor. What more could any man desire? The carpenter, Herr Knoblock, spoke some German; his son, Ludwig, Mr. Wolley's servant, also looked after our needs; and the daughter, a fair, blooming girl of about nineteen, brought us coffee before we were out of bed, and kept our fire in order. Why, Lapland was a very Sybaris in comparison with what I had expected.

Mr. Wolley proposed to us another luxury, in the shape of a vapour-bath, as Herr Forström had one of those bathing-houses which are universal in Finland. It was a little wooden building without windows. A Finnish servant-girl who had been for some time engaged in getting it in readiness, opened the door for us. The interior was very hot and moist, like an Oriental bathing-hall. In the centre was a pile of hot stones, covered with birch boughs, the leaves of which gave out an agreeable smell, and a large tub of water. The floor was strewn with straw, and under the roof was a platform extending across one end of the building. This was covered with soft hay, and reached by means of a ladder, for the purpose of getting the full effect of the steam. Some stools, and a bench for our clothes, completed the arrangements. There was also in one corner a pitcher of water, standing in a little heap of snow to keep it cool.

The servant-girl came in after us, and Mr. W. quietly proceeded to undress, informing us that the girl was bathing-master, and would do the usual scrubbing and shampooing. This, it seems, is the general practice in Finland, and is but another example of the unembarrassed habits of the people in this part of the world. The poorer families go into their bathing-rooms together—father, mother, and children—and take turns in polishing each other's backs. It would have been ridiculous to have shown any hesitation under the circumstances—in fact, an indignity to the honest simple-hearted, virtuous girl—and so we deliberately undressed also. When at last we stood, like our first parents in Paradise, "naked and not ashamed," she handed us bunches of birch-twigs with the leaves on, the use of which was suggested by the leaf of sculpture. We mounted to the platform and lay down upon our backs, whereupon she increased the temperature by throwing water upon the hot stones, until the heat was rather oppressive, and we began to sweat profusely. She then took up a bunch of birch-twigs which had been dipped in hot water, and switched us smartly from head to foot. When we had become thoroughly parboiled and lax, we descended to the floor, seated ourselves upon the stools, and were scrubbed with soap as thoroughly as propriety permitted. The girl was an admirable bather, the result of long practice in the business. She finished by pouring hot water over us, and then drying us with warm towels. The Finns frequently go out and roll in the snow during the progress of the bath. I ventured so far as to go out and stand a few seconds in the open air. The mercury was at zero, and the effect of the cold on my heated skin was delightfully refreshing.

I dressed in a violent perspiration, and then ran across to Herr Forström's house, where tea was already waiting for us. Here we found the länsman or magistrate of the Russian district opposite, a Herr Bràxen, who was decorated with the order of Stanislaus for his services in Finland during the recent war. He was a tall, dark-haired man, with a restless light in his deep-set eyes, and a gentleman in his demeanor. He entered into our plans with interest, and the evening was spent in consultation concerning them. Finally, it was decided that Herr Forström should send a messenger up the river to Palajoki (forty miles off), to engage Lapps and reindeer to take us across the mountains to Kautokeino, in Norway. As the messenger would be absent three or four days, we had a comfortable prospect of rest before us, and I went to bed with a light heart, to wake to the sixth birthday I have passed in strange lands.

In the morning, I went with Mr. Wolley to call upon a Finn, one of whose children was suffering from inflamed eyes, or snowthalmia, as it might be called. The family were prolific, as usual—children of all sizes, with a regular gradation of a year between. The father, a short, shock-headed fellow, sat in one corner; the mother, who, like nine-tenths of all the matrons we had seen between Lapland and Stockholm, gave promise of additional humanity, greeted us with a comical, dipping courtesy—a sudden relaxing and stiffening again of the muscles of the knees—which might be introduced as a novelty into our fashionable circles. The boy's eyes were terribly blood-shot, and the lids swollen, but a solution of nitrate of silver, which Mr. W. applied, relieved him greatly in the course of a day or two. We took occasion to visit the stable, where half a dozen cows lay in darkness, in their warm stalls, on one side, with two bulls and some sheep on the other. There was a fire in one corner, over which hung a great kettle filled with a mixture of boiled hay and reindeer moss. Upon this they are fed, while the sheep must content themselves with bunches of birch, willow and aspen twigs, gathered with the leaves on. The hay is strong and coarse, but nourishing, and the reindeer moss, a delicate white lichen, contains a glutinous ingredient, which probably increases the secretion of milk. The stable, as well as Forström's, which we afterwards inspected, was kept in good order. It was floored, with a gutter past each row of stalls, to carry off the manure. The cows were handsome white animals, in very good condition.

Mr. Wolley sent for his reindeer in the course of the morning, in order to give us a lesson in driving. After lunch, accordingly, we prepared ourselves for the new sensation. I put on a poesk of reindeer skin, and my fur-lined Russian boots. Ludwig took a pulk also, to assist us in case of need. These pulks are shaped very much like a canoe; they are about five feet long, one foot deep, and eighteen inches wide, with a sharp bow and a square stern. You sit upright against the stern-board, with your legs stretched out in the bottom. The deer's harness consists only of a collar of reindeer skin around the neck, with a rope at the bottom, which passes under the belly, between the legs, and is fastened to the bow of the pulk. He is driven by a single rein, attached to the base of the left horn, and passing over the back to the right hand of the driver, who thrusts his thumb into a loop at the end, and takes several turns around his wrist. The rein is held rather slack, in order that it may be thrown over to the right side when it slips to the left, which it is very apt to do.

I seated myself, took proper hold of the rein, and awaited the signal to start. My deer was a strong, swift animal, who had just shed his horns. Ludwig set off first; my deer gave a startling leap, dashed around the corner of the house, and made down the hill. I tried to catch the breath which had been jerked out of me, and to keep my balance, as the pulk, swaying from side to side, bounced over the snow. It was too late; a swift presentiment of the catastrophe flashed across my mind, but I was powerless to avert it. In another second I found myself rolling in the loose snow, with the pulk bottom upward beside me. The deer, who was attached to my arm, was standing still, facing me, with an expression of stupid surprise (but no sympathy) on his face. I got up, shook myself, righted the pulk, and commenced again. Off we went, like the wind, down the hill, the snow flying in my face and blinding me. My pulk made tremendous leaps, bounding from side to side, until, the whirlwind suddenly subsiding, I found myself off the road, deep overhead in the snow, choked and blinded, and with small snow-drifts in my pockets, sleeves and bosom. My beard and eyebrows became instantly a white, solid mass, and my face began to tingle from its snow-bath; but, on looking back, I saw as white a beard suddenly emerge from a drift, followed by the stout body of Braisted, who was gathering himself up after his third shipwreck.

We took a fresh start, I narrowly missing another overturn, as we descended the slope below the house, but on reaching the level of the Muonio, I found no difficulty in keeping my balance, and began to enjoy the exercise. My deer struck out, passed the others, and soon I was alone on the track. In the grey Arctic twilight, gliding noiselessly and swiftly over the snow, with the low huts of Muonioniska dimly seen in the distance before me, I had my first true experience of Lapland travelling. It was delightfully novel and exhilarating; I thought of "Afraja," and the song of "Kulnasatz, my reindeer!" and Bryant's "Arctic Lover," and whatever else there is of Polar poetry, urged my deer with shouts, and never once looked behind me until I had climbed the opposite shore and reached the village. My companions were then nowhere to be seen. I waited some time before they arrived, Braisted's deer having become fractious and run back with him to the house. His crimson face shone out from its white frame of icy hair as he shouted to me, "There is nothing equal to this, except riding behind a right whale when he drives to windward, with every man trimming the boat, and the spray flying over your bows!"

We now turned northward through the village, flying around many sharp corners, but this I found comparatively easy work. But for the snow I had taken in, which now began to melt, I got on finely in spite of the falling flakes, which beat in our faces. Von Buch, in his journey through Lapland in 1807, speaks of Muonioniska as "a village with an inn where they have silver spoons." We stopped at a house which Mr. Wolley stated was the very building, but it proved to be a more recent structure on the site of the old inn. The people looked at us with curiosity on hearing we were Americans. They had heard the name of America, but did not seem to know exactly where it was. On leaving the house, we had to descend the steep bank of the river. I put out my feet to steady the pulk, and thereby ploughed a cataract of fine snow into my face, completely blinding me. The pulk gave a flying leap from the steepest pitch, flung me out, and the deer, eager to make for home, dragged me by the arm for about twenty yards before I could arrest him. This was the worst upset of all, and far from pleasant, although the temperature was only zero. I reached home again without further mishap, flushed, excited, soaked with melted snow, and confident of my ability to drive reindeer with a little more practice.

During the first three days, the weather was raw, dark, and lowering, with a temperature varying from 9° above to 13° below zero. On the morning of the 14th, however, the sky finally cleared, with a cold south wind, and we saw, for the first time, the range of snowy mountains in the east. The view from our hill, before so dismally bleak and dark, became broad and beautiful, now that there was a little light to see it by. Beyond the snowy floor of the lake and the river Muonio stretched the scattering huts of Muonioniska, with the church overlooking them, and the round, white peak of Ollastyntre rising above his belt of black woods to the south. Further to the east extended alternate streaks of dark forest and frozen marsh for eighteen miles, to the foot of the mountain range of Palastyntre, which stood like a line of colossal snow-drifts against the soft violet sky, their sides touched by the rosily-golden beams of the invisible sun. This and the valley of the Torneå, at Avasaxa, are two of the finest views in Lapland.

I employed part of my time in making some sketches of characteristic faces. Mr. Wolley, finding that I wished to procure good types of the Finns and Lapps, kindly assisted me—his residence of three years in Muoniovara enabling him to know who were the most marked and peculiar personages. Ludwig was despatched to procure an old fellow by the name of Niemi, a Finn, who promised to comply with my wishes; but his ignorance made him suspicious, and it was necessary to send again. "I know what travellers are," said he, "and what a habit they have of getting people's skulls to carry home with them. Even if they are arrested for it, they are so rich, they always buy over the judges. Who knows but they might try to kill me for the sake of my skull?" After much persuasion, he was finally induced to come, and, seeing that Ludwig supposed he was still afraid, he said, with great energy: "I have made up my mind to go, even if a shower of knives should fall from heaven!" He was seventy-three years old, though he did not appear to be over sixty— his hair being thick and black, his frame erect and sturdy, and his colour crimson rather than pale. His eyebrows were jet-black and bushy, his eyes large and deep set, his nose strong and prominent, and the corners of his long mouth drawn down in a settled curve, expressing a melancholy grimness. The high cheek-bones, square brow, and muscular jaw belonged to the true Finnish type. He held perfectly still while I drew, scarcely moving a muscle of his face, and I succeeded in getting a portrait which everybody recognised.

I gave him a piece of money, with which he was greatly delighted; and, after a cup of coffee, in Herr Knoblock's kitchen, he went home quite proud and satisfied. "They do not at all look like dangerous persons," said he to the carpenter; "perhaps they do not collect skulls. I wish they spoke our language, that I might ask them how people live in their country. America is a very large, wild place. I know all about it, and the discovery of it. I was not there myself at the time, but Jenis Lampi, who lives in Kittila, was one of the crew of the ship, and he told me how it happened. Jenis Lampi said they were going to throw the captain overboard, but he persuaded them to give him three days, and on the third day they found it. Now I should like to know whether these people, who come from that country, have laws as we have, and whether they live as comfortably." So saying, Isaaki Anderinpoika Niemi departed.

No sooner had he gone than the old Lapp woman, Elsa, who had been sent for, drove up in her pulk, behind a fast reindeer. She was in complete Lapp costume—a blue cloth gown with wide sleeves, trimmed with scarlet, and a curious pear-shaped cap of the same material, upon her head. She sat upon the floor, on a deerskin, and employed herself in twisting reindeer sinews, which she rolled upon her cheek with the palm of her hand, while I was sketching her. It was already dark, and I was obliged to work by candle light, but I succeeded in catching the half-insane, witch-like expression of her face. When I took the candle to examine her features more closely, she cried out, "Look at me, O son of man!" She said that I had great powers, and was capable of doing everything, since I had come so far, and could make an image of her upon paper. She asked whether we were married, saying we could hardly travel so much if we were; yet she thought it much better to be married and stay at home. I gave her a rigsdaler, which she took with joyful surprise, saying, "What! am I to get my coffee and tobacco, and be paid too? Thanks, O son of man, for your great goodness!" She chuckled very much over the drawing, saying that the dress was exactly right.

In the afternoon we took another reindeer drive to Muonioniska, paying a visit to Pastor Fali, the clergyman whom we had met at Forström's. This time I succeeded very well, making the trip without a single overturn, though with several mishaps. Mr. Wolley lost the way, and we drove about at random for some time. My deer became restive, and whirled me around in the snow, filling my pulk. It was so dark that we could scarcely see, and, without knowing the ground, one could not tell where the ups and down were. The pastor received us courteously, treated us to coffee and pipes, and conversed with us for some time. He had not, as he said, a Swedish tongue, and I found it difficult to understand him. On our way back, Braisted's and Ludwig's deers ran together with mine, and, while going at full speed, B.'s jumped into my pulk. I tried in vain either to stop or drive on faster; he trampled me so violently that I was obliged to throw myself out to escape his hoofs. Fortunately the animals are not heavy enough to do any serious harm. We reached Forström's in season for a dinner of fat reindeer steak, cranberries, and a confect of the Arctic raspberry.

After an absence of three days Salomon, the messenger who had been sent up the river to engage reindeer for us, returned, having gone sixty miles before he could procure them. He engaged seven, which arrived the next evening, in the charge of a tall, handsome Finn, who was to be our conductor. We had, in the meantime, supplied ourselves with reindeer poesks, such as the Lapps wear,—our own furs being impracticable for pulk travelling— reindeer mittens, and boas of squirrel tails strung on reindeer sinews. The carpenter's second son, Anton, a lad of fifteen, was engaged to accompany us as an interpreter.

CHAPTER X. A REINDEER JOURNEY ACROSS LAPLAND.

We left Muoniovara at noon on the 15th, fully prepared for a three days' journey across the wilds of Lapland. We were about to traverse the barren, elevated table-land, which divides the waters of the Bothnian Gulf from those of the Northern Ocean,—a dreary, unfriendly region, inhabited only by a few wandering Lapps. Even without the prevalence of famine, we should have had difficulty in procuring food from them, so we supplied ourselves with a saddle of reindeer, six loaves of rye bread, sugar, and a can of coffee. The carpenter lent us a cup and saucer, and Anton, who felt all the responsibility of a boy who is employed for the first time, stowed everything away nicely in the broad baggage pulk. We found it impossible to procure Lapp leggings and shoes at Muoniovara, but our Russian boots proved an admirable substitute. The poesk of reindeer skin is the warmest covering for the body which could be devised. It is drawn over the head like a shirt, fitting closely around the neck and wrists, where it is generally trimmed with ermine, and reaching half-way below the knee. A thick woollen sash, wrapped first around the neck, the ends then twisted together down to the waist, where they are passed tightly around the body and tied in front, not only increases the warmth and convenience of the garment, but gives it a highly picturesque air. Our sea-otter caps, turned down so as to cover the ears and forehead, were fastened upon our heads with crimson handkerchiefs, and our boas, of black and red squirrel tails, passed thrice around the neck, reached to the tips of our noses. Over our dog-skin mittens we drew gauntlets of reindeer skin, with which it was difficult to pick up or take hold of anything; but as the deer's rein is twisted around one's wrist, their clumsiness does not interfere with the facility of driving. It would seem impossible for even Arctic cold to penetrate through such defences—and yet it did.

Herr Forström prepared us for the journey by a good breakfast of reindeer's marrow, a justly celebrated Lapland delicacy, and we set out with a splendidly clear sky and a cold of 12° below zero. The Muonio valley was superb, towards sunrise, with a pale, creamy, saffron light on the snow, the forests on the tops of the hills burning like jagged masses of rough opal, and the distant range of Palastyntre bathed in pink light, with pure sapphire shadows on its northern slopes. These Arctic illuminations are transcendent; nothing can equal them, and neither pen nor pencil can describe them. We passed through Muonioniska, and kept up the Russian side, over an undulating, wooded country. The road was quite good, but my deer, in spite of his size and apparent strength, was a lazy beast, and gave me much trouble. I was obliged to get out of the pulk frequently and punch him in the flanks, taking my chance to tumble in headlong as he sprang forward again. I soon became disgusted with reindeer travelling, especially when, after we had been on the road two hours and it was nearly dark, we reached Upper Muonioniska, only eight miles. We there took the river again, and made better progress to Kyrkessuando, the first station, where we stopped an hour to feed the deer. Here there was a very good little inn, with a bed for travellers.

We had seven reindeer, two of which ran loose, so that we could change occasionally on the road. I insisted on changing mine at once, and received in return a smaller animal, which made up in spirit what he lacked in strength. Our conductor was a tall, handsome Finn, with blue eyes and a bright, rosy complexion. His name was Isaac, but he was better known by his nickname of Pitka Isaaki, or Long Isaac. He was a slow, good-humoured, prudent, careful fellow, and probably served our purpose as well as anybody we could have found. Anton, however, who made his first journey with us, was invaluable. His father had some misgivings on account of his timidity, but he was so ambitious to give satisfaction that we found him forward enough.

I have already described the country through which we passed, as it was merely a continuation of the scenery below Muonioniska—low, wooded hills, white plains, and everywhere snow, snow, snow, silence and death. The cold increased to 33° below zero, obliging me to bury my nose in my boa and to keep up a vigorous exercise of my toes to prevent them from freezing, as it is impossible to cover one's boots in a pulk. The night was calm, clear, and starry; but after an hour a bank of auroral light gradually arose in the north, and formed a broad arch, which threw its lustre over the snow and lighted up our path. Almost stationary at first, a restless motion after a time agitated the gleaming bow; it shot out broad streamers of yellow fire, gathered them in and launched them forth again, like the hammer of Thor, which always returned to his hand, after striking the blow for which it had been hurled. The most wonderful appearance, however, was an immense square curtain, which fell from all the central part of the arch. The celestial scene-shifters were rather clumsy, for they allowed one end to fall lower than the other, so that it over-lapped and doubled back upon itself in a broad fold. Here it hung for probably half an hour, slowly swinging to and fro, as if moved by a gentle wind. What new spectacle was in secret preparation behind it we did not learn, for it was hauled up so bunglingly that the whole arch broke and fell in, leaving merely a pile of luminous ruins under the Polar Star.

Hungry and nearly frozen, we reached Palajoki at half-past nine, and were at once ushered into the guests' room, a little hut separated from the main building. Here, barring an inch of ice on the windows and numerous windy cracks in the floor, we felt a little comfort before an immense fire kindled in the open chimney. Our provisions were already adamantine; the meat was transformed into red Finland granite, and the bread into mica-slate. Anton and the old Finnish landlady, the mother of many sons, immediately commenced the work of thawing and cooking, while I, by the light of fir torches, took the portrait of a dark-haired, black-eyed, olive-skinned, big-nosed, thick-lipped youth, who gave his name as Eric Johan Sombasi. When our meal of meat, bread, and coffee had been despatched, the old woman made a bed of reindeer skins for us in one corner, covered with a coarse sheet, a quilt, and a sheepskin blanket. She then took her station near the door, where several of the sons were already standing, and all appeared to be waiting in silent curiosity to see us retire. We undressed with genuine Finnish freedom of manner, deliberately enough for them to understand the peculiarities of our apparel, and they never took their eyes from us until we were stowed away for the night in our warm nest.

It was snowing and blowing when we arose. Long Isaac had gone to the woods after the reindeer, and we employed the delay in making a breakfast off the leavings of our supper. Crossing the Muonio at starting, we entered the Russian territory and drove up the bed of the Palajok, a tributary stream which comes down from the north. The sky became clearer as the dawn increased; the road was tolerably broken, and we sped merrily along the windings of the river, under its tall banks fringed with fir trees, which, loaded with snow, shone brilliantly white against the rosy sky. The temperature was 8° below zero, which felt unpleasantly warm, by contrast with the previous evening.

After a time we left the river and entered a rolling upland—alternate thickets of fir and birch, and wastes of frozen marsh, where our path was almost obliterated. After more than two hours' travel we came upon a large lake, at the further end of which, on the southern side of a hill, was the little hamlet of Suontajärvi. Here we stopped to bait the deer, Braisted's and mine being nearly fagged out. We entered one of the huts, where a pleasant woman was taking charge of a year-old baby. There was no fire on the hearth, and the wind whistled through the open cracks of the floor. Long Isaac and the woman saluted each other by placing their right arms around each other's waists, which is the universal manner of greeting in Finland. They only shake hands as a token of thanks for a favour.

We started again at noon, taking our way across a wilderness of lakes and snow-covered marshes, dotted with stunted birch-thickets. The road had entirely disappeared, but Eric of Palajoki, who accompanied us as an extra guide, went ahead with a strong reindeer and piloted us. The sagacity with which these animals find the track under a smooth covering of loose snow, is wonderful. They follow it by the feet, of course, but with the utmost ease and rapidity, often while going at full speed. I was struck by the sinuous, mazy character of our course, even where the ground was level, and could only account for it by the supposition that the first track over the light snow had followed the smoothest and firmest ridges of the marshes. Our progress was now slow and toilsome, and it was not long before my deer gave up entirely. Long Isaac, seeing that a change must be made, finally decided to give me a wild, powerful animal, which he had not yet ventured to intrust to either of us.

The deer was harnessed to my pulk, the rein carefully secured around my wrist, and Long Isaac let go his hold. A wicked toss of the antlers and a prodigious jump followed, and the animal rushed full tilt upon Braisted, who was next before me, striking him violently upon the back. The more I endeavored to rein him in, the more he plunged and tore, now dashing against the led deer, now hurling me over the baggage pulk, and now leaping off the track into bottomless beds of loose snow. Long Isaac at last shouted to me to go ahead and follow Eric, who was about half a mile in advance. A few furious plunges carried me past our little caravan, with my pulk full of snow, and my face likewise. Now, lowering his neck and thrusting out his head, with open mouth and glaring eyes, the deer set off at the top of his speed.

Away I went, like a lance shot out from the auroral armoury; the pulk slid over the snow with the swiftness of a fish through the water; a torrent of snow-spray poured into my lap and showered against my face, until I was completely blinded. Eric was overtaken so quickly that he had no time to give me the track, and as I was not in a condition to see or hear anything, the deer, with the stupidity of his race, sprang directly upon him, trampled him down, and dragged me and my pulk over him. We came to a stand in the deep snow, while Eric shook himself and started again. My deer now turned and made for the caravan, but I succeeded in pulling his head around, when he charged a second time upon Eric, who threw himself out of his pulk to escape. My strength was fast giving way, when we came to a ridge of deep, loose snow, in which the animals sank above their bellies, and up which they could hardly drag us. My deer was so exhausted when we reached the top, that I had no further difficulty in controlling him.

Before us stretched a trackless plain, bounded by a low mountain ridge. Eric set off at a fast trot, winding hither and thither, as his deer followed the invisible path. I kept close behind him, white as a Polar bear, but glowing like a volcano under my furs. The temperature was 10° below zero, and I could have wished it ten degrees colder. My deer, although his first savage strength was spent, was still full of spirit, and I began to enjoy this mode of travel. We soon entered the hills, which were covered with thickets of frozen birch, with here and there a tall Scotch fir, completely robed in snow. The sun, which had showed about half his disc at noon, was now dipping under the horizon, and a pure orange glow lighted up the dazzling masses of the crystal woods. All was silver-clear, far and near, shining, as if by its own light, with an indescribable radiance. We had struck upon a well-beaten track on entering the hills, and flew swiftly along through this silent splendour, this jewelled solitude, under the crimson and violet mode of the sky. Here was true Northern romance; here was poetry beyond all the Sagas and Eddas that ever were written.

We passed three Lapps, with heavy hay-sleds, drawn by a reindeer apiece, and after a time issued from the woods upon a range of hills entirely bare and white. Before us was the miserable hamlet of Lappajärvi, on the western side of the barren mountain of Lippavara, which is the highest in this part of Lapland, having an altitude of 1900 feet above the sea. I have rarely seen anything quite so bleak and God-forsaken as this village. A few low black huts, in a desert of snow—that was all. We drove up to a sort of station-house, where an old, white-headed Finn received me kindly, beat the snow off my poesk with a birch broom, and hung my boa near the fire to dry. There was a wild, fierce-looking Lapp in the room, who spoke some Norwegian, and at once asked who and what I was. His head was covered with a mop of bright brown hair, his eyes were dark blue and gleamed like polished steel, and the flushed crimson of his face was set off by the strong bristles of a beard of three weeks growth. There was something savage and ferocious in his air, as he sat with his clenched fists planted upon his knees, and a heavy knife in a wooden scabbard hanging from his belt. When our caravan arrived I transferred him to my sketch-book. He gave me his name as Ole Olsen Thore, and I found he was a character well known throughout the country.

Long Isaac proposed waiting until midnight, for moon-rise, as it was already dark, and there was no track beyond Lippajärvi. This seemed prudent, and we therefore, with the old woman's help, set about boiling our meat, thawing bread, and making coffee. It was necessary to eat even beyond what appetite demanded, on account of the long distances between the stations. Drowsiness followed repletion, as a matter of course, and they gave us a bed of skins in an inner-room. Here, however, some other members of the family were gathered around the fire, and kept up an incessant chattering, while a young married couple, who lay in one corner, bestowed their endearments on each other, so that we had but little benefit of our rest. At midnight all was ready, and we set out. Long Isaac had engaged a guide, and procured fresh deer in place of those which were fatigued. There was a thick fog, which the moon scarcely brightened, but the temperature had risen to zero, and was as mild as a May morning. For the first time in many days our beards did not freeze.

We pursued our way in complete silence. Our little caravan, in single file, presented a strange, shadowy, mysterious appearance as it followed the winding path, dimly seen through the mist, first on this side and then on that; not a sound being heard, except the crunching of one's own pulk over the snow. My reindeer and myself seemed to be the only living things, and we were pursuing the phantoms of other travellers and other deer, who had long ago perished in the wilderness. It was impossible to see more than a hundred yards; some short, stunted birches, in their spectral coating of snow, grew along the low ridges of the deep, loose snow, which separated the marshes, but nothing else interrupted the monotony of the endless grey ocean, through which we went floundering, apparently at haphazard. How our guides found the way was beyond my comprehension, for I could discover no distinguishable landmarks. After two hours or more we struck upon a cluster of huts called Palajärvi, seven miles from Lippajärvi, which proved that we were on the right track.

The fog now became thicker than ever. We were upon the water-shed between the Bothnian Gulf and the Northern Ocean, about 1400 feet above the sea. The birches became mere shrubs, dotting the low mounds which here and there arose out of the ocean of snow. The pulks all ran in the same track and made a single furrow, so that our gunwales were generally below the sea-level. The snow was packed so tight, however, that we rarely shipped any. Two hours passed, and I was at length roused from a half-sleep by the evidence of our having lost the way. Long Isaac and the guide stopped and consulted every few minutes, striking sometimes in one direction and sometimes in another, but without any result. We ran over ridges of heavy, hard tussocks, blown bare of snow, which pitched our pulks right and left, just as I have bumped over the coral reefs of Loo-Choo in a ship's cutter. Then followed deep beds of snow-drifts, which tasked the utmost strength of our deer, low birch thickets and hard ridges again, over which we plunged in the wildest way possible.

After wandering about for a considerable time, we suddenly heard the barking of a dog at some distance on our left. Following the welcome sound, we reached a scrubby ridge, where we were saluted with a whole chorus of dogs, and soon saw the dark cone of a Lapp tent. Long Isaac aroused the inmates, and the shrill cry of a baby proclaimed that there was life and love, even here. Presently a clumsy form, enveloped in skins, waddled out, and entered into conversation with our men. I proposed at once to engage a Lapp to guide us as far as Eitajärvi, which they informed us was two Norwegian (fourteen English) miles farther. The man agreed, but must first go off to the woods for his deer, which would detain us two hours. He put on his snow-skates and started, and I set about turning the delay to profit by making acquaintance with the inmates of the tents. We had now reached the middle of the village; the lean, wolfish dogs were yelling on all sides, and the people began to bestir themselves. Streams of sparks issued from the open tops of the tents, and very soon we stood as if in the midst of a group of volcanic cones.

The Lapps readily gave us permission to enter. We lifted the hanging door of reindeer hide, crept in, stumbling over a confused mixture of dogs and deerskins, until we found room to sit down. Two middle-aged women, dressed in poesks, like the men, were kindling a fire between some large stones in the centre, but the air inside was still as cold as outside. The damp birch sticks gave out a thick smoke, which almost stifled us, and for half an hour we could scarcely see or breathe. The women did not appear to be incommoded in the least, but I noticed that their eyes were considerably inflamed. After a time our company was increased by the arrival of two stout, ruddy girls of about seventeen, and a child of two years old, which already wore a complete reindeer costume. They were all very friendly and hospitable in their demeanour towards us, for conversation was scarcely possible. The interior of the tent was hung with choice bits of deer's hide, from the inside of the flanks and shoulders, designed, apparently, for mittens. Long Isaac at once commenced bargaining for some of them, which he finally purchased. The money was deposited in a rather heavy bag of coin, which one of the women drew forth from under a pile of skins. Our caps and Russian boots excited their curiosity, and they examined them with the greatest minuteness.

These women were neither remarkably small nor remarkably ugly, as the Lapps are generally represented. The ground-tone of their complexion was rather tawny, to be sure, but there was a glowing red on their cheeks, and their eyes were a dark bluish-grey. Their voices were agreeable, and the language (a branch of the Finnish) had none of that barbaric harshness common to the tongues of nomadic tribes. These favorable features, nevertheless, were far from reconciling me to the idea of a trial of Lapp life. When I saw the filth, the poverty, and discomfort in which they lived, I decided that the present experience was all-sufficient. Roasting on one side and freezing on the other, with smarting eyes and asphyxiated lungs, I soon forgot whatever there was of the picturesque in my situation, and thought only of the return of our Lapp guide. The women at last cleared away several dogs, and made room for us to lie down—a more tolerable position, in our case; though how a whole family, with innumerable dogs, stow themselves in the compass of a circle eight feet in diameter, still remains a mystery.

The Lapp returned with his reindeer within the allotted time, and we took our leave of the encampment. A strong south wind had arisen, but did not dissipate the fog, and for two hours we had a renewal of our past experiences, in thumping over hard ridges and ploughing through seas of snow. Our track was singularly devious, sometimes doubling directly back upon itself without any apparent cause. At last, when a faint presentiment of dawn began to glimmer through the fog, the Lapp halted and announced that he had lost the way. Bidding us remain where we were, he struck off into the snow and was soon lost to sight. Scarcely a quarter of an hour had elapsed, however, before we heard his cries at a considerable distance. Following, as we best could, across a plain nearly a mile in diameter, we found him at last in a narrow dell between two hills. The ground now sloped rapidly northward, and I saw that we had crossed the water-shed, and that the plain behind us must be the lake Jedeckejaure, which, according to Von Buch, is 1370 feet above the sea.

On emerging from the dell we found a gentle slope before us, covered with hard ice, down which our pulks flew like the wind. This brought us to another lake, followed by a similar slope, and so we descended the icy terraces, until, in a little more than an hour, some covered haystacks gave evidence of human habitation, and we drew up at the huts of Eitajärvi, in Norway. An old man, who had been watching our approach, immediately climbed upon the roof and removed a board from the chimney, after which he ushered us into a bare, cold room, and kindled a roaring fire on the hearth. Anton unpacked our provisions, and our hunger was so desperate, after fasting for twenty hours, that we could scarcely wait for the bread to thaw and the coffee to boil. We set out again at noon, down the frozen bed of a stream which drains the lakes, but had not proceeded far before both deers and pulks began to break through the ice, probably on account of springs under it. After being almost swamped, we managed to get up the steep snow-bank and took to the plain again, making our own road over ridge and through hollow. The caravan was soon stopped, that the pulks might be turned bottom upwards and the ice scraped off, which, like the barnacles on a ship's hull, impeded their progress through the snow. The broad plain we were traversing stretched away to the north without a break or spot of color to relieve its ghastly whiteness; but toward the south-west, where the sunset of an unrisen sun spread its roseate glow through the mist, arose some low mounds, covered with drooping birches, which shone against the soft, mellow splendor, like sprays of silver embroidered on rose-colored satin.

Our course, for about fifteen miles, lay alternately upon the stream (where the ice was sufficiently strong) and the wild plain. Two or three Lapp tents on the bank exhibited the usual amount of children and dogs, but we did not think it worth while to extend the circle of our acquaintance in that direction. At five o'clock, after it had long been dark, we reached half a dozen huts called Siepe, two Norwegian miles from Kautokeino. Long Isaac wished to stop here for the night, but we resolutely set ourselves against him. The principal hut was filthy, crowded with Lapps, and filled with a disagreeable smell from the warm, wet poesks hanging on the rafters. In one corner lay the carcases of two deer-calves which had been killed by wolves. A long bench, a table, and a rude frame covered with deerskins, and serving as a bed, comprised all the furniture. The usual buckets of sour milk, with wooden ladles, stood by the door. No one appeared to have any particular occupation, if we except the host's wife, who was engaged with an infant in reindeer breeches. We smoked and deliberated while the deers ate their balls of moss, and the result was, that a stout yellow-haired Lapp youngster was engaged to pilot us to Kautokeino.

Siepe stands on a steep bank, down which our track led to the stream again. As the caravan set off, my deer, which had behaved very well through the day, suddenly became fractious, sprang off the track, whirled himself around on his hind legs, as if on a pivot, and turned the pulk completely over, burying me in the snow. Now, I had come from Muoniovara, more than a hundred miles, without being once overturned, and was ambitious to make the whole journey with equal success. I therefore picked myself up, highly disconcerted, and started afresh. The very same thing happened a second and a third time, and I don't think I shall be considered unreasonable for becoming furiously angry. I should certainly have committed cervicide had any weapon been at hand. I seized the animal by the horns, shook, cuffed, and kicked him, but all to no purpose. Long Isaac, who was passing in his pulk, made some remark, which Anton, with all the gravity and conscientiousness of his new position of interpreter, immediately translated.

"Long Isaac says," he shouted, "that the deer will go well enough, if you knew how to drive him." "Long Isaac may go to the devil!" was, I am sorry to say, my profane reply, which Anton at once translated to him.

Seating myself in the pulk again, I gave the deer the rein, and for a time kept him to the top of his speed, following the Lapp, who drove rapidly down the windings of the stream. It was quite dark, but our road was now somewhat broken, and for three hours our caravan swiftly and silently sped on its way. Then, some scattered lights appeared in the distance; our tired deers leaped forward with fresher spirit, and soon brought us to the low wooden huts of Kautokeino. We had travelled upwards of sixty miles since leaving Lippajärvi, breaking our own road through deep snow for a great part of the way. During this time our deers had not been changed. I cannot but respect the provoking animals after such a feat.

CHAPTER XI. KAUTOKEINO.—A DAY WITHOUT A SUN.

While in Dresden, my friend Ziegler had transferred to me a letter of introduction from Herr Berger, a merchant of Hammerfest, to his housekeeper in Kautokeino. Such a transfer might be considered a great stretch of etiquette in those enlightened regions of the world where hospitality requires certificates of character; but, in a benighted country like Lapland, there was no danger of very fine distinctions being drawn, and Ziegler judged that the house which was to have been placed at his disposal had he made the journey, would as readily open its doors to me. At Muoniovara, I learned that Berger himself was now in Kautokeino, so that I needed only to present him with his own letter. We arrived so late, however, that I directed Long Isaac to take us to the inn until morning. He seemed reluctant to do this, and I could not fathom the reason of his hesitation, until I had entered the hovel to which we were conducted. A single room, filled with smoke from a fire of damp birch sticks, was crammed with Lapps of all sizes, and of both sexes. There was scarcely room to spread a deerskin on the floor while the smell exhaled from their greasy garments and their unwashed bodies was absolutely stifling. I have travelled too much to be particularly nice in my choice of lodgings, but in this instance I instantly retreated, determined to lie on the snow, under my overturned pulk, rather than pass the night among such bed-fellows.

We drove on for a short distance, and drew up before a large, substantial log-house, which Long Isaac informed me was the residence of the Länsman, or magistrate of the district. I knocked at the door, and inquired of the Norwegian servant girl who opened it, where Herr Berger lived. Presently appeared a stout, ruddy gentleman—no less than Herr Berger himself—who addressed me in fluent English. A few words sufficed to explain everything, and in ten minutes our effects were deposited in the guest's room of the Länsman's house, and ourselves, stripped of our Polar hides, were seated on a sofa, in a warm, carpeted room, with a bountiful supper-table before us. Blessed be civilisation! was my inward ejaculation. Blessed be that yearning for comfort in Man, which has led to the invention of beds, of sofas, and easy chairs: which has suggested cleanliness of body and of habitation, and which has developed the noble art of cooking! The dreary and perilous wastes over which we had passed were forgotten. With hearts warmed in both senses, and stomachs which reacted gratefully upon our hearts, we sank that night into a paradise of snowy linen, which sent a consciousness of pleasure even into the oblivion of sleep.

The Länsman, Herr Lie, a tall handsome man of twenty-three, was a native of Altengaard, and spoke tolerable English. With him and Herr Berger, we found a third person, a theological student, stationed at Kautokeino to learn the Lapp tongue. Pastor Hvoslef, the clergyman, was the only other Norwegian resident. The village, separated from the Northern Ocean, by the barren, uninhabited ranges of the Kiölen Mountains, and from the Finnish settlements on the Muonio by the swampy table-lands we had traversed, is one of the wildest and most forlorn places in all Lapland. Occupying, as it does, the centre of a large district, over which the Lapps range with their reindeer herds during the summer, it is nevertheless a place of some importance, both for trade and for the education, organization, and proper control of the barely-reclaimed inhabitants. A church was first built here by Charles XI. of Sweden, in 1660, although, in the course of subsequent boundary adjustments, the district was made over to Norway. Half a century afterwards, some families of Finns settled here; but they appear to have gradually mixed with the Lapps, so that there is little of the pure blood of either race to be found at present. I should here remark that throughout Norwegian Lapland the Lapps are universally called Finns, and the Finns, Quäns. As the change of names, however, might occasion some confusion, I shall adhere to the more correct Swedish manner of designating them, which I have used hitherto.

Kautokeino is situated in a shallow valley, or rather basin, opening towards the north-east, whither its river flows to join the Alten. Although only 835 feet above the sea, and consequently below the limits of the birch and the fir in this latitude, the country has been stripped entirely bare for miles around, and nothing but the scattering groups of low, dark huts, breaks the snowy monotony. It is with great difficulty that vegetables of any kind can be raised. Potatoes have once or twice been made to yield eight-fold, but they are generally killed by the early autumn frosts before maturity. On the southern bank of the river, the ground remains frozen the whole year round, at a depth of only nine feet. The country furnishes nothing except reindeer meat, milk, and cheese. Grain, and other supplies of all kinds, must be hauled up from the Alten Fjord, a distance of 112 miles. The carriage is usually performed in winter, when, of course, everything reaches its destination in a frozen state. The potatoes are as hard as quartz pebbles, sugar and salt become stony masses, and even wine assumes a solid form. In this state they are kept until wanted for use, rapidly thawed, and immediately consumed, whereby their flavour is but little impaired. The potatoes, cabbage, and preserved berries on the Länsman's table were almost as fresh as if they had never been frozen.

Formerly, the place was almost entirely deserted during the summer months, and the resident missionary and Länsman returned to Alten until the Lapps came back to their winter huts; but, for some years past, the stationary population has increased, and the church is kept open the whole year. Winter, however, is the season when the Lapps are found at home, and when their life and habits are most characteristic and interesting. The population of Kautokeino is then, perhaps, about 800; in summer it is scarcely one-tenth of this number. Many of the families—especially those of mixed Finnish blood—live in wooden huts, with the luxury of a fireplace and chimney, and a window or two; but the greater part of them burrow in low habitations of earth, which resemble large mole hills raised in the crust of the soil. Half snowed over and blended with the natural inequalities of the earth, one would never imagine, but for the smoke here and there issuing from holes, that human beings existed below. On both sides of the stream are rows of storehouses, wherein the Lapps deposit their supplies and household articles during their summer wanderings. These structures are raised upon birch posts, each capped with a smooth, horizontal board, in order to prevent the rats and mice from effecting an entrance. The church is built upon a slight eminence to the south, with its low red belfry standing apart, as in Sweden, in a small grove of birches, which have been spared for a summer ornament to the sanctuary.

We awoke at eight o'clock to find a clear twilight and a cold of 10°

below zero. Our stay at Muoniovara had given the sun time to increase his altitude somewhat, and I had some doubts whether we should succeed in beholding a day of the Polar winter. The Länsman, however, encouraged us by the assurance that the sun had not yet risen upon his residence, though nearly six weeks had elapsed since his disappearance, but that his return was now looked for every day, since he had already begun to shine upon the northern hills. By ten o'clock it was light enough to read; the southern sky was a broad sea of golden orange, dotted with a few crimson cloud-islands, and we set ourselves to watch with some anxiety the gradual approach of the exiled god. But for this circumstance, and two other drawbacks, I should have gone to church to witness the Lapps at their religious exercises. Pastor Hvoslef was ill, and the service consisted only of the reading of some prayers by the Lapp schoolmaster; added to which, the church is never warmed, even in the coldest days of winter. One cause of this may, perhaps, be the dread of an accidental conflagration; but the main reason is, the inconvenience which would arise from the thawing out of so many antiquated reindeer garments, and the effluvia given out by the warmed bodies within them. Consequently, the temperature inside the church is about the same as outside, and the frozen moisture of the worshippers' breath forms a frosty cloud so dense as sometimes to hide the clergyman from the view of his congregation. Pastor Hvoslef informed me that he had frequently preached in a temperature of 35° below zero. "At such times," said he, "the very words seem to freeze as they issue from my lips, and fall upon the heads of my hearers like a shower of snow." "But," I ventured to remark, "our souls are controlled to such a degree by the condition of our bodies, that I should doubt whether any true devotional spirit could exist at such a time. Might not even religion itself be frozen?" "Yes," he answered, "there is no doubt that all the better feelings either disappear, or become very faint, when the mercury begins to freeze." The pastor himself was at that time suffering the penalty of indulging a spirit of reverence which for a long time led him to officiate with uncovered head.

The sky increased in brightness as we watched. The orange flushed into rose, and the pale white hills looked even more ghastly against the bar of glowing carmine which fringed the horizon. A few long purple streaks of cloud hung over the sun's place, and higher up in the vault floated some loose masses, tinged with fiery crimson on their lower edges. About half-past eleven, a pencil of bright red light shot up—a signal which the sun uplifted to herald his coming. As it slowly moved westward along the hills, increasing in height and brilliancy until it became a long tongue of flame, playing against the streaks of cloud we were apprehensive that the near disc would rise to view. When the Länsman's clock pointed to twelve, its base had become so bright as to shine almost like the sun itself; but after a few breathless moments the unwelcome glow began to fade. We took its bearing with a compass, and after making allowance for the variation (which is here very slight) were convinced that it was really past meridian, and the radiance, which was that of morning a few minutes before, belonged to the splendours of evening now. The colours of the firmament began to change in reverse order, and the dawn, which had almost ripened to sunrise, now withered away to night without a sunset. We had at last seen a day without a sun.

The snowy hills to the north, it is true, were tinged with a flood of rosy flame, and the very next day would probably bring down the tide-mark of sunshine to the tops of the houses. One day, however, was enough to satisfy me. You, my heroic friend,[A] may paint with true pencil, and still truer pen, the dreary solemnity of the long Arctic night: but, greatly as I enjoy your incomparable pictures, much as I honour your courage and your endurance, you shall never tempt me to share in the experience. The South is a cup which one may drink to inebriation; but one taste from the icy goblet of the North is enough to allay curiosity and quench all further desire. Yet the contrast between these two extremes came home to me vividly but once during this journey. A traveller's mind must never stray too far from the things about him, and long habit has enabled me to throw myself entirely into the conditions and circumstances of each separate phase of my wandering life, thereby preserving distinct the sensations and experiences of each, and preventing all later confusion in the memory. But one day, at Muoniovara, as I sat before the fire in the afternoon darkness, there flashed across my mind a vision of cloudless Egypt—trees rustling in the hot wind, yellow mountain-walls rising beyond the emerald plain of the Nile, the white pencils of minarets in the distance, the creamy odour of bean-blossoms in the air—a world of glorious vitality, where Death seemed an unaccountable accident. Here, Life existed only on sufferance, and all Nature frowned with a robber's demand to give it up. I flung my pipe across the room and very soon, behind a fast reindeer, drove away from the disturbing reminiscence.

I went across the valley to the schoolmaster's house to make a sketch of Kautokeino, but the frost was so thick on the windows that I was obliged to take a chair in the open air and work with bare hands. I soon learned the value of rapidity in such an employment. We spent the afternoon in the Länsman's parlor, occasionally interrupted by the visits of Lapps, who, having heard of our arrival, were very curious to behold the first Americans who ever reached this part of the world. They came into the room with the most perfect freedom, saluted the Länsman, and then turned to stare at us until they were satisfied, when they retired to give place to others who were waiting outside. We were obliged to hold quite a levee during the whole evening. They had all heard of America, but knew very little else about it, and many of them questioned us, through Herr Berger, concerning our religion and laws. The fact of the three Norwegian residents being able to converse with us astonished them greatly. The Lapps of Kautokeino have hitherto exalted themselves over the Lapps of Karasjok and Karessuando, because the Länsman, Berger, and Pastor Hvoslef could speak with English and French travellers in their own language, while the merchants and pastors of the latter places are acquainted only with Norwegian and Swedish; and now their pride received a vast accession. "How is it possible?" said they to Herr Berger, "these men come from the other side of the world, and you talk with them as fast in their own language as if you had never spoken any other!" The schoolmaster, Lars Kaino, a one-armed fellow, with a more than ordinary share of acuteness and intelligence, came to request that I would take his portrait, offering to pay me for my trouble. I agreed to do it gratuitously, on condition that I should keep it myself, and that he should bring his wife to be included in the sketch.

He assented, with some sacrifice of vanity, and came around the next morning, in his holiday suit of blue cloth, trimmed with scarlet and yellow binding. His wife, a short woman of about twenty-five, with a face as flat and round as a platter, but a remarkably fair complexion, accompanied him, though with evident reluctance, and sat with eyes modestly cast down while

I sketched her features. The circumstance of my giving Lars half a dollar at the close of the sitting was immediately spread through Kautokeino, and before night all the Lapps of the place were ambitious to undergo the same operation. Indeed, the report reached the neighboring villages, and a Hammerfest merchant, who came in the following morning from a distance of seven miles, obtained a guide at less than the usual price, through the anxiety of the latter to arrive in time to have his portrait taken. The shortness of the imperfect daylight, however, obliged me to decline further offers, especially as there were few Lapps of pure, unmixed blood among my visitors.

Kautokeino was the northern limit of my winter journey. I proposed visiting Altengaard in the summer, on my way to the North Cape, and there is nothing in the barren tract between the two places to repay the excursion. I had already seen enough of the Lapps to undeceive me in regard to previously-formed opinions respecting them, and to take away the desire for a more intimate acquaintance. In features, as in language, they resemble the Finns sufficiently to indicate an ethnological relationship. I could distinguish little, if any, trace of the Mongolian blood in them. They are fatter, fairer, and altogether handsomer than the nomadic offshoots of that race, and resemble the Esquimaux (to whom they have been compared) in nothing but their rude, filthy manner of life. Von Buch ascribes the difference in stature and physical stamina between them and the Finns to the use of the vapor bath by the latter and the aversion to water of the former. They are a race of Northern gipsies, and it is the restless blood of this class rather than any want of natural capacity which retards their civilisation. Although the whole race has been converted to Christianity, and education is universal among them—no Lapp being permitted to marry until he can read—they have but in too many respects substituted one form of superstition for another. The spread of temperance among them, however, has produced excellent results, and, in point of morality, they are fully up to the prevailing standard in Sweden and Norway. The practice, formerly imputed to them, of sharing their connubial rights with the guests who visited them, is wholly extinct,—if it ever existed. Theft is the most usual offence, but crimes of a more heinous character are rare.

Whatever was picturesque in the Lapps has departed with their paganism.

No wizards now ply their trade of selling favorable winds to the Norwegian coasters, or mutter their incantations to discover the concealed grottoes of silver in the Kiölen mountains. It is in vain, therefore, for the romantic traveller to seek in them the materials for weird stories and wild adventures. They are frightfully pious and commonplace. Their conversion has destroyed what little of barbaric poetry there might have been in their composition, and, instead of chanting to the spirits of the winds, and clouds, and mountains, they have become furious ranters, who frequently claim to be possessed by the Holy Ghost. As human beings, the change, incomplete as it is, is nevertheless to their endless profit; but as objects of interest to the traveller, it has been to their detriment. It would be far more picturesque to describe a sabaoth of Lapland witches than a prayer-meeting of shouting converts, yet no friend of his race could help rejoicing to see the latter substituted for the former. In proportion, therefore, as the Lapps have become enlightened (like all other savage tribes), they have become less interesting. Retaining nearly all that is repulsive in their habits of life, they have lost the only peculiarities which could persuade one to endure the inconveniences of a closer acquaintance.

I have said that the conversion of the Lapps was in some respects the substitution of one form of superstition for another. A tragic exemplification of this fact, which produced the greatest excitement throughout the North, took place in Kautokeino four years ago. Through the preaching of Lestadius and other fanatical missionaries, a spiritual epidemic, manifesting itself in the form of visions, trances, and angelic possessions, broke out among the Lapps. It infected the whole country, and gave rise to numerous disturbances and difficulties in Kautokeino. It was no unusual thing for one of the congregation to arise during church service, declare that he was inspired by the Holy Ghost, and call upon those present to listen to his revelations. The former Länsman arrested the most prominent of the offenders, and punished them with fine and imprisonment. This begat feelings of hatred on the part of the fanatics, which soon ripened into a conspiracy. The plot was matured during the summer months, when the Lapps descended towards the Norwegian coast with their herds of reindeer.

I have the account of what followed from the lips of Pastor Hvoslef, who

106

was then stationed here, and was also one of the victims of their resentment. Early one morning in October, when the inhabitants were returning from their summer wanderings, he was startled by the appearance of the resident merchant's wife, who rushed into his house in a frantic state, declaring that her husband was murdered. He fancied that the woman was bewildered by some sudden fright, and, in order to quiet her, walked over to the merchant's house. Here he found the unfortunate man lying dead upon the floor, while a band of about thirty Lapps, headed by the principal fanatics, were forcing the house of the Länsman, whom they immediately dispatched with their knives and clubs. They then seized the pastor and his wife, beat them severely with birch-sticks, and threatened them with death unless they would acknowledge the divine mission of the so-called prophets.

The greater part of the day passed in uncertainty and terror, but towards evening appeared a crowd of friendly Lapps from the neighbouring villages, who, after having received information, through fugitives, of what had happened, armed themselves and marched to the rescue. A fight ensued, in which the conspirators were beaten, and the prisoners delivered out of their hands. The friendly Lapps, unable to take charge of all the criminals, and fearful lest some of them might escape during the night, adopted the alternative of beating every one of them so thoroughly that they were all found the next morning in the same places where they had been left the evening before. They were tried at Alten, the two ringleaders executed, and a number of the others sent to the penitentiary at Christiania. This summary justice put a stop to all open and violent manifestations of religious frenzy, but it still exists to some extent, though only indulged in secret.

We paid a visit to Pastor Hvoslef on Monday, and had the pleasure of his company to dinner in the evening. He is a Christian gentleman in the best sense of the term, and though we differed in matters of belief, I was deeply impressed with his piety and sincerity. Madame Hvoslef and two rosy little Arctic blossoms shared his exile—for this is nothing less than an exile to a man of cultivation and intellectual tastes. In his house I saw—the last thing one would have expected to find in the heart of Lapland—a piano. Madame Hvoslef, who is an accomplished performer, sat down to it, and gave us the barcarole from Massaniello. While in the midst of a maze of wild Norwegian melodies, I saw the Pastor whisper something in her ear. At once, to our infinite amazement, she boldly struck up "Yankee Doodle!" Something like an American war-whoop began to issue from Braisted's mouth, but was smothered in time to prevent an alarm. "How on earth did that air get into Lapland!" I asked. "I heard Ole Bull play it at Christiania," said Madame Hvoslef, "and learned it from memory afterwards."

The weather changed greatly after our arrival. From 23° below zero on Sunday evening, it rose to 8-1/2° above, on Monday night, with a furious hurricane of snow from the north. We sent for our deer from the hills early on Tuesday morning, in order to start on our return to Muoniovara. The Lapps, however, have an Oriental disregard of time, and as there was no chance of our getting off before noon, we improved part of the delay in visiting the native schools and some of the earthen huts, or, rather, dens, in which most of the inhabitants live. There were two schools, each containing about twenty scholars—fat, greasy youngsters, swaddled in reindeer skins, with blue eyes, light brown or yellow hair, and tawny red cheeks, wherever the original colour could be discerned. As the rooms were rather warm, the odour of Lapp childhood was not quite as fresh as a cowslip, and we did not tarry long among them.

Approaching the side of a pile of dirt covered with snow, we pushed one after another, against a small square door, hung at such a slant that it closed of itself, and entered an ante-den used as a store-room. Another similar door ushered us into the house, a rude, vaulted space, framed with poles, sticks and reindeer hides, and covered compactly with earth, except a narrow opening in the top to let out the smoke from a fire kindled in the centre. Pieces of reindeer hide, dried flesh, bags of fat, and other articles, hung from the frame and dangled against our heads as we entered. The den was not more than five feet high by about eight feet in diameter. The owner, a jolly, good-humoured Lapp, gave me a low wooden stool, while his wife, with a pipe in her mouth, squatted down on the hide which served for a bed and looked at me with amiable curiosity. I contemplated them for a while with my eyes full of tears (the smoke being very thick,) until finally both eyes and nose could endure no more, and I sought the open air again.

FOOTNOTES:

[A] This was written in Lapland; and at the same time my friend Dr. Elisha Kent Kane, of immortal memory, lay upon his death-bed, in Havana. I retain the words, which I then supposed would meet his eye, that I may add my own tribute of sorrow for the untimely death of one of the truest, bravest, and noblest-hearted men I ever knew.

CHAPTER XII. THE RETURN TO MUONIOVARA.

While at Kautokeino I completed my Lapp outfit by purchasing a scarlet cap, stuffed with eider down, a pair of bœllinger, or reindeer leggings, and the komager, or broad, boat-shaped shoes, filled with dry soft hay, and tightly bound around the ankles, which are worn by everybody in Lapland. Attired in these garments, I made a very passable Lapp, barring a few superfluous inches of stature, and at once realized the prudence of conforming in one's costume to the native habits. After the first feeling of awkwardness is over, nothing can be better adapted to the Polar Winter than the Lapp dress. I walked about at first with the sensation of having each foot in the middle of a large feather bed, but my blood preserved its natural warmth even after sitting for hours in an open pulk. The bœllinger, fastened around the thighs by drawing-strings of reindeer sinew, are so covered by the poesk that one becomes, for all practical purposes, a biped reindeer, and may wallow in the snow as much as he likes without the possibility of a particle getting through his hide.

The temperature was, nevertheless, singularly mild when we set out on our return. There had been a violent storm of wind and snow the previous night, after which the mercury rose to 16° above zero. We waited until noon before our reindeers could be collected, and then set off, with the kind farewell wishes of the four Norwegian inhabitants of the place. I confess to a feeling of relief when we turned our faces southward, and commenced our return to daylight. We had at last seen the Polar night, the day without a sunrise; we had driven our reindeer under the arches of the aurora borealis; we had learned enough of the Lapps to convince us that further acquaintance would be of little profit; and it now seemed time to attempt an escape from the limbo of Death into which we had ventured. Our faces had already begun to look pale and faded from three weeks of alternate darkness and twilight, but the novelty of our life preserved us from any feeling of depression and prevented any perceptible effect upon our bodily health, such as would assuredly have followed a protracted experience of the Arctic Winter. Every day now would bring us further over the steep northern shoulder of the Earth, and nearer to that great heart of life in the south, where her blood pulsates with eternal warmth. Already there was a perceptible increase of the sun's altitude, and at noonday a thin upper slice of his disc was visible for about half an hour.

By Herr Berger's advice, we engaged as guide to Lippajärvi, a Lapp, who had formerly acted as postman, and professed to be able to find his way in the dark. The wind had blown so violently that it was probable we should have to break our own road for the whole distance. Leaving Kautokeino, we travelled up the valley of a frozen stream, towards desolate ranges of hills, or rather shelves of the table-land, running north-east and south-west. They were spotted with patches of stunted birch, hardly rising above the snow. Our deer were recruited, and we made very good progress while the twilight lasted. At some Lapp tents, where we stopped to make inquiries about the ice, I was much amused by the appearance of a group of children, who strikingly resembled bear-cubs standing on their hind legs. They were coated with reindeer hide from head to foot, with only a little full-moon of tawny red face visible.

We stopped at Siepe an hour to bait the deer. The single wooden hut was crowded with Lapps, one of whom, apparently the owner, spoke a little Norwegian. He knew who we were, and asked me many questions about America. He was most anxious to know what was our religion, and what course the Government took with regard to different sects. He seemed a little surprised, and not less pleased, to hear that all varieties of belief were tolerated, and that no one sect possessed any peculiar privileges over another. (It is only very recently that dissenters from the Orthodox Church have been allowed to erect houses of worship in Norway.) While we were speaking on these matters, an old woman, kneeling near us, was muttering prayers to herself, wringing her hands, sobbing, and giving other evidences of violent religious excitement. This appeared to be a common occurrence, as none of the Lapps took the slightest notice of it. I have no doubt that much of that hallucination which led to the murders at Kautokeino still exists among the people, kept alive by secret indulgence. Those missionaries have much to answer for who have planted the seeds of spiritual disease among this ignorant and impressible race.

The night was cold and splendidly clear. We were obliged to leave the river on account of rotten ice, and took to the open plains, where our deers sank to their bellies in the loose snow. The leading animals became fractious, and we were obliged to stop every few minutes, until their paroxysms subsided. I could not perceive that the Lapps themselves exercised much more control over them than we, who were new to the business. The domesticated reindeer still retains his wild instincts, and never fails to protest against the necessity of labour. The most docile will fly from the track, plunge, face about and refuse to draw, when you least expect it. They are possessed by an incorrigible stupidity. Their sagacity applies only to their animal wants, and they seem almost totally deficient in memory. They never become attached to men, and the only sign of recognition they show, is sometimes to allow certain persons to catch them more easily than others. In point of speed they are not equal to the horse, and an hour's run generally exhausts them. When one considers their size, however, their strength and power of endurance seem marvellous. Herr Berger informed me that he had driven a reindeer from Alten to Kautokeino, 112 miles, in twenty-six hours, and from the latter place to Muoniovara in thirty. I was also struck by the remarkable adaptation of the animal to its uses. Its hoof resembles that of the camel, being formed for snow, as the latter for sand. It is broad, cloven and flexible, the separate divisions spreading out so as to present a resisting surface when the foot is set down, and falling together when it is lifted. Thus in snow where a horse would founder in the space of a hundred yards, the deer easily works his way, mile after mile, drawing the sliding, canoe-like pulk, burdened with his master's weight, after him.

The Lapps generally treat their animals with the greatest patience and forbearance, but otherwise do not exhibit any particular attachment for them. They are indebted to them for food, clothing, habitation and conveyance, and their very existence may therefore almost be said to depend on that of their herds. It is surprising, however, what a number of deer are requisite for the support of a family. Von Buch says that a Lapp who has a hundred deer is poor, and will be finally driven to descend to the coast, and take to fishing. The does are never made to labour, but are kept in the woods for milking and

112

breeding. Their milk is rich and nourishing, but less agreeable to the taste than that of the cow. The cheese made from it is strong and not particularly palatable. It yields an oil which is the sovereign specific for frozen flesh. The male deer used for draft are always castrated, which operation the old Lapp women perform by slowly chewing the glands between their teeth until they are reduced to a pulp, without wounding the hide.

During this journey I had ample opportunity of familiarising myself with reindeer travel. It is picturesque enough at the outset, but when the novelty of the thing is worn off nothing is left but a continual drain upon one's patience. Nothing can exceed the coolness with which your deer jumps off the track, slackens his tow-rope, turns around and looks you in the face, as much as to say: "What are you going to do about it?" The simplicity and stupidity of his countenance seem to you to be admirably feigned, and unless you are an old hand you are inevitably provoked. This is particularly pleasant on the marshy table-lands of Lapland, where, if he takes a notion to bolt with you, your pulk bounces over the hard tussocks, sheers sideways down the sudden pitches, or swamps itself in beds of loose snow. Harness a frisky sturgeon to a "dug-out," in a rough sea, and you will have some idea of this method of travelling. While I acknowledge the Providential disposition of things which has given the reindeer to the Lapp, I cannot avoid thanking Heaven that I am not a Lapp, and that I shall never travel again with reindeer.

The aberrations of our deer obliged us to take a very sinuous course. Sometimes we headed north, and sometimes south, and the way seemed so long that I mistrusted the quality of our guide; but at last a light shone ahead. It was the hut of Eitajärvi. A lot of pulks lay in front of it, and the old Finn stood already with a fir torch, waiting to light us in. On arriving, Anton was greeted by his sister Caroline, who had come thus far from Muoniovara, on her way to visit some relatives at Altengaard. She was in company with some Finns, who had left Lippajärvi the day previous, but losing their way in the storm, had wandered about for twenty-four hours, exposed to its full violence. Think of an American girl of eighteen sitting in an open pulk, with the thermometer at zero, a furious wind and blinding snow beating upon her, and neither rest nor food for a day! There are few who would survive twelve hours, yet Caroline was as fresh, lively, and cheerful as ever, and immediately set about cooking our supper. We found a fire in the cold guest's room, the place swept and cleaned, and a good bed of deerskins in one corner. The temperature had sunk to 12° below zero, and the wind blew through wide cracks in the floor, but between the fire and the reciprocal warmth of our bodies we secured a comfortable sleep—a thing of the first consequence in such a climate.

Our deer started well in the morning, and the Lapp guide knew his way perfectly. The wind had blown so strongly that the track was cleared rather than filled, and we slipped up the long slopes at a rapid rate. I recognised the narrow valley where we first struck the northern streams, and the snowy plain beyond, where our first Lapp guide lost his way. By this time it was beginning to grow lighter, showing us the dreary wastes of table-land which we had before crossed in the fog. North of us was a plain of unbroken snow, extending to a level line on the horizon, where it met the dark violet sky. Were the colour changed, it would have perfectly represented the sandy plateaus of the Nubian Desert, in so many particulars does the extreme North imitate the extreme South. But the sun, which never deserts the desert, had not yet returned to these solitudes. Far, far away, on the edge of the sky, a dull red glimmer showed where he moved. Not the table-land of Pamir, in Thibet, the cradle of the Oxus and the Indus, but this lower Lapland terrace, is entitled to the designation of the "Roof of the World." We were on the summit, creeping along her mountain rafters, and looking southward, off her shelving eaves, to catch a glimpse of the light playing on her majestic front. Here, for once, we seemed to look down on the horizon, and I thought of Europe and the Tropics as lying below. Our journey northward had been an ascent but now the world's steep sloped downward before us into sunshine and warmer air. In ascending the Andes or the Himalayas, you pass through all climates and belts of vegetation between the Equator and the Pole, and so a journey due north, beyond the circle of the sun, simply reverses the phenomenon, and impresses one like the ascent of a mountain on the grandest possible scale.

In two hours from the time we left Eitajärvi we reached the Lapp encampment. The herds of deer had been driven in from the woods, and were clustered among the birch bushes around the tents. We had some difficulty in getting our own deer past them, until the Lapps came to our assistance. We made no halt, but pushed on, through deeper snows than before, over the desolate plain. As far as Palajärvi we ran with our gunwales below the snow-level, while the foremost pulks were frequently swamped under the white waves that broke over them. We passed through a picturesque gorge between two hills about 500 feet high, and beyond it came upon wide lakes covered deep with snow, under which there was a tolerable track, which the leading deer was able to find with his feet. Beyond these lakes there was a ridge, which we had no sooner crossed than a dismally grand prospect opened before us. We overlooked a valley-basin, marked with belts of stunted birch, and stretching away for several miles to the foot of a bleak snowy mountain, which I at once recognised as Lippavara. After rounding its western point and turning southward again, we were rejoiced with the sight of some fir trees, from which the snow had been shaken, brightening even with their gloomy green the white monotony of the Lapland wilderness. It was like a sudden gleam of sunshine.

We reached Lippajärvi at twelve, having made twenty-eight miles of hard travel in five hours. Here we stopped two hours to cook a meal and change our deer, and then pushed on to reach Palajoki the same night. We drove through the birch woods, no longer glorious as before, for the snow had been shaken off, and there was no sunset light to transfigure them. Still on, ploughing through deep seas in the gathering darkness, over marshy plains, all with a slant southward, draining into the Muonio, until we reached the birchen ridge of Suontajärvi, with its beautiful firs rising here and there, silent and immovable. Even the trees have no voices in the North, let the wind blow as it will. There is nothing to be heard but the sharp whistle of the dry snow—the same dreary music which accompanies the African simoom. The night was very dark, and we began to grow exceedingly tired of sitting flat in our pulks. I looked sharp for the Palajok Elv, the high fir-fringed banks of which I remembered, for they denoted our approach to the Muonio; but it was long, long before we descended from the marshes upon the winding road of snow-covered ice. In vain I shifted my aching legs and worked my benumbed hands, looking out ahead for the embouchure of the river. Braisted and I encouraged

115

each other, whenever we were near enough to hear, by the reminder that we had only one more day with reindeer. After a long time spent in this way, the high banks flattened, level snows and woods succeeded, and we sailed into the port of Palajoki.

The old Finnish lady curtsied very deeply as she recognised us, and hastened to cook our coffee and reindeer, and to make us a good bed with sheets. On our former visit the old lady and her sons had watched us undress and get into bed, but on this occasion three buxom daughters, of ages ranging from sixteen to twenty-two, appeared about the time for retiring, and stationed themselves in a row near the door, where they watched us with silent curiosity. As we had shown no hesitation in the first case, we determined to be equally courageous now, and commenced removing our garments with great deliberation, allowing them every opportunity of inspecting their fashion and the manner of wearing them. The work thus proceeded in mutual silence until we were nearly ready for repose, when Braisted, by pulling off a stocking and displaying a muscular calf, suddenly alarmed the youngest, who darted to the door and rushed out. The second caught the panic, and followed, and the third and oldest was therefore obliged to do likewise, though with evident reluctance. I was greatly amused at such an unsophisticated display of curiosity. The perfect composure of the girls, and the steadiness with which they watched us, showed that they were quite unconscious of having committed any impropriety.

The morning was clear and cold. Our deer had strayed so far into the woods that we did not get under way before the forenoon twilight commenced. We expected to find a broken road down the Muonio, but a heavy snow had fallen the day previous, and the track was completely filled. Long Isaac found so much difficulty in taking the lead, his deer constantly bolting from the path, that Anton finally relieved him, and by standing upright in the pulk and thumping the deer's flanks, succeeded in keeping up the animal's spirits and forcing a way. It was slow work, however, and the sun, rolling his whole disc above the horizon, announced midday before we reached Kyrkessuando. As we drove up to the little inn, we were boisterously welcomed by Häl, Herr Forström's brown wolf-dog, who had strayed thus far from home. Our deer were beginning to give out, and we were very anxious to reach Muoniovara in time for dinner, so we only waited long enough to give the animals a feed of moss and procure some hot milk for ourselves.

The snow-storm, which had moved over a narrow belt of country, had not extended below this place, and the road was consequently well broken. We urged our deer into a fast trot, and slid down the icy floor of the Muonio, past hills whose snows flashed scarlet and rose-orange in the long splendour of sunset. Hunger and the fatigue which our journey was producing at last, made us extremely sensitive to the cold, though it was not more than 20° below zero. My blood became so chilled, that I was apprehensive the extremities would freeze, and the most vigorous motion of the muscles barely sufficed to keep at bay the numbness which attacked them. At dusk we drove through Upper Muonioniska, and our impatience kept the reindeers so well in motion that before five o'clock (although long after dark,) we were climbing the well-known slope to Herr Forström's house at Muoniovara. Here we found the merchant, not yet departed to the Lapp fair at Karessuando, and Mr. Wolley, who welcomed us with the cordiality of an old friend. Our snug room at the carpenter's was already warmed and set in order, and after our reindeer drive of 250 miles through the wildest parts of Lapland, we felt a home-like sense of happiness and comfort in smoking our pipes before the familiar iron stove.

The trip to Kautokeino embraced about all I saw of Lapp life during the winter journey. The romance of the tribe, as I have already said, has totally departed with their conversion, while their habits of life scarcely improved in the least, are sufficiently repulsive to prevent any closer experience than I have had, unless the gain were greater. Mr. Wolley, who had been three years in Lapland, also informed me that the superstitious and picturesque traditions of the people have almost wholly disappeared, and the coarse mysticism and rant which they have engrafted upon their imperfect Christianity does not differ materially from the same excrescence in more civilised races. They have not even (the better for them, it is true) any characteristic and picturesque vices—but have become, certainly to their own great advantage, a pious, fanatical, moral, ignorant and commonplace people. I have described them exactly as I found them, and as they have been described to me by those who knew them well. The readers of "Afraja" may be a little disappointed with the picture, as I confess I have been (in an artistic sense, only) with the reality; but the Lapps have lost many vices with their poetic diablerie, and nobody has a right to complain.

It is a pity that many traits which are really characteristic and interesting in a people cannot be mentioned on account of that morbid prudery so prevalent in our day, which insults the unconscious innocence of nature. Oh, that one could imitate the honest unreserve of the old travellers—the conscientiousness which insisted on telling not only the truth, but the whole truth! This is scarcely possible, now; but at the same time I have not been willing to emasculate my accounts of the tribes of men to the extent perhaps required by our ultra-conventionalism, and must insist, now and then, on being allowed a little Flemish fidelity to nature. In the description of races, as in the biography of individuals, the most important half of life is generally omitted.

CHAPTER XIII. ABOUT THE FINNS.

We remained but another day in Muoniovara, after our return from Kautokeino, and this was devoted to preparations for the return journey to Haparanda. My first intention had been to make an excursion across the country to the iron mountains of Gellivara, thence to Quickjock, at the foot of the Northern Alp, Sulitelma, "Queen of Snows," and so southward through the heart of Swedish Lappmark; but I found that such a journey would be attended with much difficulty and delay. In the first place, there were no broken roads at this season, except on the routes of inland trade; much of the intermediate country is a wilderness, where one must camp many nights in the snow; food was very scarce, the Lapps having hardly enough for their own necessities, and the delays at every place where guides and reindeer must be changed, would have prolonged the journey far beyond the time which I had allotted to the North. I began to doubt, also, whether one would be sufficiently repaid for the great fatigue and danger which such a trip would have involved. There is no sensation of which one wearies sooner than disgust; and, much as I enjoy a degree of barbarism in milder climates, I suspected that a long companionship with Lapps in a polar winter would be a little too much for me. So I turned my face toward Stockholm, heartily glad that I had made the journey, yet not dissatisfied that I was looking forward to its termination.

Before setting out on our return, I shall devote a few pages to the Finns. For the principal facts concerning them, I am mostly indebted to Mr. Wolley, whose acquaintance with the language, and residence of three years in Lapland, have made him perfectly familiar with the race. As I have already remarked, they are a more picturesque people than the Swedes, with stronger lights and shades of character, more ardent temperaments, and a more deeply-rooted national feeling. They seem to be rather clannish and exclusive, in fact, disliking both Swedes and Russians, and rarely intermarrying with them. The sharply-defined boundaries of language and race, at the head of the Bothnian Gulf, are a striking evidence of this. Like their distant relatives, the Hungarian

Magyars, they retain many distinct traces of their remote Asiatic origin. It is partly owing to this fact, and partly to that curious approach of extremes which we observe in nature no less than in humanity, that all suggestive traits of resemblance in these regions point to the Orient rather than to Europe.

I have already described the physical characteristics of the Finns, and have nothing to add, except that I found the same type everywhere, even among the mixed-blooded Quäns of Kautokeino—high cheek-bones, square, strong jaws, full yet firm lips, low, broad foreheads, dark eyes and hair, and a deeper, warmer red on the cheeks than on those of the rosy Swedes. The average height is, perhaps, not quite equal to that of the latter race, but in physical vigor I can see no inferiority, and there are among them many men of splendid stature, strength, and proportion. Von Buch ascribes the marked difference of stature between the Finns and the Lapps, both living under precisely the same influences of climate, to the more cleanly habits of the former and their constant use of the vapor-bath; but I have always found that blood and descent, even where the variation from the primitive stock is but slight, are more potent than climate or custom. The Finns have been so long christianised and civilised (according to the European idea of civilisation), that whatever peculiar characteristic they retain must be looked for mainly in those habits which illustrate their mental and moral natures. In their domestic life, they correspond in most particulars to the Swedes of the same class.

They are passionate, and therefore prone to excesses—imaginative, and therefore, owing to their scanty education, superstitious. Thus the religious element, especially the fantastic aberrations thereof engendered by Lestadius and other missionaries, while it has tended greatly to repress the vice, has in the same proportion increased the weakness. Drunkenness, formerly so prevalent as to be the curse of Lapland, is now exceedingly rare, and so are the crimes for which it is responsible. The most flagrant case which has occurred in the neighborhood of Muoniovara for some years past, was that of a woman who attempted to poison her father-in-law by mixing the scrapings of lucifer matches with his coffee, in order to get rid of the burden of supporting him. Although the evidence was very convincing, the matter was hushed up, in order to avoid a scandal upon the Church, the woman being a steadfast member. In regard to drunkenness, I have heard it stated that, while it was formerly no unusual thing for a Finn to be frozen to death in this condition, the same catastrophe never befell a Lapp, owing to his mechanical habit of keeping his arms and feet in motion—a habit which he preserves even while utterly stupefied and unconscious.

A singular spiritual epidemic ran through Polar Finland three or four years ago, contemporary with the religious excitement in Norwegian Lapland, and partly occasioned by the same reckless men. It consisted of sobbings, strong nervous convulsions, and occasional attacks of that state of semi-consciousness called trance, the subjects of which were looked upon as having been possessed by the Spirit, and transported to the other world, where visions like those of John on Patmos, were revealed to them. The missionaries, instead of repressing this unhealthy delusion, rather encouraged it, and even went so far as to publish as supernatural revelations, the senseless ravings of these poor deluded people. The epidemic spread until there was scarcely a family some member of which was not affected by it, and even yet it has not wholly subsided. The fit would come upon the infected persons at any time, no matter where they were, or how employed. It usually commenced with a convulsive catching of the breath, which increased in violence, accompanied by sobbing, and sometimes by cries or groans, until the victim was either exhausted or fell into a trance, which lasted some hours. The persons who were affected were always treated with the greatest respect during the attack no one ventured to smile, no matter how absurd a form the visitation might take. The principle of abstinence from strong drinks was promulgated about the same time, and much of the temperance of the Finns and Lapps is undoubtedly owing the impression made upon their natures by these phenomena.

The same epidemic has often prevailed in the United States, England and Germany. The barking and dancing mania which visited Kentucky thirty or forty years ago, and the performances of the "Holy Rollers," were even more ludicrous and unnatural. Such appearances are a puzzle alike to the physiologist and the philosopher; their frequency shows that they are based on some weak spot in human nature; and in proportion as we pity the victims we have a right to condemn those who sow the seeds of the pestilence. True religion is never spasmodic; it is calm as the existence of God. I know of nothing more shocking than such attempts to substitute rockets and blue lights for Heaven's eternal sunshine.

So far as regards their moral character, the Finns have as little cause for reproach as any other people. We found them as universally honest and honourable in their dealings as the Northern Swedes, who are not surpassed in the world in this respect. Yet their countenances express more cunning and reserve, and the virtue may be partly a negative one, resulting from that indolence which characterises the frigid and the torrid zone. Thus, also, notwithstanding physical signs which denote more ardent animal passions than their neighbors, they are equally chaste, and have as high a standard of sexual purity. Illegitimate births are quite rare, and are looked upon as a lasting shame and disgrace to both parties. The practice of "bundling" which, until recently, was very common among Finnish lovers, very seldom led to such results, and their marriage speedily removed the dishonour. Their manners, socially, in this respect, are curiously contradictory. Thus, while both sexes freely mingle in the bath, in a state of nature, while the women unhesitatingly scrub, rub and dry their husbands, brothers or male friends, while the salutation for both sexes is an embrace with the right arm, a kiss is considered grossly immodest and improper. A Finnish woman expressed the greatest astonishment and horror, at hearing from Mr. Wolley that it was a very common thing in England for a husband and wife to kiss each other. "If my husband were to attempt such a thing," said she, "I would beat him about the ears so that he would feel it for a week." Yet in conversation they are very plain and unreserved, though by no means gross. They acknowledge that such things as generation, gestation and parturition exist, and it may be that this very absence of mystery tends to keep chaste so excitable and imaginative a race.

Notwithstanding their superstition, their love of poetry, and the wild, rich, musical character of their language, there is a singular absence of legendary lore in this part of Finland. Perhaps this is owing to the fact that their ancestors have emigrated hither, principally within the last two centuries, from the early home of the race—Tavastland, the shores of the

Pajana Lake, and the Gulf of Finland. It is a difficult matter to preserve family traditions among them, or even any extended genealogical record, from the circumstance that a Finn takes his name, not only from his father's surname, but from his residence. Thus, Isaaki takes the name of "Anderinpoika" from his father Anderi, and adds "Niemi," the local name of his habitation. His son Nils will be called Nils Isakipoika, with the addition of the name of his residence, wherever that may be; and his family name will be changed as often as his house. There may be a dozen different names in the course of one generation, and the list soon becomes too complicated and confused for an uneducated memory. It is no wonder, therefore, that the Finn knows very little except about what happened during his own life, or, at best, his father's. I never heard the Kalewala spoken of, and doubt very much whether it is known to the natives of this region. The only songs we heard, north of Haparanda, were hymns—devout, but dismal. There must be ballads and household songs yet alive, but the recent spiritual fever has silenced them for the time.

I was at first a little surprised to find the natives of the North so slow, indolent and improvident. We have an idea that a cold climate is bracing and stimulating—ergo, the further north you go, the more active and energetic you will find the people. But the touch of ice is like that of fire. The tropics relax, the pole benumbs, and the practical result is the same in both cases. In the long, long winter, when there are but four hours of twilight to twenty of darkness—when the cows are housed, the wood cut, the hay gathered, the barley bran and fir bark stowed away for bread, and the summer's catch of fish salted—what can a man do, when his load of wood or hay is hauled home, but eat, gossip and sleep? To bed at nine, and out of it at eight in the morning, smoking and dozing between the slow performance of his few daily duties, he becomes at last as listless and dull as a hibernating bear. In the summer he has perpetual daylight, and need not hurry. Besides, why should he give himself special trouble to produce an unusually large crop of flax or barley, when a single night may make his labours utterly profitless? Even in midsummer the blighting frost may fall: nature seems to take a cruel pleasure in thwarting him: he is fortunate only through chance; and thus a sort of Arab fatalism and acquiescence in whatever happens, takes possession of him.

His improvidence is also to be ascribed to the same cause. Such fearful famine and suffering as existed in Finland and Lapland during the winter of 1856-7 might no doubt have been partially prevented, but no human power could have wholly forestalled it.

The polar zone was never designed for the abode of man. In the pre-Adamite times, when England was covered with palm-forests, and elephants ranged through Siberia, things may have been widely different, and the human race then (if there was any) may have planted vineyards on these frozen hills and lived in bamboo huts. But since the geological émeutes and revolutions, and the establishment of the terrestrial régime, I cannot for the life of me see whatever induced beings endowed with human reason, to transplant themselves hither and here take root, while such vast spaces lie waste and useless in more genial climes. A man may be pardoned for remaining where the providences of birth and education have thrown him, but I cannot excuse the first colonists for inflicting such a home upon centuries of descendants. Compare even their physical life—the pure animal satisfaction in existence, for that is not a trifling matter after all—with that of the Nubians, or the Malays, or the Polynesians! It is the difference between a poor hare, hunted and worried year after year by hounds and visions of hounds and the familiar, confiding wren, happiest of creatures, because secure of protection everywhere. Oh that the circle of the ecliptic would coincide with that of the equator! That the sun would shine from pole to pole for evermore, and all lands be habitable and hospitable, and the Saharan sands (according to Fourier) be converted into bowers of the Hesperides, and the bitter salt of the ocean brine (vide the same author) become delicious champagne punch, wherein it would be pleasure to drown! But I am afraid that mankind is not yet fit for such a millennium.

Meanwhile it is truly comforting to find that even here, where men live under such discouraging circumstances that one would charitably forgive them the possession of many vices, they are, according to their light, fully as true, and honest, and pure, as the inhabitants of the most favoured countries in the world. Love for each other, trust in each other, faith in God, are all vital among them; and their shortcomings are so few and so easily accounted for, that one must respect them and feel that his faith in man is not lessened in knowing them. You who spend your lives at home can never know how much good there is in the world. In rude unrefined races, evil naturally rises to the surface, and one can discern the character of the stream beneath its scum. It is only in the highest civilisation where the outside is goodly to the eye, too often concealing an interior foul to the core.

But I have no time to moralise on these matters. My duty is that of a chronicler; and if I perform that conscientiously, the lessons which my observations suggest will need no pointing out. I cannot close this chapter, however, without confessing my obligations to Mr. Wolley, whose thorough knowledge of the Lapps and Finns enabled me to test the truth of my own impressions, and to mature opinions which I should otherwise, from my own short experience, have hesitated in stating. Mr. Wolley, with that pluck and persistence of English character which Emerson so much admires, had made himself master of all that Lapland can furnish to the traveller, but intended remaining another year for scientific purposes. If he gives to the world—as I hope and trust he will—the result of this long and patient inquiry and investigation, we shall have at last a standard authority for this little-known corner of Europe. We were also indebted to Mr. Wolley for much personal kindness, which I take pleasure in acknowledging in the only way he cannot prevent.

CHAPTER XIV. EXPERIENCES OF ARCTIC WEATHER.

We bade a final adieu to Muoniovara on the afternoon of the 24th of January, leaving Mr. Wolley to wait for June and the birds in that dismal seclusion. Instead of resuming skjuts, we engaged horses as far as Kengis from Herr Forström and a neighbouring Finn, with a couple of shock-headed natives as postillions. Our sleds were mounted upon two rough Finnish sledges, the only advantage of which was to make harder work for the horses—but the people would have it so. The sun was down, but a long, long twilight succeeded, with some faint show of a zodiacal light. There was a tolerable track on the river, but our Finns walked their horses the whole way, and we were nearly seven hours in making Parkajoki. The air was very sharp; my nose, feet and hands kept me busily employed, and I began to fear that I was becoming unusually sensitive to cold, for the thermometer indicated but 15° below zero when we started. At Parkajoki, however, my doubts were removed and my sensations explained, on finding that the temperature had fallen to 44° below.

We slept warmly and well on our old bed of reindeer skins, in one corner of the milk-room. When Braisted, who rose first, opened the door, a thick white mist burst in and rolled heavily along the floor. I went out, attired only in my shirt and drawers, to have a look at the weather. I found the air very still and keen, though not painfully cold—but I was still full of the warmth of sleep. The mercury, however, had sunk into the very bulb of the thermometer, and was frozen so solid that I held it in the full glare of the fire for about a minute and a half before it thawed sufficiently to mount. The temperature was probably 50° below zero, if not more—greater than any we had yet experienced. But it was six o'clock, and we must travel. Fortifying ourselves with coffee and a little meat, and relying for defence in case of extremity on a bottle of powerful rum with which we had supplied ourselves, we muffled up with more than usual care, and started for Kihlangi.

We devoted ourselves entirely to keeping warm, and during the ride of six hours suffered very little except from the gradual diminution of our bodily temperature. It was a dreary journey, following the course of the Muonio between black, snow-laden forests. The sun rose to a height of seven or eight degrees at meridian; when we came over the same road, on our way north, he only showed half his disc. At Kihlangi the people recognised us, and were as well disposed as their stupidity would allow. The old woman cooked part of our reindeer joint, which, with half a dozen cups of strong coffee, brought back a comfortable warmth to our extremities. There were still twenty-four miles to be traversed; the horses were already exhausted, and the temperature only rose to -42° at midday, after which it fell again. We had a terrible journey. Step by step the horses slowly pulled us through the snow, every hour seeming lengthened to a day, as we worked our benumbed fingers and toes until the muscles were almost powerless, and yet it was dangerous to cease. Gradually the blood grew colder in the main channels; insidious chills succeeded, followed by a drowsy torpor, like that which is produced by a heavy dose of opium, until we were fain to have recourse to the rum, a horrid, vitriolic beverage, which burned our throats and stomachs like melted lead, yet gave us a temporary relief.

We almost despaired of reaching Jokijalka, on finding, about ten o'clock at night, that our postillions had taken us to the village of Kolare, and stopped before a large log house, where they seemed to think we would spend the night. Everybody had gone to bed, we knew not where we were, and had set our hearts upon the comfortable guest's room at Jokijalka. It was impossible to make the fellows understand me, but they saw that we were angry, and after a short consultation passed on. We again entered the snowy woods, which were dimly lighted up by an aurora behind us—a strange, mysterious, ghastly illumination, like the phosphorescent glow of a putrefying world. We were desperately cold, our very blood freezing in our veins, and our limbs numb and torpid. To keep entirely awake was impossible. We talked incessantly, making random answers, as continual fleeting dreams crossed the current of our consciousness. A heavy thump on the back was pardoned by him who received it, and a punch between the eyes would have been thankfully accepted had it been necessary.

At last, at last, Kolare church on the river bank came in sight; we crossed to the Russian side, and drove into the yard of the inn. It was nearly midnight, 47° below zero, and we had been for seventeen hours exposed to such a temperature. Everybody had long been asleep. Locks and bolts are unknown, however, so we rushed into the family room, lit fir splinters, and inspected the faces of the sleeping group until we found the landlord, who arose and kindled a fresh fire in the milk-room. They made us coffee and a small bed, saying that the guest's room was too cold, which indeed it was, being little less than the outside temperature. On opening the door in the morning, the cold air rushed in as thick and white as steam. We had a little meat cooked, but could not eat enough, at such an early hour, to supply much fuel. As for taking anything with us for refreshment on the road, it was out of the question. One of our Finns turned back to Muoniovara with the laziest horse, and we got another from our Russian landlord. But it was a long, long journey to the next station (twenty miles), and the continuance of the extreme cold began to tell upon us. This part of the road was very heavy, as on the journey up—seemingly a belt of exposed country where the snow drifts more than elsewhere.

At Kexisvara we found two of the three pleasant women, who cooked our last fragment of reindeer meat, and sent off for horses to Kardis. We here parted with our other Finn, very glad to get rid of his horse, and take a fresh start. We had no difficulty now in making our way with the people, as they all recognised us and remembered our overpayments; besides which, I had enlarged my Finnish vocabulary at Muoniovara. Our horses were better, our sledges lighter and we were not long in reaching the iron-works at Kengis, which we passed at dusk. I should willingly have called upon the hospitable bruk-patron, but we were in too great a hurry to get out of the frigid zone. We were warmed by our meal, and sang lustily as we slid down the Torneå, finding its dreary, sparsely-settled banks cheerful and smiling by contrast with the frightful solitudes we had left. After some hours the postillion stopped before a house on the Swedish bank to hay his horses. We went up and found a single inhabitant, a man who was splitting fir for torches, but the conversation was limited to alternate puffs from our pipes. There was a fine aurora behind us—a low arch of white fire, with streamers radiating outward, shifting and dancing along its curve.

It was nearly ten o'clock before we reached Kardis, half unconscious from the cold. Our horse ran into the wrong place, and we lost sight of the baggage-sled, our only guide in the darkness. We could no longer trust the animal's instinct, but had to depend on our own, which is perhaps truer: at least, I have often found in myself traces of that blind, unreasoning faculty which guides the bee and the bird, and have never been deceived in trusting to it. We found the inn, and carried a cloud of frozen vapor into the kitchen with us, as we opened the door. The graceful wreaths of ice-smoke rolled before our feet, as before those of ascending saints in the old pictures, but ourselves, hair from head to foot, except two pairs of eyes, which looked out through icy loop-holes, resembled the reverse of saints. I told the landlord in Finnish that we wanted to sleep—"mia tarvi nuku á." He pointed to a bed in the corner, out of which rose a sick girl, of about seventeen, very pale, and evidently suffering. They placed some benches near the fire, removed the bedding, and disposed her as comfortably as the place permitted. We got some hot milk and hard bread, threw some reindeer skins on the vacant truck, and lay down, but not to sleep much. The room was so close and warm, and the dozen persons in it so alternately snoring and restless, that our rest was continually disturbed. We, therefore, rose early and aroused the lazy natives.

The cold was still at 47° below zero. The roads were so much better, however, that we descended again to our own runners, and our lively horses trotted rapidly down the Torneå. The signs of settlement and comparative civilisation which now increased with every mile were really cheering. Part of our way lay through the Swedish woods and over the intervening morasses, where the firs were hung with weepers of black-green moss, and stood solid and silent in their mantles of snow, lighted with a magnificent golden flush at sunrise. The morning was icy-clear and dazzling. There was not the least warmth in the sun's rays, but it was pleasant to see him with a white face once more. We could still stare at him without winking, but the reflection from the jewelled snow pained our eyes. The cold was so keen that we were obliged to keep our faces buried between our caps and boas, leaving only the smallest possible vacancy for the eyes. This was exceedingly disagreeable, on account of the moisture from the breath, which kept the squirrel tails constantly wet and sticky. Nevertheless, the cold penetrated through the little aperture; my eyes and forehead were like marble, the eyeballs like lumps of ice, sending a sharp pang of cold backward into the brain. I realised distinctly how a statue must feel.

Beyond Pello, where we stopped to "fire up," our road lay mostly on the Russian side. While crossing the Torneå at sunset, we met a drove of seventy or eighty reindeer, in charge of a dozen Lapps, who were bringing a cargo from Haparanda. We were obliged to turn off the road and wait until they had passed. The landlord at Juoxengi, who was quite drunk, hailed us with a shout and a laugh, and began talking about Kautokeino. We had some difficulty in getting rid of his conversation, and his importunities for us to stay all night. This was the place where they tried to make us leave, on the way up. I replied to the landlord's torrent of Finnish with some choice specimens of Kentucky oratory, which seemed to make but little impression on him. He gave us excellent horses, however, and we sped away again, by the light of another brilliant auroral arch.

Our long exposure to the extreme cold, coupled as it was with lack of rest and nourishment, now began to tell upon us. Our temperature fell so low that we again had recourse to the rum, which alone, I verily believe, prevented us from freezing bodily. One is locked in the iron embrace of the polar air, until the very life seems to be squeezed out of him. I huddled myself in my poesk, worked my fingers and toes, buried my nose in the damp, frozen fur, and laboured like a Hercules to keep myself awake and alive—but almost in vain. Braisted and I kept watch over each other, or attempted it, for about the only consciousness either of us had was that of the peril of falling asleep. We talked of anything and everything, sang, thumped each other, but the very next minute would catch ourselves falling over the side of the sled. A thousand dreams worried my brain and mixed themselves with my talk; and the absurdities thus created helped to arouse me. Speaking of seeing some wolves in the woods of California, I gravely continued: "I took out my sword, sharpened it on the grindstone and dared him to come on," when a punch in the ribs stopped me. Another time, while talking of hippopotami in the White Nile, I said: "If you want any skins, you must go to the Hudson's Bay Company. They have a depôt of them on Vancouver's Island." Braisted gave me much trouble, by assuring me in the most natural wide-awake voice that he was not in the least sleepy, when the reins had dropped from his hands and his head rocked on his shoulder. I could never be certain whether he was asleep or awake. Our only plan was not to let the conversation flag a minute.

At Torakankorwa we changed horses without delay, and hurried on to Matarengi. On turning out of the road to avoid a hay-sled, we were whirled completely over. There was no fun in this, at such a time. I fell head foremost into deep snow, getting a lump in my right eye, which completely blinded me for a time. My forehead, eyebrows, and the bridge of my nose were insufferably painful. On reaching Matarengi I found my nose frozen through, and considerably swollen. The people were in bed, but we went into the kitchen, where a dozen or more were stowed about, and called for the landlord. Three young girls, who were in bed in one corner, rose and dressed themselves in our presence without the least hesitation, boiled some milk, and gave us bread and butter. We had a single small bed, which kept us warm by obliging us to lie close. Sometime in the night, two Swedes arrived, who blustered about and made so much noise, that Braisted finally silenced them by threats of personal violence, delivered in very good English.

In the morning the mercury froze, after showing 49° below zero. The cold was by this time rather alarming, especially after our experiences of the previous day. The air was hazy with the fine, frozen atoms of moisture, a raw wind blew from the north, the sky was like steel which has been breathed upon—in short, the cold was visible to the naked eye. We warmed our gloves and boots, and swathed our heads so completely that not a feature was to be seen. I had a little loophole between my cap and boa, but it was soon filled up with frost from my breath, and helped to keep in the warmth. The road was hard and smooth as marble. We had good horses, and leaving Avasaxa and the polar circle behind us, we sped down the solid bed of the Torneå to Niemis. On the second stage we began to freeze for want of food. The air was really terrible; nobody ventured out of doors who could stay in the house. The smoke was white and dense, like steam; the wind was a blast from the Norseman's hell, and the touch of it on your face almost made you scream. Nothing can be more severe—flaying, branding with a hot iron, cutting with a dull knife, &c., may be something like it, but no worse.

The sun rose through the frozen air a little after nine, and mounted quite high at noon. At Päckilä we procured some hot milk and smoked reindeer, tolerable horses and a stout boy of fourteen to drive our baggage-sled. Every one we met had a face either frozen, or about to freeze. Such a succession of countenances, fiery red, purple, blue, black almost, with white frost spots, and surrounded with rings of icy hair and fur, I never saw before. We thanked God again and again that our faces were turned southward, and that the deadly wind was blowing on our backs. When we reached Korpikilä, our boy's face, though solid and greasy as a bag of lard, was badly frozen. His nose was quite white and swollen, as if blistered by fire, and there were frozen blotches on both cheeks. The landlord rubbed the parts instantly with rum, and performed the same operation on our noses.

On this day, for the first time in more than a month, we saw daylight, and I cannot describe how cheering was the effect of those pure, white, brilliant rays, in spite of the iron landscape they illumined. It was no longer the setting light of the level Arctic sun; not the twilight gleams of shifting colour, beautiful, but dim; not the faded, mock daylight which sometimes glimmered for a half-hour at noon; but the true white, full, golden day, which we had almost forgotten. So nearly, indeed, that I did not for some time suspect the cause of the unusual whiteness and brightness. Its effect upon the trees was superb. The twigs of the birch and the needles of the fir were coated with crystal, and sparkled like jets of jewels spouted up from the immaculate snow. The clumps of birches can be compared to nothing but frozen fountains—frozen in full action, with their showery sheaves of spray arrested before they fell. It was a wonderful, a fairy world we beheld—too beautiful to be lifeless, but every face we met reminded us the more that this was the chill beauty of Death—of dead Nature. Death was in the sparkling air, in the jewelled trees, in the spotless snow. Take off your mitten, and his hand will grasp yours like a vice; uncover your mouth, and your frozen lips will soon acknowledge his kiss.

Even while I looked the same icy chills were running through my blood, precursors of that drowsy torpor which I was so anxious to avoid. But no; it would come, and I dozed until both hands became so stiff that it was barely possible to restore their powers of motion and feeling. It was not quite dark when we reached Kuckula, the last station, but thence to Haparanda our horses were old and lazy, and our postillion was a little boy, whose weak voice had no effect. Braisted kept his hands warm in jerking and urging, but I sat and froze. Village after village was passed, but we looked in vain for the lights of Torneå. We were thoroughly exhausted with our five days' battle against the dreadful cold, when at last a row of lights gleamed across the river, and we drove up to the inn. The landlord met us with just the same words as on the first visit, and, strange enough, put us into the same room, where the same old Norrland merchant was again quartered in the same stage of tipsiness. The kind Fredrika did not recognise us in our Lapp dresses, until I had unrobed, when she cried out in joyful surprise, "Why, you were here before!"

We had been so completely chilled that it was a long time before any perceptible warmth returned. But a generous meal, with a bottle of what was called "gammal scherry" (though the Devil and his servants, the manufacturers of chemical wines, only knew what it was), started the flagging circulation. We then went to bed, tingling and stinging in every nerve from the departing cold. Every one complained of the severity of the weather, which, we were told, had not been equalled for many years past. But such a bed, and such a rest as I had! Lying between clean sheets, with my feet buried in soft fur, I wallowed in a flood of downy, delicious sensations until sunrise. In the morning we ventured to wash our faces and brush our teeth for the first time in five days, put on clean shirts, and felt once more like responsible beings. The natives never wash when the weather is so cold, and cautioned us against it. The wind had fallen but the mercury again froze at 47° below zero. Nevertheless, we went out after breakfast to call upon Dr. Wretholm, and walk over the Torneå.

The old Doctor was overjoyed to see us again. "Ah!" said he, "it is a good fortune that you have got back alive. When the weather was so cold, I thought of you, travelling over the Norwegian fjeller, and thought you must certainly be frozen to death." His wife was no less cordial in her welcome. They brought us ale and Swedish punch, with reindeer cheese for our frozen noses, and insisted on having their horse put into the sled to take us over to Torneå and bring us back to dinner. The doctor's boy drove us, facing the wind with our faces exposed, at -42°, but one night's rest and good food enabled us to bear it without inconvenience. Torneå is a plain Swedish town, more compactly built than Haparanda, yet scarcely larger. The old church is rather picturesque, and there were some tolerable houses, which appeared to be government buildings, but the only things particularly Russian which we noticed were a Cossack sentry, whose purple face showed that he was nearly frozen, and a guide-post with "150 versts to Uleaborg" upon it. On returning to the Doctor's we found a meal ready, with a capital salad of frozen salmon, bouillon, ale, and coffee. The family were reading the Swedish translation of "Dred" in the Aftonblad, and were interested in hearing some account of Mrs. Beecher Stowe. We had a most agreeable and interesting visit to these kind, simple-hearted people.

I made a sunset sketch of Torneå. I proposed also to draw Fredrika, but she at once refused, in great alarm. "Not for anything in the world," said she, "would I have it done!" What superstitious fears possessed her I could not discover. We made arrangements to start for Kalix the next day, on our way to Stockholm. The extreme temperature still continued. The air was hazy with the frozen moisture—the smoke froze in solid masses—the snow was brittle and hard as metal—iron stuck like glue—in short, none of the signs of an Arctic winter were wanting. Nevertheless, we trusted to the day's rest and fatter fare on the road for strength to continue the battle.

CHAPTER XV. INCIDENTS OF THE RETURN JOURNEY.

We left Haparanda on the 30th of January. After six days of true Arctic weather—severer than any registered by De Haven's expedition, during a winter in the polar ice—the temperature rose suddenly to 26° below zero. We were happy and jolly at getting fairly started for Stockholm at last, and having such mild (!) weather to travel in. The difference in our sensations was remarkable. We could boldly bare our faces and look about us; our feet kept warm and glowing, and we felt no more the hazardous chill and torpor of the preceding days. On the second stage the winter road crossed an arm of the Bothnian Gulf. The path was well marked out with fir-trees—a pretty avenue, four or five miles in length, over the broad, white plain. On the way we saw an eruption of the ice, which had been violently thrown up by the confined air. Masses three feet thick and solid as granite were burst asunder and piled atop of each other.

We travelled too fast this day for the proper enjoyment of the wonderful scenery on the road. I thought I had exhausted my admiration of these winter forests—but no, miracles will never cease. Such fountains, candelabra, Gothic pinnacles, tufts of plumes, colossal sprays of coral, and the embodiments of the fairy pencillings of frost on window panes, wrought in crystal and silver, are beyond the power of pen or pencil. It was a wilderness of beauty; we knew not where to look, nor which forms to choose, in the dazzling confusion. Silent and all unmoved by the wind they stood, sharp and brittle as of virgin ore—not trees of earth, but the glorified forests of All-Father Odin's paradise, the celestial city of Asgaard. No living forms of vegetation are so lovely. Tropical palms, the tree-ferns of Penang, the lotus of Indian rivers, the feathery bamboo, the arrowy areca—what are they beside these marvellous growths of winter, these shining sprays of pearl, ivory and opal, gleaming in the soft orange light of the Arctic sun?

At Sängis we met a handsome young fellow with a moustache, who proved to be the Länsman of Kalix. I was surprised to find that he knew all about us. He wondered at our coming here north, when we might stay at home thought once would be enough for us, and had himself been no further than Stockholm. I recognised our approach to Näsby by the barrels set in the snow—an ingenious plan of marking the road in places where the snow drifts, as the wind creates a whirl or eddy around them. We were glad to see Näsby and its two-story inn once more. The pleasant little handmaiden smiled all over her face when she saw us again. Näsby is a crack place: the horses were ready at once, and fine creatures they were, taking us up the Kalix to Månsbyn, eight miles in one hour. The road was hard as a rock and smooth as a table, from much ploughing and rolling.

The next day was dark and lowering, threatening snow, with a raw wind from the north-west, and an average temperature of 15° below zero. We turned the north-western corner of the Bothnian Gulf in the afternoon, and pushed on to Old Luleå by supper-time. At Persö, on the journey north, I had forgotten my cigar-case, an old, familiar friend of some years' standing, and was overjoyed to find that the servant-girl had carefully preserved it, thinking I might return some day. We drove through the streets of empty stables and past the massive church of Old Luleå, to the inn, where we had before met the surly landlord. There he was again, and the house was full, as the first time. However we obtained the promise of a bed in the large room, and meanwhile walked up and down to keep ourselves warm. The guests' rooms were filled with gentlemen of the neighborhood, smoking and carousing. After an hour had passed, a tall, handsome, strong fellow came out of the rooms, and informed us that as we were strangers he would give up the room to us and seek lodgings elsewhere. He had drunk just enough to be mellow and happy, and insisted on delaying his own supper to let us eat first. Who should come along at this juncture but the young fellow we had seen in company with Brother Horton at Månsbyn, who hailed us with: "Thank you for the last time!" With him was a very gentlemanly man who spoke English. They were both accompanied by ladies, and were returning from the ball of Piteå. The guests all treated us with great courtesy and respect, and the landlord retired and showed his surly face no more. Our first friend informed me that he had been born and brought up in the neighborhood, but could not recollect such a severe winter.

136

As we descended upon the Luleå River in the morning we met ten sleighs coming from the ball. The horses were all in requisition at the various stations, but an extra supply had been provided, and we were not detained anywhere. The Norrland sleds are so long that a man may place his baggage in the front part and lie down at full length behind it. A high back shields the traveller from the wind, and upon a step in the rear stands the driver, with a pair of reins as long as a main-top-bowline, in order to reach the horse, who is at the opposite end of a very long pair of shafts. In these sleds one may travel with much comfort, and less danger of overturning, though not so great speed as in the short, light, open frames we bought in Sundsvall. The latter are seldom seen so far north, and were a frequent object of curiosity to the peasants at the stations. There is also a sled with a body something like a Hansom cab, entirely closed, with a window in front, but they are heavy, easily overturned, and only fit for luxurious travellers.

We approached Piteå at sunset. The view over the broad embouchure of the river, studded with islands, was quite picturesque, and the town itself, scattered along the shore and over the slopes of the hills made a fair appearance. It reminded me somewhat of a small New-England country town, with its square frame houses and an occasional garden. Here I was rejoiced by the sight of a cherry-tree, the most northern fruit-tree which I saw. On our way up, we thought Piteå, at night and in a snow-storm, next door to the North Pole. Now, coming from the north, seeing its snowy hills and house-roofs rosy with the glow of sunset, it was warm and southern by contrast. The four principal towns of West and North Bothnia are thus characterised in an old verse of Swedish doggerel: Umeå, the fine; Piteå, the needle-making; Luleå, the lazy; and in Torneå, everybody gets drunk.

We took some refreshment, pushed on and reached Abyn between nine and ten o'clock, having travelled seventy miles since morning. The sleighing was superb. How I longed for a dashing American cutter, with a span of fast horses, a dozen strings of bells and an ebony driver! Such a turnout would rather astonish the northern solitudes, and the slow, quaint northern population. The next day we had a temperature of 2° above zero, with snow falling, but succeeded in reaching Skellefteå for breakfast. For the last two or three miles we travelled along a hill-side overlooking a broad, beautiful valley, cleared and divided into cultivated fields, and thickly sprinkled with villages and farm-houses. Skellefteå itself made an imposing appearance, as the lofty dome of its Grecian church came in sight around the shoulder of the hill. We took the wrong road, and in turning about split one of our shafts, but Braisted served it with some spare rope, using the hatchet-handle as a marlingspike, so that it held stoutly all the rest of the way to Stockholm.

We went on to Burea that night, and the next day to Djekneboda, sixty miles farther. The temperature fluctuated about the region of zero, with a heavy sky and light snow-falls. As we proceeded southward the forests became larger, and the trees began to show a dark green foliage where the wind had blown away the snow, which was refreshing to see, after the black or dark indigo hue they wear farther north. On the 4th of February, at noon, we passed through Umeå, and congratulated ourselves on getting below the southern limit of the Lapland climate. There is nothing to say about these towns; they are mere villages with less than a thousand inhabitants each, and no peculiar interest, either local or historical, attaching to any of them. We have slept in Luleå, and Piteå, and dined in Umeå,—and further my journal saith not.

The 5th, however, was a day to be noticed. We started from Angersjö, with a violent snow storm blowing in our teeth—thermometer at zero. Our road entered the hilly country of Norrland, where we found green forests, beautiful little dells, pleasant valleys, and ash and beech intermingled with the monotonous but graceful purple birch. We were overwhelmed with gusts of fine snow shaken from the trees as we passed. Blinding white clouds swept the road, and once again we heard the howl of the wind among boughs that were free to toss. At Afwa, which we reached at one o'clock, we found a pale, weak, sickly young Swede, with faded moustaches, who had decided to remain there until next day. This circumstance induced us to go on, but after we had waited half an hour and were preparing to start, the weather being now ten times worse than before, he announced his resolution to start also. He had drunk four large glasses of milk and two cups of coffee during the half hour.

We went ahead, breaking through drifts of loose snow which overtopped our sleds, and lashed by the furious wind, which drove full in our faces. There were two or three plows at work but we had no benefit from them, so long as we were not directly in their wake. Up and down went our way, over dark hills and through valleys wild with the storm, and ending in chaos as they opened toward the Bothnian Gulf. Hour after hour passed by, the storm still increased, and the snow beat in our eyes so that we were completely blinded. It was impossible to keep them open, and yet the moment we shut them the lashes began to freeze together. I had a heavy weight of ice on my lids, and long icicles depending from every corner of my beard. Yet our frozen noses appeared to be much improved by the exposure, and began to give promise of healing without leaving a red blotch as a lasting record of what they had endured. We finally gave up all attempts to see or to guide the horse, but plunged along at random through the chaos, until the postillion piloted our baggage-sled into the inn-yard of Onska, and our horse followed it. The Swede was close upon our heels, but I engaged a separate room, so that we were freed from the depressing influence of his company. He may have been the best fellow in the world, so far as his heart was concerned, but was too weak in the knees to be an agreeable associate. There was no more stiffness of fibre in him than in a wet towel, and I would as soon wear a damp shirt as live in the same room with such a man. After all, it is not strange that one prefers nerve and energy, even when they are dashed with a flavour of vice, to the negative virtues of a character too weak and insipid to be tempted.

Our inn, in this little Norrland village, was about as comfortable and as elegant as three-fourths of the hotels in Stockholm. The rooms were well furnished; none of the usual appliances were wanting; the attendance was all that could be desired; the fare good and abundant, and the charges less than half of what would be demanded in the capital. Yet Stockholm, small as it is, claims to be for Sweden what Paris is to France, and its inhabitants look with an eye of compassion on those of the provinces. Norrland, in spite of its long winter, has a bracing, healthy climate, and had it not been for letters from home, facilities for studying Swedish, occasional recreation and the other attractions of a capital, I should have preferred waiting in some of those wild valleys for the spring to open. The people, notwithstanding their seclusion from the world, have a brighter and more intelligent look than the peasants of Uppland, and were there a liberal system of common school education in Sweden, the raw material here might be worked up into products alike honourable and useful to the country.

The Norrlanders seem to me to possess an indolent, almost phlegmatic temperament, and yet there are few who do not show a latent capacity for exertion. The latter trait, perhaps, is the true core and substance of their nature; the former is an overgrowth resulting from habits and circumstances. Like the peasants, or rather small farmers, further north, they are exposed to the risk of seeing their summer's labours rendered fruitless by a single night of frost. Such a catastrophe, which no amount of industry and foresight can prevent, recurring frequently (perhaps once in three years on an average), makes them indifferent, if not reckless; while that patience and cheerfulness which is an integral part of the Scandinavian as of the Saxon character, renders them contented and unrepining under such repeated disappointments. There is the stuff here for a noble people, although nature and a long course of neglect and misrule have done their best to destroy it.

The Norrlanders live simply, perhaps frugally, but there seems to be little real destitution among them. We saw sometimes in front of a church, a representation of a beggar with his hat in his hand, under which was an iron box, with an appeal to travellers to drop something in for the poor of the parish; but of actual beggars we found none. The houses, although small, are warm and substantial, mostly with double windows, and a little vestibule in front of the door, to create an intermediate temperature between the outer and inner air. The beds, even in many of the inns, are in the family room, but during the day are either converted into sofas or narrow frames which occupy but little space. At night, the bedstead is drawn out to the required breadth, single or double, as may be desired. The family room is always covered with a strong home-made rag carpet, the walls generally hung with colored prints and lithographs, illustrating religion or royalty, and as many greenhouse plants as the owner can afford to decorate the windows. I have seen, even beyond Umeå, some fine specimens of cactus, pelargonium, calla, and other exotics. It is singular that, with the universal passion of the Swedes for flowers and for music, they have produced no distinguished painters or composers—but, indeed, a Linnæus.

We spent the evening cosily in the stately inn's best room, with its white curtains, polished floor, and beds of sumptuous linen. The great clipper-plows were out early in the morning, to cut a path through the drifts of the storm, but it was nearly noon before the road was sufficiently cleared to enable us to travel. The temperature, by contrast with what we had so recently endured, seemed almost tropical—actually 25° above zero, with a soft, southern breeze, and patches of brilliant blue sky between the parting clouds. Our deliverance from the Arctic cold was complete.

CHAPTER XVI. CONCLUSION OF THE ARCTIC TRIP.

On leaving Onska, we experienced considerable delay on account of the storm. The roads were drifted to such an extent that even the ploughs could not be passed through in many places, and the peasants were obliged to work with their broad wooden spades. The sky, however, was wholly clear and of a pure daylight blue, such as we had not seen for two months. The sun rode high in the firmament, like a strong healthy sun again, with some warmth in his beams as they struck our faces, and the air was all mildness and balm. It was heavenly, after our Arctic life. The country, too, boldly undulating, with fir-forested hills, green and warm in the sunshine, and wild, picturesque valleys sunk between, shining in their covering of snow, charmed us completely. Again we saw the soft blue of the distant ranges as they melted away behind each other, suggesting space, and light, and warmth. Give me daylight and sunshine, after all! Our Arctic trip seems like a long, long night full of splendid dreams, but yet night and not day.

On the road, we bought a quantity of the linen handkerchiefs of the country, at prices varying from twenty-five to forty cents a piece, according to the size and quality. The bedding, in all the inns, was of home-made linen, and I do not recollect an instance where it was not brought out, fresh and sweet from the press, for us. In this, as in all other household arrangements, the people are very tidy and cleanly, though a little deficient as regards their own persons. Their clothing, however, is of a healthy substantial character, and the women consult comfort rather than ornament. Many of them wear cloth pantaloons under their petticoats, which, therefore, they are able to gather under their arms in wading through snow-drifts. I did not see a low-necked dress or a thin shoe north of Stockholm.

"The damsel who trips at daybreak

Is shod like a mountaineer."

Yet a sensible man would sooner take such a damsel to wife than any delicate Cinderella of the ball-room. I protest I lose all patience when I think of the habits of our American women, especially our country girls. If ever the Saxon race does deteriorate on our side of the Atlantic, as some ethnologists anticipate, it will be wholly their fault.

We stopped for the night at Hörnäs, and had a charming ride the next day among the hills and along the inlets of the Gulf. The same bold, picturesque scenery, which had appeared so dark and forbidding to us on our way north, now, under the spring-like sky, cheered and inspired us. At the station of Docksta, we found the peasant girls scrubbing the outer steps, barefooted. At night, we occupied our old quarters at Weda, on the Angermann river. The next morning the temperature was 25° above zero, and at noon rose to 39°. It was delightful to travel once more with cap-lappets turned up, fur collar turned down, face and neck free, and hands bare. On our second stage we had an overgrown, insolent boy for postillion, who persisted in driving slow, and refused to let us pass him. He finally became impertinent, whereupon Braisted ran forward and turned his horse out of the road, so that I could drive past. The boy then seized my horse by the head; B. pitched him into a snow-bank, and we took the lead. We had not gone far before we took the road to Hernösand, through mistake, and afterwards kept it through spite, thus adding about seven miles to our day's journey. A stretch of magnificent dark-green forests brought us to a narrow strait which separates the island of Hernösand from the main land. The ice was already softening, and the upper layer repeatedly broke through under us.

Hernösand is a pretty town, of about 2000 inhabitants, with a considerable commerce. It is also the capital of the most northern bishopric of Sweden. The church, on an eminence above the town, is, next to that of Skellefteå, the finest we saw in the north. We took a walk while breakfast was preparing, and in the space of twenty minutes saw all there was to be seen. By leaving the regular road, however, we had incurred a delay of two hours, which did not add to our amiability. Therefore, when the postillion, furiously angry now as well as insolent, came in to threaten us with legal prosecution in case we did not pay him heavy damages for what he called an assault, I cut the discussion short by driving him out of the room, and that was the last we saw of him. We reached Fjäl as the moon rose,—a globe of silver fire in a perfect violet sky. Two merry boys, who sang and shouted the whole way, drove us like the wind around the hay to Wifsta. The moonlight was as bright as the Arctic noonday, and the snowy landscape flashed and glittered under its resplendent shower. From the last hill we saw Sundsvall, which lay beneath us, with its wintry roofs, like a city of ivory and crystal, shining for us with the fairy promise of a warm supper and a good bed.

On the 9th, we drove along the shores of the magnificent bay of Sundsvall. Six vessels lay frozen in, at a considerable distance from the town. Near the southern extremity of the bay, we passed the village of Svartvik, which, the postillion informed us, is all owned by one person, who carries on ship-building. The appearance of the place justified his statements. The labourers' houses were mostly new, all built on precisely the same model, and with an unusual air of comfort and neatness. In the centre of the village stood a handsome white church, with a clock tower, and near it the parsonage and school-house. At the foot of the slope were the yards, where several vessels were on the stocks, and a number of sturdy workmen busy at their several tasks. There was an air of "associated labour" and the "model lodging-house" about the whole place, which was truly refreshing to behold, except a touch of barren utilitarianism in the cutting away of the graceful firs left from the forest, and thus depriving the houses of all shade and ornament. We met many wood-teams, hauling knees and spars, and were sorely troubled to get out of their way. Beyond the bay, the hills of Norrland ceased, sinking into those broad monotonous undulations which extend nearly all the way to Stockholm. Gardens with thriving fruit-trees now began to be more frequent, giving evidence of a climate where man has a right to live. I doubt whether it was ever meant that the human race should settle in any zone so frigid that fruit cannot ripen.

Thenceforth we had the roughest roads which were ever made upon a foundation of snow. The increase in travel and in the temperature of the air, and most of all, the short, loosely-attached sleds used to support the ship-timber, had worn them into a succession of holes, channels, and troughs, in and out of which we thumped from morning till night. On going down hill, the violent shocks frequently threw our runners completely into the air, and the wrench was so great that it was a miracle how the sled escaped fracture. All the joints, it is true, began to work apart, and the ash shafts bent in the most ticklish way; but the rough little conveyance which had already done us such hard service held out gallantly to the end. We reached Mo Myskie on the second night after leaving Sundsvall, and I was greeted with "Salaam aleikoom, ya Sidi!" from the jolly old Tripolitan landlord. There was an unusual amount of travel northward on the following day, and we were detained at every station, so that it was nearly midnight before we reached the extortionate inn at Gefle. The morning dawned with a snow-storm, but we were within 120 miles of Stockholm, and drove in the teeth of it to Elfkarleby. The renowned cascades of the Dal were by no means what I expected, but it was at least a satisfaction to see living water, after the silent rivers and fettered rapids of the North.

The snow was now getting rapidly thinner. So scant was it on the exposed Upsala plain that we fully expected being obliged to leave our sleds on the way. Even before reaching Upsala, our postillions chose the less-travelled field-roads whenever they led in the same direction, and beyond that town we were charged additional post-money for the circuits we were obliged to make to keep our runners on the snow. On the evening of the 13th we reached Rotebro, only fourteen miles from Stockholm, and the next morning, in splendid sunshine, drove past Haga park and palace, into the North-Gate, down the long Drottning-gatan, and up to Kahn's Hotel, where we presented our sleds to the valet-de-place, pulled off our heavy boots, threw aside our furs for the remainder of the winter, and sat down to read the pile of letters and papers which Herr Kahn brought us. It was precisely two months since our departure in December, and in that time we had performed a journey of 2200 miles, 250 of which were by reindeer, and nearly 500 inside of the Arctic Circle. Our frozen noses had peeled off, and the new skin showed no signs of the damage they had sustained—so that we had come out of the fight not only without a scar, but with a marked increase of robust vitality.

I must confess, however, that, interesting as was the journey, and happily as we endured its exposures, I should not wish to make it again. It is well to see the North, even after the South; but, as there is no one who visits the tropics without longing ever after to return again, so, I imagine, there is no one who, having once seen a winter inside the Arctic Circle, would ever wish to see another. In spite of the warm, gorgeous, and ever-changing play of colour hovering over the path of the unseen sun, in spite of the dazzling auroral dances and the magical transfiguration of the forests, the absence of true daylight and of all signs of warmth and life exercises at last a depressing influence on the spirits. The snow, so beautiful while the sunrise setting illumination lasts, wears a ghastly monotony at all other times, and the air, so exhilarating, even at the lowest temperature, becomes an enemy to be kept out, when you know its terrible power to benumb and destroy. To the native of a warmer zone, this presence of an unseen destructive force in nature weighs like a nightmare upon the mind. The inhabitants of the North also seem to undergo a species of hibernation, as well as the animals. Nearly half their time is passed in sleep; they are silent in comparison with the natives of the other parts of the world; there is little exuberant gaiety and cheerfulness, but patience, indifference, apathy almost. Aspects of nature which appear to be hostile to man, often develop and bring into play his best energies, but there are others which depress and paralyse his powers. I am convinced that the extreme North, like the Tropics, is unfavourable to the best mental and physical condition of the human race. The proper zone of man lies between 30° and 55° North.

To one who has not an unusual capacity to enjoy the experiences of varied travel, I should not recommend such a journey. With me, the realization of a long-cherished desire, the sense of novelty, the opportunity for contrasting extremes, and the interest with which the people inspired me, far outweighed all inconveniences and privations. In fact, I was not fully aware of the gloom and cold in which I had lived until we returned far enough southward to enjoy eight hours of sunshine, and a temperature above the freezing point. It was a second birth into a living world. Although we had experienced little positive suffering from the intense cold, except on the return from Muoniovara to Haparanda, our bodies had already accommodated themselves to a low temperature, and the sudden transition to 30° above zero came upon us like the warmth of June. My friend, Dr. Kane, once described to me the comfort he felt when the mercury rose to 7° below zero, making it pleasant to be on deck. The circumstance was then incomprehensible to me, but is now quite plain. I can also the better realise the terrible sufferings of himself and his men, exposed to a storm in a temperature of -47°, when the same degree of cold, with a very light wind, turned my own blood to ice.

Most of our physical sensations are relative, and the mere enumeration of so many degrees of heat or cold gives no idea of their effect upon the system. I should have frozen at home in a temperature which I found very comfortable in Lapland, with my solid diet of meat and butter, and my garments of reindeer. The following is a correct scale of the physical effect of cold, calculated for the latitude of 65° to 70° North:

15° above zero—Unpleasantly warm.

Zero—Mild and agreeable.

10° below zero—Pleasantly fresh and bracing.

20° below zero—Sharp, but not severely cold. Keep your fingers and toes in motion, and rub your nose occasionally.

30° below zero—Very cold; take particular care of your nose and extremities: eat the fattest food, and plenty of it 40° below—Intensely cold; keep awake at all hazards, muffle up to the eyes, and test your circulation frequently, that it may not stop somewhere before you know it.

50° below—A struggle for life.

* We kept a record of the temperature from the time we left Sundsvall (Dec. 21) until our return to Stockholm. As a matter of interest, I subjoin it, changing the degrees from Reaumur to Fahrenheit. We tested the thermometer repeatedly on the way, and found it very generally reliable, although in extremely low temperature it showed from one to two degrees more than a spirit thermometer. The observations were taken at from 9 to 8 A. M., 12 to 2 P. M., and 7 to 11 P. M., whenever it was possible.

	Morning.	*Noon.*	*Evening.*
December 21	+ 6	--	zero.
December 22	+ 6	--	- 3
December 23	-22	-29	-22
December 24	- 6	-22	-22
December 25	-35	-38	mer. frozen.
December 26	-30	-24	-31
December 27 (storm)	-18	-18	-18
December 28 (storm)	zero.	zero.	zero.
December 29	- 6	-13	-13
December 30	- 6	-13	-22
December 31 (storm)	- 3	+ 9	+ 9
January 1, 1857	+ 3	+ 3	+ 3
January 2	- 6	- 6	- 6
January 3	-30	-22	-22
January 4	-18	--	-22
January 5	-31	-30	-33
January 6	-20	- 4	zero.
January 7	+ 4	+18	+25
January 8	+18	--	-11
January 9	-28	-44	-44
January 10 (storm)	- 5	--	- 2
January 11 (storm)	- 2	zero.	- 5
January 12 (storm)	- 5	- 4	- 4
January 13 (storm)	+ 5	+ 5	+ 5
January 14	- 6	-13	- 64
January 15	- 8	-13	-33
January 16	- 9	-10	-11
January 17 (fog)	zero.	zero.	zero.

January 18	-10	-18	-23
January 19 (storm)	- 3	- 3	- 9
January 20	+20	--	+ 6
January 21	- 4	zero.	zero.
January 22	+ 2	- 6	-13
January 23	-13	- 3	-13
January 24	-15	-22	-44
January 25 mer. froz.	-50?	-42	mer. frozen
January 26	-45	-35	-39
January 27 frozen	-47?	-45	-35
January 28 frozen	-49?	-47	-44
January 29	-47?	-43	-43
January 30	-27	-11	-35
January 31	-17	-16	- 7
February 1	zero.	- 9	-13
February 2	+ 2	+ 6	zero
February 3	zero.	zero.	zero.
February 4	- 9	zero.	- 3
February 5 (storm)	+ 3	+ 3	+ 3
February 6	+25	+25	+18
February 7	+14	+18	+25
February 8	+25	+39	+22
February 9	+ 5	+22	+16
February 10	+25	+37	+37
February 11	+34	+34	+32
February 12	+32	+37	+23
February 13	+16	+30	+21
February 14	+25	+30	+25

CHAPTER XVII. LIFE IN STOCKHOLM.

The Swedes are proud of Stockholm, and justly so. No European capital, except Constantinople, can boast such picturesque beauty of position, and none whatever affords so great a range of shifting yet ever lovely aspects. Travellers are fond of calling it, in the imitative nomenclature of commonplace, the "Venice of the North"—but it is no Venice. It is not that swan of the Adriatic, singing her death-song in the purple sunset, but a northern eaglet, nested on the islands and rocky shores of the pale green Mälar lake. The Stad, or city proper, occupies three islands, which lie in the mouth of the narrow strait, by which the waters of the lake, after having come a hundred miles from the westward, and washed in their course the shores of thirteen hundred islands, pour themselves into the outer archipelago which is claimed by the Baltic Sea. On the largest of these islands, according to tradition, Agne, King of Sweden, was strangled with his own golden chain, by the Finnish princess Skiolfa, whom he had taken prisoner. This was sixteen hundred years ago, and a thousand years later, Birger Jarl, on the same spot, built the stronghold which was the seed out of which Stockholm has grown.

This island, and the adjoining Riddarholm, or Island of the Knights, contain all the ancient historic landmarks of the city, and nearly all of its most remarkable buildings. The towers of the Storkyrka and the Riddarholm's Church lift themselves high into the air; the dark red mass of the Riddarhus, or House of Nobles, and the white turrets and quadrangles of the penitentiary are conspicuous among the old white, tile-roofed blocks of houses; while, rising above the whole, the most prominent object in every view of Stockholm, is the Slot, or Royal Palace. This is one of the noblest royal residences in Europe. Standing on an immense basement terrace of granite, its grand quadrangle of between three and four hundred feet square, with wings (resembling, in general design, the Pitti Palace at Florence), is elevated quite above the rest of the city, which it crowns as with a mural diadem. The chaste and simple majesty of this edifice, and its admirable proportions, are a perpetual gratification to the eye, which is always drawn to it, as a central point, and thereby prevented from dwelling on whatever inharmonious or unsightly features there may be in the general view.

Splendid bridges of granite connect the island with the northern and southern suburbs, each of which is much greater in extent than the city proper. The palace fronts directly upon the Norrbro, or Northern Bridge, the great thoroughfare of Stockholm, which leads to the Square of Gustavus Adolphus, flanked on either side by the palace of the Crown Prince and the Opera House. The northern suburb is the fashionable quarter, containing all the newest streets and the handsomest private residences. The ground rises gradually from the water, and as very little attention is paid to grading, the streets follow the undulations of the low hills over which they spread, rising to the windmills on the outer heights and sinking into the hollows between. The southern suburb, however, is a single long hill, up the steep side of which the houses climb, row after row, until they reach the Church of St. Catherine, which crowns the very summit. In front of the city (that is eastward, and toward the Baltic), lie two other islands, connected by bridges with the northern suburb. Still beyond is the Djurgård, or Deer-Park, a singularly picturesque island, nearly the whole of which is occupied by a public park, and the summer villas of the wealthy Stockholmers. Its natural advantages are superior to those of any other park in Europe. Even in April, when there was scarcely a sign of spring, its cliffs of grey rock, its rolling lawns of brown grass, and its venerable oaks, with their iron trunks and gnarled, contorted boughs, with blue glimpses of ice-free water on all sides, attracted hundreds of visitors daily.

The streets of Stockholm are, with but two or three exceptions, narrow and badly paved. The municipal regulations in regard to them appear to be sadly deficient. They are quite as filthy as those of New-York, and the American reader will therefore have some idea of their horrid condition. A few trottoirs have been recently introduced, but even in the Drottning-gatan, the principal street, they are barely wide enough for two persons to walk abreast. The pavements are rough, slippery, and dangerous both to man and beast. I have no doubt that the great number of cripples in Stockholm is owing to this cause. On the other hand, the houses are models of solidity and stability. They are all of stone, or brick stuccoed over, with staircases of stone or iron, wood being prohibited by law, and roofs of copper, slate or tiles. In fact, the Swedes have singularly luxurious ideas concerning roofs, spending much more money upon them, proportionately, than on the house itself. You even see wooden shanties with copper roofs, got up regardless of expense. The houses are well lighted (which is quite necessary in the dark streets), and supplied with double windows against the cold. The air-tight Russian stove is universal. It has the advantage of keeping up sufficient warmth with a very small supply of fuel, but at the expense of ventilation. I find nothing yet equal to the old-fashioned fireplace in this respect, though I must confess I prefer the Russian stove to our hot-air furnaces. Carpets are very common in Sweden, and thus the dwellings have an air of warmth and comfort which is not found in Germany and other parts of the Continent. The arrangements for sleeping and washing are tolerable, though scanty, as compared with England, but the cleanliness of Swedish houses makes amends for many deficiencies.

The manner of living in Stockholm, nevertheless, is not very agreeable to the stranger. There is no hotel, except Kahn's, where one can obtain both beds and meals. The practice is to hire rooms, generally with the privilege of having your coffee in the morning, and to get your meals at a restaurant, of which there are many, tolerably cheap and not particularly good. Even Davison's, the best and most fashionable, has but an ordinary cuisine. Rooms are quite dear—particularly during our sojourn, when the Diet was in session and the city crowded with country visitors—and the inclusive expenses of living were equal to Berlin and greater than in Paris. I found that it cost just about as much to be stationary here, as to travel with post-horses in the Northern provinces. The Swedes generally have a cup of coffee on getting out of bed, or before, a substantial breakfast at nine, dinner at three, and tea in the evening. The wealthier families dine an hour or two later, but the crowds at the restaurants indicate the prevailing time. Dinner, and frequently breakfast, is prefaced with a smörgås (butter-goose), consisting of anchovies, pickled herrings, cheese and brandy. Soup which is generally sweet, comes in the middle and sometimes at the end of dinner, and the universal dessert is preserved fruit covered with whipped cream. I have had occasion to notice the fondness of the Swedes for sugar, which some persons seem to apply to almost every dish, except fish and oysters. I have often seen them season crab soup with powdered sugar. A favourite dish is raw salmon, buried in the earth until it is quite sodden—a great delicacy, they say, but I have not yet been hungry enough to eat it. Meat, which is abundant, is rarely properly cooked, and game, of which Sweden has a great variety, is injured by being swamped in sauces. He must be very fastidious, however, who cannot live passably well in Stockholm, especially if he has frequent invitations to dine with private families, many of whom have very excellent cooks.

My Swedish friends all said, "You should see Stockholm in summer! You have passed the worst part of the whole year among us, and you leave just when our fine days begin." I needed no assurance, however, of the summer charm of the place. In those long, golden evenings, which give place to an unfading twilight, when the birch is a network of silver and green, and the meadows are sown with the bright wild flowers of the North, those labyrinths of land and water must be truly enchanting. But were the glories of the Northern Summer increased tenfold, I could not make my home where such a price must be paid for them. From the time of our arrival, in February, until towards the close of April, the weather was of that kind which aggravates one to the loss of all patience. We had dull, raw, cloudy skies, a penetrating, unnerving, and depressing atmosphere, mud under foot, alternating with slushy snow,—in short, everything that is disagreeable in winter, without its brisk and bracing qualities. I found this season much more difficult to endure than all the cold of Lapland, and in spite of pleasant society and the charms of rest after a fatiguing journey, our sojourn in Stockholm was for a time sufficiently tedious.

At first, we lived a rather secluded life in our rooms in the Beridarebansgatan, in the northern suburb, devoting ourselves principally to gymnastics and the study of the Swedish language,—both of which can be prosecuted to more advantage in Stockholm than anywhere else. For, among the distinguished men of Sweden may be reckoned Ling, the inventor of what may be termed anatomical gymnastics. His system not only aims at reducing to a science the muscular development of the body, but, by means of both active and passive movements, at reaching the seat of disease and stimulating the various organs to healthy action. In the former of these objects, Ling has certainly succeeded; there is no other system of muscular training that will bear comparison with his; and if he has to some extent failed in the latter, it is because, with the enthusiasm of a man possessed by a new discovery, he claimed too much. His successor, Prof. Branting, possesses equal enthusiasm, and his faith in gymnastics, as a panacea for all human infirmities, is most unbounded. The institution under his charge is supported by Government, and, in addition to the officers of the army and navy, who are obliged to make a complete gymnastic course, is largely attended by invalids of all ages and classes.

Neither of us required the system as a medical application. I wished to increase the girth of my chest, somewhat diminished by a sedentary life, and Braisted needed a safety-valve for his surplus strength. However, the professor, by dint of much questioning, ascertained that one of us was sometimes afflicted with cold feet, and the other with headaches, and thereupon clapped us both upon the sick list. On entering the hall, on the first morning of our attendance, a piece of paper containing the movements prescribed for our individual cases, was stuck in our bosoms. On inspecting the lists, we found we had ten movements apiece, and no two of them alike. What they were we could only dimly guess from such cabalistic terms as "Stödgångst," "Krhalfligg," "Simhäng," or "Högstrgrsitt." The hall, about eighty feet in length by thirty in height, was furnished with the usual appliances for gymnastic exercises. Some fifty or sixty patients were present, part of whom were walking up and down the middle passage with an air of great solemnity, while the others, gathered in various little groups on either side, appeared to be undergoing uncouth forms of torture. There was no voluntary exercise, if I except an old gentleman in a black velvet coat, who repeatedly suspended himself by the hands, head downwards, and who died of apoplexy not long afterwards; every one was being exercised upon. Here, a lathy young man, bent sideways over a spar, was struggling, with a very red face, to right himself, while a stout teacher held him down; there, a corpulent gentleman, in the hands of five robust assistants, was having his body violently revolved upon the base of his hip joints, as if they were trying to unscrew him from his legs; and yonder again, an individual, suspended by his arms from a cross-bar, had his feet held up and his legs stretched apart by another, while a third pounded vigorously with closed fists upon his seat of honour. Now and then a prolonged yell, accompanied with all sorts of burlesque variations, issued from the throats of the assembly. The object of this was at first not clear to me, but I afterwards discovered that the full use of the lungs was considered by Ling a very important part of the exercises. Altogether, it was a peculiar scene, and not without a marked grotesque character.

On exhibiting my matsedel, or "bill of fare," to the first teacher who happened to be disengaged, I received my first movement, which consisted in being held with my back against a post, while I turned my body from side to side against strong resistance, employing the muscles of the chest only. I was then told to walk for five minutes before taking the second movement. It is unnecessary to recapitulate the various contortions I was made to perform; suffice it to say, that I felt very sore after them, which Professor Branting considered a promising sign, and that, at the end of a month, I was taken off the sick list and put among the friskas, or healthy patients, to whom more and severer movements, in part active, are allotted. This department was under the special charge of Baron Vegesach, an admirable teacher, and withal a master of fencing with the bayonet, a branch of defensive art which the Swedes have the honour of originating. The drill of the young officers in bayonet exercise was one of the finest things of the kind I ever saw. I prospered so well under the Baron's tuition, that at the end of the second month I was able to climb a smooth mast, to run up ropes with my hands, and to perform various other previous impossibilities, while my chest had increased an inch and a half in circumference, the addition being solid muscle.

During the time of my attendance I could not help but notice the effect of the discipline upon the other patients, especially the children. The weak and listless gradually straightened themselves; the pale and sallow took colour and lively expression; the crippled and paralytic recovered the use of their limbs; in short, all, with the exception of two or three hypochondriacs, exhibited a very marked improvement. The cheerfulness and geniality which pervaded the company, and of which Professor Branting himself was the best example, no doubt assisted the cure. All, both teachers and pupils, met on a platform of

155

the most absolute equality, and willingly took turns in lending a hand wherever it was needed. I have had my feet held up by a foreign ambassador, while a pair of Swedish counts applied the proper degree of resistance to the muscles of my arms and shoulders. The result of my observation and experience was, that Ling's system of physical education is undoubtedly the best in the world, and that, as a remedial agent in all cases of congenital weakness or deformity, as well as in those diseases which arise from a deranged circulation, its value can scarcely be over-estimated. It may even afford indirect assistance in more serious organic diseases, but I do not believe that it is of much service in those cases where chemical agencies are generally employed. Professor Branting, however, asserts that it is a specific for all diseases whatsoever, including consumption, malignant fevers, and venereal affections. One thing at least is certain—that in an age when physical training is most needed and most neglected, this system deserves to be introduced into every civilised country, as an indispensable branch in the education of youth.

I found the Swedish language as easy to read as it is difficult to speak correctly. The simplicity of its structure, which differs but slightly from English, accounts for the former quality, while the peculiar use of the definite article as a terminal syllable, attached to the noun, is a great impediment to fluent speaking. The passive form of the verb also requires much practice before it becomes familiar, and the mode of address in conversation is awkward and inconvenient beyond measure. The word you, or its correspondent, is never used, except in speaking to inferiors; wherever it occurs in other languages, the title of the person addressed must be repeated; as, for example: "How is the Herr Justizråd? I called at the Herr Justizråd's house this morning, but the Herr Justizråd was not at home." Some of the more progressive Swedes are endeavouring to do away with this absurdity, by substituting the second person plural, ni, which is already used in literature, but even they only dare to use it in their own private circle. The Swedes, especially in Stockholm, speak with a peculiar drawl and singing accent, exactly similar to that which is often heard in Scotland. It is very inferior to the natural, musical rhythm of Spanish, to which, in its vocalisation, Swedish has a great resemblance. Except Finnish, which is music itself, it is the most melodious of northern languages, and the mellow flow of its poetry is often scarcely surpassed by the

Italian. The infinitive verb always ends in a, and the language is full of soft, gliding iambics, which give a peculiar grace to its poetry.

It is rather singular that the Swedish prose, in point of finish and elegance, is far behind the Swedish poetry. One cause of this may be, that it is scarcely more than fifty years since the prose writers of the country began to use their native language. The works of Linnæus, Swedenborg, and other authors of the past century must now be translated into Swedish. Besides, there are two prose dialects—a conversational and a declamatory, the latter being much more artificial and involved than the former. All public addresses, as well as prose documents of a weighty or serious character, must be spoken or written in this pompous and antiquated style, owing to which, naturally, the country is almost destitute of orators. But the poets,—especially men of the sparkling fancy of Bellman, or the rich lyrical inspiration of Tegner, are not to be fettered by such conventionalities; and they have given the verse of Sweden an ease, and grace, and elegance, which one vainly seeks in its prose. In Stockholm, the French taste, so visible in the manners of the people, has also affected the language, and a number of French words and forms of expression, which have filtered through society, from the higher to the lower classes, are now in general use. The spelling, however, is made to conform to Swedish pronunciation, and one is amused at finding on placards such words as "trottoar," "salong," and "paviljong."

No country is richer in song-literature than Sweden. The popular songs and ballads of the different provinces, wedded to airs as original and characteristic as the words, number many hundreds. There are few Swedes who cannot sing, and I doubt whether any country in Europe would be able to furnish so many fine voices. Yet the taste for what is foreign and unaccustomed rules, and the minstrels of the cafes and the Djurgård are almost without exception German. Latterly, two or three bands of native singers have been formed, who give concerts devoted entirely to the country melodies of Sweden; and I believe they have been tolerably successful.

In these studies, relieved occasionally by rambles over the hills, whenever there was an hour's sunshine, and by occasional evenings with Swedish, English, and American friends, we passed the months of March and April, waiting for the tardy spring. Of the shifting and picturesque views which Stockholm presents to the stranger's eye, from whatever point he beholds her, we never wearied; but we began at last to tire of our ice-olation, and to look forward to the reopening of the Gotha Canal, as a means of escape. Day after day it was a new satisfaction to behold the majestic palace crowning the island-city and looking far and wide over the frozen lakes; the tall, slender spire of the Riddarholm, soaring above the ashes of Charles XII. and Gustavus Adolphus, was always a welcome sight; but we had seen enough of the hideous statues which ornament the public squares, (Charles XII. not among them, and the imbecile Charles XIII. occupying the best place); we grew tired of the monotonous perambulators on the Forrbro, and the tameness and sameness of Stockholm life in winter: and therefore hailed the lengthening days which heralded our deliverance.

As to the sights of the capital, are they not described in the guide-books? The champion of the Reformation lies in his chapel, under a cloud of his captured banners: opposite to him, the magnificent madman of the North, with hundreds of Polish and Russian ensigns rustling above his heads. In the royal armory you see the sword and the bloody shirt of the one, the bullet-pierced hat and cloak of the other, still coated with the mud of the trench at Fredrickshall. There are robes and weapons of the other Carls and Gustavs, but the splendour of Swedish history is embodied in these two names, and in that of Gustavus Vasa, who lies entombed in the old cathedral at Upsala. When I had grasped their swords, and the sabre of Czar Peter, captured at Narva, I felt that there were no other relics in Sweden which could make my heart throb a beat the faster.

CHAPTER XVIII. MANNERS AND MORALS OF STOCKHOLM.

As a people, the Swedes are very hospitable, and particularly so toward foreigners. There is perhaps no country in Europe where travellers are treated with so much kindness and allowed so many social privileges. This is fortunate, as the conventionalities of the country are more rigid than the laws of the Medes and Persians. Nothing excites greater scandal than an infraction of the numberless little formalities with which the descendants of the honest, spontaneous, impulsive old Scandinavians have, somehow or other, allowed themselves to be fettered, and were not all possible allowance made for the stranger, he would have but a dismal time of it. Notwithstanding these habits have become a second nature, they are still a false nature, and give a painfully stiff and constrained air to society. The Swedes pride themselves on being the politest people in Europe. Voltaire called them the "Frenchmen of the North," and they are greatly flattered by the epithet. But how much better, to call themselves Swedes?—to preserve the fine, manly characteristics of their ancient stock, rather than imitate a people so alien to them in blood, in character, and in antecedents. Those meaningless social courtesies which sit well enough upon the gay, volatile, mercurial Frenchman, seem absurd affectations when practiced by the tall, grave, sedate Scandinavian. The intelligent Swedes feel this, but they are powerless to make headway against the influence of a court which was wholly French, even before Bernadotte's time. "We are a race of apes," said one of them to me bitterly. Gustavus III. was thoroughly French in his tastes, but the ruin of Swedish nationality in Stockholm was already commenced when he ascended the throne.

Stockholm manners, at present, are a curious mixture of English and French, the latter element, of course, being predominant. In costume, the gentlemen are English, with exaggeration. Nowhere are to be seen such enormously tall and stiff black chimney-pots (misnamed hats), nowhere such straight-cut overcoats, descending to the very heels. You might stick all the men you see into pasteboard cards, like a row of pins, so precisely are they clothed upon the same model. But when you meet one of these grim, funereal figures, he pulls off his hat with a politeness which is more than French; he keeps it off, perhaps, while he is speaking; you shake hands and accept his invitation to enter his house. After you are within, he greets you a second time with the same ceremonies, as if you had then first met; he says, "Tak for sist!" (equivalent to; "thank you for the pleasure of your company the last time we met!") and, after your visit is over, you part with equal formality. At dinner the guests stand gravely around the table with clasped hands, before sitting down. This is repeated on rising, after which they bow to each other and shake hands with the host and hostess. Formerly they used to say "I thank you for the meal," a custom still retained in Denmark and Norway. Not long ago the guests were obliged to make a subsequent visit of ceremony to thank the host for his entertainment, and he was obliged to invite them all to a second dinner, in consequence thereof; so that giving one dinner always involved giving two. Fortunately the obligation was cancelled by the second, or the visits and dinners might have gone on alternately, ad infinitum.

At dinners and evening parties, white gloves and white cravats are invariably worn, and generally white vests. The same custom is observed at funerals, even the drivers of the hearse and carriages being furnished with resplendent white gloves for the occasion. I have a horror of white cravats, and took advantage of the traveller's privilege to wear a black one. I never could understand why, in England, where the boundaries of caste are so distinctly marked, a gentleman's full dress should be his servant's livery. The chimney-pots are no protection to the head in raw or very cold weather, and it required no little courage in me to appear in fur or felt. "I wish I could wear such a comfortable hat," said a Swede to me; "but I dare not; you are a traveller, and it is permitted; but a Swede would lose his position in society, if he were to do so." Another gentleman informed me that his own sisters refused to appear in the streets with him, because he wore a cap. A former English Consul greatly shocked the people by carrying home his own marketing. A few gentlemen have independence enough to set aside, in their own houses, some of the more disagreeable features of this conventionalism, and the success of two or three, who held weekly soirees through the winter, on a more free and unrestrained plan, may in the end restore somewhat of naturalness and spontaneity to the society of Stockholm.

The continual taking off of your hat to everybody you know, is a great annoyance to many strangers. A lift of the hat, as in Germany, is not sufficient. You must remove it entirely, and hold it in the air a second or two before you replace it. King Oscar once said to an acquaintance of mine, who was commiserating him for being obliged to keep his hat off, the whole length of the Drottning-gatan, in a violent snow-storm: "You are quite right; it was exceedingly disagreeable, and I could not help wishing that instead of being king of Sweden, I were king of Thibet, where, according to Huc, the polite salutation is simply to stick out your tongue." The consideration extended to foreigners is, I am told, quite withdrawn after they become residents; so that, as an Englishman informed me, Stockholm is much more pleasant the first year than the second. The principle, on the whole, is about the same as governs English, and most American society, only in Sweden its tyranny is more severely felt, on account of the French imitations which have been engrafted upon it.

I do not wish to be understood as saying a word in censure of that genial courtesy which is characteristic of the Swedes, not less of the bonder, or country farmers, than of the nobility. They are by nature a courteous people, and if, throughout the country, something of the primness and formality of ancient manners has been preserved, it the rather serves to give a quaint and picturesque grace to society. The affectation of French manners applies principally to the capital, which, both in manners and morals, can by no means be taken as a standard for the whole country. The Swedes are neither licentious, nor extravagantly over-mannered: the Stockholmers are both. During the whole of our journey to Lapland, we were invariably treated with a courtesy which bordered on kindness, and had abundant opportunities of noticing the general amenity which exists in the intercourse even of the poorest classes. The only really rude people we saw, were travelling traders, especially those from the capital, who thought to add to their importance by a little swaggering.

I recollect hearing of but a single instance in which the usual world-wide rules of hospitality were grossly violated. This occurred to an English traveller, who spent some time in the interior of the country. While taking tea one evening with a prominent family of the province, he happened to make use of his thumb and fore-finger in helping himself to a lump of sugar. The mistress of the house immediately sent out the servant, who reappeared after a short time with another sugar-bowl, filled with fresh lumps. Noticing this, the traveller, in order to ascertain whether his harmless deviation from Swedish customs had really contaminated the whole sugar-bowl, sweetened his second cup in the same manner. The result was precisely the same: the servant was again sent out, and again returned with a fresh supply. The traveller, thereupon, coolly walked to the stove, opened the door, and threw in his cup, saucer, and tea-spoon, affecting to take it for granted that they never could be used again.

Speaking of King Oscar reminds me that I should not fail to say a word about this liberal and enlightened monarch. There is probably no king in Europe at present, who possesses such extensive acquirements, or is animated by a more genuine desire for the good of his kingdom. The slow progress which Sweden has made in introducing needful reforms is owing to the conservative spirit of the nobility and the priesthood, who possess half the legislative power. I do not believe there is a greater enemy to progress than an established church. Oscar is deservedly popular throughout Sweden, and I wish I could believe that his successor will exhibit equal intelligence and liberality. During my stay I saw all the members of the Royal Family frequently, and once had an informal self-presentation to the whole of them. I was descending the stairway of Kahn's Hotel one afternoon, when a tall, black-bearded, Frenchy gentleman coming up, brushed so close to me in the narrow passage that he received the full benefit of a cloud of smoke which I was ejaculating. It was the Crown Prince, as a servant whispered to me, but as my cigar was genuine Havana, and he is said to be a connoisseur of the article, there was no harm done. As I reached the street door a dragoon dashed up, preceding the carriages containing the Royal Family, who were coming to view Professor Enslen's panoramas. First, the Crown Princess, with her children; she bowed gracefully in answer to my greeting. The Princess Eugenia, a lady of twenty-seven, or thereabouts, with a thoroughly cheerful and amiable face, came next and nodded, smiling. With her was the Queen, a daughter of Eugene Beauharnais, a handsome woman for her years, with the dark hair and eyes of her grandmother, Josephine. King Oscar followed, at the head of a company of officers and nobles, among whom was his second son, Prince Oscar, the handsomest young man in Stockholm. He wore his Admiral's uniform, and made me a naval salute as he passed. The King is about medium height, with a symmetrical head, a bold, finely-cut nose, keen, intelligent eyes, and a heavy grey moustache. There was something gallant, dashing, and manly in his air, despite his fifty-seven years. He gave me the impression of an honest, energetic and thoroughly accomplished man; and this is the character he bears throughout Sweden, except with a small class, who charge him with being insincere, and too much under the influence of the Queen, against whom, however, they can find no charge, except that of her Catholicism.

I was sorry to notice, not only in Stockholm, but more or less throughout Sweden, a spirit of detraction in regard to everything Swedish. Whenever I mentioned with admiration the name of a distinguished Swede, I was almost always sure to hear, in return, some disparaging remark, or a story to his disadvantage. Yet, singularly enough, the Swedes are rather sensitive to foreign criticism, seeming to reserve for themselves the privilege of being censorious. No amount of renown, nor even the sanctity which death gives to genius, can prevent a certain class of them from exhibiting the vices and weaknesses of their countrymen. Much the severest things which I heard said about Sweden, were said by Swedes themselves, and I was frequently obliged to rely upon my own contrary impressions, to protect me from the chance of being persuaded to paint things worse than they really are.

Just before leaving Stockholm I made application, through the Hon. Mr. Schroeder, our Minister Resident, and Baron Lagerheim, for the privilege of an interview with the king. A few days previously, however, he had been attacked with that illness which has obliged him to withdraw from the labours of government, and was advised by his physicians to receive no one. He sent me a very kind message, with an invitation to renew my request as soon as his health should be restored. Gentlemen who had opportunities of knowing the fact, assured me that his health broke down under an accumulation of labour and anxiety, in his endeavours to bring the question of religious liberty before the Diet—a measure in which he had to contend with the united influence of the clergy, the House of Peasants, whom the clergy rule to a great extent, and a portion of the House of Nobles. It is not often that a king is in advance of the general sentiment of his people, and in losing the services of Oscar, I fear that Sweden has lost her best man. The Crown Prince, now Prince Regent, is said to be amiably weak in his character, rather reactionary in his views, and very ambitious of military glory. At least, that is the average of the various opinions which I heard expressed concerning him.

After speaking of the manners of Stockholm, I must not close this chapter without saying a few words about its morals. It has been called the most licentious city in Europe, and, I have no doubt, with the most perfect justice. Vienna may surpass it in the amount of conjugal infidelity, but certainly not in general incontinence. Very nearly half the registered births are illegitimate, to say nothing of the illegitimate children born in wedlock. Of the servant-girls, shop-girls, and seamstresses in the city, it is very safe to say that scarcely ten out of a hundred are chaste, while, as rakish young Swedes have coolly informed me, many girls of respectable parentage, belonging to the middle class, are not much better. The men, of course, are much worse than the women, and even in Paris one sees fewer physical signs of excessive debauchery. Here, the number of broken-down young men, and blear-eyed, hoary sinners, is astonishing. I have never been in any place where licentiousness was so open and avowed—and yet, where the slang of a sham morality was so prevalent. There are no houses of prostitution in Stockholm, and the city would be scandalised at the idea of allowing such a thing. A few years ago two were established and the fact was no sooner known than a virtuous mob arose and violently pulled them down! At the restaurants, young blades order their dinners of the female waiters, with an arm around their waists, while the old men place their hands unblushingly upon their bosoms. All the baths in Stockholm are attended by women (generally middle-aged and hideous, I must confess), who perform the usual scrubbing and shampooing with the greatest nonchalance. One does not wonder when he is told of young men who have passed safely through the ordeals of Berlin and Paris, and have come at last to Stockholm to be ruined.[B]

It is but fair to say that the Swedes account for the large proportion of illegitimate births, by stating that many unfortunate females come up from the country to hide their shame in the capital, which is no doubt true. Everything that I have said has been derived from residents of Stockholm, who, proud as they are, and sensitive, cannot conceal this glaring depravity. The population of Stockholm, as is proved by statistics, has only been increased during the last fifty years by immigration from the country, the number of deaths among the inhabitants exceeding the births by several hundreds every year. I was once speaking with a Swede about these facts, which he seemed inclined to doubt. "But," said I, "they are derived from your own statistics." "Well," he answered, with a naïve attempt to find some compensating good, "you must at least admit that the Swedish statistics are as exact as any in the world!"

Drunkenness is a leading vice among the Swedes, as we had daily evidence. Six years ago the consumption of brandy throughout the kingdom was nine gallons for every man, woman, and child annually; but it has decreased considerably since then, mainly through the manufacture of beer and porter. "Bajerskt öl" (Bavarian beer) is now to be had everywhere, and is rapidly becoming the favourite drink of the people. Sweden and the United States will in the end establish the fact that lager beer is more efficacious in preventing intemperance than any amount of prohibitory law. Brandy-drinking is still, nevertheless, one of the greatest curses of Sweden. It is no unusual thing to see boys of twelve or fourteen take their glass of fiery finkel before dinner. The celebrated Swedish punch, made of arrack, wine, and sugar, is a universal evening drink, and one of the most insidious ever invented, despite its agreeable flavor. There is a movement in favor of total abstinence, but it seems to have made but little progress, except as it is connected with some of the new religious ideas, which are now preached throughout the country.

I have rarely witnessed a sadder example of ruin, than one evening in a Stockholm café. A tall, distinguished-looking man of about forty, in an advanced state of drunkenness, was seated at a table opposite to us. He looked at me awhile, apparently endeavoring to keep hold of some thought with which his mind was occupied. Rising at last he staggered across the room, stood before me, and repeated the words of Bellman:

"Så vandra våra stora män'

Från ljuset ned til skuggan."[C]

A wild, despairing laugh followed the lines, and he turned away, but came back again and again to repeat them. He was a nobleman of excellent family, a man of great intellectual attainments, who, a few years ago, was considered one of the most promising young men in Sweden. I saw him frequently afterwards, and always in the same condition, but he never accosted me again. The Swedes say the same thing of Bellman himself, and of Tegner, and many others, with how much justice I care not to know, for a man's faults are to be accounted for to God, and not to a gossiping public.

FOOTNOTES:

[B] The substance of the foregoing paragraph was contained in a letter published in The New-York Tribune during my travels in the North, and which was afterwards translated and commented upon by the Swedish papers. The latter charged me with having drawn too dark a picture and I therefore took some pains to test my statements, both by means of the Government statistics, and the views of my Swedish friends. I see no reason to change my first impression: had I accepted all that was told me by natives of the capital, I should have made the picture much darker. The question is simply whether there is much difference between the general adoption of illicit connections, or the existence of open prostitution. The latter is almost unknown; the former is almost universal, the supply being kept up by the miserable rates of wages paid to female servants and seamstresses. The former get, on an average, fifty rigsdaler ($13) per year, out of which they must clothe themselves: few of the latter can make one rigsdaler a day. These connections are also encouraged by the fact, that marriage legitimates all the children previously born. In fact, during the time of my visit to Stockholm, a measure was proposed in the House of Clergy, securing to bastards the same right of inheritance, as to legitimate children. Such measures, however just they may be so far as the innocent offspring of a guilty connection are concerned, have a direct tendency to impair the sanctity of marriage, and consequently the general standard of morality.

This, the most vital of all the social problems, is strangely neglected. The diseases and excesses which it engenders are far more devastating than those which spring from any other vice, and yet no philanthropist is bold enough to look the question in the face. The virtuous shrink from it, the vicious don't care about it, the godly simply condemn, and the ungodly indulge—and so the world rolls on, and hundreds of thousands go down annually to utter ruin. It is useless to attempt the extirpation of a vice which is inherent in the very nature of man, and the alternative of either utterly ignoring, or of attempting to check and regulate it, is a question of the most vital importance to the whole human race.

[C] "Thus our great men wander from the light down into the shades."

CHAPTER XIX. JOURNEY TO GOTTENBURG AND COPENHAGEN.

I never knew a more sudden transition from winter to summer than we experienced on the journey southward from Stockholm. When we left that city on the evening of the 6th of May, there were no signs of spring except a few early violets and anemones on the sheltered southern banks in Haga Park; the grass was still brown and dead, the trees bare, and the air keen; but the harbour was free from ice and the canal open, and our winter isolation was therefore at an end. A little circulation entered into the languid veins of society; steamers from Germany began to arrive; fresh faces appeared in the streets, and less formal costumes—merchants and bagmen only, it is true, but people of a more dashing and genial air. We were evidently, as the Swedes said, leaving Stockholm just as it began to be pleasant and lively.

The steamer left the Riddarholm pier at midnight, and took her way westward up the Mälar Lake to Södertelje. The boats which ply on the Gotha canal are small, but neat and comfortable. The price of a passage to Gottenburg, a distance of 370 miles, is about $8.50. This, however, does not include meals, which are furnished at a fixed price, amounting to $6 more. The time occupied by the voyage varies from two and a half to four days. In the night we passed through the lock at Södertelje, where St. Olaf, when a heathen Viking, cut a channel for his ships into the long Baltic estuary which here closely approaches the lake, and in the morning found ourselves running down the eastern shore of Sweden, under the shelter of its fringe of jagged rocky islets. Towards noon we left the Baltic, and steamed up the long, narrow Bay of Söderköping, passing, on the way, the magnificent ruins of Stegeborg Castle, the first mediæval relic I had seen in Sweden. Its square massive walls, and tall round tower of grey stone, differed in no respect from those of contemporary ruins in Germany.

Before reaching Söderköping, we entered the canal, a very complete and substantial work of the kind, about eighty feet in breadth, but much more crooked than would seem to be actually necessary. For this reason the boats make but moderate speed, averaging not more than six or seven miles an hour, exclusive of the detention at the locks. The country is undulating, and neither rich nor populous before reaching the beautiful Roxen Lake, beyond which we entered upon a charming district. Here the canal rises, by eleven successive locks, to the rich uplands separating the Roxen from the Wetter, a gently rolling plain, chequered, so far as the eye could reach, with green squares of springing wheat and the dark mould of the newly ploughed barley fields. While the boat was passing the locks, we walked forward to a curious old church, called Vreta Kloster. The building dates from the year 1128, and contains the tombs of three Swedish kings, together with that of the Count Douglas, who fled hither from Scotland in the time of Cromwell. The Douglas estate is in this neighbourhood, and is, I believe, still in the possession of the family. The church must at one time have presented a fine, venerable appearance: but all its dark rich colouring and gilding are now buried under a thick coat of white-wash.

We had already a prophecy of the long summer days of the North, in the perpetual twilight which lingered in the sky, moving around from sunset to sunrise. During the second night we crossed the Wetter Lake, which I did not see; for when I came on deck we were already on the Viken, the most beautiful sheet of water between Stockholm and Gottenburg. Its irregular shores, covered with forests of fir and birch, thrust out long narrow headlands which divide it into deep bays, studded with wild wooded islands. But the scenery was still that of winter, except in the absence of ice and snow. We had not made much southing, but we expected to find the western side of Sweden much warmer than the eastern. The highest part of the canal, more than 300 feet above the sea, was now passed, however, and as we descended the long barren hills towards the Wener Lake I found a few early wild flowers in the woods. In the afternoon we came upon the Wener, the third lake in Europe, being one hundred miles in extent by about fifty in breadth. To the west, it spread away to a level line against the sky; but, as I looked southward, I perceived two opposite promontories, with scattered islands between, dividing the body of water into almost equal portions. The scenery of the Wener has great resemblance to that of the northern portion of Lake Michigan. Further down on the eastern shore, the hill of Kinnekulle, the highest land in Southern Sweden, rises to the height of nearly a thousand feet above the water, with a graceful and very gradual sweep; but otherwise the scenery is rather tame, and, I suspect, depends for most of its beauty upon the summer foliage.

There were two or three intelligent and agreeable passengers on board, who showed a more than usual knowledge of America and her institutions. The captain, however, as we walked the deck together, betrayed the same general impression which prevails throughout the Continent (Germany in particular), that we are a thoroughly material people, having little taste for or appreciation of anything which is not practical and distinctly utilitarian. Nothing can be further from the truth; yet I have the greatest difficulty in making people comprehend that a true feeling for science, art, and literature can co-exist with our great practical genius. There is more intellectual activity in the Free States than in any other part of the world, a more general cultivation, and, taking the collective population, I venture to say, a more enlightened taste. Nowhere are greater sums spent for books and works of art, or for the promotion of scientific objects. Yet this cry of "Materialism" has become the cant and slang of European talk concerning America, and is obtruded so frequently and so offensively that I have sometimes been inclined to doubt whether the good breeding of Continental society has not been too highly rated.

While on the steamer, I heard an interesting story of a Swedish nobleman, who is at present attempting a practical protest against the absurd and fossilised ideas by which his class is governed. The nobility of Sweden are as proud as they are poor, and, as the father's title is inherited by each of his sons, the country is overrun with Counts and Barons, who, repudiating any means of support that is not somehow connected with the service of the government, live in a continual state of debt and dilapidation. Count R——, however, has sense enough to know that honest labour is always honourable, and has brought up his eldest son to earn his living by the work of his own hands. For the past three years, the latter has been in the United States, working as a day-labourer on farms and on Western railroads. His experiences, I learn, have not been agreeable, but he is a young man of too

170

much spirit and courage to give up the attempt, and has hitherto refused to listen to the entreaties of his family, that he shall come home and take charge of one of his father's estates. The second son is now a clerk in a mercantile house in Gottenburg, while the Count has given his daughter in marriage to a radical and untitled editor, whose acquaintance I was afterwards so fortunate as to make, and who confirmed the entire truth of the story.

We were to pass the locks at Trollhätta in the middle of the night, but I determined to visit the celebrated falls of the Gotha River, even at such a time, and gave orders that we should be called. The stupid boy, however, woke up the wrong passenger, and the last locks were reached before the mistake was discovered. By sunrise we had reached Lilla Edet, on the Gotha River, where the buds were swelling on the early trees, and the grass, in sunny places, showed a little sprouting greenness. We shot rapidly down the swift brown stream, between brown, bald, stony hills, whose forests have all been stripped off to feed the hostile camp-fires of past centuries. Bits of bottom land, held in the curves of the river, looked rich and promising, and where the hills fell back a little, there were groves and country-houses—but the scenery, in general, was bleak and unfriendly, until we drew near Gottenburg. Two round, detached forts, built according to Vauban's ideas (which the Swedes say he stole from Sweden, where they were already in practice) announced our approach, and before noon we were alongside the pier. Here, to my great surprise, a Custom-house officer appeared and asked us to open our trunks. "But we came by the canal from Stockholm!" "That makes no difference," he replied; "your luggage must be examined." I then appealed to the captain, who stated that, in consequence of the steamer's being obliged to enter the Baltic waters for two or three hours between Södertelje and Söderköping, the law took it for granted that we might have boarded some foreign vessel during that time and procured contraband goods. In other words, though sailing in a narrow sound, between the Swedish islands and the Swedish coast, we had virtually been in a foreign country! It would scarcely be believed that this sagacious law is of quite recent enactment.

We remained until the next morning in Gottenburg. This is, in every respect, a more energetic and wide-awake place than Stockholm. It has not the same unrivalled beauty of position, but is more liberally laid out and kept in better order. Although the population is only about 40,000, its commerce is much greater than that of the capital, and so are, proportionately, its wealth and public spirit. The Magister Hedlund, a very intelligent and accomplished gentleman, to whom I had a letter from Mügge, the novelist, took me up the valley a distance of five or six miles, to a very picturesque village among the hills, which is fast growing into a manufacturing town. Large cotton, woollen and paper mills bestride a strong stream, which has such a fall that it leaps from one mill-wheel to another for the distance of nearly half a mile. On our return, we visited a number of wells hollowed in the rocky strata of the hills, to which the country people have given the name of "The Giant's Pots." A clergyman of the neighbourhood, even, has written a pamphlet to prove that they were the work of the antediluvian giants, who excavated them for the purpose of mixing dough for their loaves of bread and batter for their puddings. They are simply those holes which a pebble grinds in a softer rock, under the rotary action of a current of water, but on an immense scale, some of them being ten feet in diameter, by fifteen or eighteen in depth. At Herr Hedlund's house, I met a number of gentlemen, whose courtesy and intelligence gave me a very favourable impression of the society of the place.

The next morning, at five o'clock, the steamer Viken, from Christiania, arrived, and we took passage for Copenhagen. After issuing from the Skärgaard, or rocky archipelago which protects the approach to Gottenburg from the sea, we made a direct course to Elsinore, down the Swedish coast, but too distant to observe more than its general outline. This part of Sweden, however—the province of Halland—is very rough and stony, and not until after passing the Sound does one see the fertile hills and vales of Scania. The Cattegat was as smooth as an inland sea, and our voyage could not have been pleasanter. In the afternoon Zealand rose blue from the wave, and the increase in the number of small sailing craft denoted our approach to the Sound. The opposite shores drew nearer to each other, and finally the spires of Helsingborg, on the Swedish shore, and the square mass of Kronborg Castle, under the guns of which the Sound dues have been so long demanded, appeared in sight. In spite of its bare, wintry aspect, the panorama was charming. The picturesque Gothic buttresses and gables of Kronborg rose above the zigzag of its turfed outworks; beyond were the houses and gardens of Helsingör (Elsinore)—while on the glassy breast of the Sound a fleet of merchant vessels lay at anchor, and beyond, the fields and towns of Sweden gleamed in the light of the setting sun. Yet here, again, I must find fault with Campbell, splendid lyrist as he is. We should have been sailing

"By thy *wild and stormy steep,*

Elsinore!"

only that the level shore, with its fair gardens and groves wouldn't admit the possibility of such a thing. The music of the line remains the same, but you must not read it on the spot.

There was a beautiful American clipper at anchor off the Castle. "There," said a Danish passenger to me, "is one of the ships which have taken from us the sovereignty of the Sound." "I am very glad of it," I replied; "and I can only wonder why the maritime nations of Europe have so long submitted to such an imposition." "I am glad, also," said he, "that the question has at last been settled, and our privilege given up—and I believe we are all, even the Government itself, entirely satisfied with the arrangement." I heard the same opinion afterwards expressed in Copenhagen, and felt gratified, as an American, to hear the result attributed to the initiative taken by our Government; but I also remembered the Camden and Amboy Railroad Company, and could not help wishing that the same principle might be applied at home. We have a Denmark, lying between New-York and Philadelphia, and I have often paid sand dues for crossing her territory.

At dusk, we landed under the battlements of Copenhagen. "Are you travellers or merchants?" asked the Custom-house officers. "Travellers," we replied. "Then," was the answer, "there is no necessity for examining your trunks," and we were politely ushered out at the opposite door, and drove without further hindrance to a hotel. A gentleman from Stockholm had said to me: "When you get to Copenhagen, you will find yourself in Europe:" and I was at once struck with the truth of his remark. Although Copenhagen is by no means a commercial city—scarcely more so than Stockholm—its streets are gay, brilliant and bustling, and have an air of life and joyousness which contrasts strikingly with the gravity of the latter capital. From without, it makes very little impression, being built on a low, level ground, and surrounded by high earthen fortifications, but its interior is full of quaint and attractive points. There is already a strong admixture of the German element in the population, softening by its warmth and frankness the Scandinavian reserve. In their fondness for out-door recreation, the Danes quite equal the Viennese, and their Summer-garden of Tivoli is one of the largest and liveliest in all Europe. In costume, there is such a thing as individuality; in manners, somewhat of independence. The Danish nature appears to be more pliant and flexible than the Swedish, but I cannot judge whether the charge of inconstancy and dissimulation, which I have heard brought against it, is just. With regard to morals, Copenhagen is said to be an improvement upon Stockholm.

During our short stay of three days, we saw the principal sights of the place. The first, and one of the pleasantest to me, was the park of Rosenborg Palace, with its fresh, green turf, starred with dandelions, and its grand avenues of chestnuts and lindens, just starting into leaf. On the 11th of May, we found spring at last, after six months of uninterrupted winter. I don't much enjoy going the round of a new city, attended by a valet-de-place, and performing the programme laid down by a guide-book, nor is it an agreeable task to describe such things in catalogue style; so I shall merely say that the most interesting things in Copenhagen are the Museum of Northern Antiquities, the Historical Collections in Rosenborg Palace, Thorwaldsen's Museum, and the Church of our Lady, containing the great sculptor's statues of Christ and the Apostles. We have seen very good casts of the latter in New-York, but one must visit the Museum erected by the Danish people, which is also Thorwaldsen's mausoleum, to learn the number, variety and beauty of his works. Here are the casts of between three and four hundred statues, busts and bas reliefs, with a number in marble. No artist has ever had so noble a monument.

On the day after my arrival, I sent a note to Hans Christian Andersen, reminding him of the greeting which he had once sent me through a mutual friend, and asking him to appoint an hour for me to call upon him. The same afternoon, as I was sitting in my room, the door quietly opened, and a tall, loosely-jointed figure entered. He wore a neat evening dress of black, with a white cravat; his head was thrown back, and his plain, irregular features wore an expression of the greatest cheerfulness and kindly humour. I recognised him at once, and forgetting that we had never met—so much did he seem like an old, familiar acquaintance—cried out "Andersen!" and jumped up to greet him. "Ah," said he stretching out both his hands, "here you are! Now I should have been vexed if you had gone through Copenhagen and I had not known it." He sat down, and I had a delightful hour's chat with him. One sees the man so plainly in his works, that his readers may almost be said to know him personally. He is thoroughly simple and natural, and those who call him egotistical forget that his egotism is only a naïve and unthinking sincerity, like that of a child. In fact, he is the youngest man for his years that I ever knew. "When I was sixteen," said he, "I used to think to myself, 'when I am twenty-four, then will I be old indeed'—but now I am fifty-two, and I have just the same feeling of youth as at twenty." He was greatly delighted when Braisted, who was in the room with me, spoke of having read his "Improvisatore" in the Sandwich Islands. "Why, is it possible?" he exclaimed: "when I hear of my books going so far around the earth, I sometimes wonder if it can be really true that I have written them." He explained to me the plot of his new novel, "To Be, or Not To Be," and ended by presenting me with the illustrated edition of his stories. "Now, don't forget me," said he, with a delightful entreaty in his, voice, as he rose to leave, "for we shall meet again. Were it not for sea-sickness, I should see you in America; and who knows but I may come, in spite of it?" God bless you, Andersen! I said, in my thoughts. It is so cheering to meet a man whose very weaknesses are made attractive through the perfect candour of his nature!

Goldschmidt, the author of "The Jew," whose acquaintance I made, is himself a Jew, and a man of great earnestness and enthusiasm. He is the editor of the "North and South," a monthly periodical, and had just completed, as he informed me, a second romance, which was soon to be published. Like most of the authors and editors in Northern Europe, he is well acquainted with American literature.

Professor Rafn, the distinguished archæologist of Northern lore, is still

175

as active as ever, notwithstanding he is well advanced in years. After going up an innumerable number of steps, I found him at the very top of a high old building in the Kronprinzensgade, in a study crammed with old Norsk and Icelandic volumes. He is a slender old man, with a thin face, and high, narrow head, clear grey eyes, and a hale red on his cheeks. The dust of antiquity does not lie very heavily on his grey locks; his enthusiasm for his studies is of that fresh and lively character which mellows the whole nature of the man. I admired and enjoyed it, when, after being fairly started on his favourite topic, he opened one of his own splendid folios, and read me some ringing stanzas of Icelandic poetry. He spoke much of Mr. Marsh, our former minister to Turkey, whose proficiency in the northern languages he considered very remarkable.

CHAPTER XX. RETURN TO THE NORTH.—CHRISTIANIA.

I was obliged to visit both Germany and England, before returning to spend the summer in Norway. As neither of those countries comes within the scope of the present work, I shall spare the reader a recapitulation of my travels for six weeks after leaving Copenhagen. Midsummer's Day was ten days past before I was ready to resume the journey, and there was no time to be lost, if I wished to see the midnight sun from the cliffs of the North Cape. I therefore took the most direct route, from London, by the way of Hull, whence a steamer was to sail on the 3rd of July for Christiania.

We chose one of the steamers of the English line, to our subsequent regret, as the Norwegian vessels are preferable, in most respects. I went on board on Friday evening, and on asking for my berth, was taken into a small state-room, containing ten. "Oh, there's only seven gentleman goin' in here, this time," said the steward, noticing my look of dismay, "and then you can sleep on a sofa in the saloon, if you like it better." On referring to the steamer's framed certificate, I found that she was 250 tons' burden, and constructed to carry 171 cabin and 230 deck passengers! The state-room for ten passengers had a single wash-basin, but I believe we had as many as four small towels, which was a source of congratulation. "What a jolly nice boat it is!" I heard one of the English passengers exclaim. The steward, who stood up for the dignity of the vessel, said: "Oh, you'll find it very pleasant; we 'ave only twenty passengers, and we once 'ad heighty-four."

In the morning we were upon the North Sea, rolling with a short, nauseating motion, under a dismal, rainy sky. "It always rains when you leave Hull," said the mate, "and it always rains when you come back to it." I divided my time between sea sickness and Charles Reade's novel of "Never too Late to Mend," a cheery companion under such circumstances. The purposed rowdyism of the man's style shows a little too plainly, but his language is so racy and muscular, his characters so fairly and sharply drawn, that one must not be censorious. Towards evening I remembered that it was the Fourth, and so procured a specific for sea-sickness, with which Braisted and I, sitting alone on the main hatch, in the rain, privately remembered our Fatherland. There was on board an American sea-captain, of Norwegian birth, as I afterwards found, who would gladly have joined us. The other passengers were three Norwegians, three fossil Englishmen, two snobbish do., and some jolly, good-natured, free-and-easy youths, bound to Norway, with dogs, guns, rods, fishing tackle, and oil-cloth overalls.

We had a fair wind and smooth sea, but the most favourable circumstances could not get more than eight knots an hour out of our steamer. After forty-eight hours, however, the coast of Norway came in sight—a fringe of scattered rocks, behind which rose bleak hills, enveloped in mist and rain. Our captain, who had been running on this route some years, did not know where we were, and was for putting to sea again, but one of the Norwegian passengers offered his services as pilot and soon brought us to the fjord of Christiansand. We first passed through a Skärgaard—archipelago, or "garden of rocks," as it is picturesquely termed in Norsk—and then between hills of dark-red rock, covered by a sprinkling of fir-trees, to a sheltered and tranquil harbour, upon which lay the little town. By this time the rain came down, not in drops, but in separate threads or streams, as if the nozzle of an immense watering-pot had been held over us. After three months of drouth, which had burned up the soil and entirely ruined the hay-crops, it was now raining for the first time in Southern Norway. The young Englishmen bravely put on their waterproofs and set out to visit the town in the midst of the deluge; but as it contains no sight of special interest, I made up my mind that, like Constantinople, it was more attractive from without than within, and remained on board. An amphitheatre of rugged hills surrounds the place, broken only by a charming little valley, which stretches off to the westward.

The fishermen brought us some fresh mackerel for our breakfast. They are not more than half the size of ours, and of a brighter green along the back; their flavour, however, is delicious. With these mackerels, four salmons, a custom-house officer, and a Norwegian parson, we set off at noon for Christiania. The coast was visible, but at a considerable distance, all day. Fleeting gleams of sunshine sometimes showed the broken inland ranges of mountains with jagged saw-tooth peaks shooting up here and there. When night came there was no darkness, but a strong golden gleam, whereby one could read until after ten o'clock. We reached the mouth of Christiania Fjord a little after midnight, and most of the passengers arose to view the scenery. After passing the branch which leads to Drammen, the fjord contracts so as to resemble a river or one of our island-studded New England lakes. The alternation of bare rocky islets, red-ribbed cliffs, fir-woods, grey-green birchen groves, tracts of farm land, and red-frame cottages, rendered this part of the voyage delightful, although, as the morning advanced, we saw everything through a gauzy veil of rain. Finally, the watering-pot was turned on again, obliging even oil cloths to beat a retreat to the cabin, and so continued until we reached Christiania.

After a mild custom-house visitation, not a word being said about passports, we stepped ashore in republican Norway, and were piloted by a fellow-passenger to the Victoria Hotel, where an old friend awaited me. He who had walked with me in the colonnades of Karnak, among the sands of Kôm-Ombos, and under the palms of Philæ, was there to resume our old companionship on the bleak fjelds of Norway and on the shores of the Arctic Sea. We at once set about preparing for the journey. First, to the banker's who supplied me with a sufficient quantity of small money for the post-stations on the road to Drontheim; then to a seller of carrioles, of whom we procured three, at $36 apiece, to be resold to him for $24, at the expiration of two months; and then to supply ourselves with maps, posting-book, hammer, nails rope, gimlets, and other necessary helps in case of a breakdown. The carriole (carry-all, lucus a non lucendo, because it only carries one) is the national Norwegian vehicle, and deserves special mention. It resembles a reindeer-pulk, mounted on a pair of wheels, with long, flat, flexible ash shafts, and no springs. The seat, much like the stern of a canoe, and rather narrow for a traveller of large basis, slopes down into a trough for the feet, with a dashboard in front. Your single valise is strapped on a flat board behind, upon which your postillion sits. The whole machine resembles an American sulky in appearance, except that it is springless, and nearly the whole weight is forward of the axle. We also purchased simple and strong harness, which easily accommodates itself to any horse.

Christiania furnishes a remarkable example of the progress which Norway has made since its union with Sweden and the adoption of a free Constitution. In its signs of growth and improvement, the city reminds one of an American town. Its population has risen to 40,000, and though inferior to Gottenburg in its commerce, it is only surpassed by Stockholm in size. The old log houses of which it once was built have almost entirely disappeared; the streets are broad, tolerably paved, and have—what Stockholm cannot yet boast of—decent side-walks. From the little nucleus of the old town, near the water, branch off handsome new streets, where you often come suddenly from stately three-story blocks upon the rough rock and meadow land. The broad Carl-Johansgade, leading directly to the imposing white front of the Royal Palace, upon an eminence in the rear of the city, is worthy of any European capital. On the old market square a very handsome market hall of brick, in semi-Byzantine style, has recently been erected, and the only apparent point in which Christiania has not kept up with the times, is the want of piers for her shipping. A railroad, about forty miles in length, is already in operation as far as Eidsvold, at the foot of the long Miösen Lake, on which steamers ply to Lillehammer, at its head, affording an outlet for the produce of the fertile Guldbrandsdal and the adjacent country. The Norwegian Constitution is in almost all respects as free as that of any American state, and it is cheering to see what material well-being and solid progress have followed its adoption.

The environs of Christiania are remarkably beautiful. From the quiet basin of the fjord, which vanishes between blue, interlocking islands to the southward, the land rises gradually on all sides, speckled with smiling country-seats and farm-houses, which trench less and less on the dark evergreen forests as they recede, until the latter keep their old dominion and sweep in unbroken lines to the summits of the mountains on either hand. The ancient citadel of Aggershus, perched upon a rock, commands the approach to the city, fine old linden trees rising above its white walls and tiled roofs; beyond, over the trees of the palace park, in which stand the new Museum and University, towers the long palace-front, behind which commences a range of villas and gardens, stretching westward around a deep bight of the fjord, until they reach the new palace of Oscar-hall, on a peninsula facing the city. As we floated over the glassy water, in a skiff, on the afternoon following our arrival, watching the scattered sun-gleams move across the lovely panorama, we found it difficult to believe that we were in the latitude of Greenland. The dark, rich green of the foliage, the balmy odours which filled the air, the deep blue of the distant hills and islands, and the soft, warm colors of the houses, all belonged to the south. Only the air, fresh without being cold, elastic, and exciting, not a delicious opiate, was wholly northern, and when I took a swim under the castle walls, I found that the water was northern too. It was the height of summer, and the showers of roses in the gardens, the strawberries and cherries in the market, show that the summer's best gifts are still enjoyed here.

The English were off the next day with their dogs, guns, fishing tackle, waterproofs, clay pipes, and native language, except one, who became home-sick and went back in the next steamer. We also prepared to set out for Ringerike, the ancient dominion of King Ring, on our way to the Dovre-fjeld and Drontheim.

CHAPTER XXI. INCIDENTS OF CARRIOLE TRAVEL.

It is rather singular that whenever you are about to start upon a new journey, you almost always fall in with some one who has just made it, and who overwhelms you with all sorts of warning and advice. This has happened to me so frequently that I have long ago ceased to regard any such communications, unless the individual from whom they come inspires me with more than usual confidence. While inspecting our carrioles at the hotel in Christiania, I was accosted by a Hamburg merchant, who had just arrived from Drontheim, by way of the Dovre Fjeld and the Miösen Lake. "Ah," said he, "those things won't last long. That oil-cloth covering for your luggage will be torn to pieces in a few days by the postillions climbing upon it. Then they hold on to your seat and rip the cloth lining with their long nails; besides, the rope reins wear the leather off your dashboard, and you will be lucky if your wheels and axles don't snap on the rough roads." Now, here was a man who had travelled much in Norway, spoke the language perfectly, and might be supposed to know something; but his face betrayed the croaker, and I knew, moreover, that of all fretfully luxurious men, merchants—and especially North-German merchants—are the worst, so I let him talk and kept my own private opinion unchanged.

At dinner he renewed the warnings. "You will have great delay in getting horses at the stations. The only way is to be rough and swaggering, and threaten the people—and even that won't always answer." Most likely, I thought.—"Of course you have a supply of provisions with you?" he continued. "No," said I, "I always adopt the diet of the country in which I travel."—"But you can't do it here!" he exclaimed in horror, "you can't do it here! They have no wine, nor no white bread, nor no fresh meat; and they don't know how to cook anything!" "I am perfectly aware of that," I answered; "but as long as I am not obliged to come down to bread made of fir-bark and barley-straw, as last winter in Lapland, I shall not complain."—"You possess the courage of a hero if you can do such a thing; but you will not start now, in this rain?" We answered by bidding him a polite adieu, for the post-horses had come, and our carrioles were at the door. As if to reward our resolution, the rain, which had been falling heavily all the morning, ceased at that moment, and the grey blanket of heaven broke and rolled up into loose masses of cloud.

I mounted into the canoe-shaped seat, drew the leathern apron over my legs, and we set out, in single file, through the streets of Christiania. The carriole, as I have already said, has usually no springs (ours had none at least), except those which it makes in bounding over the stones. We had not gone a hundred yards before I was ready to cry out—"Lord, have mercy upon me!" Such a shattering of the joints, such a vibration of the vertebræ, such a churning of the viscera, I had not felt since travelling by banghy-cart in India. Breathing went on by fits and starts, between the jolts; my teeth struck together so that I put away my pipe, lest I should bite off the stem, and the pleasant sensation of having been pounded in every limb crept on apace. Once off the paving-stones, it was a little better; beyond the hard turnpike which followed, better still; and on the gravel and sand of the first broad hill, we found the travel easy enough to allay our fears. The two skydsbonder, or postillions, who accompanied us, sat upon our portmanteaus, and were continually jumping off to lighten the ascent of the hills. The descents were achieved at full trotting speed, the horses leaning back, supporting themselves against the weight of the carrioles, and throwing out their feet very firmly, so as to avoid the danger of slipping. Thus, no matter how steep the hill, they took it with perfect assurance and boldness, never making a stumble. There was just sufficient risk left, however, to make these flying descents pleasant and exhilarating.

Our road led westward, over high hills and across deep valleys, down which we had occasional glimpses of the blue fjord and its rocky islands. The grass and grain were a rich, dark green, sweeping into a velvety blue in the distance, and against this deep ground, the bright red of the houses showed with strong effect—a contrast which was subdued and harmonised by the still darker masses of the evergreen forests, covering the mountain ranges. At the end of twelve or thirteen miles we reached the first post-station, at the foot of the mountains which bound the inland prospect from Christiania on the west. As it was not a "fast" station, we were subject to the possibility of waiting two or three hours for horses, but fortunately were accosted on the road by one of the farmers who supply the skyds, and changed at his house. The Norwegian skyds differs from the Swedish skjuts in having horses ready only at the fast stations, which are comparatively few, while at all others you must wait from one to three hours, according to the distance from which the horses must be brought. In Sweden there are always from two to four horses ready, and you are only obliged to wait after these are exhausted. There, also, the regulations are better, and likewise more strictly enforced. It is, at best, an awkward mode of travelling—very pleasant, when everything goes rightly, but very annoying when otherwise.

We now commenced climbing the mountain by a series of terribly steep ascents, every opening in the woods disclosing a wider and grander view backward over the lovely Christiania Fjord and the intermediate valleys. Beyond the crest we came upon a wild mountain plateau, a thousand feet above the sea, and entirely covered with forests of spruce and fir. It was a black and dismal region, under the lowering sky: not a house or a grain field to be seen, and thus we drove for more than two hours, to the solitary inn of Krogkleven, where we stopped for the night in order to visit the celebrated King's View in the morning. We got a tolerable supper and good beds, sent off a messenger to the station of Sundvolden, at the foot of the mountain, to order horses for us, and set out soon after sunrise, piloted by the landlord's son, Olaf. Half an hour's walk through the forest brought us to a pile of rocks on the crest of the mountain, which fell away abruptly to the westward. At our feet lay the Tyri Fjord, with its deeply indented shores and its irregular, scattered islands, shining blue and bright in the morning sun, while away beyond it stretched a great semicircle of rolling hills covered with green farms, dotted with red farm-houses, and here and there a white church glimmering like a spangle on the breast of the landscape. Behind this soft, warm, beautiful region, rose dark, wooded hills, with lofty mountain-ridges above them, until, far and faint, under and among the clouds, streaks of snow betrayed some peaks of the Nore Fjeld, sixty or seventy miles distant. This is one of the most famous views in Norway, and has been compared to that from the Righi, but without sufficient reason. The sudden change, however, from the gloomy wilderness through which you first pass to the sunlit picture of the enchanting lake, and green, inhabited hills and valleys, may well excuse the raptures of travellers. Ringerike, the realm of King Ring, is a lovely land, not only as seen from this eagle's nest, but when you have descended upon its level. I believe the monarch's real name was Halfdan the Black. So beloved was he in life that after death his body was divided into four portions, so that each province might possess some part of him. Yet the noblest fame is transitory, and nobody now knows exactly where any one of his quarters was buried.

A terrible descent, through a chasm between perpendicular cliffs some hundreds of feet in height, leads from Krogkleven to the level of the Tyri Fjord. There is no attempt here, nor indeed upon the most of the Norwegian roads we travelled, to mitigate, by well-arranged curves, the steepness of the hills. Straight down you go, no matter of how breakneck a character the declivity may be. There are no drags to the carrioles and country carts, and were not the native horses the toughest and surest-footed little animals in the world, this sort of travel would be trying to the nerves.

Our ride along the banks of the Tyri Fjord, in the clear morning sunshine, was charming. The scenery was strikingly like that on the lake of Zug, in Switzerland, and we missed the only green turf, which this year's rainless spring had left brown and withered. In all Sweden we had seen no such landscapes, not even in Norrland. There, however, the people carried off the palm. We found no farm-houses here so stately and clean as the Swedish, no such symmetrical forms and frank, friendly faces. The Norwegians are big enough, and strong enough, to be sure, but their carriage is awkward, and their faces not only plain but ugly. The countrywomen we saw were remarkable in this latter respect, but nothing could exceed their development of waist, bosom and arms. Here is the stuff of which Vikings were made, I thought, but there has been no refining or ennobling since those times. These are the rough primitive formations of the human race—the bare granite and gneiss, from which sprouts no luxuriant foliage, but at best a few simple and hardy flowers. I found much less difficulty in communicating with the Norwegians than I anticipated. The language is so similar to the Swedish that I used the latter, with a few alterations, and easily made myself understood.

The Norwegian dialect, I imagine, stands in about the same relation to pure Danish as the Scotch does to the English. To my ear, it is less musical and sonorous than the Swedish, though it is often accented in the same peculiar sing-song way.

Leaving the Tyri Fjord, we entered a rolling, well-cultivated country, with some pleasant meadow scenery. The crops did not appear to be thriving remarkably, probably on account of the dry weather. The hay crop, which the farmers were just cutting, was very scanty; rye and winter barley were coming into head, but the ears were thin and light, while spring barley and oats were not more than six inches in height. There were many fields of potatoes, however, which gave a better promise. So far as one could judge from looking over the fields, Norwegian husbandry is yet in a very imperfect state, and I suspect that the resources of the soil are not half developed. The whole country was radiant with flowers, and some fields were literally mosaics of blue, purple, pink, yellow, and crimson bloom. Clumps of wild roses fringed the road, and the air was delicious with a thousand odours. Nature was throbbing with the fullness of her short midsummer life, with that sudden and splendid rebound from the long trance of winter which she nowhere makes except in the extreme north.

At Kläkken, which is called a lilsigelse station, where horses must be specially engaged, we were obliged to wait two hours and a half, while they were sent for from a distance of four miles. The utter coolness and indifference of the people to our desire to get on faster was quite natural, and all the better for them, no doubt, but it was provoking to us. We whiled away a part of the time with breakfast, which was composed mainly of boiled eggs and an immense dish of wild strawberries, of very small size but exquisitely fragrant flavour. The next station brought us to Vasbunden, at the head of the beautiful Randsfjord, which was luckily a fast station, and the fresh horses were forthcoming in two minutes. Our road all the afternoon lay along the eastern bank of the Fjord, coursing up and down the hills through a succession of the loveliest landscape pictures. This part of Norway will bear a comparison with the softer parts of Switzerland, such as the lakes of Zurich and Thun. The hilly shores of the Fjord were covered with scattered farms, the villages being merely churches with half a dozen houses clustered about them.

At sunset we left the lake and climbed a long wooded mountain to a height of more than two thousand feet. It was a weary pull until we reached the summit, but we rolled swiftly down the other side to the inn of Teterud, our destination, which we reached about 10 P.M. It was quite light enough to read, yet every one was in bed, and the place seemed deserted, until we remembered what latitude we were in. Finally, the landlord appeared, followed by a girl, whom, on account of her size and blubber, Braisted compared to a cow-whale. She had been turned out of her bed to make room for us, and we two instantly rolled into the warm hollow she had left, my Nilotic friend occupying a separate bed in another corner. The guests' room was an immense apartment; eight sets of quadrilles might have been danced in it at one time. The walls were hung with extraordinary pictures of the Six Days of Creation, in which the Almighty was represented as an old man dressed in a long gown, with a peculiarly good-humoured leer, suggesting a wink, on his face. I have frequently seen the same series of pictures in the Swedish inns. In the morning I was aroused by Braisted exclaiming, "There she blows!" and the whale came up to the surface with a huge pot of coffee, some sugar candy, excellent cream, and musty biscuit.

It was raining when we started, and I put on a light coat, purchased in London, and recommended in the advertisement as being "light in texture, gentlemanly in appearance, and impervious to wet," with strong doubts of its power to resist a Norwegian rain. Fortunately, it was not put to a severe test; we had passing showers only, heavy, though short. The country, between the Randsfjord and the Miösen Lake was open and rolling, everywhere under cultivation, and apparently rich and prosperous. Our road was admirable, and we rolled along at the rate of one Norsk mile (seven miles) an hour, through a land in full blossom, and an atmosphere of vernal odours. At the end of the second station we struck the main road from Christiania to Drontheim. In the station-house I found translations of the works of Dickens and Captain Chamier on the table. The landlord was the most polite and attentive Norwegian we had seen; but he made us pay for it, charging one and a half marks apiece for a breakfast of boiled eggs and cheese.

Starting again in a heavy shower, we crossed the crest of a hill, and saw all at once the splendid Miösen Lake spread out before us, the lofty Island of Helge, covered with farms and forests, lying in the centre of the picture. Our road went northward along the side of the vast, sweeping slope of farm-land which bounds the lake on the west. Its rough and muddy condition showed how little land-travel there is at present, since the establishment of a daily line of steamers on the lake. At the station of Gjövik, a glass furnace, situated in a wooded little dell on the shore, I found a young Norwegian who spoke tolerable English, and who seemed astounded at our not taking the steamer in preference to our carrioles. He hardly thought it possible that we could be going all the way to Lillehammer, at the head of the lake, by the land road. When we set out, our postillion took a way leading up the hills in the rear of the place. Knowing that our course was along the shore, we asked him if we were on the road to Sveen, the next station. "Oh, yes; it's all right," said he, "this is a new road." It was, in truth, a superb highway; broad and perfectly macadamised, and leading along the brink of a deep rocky chasm, down which thundered a powerful stream. From the top of this glen we struck inland, keeping more and more to the westward. Again we asked the postillion, and again received the same answer. Finally; when we had travelled six or seven miles, and the lake had wholly disappeared, I stopped and demanded where Sveen was. "Sveen is not on this road," he answered; "we are going to Mustad!" "But," I exclaimed, "we are bound for Sveen and Lillehammer!" "Oh," said he, with infuriating coolness, "you can go there afterwards!" You may judge that the carrioles were whirled around in a hurry, and that the only answer to the fellow's remonstrances was a shaking by the neck which frightened him into silence.

We drove back to Gjövik in a drenching shower, which failed to cool our anger. On reaching the station I at once made a complaint against the postillion, and the landlord called a man who spoke good English, to settle the matter. The latter brought me a bill of $2 for going to Mustad and back. Knowing that the horses belonged to farmers, who were not to blame in the least, we had agreed to pay for their use; but I remonstrated against paying the full price when we had not gone the whole distance, and had not intended to go at all. "Why, then, did you order horses for Mustad?" he asked. "I did no such thing!" I exclaimed, in amazement. "You did!" he persisted, and an investigation ensued, which resulted in the discovery that the Norwegian who had advised us to go by steamer, had gratuitously taken upon himself to tell the landlord to send us to the Randsfjord, and had given the postillion similar directions! The latter, imagining, perhaps, that we didn't actually know our own plans, had followed his instructions. I must say that I never before received such an astonishing mark of kindness. The ill-concealed satisfaction of the people at our mishap made it all the more exasperating. The end of it was that two or three marks were taken off the account, which we then paid, and in an hour afterwards shipped ourselves and carrioles on board a steamer for Lillehammer. The Norwegian who had caused all this trouble came along just before we embarked, and heard the story with the most sublime indifference, proffering not a word of apology, regret, or explanation. Judging from this specimen, the King of Sweden and Norway has good reason to style himself King of the Goths and Vandals.

I was glad, nevertheless, that we had an opportunity of seeing the Miösen, from the deck of a steamer. Moving over the glassy pale-green water, midway between its shores, we had a far better exhibition of its beauties than from the land-road. It is a superb piece of water, sixty miles in length by from two to five in breadth, with mountain shores of picturesque and ever-varying outline. The lower slopes are farm land, dotted with the large gaards, or mansions of the farmers, many of which have a truly stately air; beyond them are forests of fir, spruce, and larch, while in the glens between, winding groves of birch, alder, and ash come down to fringe the banks of the lake. Wandering gleams of sunshine, falling through the broken clouds, touched here and there the shadowed slopes and threw belts of light upon the water—and these illuminated spots finely relieved the otherwise sombre depth of colour. Our boat was slow, and we had between two and three hours of unsurpassed scenery before reaching our destination. An immense raft of timber, gathered from the loose logs which are floated down the Lougen Elv, lay at the head of the lake, which contracts into the famous Guldbrandsdal. On the brow of a steep hill on the right lay the little town of Lillehammer, where we were ere long quartered in a very comfortable hotel.

CHAPTER XXII. GULDBRANDSDAL AND THE DOVRE FJELD.

We left Lillehammer on a heavenly Sabbath morning. There was scarcely a cloud in the sky, the air was warm and balmy, and the verdure of the valley, freshened by the previous day's rain, sparkled and glittered in the sun. The Miösen Lake lay blue and still to the south, and the bald tops of the mountains which inclose Guldbrandsdal stood sharp and clear, and almost shadowless, in the flood of light which streamed up the valley. Of Lillehammer, I can only say that it is a commonplace town of about a thousand inhabitants. It had a cathedral and bishop some six hundred years ago, no traces of either of which now remain. We drove out of it upon a splendid new road, leading up the eastern bank of the river, and just high enough on the mountain side to give the loveliest views either way. Our horses were fast and spirited, and the motion of our carrioles over the firmly macadamised road was just sufficient to keep the blood in nimble circulation. Rigid Sabbatarians may be shocked at our travelling on that day; but there were few hearts in all the churches of Christendom whose hymns of praise were more sincere and devout than ours. The Lougen roared an anthem for us from his rocky bed; the mountain streams, flashing down their hollow channels, seemed hastening to join it; the mountains themselves stood silent, with uncovered heads; and over all the pale-blue northern heaven looked lovingly and gladly down—a smile of God upon the grateful earth. There is no Sabbath worship better than the simple enjoyment of such a day.

Toward the close of the stage, our road descended to the banks of the Lougen, which here falls in a violent rapid—almost a cataract—over a barrier of rocks. Masses of water, broken or wrenched from the body of the river, are hurled intermittently high into the air, scattering as they fall, with fragments of rainbows dancing over them. In this scene I at once recognised the wild landscape by the pencil of Dahl, the Norwegian painter, which had made such an impression upon me in Copenhagen. In Guldbrandsdal, we found at once what we had missed in the scenery of Ringerike—swift, foaming streams. Here they leapt from every rift of the upper crags, brightening the gloom of the fir-woods which clothed the mountain-sides, like silver braiding upon a funeral garment. This valley is the pride of Norway, nearly as much for its richness as for its beauty and grandeur. The houses were larger and more substantial, the fields blooming, with frequent orchards of fruit-trees, and the farmers, in their Sunday attire showed in their faces a little more intelligence than the people we had seen on our way thither. Their countenances had a plain, homely stamp; and of all the large-limbed, strong-backed forms I saw, not one could be called graceful, or even symmetrical. Something awkward and uncouth stamps the country people of Norway. Honest and simple-minded they are said to be, and probably are; but of native refinement of feeling they can have little, unless all outward signs of character are false.

We changed horses at Moshûûs, and drove up a level splendid road to Holmen, along the river-bank. The highway, thus far, is entirely new, and does great credit to Norwegian enterprise. There is not a better road in all Europe; and when it shall be carried through to Drontheim, the terrors which this trip has for timid travellers will entirely disappear. It is a pity that the skyds system should not be improved in equal ratio, instead of becoming even more inconvenient than at present. Holmen, hitherto a fast station, is now no longer so; and the same retrograde change is going on at other places along the road. The waiting at the tilsigelse stations is the great drawback to travelling by skyds in Norway. You must either wait two hours or pay fast prices, which the people are not legally entitled to ask. Travellers may write complaints in the space allotted in the post-books for such things, but with very little result, if one may judge from the perfect indifference which the station-masters exhibit when you threaten to do so. I was more than once tauntingly asked whether I would not write a complaint. In Sweden, I found but one instance of inattention at the stations, during two months' travel, and expected, from the boasted honesty of the Norwegians, to meet with an equally fortunate experience. Travellers, however, and especially English, are fast teaching the people the usual arts of imposition. Oh, you hard-shelled, unplastic, insulated Englishmen! You introduce towels and fresh water, and tea, and beefsteak, wherever you go, it is true; but you teach high prices, and swindling, and insolence likewise!

A short distance beyond Holmen, the new road terminated, and we took the old track over steep spurs of the mountain, rising merely to descend and rise again. The Lougen River here forms a broad, tranquil lake, a mile in width, in which the opposite mountains were splendidly reflected. The water is pale, milky-green colour, which, under certain effects of light, has a wonderful aerial transparency. As we approached Lösnäs, after this long and tedious stage, I was startled by the appearance of a steamer on the river. It is utterly impossible for any to ascend the rapids below Moshûûs; and she must therefore have been built there. We could discover no necessity for such an undertaking in the thin scattered population and their slow, indifferent habits. Her sudden apparition in such a place was like that of an omnibus in the desert.

The magnificent vista of the valley was for a time closed by the snowy peaks of the Rundan Fjeld; but as the direction of the river changed they disappeared, the valley contracted, and its black walls, two thousand feet high, almost overhung us. Below, however, were still fresh meadows, twinkling birchen groves and comfortable farm-houses. Out of a gorge on our right, plunged a cataract from a height of eighty or ninety feet, and a little further on, high up the mountain, a gush of braided silver foam burst out of the dark woods, covered with gleaming drapery the face of a huge perpendicular crag, and disappeared in the woods again, My friend drew up his horse in wonder and rapture. "I know all Switzerland and the Tyrol," he exclaimed, "but I have never seen a cataract so wonderfully framed in the setting of a forest." In the evening, as we approached our destination, two streams on the opposite side of the valley, fell from a height of more than a thousand feet, in a series of linked plunges, resembling burnished chains hanging dangling from the tremendous parapet of rock. On the meadow before us, commanding a full view of this wild and glorious scene, stood a stately gaard, entirely deserted, its barns, out-houses and gardens utterly empty and desolate. Its aspect saddened the whole landscape.

We stopped at the station of Lillehaave, which had only been established the day before, and we were probably the first travellers who had sojourned there. Consequently the people were unspoiled, and it was quite refreshing to be courteously received, furnished with a trout supper and excellent beds, and to pay therefor an honest price. The morning was lowering, and we had rain part of the day; but, thanks to our waterproofs and carriole aprons, we kept comfortably dry. During this day's journey of fifty miles, we had very grand scenery, the mountains gradually increasing in height and abruptness as we ascended the Guldbrandsdal, with still more imposing cataracts "blowing their trumpets from the steeps." At Viik, I found a complaint in the post-book, written by an Englishman who had come with us from Hull, stating that the landlord had made him pay five dollars for beating his dog off his own. The complaint was written in English, of course, and therefore useless so far as the authorities were concerned. The landlord whom I expected, from this account, to find a surly, swindling fellow, accosted us civilly, and invited us into his house to see some old weapons, principally battle-axes. There was a cross-bow, a battered, antique sword, and a buff coat, which may have been stripped from one of Sinclair's men in the pass of Kringelen. The logs of his house, or part of them, are said to have been taken from the dwelling in which the saint-king Olaf—the apostle of Christianity in the North,—was born. They are of the red Norwegian pine, which has a great durability; and the legend may be true, although this would make them eight hundred and fifty years old.

Colonel Sinclair was buried in the churchyard at Viik, and about fifteen miles further we passed the defile of Kringelen, where his band was cut to pieces. He landed in Romsdal's Fjord, on the western coast, with 900 men intending to force his way across the mountains to relieve Stockholm, which was then (1612) besieged by the Danes. Some three hundred of the peasants collected at Kringelen, gathered together rocks and trunks of trees on the brow of the cliff, and, at a concerted signal, rolled the mass down upon the Scotch, the greater part of whom were crushed to death or hurled into the river. Of the whole force only two escaped. A wooden tablet on the spot says, as near as I could make it out, that there was never such an example of courage and valour known in the world, and calls upon the people to admire this glorious deed of their fathers. "Courage and valour;" cried Braisted, indignantly; "it was a cowardly butchery! If they had so much courage, why did they allow 900 Scotchmen to get into the very heart of the country before they tried to stop them?" Well, war is full of meanness and cowardice. If it were only fair fighting on an open field, there would be less of it.

Beyond Laurgaard, Guldbrandsdal contracts to a narrow gorge, down which the Lougen roars in perpetual foam. This pass is called the Rusten; and the road here is excessively steep and difficult. The forests disappear; only hardy firs and the red pine cling to the ledges of the rocks; and mountains, black, grim, and with snow-streaked summits, tower grandly on all sides. A broad cataract, a hundred feet high, leaped down a chasm on our left, so near to the road that its sprays swept over us, and then shot under a bridge to join the seething flood in the frightful gulf beneath. I was reminded of the Valley of the Reuss, on the road to St. Gothard, like which, the pass of the Rusten leads to a cold and bleak upper valley. Here we noticed the blight of late frost on the barley fields, and were for the first time assailed by beggars. Black storm-clouds hung over the gorge, adding to the savage wildness of its scenery; but the sun came out as we drove up the Valley of Dovre, with its long stretch of grain-fields on the sunny sweep of the hill-side, sheltered by the lofty Dovre Fjeld behind them. We stopped for the night at the inn of Toftemoen, long before sunset, although it was eight o'clock, and slept in a half-daylight until morning.

The sun was riding high in the heavens when we left, and dark lowering clouds slowly rolled their masses across the mountain-tops. The Lougen was now an inconsiderable stream, and the superb Guldbrandsdal narrowed to a bare, bleak dell, like those in the high Alps. The grain-fields had a chilled, struggling appearance; the forests forsook the mountain-sides and throve only in sheltered spots at their bases; the houses were mere log cabins, many of which were slipping off their foundation-posts and tottering to their final fall; and the people, poorer than ever, came out of their huts to beg openly and shamelessly as we passed. Over the head of the valley, which here turns westward to the low water-shed dividing it from the famous Romsdal, rose two or three snow-streaked peaks of the Hurunger Fjeld; and the drifts filling the ravines of the mountains on our left descended lower and lower into the valley.

At Dombaas, a lonely station at the foot of the Dovre Fjeld, we turned northward into the heart of the mountains. My postillion, a boy of fifteen, surprised me by speaking very good English. He had learned it in the school at Drontheim. Sometimes, he said, they had a schoolmaster in the house, and sometimes one at Jerkin, twenty miles distant. Our road ascended gradually through half-cut woods of red pine, for two or three miles, after which it entered a long valley, or rather basin, belonging to the table land of the Dovre Fjeld. Stunted heath and dwarfed juniper-bushes mixed with a grey, foxy shrub-willow, covered the soil, and the pale yellow of the reindeer moss stained the rocks. Higher greyer and blacker ridges hemmed in the lifeless landscape; and above them, to the north and west, broad snow-fields shone luminous under the heavy folds of the clouds. We passed an old woman with bare legs and arms, returning from a söter, or summer châlet of the shepherds. She was a powerful but purely animal specimen of humanity,—"beef to the heel," as Braisted said. At last a cluster of log huts, with a patch of green pasture-ground about them, broke the monotony of the scene. It was Fogstuen, or next station, where we were obliged to wait half an hour until the horses had been caught and brought in. The place had a poverty stricken air; and the slovenly woman who acted as landlady seemed disappointed that we did not buy some horridly coarse and ugly woolen gloves of her own manufacture.

Our road now ran for fourteen miles along the plateau of the Dovre, more than 3000 feet above the level of the sea. This is not a plain or table land, but an undulating region, with hills, valleys, and lakes of its own; and more desolate landscapes one can scarcely find elsewhere. Everything is grey, naked, and barren, not on a scale grand enough to be imposing, nor with any picturesqueness of form to relieve its sterility. One can understand the silence and sternness of the Norwegians, when he has travelled this road. But I would not wish my worst enemy to spend more than one summer as a solitary herdsman on these hills. Let any disciple of Zimmerman try the effect of such a solitude. The statistics of insanity in Norway exhibit some of its effects, and that which is most common is most destructive. There never was a greater humbug than the praise of solitude: it is the fruitful mother of all evil, and no man covets it who has not something bad or morbid in his nature.

By noon the central ridge or comb of the Dovre Fjeld rose before us, with the six-hundred-year old station of Jerkin in a warm nook on its southern side. This is renowned as the best post-station in Norway, and is a favourite resort of English travellers and sportsmen, who come hither to climb the peak of Snæhätten, and to stalk reindeer. I did not find the place particularly inviting. The two women who had charge of it for the time were unusually silent and morose, but our dinner was cheap and well gotten up, albeit the trout were not the freshest. We admired the wonderful paintings of the landlord, which although noticed by Murray, give little promise for Norwegian art in these high latitudes. His cows, dogs, and men are all snow-white, and rejoice in an original anatomy.

The horses on this part of the road were excellent, the road admirable, and our transit was therefore thoroughly agreeable. The ascent of the dividing ridge, after leaving Jerkin, is steep and toilsome for half a mile, but with this exception the passage of the Dovre Fjeld is remarkably easy. The highest point which the road crossed is about 4600 feet above the sea, or a little higher than the Brenner Pass in the Tyrol. But there grain grows and orchards bear fruit, while here, under the parallel of 62°, nearly all vegetation ceases, and even the omnivorous northern sheep can find no pasturage. Before and behind you lie wastes of naked grey mountains, relieved only by the snow-patches on their summits. I have seen as desolate tracts of wilderness in the south made beautiful by the lovely hues which they took from the air; but Nature has no such tender fancies in the north. She is a realist of the most unpitying stamp, and gives atmospheric influences which make that which is dark and bleak still darker and bleaker. Black clouds hung low on the horizon, and dull grey sheets of rain swept now and then across the nearer heights. Snæhätten, to the westward, was partly veiled, but we could trace his blunt mound of alternate black rock and snow nearly to the apex. The peak is about 7700 feet above the sea, and was until recently considered the highest in Norway, but the Skagtolstind has been ascertained to be 160 feet higher, and Snæhätten is dethroned.

The river Driv came out of a glen on our left, and entered a deep gorge in front, down which our road lay, following the rapid descent of the foaming stream. At the station of Kongsvold, we had descended to 3000 feet again, yet no trees appeared. Beyond this, the road for ten miles has been with great labour hewn out of the solid rock, at the bottom of a frightful defile, like some of those among the Alps. Formerly, it climbed high up on the mountain-side, running on the brink of almost perpendicular cliffs, and the Vaarsti, as it is called, was then reckoned one of the most difficult and dangerous roads in the country. Now it is one of the safest and most delightful. We went down the pass on a sharp trot, almost too fast to enjoy the wild scenery as it deserved. The Driv fell through the cleft in a succession of rapids, while smaller streams leaped to meet him in links of silver cataract down a thousand feet of cliff. Birch and fir now clothed the little terraces and spare corners of soil, and the huge masses of rock, hanging over our heads, were tinted with black, warm brown, and russet orange, in such a manner as to produce the most charming effects of colour. Over the cornices of the mountain-walls, hovering at least two thousand feet above, gleamed here and there the scattered snowy jötuns of the highest fjeld.

The pass gradually opened into a narrow valley, where we found a little cultivation again. Here was the post of Drivstuen, kept by a merry old lady. Our next stage descended through increasing habitation and culture to the inn of Rise, where we stopped for the night, having the Dovre Fjeld fairly behind us. The morning looked wild and threatening, but the clouds gradually hauled off to the eastward, leaving us the promise of a fine day. Our road led over hills covered with forests of fir and pine, whence we looked into a broad valley clothed with the same dark garment of forest, to which the dazzling white snows of the fjeld in the background made a striking contrast. We here left the waters of the Driv and struck upon those of the Orkla, which flow into Drontheim Fjord. At Stuen, we got a fair breakfast of eggs, milk, cheese, bread and butter. Eggs are plentiful everywhere, yet, singularly enough, we were nearly a fortnight in Norway before we either saw or heard a single fowl. Where they were kept we could not discover, and why they did not crow was a still greater mystery. Norway is really the land of silence. For an inhabited country, it is the quietest I have ever seen. No wonder that anger and mirth, when they once break through the hard ice of Norwegian life, are so furious and uncontrollable. These inconsistent extremes may always be reconciled, when we understand how nicely the moral nature of man is balanced.

Our road was over a high, undulating tract for two stages, commanding wide views of a wild wooded region, which is said to abound with game. The range of snowy peaks behind us still filled the sky, appearing so near at hand as to deceive the eye in regard to their height. At last, we came upon the brink of a steep descent, overlooking the deep glen of the Orkla, a singularly picturesque valley, issuing from between the bases of the mountains, and winding away to the northward. Down the frightful slant our horses plunged and in three minutes we were at the bottom, with flower-sown meadows on either hand, and the wooded sides of the glen sweeping up to a waving and fringed outline against the sky. After crossing the stream, we had an ascent as abrupt, on the other side; but half-way up stood the station of Bjærkager, where we left our panting horses. The fast stations were now at an end, but by paying fast prices we got horses with less delay. In the evening, a man travelling on foot offered to carry förbud notices for us to the remaining stations, if we would pay for his horse. We accepted; I wrote the orders in my best Norsk, and on the following day we found the horses in readiness everywhere.

The next stage was an inspiring trot through a park-like country, clothed with the freshest turf and studded with clumps of fir, birch, and ash. The air was soft and warm, and filled with balmy scents from the flowering grasses, and the millions of blossoms spangling the ground. In one place, I saw half an acre of the purest violet hue, where the pansy of our gardens grew so thickly that only its blossoms were visible. The silver green of the birch twinkled in the sun, and its jets of delicate foliage started up everywhere with exquisite effect amid the dark masses of the fir. There was little cultivation as yet, but these trees formed natural orchards, which suggested a design in their planting and redeemed the otherwise savage character of the scenery. We dipped at last into a hollow, down which flowed one of the tributaries of the Gûûl Elv, the course of which we thence followed to Drontheim.

One of the stations was a lonely gaard, standing apart from the road, on a high hill. As we drove up, a horrid old hag came out to receive us. "Can I get three horses soon?" I asked. "No," she answered with a chuckle. "How soon?" "In a few hours," was her indifferent reply, but the promise of paying fast rates got them in less than one. My friend wanted a glass of wine, but the old woman said she had nothing but milk. We were sitting on the steps with our pipes, shortly afterwards, when she said: "Why don't you go into the house?" "It smells too strongly of paint," I answered. "But you had better go in," said she, and shuffled off. When we entered, behold! there were three glasses of very good Marsala on the table. "How do you sell your milk?" I asked her. "That kind is three skillings a dram," she answered. The secret probably was that she had no license to sell wine. I was reminded of an incident which occurred to me in Maine, during the prevalence of the prohibitory law. I was staying at an hotel in a certain town, and jestingly asked the landlord: "Where is the Maine Law? I should like to see it." "Why," said he, "I have it here in the house;'" and he unlocked a back room and astonished me with the sight of a private bar, studded with full decanters.

The men folks were all away at work, and our postillion was a strapping girl of eighteen, who rode behind Braisted. She was gotten up on an immense scale, but nature had expended so much vigour on her body that none was left for her brain. She was a consummate representation of health and stupidity. At the station where we stopped for the night I could not help admiring the solid bulk of the landlady's sister. Although not over twenty four she must have weighed full two hundred. Her waist was of remarkable thickness, and her bust might be made into three average American ones. I can now understand why Mügge calls his heroine Ilda "the strong maiden."

A drive of thirty-five miles down the picturesque valley of the Gûûl brought us to Drontheim the next day—the eighth after leaving Christiania.

CHAPTER XXIII. DRONTHEIM.—VOYAGE UP THE COAST OF NORWAY.

Our first view of Drontheim (or Trondhjem, as it should properly be written) was from the top of the hill behind the town, at the termination of six miles of execrable road, and perhaps the relief springing from that circumstance heightened the agreeable impression which the scene made upon our minds. Below us, at the bottom of a crescent-shaped bay, lay Drontheim—a mass of dark red, yellow, and brown buildings, with the grey cathedral in the rear. The rich, well cultivated valley of the Nid stretched behind it, on our right, past the Lierfoss, whose column of foam was visible three miles away, until the hills, rising more high and bleak behind each other, completely enclosed it. The rock-fortress of Munkholm, in front of the city, broke the smooth surface of the fjord, whose further shores, dim with passing showers, swept away to the north-east, hiding the termination of this great sea-arm, which is some fifty miles distant. The panorama was certainly on a grand scale, and presented very diversified and picturesque features; but I can by no means agree with Dr. Clarke, who compares it to the Bay of Naples. Not only the rich colours of the Mediterranean are wanting, but those harmonic sweeps and curves of the Italian shores and hills have nothing in common with these rude, ragged, weather beaten, defiant forms.

Descending the hill between rows of neat country-houses, we passed a diminutive fortification, and entered the city. The streets are remarkably wide and roughly paved, crossing each other at right angles, with a Philadelphian regularity. The houses are all two stories high, and raised upon ample foundations, so that the doors are approached by flights of steps—probably on account of the deep snows during the winter. They are almost exclusively of wood, solid logs covered with neat clap-boards, but a recent law forbids the erection of any more wooden houses, and in the course of time, the town, like Christiania, will lose all that is peculiar and characteristic in its architecture. A cleaner place can scarcely be found, and I also noticed, what is quite rare in the North, large square fountains or wells, at the intersection of all the principal streets. The impression which Drontheim makes upon the stranger is therefore a cheerful and genial one. Small and unpretending though it be, it is full of pictures; the dark blue fjord closes the vista of half its streets; hills of grey rock, draped with the greenest turf, overlook it on either side, and the beautiful valley of the Nid, one of the loveliest nooks of Norway, lies in its rear.

We drove to the Hotel de Belle-Vue, one of the two little caravanserais of which the town boasts, and were fortunate in securing the two vacant rooms. The hotel business in Norway is far behind that of any other country, except in regard to charges, where it is far in advance. Considering what one gets for his money, this is the most expensive country in the world for foreigners. Except where the rates are fixed by law, as in posting, the natives pay much less; and here is an instance of double-dealing which does not harmonise with the renowned honesty of the Norwegians. At the Belle-Vue, we were furnished with three very meagre meals a day, at the rate of two dollars and a half. The attendance was performed by two boys of fourteen or fifteen, whose services, as may be supposed, were quite inadequate to the wants of near twenty persons. The whole business of the establishment devolved on these two fellows, the landlady, though good-humoured and corpulent, as was meet, knowing nothing about the business, and, on the whole, it was a wonder that matters were not worse. It is singular that in a pastoral country like Norway one gets nothing but rancid butter, and generally sour cream, where both should be of the finest quality. Nature is sparing of her gifts, to be sure; but what she does furnish is of the best, as it comes from her hand. Of course, one does not look for much culinary skill, and is therefore not disappointed, but the dairy is the primitive domestic art of all races, and it is rather surprising to find it in so backward a state.

My friend, who received no letters, and had no transatlantic interests to claim his time, as I had, applied himself to seeing the place, which he accomplished, with praiseworthy industry, in one day. He walked out to the falls of the Nid, three miles up the valley, and was charmed with them. He then entered the venerable cathedral, where he had the satisfaction of seeing a Protestant clergyman perform high mass in a scarlet surplice, with a gold cross on his back. The State Church of Norway, which, like that of Sweden, is Lutheran of a very antiquated type, not only preserves this ritual, but also the form of confession (in a general way, I believe, and without reference to particular sins) and of absolution. Of course, it is violently dogmatic and illiberal, and there is little vital religious activity in the whole country. Until within a very few years, no other sects were tolerated, and even yet there is simply freedom of conscience, but not equal political rights, for those of other denominations. This concession has perhaps saved the church from becoming a venerable fossil, yet one still finds persons who regret that it should have been made, not knowing that all truth, to retain its temper, must be whetted against an opposing blade. According to the new constitution of Norway, the king must be crowned in the cathedral of Drontheim. Bernadotte received the proper consecration, but Oscar, though King of Norway, has not yet seen fit to accept it. I once heard a Norwegian exclaim, with a sort of jealous satisfaction: "Oscar calls himself King of Norway, but he is a king without a crown!" I cannot see, however, that this fact lessens his authority as sovereign, in the least.

There is a weekly line of steamers, established by the Storthing (Legislative Assembly), to Hammerfest and around the North Cape. The "Nordkap," the largest and best of these boats, was to leave Drontheim on Saturday evening, the 18th of July, and we lost no time in securing berths, as another week would have made it too late for the perpetual sunshine of the northern summer. Here again, one is introduced to a knowledge of customs and regulations unknown elsewhere. The ticket merely secures you a place on board the steamer, but neither a berth nor provisions. The latter you obtain from a restaurateur on board, according to fixed rates; the former depends on the will of the captain, who can stow you where he chooses. On the "Nordkap" the state-rooms were already occupied, and there remained a single small saloon containing eight berths. Here we did very well so long as there were only English and American occupants, who at once voted to have the skylight kept open; but after two Norwegians were added to our company, we lived in a state of perpetual warfare, the latter sharing the national dread of fresh air; and yet one of them was a professor from the University of Christiania, and the other a physician, who had charge of the hospital in Bergen! With this exception, we had every reason to be satisfied

202

with the vessel. She was very stanch and steady-going, with a spacious airy saloon on deck; no captain could have been more kind and gentlemanly, and there was quite as much harmony among the passengers as could reasonably have been expected. Our party consisted of five Americans, three English, two Germans, and one Frenchman (M. Gay, Membre de l'Academie), besides a variety of Norwegians from all parts of the country.

Leaving our carrioles and part of our baggage behind us, we rowed out to the steamer in a heavy shower. The sun was struggling with dark grey rain-clouds all the evening, and just as we hove anchor, threw a splendid triumphal iris across the bay, completely spanning the town, which, with the sheltering hills, glimmered in the rosy mist floating within the bow. Enclosed by such a dazzling frame the picture of Drontheim shone with a magical lustre, like a vision of Asgaard, beckoning to us from the tempestuous seas. But we were bound for the north, the barriers of Niflhem, the land of fog and sleet, and we disregarded the celestial token, though a second perfect rainbow overarched the first, and the two threw their curves over hill and fortress and the bosom of the rainy fjord, until they almost touched our vessel on either side. In spite of the rain, we remained on deck until a late hour, enjoying the bold scenery of the outer fjord—here, precipitous woody shores, gashed with sudden ravines; there, jet-black rocky peaks, resembling the porphyry hills of the African deserts; and now and then, encircling the sheltered coves, soft green fields glowing with misty light, and the purple outlines of snow-streaked mountains in the distance.

The morning was still dark and rainy. We were at first running between mountain-islands of bare rock and the iron coast of the mainland, after which came a stretch of open sea for two hours, and at noon we reached Björö, near the mouth of the Namsen Fjord. Here there was half a dozen red houses on a bright green slope, with a windmill out of gear crowning the rocky hill in the rear. The sky gradually cleared as we entered the Namsen Fjord, which charmed us with the wildness and nakedness of its shores, studded with little nooks and corners of tillage, which sparkled like oases of tropical greenness, in such a rough setting. Precipices of dark-red rock, streaked with foamy lines of water from the snows melting upon their crests, frowned over the narrow channels between the islands, and through their gaps and gorges we caught sight of the loftier ranges inland. Namsos, at the head of the fjord, is a red-roofed town of a few hundred inhabitants, with a pleasant background of barley-fields and birchen groves. The Namsen valley, behind it, is one of the richest in this part of Norway, and is a great resort of English salmon-fishers. There was a vessel of two hundred tons on the stocks, and a few coasting crafts lying at anchor.

We had a beautiful afternoon voyage out another arm of the fjord, and again entered the labyrinth of islands fringing the coast. Already, the days had perceptibly lengthened, and the increased coldness of the air at night indicated our approach to the Arctic Circle. I was surprised at the amount of business done at the little stations where we touched. Few of these contained a dozen houses, yet the quantity of passengers and freight which we discharged and took on board, at each, could only be explained by the fact that these stations are generally outlets for a tolerably large population, hidden in the valleys and fjords behind, which the steamer does not visit. Bleak and desolate as the coast appears, the back country has its fertile districts—its pasture-ground, its corn-land and forests, of which the voyager sees nothing, and thus might be led to form very erroneous conclusions. Before we had been twenty-four hours out from Drontheim, there was a marked change in the appearance of the people we took on board. Not even in the neighborhood of Christiania or in the rich Guldbrandsdal were the inhabitants so well-dressed, so prosperous (judging from outward signs, merely), or so intelligent. They are in every respect more agreeable and promising specimens of humanity than their brothers of Southern Norway, notwithstanding the dark and savage scenery amidst which their lot is cast.

Toward midnight, we approached the rock of Torghätten, rising 1200 feet high, in the shape of a tall-crowned, battered "wide-awake," above the low, rocky isles and reefs which surround it. This rock is famous for a natural tunnel, passing directly through its heart—the path of an arrow which the Giant Horseman (of whom I shall speak presently) shot at a disdainful maiden, equally colossal, in the old mythological times, when Odin got drunk nightly in Walhalla. We were all on the look-out for this tunnel, which, according

204

to Murray, is large enough for a ship to go through—if it were not some six hundred feet above the sea-level. We had almost passed the rock and nothing of the kind could be seen; but Capt. Riis, who was on deck, encouraged us to have a little patience, changed the steamer's course, and presently we saw a dark cavern yawning in the face of a precipice on the northern side. It was now midnight, but a sunset light tinged the northern sky, and the Torghätten yet stood in twilight. "Shall we see through it?" was the question; but while we were discussing the chances, a faint star sparkled in the midst of the cavernous gloom. "You see it because you imagine it," cried some; yet, no, it was steadfast, and grew broad and bright, until even the most sceptical recognised the pale midnight sky at the bottom of the gigantic arch.

My friend aroused me at five in the morning to see the Seven Sisters— seven majestic peaks, 4000 feet high, and seated closely side by side, with their feet in the sea. They all wore nightcaps of gray fog, and had a sullen and sleepy [Pg 277]air. I imagined they snored, but it was a damp wind driving over the rocks. They were northern beauties, hard-featured and large-boned, and I would not give a graceful southern hill, like Monte Albano or the Paphian Olympus, for the whole of them. So I turned in again, and did not awake until the sun had dried the decks, and the split, twisted and contorted forms of the islands gave promise of those remarkable figures which mark the position of the Arctic Circle. There was already a wonderful change in the scenery. The islands were high and broken, rising like towers and pyramids from the water, and grouped together in the most fantastic confusion. Between their jagged pinnacles, and through their sheer walls of naked rock, we could trace the same formation among the hills of the mainland, while in the rear, white against the sky, stretched the snowy table-land which forms a common summit for all. One is bewildered in the attempt to describe such scenery. There is no central figure, no prevailing character, no sharp contrasts, which may serve as a guide whereby to reach the imagination of the reader. All is confused, disordered, chaotic. One begins to understand the old Norse myth of these stones being thrown by the devil in a vain attempt to prevent the Lord from finishing the world. Grand as they are, singly, you are so puzzled by their numbers and by the fantastic manner in which they seem to dance around you, as the steamer threads the watery labyrinth, that you scarcely appreciate them as they deserve. Take almost any one of these hundreds, and place it inland, anywhere in Europe or America, and it will be visited, sketched and sung to distraction.

At last we saw in the west, far out at sea, the four towers of Threnen, rising perpendicularly many hundred feet from the water. Before us was the Hestmand, or Horseman, who bridles his rocky steed with the polar circle. At first, he appeared like a square turret crowning an irregular mass of island-rock, but, as we approached a colossal head rounded itself at the top, and a sweeping cloak fell from the broad shoulder, flowing backward to the horse's flanks. Still, there was no horse; but here again our captain took the steamer considerably out of her course, so that, at a distance of a mile the whole enormous figure, 1500 feet in height, lay clearly before us. A heavy beard fell from the grand, Jupitolian head; the horse, with sharp ears erect and head bent down, seemed to be plunging into the sea, which was already above his belly; the saddle had slipped forward, so that the rider sat upon his shoulders, but with his head proudly lifted, as if conscious of his fate, and taking a last look at the world. Was it not All-Father Odin, on his horse Sleipner, forsaking the new race which had ceased to worship him? The colossi of the Orient— Rameses and Brahma and Boodh—dwindle into insignificance before this sublime natural monument to the lost gods of the North.

At the little fishing-village of Anklakken, near the Horseman, a fair was being held, and a score or more of coasting craft, gay with Norwegian flags, lay at anchor. These jægts, as they are called, have a single mast, with a large square sail, precisely like those of the Japanese fishing junks, and their hulls are scarcely less heavy and clumsy. They are the Norwegian boats of a thousand years ago; all attempt to introduce a better form of ship-building having been in vain. But the romantic traveller should not suppose that he beholds the "dragons" of the Vikings, which were a very different craft, and have long since disappeared. The jægts are slow, but good seaboats, and as the article haste is not in demand anywhere in Norway, they probably answer every purpose as well as more rational vessels. Those we saw belonged to traders who cruise along the coast during the summer, attending the various fairs, which appear to be the principal recreation of the people. At any rate, they bring some life and activity into these silent solitudes. We had on board the effects of an Englishman who went on shore to see a fair and was left behind by a previous steamer. He had nothing with him but the clothes on his back, and spoke no Norsk: so the captain anxiously looked out for a melancholy, dilapidated individual at every station we touched at—but he looked in vain, for we neither saw nor heard anything of the unfortunate person.

All the afternoon, we had a continuation of the same wonderful scenery—precipices of red rock a thousand feet high, with snowy, turreted summits, and the loveliest green glens between. To the east were vast snow-fields, covering the eternal glaciers of the Alpine range. As we looked up the Salten Fjord, while crossing its mouth, the snows of Sulitelma, the highest mountain in Lappmark, 6000 feet above the sea, were visible, about fifty miles distant. Next came the little town of Bodö where we stopped for the night. It is a cluster of wooden houses, with roofs of green sod, containing about three hundred inhabitants. We found potatoes in the gardens, some currant bushes, and a few hardy vegetables, stunted ash trees and some patches of barley. The sun set a little before eleven o'clock, but left behind him a glory of colours which I have never seen surpassed. The snowy mountains of Lappmark were transmuted into pyramids of scarlet flame, beside which the most gorgeous sunset illuminations of the Alps would have been pale and tame. The sky was a sheet of saffron, amber and rose, reduplicated in the glassy sea, and the peaked island of Landegode in the west, which stood broad against the glow, became a mass of violet hue, topped with cliffs of crimson fire. I sat down on deck and tried to sketch this superb spectacle, in colours which nobody will believe to be real. Before I had finished, the sunset which had lighted one end of Landegode became sunrise at the other, and the fading Alps burned anew with the flames of morning.

CHAPTER XXIV. THE LOFODEN ISLES.

The northern summer soon teaches one fashionable habits of life. Like the man whose windows Sidney Smith darkened, and who slept all day because he thought it was night, you keep awake all night because you forget that it is not day. One's perception of time contracts in some mysterious way, and the sun, setting at eleven, seems to be no later than when he set at seven. You think you will enjoy the evening twilight an hour or two before going to bed, and lo! the morning begins to dawn. It seems absurd to turn in and sleep by daylight, but you sleep, nevertheless, until eight or nine o'clock, and get up but little refreshed with your repose. You miss the grateful covering of darkness, the sweet, welcome gloom, which shuts your senses, one after one, like the closing petals of a flower, in the restoring trance of the night. The light comes through your eyelids as you sleep, and a certain nervous life of the body that should sleep too keeps awake and active. I soon began to feel the wear and tear of perpetual daylight, in spite of its novelty and the many advantages which it presents to the traveller.

At Bodö we were in sight of the Lofoden Islands, which filled up all the northern and western horizon, rising like blue saw-teeth beyond the broad expanse of the West Fjord, which separates them from the group of the shore islands. The next morning, we threaded a perfect labyrinth of rocks, after passing Grotö, and headed across the fjord, for Balstad, on West-Vaagöe, one of the outer isles. This passage is often very rough, especially when the wind blows from the south-west, rolling the heavy swells of the Atlantic into the open mouth of the fjord. We were very much favoured by the weather, having a clear sky, with a light north wind and smooth sea. The long line of jagged peaks, stretching from Væröe in the south west to the giant ridges of Hindöe in the north east, united themselves in the distance with the Alpine chain of the mainland behind us, forming an amphitheatre of sharp, snowy summits, which embraced five-sixths of the entire circle of the horizon, and would have certainly numbered not less than two hundred. Von Buch compares the Lofodens to the jaws of a shark, and most travellers since his time have resuscitated the comparison, but I did not find it so remarkably applicable. There are shark tooth peaks here and there, it is true, but the peculiar conformation of Norway—extensive plateaus, forming the summit-level of the mountains—extends also to these islands, whose only valleys are those which open to the sea, and whose interiors are uninhabitable snowy tracts, mostly above the line of vegetation.

On approaching the islands, we had a fair view of the last outposts of the group—the solid barriers against which the utmost fury of the Atlantic dashes in vain. This side of Væröe lay the large island of Mosköe, between which and a large solitary rock in the middle of the strait dividing them, is the locality of the renowned Maelström—now, alas! almost as mythical as the kraaken or great sea snake of the Norwegian fjords. It is a great pity that the geographical illusions of our boyish days cannot retrain. You learn that the noise of Niagara can be heard 120 miles off, and that "some Indians, in their canoes, have ventured down it, with safety." Well, one could give up the Indians without much difficulty; but it is rather discouraging to step out of the Falls Depôt for the first time, within a quarter of a mile of the cataract, and hear no sound except "Cab sir?" "Hotel, sir?" So of the Maelström, denoted on my schoolboy map by a great spiral twist, which suggested to me a tremendous whirl of the ocean currents, aided by the information that "vessels cannot approach nearer than seven miles." In Olney, moreover, there was a picture of a luckless bark, half-way down the vortex. I had been warming my imagination, as we came up the coast, with Campbell's sonorous lines:

"Round the shores where runic Odin

Howls his war-song to the gale;

Round the isles where loud Lofoden

Whirls to death the roaring whale;"

and, as we looked over the smooth water towards Mosköe, felt a renewed desire to make an excursion thither on out return from the north. But, according to Captain Riis, and other modern authorities which I consulted, the Maelström has lost all its terrors and attractions. Under certain conditions of wind and tide, an eddy is formed in the strait it is true, which may be dangerous to small boats—but the place is by no means so much dreaded as the Salten Fjord, where the tide, rushing in, is caught in such a manner as to form a bore, as in the Bay of Fundy, and frequently proves destructive to the fishing craft. It is the general opinion that some of the rocks which formerly made the Maelström so terrible have been worn away, or that some submarine convulsion has taken place which has changed the action of the waters; otherwise it is impossible to account for the reputation it once possessed.

It should also be borne in mind that any accident to a boat among these islands is more likely to prove disastrous than elsewhere, since there are probably not a score out of the twenty thousand Lofoden fishermen who pass half their lives on the water, who know how to swim. The water is too cold to make bathing a luxury, and they are not sufficiently prepossessed in favour of cleanliness to make it a duty. Nevertheless, they are bold sailors, in their way, and a tougher, hardier, more athletic class of men it would be difficult to find. Handsome they are not, but quite the reverse, and the most of them have an awkward and uncouth air; but it is refreshing to look at their broad shoulders, their brawny chests, and the massive muscles of their legs and arms. During the whole voyage, I saw but one man who appeared to be diseased. Such men, I suspect, were the Vikings—rough, powerful, ugly, dirty fellows, with a few primitive virtues, and any amount of robust vices. We noticed, however, a marked change for the better in the common people, as we advanced northward. They were altogether better dressed, better mannered, and more independent and intelligent, but with a hard, keen, practical expression of face, such as one finds among the shoremen of New-England. The school system of Norway is still sadly deficient, but there is evidently no lack of natural capacity among these people. Their prevailing vice is intemperance, which here, as in all other parts of the country, is beginning to diminish since restrictions have been placed upon the manufacture and sale of spirituous liquors, simultaneously with the introduction of cheap and excellent fermented drinks. The statistics of their morality also show a better state of things than in the South. There is probably no country population in the world where licentiousness prevails to such an extent as in the districts of

Guldbrandsdal and Hedemark.

A voyage of four hours across the West Fjord brought us to the little village of Balstad, at the southern end of West-Vaagöe. The few red, sod-roofed houses were built upon a rocky point, behind which were some patches of bright green pasture, starred with buttercups, overhung by a splendid peak of dark-red rock, two thousand feet in height. It was a fine frontispiece to the Lofoden scenery which now opened before us. Running along the coast of West and East Vaagöe, we had a continual succession of the wildest and grandest pictures—thousand feet precipices, with turrets and needles of rock piercing the sky, dazzling snow-fields, leaking away in cataracts which filled the ravines with foam, and mazes of bald, sea-worn rocks, which seem to have been thrown down from the scarred peaks in some terrible convulsion of nature. Here and there were hollows, affording stony pasturage for a few sheep and cows and little wooden fisher-huts stood on the shore in the arms of sheltered coves. At the village of Svolvær, which is built upon a pile of bare stones, we took on board a number of ladies in fashionable dresses, with bonnets on the backs of their heads and a sufficiency of cumbrous petticoats to make up for the absence of hoops, which have not yet got further north than Drontheim. In seeing these unexpected apparitions emerge from such a wild corner of chaos I could not but wonder at the march of modern civilisation. Pianos in Lapland, Parisian dresses among the Lofodens, billiard-tables in Hammerfest—whither shall we turn to find the romance of the North!

We sailed, in the lovely nocturnal sunshine, through the long, river-like channel—the Rasksund, I believe, it is called—between the islands of East-Vaagöe and Hindöe, the largest of the Lofodens. For a distance of fifteen miles the strait was in no place more than a mile in breadth, while it was frequently less than a quarter. The smooth water was a perfect mirror, reflecting on one side the giant cliffs, with their gorges choked with snow, their arrowy pinnacles and white lines of falling water—on the other, hills turfed to the summit with emerald velvet, sprinkled with pale groves of birch and alder, and dotted, along their bases, with the dwellings of the fishermen. It was impossible to believe that we were floating on an arm of the Atlantic—it was some unknown river, or a lake high up among the Alpine peaks. The silence of these shores added to the impression. Now and then a white sea-gull fluttered about the cliffs, or an eider duck paddled across some glassy cove, but no sound was heard: there was no sail on the water, no human being on the shore. Emerging at last from this wild and enchanting strait, we stood across a bay, opening southward to the Atlantic, to the port of Steilo, on one of the outer islands. Here the broad front of the island, rising against the roseate sky, was one swell of the most glorious green, down to the very edge of the sea, while the hills of East-Vaagöe, across the bay, showed only naked and defiant rock, with summit-fields of purple-tinted snow. In splendour of coloring, the tropics were again surpassed, but the keen north wind obliged us to enjoy it in an overcoat.

Toward midnight, the sun was evidently above the horizon, though hidden by intervening mountains. Braisted and another American made various exertions to see it, such as climbing the foremast, but did not succeed until about one o'clock, when they were favoured by a break in the hills. Although we had daylight the whole twenty-four hours, travellers do not consider that their duty is fulfilled unless they see the sun itself, exactly at midnight. In the morning, we touched at Throndenaes, on the northern side of Hindöe, a beautiful bay with green and wooded shores, and then, leaving the Lofodens behind us, entered the archipelago of large islands which lines the coast of Finmark. Though built on the same grand and imposing scale as the Lofodens, these islands are somewhat less jagged and abrupt in their forms, and exhibit a much more luxuriant vegetation. In fact, after leaving the Namsen Fjord, near Drontheim, one sees very little timber until he reaches the parallel of 69°. The long straits between Senjen and Qvalö and the mainland are covered with forests of birch and turfy slopes greener than England has ever shown. At the same time the snow level was not more than 500 feet above the sea, and broad patches lay melting on all the lower hills. This abundance of snow seems a singular incongruity, when you look upon the warm summer sky and the dark, mellow, juicy green of the shores. One fancies that he is either sailing upon some lofty inland lake, or that the ocean-level in these latitudes must be many thousand feet higher than in the temperate zone. He cannot believe that he is on the same platform with Sicily and Ceylon.

After a trip up the magnificent Maans Fjord, and the sight of some sea-green glaciers, we approached Tromsöe, the capital of Finmark. This is a town of nearly 3000 inhabitants, on a small island in the strait between Qvalö and the mainland. It was just midnight when we dropped anchor, but, although the sun was hidden by a range of snowy hills in the north, the daylight was almost perfect. I immediately commenced making a sketch of the harbour, with its fleet of coasting vessels. Some Russian craft from Archangel, and a Norwegian cutter carrying six guns, were also at anchor before the town. Our French traveller, after amusing himself with the idea of my commencing a picture at sunset and finishing it at sunrise, started for a morning ramble over the hills. Boats swarmed around the steamer; the coal-lighters came off, our crew commenced their work, and when the sun's disc appeared, before one o'clock, there was another day inaugurated. The night had vanished mysteriously, no one could tell how.

CHAPTER XXV. FINMARK AND HAMMERFEST.

The steamer lay at Tromsöe all day, affording us an opportunity to visit an encampment of Lapps in Tromsdal, about four miles to the eastward. So far as the Lapps were concerned, I had seen enough of them, but I joined the party for the sake of the northern summer. The captain was kind enough to despatch a messenger to the Lapps, immediately on our arrival, that their herd of reindeer, pasturing on the mountains, might be driven down for our edification, and also exerted himself to procure a horse for the American lady. The horse came, in due time, but a side saddle is an article unknown in the arctic regions, and the lady was obliged to trust herself to a man's saddle and the guidance of a Norseman of the most remarkable health, strength, and stupidity.

Our path led up a deep valley, shut in by overhanging cliffs, and blocked up at the eastern end by the huge mass of the fjeld. The streams, poured down the crags from their snowy reservoirs, spread themselves over the steep side of the hill, making a succession of quagmires, over which we were obliged to spring and scramble in breakneck style. The sun was intensely hot in the enclosed valley, and we found the shade of the birchen groves very grateful. Some of the trees grew to a height of forty feet, with trunks the thickness of a man's body. There were also ash and alder trees, of smaller size, and a profusion of brilliant wild flowers. The little multeberry was in blossom; the ranunculus, the globe-flower, the purple geranium, the heath, and the blue forget-me-not spangled the ground, and on every hillock the young ferns unrolled their aromatic scrolls written with wonderful fables of the southern spring. For it was only spring here, or rather the very beginning of summer. The earth had only become warm enough to conceive and bring forth flowers, and she was now making the most of the little maternity vouchsafed to her. The air was full of winged insects, darting hither and thither in astonishment at finding themselves alive; the herbage seemed to be visibly growing under your eyes; even the wild shapes of the trees were expressive of haste, lest the winter might come on them unawares; and I noticed that the year's growth had been shot out at once, so that the young sprays might have time to harden and to protect the next year's buds. There was no lush, rollicking out-burst of foliage, no mellow, epicurean languor of the woods, no easy unfolding of leaf on leaf, as in the long security of our summers; but everywhere a feverish hurry on the part of nature to do something, even if it should only be half done. And above the valley, behind its mural ramparts, glowered the cold white snows, which had withdrawn for a little while, but lay in wait, ready to spring down as soon as the protecting sunshine should fail.

The lady had one harmless tumble into the mud, and we were all pretty well fatigued with our rough walk, when we reached the Lapp encampment. It consisted only of two families, who lived in their characteristic gammes, or huts of earth, which serve them also for winter dwellings. These burrows were thrown up on a grassy meadow, beside a rapid stream which came down from the fjeld; and at a little distance were two folds, or corrals for their reindeer, fenced with pickets slanting outward. A number of brown-haired, tailless dogs, so much resembling bear-cubs that at first sight we took them for such, were playing about the doors. A middle-aged Lapp, with two women and three or four children, were the inmates. They scented profit, and received us in a friendly way, allowing the curious strangers to go in and out at pleasure, to tease the dogs, drink the reindeer milk, inspect the children, rock the baby, and buy horn spoons to the extent of their desire. They were smaller than the Lapps of Kautokeino—or perhaps the latter appeared larger in their winter dresses—and astonishingly dirty. Their appearance is much more disgusting in summer than in winter, when the snow, to a certain extent, purifies everything. After waiting an hour or more, the herd appeared descending the fjeld, and driven toward the fold by two young Lapps, assisted by their dogs. There were about four hundred in all, nearly one-third being calves. Their hoarse bleating and the cracking noise made by their knee-joints, as they crowded together into a dense mass of grey, mossy backs, made a very peculiar sound; and this combined with their ragged look, from the process of shedding their coats of hair, did not very favourably impress those of our party who saw them for the first time. The old Lapp and his boy, a strapping fellow of fifteen, with a ruddy, olive complexion and almost Chinese features, caught a number of the cows with lassos, and proceeded to wean the young deer by anointing the mothers' dugs with cow-dung, which they carried in pails slung over their shoulders. In this delightful occupation we left them, and returned to Tromsöe.

As we crossed the mouth of the Ulvsfjord, that evening we had an open sea horizon toward the north, a clear sky, and so much sunshine at eleven o'clock that it was evident the Polar day had dawned upon us at last. The illumination of the shores was unearthly in its glory, and the wonderful effects of the orange sunlight, playing upon the dark hues of the island cliffs, can neither be told nor painted. The sun hung low between Fuglöe, rising like a double dome from the sea, and the tall mountains of Arnöe, both of which islands resembled immense masses of transparent purple glass, gradually melting into crimson fire at their bases. The glassy, leaden-coloured sea was powdered with a golden bloom, and the tremendous precipices at the mouth of the Lyngen Fjord, behind us, were steeped in a dark red, mellow flush, and touched with pencillings of pure, rose-coloured light, until their naked ribs seemed to be clothed in imperial velvet. As we turned into the Fjord and ran southward along their bases, a waterfall, struck by the sun, fell in fiery orange foam down the red walls, and the blue ice-pillars of a beautiful glacier filled up the ravine beyond it. We were all on deck, and all faces, excited by the divine splendour of the scene, and tinged by the same wonderful aureole, shone as if transfigured. In my whole life I have never seen a spectacle so unearthly beautiful.

Our course brought the sun rapidly toward the ruby cliffs of Arnöe, and it was evident that he would soon be hidden from sight. It was not yet half-past eleven, and an enthusiastic passenger begged the captain to stop the vessel until midnight. "Why," said the latter, "it is midnight now, or very near it; you have Drontheim time, which is almost forty minutes in arrears." True enough, the real time lacked but five minutes of midnight, and those of us who had sharp eyes and strong imaginations saw the sun make his last dip and rise a little, before he vanished in a blaze of glory behind Arnöe. I turned away with my eyes full of dazzling spheres of crimson and gold, which danced before me wherever I looked, and it was a long time before they were blotted out by the semi-oblivion of a daylight sleep.

The next morning found us at the entrance of the long Alten Fjord. Here the gashed, hacked, split, scarred and shattered character of the mountains ceases, and they suddenly assume a long, rolling outline, full of bold features, but less wild and fantastic. On the southern side of the fjord many of them are clothed with birch and fir to the height of a thousand feet. The valleys here are cultivated to some extent, and produce, in good seasons, tolerable crops of potatoes, barley, and buckwheat. This is above lat. 70°, or parallel with the northern part of Greenland, and consequently the highest cultivated land in the world. In the valley of the Alten River, the Scotch fir sometimes reaches a height of seventy or eighty feet. This district is called the Paradise of Finmark, and no doubt floats in the imaginations of the settlers on Mageröe and the dreary Porsanger Fjord, as Andalusia and Syria float in ours. It is well that human bliss is so relative in its character.

At Talvik, a cheerful village with a very neat, pretty church, who should come on board but Pastor Hvoslef, our Kautokeino friend of the last winter! He had been made one of a Government Commission of four, appointed to investigate and report upon the dissensions between the nomadic Lapps and those who have settled habitations. A better person could not have been chosen than this good man, who has the welfare of the Lapps truly at heart, and in whose sincerity every one in the North confides.

We had on board Mr. Thomas, the superintendent of the copper works at Kaafjord, who had just resigned his seat in the Storthing and given up his situation for the purpose of taking charge of some mines at Copiapo, in Chili. Mr. Thomas is an Englishman, who has been for twenty years past one of the leading men of Finmark, and no other man, I venture to say, has done more to improve and enlighten that neglected province. His loss will not be easily replaced. At Talvik, his wife, a pleasant, intelligent Norwegian lady, came on board; and, as we passed the rocky portals guarding the entrance to the little harbour of Kaafjord, a gun, planted on a miniature battery above the landing-place, pealed forth a salute of welcome. I could partly understand Mr. Thomas's long residence in those regions, when I saw what a wild, picturesque spot he had chosen for his home. The cavernous entrances to the copper mines yawned in the face of the cliff above the outer bay below, on the water's edge, stood the smelting works, surrounded by labourers' cottages; a graceful white church crowned a rocky headland a little further on; and beyond, above a green lawn, decked with a few scattering birches, stood a comfortable mansion, with a garden in the rear. The flag of Norway and the cross of St. George floated from separate staffs on the lawn. There were a number of houses, surrounded with potato-fields on the slope stretching around the bay, and an opening of the hills at its head gave us a glimpse of the fir forests of the inland valleys. On such a cloudless day as we had, it was a cheerful and home-like spot.

We took a friendly leave of Mr. Thomas and departed, the little battery giving us I don't know how many three-gun salutes as we moved off. A number of whales spouted on all sides of us as we crossed the head of the fjord to Bosekop, near the mouth of the Alten River. This is a little village on a bare rocky headland, which completely shuts out from view the rich valley of the Alten, about which the Finmarkers speak with so much enthusiasm. "Ah, you should see the farms on the Alten," say they; "there we have large houses, fields, meadows, cattle, and the finest timber." This is Altengaard, familiar to all the readers of Mügge's "Afraja." The gaard, however, is a single large estate, and not a name applied to the whole district, as those unfamiliar with Norsk nomenclature might suppose. Here the Catholics have established a mission— ostensibly a missionary boarding-house, for the purpose of acclimating arctic apostles; but the people, who regard it with the greatest suspicion and distrust, suspect that the ultimate object is the overthrow of their inherited, venerated, and deeply-rooted Lutheran faith. At Bosekop we lost Pastor Hvoslef, and took on board the chief of the mission, the Catholic Bishop of the Arctic Zone—for I believe his diocese includes Greenland, Spitzbergen, and Polar America. Here is a Calmuck Tartar, thought I, as a short, strongly-built man, with sallow complexion, deep-set eyes, broad nostrils, heavy mouth, pointed chin, and high cheek-bones, stepped on board; but he proved to be a Russian baron, whose conversion cost him his estates. He had a massive head, however, in which intellect predominated, and his thoroughly polished manners went far to counteract the effect of one of the most unprepossessing countenances I ever saw.

M. Gay, who had known the bishop at Paris, at once entered into conversation with him. A short time afterwards, my attention was drawn to the spot where they stood by loud and angry exclamations. Two of our Norwegian savans stood before the bishop, and one of them, with a face white with rage, was furiously vociferating: "It is not true! it is not true! Norway is a free country!" "In this respect, it is not free," answered the bishop, with more coolness than I thought he could have shown, under such circumstances: "You know very well that no one can hold office except those who belong to your State Church—neither a Catholic, nor a Methodist, nor a Quaker: whereas in France, as I have said, a Protestant may even become a minister of the Government." "But we do not believe in the Catholic faith:—we will have nothing to do with it!" screamed the Norwegian. "We are not discussing our creeds," answered the bishop: "I say that, though Norway is a free country, politically, it does not secure equal rights to all its citizens, and so far as the toleration of religious beliefs is concerned, it is behind most other countries of Europe." He thereupon retreated to the cabin, for a crowd had gathered about the disputants, and the deck-passengers pressing aft, seemed more than usually excited by what was going on. The Norwegian shaking with fury, hissed through his set teeth: "How dare he come here to insult our national feeling!" Yes, but every word was true; and the scene was only another illustration of the intense vanity of the Norwegians in regard to their country. Woe to the man who says a word against Norway, though he say nothing but what everybody knows to be true! So long as you praise everything—scenery, people, climate, institutions, and customs—or keep silent where you cannot praise, you have the most genial conversation; but drop a word of honest dissent or censure, and you will see how quickly every one draws back into his shell. There are parts of our own country where a foreigner might make the same observation. Let a Norwegian travel in the Southern States, and dare to say a word in objection to slavery!

There is nothing of interest between Alten and Hammerfest, except the old sea-margins on the cliffs and a small glacier on the island of Seiland. The coast is dismally bleak and barren. Whales were very abundant; we sometimes saw a dozen spouting at one time. They were of the hump-backed species, and of only moderate size; yet the fishery would doubtless pay very well, if the natives had enterprise enough to undertake it. I believe, however, there is no whale fishery on the whole Norwegian coast. The desolate hills of Qvalö surmounted by the pointed peak of the Tjuve Fjeld, or "Thief Mountain,"— so called because it steals so much of the winter sunshine,—announced our approach to Hammerfest, and towards nine o'clock in the evening we were at anchor in the little harbour. The summer trade had just opened, and forty Russian vessels, which had arrived from the White Sea during the previous week or two, lay crowded before the large fish warehouses built along the water. They were all three-masted schooners, the main and mizen masts set close together, and with very heavy, square hulls. Strong Muscovite faces, adorned with magnificent beards, stared at us from the decks, and a jabber of Russian, Finnish, Lapp, and Norwegian, came from the rough boats crowding about our gangways. The north wind, blowing to us off the land, was filled with the perfume of dried codfish, train oil, and burning whale-"scraps," with which, as we soon found, the whole place is thoroughly saturated.

There is one hotel in the place, containing half a dozen chambers of the size of a state-room. We secured quarters here with a great deal of difficulty, owing to slowness of comprehension on the part of an old lady who had charge of the house. The other American, who at first took rooms for himself and wife, gave them up again very prudently; for the noises of the billiard-room penetrated through the thin wooden partitions, and my bed, at least, had been slept in by one of the codfish aristocracy, for the salty odour was so pungent that it kept me awake for a long time. With our fare, we had less reason to complain. Fresh salmon, arctic ptarmigan, and reindeer's tongue were delicacies which would have delighted any palate, and the wine had really seen Bordeaux, although rainy weather had evidently prevailed during the voyage thence to Hammerfest. The town lies in a deep bight, inclosed by precipitous cliffs, on the south-western side of the island, whence the sun, by this time long past his midsummer altitude, was not visible at midnight. Those of our passengers who intended returning by the Nordkap climbed the hills to get another view of him, but unfortunately went upon the wrong summit, so that they did not see him after all. I was so fatigued, from the imperfect sleep of the sunshiny nights and the crowd of new and exciting impressions which the voyage had given me, that I went to bed; but my friend sat up until long past midnight, writing, with curtains drawn.

CHAPTER XXVI. THE MIDNIGHT SUN.

Most of the travellers who push as far north as Hammerfest content themselves with one experience of the midnight sun, and return with the same steamer to Drontheim. A few extend their journey to the North Cape, and, once a year, on an average, perhaps, some one is adventurous enough to strike across Lapland to Torneå. The steamers, nevertheless, pass the North Cape, and during the summer make weekly trips to the Varanger Fjord, the extreme eastern limit of the Norwegian territory. We were divided in opinion whether to devote our week of sunshine to the North Cape, or to make the entire trip and see something of the northern coast of Europe, but finally decided that the latter, on the whole, as being unfamiliar ground, would be most interesting. The screw-steamer Gyller (one of Odin's horses) was lying in the harbour when we arrived, and was to leave in the course of the next night; so we lost no time in securing places, as she had but a small cabin and no state-rooms. Nevertheless, we found her very comfortable, and in every respect far superior to the English vessels which ply between Hull and Christiania. Our fellow travellers were all returning to Drontheim—except three Norwegian officers on their way to make an official inspection of the fortress of Wardöhuus—and the last we saw of them was their return, an hour past midnight, from making a second attempt to see the sun from the hills. The night was somewhat obscured, and I doubt if they were successful.

When I went on deck on the morning after our departure, we were in the narrow strait between the island of Mageröe, the northern extremity of which forms the North Cape, and the mainland. On either side, the shores of bare bleak rock, spotted with patches of moss and stunted grass, rose precipitously from the water, the snow filling up their ravines from the summit to the sea. Not a tree nor a shrub, nor a sign of human habitation was visible; there was no fisher's sail on the lonely waters, and only the cries of some sea-gulls, wheeling about the cliffs, broke the silence. As the strait opened to the eastward, a boat appeared, beating into Kjelvik, on the south-eastern corner of the island; but the place itself was concealed from us by an intervening cape. This is the spot which Von Buch visited in the summer of 1807, just fifty years ago, and his description would be equally correct at the present day. Here, where the scurvy carries off half the inhabitants,—where pastors coming from Southern Norway die within a year,—where no trees grow, no vegetables come to maturity, and gales from every quarter of the Icy Sea beat the last faint life out of nature, men will still persist in living, in apparent defiance of all natural laws. Yet they have at least an excuse for it, in the miraculous provision which Providence has made for their food and fuel. The sea and fjords are alive with fish, which are not only a means of existence but of profit to them, while the wonderful Gulf Stream, which crosses 5000 miles of the Atlantic to die upon this Ultima Thule in a last struggle with the Polar Sea, casts up the spoils of tropical forests to feed their fires. Think of arctic fishers burning upon their hearths the palms of Hayti, the mahogany of Honduras, and the precious woods of the Amazon and the Orinoco!

In the spring months, there are on an average 800 vessels on the northern coast, between the North Cape and Vadsö, with a fishing population of 5000 men on board, whose average gains, even at the scanty prices they receive amount to $30 apiece, making a total yield of $150,000. It is only within a very few years that the Norwegian Government has paid any attention to this far corner of the peninsula. At present, considering the slender population, the means of communication are well kept up during eight months in the year, and the result is an increase (perceptible to an old resident, no doubt) in the activity and prosperity of the country.

On issuing from the strait, we turned southward into the great Porsanger Fjord, which stretches nearly a hundred miles into the heart of Lapland, dividing Western from Eastern Finmark. Its shores are high monotonous hills, half covered with snow, and barren of vegetation except patches of grass and moss. If once wooded, like the hills of the Alten Fjord, the trees have long since disappeared, and now nothing can be more bleak and desolate. The wind blew violently from the east, gradually lifting a veil of grey clouds from the cold pale sky, and our slow little steamer with jib and fore-topsail set, made somewhat better progress. Toward evening (if there is such a time in the arctic summer), we reached Kistrand, the principal settlement on the fjord.

It has eight or nine houses, scattered along a gentle slope a mile in length, and a little red church, but neither gardens, fields, nor potato patches. A strip of grazing ground before the principal house was yellow with dandelions, the slope behind showed patches of brownish green grass, and above this melancholy attempt at summer stretched the cold, grey, snow-streaked ridge of the hill. Two boats, manned by sea-Lapps, with square blue caps, and long ragged locks of yellow hair fluttering in the wind, brought off the only passenger and the mails, and we put about for the mouth of the fjord.

Running along under the eastern shore, we exchanged the dreadful monotony through which we had been sailing for more rugged and picturesque scenery. Before us rose a wall of dark cliff, from five to six hundred feet in height, gaping here and there with sharp clefts or gashes, as if it had cracked in cooling, after the primeval fires. The summit of these cliffs was the average level of the country; and this peculiarity, I found, applies to all the northern shore of Finmark, distinguishing the forms of the capes and islands from those about Alten and Hammerfest, which, again, are quite different from those of the Lofodens. "On returning from Spitzbergen," said a Hammerfest merchant to me, "I do not need to look at chart or compass, when I get sight of the coast; I know, from the formation of the cliffs, exactly where I am." There is some general resemblance to the chalk bluffs of England, especially about Beachy Head, but the rock here appears to be mica-slate, disposed in thin, vertical strata, with many violent transverse breaks.

As we approached the end of the promontory which divides the Porsanger from the Laxe Fjord, the rocks became more abrupt and violently shattered. Huge masses, fallen from the summit, lined the base of the precipice, which was hollowed into cavernous arches, the home of myriads of sea-gulls. The rock of Sværholtklub, off the point, resembled a massive fortress in ruins. Its walls of smooth masonry rested on three enormous vaults, the piers of which were buttressed with slanting piles of rocky fragments. The ramparts, crenelated in some places, had mouldered away in others, and one fancied he saw in the rents and scars of the giant pile the marks of the shot and shell which had wrought its ruin. Thousands of white gulls, gone to their nightly roost, rested on every ledge and cornice of the rock; but preparations were already made to disturb their slumbers. The steamer's cannon was directed towards the largest vault, and discharged. The fortress shook with the crashing reverberation; "then rose a shriek, as of a city sacked"—a wild, piercing, maddening, myriad-tongued cry, which still rings in my ears. With the cry, came a rushing sound, as of a tempest among the woods; a white cloud burst out of the hollow arch-way, like the smoke of an answering shot, and, in the space of a second, the air was filled with birds, thicker than autumn leaves, and rang with one universal, clanging shriek. A second shot, followed by a second outcry and an answering discharge from the other caverns, almost darkened the sky. The whirring, rustling and screaming, as the birds circled overhead, or dropped like thick scurries of snow-flakes on the water, was truly awful. There could not have been less than fifty thousand in the air at one time, while as many more clung to the face of the rock, or screamed from the depth of the vaults. Such an indignation meeting I never attended before; but, like many others I have heard of, the time for action was passed before they had decided what to do.

It was now eleven o'clock, and Sværholt glowed in fiery bronze lustre as we rounded it, the eddies of returning birds gleaming golden in the nocturnal sun, like drifts of beech leaves in the October air. Far to the north, the sun lay in a bed of saffron light over the clear horizon of the Arctic Ocean. A few bars of dazzling orange cloud floated above him, and still higher in the sky, where the saffron melted through delicate rose-colour into blue, hung light wreaths of vapour, touched with pearly, opaline flushes of pink and golden grey. The sea was a web of pale slate-colour, shot through and through with threads of orange and saffron, from the dance of a myriad shifting and twinkling ripples. The air was filled and permeated with the soft, mysterious glow, and even the very azure of the southern sky seemed to shine through a net of golden gauze. The headlands of this deeply-indented coast—the capes of the Laxe and Porsanger Fjords, and of Mageröe—lay around us, in different degrees of distance, but all with foreheads touched with supernatural glory. Far to the north-east was Nordkyn, the most northern point of the mainland of Europe, gleaming rosily and faint in the full beams of the sun, and just as our watches denoted midnight the North Cape appeared to the westward—a long line of purple bluff, presenting a vertical front of nine hundred feet in height to the Polar Sea. Midway between those two magnificent headlands stood the Midnight Sun, shining on us with subdued fires, and with the gorgeous colouring of an hour for which we have no name, since it is neither sunset nor sunrise, but the blended loveliness of both—but shining at the same moment, in the heat and splendour of noonday, on the Pacific Isles.

This was the midnight sun as I had dreamed it—as I had hoped to see it.

Within fifteen minutes after midnight, there was a perceptible increase of altitude, and in less than half an hour the whole tone of the sky had changed, the yellow brightening into orange, and the saffron melting into the pale vermilion of dawn. Yet it was neither the colours, nor the same character of light as we had had, half an hour before midnight. The difference was so slight as scarcely to be described; but it was the difference between evening and morning. The faintest transfusion of one prevailing tint into another had changed the whole expression of heaven and earth, and so imperceptibly and miraculously that a new day was already present to our consciousness. Our view of the wild cliffs of Sværholt, less than two hours before, belonged to yesterday, though we had stood on deck, in full sunshine, during all the intervening time. Had the sensation of a night slipped through our brains in the momentary winking of the eyes? Or was the old routine of consciousness so firmly stereotyped in our natures, that the view of a morning was sufficient proof to them of the preëxistence of a night? Let those explain the phenomenon who can—but I found my physical senses utterly at war with those mental perceptions wherewith they should harmonise. The eye saw but one unending day; the mind notched the twenty-four hours on its calendar, as before.

Before one o'clock we reached the entrance of the Kiöllefjord, which in the pre-diluvial times must have been a tremendous mountain gorge, like that of Gondo, on the Italian side of the Simplon. Its mouth is about half a mile in breadth, and its depth is not more than a mile and a half. It is completely walled in with sheer precipices of bare rock, from three to five hundred feet in height, except at the very head, where they subside into a stony heap, upon which some infatuated mortals have built two or three cabins. As we neared the southern headland, the face of which was touched with the purest orange

225

light, while its yawning fissures lay in deep-blue gloom, a tall ruin, with shattered turrets and crumbling spires, detached itself from the mass, and stood alone at the foot of the precipice. This is the Finnkirka, or "Church of the Lapps," well known to all the northern coasters. At first it resembles a tall church with a massive square spire; but the two parts separate again, and you have a crag-perched castle of the middle-ages, with its watch-tower—the very counterpart of scores in Germany—and a quaint Gothic chapel on the point beyond. The vertical strata of the rock, worn into sharp points at the top and gradually broadening to the base, with numberless notched ornaments and channels fluted by the rain, make the resemblance marvellous, when seen under the proper effects of light and shade. The lustre in which we saw it had the effect of enchantment. There was a play of colours upon it, such as one sees in illuminated Moorish halls, and I am almost afraid to say how much I was enraptured by a scene which has not its equal on the whole Norwegian coast, yet of which none of us had ever heard before.

We landed a single passenger—a government surveyor apparently—on the heap of rocks beyond, and ran out under the northern headland, which again charmed us with a glory peculiarly its own. Here the colours were a part of the substance of the rock, and the sun but heightened and harmonised their tones. The huge projecting masses of pale yellow had a mellow gleam, like golden chalk; behind them were cliffs, violet in shadow; broad strata of soft red, tipped on the edges with vermilion; thinner layers, which shot up vertically to the height of four or five hundred feet, and striped the splendid sea-wall with lines of bronze, orange, brown, and dark red, while great rents and breaks interrupted these marvellous frescoes with their dashes of uncertain gloom. I have seen many wonderful aspects of nature, in many lands, but rock-painting such as this I never beheld. A part of its effect may have been owing to atmospheric conditions which must be rare, even in the North; but, without such embellishments, I think the sight of this coast will nobly repay any one for continuing his voyage beyond Hammerfest.

We lingered on deck, as point after point revealed some change in the dazzling diorama, uncertain which was finest, and whether something still grander might not be in store. But at last Nordkyn drew nigh, and at three

226

o'clock the light became that of day, white and colourless. The north-east wind blew keenly across the Arctic Ocean, and we were both satisfied and fatigued enough to go to bed. It was the most northern point of our voyage—about 71° 20', which is further north than I ever was before, or ever wish to be again.

CHAPTER XXVII. THE VARANGER FJORD.—ARCTIC LIFE.

When we awoke, after six hours' sleep, with curtains drawn to keep out the daylight, our steamer was deep in the Tana Fjord, which receives the waters of the Tana River, the largest Lapland stream flowing into the Arctic Ocean. The greater part of the day was consumed in calling at two settlements of three houses each, and receiving and delivering mails of one letter, or less. The shores of this fjord are steep hills of bare rock, covered with patches of snow to the water's edge. The riven walls of cliff, with their wonderful configuration and marvellous colouring, were left behind us, and there was nothing of the grand or picturesque to redeem the savage desolation of the scenery. The chill wind, blowing direct from Nova Zembla, made us shiver, and even the cabin saloon was uncomfortable without a fire. After passing the most northern point of Europe, the coast falls away to the south-east, so that on the second night we were again in the latitude of Hammerfest, but still within the sphere of perpetual sunshine. Our second night of sun was not so rich in colouring as the first, yet we remained on deck long enough to see the orb rise again from his lowest dip, and change evening into morning by the same incomprehensible process. There was no golden transfiguration of the dreadful shore; a wan lustre played over the rocks—pictures of eternal death—like a settled pallor of despair on Nature's stony face.

One of the stations on this coast, named Makur, consisted of a few fishermen's huts, at the bottom of a dismal rocky bight. There was no grass to be seen, except some tufts springing from the earth with which the roofs were covered, and it was even difficult to see where so much earth had been scraped together. The background was a hopelessly barren hill, more than half enveloped in snow. And this was midsummer—and human beings passed their lives here! "Those people surely deserve to enter Paradise when they die," I remarked to my friend, "for they live in hell while upon earth." "Not for that," he answered, "but because it is impossible for them to commit sin. They cannot injure their neighbours, for they have none. They cannot steal, for there is nothing to tempt them. They cannot murder, for there are none of the usual incentives to hate and revenge. They have so hard a struggle merely to live, that they cannot fall into the indulgences of sense; so that if there is nothing recorded in their favour, there is also nothing against them, and they commence the next life with blank books."

"But what a life!" I exclaimed. "Men may be happy in poverty, in misfortune, under persecution, in life-long disease even, so that they are not wholly deprived of the genial influences of society and Nature—but what is there here?" "They know no other world," said he, "and this ignorance keeps them from being miserable. They do no more thinking than is necessary to make nets and boats, catch fish and cook them, and build their log-houses. Nature provides for their marrying and bringing up their children, and the pastor, whom they see once in a long time, gives them their religion ready made." God keep them ignorant, then! was my involuntary prayer. May they never lose their blessed stupidity, while they are chained to these rocks and icy seas! May no dreams of summer and verdure, no vision of happier social conditions, or of any higher sphere of thought and action, flash a painful light on the dumb-darkness of their lives!

The next day, we were in the Varanger Fjord, having passed the fortress of Vardöhuus and landed our military committee. The Norwegian shore was now low and tame, but no vegetation, except a little brown grass, was to be seen. The Russian shore, opposite, and some twenty-five or thirty miles distant, consisted of high, bold hills, which, through a glass, appeared to be partially wooded. The Varanger Fjord, to which so important a political interest has attached within the last few years, is about seventy miles in depth, with a general direction towards the south-west. The boundary-line between Norwegian and Russian Finmark strikes it upon the southern side, about half-way from the mouth, so that three-fourths, or more, of the waters of the fjord belong to Norway. There is, however, a wonderful boundary-line, in addition, drawn by Nature between the alien waters. That last wave of the Gulf Stream which washes the North Cape and keeps the fjords of Finmark open and unfrozen the whole year through, sweeps eastward along the coast, until it reaches the head of Varanger Fjord. Here its power is at last spent, and from this point commences that belt of solid ice which locks up the harbours of the northern coast of Russia for six months in the year. The change from open water to ice is no less abrupt than permanent. Pastor Hvoslef informed me that in crossing from Vadsö, on the northern coast, to Pasvik, the last Norwegian settlement, close upon the Russian frontier, as late as the end of May, he got out of his boat upon the ice, and drove three or four miles over the frozen sea, to reach his destination.

The little fort of Vardöhuus, on an island at the northern entrance of the fjord, is not a recent defence, meant to check Russian plans in this quarter. It was established by Christian IV. nearly two and a half centuries ago. The king himself made a voyage hither, and no doubt at that time foresaw the necessity of establishing, by military occupation, the claims of Denmark to this part of the coast. The little fortress has actually done this service; and though a single frigate might easily batter it to pieces, its existence has kept Russia from the ownership of the Varanger Fjord and the creation (as is diplomatically supposed,) of an immense naval station, which, though within the Arctic waters, would at all times of the year be ready for service. It is well known that Russia has endeavoured to obtain possession of the northern side of the fjord, as well as of the Lyngen Fjord, near Tromsöe, towards which her Lapland territory stretches out a long arm. England is particularly suspicious of these attempts, and the treaty recently concluded between the Allied Powers and Sweden had a special reference thereto. The importance of such an acquisition to Russia is too obvious to be pointed out, and the jealous watchfulness of England is, therefore, easy to understand. But it is a singular thing that the conflicting forces of Europe find a fulcrum on a little corner of this dead, desolate, God-forsaken shore.

About ten o'clock we reached Vadsö, the limit of the steamer's route. Here we had intended taking a boat, continuing our voyage to Nyborg, at the head of the fjord, crossing thence to the Tana, and descending that river in season to meet the steamer in the Tana Fjord on her return. We were behind time, however, and the wind was light; the people informed us that we could scarcely carry out the project; so we reluctantly gave it up, and went ashore to spend the day. Vadsö is a town of about 800 inhabitants, with a secure though shallow harbour, which was crowded with fishing vessels and Russian traders

230

from the White Sea. It lies on the bleak hill-side, without a tree or bush, or a patch of grass large enough to be seen without close inspection, and its only summer perfume is that of dried fish. I saw in gardens attached to one or two houses a few courageous radishes and some fool-hardy potatoes, which had ventured above ground without the least chance of living long enough to blossom. The snow had been four feet deep in the streets in the beginning of June, and in six weeks it would begin to fall again. A few forlorn cows were hunting pasture over the hills, now and then looking with melancholy resignation at the strings of codfish heads hanging up to dry, on the broth of which they are fed during the winter. I took a walk and made a sketch during the afternoon, but the wind was so chill that I was glad to come back shivering to our quarters.

We obtained lodgings at the house of a baker, named Aas, who had learned the art of charging, and was therefore competent to conduct a hotel. In order to reach our room, we were obliged to pass successively through the family dwelling-room, kitchen, and a carpenter's workshop, but our windows commanded a full view of a grogshop across the way, where drunken Lapps were turned out with astonishing rapidity. It was the marriage month of the Lapps, and the town was full of young couples who had come down to be joined, with their relatives and friends, all in their gayest costumes. Through the intervention of the postmaster, I procured two women and a child, as subjects for a sketch. They were dressed in their best, and it was impossible not to copy the leer of gratified vanity lurking in the corners of their broad mouths. The summer dress consisted of a loose gown of bright green cloth, trimmed on the neck and sleeves with bands of scarlet and yellow, and a peculiar head-dress, shaped like a helmet, but with a broader and flatter crest, rounded in front. This, also, was covered with scarlet cloth, and trimmed with yellow and blue. They were greatly gratified with the distinction, and all the other Lapps, as in Kautokeino, would have willingly offered themselves. I found the same physical characteristics here as there—a fresh, ruddy complexion, inclining to tawny; bright blue eyes, brown hair, high cheek-bones, and mouths of enormous width. They are not strikingly below the average size, Heine says, in one of his mad songs:

"In Lapland the people are dirty,

Flat-headed, and broad-mouthed, and small

They squat round the fire while roasting

Their fishes, and chatter and squall;"

which is as good a description of them as can be packed into a stanza. On the present occasion they were all drunk, in addition. One of them lay for a long time at the door, with his legs doubled under him as he fell, the others stepping over his body as they went in and out. These poor creatures were openly and shamelessly allowed to drug themselves, as long as their money lasted. No wonder the race is becoming extinct, when the means of destruction is so freely offered.

Vadsö, although only forty miles from Vardö, at the mouth of the fjord, has a much drier and more agreeable climate, and the inhabitants are therefore loud in praise of their place. "We have no such fogs as at Vardö," say they; "our fish dry much better, and some years we can raise potatoes." For the last four or five years, however, the winters have been getting more and more severe, and now it is impossible to procure hay enough to keep their few cattle through the winter. We had on board a German who had been living there five years, and who appeared well satisfied with his lot. "I have married here," said he; "I make a good living with less trouble than in Germany, and have no wish to return." Singularly enough, there were also two Italian organ grinders on board, whom I accosted in their native language; but they seemed neither surprised nor particularly pleased. They dropped hints of having been engaged in some political conspiracy; and one of them said, with a curious mixture of Italian and Norsk words "Jeg voglio ikke ritornare." I said the same thing ("I shall not return") as I left Vadsö.

We sailed early the next morning, and in the afternoon reached Vardö, where we lay three hours. Here we took on board the three officers, who had in the meantime made their inspection. Vardöhuus is a single star-shaped fort, with six guns and a garrison of twenty-seven men. During the recent war, the garrison was increased to three hundred—an unnecessary precaution, if there was really any danger of an attack to be apprehended, so long as the defences of the place were not strengthened. One of the officers, who had gone out fishing the night previous, caught eighty-three splendid cod in the space of two hours. It was idle sport, however, for no one would take his fish as a gift, and they were thrown on the shore to rot. The difficulty is not in catching but in curing them. Owing to the dampness of the climate they cannot be hung up on poles to dry slowly, like the stock-fish of the Lofodens, but must be first salted and then laid on the rocks to dry, whence the term klip (cliff) fish, by which they are known in trade.

At the mouth of the Tana we picked up four Englishmen, who had been salmon fishing on the river. They were sunburnt, spotted with mosquito bites, and had had little luck, the river being full of nets and the fjord of seals, between which the best of the salmon are either caught or devoured; but they spoke of their experience with true English relish. "Oh, it was very jolly!" said one: "we were so awfully bitten by mosquitoes. Then our interpreter always lost everything just before we wanted it—think of his losing our frying-pan, so that we had to fry in the lids of our kettles; He had a habit of falling overboard and getting nearly drowned before we could pull him in. We had a rough time of it, but it was very jolly, I assure you!" The young fellows meant what they said; they were all the better for their roughing, and I wish the spindle-shanked youths who polk and flirt at Newport and Saratoga had manliness enough for such undertakings.

We reached Hammerfest on the last day of July, and re-occupied our old quarters. That night the sun went below the horizon for the first time in eight days, but his depth was too slight to make any darkness visible. I was quite tired of the unending daylight, and would willingly have exchanged the pomp of the arctic midnight for the starlit darkness of home. We were confused by the loss of night; we lost the perception of time. One is never sleepy, but simply tired, and after a sleep of eight hours by sunshine, wakes up as tired as ever. His sleep at last is broken and irregular; he substitutes a number of short naps, distributed through the twenty-four hours, for the one natural repose, and finally gets into a state of general uneasiness and discomfort. A Hammerfest merchant, who has made frequent voyages to Spitzbergen, told me that in the latitude of 80° he never knew certainly whether it was day or night, and the cook was the only person on board who could tell him.

At first the nocturnal sunshine strikes you as being wonderfully convenient. You lose nothing of the scenery; you can read and write as usual; you never need be in a hurry, because there is time enough for everything. It is not necessary to do your day's work in the daytime, for no night cometh. You are never belated, and somewhat of the stress of life is lifted from your shoulders; but, after a time, you would be glad of an excuse to stop seeing, and observing, and thinking, and even enjoying. There is no compulsive rest such as darkness brings—no sweet isolation, which is the best refreshment of sleep. You lie down in the broad day, and the summons, "Arise!" attends on every reopening of your eyes. I never went below and saw my fellow-passengers all asleep around me without a sudden feeling that something was wrong: they were drugged, or under some unnatural influence, that they thus slept so fast while the sunshine streamed in through the port-holes.

There are some advantages of this northern summer which have presented themselves to me in rather a grotesque light. Think what an aid and shelter is removed from crime—how many vices which can only flourish in the deceptive atmosphere of night, must be checked by the sober reality of daylight! No assassin can dog the steps of his victim; no burglar can work in sunshine; no guilty lover can hold stolen interviews by moonlight—all concealment is removed, for the sun, like the eye of God, sees everything, and the secret vices of the earth must be bold indeed, if they can bear his gaze. Morally, as well as physically, there is safety in light and danger in darkness; and yet give me the darkness and the danger! Let the patrolling sun go off his beat for awhile, and show a little confidence in my ability to behave properly, rather than worry me with his sleepless vigilance.

I have described the smells of Hammerfest, which are its principal characteristic. It seemed to me the dreariest place in the world on first landing, a week previous; but, by contrast with what we had in the meantime seen, it became rather cheerful and comfortable. I was visiting a merchant after our return, and noticed with pleasure a stunted ash about eight feet high, in an adjoining garden. "Oh!" said he, in a tone of irritated pride, "we have plenty of trees here; there is quite a forest up the valley." This forest, after some search, I found. The trees were about six feet high, and some of them might have been as thick as my wrist. In the square before the merchant's house lay a crowd of drunken Lapps, who were supplied with as much bad brandy as they wanted by a licensed grogshop. The Russian sailors made use of the same privilege, and we frequently heard them singing and wrangling on board their White Sea junks. They were unapproachably picturesque, especially after the day's work was over, when they generally engaged in hunting in the extensive forests of their beards, and exercised the law of retaliation on all the game they caught.

A long street of turf-roofed houses, whose inhabitants may be said to be under the sod even before they die, leads along the shore of the bay to a range of flakes redolent of drying codfish. Beyond this you clamber over rocks and shingles to a low grassy headland, whereon stands a pillar commemorating the measurement of a meridian line of 25° 20', from the Danube to the Polar Sea, which was accomplished by the Governments of Austria, Russia, and Sweden, between the years 1816 and 1852. The pillar marks the northern terminus of the line, and stands in lat. 70° 40' 11.3". It is a plain shaft of polished red granite, standing on a base of grey granite, and surmounted by a bronze globe, on which a map of the earth is roughly outlined.

CHAPTER XXVIII. THE RETURN TO DARKNESS.—NORWEGIAN CHARACTER.

I do not intend to trace our return, step by step, down the Norwegian coast. The splendid weather which prevailed during our upward voyage, enabled us to see all the interesting points, leaving only those parts which we missed in the few hours devoted to sleep, to give a little novelty to our return. During the whole trip we had not a drop of rain,—the rarest good fortune in these latitudes,—and were therefore twice enabled to enjoy, to the fullest extent, the sublime scenery of the Lofoden Isles and the coast of Nordland. This voyage has not its like in the world. The traveller, to whom all other lands are familiar, has here a new volume of the most wonderful originality and variety, opened to him. The days are illuminated pages, crowded with pictures, the forms and hues of which he can never forget. After I returned to the zone of darkness, and recovered from the stress and tension of three weeks of daylight, I first fully appreciated the splendours of the arctic sun. My eyes were still dazzled with the pomp of colour, and the thousand miles of coast, as I reviewed them in memory, with their chaos of island-pyramids of shattered rock, their colossal cliffs, their twisted fjords, and long field-levels of eternal snow, swam in a sea of saffron and rosy light, in comparison with which the pale blue day around me seemed dull and dead. My dream of the North, in becoming a reality, has retained the magical atmosphere of dreams, and basks in the same gorgeous twilight which irradiates the Scandinavian sagas.

I was particularly struck during the return, with the rapid progress of summer—the flying leaps with which she clears her short course. Among the Lofodens, the potatoes were coming into blossom, and the rye and barley into head; the grass was already cut, in many places, and drying on poles, and the green of the woods and meadows showed the dark, rich character of southern lands. Owing to this rapidity of growth, all the more hardy varieties of vegetables may be successfully cultivated. Mr. Thomas informed me that his peas and beans at Kaafjord (lat. 70° N.) grew three inches in twenty-four hours, and, though planted six weeks later than those about Christiania, came to maturity at the same time. He has even succeeded in raising excellent cauliflowers. But very few of the farmers have vegetable gardens, and those which I saw contained only radishes and lettuce, with a few useful herbs. One finds the same passion for flowers, however, as in Northern Sweden, and the poorest are rarely without a rose or a geranium in their windows.

Pastor Hvoslef, who was again our fellow-traveller for a few hours, gave me some interesting information concerning the Lapps. They are, it seems, entitled to the right of suffrage, and to representation in the Storthing, equally with the Norwegians. The local jurisdiction repeats on a small scale what the Storthing transacts on a large one, being entirely popular in its character, except that the vogts and länsmen (whose powers are somewhat similar to those of our judges and country magistrates) are not elected. But each district chooses from among its inhabitants a committee to confer upon and arrange all ordinary local matters. These committees, in turn, choose persons to constitute a higher body, who control the reciprocal relations of the several districts, and intervene in case of difficulties between them. The system is necessarily simpler and somewhat more primitive in its character than our local organisations in America; but it appears at present to answer every purpose. The heavy responsibility resting upon judges in Norway— the severity of the checks and penalties by which their probity is insured— probably contributes to make the administration of the laws more efficacious and easy. The Lapps are not a difficult people to govern, and much of the former antagonism between them and the poorer classes of the Norwegians has passed away. There is little, if any, amalgamation of the two races, nor will there ever be, but there is probably as little conflict between them as is compatible with the difference of blood.

At Tromsöe, a tall, strong, clerical gentleman came on board, who proved to be the noted Pastor Lamers, one of the first if not the very first Clergyman in Norway, who has refused to receive the government support— or, in other words, has seceded from the Church, as a State establishment, while adhering to all its fundamental doctrines. It is the first step towards the separation of Church and State, which must sooner or later come, in Norway and in Sweden. He has a congregation of three hundred members, in Tromsöe, and is about organising a church at Gibostad, on the island of Senjen. He has some peculiar views, I believe, in relation to the baptism of children, and insists that the usual absolution dealt out by the Pastors is of no effect without full confession and the specification of particular sins—but in other respects he is entirely orthodox, retaining even the ceremonial of the Eucharist. This, in the Lutheran church of Norway, comes so near to the Roman Catholic doctrine of transubstantiation, that one cannot easily perceive any difference. Instead of bread, an unleavened wafer is administered to the communicants, the priest saying, as he gives it, "This is the true body and blood of Jesus Christ." Mr. Forrester, a devout admirer of the Church, which he thinks identical with that of England in all its essentials, says, "The Lutherans reject the Romish doctrine of transubstantiation, but they hold that of a spiritual and ineffable union of the divine nature with the elements, the substance of which remains unchanged. This is called consubstantiation." Verily, the difference between tweedledum and tweedledee—one being as absurd as the other.

No one, coming from a land where all sects stand upon an equal footing, and where every church must depend for existence on its own inherent vitality, can fail to be struck with the effete and decrepit state of religion in Sweden and Norway. It is a body of frigid mechanical forms and ceremonies, animated here and therewith a feeble spark of spiritual life, but diffusing no quickening and animating glow. I have often been particularly struck with the horror with which the omission of certain forms was regarded by persons in whom I could discover no trace of any religious principle. The Church has a few dissensions to combat; she has not been weakened by schism; but she is slowly ossifying from sheer inertia. The Reformation needs to be reformed again, and perhaps the tardy privileges granted to the Haugianer and Läsare—the northern Methodists—may result in producing a body of Dissenters large enough to excite emulation, action, and improvement. In Norway, the pastors have the best salaries and the easiest places of all government officials. Those who conscientiously discharge their duties have enough to do; but were this universally the case, one would expect to find the people less filthy, stupid, and dishonest than they are in many parts of the country. A specimen of the intelligence of one, who is now a member of the Storthing, was communicated to me by a gentleman who heard it. The clergyman advocated the establishment of telegraph lines in Norway, "not for the sake of sending news," said he, "that is of no consequence. But it is well known that no wolf can pass under a telegraph wire, and if we can get lines put up throughout the country, all the wolves will be obliged to leave!" Of course, I do not mean to assert that the Norwegian clergymen, as a body, are not sincere, zealous, well-informed men. The evil lies rather in that system which makes religion as much a branch of government service as law or diplomacy; and which, until very recently, has given one sect an exclusive monopoly of the care of human souls.

I had a strong desire to converse with Pastor Lamers in relation to the stand he has taken, but he was surrounded by a crowd of persons during his stay on board, and no opportunity presented itself. The sensation which his presence produced, showed that there are restless elements at work in the mind of the people. The stony crust is beginning to heave and split at last. Even the deck-passengers gathered into little groups and talked earnestly. Two gentlemen near me were discussing the question of an Established Church, one contending, that a variety of sects tended only to confuse, perplex, and unchristianise the uneducated, unthinking class, while the other asserted that this very class adhered most tenaciously to whatever faith had been taught them. At this moment a woman standing near us exclaimed: "There were false prophets in all times, and there are false prophets now! We must beware of them!"—the earnestness of her speech affording a good comment on the argument just produced. Whatever may be the popular opinion concerning the course of Pastor Lamers, I could not but notice the marked respect displayed by every one who approached him.

In passing Hindöe we saw two magnificent golden eagles wheeling around one of the loftiest cliffs. The wind blew strongly from the south-west, increasing until we had what sailors call a dry gale in crossing the West Fjord, but it abated the next day and by the late twilight we recrossed the arctic circle. This night there was great rejoicing on board, at the discovery of a star. We had not seen one for a month, and some of the passengers coming from Finmark had been more than two months in daylight. While we were all gazing upon it as upon some extraordinary phenomenon, a flood of yellow lamp-light suddenly streamed through the cabin skylight. The sky was still brilliant with sunset in the north, but it was dark enough to see to sleep. We could not yet cover ourselves all over, even as with a cloak; still there was a shelter and friendly covering for the helpless body. Our sleep became sound and regular, and its old power of restoration was doubly sweet, since we had known what it was to be deprived of it.

Our fellow-passengers, after leaving Carlsoe, where the young Englishmen stopped to hunt, were almost exclusively Norwegian, and this gave us further opportunities of becoming acquainted with some peculiarities of the national character. Intelligent Norwegians, especially those who have travelled, are exceedingly courteous, gentlemanly, and agreeable persons. The three officers on board were men of unusual intelligence and refinement, and we considered ourselves fortunate in having their company during the entire voyage. The landhand lare, or country merchants, and government officials of the lower ranks, exhibit more reserve, and not unfrequently a considerable amount of ignorance and prejudice. Perhaps the most general feature of the Norwegian character is an excessive national vanity, which is always on the alert, and fires up on the slightest provocation. Say everything you like, except that Norway in any respect is surpassed by any other country. One is assailed with questions about his impressions of the scenery, people, government, &c.—a very natural and pardonable curiosity, it is true, and one only demands in return that his candour be respected, and no offence taken. This, however, is rarely the case. If there is no retaliatory answer on the spot, you hear a remark days afterwards which shows how your mild censure has rankled in the mind of the hearer. My friend was asked by a passenger whether he did not think the women of Finmark very beautiful. It was impossible to answer in the affirmative: the questioner went off in high dudgeon, and did not speak to him again for several days.

In the Varanger Fjord, we had pretty freely expressed our impressions of the desolate coast. Afterwards on returning past the grand cliff scenery of Nordkyn, we were admiring some bold formation of the rocks, when a Norwegian came up and said, in a tone of angry irony: "Ah, you find a little

240

to admire at last, do you? You find some beauty in our country, after all?" So in regard to the government. The Norwegians may be justly proud of their constitution, which is as republican in its character as our own. There is so much in the administration of the government which every one must heartily commend, that they should be less sensitive in regard to minor faults. This sensitiveness, however, is partly accounted for, when we remember that for four hundred years Norway was a Danish province, and that only forty-three years ago she leaped at once from subjection to a freedom such as no other country in Europe enjoys. The intense pride and self-glorification of the people resembles that of a youth who for the first time assumes a dress-coat and standing collar. King Oscar, on his accession to the throne, gave the country a separate national flag, and nowhere does one see such a display of flags. All over the land and all along the shores, the colours of Norway are flying.

Jealousy of Sweden and dislike of the Swedes are inherited feelings, and are kept alive by a mutual prejudice on the part of the latter people. One cannot but smile a little at the present union of Sweden and Norway, when he finds that the countries have separate currencies, neither of which will pass at its full value in the other—separate tariffs, and of course Custom-house examinations between the two, and, if the Norwegians had their way, would have separate diplomatic representatives abroad. Yet the strength of Norway is undoubtedly in her alliance with Sweden: alone, she would be but a fourth-rate power. Enough has been done to satisfy her national feeling and secure her liberties against assault, and it is now time that this unnecessary jealousy and mistrust of a kindred race should cease. The Swedes have all the honesty which the Norwegians claim for themselves, more warmth and geniality of character, and less selfish sharpness and shrewdness. Mügge tells a story of a number of Swedes who were at a dinner party in Paris, where the health of "the King of Sweden and Norway" was proposed and drunk with great enthusiasm. One glass was observed to be untouched. It belonged to a Norwegian, who, when called upon for an explanation, said: "I cannot drink such a toast as this, but I will drink the health of the King of Norway, who is also King of Sweden!"

One cannot find fault with a people for their patriotism. I have always admired that love of Gamle Norge which shines through Norwegian history, song, and saga—but when it is manifested in such ridiculous extremes, one doubts the genuineness of the feeling, and suspects it of being alloyed with some degree of personal vanity. There are still evils to be eradicated,—reproaches to be removed,—reforms to be achieved, which claim all the best energies of the best men of the country, and positive harm is done by concealing or denying the true state of things.

CHAPTER XXIX. DRONTHEIM AND BERGEN.

We spent another day and a half in Drontheim, before reshipping in the steamer for Bergen. With the exception of a trip to the Lierfoss, or falls of the Nid, however, it was by no means a satisfactory sojourn. The hotel was full, and we could only get quarters in the billiard-room, through which other guests were continually passing and repassing. Two small boys were quite inadequate to the service; the table d'hote was the scantiest I ever saw, and the charges at the rate of three dollars a day. The whole of Sunday was consumed in an attempt to recover our carrioles, which we left behind us on embarking for Hammerfest. The servants neglected to get them on Saturday evening, as we had ordered, and in the morning the man who had the key of the warehouse went into the country, taking it with him. The whole day was spent in searching and waiting, and it was only by unremitting exertions that we succeeded in putting them on board in the evening. Owing to this annoyance, I was unable to attend service in the cathedral, or even to see the inside of it.

Our drive to the Lierfoss, in the evening, was an exquisite enjoyment. The valley of the Nid, behind Drontheim, is one of the most carefully cultivated spots in Norway. Our road led up the stream, overlooking rich levels of grain and hay fields, studded with large and handsome farm-houses, while the lower slopes of the hills and the mound-like knolls scattered along their bases, were framed to the very summit, steep as they were. The whole scene was like a piece of landscape gardening, full of the loveliest effects, which were enhanced by the contrast of the grey, sterile mountains by which the picture was framed. The soft, level sunshine, streaming through the rifts of broken thunder-clouds in the west, slowly wandered over the peaceful valley, here lighting up a red-roofed homestead, there a grove in full summer foliage, or a meadow of so brilliant an emerald that it seemed to shine by its own lustre. As we approached the Lierfoss, the road was barred with a great number of gates, before which waited a troop of ragged boys, who accompanied us the whole of the way, with a pertinacity equal to that of the little Swiss beggars.

The Nid here makes two falls about half a mile apart, the lower one being eighty, and the upper one ninety feet in height. The water is of a dark olive-green colour, and glassy transparency, and so deep that at the brink it makes huge curves over the masses of rock in its bed without breaking into the faintest ripple. As you stand on a giant boulder above it, and contrast the swift, silent rush with the thundering volume of amber-tinted spray which follows, you feel in its full force the strange fascination of falling water—the temptation to plunge in and join in its headlong revelry. Here, however, I must admit that the useful is not always the beautiful. The range of smoky mills driven by a sluice from the fall had better be away. The upper fall is divided in the centre by a mass of rock, and presents a broader and more imposing picture, though the impetus of the water is not so great.

The coast between Drontheim and Bergen is, on the whole, much less striking than that further north; but it has some very grand features. The outer islands are, with few exceptions, low and barren, but the coast, deeply indented with winding fjords, towers here and there into sublime headlands, and precipitous barriers of rock. Christiansund, where we touched the first afternoon, is a singularly picturesque place, built on four islands, separated by channels in the form of a cross. The bare, rounded masses of grey rock heave up on all sides behind the houses, which are built along the water's edge; here and there a tree of superb greenness shines against the colourless background, and the mountains of the mainland, with their tints of pink and purple, complete the picture. The sun was burningly hot, and the pale-green water reflected the shores in its oily gloss; but in severe storms, I was told, it is quite impossible to cross from one island to another, and the different parts of the town sometimes remain for days in a state of complete isolation. I rose very early next morning, to have a view of Molde and the enchanting scenery of the Romsdals-fjord. The prosperous-looking town, with its large square houses, its suburban cottages and gardens, on the slope of a long green hill, crowned with woods, was wholly Swiss in its appearance, but the luminous morning vapors hovering around the Alpine peaks in the east, entirely hid them from our view. In this direction lies the famous Romsdal, which many travellers consider the grandest specimen of Norwegian scenery. Unfortunately we could not have visited it without taking an entire week, and we were apprehensive lest the fine weather, which we had now enjoyed for twenty-four days, should come to an end before we were done with the Bergenstift. It is almost unexampled that travellers make the voyage from Drontheim to the Varanger Fjord and back without a cloudy day. While we had perpetual daylight, the tourists whom we left behind were drenched with continual rains.

Aalesund is another island port, smaller than Christiansund, but full as picturesque. The intense heat and clearness of the day, the splendour of the sunshine, which turned the grassy patches on the rocks into lustrous velvet, and the dark, dazzling blue of the sea belonged rather to southern Italy than to Norway. As we approached Bergen, however, the sky became gradually overcast, and the evening brought us clouds and showers. Not far from Aalesund was the castle of Rollo, the conqueror of Normandy. All this part of the coast is Viking ground: from these fjords went forth their piratical dragons, and hither they returned, laden with booty, to rest and carouse in their strongholds. They were the buccaneers of the north in their time, bold, brave, with the virtues which belong to courage and hardihood, but coarse, cruel, and brutal. The Viking of Scandinavian song is a splendid fellow; but his original, if we may judge from his descendants, was a stupid, hard-headed, lustful, and dirty giant, whom we should rather not have had for a companion. Harold Haarfager may have learnt in Constantinople to wash his face, and comb his beautiful hair, but I doubt if many of his followers imitated him. Let us hope that Ingeborg changed her dress occasionally, and that Balder's temple was not full of fleas; that Thorsten Vikingsson placed before his guests something better than fladbröd and rancid butter; and that Björn and Frithiof acted as honestly towards strangers as towards each other. The Viking chiefs, undoubtedly, must have learned the comfort of cleanliness and the delights of good living, but if such habits were general, the nation has greatly degenerated since their time.

We stayed on deck until midnight, notwithstanding the rain, to see the grand rock of Hornelen, a precipice 1200 feet high. The clouds lifted a little, and there was a dim, lurid light in the sky as our steamer swept under the awful cliff. A vast, indistinct mass, reaching apparently to the zenith, the summit crowned with a pointed tour, resembling the Cathedral of Drontheim, and the sides scarred with deep fissures, loomed over us. Now a splintered spire disengaged itself from the gloom, and stood defined against the sky; lighter streaks marked the spots where portions had slid away; but all else was dark, uncertain, and sublime. Our friendly captain had the steamer's guns discharged as we were abreast of the highest part. There were no separate echoes, but one tremendous peal of sound, prolonged like the note of an organ-pipe, and gradually dying away at the summit in humming vibrations.

Next morning, we were sailing in a narrow strait, between perpendicular cliffs, fluted like basaltic pillars. It was raining dismally, but we expected nothing else in the neighbourhood of Bergen. In this city the average number of rainy days in a year is two hundred. Bergen weather has become a by-word throughout the north, and no traveller ventures to hope for sunshine when he turns his face thither. "Is it still raining at Bergen?" ask the Dutch skippers when they meet a Norwegian captain. "Yes, blast you; is it still blowing at the Texel?" is generally the response.

We took on board four or five lepers, on their way to the hospital at Bergen. A piece of oil-cloth had been thrown over some spars to shield them from the rain, and they sat on deck, avoided by the other passengers, a melancholy picture of disease and shame. One was a boy of fourteen, upon whose face wart-like excrescences were beginning to appear; while a woman, who seemed to be his mother, was hideously swollen and disfigured. A man, crouching down with his head between his hands, endeavoured to hide the seamed and knotted mass of protruding blue flesh, which had once been a human face. The forms of leprosy, elephantiasis, and other kindred diseases, which I have seen in the East, and in tropical countries, are not nearly so horrible. For these unfortunates there was no hope. Some years, more or less, of a life which is worse than death, was all to which they could look forward. No cure has yet been discovered for this terrible disease. There are two hospitals in Bergen, one of which contains about five hundred patients; while the other, which has recently been erected for the reception of cases in the earlier stages, who may be subjected to experimental courses of treatment, has already one hundred. This form of leprosy is supposed to be produced partly

246

by an exclusive diet of salt fish, and partly by want of personal cleanliness. The latter is the most probable cause, and one does not wonder at the result, after he has had a little experience of Norwegian filth. It is the awful curse which falls upon such beastly habits of life. I wish the Norwegians could be made Mussulmen for awhile, for the sake of learning that cleanliness is not only next to godliness, but a necessary part of it. I doubt the existence of filthy Christians, and have always believed that St. Jerome was atrociously slandered by the Italian painters. But is there no responsibility resting upon the clergymen of the country, who have so much influence over their flocks, and who are themselves clean and proper persons?

Bergen is also, as I was informed, terribly scourged by venereal diseases. Certainly, I do not remember a place, where there are so few men—tall, strong, and well-made as the people generally are—without some visible mark of disease or deformity. A physician of the city has recently endeavoured to cure syphilis in its secondary stage, by means of inoculation, having first tried the experiment upon himself; and there is now a hospital where this form of treatment is practiced upon two or three hundred patients, with the greatest success, as another physician informed me. I intended to have visited it, as well as the hospital for lepers; but the sight of a few cases, around the door of the latter establishment, so sickened me, that I had no courage to undertake the task.

Let me leave these disagreeable themes, and say that Bergen is one of the most charmingly picturesque towns in all the North. Its name, "The Mountain," denotes one of its most striking features. It is built upon two low capes, which project from the foot of a low mountain, two thousand feet high, while directly in its rear lies a lovely little lake, about three miles in circumference. On the end of the northern headland stands the fortress of Berghenhuus, with the tall square mass of Walkendorf's Tower, built upon the foundations of the former palace of King Olaf Kyrre, the founder of the city. The narrow harbour between is crowded with fishing-vessels,—during the season often numbering from six to eight hundred,—and beyond it the southern promontory, quite covered with houses, rises steeply from the water. A public grove, behind the fortress, delights the eye with its dark-green mounds of foliage; near it rise the twin towers of the German Church, which boasts an age of nearly seven hundred years, and the suburbs on the steep mountain-sides gradually vanish among gardens and country-villas, which are succeeded by farms and grazing fields, lying under the topmost ridges of the bare rock. The lake in the rear is surrounded with the country residences of the rich merchants—a succession of tasteful dwellings, each with its garden and leafy arbours, its flowers and fountains, forming a rich frame to the beautiful sheet of water. Avenues of fine old lindens thread this suburban paradise, and seats, placed at the proper points, command views of which one knows not the loveliest. Everything has an air of ancient comfort, taste, and repose. One sees yet, the footsteps of mighty Hansa, who for three centuries reigned here supreme. The northern half of Bergen is still called the "German Quarter," and there are very few citizens of education who do not speak the language.

With one or two exceptions, the streets are rough and narrow. There are no quaint peculiarities in the architecture, the houses being all of wood, painted white or some light colour. At every door stands a barrel filled with water, to be ready in case of fire. Owing to the great number of fishing-vessels and its considerable foreign trade, Bergen is a much more lively and bustling place than either Christiania or Drontheim. The streets are well populated, and the great square at the head of the harbour is always thronged with a motley concourse of fishermen, traders, and country people. Drunkenness seems to be a leading vice. I saw, at least, fifty people, more or less intoxicated, in the course of a short walk, one afternoon. The grog shops, however, are rigidly closed at six o'clock on Saturday evening, and remain so until Monday morning, any violation or evasion of the law being severely punished. The same course has been adopted here as in Sweden; the price of brandy has been doubled, by restrictions on its manufacture, and every encouragement has been afforded to breweries. The beer of Christiania is equal in flavour and purity to any in the world, and it is now in great demand all over Norway.

The day after our arrival the sky cleared again, and we were favoured with superb weather; which might well be the case, as the people told me it had previously been raining every day for a month. The gardens, groves, and lawns of velvet turf, so long moistened, now blazed out with splendid effect in the hot August sunshine. "Is there such a green anywhere else in the world?" asked my friend. "If anywhere, only in England—but scarcely there," I was obliged to confess. Yet there was an acquaintance of mine in Bergen, a Hammerfest merchant, who, in this rare climax of summer beauty, looked melancholy and dissatisfied. "I want to get back to the north," said he, "I miss our Arctic summer. These dark nights are so disagreeable, that I am very tired of them. There is nothing equal to our three months of daylight, and they alone reconcile us to the winter." Who will say, after this, that anything more than the fundamental qualities of human nature are the same in all climates? But from the same foundation you may build either a Grecian temple or a Chinese pagoda.

The lions of Bergen are soon disposed of. After you have visited the fortress and admired the sturdy solidity of Walkendorf's Tower, you may walk into the German church which stands open (or did, when we were there), without a soul to prevent you from carrying off some of the queer old carved work and pictures. The latter are hideous enough to be perfectly safe, and the church, though exceedingly quaint and interesting, is not beautiful. Then you may visit the museum, which contains an excellent collection of northern fish, and some very curious old furniture. The collection of antiquities is not remarkable; but it should be remembered that the museum has been created within the last twenty years, and is entirely the result of private taste and enterprise. One of the most singular things I saw was a specimen (said to be the only one in existence) of a fish called the "herring-king," about twelve feet in length by one in thickness, and with something of the serpent in its appearance. The old Kraaken has not shown himself for a number of years, possibly frightened away by the appearance of steamers in his native waters. In spite of all the testimony which Capell Brooke has collected in favour of his existence, he is fast becoming a myth.

Bergen, we found, is antiquated in more respects than one. On sending for horses, on the morning fixed for our departure, we were coolly told that we should have to wait twenty-four hours; but after threatening to put the law in force against the skyds-skaffer, he promised to bring them by one o'clock in the afternoon. In this city of 30,000 inhabitants, no horses are kept in readiness at the post-station; but are furnished by farmers somewhere at a distance. In the matter of hotels, however, Bergen stands in the front rank of progress, rivalling Christiania and Drontheim. The fare is not so good, and the charges are equally high. There are two little inns, with five or six rooms each, and one boarding-house of the same size. We could only get one small room, into which all three were packed, at a charge of a dollar and a quarter per day; while for two wretched meals we paid a dollar and a half each. The reader may judge of our fare from the fact that one day our soup was raspberry juice and water, and another time, cold beer, flavoured with pepper and cinnamon. Add tough beafsteaks swimming in grease and rancid butter, and you have the principal ingredients. For the first time in my life I found my digestive powers unequal to the task of mastering a new national diet.

CHAPTER XXX. A TRIP TO THE VÖRING-FOSS.

After waiting only five hours, we obtained three horses and drove away from Bergen. It was a superb afternoon, spotlessly blue overhead, with still bluer water below, and hills of dark, velvety verdure throbbing and sparkling in the sunshine, and the breezes from off the fjord. We sped past the long line of suburban gardens, through the linden avenues, which, somehow or other, suggested to me the days of the Hanseatic League, past Tivoli, the Hoboken of Bergen, and on the summit of the hill beyond stopped to take a parting look at the beautiful city. She sat at the foot of her guardian mountain, across the lake, her white towers and red roofs rising in sharp relief against the purple background of the islands which protect her from the sea. In colour, form, and atmospheric effect, the picture was perfect. Norway is particularly fortunate in the position and surroundings of her three chief cities. Bergen bears away the palm, truly, but either of them has few rivals in Europe.

Our road led at first over well-cultivated hills dotted with comfortable farmhouses—a rolling, broken country enclosed by rugged and sterile groups of hills. After some miles we turned northward into a narrow valley running parallel to the coast line. The afternoon sun, shining over the shoulder of the mountain-ridge on our left, illuminated with dazzling effect the green pastures in the bosom of the valley, and the groves of twinkling birch and sombre fir on the opposite slope. I have never seen purer tints in the sunshine— never a softer transparency in the shadows. The landscape was ideal in its beauty, except the houses, whose squalor and discomfort were real. Our first station lay off the road, on a hill. A very friendly old man promised to get us horses as soon as possible, and his wife set before us the best fare the house afforded—milk, oaten shingles, and bad cheese. The house was dirty, and the aspect of the family bed, which occupied one end of the room, merely divided by boards into separate compartments for the parents, children and servants was sufficient to banish sleep. Notwithstanding the poverty of the place, the old woman set a good value upon her choice provender. The horses were soon forthcoming, and the man, whose apparent kindness increased every moment, said to me, "Have I not done well? Is it not very well that I have brought you horses so soon?" I assented cheerfully, but he still repeated the same questions, and I was stupid enough not to discover their meaning, until he added; "I have done everything so well, that you ought to give me something for it." The naïve manner of this request made it seem reasonable, and I gave him something accordingly, though a little disappointed, for I had congratulated myself on finding at last a friendly and obliging skyds-skaffer (Postmaster) in Norway.

Towards evening we reached a little village on the shore of the Osterfjord. Here the road terminated, and a water station of eighteen miles in length lay before us. The fjords on the western coast of Norway are narrow, shut in by lofty and abrupt mountains, and penetrate far into the land— frequently to the distance of a hundred miles. The general direction of the valleys is parallel to the line of the coast, intersecting the fjords at nearly a right angle, so that they, in connection with these watery defiles, divide the mountains into immense irregular blocks, with very precipitous sides and a summit table-land varying from two to four thousand feet above the sea level. For this reason there is no continuous road in all western Norway, but alternate links of land and water—boats and post-horses. The deepest fjords reach very nearly to the spinal ridge of the mountain region, and a land-road from Bergen to this line would be more difficult to construct than any of the great highways across the Alps. In proportion to her population and means, Norway has done more for roads than any country in the world. Not only her main thoroughfares, but even her by-ways, give evidence of astonishing skill, industry, and perseverance. The Storthing has recently appropriated a sum of $188,000 for the improvement of roads, in addition to the repairs which the farmers are obliged to make, and which constitute almost their only tax, as there is no assessment whatever upon landed property. There seems a singular incongruity, however, in finding such an evidence of the highest civilisation, in connection with the semi-barbaric condition of the people. Generally, the improvement of the means of communication in a country is in the ratio of its social progress.

As we were obliged to wait until morning before commencing our voyage, we set about procuring supper and lodging. Some dirty beds in a dirty upper room constituted the latter, but the former was a doubtful affair. The landlord, who persisted in calling me "Dock," made a foraging excursion among the houses, and, after some time, laid before us a salted and smoked leg of mutton, some rancid butter, hard oaten bread, and pestilential cheese. I ate as a matter of duty towards my body, but my companions were less conscientious. We deserve no credit for having risen early the next morning, neither was there any self-denial in the fact of our being content with a single cup of coffee. The boatmen, five in number, who had been engaged the evening before, took our carrioles apart and stowed them in the stern, while we three disposed ourselves very uneasily in the narrow bow. As we were about pushing off, one of the men stepped upon a stone and shouted in a loud voice, "Come and help us, fairies!"—whereat the others laughed heartily. The wind was against us, but I thought the men hugged the shore much more than was necessary. I noticed the same thing afterwards, and spoke of it, but they stated that there were strong currents in these fjords, setting towards the sea. The water, in fact, is but slightly brackish, and the ebb and flow of the tides is hardly felt.

The scenery in the Osterfjord is superb. Mountains, 2000 feet high, inclose and twist it between their interlocking bases. Cliffs of naked rock overhang it, and cataracts fall into it in long zigzag chains of foam. Here and there a little embayed dell rejoices with settlement and cultivation, and even on the wildest steeps, where it seems almost impossible for a human foot to find hold, the people scramble at the hazard of their lives, to reap a scanty harvest of grass for the winter. Goats pasture everywhere, and our boatmen took delight in making the ewes follow us along the cliffs, by imitating the bleating of kids. Towards noon we left the main body of the fjord and entered a narrow arm which lay in eternal shadow under tremendous walls of dark rock. The light and heat of noonday were tropical in their silent intensity, painting the summits far above with dashes of fierce colour, while their bases sank in blue gloom to meet the green darkness of the water. Again and again the heights enclosed us, so that there was no outlet; but they opened as if purposely to make way for us, until our keel grated the pebbly barrier of a narrow valley, where the land road was resumed. Four miles through this gap brought us to another branch of the same fjord, where we were obliged to have our carrioles taken to pieces and shipped for a short voyage.

At its extremity the fjord narrowed, and still loftier mountains overhung it. Shut in by these, like some palmy dell in the heart of the porphyry mountains of the Sahara, lay Bolstadören, a miracle of greenness and beauty. A mantle of emerald velvet, falling in the softest slopes and swells to the water's edge, was thrown upon the valley; the barley had been cut and bound to long upright poles to dry, rising like golden pillars from the shaven stubble; and, to crown all, above the landing-place stood a two-story house, with a jolly fat landlord smoking in the shade, and half-a-dozen pleasant-looking women gossiping in-doors. "Can we get anything to eat?" was the first question. "The gentlemen can have fresh salmon and potatoes, and red wine if they wish it," answered the mistress. Of course we wished it; we wished for any food clean enough to be eatable, and the promise of such fare was like the falling of manna in the desert. The salmon, fresh from the stream, was particularly fine; the fish here is so abundant that the landlord had caught 962, as he informed us, in the course of one season.

We had but two miles of land before another sheet of water intervened, and our carrioles were again taken to pieces. The postillions and boatmen along this route were great scamps, frequently asking more than the legal fare, and in one instance threatened to prevent us from going on unless we paid it. I shall not bore the reader with accounts of our various little squabbles on the road, all of which tended more and more to convince us, that unless the Norwegians were a great deal more friendly, kind, and honest a few years ago than they are now, they have been more over-praised than any people in the world. I must say, however, that they are bungling swindlers, and could only be successful with the greenest of travellers. The moment an imposition is resisted, and the stranger shows himself familiar with the true charges and methods of travel, they give up the attempt; but the desire to cheat is only less annoying to one than cheating itself. The fees for travelling by skyds are, it is true, disproportionably low, and in many instances the obligation to furnish horses is no doubt an actual loss to the farmer. Very often we would have willingly paid a small increase upon the legal rates if it had been asked for as a favour; but when it was boldly demanded as a right, and backed by a falsehood, we went not a stiver beyond the letter of the law.

Landing at Evanger, an intelligent landlord, who had four brothers in America, gave us return horses to Vossevangen, and we enjoyed the long twilight of the warm summer evening, while driving along the hills which overlook the valley connecting the lakes of Vossevangen and Evanger. It was a lovely landscape, ripe with harvest, and the air full of mellow, balmy odours from the flowers and grain. The black spire of Vossevangen church, standing dark against the dawning moonlight, was the welcome termination of our long day's journey, and not less welcome were our clean and comfortable quarters in the house of a merchant there. Here we left the main road across Norway, and made an excursion to the Vöring-Foss, which lies beyond the Hardanger Fjord, about fifty miles distant, in a south-eastern direction.

Vossevangen, in the splendour of a cloudless morning, was even more beautiful than as a moonlit haven of repose. The compact little village lay half buried in trees, clustered about the massive old church, with its black, pointed tower, and roof covered with pitched shingles, in the centre of the valley, while the mountains around shone bald and bright through floating veils of vapour which had risen from the lake. The people were all at work in the fields betimes, cutting and stacking the barley. The grass-fields, cut smooth and close, and of the softest and evenest green, seemed kept for show rather than for use. The bottom of the valley along which we drove, was filled with an unbroken pine forest, inclosing here and there a lake,

"Where Heaven itself, brought down to Earth,

Seemed fairer than above;"

while the opposite mountain rose rich with harvest fields and farmhouses. There are similar landscapes between Fribourg and Vevay, in Switzerland— finer, perhaps, except that all cultivated scenery in Norway gains wonderfully in effect from the savage environment of the barren fjelds. Here, cultivation is somewhat of a phenomenon, and a rich, thickly settled valley strikes one with a certain surprise. The Norwegians have been accused of neglecting agriculture; but I do not see that much more could be expected of them. The subjugation of virgin soil, as we had occasion to notice, is a serious work. At the best, the grain harvests are uncertain, while fish are almost as sure as the season; and so the surplus agricultural population either emigrates or removes to the fishing grounds on the coast. There is, undoubtedly, a considerable quantity of wild land which could be made arable, but the same means, applied to the improvement of that which is at present under cultivation, would accomplish far more beneficent results.

Leaving the valley, we drove for some time through pine forests, and here, as elsewhere, had occasion to notice the manner in which this source of wealth has been drained of late years. The trees were very straight and beautiful, but there were none of more than middle age. All the fine old timber had been cut away; all Norway, in fact, has been despoiled in like manner, and the people are but just awaking to the fact, that they are killing a goose which lays golden eggs. The government, so prudently economical that it only allows $100,000 worth of silver to be quarried annually in the mines of Kongsberg, lest the supply should be exhausted, has, I believe, adopted measures for the preservation of the forests; but I am not able to state their precise character. Except in valleys remote from the rivers and fjords, one now finds very little mature timber.

> "The tallest pine,
>
> Hewn on Norwegian hills, to be the mast
>
> Of some great admiral,"

I have not yet seen.

We at last came upon a little lake, in a close glen with walls 1000 feet high. Not suspecting that we had ascended much above the sea-level, we were surprised to see the gorge all at once open below us, revealing a dark-blue lake, far down among the mountains. We stood on the brink of a wall, over which the stream at our side fell in a "hank" of divided cataracts. Our road was engineered with great difficulty to the bottom of the steep, whence a gentler descent took us to the hamlet of Vasenden, at the head of the lake. Beyond this there was no road for carrioles, and we accordingly gave ours in charge of a bright, active and intelligent little postmaster, twelve years old. He and his mother then rowed us across the lake to the village of Graven, whence there was a bridle-road across the mountains to a branch of the Hardanger Fjord. They demanded only twelve skillings (ten cents) for the row of three miles, and then posted off to a neighbouring farmhouse to engage horses for us.

There was a neat white dwelling on the hill, which we took to be the parsonage, but which proved to be the residence of an army captain on leave, whom we found sitting in the door, cleaning his gun, as we approached. He courteously ushered us into the house, and made his appearance soon afterwards in a clean shirt, followed by his wife, with wine and cakes upon a tray. I found him to be a man of more than ordinary intelligence, and of an earnest and reflective turn of mind, rare in men of his profession. He spoke chiefly of the passion for emigration which now possesses the Norwegian farmers, considering it not rendered necessary by their actual condition, but rather one of those contagions which spread through communities and nations, overcoming alike prudence and prejudice. He deplored it as retarding the development of Norway. Personal interest, however, is everywhere stronger than patriotism, and I see no signs of the emigration decreasing for some years to come.

After waiting a considerable time, we obtained two horses and a strapping farmer's son for guide. The fellow was delighted to find out where we came from, and was continually shouting to the people in the fields: "Here these are Americans: they were born there!" whereat the people stared, saluted, and then stared again. He shouldered our packs and marched beside the horses with the greatest ease. "You are strong," I remarked. "Yes," he replied, "I am a strong Normand," making his patriotism an excuse for his personal pride. We had a terribly tough pull up the mountain, through fine woods, to the summit level of the fjeld. The view backwards, over the lake, was enchanting, and we lingered long on the steep, loth to lose it. Turning again, a desolate lake lay before us, heathery swells of the bleak table-land and distant peaks, touched with snow. Once upon the broad, level summit of a Norwegian fjeld, one would never guess what lovely valleys lie under those misty breaks which separate its immense lobes—what gashes of life and beauty penetrate its stony heart. There are, in fact, two Norways: one above—a series of detached, irregular masses, bleak, snowy, wind-swept and heather-grown, inhabited by herdsmen and hunters: and one below—a ramification of narrow veins of land and water, with fields and forests, highways and villages.

So, when we had traversed the upper land for several miles, we came to a brink overlooking another branch of the lower land, and descended through thick woods to the farms of Ulvik, on the Eyfjord, an arm of the Hardanger. The shores were gloriously beautiful; slopes of dazzling turf inclosed the bright blue water, and clumps of oak, ash, and linden, in park-like groups, studded the fields. Low red farmhouses, each with its hollow square of stables and granaries, dotted the hill-sides, and the people, male and female, were everywhere out reaping the ripe barley and piling it, pillar-wise, upon tall stakes. Owing to this circumstance we were obliged to wait some time for oarsmen. There was no milk to be had, nor indeed anything to eat, notwithstanding the signs of plenty on all sides. My friend, wandering from house to house, at last discovered an old man, who brought him a bowl of mead in exchange for a cigar. Late in the afternoon two men came, put us into a shabby and leaky boat, and pulled away slowly for Vik, ten miles distant.

The fjord was shut in by lofty and abrupt mountains, often interrupted by deep lateral gorges. This is the general character of the Hardanger Fjord, a broad winding sheet of water, with many arms, but whose extent is diminished to the eye by the grandeur of its shores. Nothing can be wilder or more desolate than this scenery, especially at the junction of the two branches, where all signs of habitation are shut out of sight, and one is surrounded by mighty precipices of dark-red rock, vanishing away to the eastward in a gloomy defile. It was three hours and a half before we reached Vik, at the head of a bay on the southern side. Here, however, some English fishermen were quartered and we made sure of a supper. The landlord, of course, received their superfluous salmon, and they were not the men to spare a potato-field, so both were forthcoming, and in the satisfaction of appeased hunger, we were willing to indorse the opinion of a former English traveller in the guest's book: "This place seems to me a paradise, although very probably it is not one." The luxury of fishing, which I never could understand, has taught the Norwegians to regard travellers as their proper prey. Why should a man, they think, pay 50l. for the privilege of catching fish, which he gives away as soon as caught, unless he don't know how else to get rid of his money? Were it not that fishing in Norway includes pure air, hard fare, and healthy exercise, I should agree with somebody's definition of angling, "a rod with a fly at one end and a fool at the other;" but it is all that, and besides furnished us with a good meal more than once; wherefore I respect it.

We were now but eight miles from the Vöring-Foss, and set out betimes the next morning, taking with us a bottle of red wine, some dry bread, and Peder Halstensen as guide. I mention Peder particularly, because he is the only jolly, lively, wide-awake, open-hearted Norwegian I have ever seen. As rollicking as a Neapolitan, as chatty as an Andalusian, and as frank as a Tyrolese, he formed a remarkable contrast to the men with whom we had hitherto come in contact. He had long black hair, wicked black eyes, and a mouth which laughed even when his face was at rest. Add a capital tenor voice, a lithe, active frame, and something irresistibly odd and droll in his motions, and you have his principal points. We walked across the birch-wooded isthmus behind Vik to the Eyfjordsvand, a lake about three miles long, which completely cuts off the further valley, the mountains on either side falling to it in sheer precipices 1000 feet high.

We embarked in a crazy, leaky boat, Peder pulling vigorously and singing. "Frie dig ved lifvet" ("Life let us cherish"), with all the contentment on his face which is expressed in Mozart's immortal melody. "Peder," said I, "do you know the national song of Norway?" "I should think so," was his answer, stopping short in the midst of a wild fjeld-song, clearing his throat, and singing with a fervour and enthusiasm which rang wide over the lonely lake:—

> "Minstrel, awaken the harp from its slumbers,
>
> Strike for old Norway, the land of the free!
>
> High and heroic, in soul-stirring numbers,
>
> Clime of our fathers, we strike it for thee!

Old recollections awake our affections—

Hallow the name of the land of our birth;

Each heart beats its loudest, each cheek glows its proudest,

For Norway the ancient, the throne of the earth!"[D]

"Dost thou know," said he, becoming more familiar in his address, "that a lawyer (by the name of Bjerregaard) wrote this song, and the Storthing at Christiania gave him a hundred specie dollars for it. That was not too much, was it?" "No," said I, "five hundred dollars would have been little enough for such a song." "Yes, yes, that it would," was his earnest assent; and as I happened at that moment to ask whether we could see the peaks of the Halling Jökeln, he commenced a sœter-song of life on the lofty fjeld—a song of snow, and free winds, and blue sky. By this time we had reached the other end of the lake, where, in the midst of a little valley of rich alluvial soil, covered with patches of barley and potatoes, stood the hamlet of Sæbö. Here Peder procured a horse for my friend, and we entered the mouth of a sublime gorge which opened to the eastward—a mere split in the mighty ramparts of the Hardanger-Fjeld. Peder was continually shouting to the people in the fields: "Look here! These are Americans, these two, and the other one is a German! This one talks Norsk, and the others don't."

We ascended the defile by a rough footpath, at first through alder thickets, but afterwards over immense masses of rocky ruin, which had tumbled from the crags far above, and almost blocked up the valley. For silence, desolation, and awful grandeur, this defile equals any of the Alpine passes. In the spring, when the rocks, split by wedges of ice, disengage themselves from the summit, and thunder down upon the piled wrecks of ages, it must be terribly sublime. A bridge, consisting of two logs spanned across abutments of loose stones, and vibrating strongly under our tread, took us over the torrent. Our road, for some distance was now a mere staircase, scrambling up, down, under, over, and between the chaos of sundered rocks. A little further, and the defile shut in altogether, forming a cul de sac of apparently perpendicular walls, from 2000 to 3000 feet high. "How are we to get out of this?" I asked Peder. "Yonder," said he, pointing to the inaccessible summit in front. "But where

260

does the stream come from?" "That you will soon see." Lo! all at once a clean split from top to bottom disclosed itself in the wall on our left, and in passing its mouth we had a glimpse up the monstrous chasm, whose dark-blue sides, falling sheer 3000 feet, vanished at the bottom in eternal gloom and spray.

Crossing the stream again, we commenced ascending over the débris of stony avalanches, the path becoming steeper and steeper, until the far-off summit almost hung over our heads. It was now a zigzag ladder, roughly thrown together, but very firm. The red mare which my friend rode climbed it like a cat, never hesitating, even at an angle of 50°, and never making a false step. The performance of this noble animal was almost incredible. I should never have believed a horse capable of such gymnastics, had I not seen it with my own eyes, had I not mounted her myself at the most difficult points, in order to test her powers. You, who have climbed the Mayenwand, in going from the glacier of the Rhone to the Grimsel, imagine a slant higher, steeper, and composed of loose rocks, and you will have an exact picture of our ascent. We climbed well; and yet it took us just an hour and a half to reach the summit.

We were now on the great plateau of the Hardanger Fjeld, 2500 feet above the sea. A wild region lay before us—great swells, covered with heather, sweeping into the distance and given up to solitude and silence. A few isolated peaks, streaked with snow, rose from this upper level; and a deep break on our left revealed the top of the chasm through which the torrent made its way. At its extremity, a mile or more distant, rose a light cloud of vapour, seeming close at hand in the thin mountain air. The thick, spongy soil, not more than two feet deep, rests on a solid bed of rock,—the entire Hardanger Fjeld, in fact, is but a single rock,—and is therefore always swampy. Whortleberries were abundant, as well as the multeberry (Rubus chamœmorus), which I have found growing in Newfoundland; and Peder, running off on the hunt of them, was continually leading us astray. But at last, we approached the wreath of whirling spray, and heard the hollow roar of the Vöring-Foss. The great chasm yawned before us; another step, and we stood on the brink. I seized the branch of a tough pine sapling as a support and leaned over. My head did not swim; the height was too great for that, the impression too grand and wonderful. The shelf of rock on which I stood projected far out over a gulf 1200 feet deep, whose opposite side rose in one great escarpment from the bottom to a height of 800 feet above my head. On this black wall, wet with eternal spray, was painted a splendid rainbow, forming two thirds of a circle before it melted into the gloom below. A little stream fell in one long thread of silver from the very summit, like a plumb-line dropped to measure the 2000 feet. On my right hand the river, coming down from the level of the fjeld in a torn, twisted, and boiling mass, reached the brink of the gulf at a point about 400 feet below me, whence it fell in a single sheet to the bottom, a depth of between 800 and 900 feet.

Could one view it from below, this fall would present one of the grandest spectacles in the world. In height, volume of water, and sublime surroundings it has no equal. The spectator, however, looks down upon it from a great height above its brink, whence it is so foreshortened that he can only guess its majesty and beauty. By lying upon your belly and thrusting your head out beyond the roots of the pines, you can safely peer into the dread abyss, and watch, through the vortex of whirling spray in its tortured womb, the starry coruscations which radiate from the bottom of the fall, like rockets of water incessantly exploding. But this view, sublime as it is, only whets your desire to stand below, and see the river, with its sprayey crest shining against the sky, make but one leap from heaven to hell. Some persons have succeeded, by entering the chasm at its mouth in the valley below, in getting far enough to see a portion of the fall, the remainder being concealed by a projecting rock; and the time will come, no doubt, when somebody will have energy enough to carry a path to its very foot. I envy the travellers who will then visit the Vöring-Foss.

A short distance above the fall there are a few cabins inhabited by sœters, or herdsmen, whither we repaired to procure some fresh milk. The house was rude and dirty; but the people received us in a friendly manner. The powerful housewife laid aside her hay-rake, and brought us milk which was actually sweet (a rare thing in Norway,) dirty, but not rancid butter, and tolerable cheese. When my friend asked for water, she dipped a pailful from a neighbouring stream, thick with decayed moss and vegetable mould, and handed it to him. He was nice enough to pick out a rotten root before drinking, which one of the children snatched up from the floor and ate. Yet these people did not appear to be in want; they were healthy, cheerful, and contented; and their filthy manner of living was the result of sheer indolence and slovenliness. There was nothing to prevent them from being neat and comfortable, even with their scanty means; but the good gifts of God are always spoiled and wasted in dirty hands.

When we opened our bottle of wine, an exquisite aroma diffused itself through the room—a mingled smell of vine blossoms and ripe grapes. How could the coarse vintage sent to the North, watered and chemically doctored as it is, produce such a miracle? We tasted—superb old Chateau Latour, from the sunniest hill of Bordeaux! By whatever accident it had wandered thither, it did not fall into unappreciative hands. Even Brita Halstendsdatter Höl, the strong housewife, smacked her lips over the glass which she drank after sitting to me for her portrait.

When the sketch was completed, we filled the empty bottle with milk and set out on our return.

FOOTNOTES:

[D] Latham's translation.

CHAPTER XXXI. SKETCHES FROM THE BERGENSTIFT.

Our return from the Vöring-Foss to the hamlet of Sæbö was accomplished without accident or particular incident. As we were crossing the Eyfjordsvand, the stillness of the savage glen, yet more profound in the dusk of evening, was broken by the sudden thunder of a slide in some valley to the eastward. Peder stopped in the midst of "Frie dig ved lifvet" and listened. "Ho!" said he, "the spring is the time when the rocks come down, but that sounds like a big fellow, too." Peder was not so lively on the way back, not because he was fatigued, for in showing us how they danced on the fjeld, he flung himself into the air in a marvellous manner, and turned over twice before coming down, but partly because he had broken our bottle of milk, and partly because there was something on his mind. I waited patiently, knowing that it would come out at last, as indeed it did. "You see," said he, hesitatingly, "some travellers give a drink-money to the guide. It isn't an obligation, you know; but then some give it. Now, if you should choose to give me anything, don't pay it to the landlord for me, because then I won't get it. You are not bound to do so you know but some travellers do it, and I don't know but you might also. Now, if you should, give it directly to me, and then I will have it." When we reached Vik, we called Peder aside and gave him three marks. "Oh, you must pay your bill to the landlord," said he. "But that is your drink-money," I explained. "That?" he exclaimed; "it is not possible! Frie dig ved lifvet," &c., and so he sang, cut a pigeon-wing or two, and proceeded to knot and double knot the money in a corner of his pocket-handkerchief.

"Come and take a swim!" said Peder, reappearing. "I can swim ever since I fell into the water. I tumbled off the pier, you must know, and down I went. Everything became black before my eyes; and I thought to myself, 'Peder, this is the end of you.' But I kicked and splashed nevertheless, until my eyes opened again, wide enough to see where a rope was. Well, after I found I could fall into the water without drowning, I was not afraid to swim." In fact, Peder now swam very well, and floundered about with great satisfaction in the ice cold water. A single plunge was all I could endure. After supper the landlady came in to talk to me about America. She had a son in California, and a daughter in Wisconsin, and showed me their daguerreotypes and some bits of gold with great pride. She was a stout, kindly, motherly body, and paid especial attention to our wants on finding where we came from. Indeed we were treated in the most friendly manner by these good people, and had no reason to complain of our reckoning on leaving. This experience confirms me in the belief that honesty and simplicity may still be characteristics of the Norwegians in the more remote parts of the country.

We bade a cordial farewell to Vik next morning, and set off on our return, in splendid sunshine. Peder was in the boat, rejoiced to be with us again; and we had no sooner gotten under way, than he began singing, "Frie dig ved lifvet." It was an intensely hot day, and the shores of Ulvik were perfectly dazzling. The turf had a silken gloss; the trees stood darkly and richly green, and the water was purest sapphire. "It is a beautiful bay, is it not?" said the farmer who furnished us with horses, after we had left the boat and were slowly climbing the fjeld. I thought I had never seen a finer; but when heaven and earth are in entire harmony, when form, colour and atmosphere accord like some rich swell of music, whatever one sees is perfect. Hence I shall not say how beautiful the bay of Ulvik was to me, since under other aspects the description would not be true.

The farmer's little daughter, however, who came along to take back one of the horses, would have been a pleasant apparition at any time and in any season. She wore her Sunday dress, consisting of a scarlet boddice over a white chemise, green petticoat, and white apron, while her shining flaxen hair was plaited into one long braid with narrow strips of crimson and yellow cloth and then twisted like a garland around her head. She was not more than twelve or thirteen years old, but tall, straight as a young pine, and beautifully formed, with the promise of early maidenhood in the gentle swell of her bosom. Her complexion was lovely—pink, brightened with sunburnt gold,—and her eyes like the blossoms of the forget-me-not, in hue. In watching her firm yet graceful tread, as she easily kept pace with the horse, I could not realise that in a few more years she would probably be no more graceful and beautiful than the women at work in the fields—coarse, clumsy shapes, with frowzy hair, leathery faces, and enormous hanging breasts.

In the Bergenstift, however, one sometimes sees a pretty face; and the natural grace of the form is not always lost. About Vossevangen, for instance, the farmers' daughters are often quite handsome; but beauty, either male or female, is in Norway the rarest apparition. The grown-up women, especially after marriage, are in general remarkably plain. Except among some of the native tribes of Africa, I have nowhere seen such overgrown, loose, pendant breasts as among them. This is not the case in Sweden, where, if there are few beauties, there are at least a great many passable faces. There are marked differences in the blood of the two nations; and the greater variety of feature and complexion in Norway seems to indicate a less complete fusion of the original stocks.

We were rowed across the Graven Lake by an old farmer, who wore the costume of the last century,—a red coat, à la Frederic the Great, long waistcoat, and white knee-breeches. He demanded double the lawful fare, which, indeed, was shamefully small; and we paid him without demur. At Vasenden we found our carrioles and harness in good condition, nothing having been abstracted except a ball of twine. Horses were in waiting, apparently belonging to some well-to-do farmer; for the boys were well dressed, and took especial care of them. We reached the merchant's comfortable residence at Vossevangen before sunset, and made amends on his sumptuous fare for the privations of the past three days.

We now resumed the main road between Christiania and Bergen. The same cloudless days continued to dawn upon us. For one summer, Norway had changed climates with Spain. Our oil-cloths were burnt up and cracked by the heat, our clothes covered with dust, and our faces became as brown as those of Bedouins. For a week we had not a cloud in the sky; the superbly clear days belied the old saying of "weather-breeders."

Our road, on leaving Vossevangen, led through pine-forests, following the course of a stream up a wild valley, enclosed by lofty mountains. Some lovely cataracts fell from the steep on our left; but this is the land of cataracts and there is many a one, not even distinguished by a name, which would be

266

renowned in Switzerland. I asked my postillion the name of the stream beside us. "Oh," said he, "it has none; it is not big enough!" He wanted to take us all the way through to Gudvangen, twenty-eight miles, on our paying double fare, predicting that we would be obliged to wait three hours for fresh horses at each intermediate station. He waited some time at Tvinde, the first station, in the hope that we would yield, but departed suddenly in a rage on seeing that the horses were already coming. At this place, a stout young fellow, who had evidently been asleep, came out of the house and stood in the door staring at us with open mouth for a full hour. The postmaster sat on the step and did likewise. It was the height of harvest-time, and the weather favourable almost to a miracle; yet most of the harvesters lay upon their backs under the trees as we passed. The women appeared to do most of the out-door, as well as the in-door work. They are certainly far more industrious than the men, who, judging from what I saw of them, are downright indolent Evidences of slow, patient, plodding toil, one sees truly; but active industry, thrift, and honest ambition, nowhere.

The scenery increased in wildness and roughness as we proceeded. The summit of Hvitnaset (White-nose) lifted its pinnacles of grey rock over the brow of the mountains on the north, and in front, pale, blue-grey peaks, 5000 feet high, appeared on either hand. The next station was a village of huts on the side of a hill. Everybody was in the fields except one woman, who remained to take charge of the station. She was a stupid creature, but had a proper sense of her duty; for she started at full speed to order horses, and we afterwards found that she must have run full three English miles in the space of half an hour. The emigration to America from this part of Bergenstift has been very great, and the people exhibited much curiosity to see and speak with us.

The scenery became at the same time more barren and more magnificent, as we approached the last station, Stalheim, which is a miserable little village at the head of the famous Naerödal. Our farmer-postillion wished to take us on to Gudvangen with the same horses, urging the same reasons as the former one. It would have been better if we had accepted his proposal; but our previous experience had made us mistrustful. The man spoke truth, however;

hour after hour passed away, and the horses came not. A few miserable people collected about us, and begged money. I sketched the oldest, ugliest and dirtiest of them, as a specimen, but regretted it afterwards, as his gratitude on receiving a trifle for sitting, obliged me to give him my hand. Hereupon another old fellow, not quite so hideous, wanted to be taken also. "Lars," said a woman to the former, "are you not ashamed to have so ugly a face as yours go to America?" "Oh," said he, "it does not look so ugly in the book." His delight on getting the money created some amusement. "Indeed," he protested, "I am poor, and want it; and you need not laugh."

The last gush of sunset was brightening the tops of the savage fjeld when the horses arrived. We had waited two hours and three quarters and I therefore wrote a complaint in the post-book in my best Norsk. From the top of a hill beyond the village, we looked down into the Naerödal. We stood on the brink of a tremendous wall about a thousand feet above the valley. On one side, the stream we had been following fell in a single cascade 400 feet; on the other, a second stream, issuing from some unseen defile, flung its several ribbons of foam from nearly an equal height. The valley, or rather gorge, disappeared in front between mountains of sheer rock, which rose to the height of 3000 feet. The road—a splendid specimen of engineering—was doubled back and forth around the edge of a spur projecting from the wall on which we stood, and so descended to the bottom. Once below, our carrioles rolled rapidly down the gorge, which was already dusky with twilight. The stream, of the most exquisite translucent azure-green colour, rolled between us; and the mountain crests towered so far above, that our necks ached as we looked upwards. I have seen but one valley which in depth and sublimity can equal the Naerödal— the pass of the Taurus, in Asia Minor, leading from Cappadocia into Cilicia. In many places the precipices were 2000 feet in perpendicular height; and the streams of the upper fjeld, falling from the summits, lost themselves in evanescent water-dust before they reached the bottom. The bed of the valley was heaped with fragments of rock; which are loosed from above with every returning spring.

It was quite dark before we reached Gudvangen, thoroughly tired and as hungry as wolves. My postillion, on hearing me complain, pulled a piece of dry mutton out of his pocket and gave it to me. He was very anxious to learn whether brandy and tobacco were as dear in America as in Norway; if so, he did not wish to emigrate. A stout girl had charge of Braisted's horse; the female postillions always fell to his lot. She complained of hard work and poor pay, and would emigrate if she had the money. At Gudvangen we had a boat journey of thirty-five miles before us, and therefore engaged two boats with eight oarsmen for the morrow. The people tried hard to make us take more, but we had more than the number actually required by law, and, as it turned out, quite as many as were necessary. Travellers generally supply themselves with brandy for the use of their boatmen, from an idea that they will be stubborn and dilatory without it. We did so in no single instance; yet our men were always steady and cheerful.

We shipped our carrioles and sent them off in the larger boat, delaying our own departure until we had fortified ourselves with a good breakfast, and laid in some hard bread and pork omelette, for the day. The Gudvangen Fjord, down which we now glided over the glassy water, is a narrow mountain avenue of glorious scenery. The unseen plateaus of the Blaa and Graa Fjelds, on either hand, spilled their streams over precipices from 1000 to 2000 feet in height, above whose cornices shot the pointed summits of bare grey rock, wreathed in shifting clouds, 4000 feet above the sea. Pine-trees feathered the less abrupt steeps, with patches of dazzling turf here and there; and wherever a gentler slope could be found in the coves, stood cottages surrounded by potato-fields and ripe barley stacked on poles. Not a breath of air rippled the dark water, which was a perfect mirror to the mountains and the strip of sky between them, while broad sheets of morning sunshine, streaming down the breaks in the line of precipices, interrupted with patches of fiery colour the deep, rich, transparent gloom of the shadows. It was an enchanted voyage until we reached the mouth of the Aurlands Fjord, divided from that of Gudvangen by a single rocky buttress 1000 feet high. Beyond this point the watery channel is much broader, and the shores diminish in grandeur as they approach the Sogne Fjord, of which this is but a lateral branch.

I was a little disappointed in the scenery of Sogne Fjord, The mountains which enclose it are masses of sterile rock, neither lofty nor bold enough in

269

their forms to make impression, after the unrivalled scenery through which we had passed. The point of Vangnæs, a short distance to the westward, is the "Framnæs" of Frithiof's Saga, and I therefore looked towards it with some interest, for the sake of that hero and his northern lily, Ingeborg. There are many bauta-stones still standing on the shore, but one who is familiar with Tegner's poem must not expect to find his descriptions verified, either in scenery or tradition. On turning eastward, around the point of Fronningen, we were surprised by the sudden appearance of two handsome houses, with orchards and gardens, on the sunny side of the bank. The vegetation, protected in some degree from the sea-winds, was wonderfully rich and luxuriant. There were now occasional pine-woods on the southern shore, but the general aspect of this fjord is bleak and desolate. In the heat and breathless silence of noonday, the water was like solid crystal. A faint line, as if drawn with a pencil along the bases of the opposite mountains, divided them from the equally perfect and palpable mountains inverted below them. In the shadows near us, it was quite impossible to detect the boundary between the substance and its counterpart. In the afternoon we passed the mouth of the northern arms of the fjord, which strike into the heart of the wildest and grandest region of Norway; the valley of Justedal, with its tremendous glaciers, the snowy teeth of the Hurunger, and the crowning peaks of the Skagtolstind. Our course lay down the other arm, to Lærdalsören, at the head of the fjord. By five o'clock it came in sight, at the mouth of a valley opening through the barren flanks on the Fille Fjeld. We landed, after a voyage of ten hours, and found welcome signs of civilisation in a neat but exorbitant inn.

Our boatmen, with the exception of stopping half an hour for breakfast, had pulled steadily the whole time. We had no cause to be dissatisfied with them, while they were delighted with the moderate gratuity we gave them. They were tough, well-made fellows, possessing a considerable amount of endurance, but less actual strength than one would suspect. Braisted, who occasionally tried his hand at an oar, could pull them around with the greatest ease. English travellers whom I have met inform me that in almost every trial they find themselves stronger than the Norwegians. This is probably to be accounted for by their insufficient nourishment. Sour milk and oaten bread never yet fed an athlete. The proportions of their bodies would admit of fine muscular development; and if they cannot do what their Viking ancestors once did, it is because they no longer live upon the spoils of other lands, as they.

CHAPTER XXXII. HALLINGDAL—THE COUNTRY-PEOPLE OF NORWAY.

There are two roads from Lærdalsören to Christiania, the eastern one passing through the districts of Valders and Hadeland, by way of the Little Miösen Lake and the Randsfjord, while the western, after crossing the Fille Fjeld, descends the long Hallingdal to Ringerike. In point of scenery there is little difference between them; but as we intended visiting the province of Tellemark, in Southern Norway, we chose the latter. The valley of the Fille Fjeld, which we entered on leaving Lærdalsören, is enclosed by wild, barren mountains, more isolated and irregular in their forms than the Hardanger and Dovre Fjelds. There were occasional precipices and dancing waterfalls, but in general the same tameness and monotony we had found on the Sogne Fjord. Down the bed of the valley flowed a large rapid stream, clear as crystal, and of a beautiful beryl tint. The cultivation was scanty; and the potato fields, utterly ruined by disease, tainted the air with sickening effluvia. The occasional forests on the hill-sides were of fir and birch, while poplar, ash, and linden grew in the valley. The only fruit-trees I saw were some sour red cherries.

But in the splendour of the day, this unfriendly valley shone like a dell of the Apennines. Not a cloud disturbed the serenity of the sky; the brown grass and yellow moss on the mountains were painted with sunny gold, and the gloss and sparkle of the foliage equalled that of the Italian ilex and laurel. On the second stage a new and superb road carried us through the rugged defile of Saltenaaset. This pass is evidently the effect of some mighty avalanche thousands of ages ago. The valley is blocked up by tremendous masses of rock, hurled one upon the other in the wildest confusion, while the shattered peaks from which they fell still tower far above. Threading this chaos in the shadow of the rocks, we looked across the glen upon a braided chain of foam, twisted together at the end into a long white cascade, which dropped into the gulf below. In another place, a rainbow meteor suddenly flashed across the face of a dark crag, betraying the dusty spray of a fall, else invisible.

On the third stage the road, after mounting a difficult steep, descended into the valley of Borgund, in which stands most probably the most ancient church in Norway. It is a singular, fantastic structure, bristling with spiky spires and covered with a scale armour of black pitched shingles. It is certainly of no more recent date than the twelfth century, and possibly of the close of the eleventh. The architecture shows the Byzantine style in the rounded choir and the arched galleries along the sides, the Gothic in the windows and pointed gables, and the horned ornaments on the roof suggest the pagan temples of the ante-Christian period. A more grotesque affair could hardly be found in Christendom; it could only be matched among the monstrosities of Chinese art. With the exception of the church of Hitterdal, in Tellemark, a building of similar date, this is the best preserved of the few antiquities of Norway. The entire absence of feudal castles is a thing to be noticed. Serfdom never existed here, and one result of this circumstance, perhaps, is the ease with which institutions of a purely republican stamp have been introduced.

Our road still proceeded up the bottom of a rough barren valley, crossing stony headlands on either side. At the station of Haug our course turned to the south-east, climbing a slope leading to the plateau of the Fille Fjeld—a severe pull for our horses in the intense heat. The birch woods gradually diminished in size until they ceased altogether, and the naked plain stretched before us. In this upper land the air was delicious and inspiring. We were more than 3000 feet above the sea, but the summits to the right and left, with their soft gleams of pale gray, lilac and purple hues in the sunshine, and pure blue in shadow, rose to the height of 6000. The heat of the previous ten days had stripped them bare of snow, and the landscape was drear and monotonous. The summits of the Norwegian Fjelds have only the charm of wildness and bleakness. I doubt whether any mountains of equal height exhibit less grandeur in their upper regions. The most imposing features of Norwegian scenery are its deep valleys, its tremendous gorges with their cataracts, flung like banners from steeps which seem to lean against the very sky, and, most of all, its winding, labyrinthine fjords—valleys of the sea, in which the phenomena of the valleys of the land are repeated. I found no scenery in the Bergenstift of so original and impressive a character as that of the Lofoden Isles.

The day was Sunday, and we, of course, expect to see some evidence of it in the appearance of the people. Yet, during the whole day, we found but one clean person—the hostess of an inn on the summit of Fille Fjeld, where we stopped to bait our horses. She was a young fresh-faced woman, in the first year of her wifehood, and her snowy chemise and tidy petticoat made her shine like a star among the dirty and frowzy creatures in the kitchen. I should not forget a boy, who was washing his face in a brook as we passed; but he was young, and didn't know any better. Otherwise the people lounged about the houses, or sat on the rocks in the sun, filthy, and something else, to judge from certain signs. At Haug, forgetting that it was a fast station, where there is no tilsigelse (money for ordering horses) to be paid, I handed the usual sum to the landlady, saying: "This is for tilsigelse." "It is quite right," said she, pocketing the coin.

Skirting an azure lake, we crossed the highest part of the pass, nearly four thousand feet above the sea, and descended a naked valley to the inn of Bjöberg. The landlord received us very cordially; and as the inn promised tolerable accommodation, he easily persuaded us to stop there for the night. His wife wore a frightful costume, which we afterwards found to prevail throughout all Hemsedal and Hallingdal. It consisted simply of a band across the shoulders, above the breasts, passing around the arms and over the back of the neck, with an immense baggy, dangling skirt hanging therefrom to the ancles. Whether she was fat or lean, straight or crooked, symmetrical or deformed, it was impossible to discern, except when the wind blew. The only thing to be said in favour of such a costume is, that it does not impede the development and expansion of the body in any direction. Hence I would strongly recommend its adoption to the advocates of reform in feminine dress at home. There is certainly none of that weight upon the hips, of which they complain in the fashionable costume. It is far more baggy, loose, and hideous than the Bloomer, with the additional advantage of making all ages and styles of beauty equally repulsive, while on the score of health and convenience, there is still less to be said against it. Do not stop at half-way measures, oh, fair reformers!

It seems incredible that, in a pastoral country like Norway, it should be almost impossible to procure sweet milk and good butter. The cattle are of good quality, there is no better grass in the world; and the only explanation of the fact is to be found in the general want of cleanliness, especially among the inhabitants of the mountain districts, which are devoted to pasturage alone. Knowing this, one wonders the less to see no measures taken for a supply of water in the richer grain-growing valleys, where it is so easily procurable. At Bjöberg, for instance, there was a stream of delicious water flowing down the hill, close beside the inn, and four bored pine-trunks would have brought it to the very door; but, instead of that, the landlady whirled off to the stream in her revolving dress, to wash the dishes, or to bring us half a pint to wash ourselves. We found water much more abundant the previous winter in Swedish Lapland.

Leaving Bjöberg betimes, we drove rapidly down Hemsedal, enjoying the pure delicious airs of the upper fjeld. The scenery was bleak and grey; and even the soft pencil of the morning sun failed to impart any charm to it, except the nameless fascination of utter solitude and silence. The valley descends so gradually that we had driven two Norsk miles before the fir-forests in its bed began to creep up the mountain-sides. During the second stage we passed the remarkable peak of Saaten, on the opposite side of the valley—the end or cape of a long projecting ridge, terminating in a scarped cliff, from the very summit of which fell a cascade from three to four hundred feet in height. Where the water came from, it was impossible to guess, unless there were a large deposit of snow in the rear; for the mountains fell away behind Saaten, and the jagged, cleft headland rose alone above the valley. It was a strange and fantastic feature of the landscape, and, to me, a new form in the repertory of mountain aspects.

We now drove, through fir-woods balmy with warm resinous odours, to Ekre, where we had ordered breakfast by förbud. The morning air had given us a healthy appetite; but our spirits sank when the only person at the station, a stupid girl of twenty, dressed in the same bulging, hideous sack, informed us that nothing was to be had. After some persuasion she promised us coffee, cheese, and bread, which came in due time; but with the best will we found it impossible to eat anything. The butter was rather black than yellow, the cheese as detestable to the taste as to the smell, the bread made apparently of saw-dust, with a slight mixture of oat-bran, and the coffee muddy dregs, with some sour cream in a cup, and sugar-candy which appeared to have been sucked and then dropped in the ashes. The original colour of the girl's hands was barely to be distinguished through their coating of dirt; and all of us, tough old travellers as we were, sickened at the sight of her. I verily believe that the poorer classes of the Norwegians are the filthiest people in Europe. They are even worse than the Lapps, for their habits of life allow them to be clean.

After passing Ekre, our view opened down the valley, over a wild stretch of wooded hills, to the blue mountain folds of the Hallingdal, which crosses the Hemsedal almost at right angles, and receives its tributary waters. The forms of the mountains are here more gradual; and those grand sweeps and breaks which constitute the peculiar charms of the scenery of the Bergenstift are met with no longer. We had a hot ride to the next station, where we were obliged to wait nearly an hour in the kitchen, our förbud not having been forwarded from the former station as soon as the law allowed us to expect. A strapping boy of eighteen acted as station master. His trowsers reached considerably above his shoulder blades, leaving barely room for a waistcoat, six inches long, to be buttoned over his collar bone. The characteristic costumes of Norway are more quaint and picturesque in the published illustrations than in the reality, particularly those of Hemsedal. My postillion to this station was a communicative fellow, and gave me some information about the value of labour. A harvest-hand gets from one mark (twenty-one cents) to one and a half daily, with food, or two marks without. Most work is paid by the job; a strong lumber-man may make two and a half marks when the days are long, at six skillings (five cents) a tree—a plowman two marks. In the winter the usual wages of labourers are two marks a week, with board. Shoemakers, tailors, and other mechanics average about the same daily. When one considers the scarcity of good food, and the high price of all luxuries, especially tobacco and brandy, it does not seem strange that the emigration fever should be so prevalent. The Norwegians have two traits in common with a large class of Americans—rampant patriotism and love of gain; but they cannot so easily satisfy the latter without sacrificing the former.

From the village of Göl, with its dark pretty church, we descended a steep of many hundred feet, into Hallingdal, whose broad stream flashed blue in the sunshine far below us. The mountains were now wooded to their very summits; and over the less abrupt slopes, ripe oats and barley-fields made yellow spots of harvest among the dark forests. By this time we were out of smoking material, and stopped at the house of a landhandlare, or country merchant, to procure a supply. A riotous sound came from the door as we approached. Six or eight men, all more or less drunk, and one woman, were inside, singing, jumping, and howling like a pack of Bedlamites. We bought the whole stock of tobacco, consisting of two cigars, and hastened out of the den. The last station of ten miles was down the beautiful Hallingdal, through a country which seemed rich by contrast with Hemsedal and the barren fjeld. Our stopping-place was the village of Næs, which we reached in a famished condition, having eaten nothing all day. There were two landhandlare in the place, with one of whom we lodged. Here we found a few signs of Christianity, such as gardens and decent dresses; but both of the merchant's shops swarmed with rum-drinkers.

I had written, and sent off from Björberg, förbud tickets for every station as far as Kongsberg. By the legal regulations, the skyds-skaffer is obliged to send forward such tickets as soon as received, the traveller paying the cost thereof on his arrival. Notwithstanding we had given our förbud twelve hours' start, and had punctually paid the expense at every station, we overtook it at Næs. The postmaster came to know whether we would have it sent on by special express, or wait until some traveller bound the same way would take it for us. I ordered it to be sent immediately, astounded at such a question, until, making the acquaintance of a Scotchman and his wife, who had arrived in advance of us, the mystery was solved. They had spent the night at the first station beyond Björberg, where our förbud tickets were given to them, with the request that they would deliver them. They had punctually done so as far as Næs, where the people had endeavoured to prevent them from stopping for the night, insisting that they were bound to go on and carry the förbud. The cool impudence of this transaction reached the sublime. At every station that day, pay had been taken for service unperformed, and it was more than once demanded twice over.

We trusted the repeated assurance of the postmaster at Næs, that our tickets had been forwarded at once, and paid him accordingly. But at the first station next morning we found that he had not done so; and this interlinked chain of swindling lasted the whole day. We were obliged to wait an hour or two at every post, to pay for messengers who probably never went, and then to resist a demand for payment at the other end of the station. What redress was there? We might indeed have written a complaint in imperfect Norsk, which would be read by an inspector a month afterwards; or perhaps it would be crossed out as soon as we left, as we saw done in several cases. Unless a traveller is very well versed in the language and in the laws relating to the skyds system, he has no defence against imposition, and even in such a case, he can only obtain redress through delay. The system can only work equitably when the people are honest; and perhaps they were so when it was first adopted.

Here I must tell an unpleasant truth. There must have been some foundation in the beginning for the wide reputation which the Norwegians have for honest simplicity of character; but the accounts given by former travellers are undeserved praise if applied at present. The people are trading on fictitious capital. "Should I have a written contract?" I asked of a landlord, in relation to a man with whom I was making a bargain. "Oh, no," said he, "everybody is honest in Norway;" and the same man tried his best to cheat me. Said Braisted, "I once heard an old sailor say,—'when a man has a reputation for honesty, watch him!'"—and there is some knowledge of human nature in the remark. Norway was a fresh field when Laing went thither opportunities for imposition were so rare, that the faculty had not been developed; he found the people honest, and later travellers have been content with echoing his opinion. "When I first came to the country," said an Irish gentleman who for ten years past has spent his summers there, "I was advised, as I did not understand the currency, to offer a handful in payment, and let the people take what was due to them." "Would you do it now?" I asked. "No, indeed," said he, "and the man who then advised me, a Norwegian merchant, now says he would not do it either." An English salmon-fisher told me very much the same thing. "I believe they are honest in their intercourse with each other," said he; "but they do not scruple to take advantage of travellers whenever they can." For my own part, I must say that in no country of Europe, except Italy, have I experienced so many attempts at imposition. Another Englishman, who has been farming in Norway for several years, and who employs about forty labourers, has been obliged to procure Swedes, on account of the peculations of native hands. I came to Norway with the popular impression concerning the people, and would not confess myself so disagreeably undeceived, could I suppose that my own experiences were exceptional. I found, however, that they tallied with those of other travellers; and the conclusion is too flagrant to be concealed.

As a general rule, I have found the people honest in proportion as they are stupid. They are quick-witted whenever the spirit of gain is aroused; and the ease with which they pick up little arts of acquisitiveness does not suggest an integrity proof against temptation. It is but a negative virtue, rather than that stable quality rooted in the very core of a man's nature. I may, perhaps, judge a little harshly; but when one finds the love of gain so strongly developed, so keen and grasping, in combination with the four capital vices of the Norwegians—indolence, filth, drunkenness, and licentiousness,—the descent to such dishonest arts as I have described is scarcely a single step. There are, no doubt, many districts where the people are still untempted by rich tourists and sportsmen, and retain the virtues once ascribed to the whole population: but that there has been a general and rapid deterioration of character cannot be denied. The statistics of morality, for instance, show that one child out of every ten is illegitimate; and the ratio has been steadily increasing for the past fifty years. Would that the more intelligent classes would seriously set themselves to work for the good of "Gamle Norge" instead of being content with the poetical flourish of her name!

The following day, from Næs to Green, was a continuation of our journey down the Hallingdal. There was little change in the scenery,—high fir-wooded mountains on either hand, the lower slopes spotted with farms. The houses showed some slight improvement as we advanced. The people were all at work in the fields, cutting the year's satisfactory harvest. A scorching sun blazed in a cloudless sky; the earth was baked and dry, and suffocating clouds of dust rose from under our horses' hoofs. Most of the women in the fields, on account of the heat, had pulled off their body-sacks, and were working in shifts made on the same principle, which reached to the knees. Other garments they had none. A few, recognising us as strangers, hastily threw on their sacks or got behind a barley-stack until we had passed; the others were quite unconcerned. One, whose garment was exceedingly short, no sooner saw us than she commenced a fjeld dance, full of astonishing leaps and whirls to the great diversion of the other hands. "Weel done, cutty sark!" I cried; but the quotation was thrown away upon her.

Green, on the Kröder Lake, which we did not reach until long after dark, was an oasis after our previous experience. Such clean, refined, friendly people, such a neat table, such excellent fare, and such delicious beds we had certainly never seen before. Blessed be decency! blessed be humanity! was our fervent ejaculation. And when in the morning we paid an honest reckoning and received a hearty "lycksame resa!" (a lucky journey!) at parting, we vowed that the place should always be green in our memories. Thence to Kongsberg we had fast stations and civilised people; the country was open, well settled, and cultivated, the scenery pleasant and picturesque, and, except the insufferable heat and dust, we could complain of nothing.

CHAPTER XXXIII. TELLEMARK AND THE RIUKAN FOSS.

Kongsberg, where we arrived on the 26th of August, is celebrated for its extensive silver mines, which were first opened by Christian IV in 1624, and are now worked by the Government. They are doubtless interesting to mineralogists; but we did not visit them. The guide-book says, "The principal entrance to the mines is through a level nearly two English miles in length; from this level you descend by thirty-eight perpendicular ladders, of the average length of five fathoms each, a very fatiguing task, and then find yourself at the bottom of the shaft, and are rewarded by the sight of the veins of native silver"—not a bit of which, after all, are you allowed to put into your pocket. Thank you! I prefer remaining above ground, and was content with having in my possession smelted specimens of the ore, stamped with the head of Oscar I.

The goal of our journey was the Riukan Foss, which lies in Upper Tellemark, on the south-eastern edge of the great plateau of the Hardanger Fjeld. This cascade disputes with the Vöring Foss the supremacy of the thousand waterfalls of Norway. There are several ways from Kongsberg thither; and in our ignorance of the country, we suffered ourselves to be guided by the landlord of our hotel. Let no traveller follow our example! The road he recommended was almost impassable for carrioles, and miserably supplied with horses, while that through Hitterdal, by which we returned, is broad, smooth, and excellent. We left on the morning after our arrival, taking a road which led up the valley of the Lauven for some distance, and then struck westward through the hills to a little station called Moen. Here, as the place was rarely visited by travellers, the people were simple, honest, and friendly. Horses could not be had in less than two hours; and my postillion, an intelligent fellow far gone in consumption, proposed taking the same horse to the next station, fifteen miles further. He accepted my offer of increased pay; but another, who appeared to be the owner of the horses, refused, demanding more than double the usual rates. "How is it?" said I, "that you were willing to bring us to Moen for one and a half marks, and will not take us to Bolkesjö for less than five?" "It was my turn," he answered, "to furnish post-horses. I am bound by law to bring you here at the price fixed by the law; but now I can make my own bargain, and I want a price that will leave me some profit." This was reasonable enough; and we finally agreed to retain two of the horses, taking the postmaster's for a third.

The region we now traversed was almost a wilderness. There were grazing-farms in the valley, with a few fields of oats or barley; but these soon ceased, and an interminable forest enclosed us. The road, terribly rough and stony, crossed spurs of the hills, slowly climbing to a wild summit-level, whence we caught glimpses of lakes far below us, and the blue mountain-ranges in the west, with the pyramidal peak of the Gousta Fjeld crowning them. Bolkesjö, which we reached in a little more than two hours, is a small hamlet on the western slope of the mountain, overlooking a wide tract of lake and forest. Most of the inhabitants were away in the harvest-fields; but the skyds-shaffer, a tall powerful fellow, with a grin of ineffable stupidity on his face, came forward as we pulled in our horses on the turfy square between the rows of magazines. "Can we get horses at once?" "Ne-e-ey!" was his drawling answer, accompanied with a still broader grin, as if the thing were a good joke. "How soon?" "In three hours." "But if we pay fast prices?" He hesitated, scratched his head, and drawled, "In a liten stund" (a "short time"), which may mean any time from five minutes to as many hours. "Can we get fresh milk?" "Ne-e-ey!" "Can we get butter?" "Ne-e-ey!" "What can we get?" "Nothing." Fortunately we had foreseen this emergency, and had brought a meal with us from Kongsberg.

We took possession of the kitchen, a spacious and tolerably clean apartment, with ponderous benches against two sides of it, and two bedsteads, as huge and ugly as those of kings, built along the third. Enormous platters of pewter, earthen and stone ware, were ranged on shelves; while a cupboard, fantastically painted, contained the smaller crockery. There was a heavy red and green cornice above the bed, upon which the names of the host and his wife, with the date of their marriage, were painted in yellow letters. The worthy couple lay so high that several steps were necessary to enable them to reach the bed, in which process their eyes encountered words of admonition,

Bayard Taylor

painted upon triangular boards, introduced to strengthen the pillars at the head and foot. One of these inscriptions ran, "This is my bed: here I take my rest in the night, and when morning comes I get up cheerfully and go to work;" and the other, "When thou liest down to sleep think on thy last hour, pray that God will guard thy sleep, and be ready for thy last hour when it comes." On the bottom of the cupboard was a representation of two individuals with chalk-white faces and inky eyes, smoking their pipes and clinking glasses. The same fondness for decorations and inscriptions is seen in all the houses in Tellemark and a great part of Hallingdal. Some of them are thoroughly Chinese in gaudy colour and grotesque design.

In the course of an hour and a half we obtained three strong and spirited stallions, and continued our journey towards the Tind-Sö. During this stage of twelve or thirteen miles, the quality of our carrioles was tested in the most satisfactory manner. Up-hill and down, over stock and stone, jolted on rock and wrenched in gulley, they were whirled at a smashing rate; but the tough ash and firmly-welded iron resisted every shock. For any other than Norwegian horses and vehicles, it would have been hazardous travelling. We were anxious to retain the same animals for the remaining stage to Tinoset, at the foot of the lake; but the postillions refused, and a further delay of two hours was the consequence. It was dark when the new horses came; and ten miles of forest lay before us. We were ferried one by one across the Tind Elv, on a weak, loose raft and got our carrioles up a frightful bank on the opposite side by miraculous luck. Fortunately we struck the post-road from Hitterdal at this place; for it would have been impossible to ride over such rocky by-ways as we had left behind us. A white streak was all that was visible in the gloom of the forest. We kept in the middle of it, not knowing whether the road went up, down, or on a level, until we had gone over it. At last, however, the forest came to an end, and we saw Tind Lake lying still and black in the starlight. All were in bed at Tinoset; but we went into the common sleeping-room, and stirred the people up promiscuously until we found the housewife, who gave us the only supper the house afforded—hard oaten bread and milk. We three then made the most of two small beds.

In the morning we took a boat, with four oarsmen, for Mael, at the

283

mouth of the Westfjord-dal, in which lies the Riukan Foss. There was no end to our wonderful weather. In rainy Norway the sky had for once forgotten its clouds. One after another dawned the bright Egyptian days, followed by nights soft, starry, and dewless. The wooded shores of the long Tind Lake were illuminated with perfect sunshine, and its mirror of translucent beryl broke into light waves under the northern breeze. Yet, with every advantage of sun and air, I found this lake undeserving of its reputation for picturesque beauty. The highest peaks rise to the height of 2000 feet, but there is nothing bold and decided in their forms, and after the splendid fjords of the western coast the scenery appears tame and commonplace. Our boatmen pulled well, and by noon brought us to Hakenaes, a distance of twenty-one miles. Here we stopped to engage horses to the Riukan Foss, as there is no post-station at Mael. While the old man put off in his boat to notify the farmers whose turn it was to supply the animals, we entered the farm-house, a substantial two-story building. The rooms were tolerably clean and well stocked with the clumsy, heavy furniture of the country, which is mostly made by the farmers themselves, every man being his own carpenter, cooper, and blacksmith. There were some odd old stools, made of segments of the trunk of a tree, the upper part hollowed out so as to receive the body, and form a support for the back. I have no doubt that this fashion of seat is as old as the time of the Vikings. The owner was evidently a man in tolerable circumstances, and we therefore cherished the hope of getting a good meal; but all that the old woman, with the best will in the world, was able to furnish, was milk, butter, oaten bread, and an egg apiece. The upper rooms were all supplied with beds, one of which displayed remarkable portraits of the Crown Prince of Denmark and his spouse, upon the head-board. In another room was a loom of primitive construction.

It was nearly two hours before the old farmer returned with the information that the horses would be at Mael as soon as we; but we lay upon the bank for some time after arriving there, watching the postillions swim them across the mouth of the Maan Elv. Leaving the boat, which was to await our return the next day, we set off up the Westfjord-dal, towards the broad cone-like mass of the Gousta-Fjeld, whose huge bulk, 6000 feet in height, loomed grandly over the valley. The houses of Mael, clustered about its little church, were scattered over the slope above the lake; and across the river, amid the fields of grass and grain, stood another village of equal size. The bed of the valley, dotted with farms and groups of farm-houses, appeared to be thickly populated; but as a farmer's residence rarely consists of less than six buildings—sometimes even eight—a stranger would naturally overrate the number of inhabitants. The production of grain, also, is much less than would be supposed from the amount of land under cultivation, owing to the heads being so light. The valley of the Maan, apparently a rich and populous region, is in reality rather the reverse. In relation to its beauty, however, there can be no two opinions. Deeply sunken between the Gousta and another bold spur of the Hardanger, its golden harvest-fields and groves of birch, ash, and pine seem doubly charming from the contrast of the savage steeps overhanging them, at first scantily feathered with fir-trees, and scarred with the tracks of cataracts and slides, then streaked only with patches of grey moss, and at last bleak and sublimely bare. The deeply-channelled cone of the Gousta, with its indented summit, rose far above us, sharp and clear in the thin ether; but its base, wrapped in forests and wet by many a waterfall—sank into the bed of blue vapour which filled the valley.

There was no Arabian, nor even Byzantine blood in our horses; and our attendants—a stout full-grown farmer and a boy of sixteen—easily kept pace with their slow rough trot. In order to reach Tinoset the next day, we had determined to push on to the Riukan Foss the same evening. Our quarters for the night were to be in the house of the old farmer, Ole Torgensen, in the village of Däl, half-way between Mael and the cataract, which we did not reach until five o'clock, when the sun was already resting his chin on the shoulder of the Gousta. On a turfy slope surrounded with groves, above the pretty little church of Däl, we found Ole's gaard. There was no one at home except the daughter, a blooming lass of twenty, whose neat dress, and graceful, friendly deportment, after the hideous feminines of Hallingdal, in their ungirdled sacks and shifts, so charmed us that if we had been younger, more sentimental, and less experienced in such matters, I should not answer for the consequences. She ushered us into the guests' room, which was neatness itself, set before us a bottle of Bavarian beer and promised to have a supper ready on our return.

There were still ten miles to the Riukan, and consequently no time to be lost. The valley contracted, squeezing the Maan between the interlocking bases of the mountains, through which, in the course of uncounted centuries, it had worn itself a deep groove, cut straight and clean into the heart of the rock. The loud, perpetual roar of the vexed waters filled the glen; the only sound except the bleating of goats clinging to the steep pastures above us. The mountain walls on either hand were now so high and precipitous, that the bed of the valley lay wholly in shadow; and on looking back, its further foldings were dimly seen through purple mist. Only the peak of the Gousta, which from this point appeared an entire and perfect pyramid, 1500 feet in perpendicular height above the mountain platform from which it rose, gleamed with a rich bronze lustre in the setting sun. The valley was now a mere ascending gorge, along the sides of which our road climbed. Before us extended a slanting shelf thrust out from the mountain, and affording room for a few cottages and fields; but all else was naked rock and ragged pine. From one of the huts we passed, a crippled, distorted form crawled out on its hands and knees to beg of us. It was a boy of sixteen, struck with another and scarcely less frightful form of leprosy. In this case, instead of hideous swellings and fungous excrescences, the limbs gradually dry up and drop off piecemeal at the joints. Well may the victims of both these forms of hopeless disease curse the hour in which they were begotten. I know of no more awful example of that visitation of the sins of the parents upon the children, which almost always attends confirmed drunkenness, filth, and licentiousness.

When we reached the little hamlet on the shelf of the mountain, the last rays of the sun were playing on the summits above. We had mounted about 2000 feet since leaving the Tind Lake, and the dusky valley yawned far beneath us, its termination invisible, as if leading downward into a lower world. Many hundreds of feet below the edge of the wild little platform on which we stood, thundered the Maan in a cleft, the bottom of which the sun has never beheld. Beyond this the path was impracticable for horses; we walked, climbed, or scrambled along the side of the dizzy steep, where, in many places, a false step would have sent us to the brink of gulfs whose mysteries we had no desire to explore. After we had advanced nearly two miles in this manner, ascending rapidly all the time, a hollow reverberation, and a glimpse of profounder abysses ahead, revealed the neighbourhood of the Riukan. All at once patches of lurid gloom appeared through the openings of the birch thicket we were threading, and we came abruptly upon the brink of the great chasm into which the river falls.

The Riukan lay before us, a miracle of sprayey splendour, an apparition of unearthly loveliness, set in a framework of darkness and terror befitting the jaws of hell. Before us, so high against the sky as to shut out the colours of sunset, rose the top of the valley—the level of the Hardanger table land, on which, a short distance further, lies the Miös-Vand, a lovely lake, in which the Maan Elv is born. The river first comes into sight a mass of boiling foam, shooting around the corner of a line of black cliffs which are rent for its passage, curves to the right as it descends, and then drops in a single fall of 500 feet in a hollow caldron of bare black rock. The water is already foam as it leaps from the summit; and the successive waves, as they are whirled into the air, and feel the gusts which for ever revolve around the abyss, drop into beaded fringes in falling, and go fluttering down like scarfs of the richest lace. It is not water, but the spirit of water. The bottom is lost in a shifting snowy film, with starry rays of foam radiating from its heart, below which, as the clouds shifts, break momentary gleams of perfect emerald light. What fairy bowers of some Northern Undine are suggested in those sudden flashes of silver and green! In that dim profound, which human eye can but partially explore, in which human foot shall never be set, what secret wonders may still lie hidden! And around this vision of perfect loveliness, rise the awful walls wet with spray which never dries, and crossed by ledges of dazzling turf, from the gulf so far below our feet, until, still further above our heads, they lift their irregular cornices against the sky.

I do not think I am extravagant when I say that the Riukan Foss is the most beautiful cataract in the world. I looked upon it with that involuntary suspension of the breath and quickening of the pulse, which is the surest recognition of beauty. The whole scene, with its breadth and grandeur of form, and its superb gloom of colouring, enshrining this one glorious flash of grace, and brightness, and loveliness, is indelibly impressed upon my mind. Not alone during that half hour of fading sunset, but day after day, and night after night, the embroidered spray wreaths of the Riukan were falling before me.

We turned away reluctantly at last, when the emerald pavement of Undine's palace was no longer visible through the shooting meteors of silver foam. The depths of Westfjord-dal were filled with purple darkness: only the perfect pyramid of the Gousta, lifted upon a mountain basement more than 4000 feet in height, shone like a colossal wedge of fire against the violet sky. By the time we reached our horses we discovered that we were hungry, and, leaving the attendants to follow at their leisure, we urged the tired animals down the rocky road. The smell of fresh-cut grain and sweet mountain hay filled the cool evening air; darkness crept under the birches and pines, and we no longer met the home-going harvesters. Between nine and ten our horses took the way to a gaard standing a little off the road; but it did not appear to be Ole Torgensen's, so we kept on. In the darkness, however, we began to doubt our memory, and finally turned back again. This time there could be no mistake: it was not Ole Torgensen's. I knocked at various doors, and hallooed loudly, until a sleepy farmer made his appearance, and started us forward again. He kindly offered to accompany us, but we did not think it necessary. Terribly fatigued and hungry, we at last saw a star of promise—the light of Ole's kitchen window. There was a white cloth on the table in the guests' house, and Ole's charming daughter—the Rose of Westfjord-dalen—did not keep us long waiting. Roast mutton, tender as her own heart, potatoes plump as her cheeks, and beer sparkling as her eyes, graced the board; but emptiness, void as our own celibate lives, was there when we arose. In the upper room there were beds, with linen fresh as youth and aromatic as spring; and the peace of a full stomach and a clear conscience descended upon our sleep.

In the morning we prepared for an early return to Mael, as the boatmen were anxious to get back to their barley-fields. I found but one expression in the guests' book—that of satisfaction with Ole Torgensen, and cheerfully added our amen to the previous declarations. Ole's bill proved his honesty, no less than his worthy face. He brightened up on learning that we were Americans. "Why," said he, "there have only been two Americans here before in all my life; and you cannot be a born American, because you speak Norsk so well." "Oh," said I, "I have learned the language in travelling." "Is it possible?" he exclaimed: "then you must have a powerful intellect." "By no means," said I, "it is a very easy thing; I have travelled much, and can speak six other languages." "Now, God help us!" cried he; "seven languages! It is truly wonderful how much comprehension God has given unto man, that he can keep seven languages in his head at one time. Here am I, and I am not a fool; yet I do not see how it would be possible for me to speak anything but Norsk; and when I think of you, it shows me what wonders God has done. Will you not make a mark under your name, in the book, so that I may distinguish you from the other two?" I cheerfully complied, and hereby notify future visitors why my name is italicised in Ole's book.

We bade farewell to the good old man, and rode down the valley of the Maan, through the morning shadow of the Gousta. Our boat was in readiness; and its couch of fir boughs in the stern became a pleasant divan of indolence, after our hard horses and rough roads. We reached Tinoset by one o'clock, but were obliged to wait until four for horses. The only refreshment we could obtain was oaten bread, and weak spruce beer. Off at last, we took the post-road to Hitterdal, a smooth, excellent highway, through interminable forests of fir and pine. Towards the close of the stage, glimpses of a broad, beautiful, and thickly-settled valley glimmered through the woods, and we found ourselves on the edge of a tremendous gully, apparently the bed of an extinct river. The banks on both sides were composed entirely of gravel and huge rounded pebbles, masses of which we loosened at the top, and sent down the sides, gathering as they rolled, until in a cloud of dust they crashed with a sound like thunder upon the loose shingles of the bottom 200 feet below. It was scarcely possible to account for this phenomenon by the action of spring torrents from the melted snow. The immense banks of gravel, which we found to extend for a considerable distance along the northern side of the valley, seemed rather to be the deposit of an ocean-flood.

Hitterdal, with its enclosed fields, its harvests, and groups of picturesque, substantial farm-houses, gave us promise of good quarters for the night; and when our postillions stopped at the door of a prosperous-looking establishment, we congratulated ourselves on our luck. But (—) never whistle until you are out of the woods. The people seemed decidedly not to like the idea of our remaining, but promised to give us supper and beds. They were stupid, but not unfriendly; and our causes of dissatisfaction were, first, that they were so outrageously filthy, and secondly, that they lived so miserably when their means evidently allowed them to do better. The family room, with its two cumbrous bedsteads built against the wall, and indescribably dirty beds, was given up to us, the family betaking themselves to the stable. As they issued thence in the morning, in single garments, we were involuntary observers of their degree of bodily neatness; and the impression was one we would willingly forget. Yet a great painted desk in the room contained, amid many flourishes, the names and character of the host and hostess, as follows:—"Andres Svennogsen Bamble, and Ragnil Thorkilsdatter Bamble, Which These Two Are Respectable People." Over the cupboard, studded with earthen-ware dishes, was an inscription in misspelt Latin: "Solli Deo Glorria." Our supper consisted of boiled potatoes and fried salt pork, which, having seen the respectable hosts, it required considerable courage to eat, although we had not seen the cooking. Fleas darkened the floor; and they, with the fear of something worse, prevented us from sleeping much. We did not ask for coffee in the morning, but, as soon as we could procure horses, drove away hungry and disgusted from Bamble-Kaasa and its respectable inhabitants.

The church of Hitterdal, larger than that of Borgund, dates from about the same period, probably the twelfth century. Its style is similar, although it has not the same horned ornaments upon the roof, and the Byzantine features being simpler, produce a more harmonious effect. It is a charmingly quaint and picturesque building, and the people of the valley are justly proud of it. The interior has been renovated, not in the best style.

Well, to make this very long chapter short, we passed the beautiful falls of the Tind Elv, drove for more than twenty miles over wild piny hills, and then descended to Kongsberg, where Fru Hansen comforted us with a good dinner. The next day we breakfasted in Drammen, and, in baking heat and stifling dust, traversed the civilised country between that city and Christiania. Our Norwegian travel was now at an end; and, as a snobby Englishman once said to me of the Nile, "it is a good thing to have gotten over."

CHAPTER XXXIV. NORWAY AND SWEDEN.

We spent four days in Christiania, after completing our Norwegian travels. The sky was still perfectly clear, and up to the day of our departure no rain fell. Out of sixty days which we had devoted to Norway, only four were rainy—a degree of good fortune which rarely falls to the lot of travellers in the North.

Christiania, from its proximity to the continent, and its character as capital of the country, is sufficiently advanced in the arts of living, to be a pleasant resting-place after the désagrémens and privations of travel in the interior. It has two or three tolerably good and very exorbitant hotels, and some bankers with less than the usual amount of conscience. One of them offered to change some Prussian thalers for my friend, at only ten per cent. less than their current value. The vognmand from whom we purchased our carrioles, endeavoured to evade his bargain, and protested that he had not money enough to repurchase them. I insisted, however, and with such good effect that he finally pulled a roll of notes, amounting to several hundred dollars out of his pocket, and paid me the amount in full. The English travellers whom I met had not fared any better; and one and all of us were obliged to recede from our preconceived ideas of Norwegian character. But enough of an unpleasant theme; I would rather praise than blame, any day, but I can neither praise nor be silent when censure is a part of the truth.

I had a long conversation with a distinguished Norwegian, on the condition of the country people. He differed with me in the opinion that the clergy were to some extent responsible for their filthy and licentious habits, asserting that, though the latter were petits seigneurs, with considerable privileges and powers, the people were jealously suspicious of any attempt to exert an influence upon their lives. But is not this a natural result of the preaching of doctrinal religion, of giving an undue value to external forms and ceremonies? "We have a stubborn people," said my informant; "their excessive self-esteem makes them difficult to manage. Besides, their morals are perhaps better than would be inferred from the statistics. Old habits have been retained, in many districts, which are certainly reprehensible, but which spring from custom rather than depravity. I wish they were less vain and sensitive, since in that case they would improve more rapidly." He stated also that the surprising number of illegitimate births is partly accounted for by the fact that there are a great number of connections which have all the character of marriage except the actual ceremony. This is an affair of considerable cost and show; and many of the poorer people, unable to afford it, live together rather than wait, hoping that a time may come when they will be able to defray the expenses, and legitimate the children who may meanwhile be born. In some cases the parties disagree, the connection is broken off, and each one seeks a new mate. Whatever palliation there may be in particular instances, the moral effect of this custom is unquestionably bad; and the volume of statistics recently published by Herr Sundt, who was appointed by the Storthing to investigate the subject, shows that there is no agricultural population in the world which stands lower in the scale of chastity, than that of Norway.

In the course of our conversation, the gentleman gave an amusing instance of the very sensitiveness which he condemned. I happened, casually, to speak of the Icelandic language. "The Icelandic language!" he exclaimed. "So you also in America call it Icelandic; but you ought to know that it is Norwegian. It is the same language spoken by the Norwegian Vikings who colonised Iceland—the old Norsk, which originated here, and was merely carried thither." "We certainly have some reason," I replied, "seeing that it now only exists in Iceland, and has not been spoken in Norway for centuries; but let me ask why you, speaking Danish, call your language Norsk." "Our language, as written and printed, is certainly pure Danish," said he; "but there is some difference of accent in speaking it." He did not add that this difference is strenuously preserved and even increased by the Norwegians, that they may not be suspected of speaking Danish, while they resist with equal zeal, any approach to the Swedish. Often, in thoughtlessly speaking of the language as Danish, I have heard the ill-humoured reply, "Our language is not Danish, but Norsk." As well might we say at home, "We speak American, not English."

I had the good fortune to find Professor Munck, the historian of Norway, at home, though on the eve of leaving for Italy. He is one of the few distinguished literary names the country has produced. Holberg the comedian was born in Bergen; but he is generally classed among the Danish authors. In art, however, Norway takes no mean rank, the names of her painters Dahl, Gude, and Tidemand having a European reputation. Professor Munck is about fifty years of age, and a fine specimen of the Viking stock. He speaks English fluently, and I regretted that the shortness of my stay did not allow me to make further drafts on his surplus intelligence. In the Museum of Northern Antiquities, which is small, as compared with that of Copenhagen, but admirably arranged, I made the acquaintance of Professor Keyser, the author of a very interesting work, on the "Religion of Northmen," a translation of which by Mr. Barclay Pennock, appeared in New York, some three years ago.

I was indebted to Professor Munck, for a sight of the Storthing, or National Legislative Assembly, which was then in session. The large hall of the University, a semi-circular room, something like our Senate Chamber, has been given up to its use, until an appropriate building shall be erected. The appearance and conduct of the body strikingly reminded me of one of our State Legislatures. The members were plain, practical-looking men, chosen from all classes, and without any distinguishing mark of dress. The speaker was quite a young man, with a moustache. Schweigaard the first jurist in Norway, was speaking as we entered. The hall is very badly constructed for sound, and I could not understand the drift of his speech, but was exceedingly struck by the dryness of his manner. The Norwegian Constitution has been in operation forty-three years, and its provisions, in most respects so just and liberal, have been most thoroughly and satisfactorily tested. The Swedes and a small conservative party in Norway, would willingly see the powers of the Storthing curtailed a little; but the people now know what they have got, and are further than ever from yielding any part of it. In the house of almost every Norwegian farmer, one sees the constitution, with the facsimile autographs of its signers, framed and conspicuously hung up. The reproach has been made, that it is not an original instrument—that it is merely a translation of the Spanish Constitution of 1812, a copy of the French Constitution of 1791,

&c.; but it is none the worse for that. Its framers at least had the wisdom to produce the right thing at the right time, and by their resolution and determined attitude to change a subject province into a free and independent state: for, carefully guarded as it is, the union with Sweden is only a source of strength and security.

One peculiarity of the Storthing is, that a majority of its members are, and necessarily must be, farmers; whence Norway is sometimes nicknamed the Farmer State. Naturally, they take very good care of their own interests, one of their first steps being to abolish all taxes on landed property; but in other respects I cannot learn that their rule is not as equitable as that of most legislative bodies. Mügge, in his recently published Nordisches Bilderbuch (Northern Picture Book), gives an account of a conversation which he had with a Swedish statesman on this subject. The latter was complaining of the stubbornness and ignorance of the Norwegian farmers. Mügge asked, (the remainder of the dialogue is too good to be omitted):—

"The Storthing, then, consists of a majority of coarse and ignorant people?"

Statesman. "I will not assert that. A certain practical understanding cannot be denied to most of these farmers, and they often bestow on their sons a good education before giving them the charge of the paternal fields. One, therefore, finds in the country many accomplished men: how could there be 700 students in Christiania, if there were not many farmers' sons among them?"

Author. "But does this majority of farmers in the Storthing commit absurdities? does it govern the country badly, burden it with debts or enact unjust laws?"

Statesman. "That cannot exactly be admitted, although this majority naturally gives its own interests the preference, and shapes the government accordingly. The state has no debts; on the contrary, its treasury is full, an abundance of silver, its bank-notes in demand, order everywhere, and, as you see, an increase of prosperity, with a flourishing commerce. Here lies a statement before me, according to which, in the last six months alone, more than a hundred vessels have been launched in different ports."

Author. "The Farmer-Legislature, then, as I remark, takes care of itself, but is niggardly and avaricious when its own interests are not concerned?"

Statesman. "It is a peculiar state of affairs. In very many respects this reproach cannot be made against the farmers. If anything is to be done for science, or for so-called utilitarian objects, they are always ready to give money. If a deserving man is to be assisted, if means are wanted for beneficial purposes, insane asylums, hospitals, schools, and such like institutions, the Council of State is always sure that it will encounter no opposition. On other occasions, however, these lords of the land are as hard and tough as Norwegian pines, and button up their pockets so tight that not a dollar drops out."

Author. "On what occasions?"

Statesman. "Why, you see (shrugging his shoulders), those farmers have not the least comprehension of statesmanship! As soon as there is any talk of appropriations for increasing the army, or the number of officers, or the pay of foreign ministers, or the salaries of high official persons, or anything of that sort, you can't do anything with them."

Author. (To himself.) "God keep them a long time without a comprehension of statesmanship! If I were a member of the Storthing, I would have as thick a head as the rest of them."

On the 5th of September, Braisted and I took passage for Gottenburg, my friend having already gone home by way of Kiel. We had a smooth sea and an agreeable voyage, and awoke the next morning in Sweden. On the day after our arrival, a fire broke out in the suburb of Haga, which consumed thirteen large houses, and turned more than two hundred poor people out of doors. This gave me an opportunity to see how fires are managed here. It was full half an hour after the alarm-bell was rung before the first engine began to play; the water had to be hauled from the canal, and the machine, of a very small and antiquated pattern, contributed little towards stopping the progress of the flames. The intervention of a row of gardens alone saved the whole suburb from destruction. There must have been from six to eight thousand spectators present, scattered all over the rocky knolls which surround Gottenburg. The fields were covered with piles of household furniture and clothing, yet no guard seemed to be necessary for their protection, and the owners showed no concern for their security.

There is a degree of confidence exhibited towards strangers in Sweden, especially in hotels, at post-stations, and on board the inland steamers, which tells well for the general honesty of the people. We went on board the steamer Werner on the morning of the 8th, but first paid our passage two days afterwards, just before reaching Carlstad. An account book hangs up in the cabin, in which each passenger enters the number of meals or other refreshments he has had, makes his own bill and hands over the amount to the stewardess. In posting, the skjutsbonder very often do not know the rates, and take implicitly what the traveller gives them. I have yet to experience the first attempt at imposition in Sweden. The only instances I heard of were related to me by Swedes themselves, a large class of whom make a point of depreciating their own country and character. This habit of detraction is carried to quite as great an extreme as the vanity of the Norwegians, and is the less pardonable vice of the two.

It was a pleasant thing to hear again the musical Swedish tongue, and to exchange the indifference and reserve of Norway for the friendly, genial, courteous manner of Sweden. What I have said about the formality and affectation of manners, and the rigidity of social etiquette, in the chapters relating to Stockholm, was meant to apply especially to the capital. Far be it from me to censure that natural and spontaneous courtesy which is a characteristic of the whole people. The more I see of the Swedes, the more I am convinced that there is no kinder, simpler, and honester people in the world. With a liberal common school system, a fairer representation, and release from the burden of a state church, they would develop rapidly and nobly.

Our voyage from Gottenburg to Carlstad, on the Wener Lake, had but one noteworthy point—the Falls of Trollhätten. Even had I not been fresh from the Riukan-Foss, which was still flashing in my memory, I should have been disappointed in this renowned cataract. It is not a single fall, but four successive descents, within the distance of half a mile, none of them being over twenty feet in perpendicular height. The Toppö Fall is the only one which at all impressed me, and that principally through its remarkable form. The huge mass of the Gotha River, squeezed between two rocks, slides down a plane with an inclination of about 50°, strikes a projecting rock at the bottom, and takes an upward curve, flinging tremendous volumes of spray, or rather broken water, into the air. The bright emerald face of the watery plane is covered with a network of silver threads of shifting spray, and gleams of pale blue and purple light play among the shadows of the rising globes of foam below.

CHAPTER XXXV. A TRAMP THROUGH WERMELAND AND DALECARLIA.

On leaving Carlstad our route lay northward up the valley of the Klar Elv, in the province of Wermeland, and thence over the hills, by way of Westerdal, in Dalecarlia, to the head of the Siljan Lake. The greater part of this region is almost unknown to travellers, and belongs to the poorest and wildest parts of Sweden. We made choice of it for this reason, that we might become acquainted with the people in their true character, and compare them with the same class in Norway. Our heavy luggage had all been sent on to Stockholm, in the charge of an Irish friend, and we retained no more than could be carried easily in two packs, as we anticipated being obliged to perform part of the journey on foot.

It rained in torrents during the day we spent in Carlstad, and some lumber merchants of Gottenburg, who were on their way to Fryxendal, to superintend the getting down of their rafts, predicted that the deluge would last an entire month. There was always a month of rainy weather at this season they said, and we had better give up our proposed journey. We trusted to our combined good luck however, and were not deceived, for, with the exception of two days, we had charming weather during the remainder of our stay in Sweden. Having engaged a two-horse cart for the first post-station, we left Carlstad on the morning of the 11th of September. The clouds were still heavy, but gradually rolled into compacter masses, giving promise of breaking away. The city is built upon a little island at the head of the lake, whence we crossed to the mainland by a strong old bridge. Our road led eastward through a slightly undulating country, where broad woods of fir and birch divided the large, well cultivated farms. The gårds, or mansions, which we passed, with their gardens and ornamental shrubbery, gave evidence of comfort and competence. The people were in the harvest-fields, cutting oats, which they piled upon stakes to dry. Every one we met saluted us courteously, with a cheerful and friendly air, which was all the more agreeable by contrast with the Norwegian reserve.

At the station, Prestegård, we procured a good breakfast of ham, eggs, and potatoes, and engaged two carts to take us further. We now turned northward over a lovely rolling country, watered with frequent streams,—a land of soft outlines, of woods and swelling knolls, to which the stately old houses gave an expression of contentment and household happiness. At Deye we left our carts, shouldered our packs, and trudged off on foot up the valley of the Klar Elv, which is here a broad lazy stream, filled with tens of thousands of pine-logs, waiting to be carried down to the Wener by the first freshet. The scenery charmed us by its rich and quiet beauty; it was without grand or striking features, but gently undulating, peaceful, and home-like. We found walking very fatiguing in the hot sun, which blazed upon us all the afternoon with a summer heat. The handsome residences and gardens, which we occasionally passed, gave evidence of taste and refinement in their possessors, and there was a pleasant grace in the courteous greetings of the country people whom we met. Towards evening we reached a post-station, and were tired enough to take horses again. It was after dark before we drew up at Ohlsäter, in the heart of Wermeland. Here we found a neat, comfortable room, with clean beds, and procured a supper of superb potatoes. The landlord was a tall, handsome fellow, whose friendly manners, and frank face, breathing honesty and kindness in every lineament, quite won my heart. Were there more such persons in the world, it would be a pleasanter place of residence.

We took horses and bone-shattering carts in the morning, for a distance of thirteen miles up the valley of the Klar Elv. The country was very picturesque and beautiful, well cultivated, and quite thickly settled. The wood in the sheltered bed of the valley was of remarkably fine growth; the birch trees were the largest I ever saw, some of them being over one hundred feet in height. Comfortable residences, with orchards and well-kept gardens attached, were quite frequent, and large sawmills along the river, which in some places was entirely concealed by floating rafts of lumber, gave an air of industry and animation to the landscape. In one place the road was spanned, for a considerable distance, with triumphal arches of foliage. I inquired the meaning of this display of the boy who accompanied us. "Why," said he, "there was a wedding a week ago, at the herregård (gentleman's residence); the young Herr got married, and these arches were put up for him and his bride." The herregård, which we passed soon afterwards, was an imposing mansion, upon an eminence overlooking the valley. Beside it was a jernbruk, or iron-works, from which a tramway, some miles in length, led to the mines.

Resuming our knapsacks, we walked on up the valley. The hills on either side increased in height, and gloomed darkly under a threatening sky. The aspect of the country gradually became wilder, though, wherever there was cultivation, it bore the same evidence of thrift and prosperity. After a steady walk of four hours, we reached the village of Råda, where our road left the beautiful Klar Elv, and struck northwards towards Westerdal, in Dalecarlia. We procured a dinner of potatoes and bacon, with excellent ale, enjoying, meanwhile, a lovely view over a lake to the eastward, which stretched away for ten miles between the wooded hills. The evening was cold and raw: we drove through pine-woods, around the head of the lake, and by six o'clock reached Asplund, a miserable little hamlet on a dreary hill. The post-station was a forlorn cottage with a single room, not of the most inviting appearance. I asked if we could get quarters for the night. "If you will stay, of course you can," said the occupant, an old woman; "but there is no bed, and I can get you horses directly to go on." It was a distance of thirteen miles to the next station, but we yielded to the old woman's hint, and set forward. The road led through woods, which seemed interminable. We were jammed together into a little two-wheeled cart, with the boy between our knees. He seemed much disinclined to hurry the horse, but soon fell asleep, and one of us held him by the collar to prevent his tumbling out, while the other took the lines, and urged on our slow beast. The night was so dark that we had great difficulty in keeping the road, but towards eleven o'clock we emerged from the woods, and found, by shaking the boy, that we were approaching the station at last. This was a little place called Laggasen, on the northern frontier of Wermeland.

Everybody had gone to bed in the hut at which we stopped. We entered the kitchen, which was at the same time the bedroom, and aroused the inmates, who consisted of a lonely woman, with two or three children. She got up in a very scanty chemise, lit a wooden splinter, and inspected us, and, in answer to our demand for a bed, informed us that we would have to lie upon the floor. We were about to do this, when she said we could get good quarters at the Nore, on the top of the hill. Her earnestness in persuading us to go made me suspect that she merely wanted to get rid of us, and I insisted that she should accompany us to show the way. After some hesitation she consented, and we set out. We first crossed a broad swamp, on a road made of loose logs, then climbed a hill, and trudged for some distance across stubble-fields, until my patience was quite worn out, and Braisted made use of some powerful maritime expressions. Finally, we reached a house, which we entered without more ado. The close, stifling atmosphere, and the sound of hard breathing on all sides, showed us that a whole family had been for some hours asleep there. Our guide thumped on the door, and hailed, and at length somebody awoke. "Can you give two travellers a bed?" she asked. "No," was the comfortable reply, followed by the yell of an aroused baby and the noises of the older children. We retreated at once, and opened a battery of reproaches on the old woman for having brought us on a fool's errand. "There is Ohlsen's," she replied, very quietly, "I think I can get you a bed there." Whereupon we entered another house in the same unceremonious manner, but with a better result. A plump, good-natured housewife jumped out of bed, went to an opposite door, and thumped upon it. "Lars!" she cried, "come out of that this minute!" As we entered, with a torch of dry fir, Lars, who proved to be a middle-aged man, got out of bed sleepily, picked up his clothes and marched off. The hostess then brought clean sheets and pillow-cases, and by midnight we were sweetly and blissfully stowed away together in the place vacated by poor Lars.

Nothing could exceed the kindness and courtesy of the good people in the morning. The hostess brought us coffee, and her son went off to get us a horse and cart. She would make no charge, as we had had so little, she said, and was quite grateful for the moderate sum I gave her. We had a wild road over hills, covered with pine forests, through the breaks in which we now and then caught a glimpse of a long lake to the westward, shining with a steel-blue gleam in the morning sun. There were but few clearings along the road, and miles frequently intervened without a sign of human habitation. We met, however, with great numbers of travellers, mostly farmers, with laden hay-carts. It was Sunday morning, and I could not help contrasting these people with those we had seen on the same day three weeks previous whilst crossing the Fille Fjeld. Here, every one had evidently been washed and combed: the men wore clean shirts and stockings, and the women chemises of snowy whiteness under their gay boddices. They were mostly Dalecarlians, in the picturesque costume of the province. We entered Dalecarlia on this stage, and the frank fresh faces of these people, their unmistakable expression of honesty and integrity, and the hearty cordiality of their greetings, welcomed us delightfully to the storied ground of Sweden.

Towards noon we reached the village of Tyngsjö, a little settlement buried in the heart of the wild woods. A mile or two of the southern slope of a hill had been cleared away, and over this a number of dark wooden farmhouses were scattered, with oats and potato-fields around them. An odd little church stood in midst, and the rich swell of a hymn, sung by sweet Swedish voices, floated to us over the fields as we drove up to the post-station. The master, a tall, slender man, with yellow locks falling upon his shoulders, and a face which might be trusted with millions, welcomed us with a fine antique courtesy, and at once sent off for horses. In a little while three farmers came, saluting us gracefully, and standing bareheaded while they spoke to us. One of them, who wore a dark brown jacket and knee-breeches, with a clean white shirt and stockings, had a strikingly beautiful head. The face was a perfect oval, the eyes large and dark, and the jet-black hair, parted on the forehead, fell in silky waves upon his shoulders. He was as handsome and graceful as one of Vandyk's cavaliers, and showed the born gentleman in his demeanour. He proposed that we should take one horse, as it could be gotten without delay, while two (which the law obliged us to take and pay for, if the farmers chose), would have detained us an hour. As the women were in church, the postmaster himself cooked us some freshly-dug potatoes, which, with excellent butter, he set before us. "I have a kind of ale," said he, "which is called porter; if you will try it, perhaps you will like it." It was, in reality, so good, that we took a second bottle with us for refreshment on the road. When I asked how much we should pay, he said: "I don't think you should pay anything, there was so little." "Well," said I, "It is worth at least half a rigsdaler." "Oh, but that may be too much," he answered, hesitatingly.

Our postillion was a fine handsome fellow, so rosy and robust that it made one feel stronger and healthier to sit beside him. He did not spare the horse, which was a big, capable animal, and we rolled along through endless forests of fir and pine as rapidly as the sandy road would allow. After we had gone about eight miles he left us, taking a shorter footpath through the woods. We guessed at our proper direction, sometimes taking the wrong road, but finally, after two hours or more, emerged from the woods into Westerdal, one of the two great valleys from which Dalecarlia (Dalarne, or The Dales) takes its name. The day was magnificent, clear, and with a cold north-east wind, resembling the latter part of October at home. The broad, level valley, with its fields and clustered villages, lay before us in the pale, cold autumnal sunshine, with low blue hills bounding it in the distance. We met many parties in carts, either returning from church, or on their way to visit neighbours. All were in brilliant Sunday costume, the men in blue jackets and knee-breeches, with vests of red or some other brilliant colour, and the women with gay embroidered boddices, white sleeves, and striped petticoats of blue, red, brown, and purple, and scarlet stockings. Some of them wore, in addition, an outer jacket of snowy sheepskin, with elaborate ornamental stitch-work on the back. Their faces were as frank and cheerful as their dresses were tidy, and they all greeted us with that spontaneous goodness of heart which recognises a brother in every man. We had again taken a wrong road, and a merry party carefully set us right again, one old lady even proposing to leave her friends and accompany us, for fear we should go astray again.

We crossed the Westerdal by a floating bridge, and towards sunset reached the inn of Rågsveden, our destination. It was a farmer's gård, standing a little distance off the road. An entrance through one of the buildings, closed with double doors, admitted us into the courtyard, a hollow square, surrounded with two story wooden dwellings, painted dark red. There seemed to be no one at home, but after knocking and calling for a time an old man made his appearance. He was in his second childhood, but knew enough to usher us into the kitchen and ask us to wait for the landlord's arrival. After half an hour our postillion arrived with four or five men in their gayest and trimmest costume, the landlord among them. They immediately asked who and what we were, and we were then obliged to give them an account of all our travels. Their questions were shrewd and intelligent, and their manner of asking, coupled as it was with their native courtesy, showed an earnest desire for information, which we were most willing to gratify. By and by the hostess came, and we were ushered into a very pleasant room, with two beds, and furnished with a supper of fresh meat, potatoes, and mead. The landlord and two or three of the neighbours sat with us before the fire until we were too sleepy to answer any more questions. A more naturally independent and manly bearing I have never seen than that of our host. He was a tall, powerful man, of middle age, with very handsome features, which were softened but not weakened in expression by his long blond hair, parted on his forehead. He had the proper pride which belongs to the consciousness of worth, and has no kinship with empty vanity. "We have come to Dalecarlia to see the descendants of the people who gave Gustavus Vasa his throne," said I, curious to see whether he would betray any signs of flattered pride. His blue eye flashed a little, as he sat with his hands clasped over one knee, gazing at the fire, a light flush ran over his temples—but he said nothing. Some time ago a proposition was made to place a portrait of Gustavus Vasa in the church at Mora. "No," said the Dalecarlians, "we will not have it: we do not need any picture to remind us of what our fathers have done."

The landlady was a little woman, who confessed to being forty-nine years old, although she did not appear to be more than forty. "I have had a great deal of headache," said she, "and I look much older than I am." Her teeth were superb, as were those of all the women we saw. I do not suppose a tooth-brush is known in the valley; yet the teeth one sees are perfect pearls. The use of so much sour milk is said to preserve them. There was a younger person in the house, whom we took to be a girl of sixteen, but who proved to be the son's wife, a woman of twenty-six, and the mother of two or three children. The Dalecarlians marry young when they are able, but even in opposite cases they rarely commit any violation of the laws of morality. Instances are frequent, I was told, where a man and woman, unable to defray the expense of marriage, live together for years in a state of mutual chastity, until they have saved a sum sufficient to enable them to assume the responsibilities of married life. I know there is no honester, and I doubt whether there is a purer, people on the earth than these Dalecarlians.

We awoke to another glorious autumnal day. The valley was white with frost in the morning, and the air deliciously keen and cold; but after sunrise heavy white vapours arose from the spangled grass, and the day gradually grew milder. I was amused at the naïve curiosity of the landlady and her daughter-in-law, who came into our room very early, that they might see the make of our garments and our manner of dressing. As they did not appear to be conscious of any impropriety, we did not think it necessary to feel embarrassed. Our Lapland journey had taught us habits of self-possession under such trying circumstances. We had coffee, paid an absurdly small sum for our entertainment, and took a cordial leave of the good people. A boy of fifteen, whose eyes, teeth and complexion kept my admiration on the stretch during the whole stage, drove us through unbroken woods to Skamhed, ten miles further down the valley. Here the inn was a little one story hut, miserable to behold externally, but containing a neat guest's room and moreover, as we discovered in the course of time—a good breakfast. While we were waiting there, a man came up who greeted us in the name of our Lord Jesus Christ, on learning that we came from America. "Are you not afraid to travel so far from home?" he asked: "how could you cross the great sea?" "Oh," I answered, "there is no more danger in one part of the world than another." "Yes," said he, "God is as near on the water as on the land"—unconsciously repeating the last words of Sir Humphrey Gilbert: "Christ walked upon the waves and quieted them, and he walks yet, for them that believe in Him." Hereupon he began repeating some hymns, mingled with texts of Scripture, which process he continued until we became heartily tired. I took him at a venture, for an over-enthusiastic Läsare, or "Reader," the name given to the Swedish dissenters.

We had a station of twenty three miles before us, to the village of Landbobyn, which lies in the wooded wilderness between Osterdal and Westerdal. Our postillion, a fine young fellow of twenty-two, over six feet in height, put on his best blue jacket and knee-breeches, with a leather apron reaching from his shoulders to below his knees. This is an article worn by almost all Dalecarlians for the purpose of saving their clothes while at work, and gives them an awkward and ungraceful air. This fellow, in spite of a little fear at the bare idea, expressed his willingness to go with us all over the world, but the spirit of wandering was evidently so easy to be kindled in him, that I rather discouraged him. We had a monotonous journey of five hours through a forest of pine, fir, and birch, in which deer and elk are frequently met with; while the wolf and the bear haunt its remoter valleys. The ground was but slightly undulating, and the scenery in general was as tame as it was savage.

Landbobyn was a wretched hamlet on the banks of a stream, with a few cleared fields about it. As the sun had not yet set, we determined to push on to Kettbo, eight or ten miles further, and engaged a boy to pilot us through the woods. The post-station was a miserable place, where we found it impossible to get anything to eat. I sat down and talked with the family while our guide recruited himself with a large dish of thick sour milk. "Why do you travel about the earth?" asked his mother: "is it that you may spy out the poverty of the people and see how miserably they live?" "No," said I, "it is that I may become acquainted with the people, whether they are poor or not." "But," she continued, "did you ever see a people poorer than we?" "Often," said I; "because you are contented, and no one can be entirely poor who does not complain." She shook her head with a sad smile and said nothing.

Our guide poled us across the river in a rickety boat, and then plunged into the woods. He was a tall, well grown boy of fifteen or sixteen, with a beautiful oval face, long fair hair parted in the middle and hanging upon his shoulders, and a fine, manly, resolute expression. With his jacket, girdle, knee-breeches, and the high crowned and broad brimmed felt hat he wore, he reminded me strongly of the picture of Gustavus Vasa in his Dalecarlian disguise, in the cathedral of Upsala. He was a splendid walker, and quite put me, old pedestrian as I am, out of countenance. The footpath we followed was terribly rough; we stumbled over stock and stone, leaped fallen trees, crossed swamps on tussocks of spongy moss, and climbed over heaps of granite boulders: yet, while we were panting and exhausted with our exertions to keep pace with him, he walked onward as quietly and easily as if the smoothest meadow turf were under his feet. I was quite puzzled by the speed he kept up on such a hard path, without seeming to put forth any extra strength. At sunset he pointed out some clearings on a hill side over the tree tops, a mile or two ahead, as our destination. Dusk was gathering as we came upon a pretty lake, with a village scattered along its hilly shore. The post-station, however, was beyond it, and after some delay the boy procured a boat and rowed us across. Telling us to go up the hill and we should find the inn, he bade us good bye and set out on his return.

We soon reached a gård, the owner whereof, after satisfying his curiosity concerning us by numerous questions, informed us that the inn was still further. After groping about in the dark for awhile, we found it. The landlord and his wife were sitting before the fire, and seemed, I thought, considerably embarrassed by our arrival. There was no bed, they said, and they had nothing that we could eat; their house was beyond the lake, and they only came over to take charge of the post-station when their turn arrived. We were devoured with hunger and thirst, and told them we should be satisfied with potatoes and a place on the floor. The wife's brother, who came in soon afterwards, was thereupon despatched across the lake to bring coffee for us, and the pleasant good-wife put our potatoes upon the fire to boil. We lit our pipes, meanwhile, and sat before the fire, talking with our host and some neighbours who came in. They had much to ask about America, none of them having ever before seen a native of that country. Their questions related principally to the cost of living, to the value of labour, the price of grain, the climate and productions, and the character of our laws. They informed me that the usual wages in Dalecarlia were 24 skillings (13 cents) a day, and that one tunne (about 480 lbs.) of rye cost 32 rigsdaler ($8.37-1/2). "No doubt you write descriptions of your travels?" asked the landlord. I assented. "And then, perhaps, you make books of them?" he continued: whereupon one of the neighbours asked, "But do you get any money for your books?"

The potatoes were finally done, and they, with some delicious milk, constituted our supper. By this time the brother had returned, bringing with him coffee, a pillow, and a large coverlet made entirely of cat-skins. A deep bed of hay was spread upon the floor, a coarse linen sheet thrown over it, and, with the soft fur covering, we had a sumptuous bed. About midnight we were awakened by an arrival. Two tailors, one of them hump-backed, on their way to Wermeland, came in, with a tall, strong woman as postillion. The fire was rekindled, and every thing which the landlord had extracted from us was repeated to the new comers, together with a very genial criticism upon our personal appearance and character. After an hour or two, more hay was brought in and the two tailors and the postillioness lay down side by side. We had barely got to sleep again, when there was another arrival. "I am the post-girl," said a female voice. Hereupon everybody woke up, and the story of the two foreign travellers was told over again. In the course of the conversation I learned that the girl carried the post twenty English miles once a week, for which she received 24 rigs ($6.25) annually. "It is a hard business," said the hump-backed tailor. "Yes; but I am obliged to do it," answered the girl. After her departure we were not again disturbed, and managed to get some sleep at last.

We all completed our toilettes in the same room, without the least embarrassment; and, with a traveller's curiosity, I may be pardoned for noticing the general bodily cleanliness of my various bed-fellows, especially as the city Swedes are in the habit of saying that the country people are shockingly dirty. We had coffee, and made arrangements with the girl who had brought the tailors to take us back in her cart. Our host would make no charge for the bed, and next to nothing for our fare, so I put a bank-note in the hand of little Pehr, his only child, telling him to take care of it, and spend it wisely when he grew up. The delight of the good people knew no bounds. Pehr must hold up his little mouth to be kissed, again and again; the mother shook us warmly by the hand, and the father harnessed his horse and started with us. May the blessing of God be upon all poor, honest, and contented people!

Our road led between wooded hills to the Siljan-Forss, a large iron-foundry upon a stream which flows into the Siljan Lake. It was a lovely morning, and our postillion who was a woman of good sense and some intelligence, chatted with me the whole way. She was delighted to find that we could so easily make ourselves understood. "When I saw you first in the night," said she, "I thought you must certainly be Swedes. All the foreigners I saw in Stockholm had something dark and cloudy in their countenances, but both of you have shining faces." She questioned me a great deal about the sacred localities of Palestine, and about the state of religion in America. She evidently belonged to the Läsare, who, she stated, were very numerous in Dalecarlia. "It is a shame," said she, "that we poor people are obliged to pay so much for the support of the Church, whether we belong to it or not. Our taxes amount to 40 rigs yearly, ten of which, in Mora parish, go to the priest. They say he has an income of half a rigs every hour of his life. King Oscar wishes to make religion free, and so it ought to be, but the clergy are all against him, and the clergy control the Bondestånd (House of Peasants), and so he can do nothing." The woman was thirty-one years old, and worn with hard labour. I asked her if she was married. "No," she answered, with a deep sigh, looking at the betrothal-ring on her finger. "Ah," she continued, "we are all poor, Sweden is a poor country; we have only iron and timber, not grain, and cotton, and silk, and sugar, like other countries."

As we descended towards the post-station of Vik we caught a glimpse of the Siljan Lake to the south, and the tall tower of Mora Church, far to the eastward. At Vik, where we found the same simple and honest race of people, we parted with the postillioness and with our host of Kettbo, who thanked us again in Pehr's name, as he shook hands for the last time. We now had fast horses, and a fine road over a long wooded hill, which was quite covered with the lingon, or Swedish cranberry. From the further slope we at last looked down upon Mora, at the head of the Siljan Lake, in the midst of a broad and fertile valley. Ten miles to the eastward arose the spire of Orsa, and southward, on an island in the lake, the tall church of Sollerön. "You can see three churches at once," said our postillion with great pride. So we could, and also the large, stately inn of Mora—a most welcome sight to us, after five days on potato diet.

CHAPTER XXXVI. LAST DAYS IN THE NORTH.

Mora, in Dalecarlia, is classic ground. It was here that Gustavus Vasa first harangued the people, and kindled that spark of revolution, which in the end swept the Danes from Sweden. In the cellar of a house which was pointed out to us, on the southern shore of the Siljan Lake, he lay hidden three days; in the barn of Ivan Elfssen he threshed corn, disguised as a peasant; and on the road by which we had travelled from Kettbo, in descending to the lake, we had seen the mounds of stone, heaped over the Danes, who were slain in his first victorious engagement. This district is considered, also, one of the most beautiful in Sweden. It has, indeed, a quiet, tranquil beauty, which gradually grows upon the eye, so that if one is not particularly aroused on first acquaintance, he at least carries away a delightful picture in his memory. But in order to enjoy properly any Swedish landscape whatsoever, one should not be too fresh from Norway.

After dinner we called at the "Parsonage of Mora," which has given Miss Fredrika Bremer the materials for one of her stories of Swedish life.

The Prost, Herr Kjelström, was not at home, but his wife received us with great cordiality, and insisted upon our remaining to tea. The magister——, who called at the same time, gave us some information concerning the porphyry quarries at Elfdal, which we were debating whether we should visit. Very little is doing at present, not more than ten men in all being employed, and in his opinion we would hardly be repaid for the journey thither; so we determined to turn southward again, and gradually make our way to Stockholm. Fru Kjelström was one of the few Swedes I met, who was really an enthusiastic admirer of Tegner; she knew by heart the greater part of his "Frithiof's Saga."

The morning after our arrival in Mora dawned dark and cloudy, with a wailing wind and dashes of rain. There were threats of the equinoctial storm, and we remembered the prediction of the lumber merchants in Carlstad. During the night, however, a little steamer belonging to an iron company arrived, offering us the chance of a passage down the lake to Leksand. While we were waiting on the shore, the magister, who had come to see us depart, gave me some information about the Läsare. He admitted that there were many in Dalecarlia, and said that the policy of persecution, which was practiced against them in the beginning, was now dropped. They were, in general, ignored by the clerical authorities. He looked upon the movement rather as a transient hallucination than as a permanent secession from the Established Church, and seemed to think that it would gradually disappear, if left to itself. He admitted that the king was in favour of religious liberty, but was so guarded in speaking of the subject that I did not ascertain his own views.

We had on board about sixty passengers, mostly peasants from Upper Elfdal, bound on a peddling excursion through Sweden, with packs of articles which they manufacture at home. Their stock consisted mostly of pocket-books, purses, boxes, and various small articles of ornament and use. The little steamer was so well laden with their solid forms that she settled into the mud, and the crew had hard poling to get her off. There was service in Mora Church, and the sound of the organ and choir was heard along the lake. Many friends and relatives of the wandering Elfdalians were on the little wooden pier to bid them adieu. "God's peace be with thee!" was a parting salutation which I heard many times repeated. At last we got fairly clear and paddled off through the sepia-coloured water, watching the softly undulating shores, which soon sank low enough to show the blue, irregular hills in the distant background. Mora spire was the central point in the landscape, and remained visible until we had nearly reached the other end of the lake. The Siljan has a length of about twenty-five miles, with a breadth of from six to ten. The shores are hilly, but only moderately high, except in the neighborhood of Rättvik, where they were bold and beautiful. The soft slopes on either hand were covered with the yellow pillars of the ripe oats, bound to upright stakes to dry. From every village rose a tall midsummer pole, yet laden with the withered garlands of Sweden's fairest festival, and bearing aloft its patriotic symbol, the crossed arrows of Dalecarlia. The threatened storm broke and dispersed as we left Mora, and strong sun-bursts between the clouds flashed across these pastoral pictures.

Soon after we left, a number of the men and women collected together on the after-deck, and commenced singing hymns, which occupation they kept up with untiring fervour during the whole voyage. The young girls were remarkable for weight and solidity of figure, ugliness of face, and sweetness of voice. The clear, ringing tones, with a bell-like purity and delicious timbre, issued without effort from between their thick, beefy lips, and there was such a contrast between sound and substance, that they attracted my attention more than I should have thought possible. Some of the men, who had heard what we were, entered into conversation with us. I soon discovered that they were all Läsare, and one of them, who seemed to exercise a kind of leadership, and who was a man of considerable intelligence, gave me a good deal of information about the sect. They met together privately, he said, to read the New Testament, trusting entirely to its inspired pages for the means of enlightenment as to what was necessary for the salvation of their souls. The clergy stood between them and the Voice of God, who had spoken not to a particular class, but to all mankind. They were liable to a fine of 200 rigs ($52) every time they thus met together, my informant had once been obliged to pay it himself. Nevertheless, he said they were not interfered with so much at present, except that they were obliged to pay tithes, as before. "The king is a good man," he continued, "he means well, and would do us justice if he had the power; but the clergy are all against him, and his own authority is limited. Now they are going to bring the question of religious freedom before the Diet, but we have not the least hope that anything will be done." He also stated—what, indeed, must be evident to every observing traveller—that the doctrines of the Läsare had spread very rapidly, and that their numbers were continually increasing.

The creation of such a powerful dissenting body is a thing that might have been expected. The Church, in Sweden, had become a system of forms and ceremonies. The pure spiritualism of Swedenborg, in the last century, was a natural and gigantic rebound to the opposite extreme, but, from its lofty intellectuality, was unfitted to be the nucleus of a popular protest. Meanwhile, the souls of the people starved on the dry husks which were portioned out to them. They needed genuine nourishment. They are an earnest, reflective race, and the religious element is deeply implanted in their nature. The present movement, so much like Methodism in many particulars, owes its success to the same genial and all-embracing doctrine of an impartial visitation of Divine grace, bringing man into nearer and tenderer relations to his Maker. In a word, it is the democratic, opposed to the aristocratic principle in religion. It is fashionable in Sweden to sneer at the Läsare; their numbers, character, and sincerity are very generally under-estimated. No doubt there is much that is absurd and grotesque in their services; no doubt they run into violent and unchristian extremes, and often merely substitute fanaticism for spiritual apathy; but I believe they will in the end be the instrument of bestowing religious liberty upon Sweden.

There was no end to the desire of these people for knowledge. They overwhelmed us with questions about our country, its government, laws, climate, productions and geographical extent. Next to America, they seemed most interested in Palestine, and considered me as specially favoured by Providence in having beheld Jerusalem. They all complained of the burdens which fall upon a poor man in Sweden, in the shape of government taxes, tithes, and the obligation of supporting a portion of the army, who are distributed through the provinces. Thus Dalecarlia, they informed me, with a population of 132,000, is obliged to maintain 1200 troops. The tax on land corresponded very nearly with the statement made by my female postillion the previous day. Dalecarlia, its mines excepted, is one of the poorest of the Swedish provinces. Many of its inhabitants are obliged to wander forth every summer, either to take service elsewhere, or to dispose of the articles they fabricate at home, in order, after some years of this irregular life, to possess enough to enable them to pass the rest of their days humbly at home. Our fellow-passengers told me of several who had emigrated to America, where they had spent five or six years. They grew home-sick at last, and returned to their chilly hills. But it was not the bleak fir-woods, the oat-fields, or the wooden huts which they missed; it was the truth, the honesty, the manliness, and the loving tenderness which dwell in Dalecarlian hearts.

We had a strong wind abeam, but our little steamer made good progress down the lake. The shores contracted, and the white church of Leksand rose over the dark woods, and between two and three o'clock in the afternoon, we were moored in the Dal River, where it issues from the Siljan. The Elfdal peddlers shouldered their immense packs and set out, bidding us a friendly adieu as we parted. After establishing ourselves in the little inn, where we procured a tolerable dinner, we called upon the Domprost Hvasser, to whom I had a letter from a countryman who made a pedestrian journey through Dalecarlia five years ago. The parsonage was a spacious building near the church, standing upon the brink of a lofty bank overlooking the outflow of the Dal. The Domprost, a hale, stout old man, with something irresistibly hearty and cheering in his manner, gave us both his hands and drew us into the room, on seeing that we were strangers. He then proceeded to read the letter. "Ho!" he exclaimed, "to think that he has remembered me all this time! And he has not forgotten that it was just midsummer when he was here!" Presently he went out, and soon returned with a basket in one hand and some plates in the other, which he placed before us and heaped with fine ripe cherries. "Now it is autumn," said he; "it is no longer midsummer, but we have a little of the summer's fruit left." He presented us to his sister and daughter, and to two handsome young magisters, who assisted him in his parochial duties.

We walked in the garden, which was laid out with some taste along the brow of the hill. A superb drooping birch, eighty feet in height, was the crowning glory of the place. The birch is the characteristic tree of Sweden, as the fir is of Norway, the beech of Denmark, the oak of England and Germany, the chestnut of Italy, and the palm of Esrypt. Of northern trees, there is none more graceful in outline, but in the cold, silvery hue of its foliage, summer can never find her best expression. The parson had a neat little bowling-alley, in a grove of pine, on a projecting spur of the hill. He did not disdain secular recreations; his religion was cheerful and jubilant; he had found something else in the Bible than the Lamentations of Jeremiah. There are so many Christians who—to judge from the settled expression of their faces—suffer under their belief, that it is a comfort to find those who see nothing heretical in the fullest and freest enjoyment of life. There was an apple-tree in the garden which was just bursting into blossoms for the second time. I called the Domprost's attention to it, remarking, in a line from Frithiof's Saga:—"Hösten bjuder sin thron til varen" (Autumn offers his

314

throne to the spring). "What!" he exclaimed in joyful surprise, "do you know Tegnér?" and immediately continued the quotation.

There was no resisting the hospitable persuasions of the family; we were obliged to take supper and spend the evening with them. The daughter and the two magisters sang for us all the characteristic songs of Wermeland and Dalecarlia which they could remember, and I was more than ever charmed with the wild, simple, original character of the native melodies of Sweden. They are mostly in the minor key, and some of them might almost be called monotonous; yet it is monotony, or rather simplicity, in the notation, which sticks to the memory. The longings, the regrets, the fidelity, and the tenderness of the people, find an echo in these airs, which have all the character of improvisations, and rekindle in the heart of the hearer the passions they were intended to relieve.

We at last took leave of the good old man and his friendly household. The night was dark and rainy, and the magisters accompanied us to the inn. In the morning it was raining dismally,—a slow, cold, driving rain, which is the climax of bad weather. We determined, however, to push onward as far as Fahlun, the capital of Dalecarlia, about four Swedish miles distant. Our road was down the valley of the Dal Elv, which we crossed twice on floating bridges, through a very rich, beautiful, and thickly settled country. The hills were here higher and bolder than in Westerdal, dark with forests of fir and pine, and swept south-eastward in long ranges, leaving a broad, open valley for the river to wander in. This valley, from three to five miles in width, was almost entirely covered with enclosed fields, owing to which the road was barred with gates, and our progress was much delayed thereby. The houses were neat and substantial, many of them with gardens and orchards attached, while the unusual number of the barns and granaries gave evidence of a more prosperous state of agriculture than we had seen since leaving the neighborhood of Carlstad. We pressed forward in the rain and raw wind, and reached Fahlun towards evening, just in time to avoid a drenching storm.

Of the celebrated copper-mines of Fahlun, some of which have been worked for 600 years, we saw nothing. We took their magnitude and richness for granted, on the strength of the immense heaps of dross through which we drove on approaching the town, and the desolate appearance of the surrounding country, whose vegetation has been for the most part destroyed by the fumes from the smelting works. In our sore and sodden condition, we were in no humour to go sight seeing, and so sat comfortably by the stove, while the rain beat against the windows, and the darkness fell. The next morning brought us a renewal of the same weather, but we set out bravely in our open cart, and jolted over the muddy roads with such perseverance, that we reached Hedemora at night. The hills diminished in height as we proceeded southward, but the scenery retained its lovely pastoral character. My most prominent recollection of the day's travel, however, is of the number of gates our numb and blue-faced boy-postillions were obliged to jump down and open.

From Hedemora, a journey of two days through the provinces of Westerås and Uppland, brought us to Upsala. After leaving Dalecarlia and crossing the Dal River for the fifth and last time, the country gradually sank into those long, slightly rolling plains, which we had traversed last winter, between Stockholm and Gefle. Here villages were more frequent, but the houses had not the same air of thrift and comfort as in Dalecarlia. The population also changed in character, the faces we now saw being less bright, cheerful, and kindly, and the forms less tall and strongly knit.

We had very fair accommodations, at all the post-stations along the road, and found the people everywhere honest and obliging. Still, I missed the noble simplicity which I had admired so much in the natives of Westerdal, and on the frontier of Wermeland,—the unaffected kindness of heart, which made me look upon every man as a friend.

The large town of Sala, where we spent a night, was filled with fugitives from Upsala, where the cholera was making great ravages. The violence of the disease was over by the time we arrived; but the students, all of whom had left, had not yet returned, and the fine old place had a melancholy air. The first thing we saw on approaching it, was a funeral. Professor Bergfalk, who had remained at his post, and to whom I had letters, most kindly gave me an entire day of his time. I saw the famous Codex argenteus, in the library, the original manuscript of Frithiof's Saga, the journals of Swedenborg and Linnæus, the Botanical Garden, and the tombs of Gustavus Vasa and John III. in the cathedral. But most interesting of all was our drive to Old Upsala, where we climbed upon the mound of Odin, and drank mead out of the silver-mounted drinking horn, from which Bernadotte, Oscar, and the whole royal family of Sweden, are in the habit of drinking when they make a pilgrimage to the burial place of the Scandinavian gods.

A cold, pale, yellow light lay upon the landscape; the towers of Upsala Cathedral, and the massive front of the palace, rose dark against the sky, in the south-west; a chill autumnal wind blew over the plains, and the yellowing foliage of the birch drifted across the mysterious mounds, like those few golden leaves of poetry, which the modern bards of the North have cast upon the grave of the grand, muscular religion of the earlier race. There was no melodious wailing in the wind, like that which proclaimed "Pan is dead!" through the groves of Greece and Ionia; but a cold rustling hiss, as if the serpent of Midgard were exulting over the ruin of Walhalla. But in the stinging, aromatic flood of the amber-coloured mead, I drank to Odin, to Balder, and to Freja.

We reached Stockholm on the 22nd of September, in the midst of a furious gale, accompanied with heavy squalls of snow—the same in which the Russian line-of-battle ship "Lefort," foundered in the Gulf of Finland. In the mild, calm, sunny, autumn days which followed, the beautiful city charmed us more than ever, and I felt half inclined to take back all I had said against the place, during the dismal weather of last spring. The trees in the Djurgård and in the islands of Mälar, were still in full foliage; the Dalecarlian boatwomen plied their crafts in the outer harbour; the little garden under the Norrbro was gay with music and lamps every evening; and the brief and jovial summer life of the Swedes, so near its close, clung to the flying sunshine, that not a moment might be suffered to pass by unenjoyed.

In another week we were standing on the deck of the Prussian steamer "Nagler," threading the rocky archipelago between Stockholm and the open Baltic on our way to Stettin. In leaving the North, after ten months of winter and summer wanderings, and with scarce a hope of returning again, I found myself repeating, over and over again, the farewell of Frithiof:—

"Farväl, J fjällar,

Der äran bor;

J runohällar,

För väldig Thor;

J blåa sjöar,

Jag känt så väl;

J skär och öar,

Farväl, farväl"

THE END.

THE LANDS OF THE SARACEN

TO WASHINGTON IRVING,

This book--the chronicle of my travels through lands once occupied by the Saracens--naturally dedicates itself to you, who, more than any other American author, have revived the traditions, restored the history, and illustrated the character of that brilliant and heroic people. Your cordial encouragement confirmed me in my design of visiting the East, and making myself familiar with Oriental life; and though I bring you now but imperfect returns, I can at least unite with you in admiration of a field so rich in romantic interest, and indulge the hope that I may one day pluck from it fruit instead of blossoms. In Spain, I came upon your track, and I should hesitate to exhibit my own gleanings where you have harvested, were it not for the belief that the rapid sketches I have given will but enhance, by the contrast, the charm of your finished picture.

Bayard Taylor.

PREFACE.

This volume comprises the second portion of a series of travels, of which the "Journey to Central Africa," already published, is the first part. I left home, intending to spend a winter in Africa, and to return during the following summer; but circumstances afterwards occurred, which prolonged my wanderings to nearly two years and a half, and led me to visit many remote and unexplored portions of the globe. To describe this journey in a single work, would embrace too many incongruous elements, to say nothing of its great length, and as it falls naturally into three parts, or episodes, of very distinct character, I have judged it best to group my experiences under three separate heads, merely indicating the links which connect them. This work includes my travels in Palestine, Syria, Asia Minor, Sicily and Spain, and will be followed by a third and concluding volume, containing my adventures in India, China, the Loo-Choo Islands, and Japan. Although many of the letters, contained in this volume, describe beaten tracks of travel, I have always given my own individual impressions, and may claim for them the merit of entire sincerity. The journey from Aleppo to Constantinople, through the heart of Asia Minor, illustrates regions rarely traversed by tourists, and will, no doubt, be new to most of my readers. My aim, throughout the work, has been to give correct pictures of Oriental life and scenery, leaving antiquarian research and speculation to abler hands. The scholar, or the man of science, may complain with reason that I have neglected valuable opportunities for adding something to the stock of human knowledge: but if a few of the many thousands, who can only travel by their firesides, should find my pages answer the purpose of a series of cosmoramic views--should in them behold with a clearer inward eye the hills of Palestine, the sun-gilded minarets of Damascus, or the lonely pine-forests of Phrygia--should feel, by turns, something of the inspiration and the indolence of the Orient--I shall have achieved all I designed, and more than I can justly hope.

New York, *October*, 1854.

Chapter I. Life in a Syrian Quarantine.

Voyage from Alexandria to Beyrout--Landing at Quarantine--The Guardiano--Our Quarters--Our Companions--Famine and Feasting--The Morning--The Holy Man of Timbuctoo--Sunday in Quarantine--Islamism--We are Registered--Love through a Grating--Trumpets--The Mystery Explained--Delights of Quarantine--Oriental vs. American Exaggeration--A Discussion of Politics--Our Release--Beyrout--Preparations for the Pilgrimage.

"The mountains look on Quarantine, And Quarantine looks on the sea."

Quarantine MS.

In Quarantine, Beyrout, *Saturday, April* 17, 1852.

Everybody has heard of Quarantine, but in our favored country there are many untravelled persons who do not precisely know what it is, and who no doubt wonder why it should be such a bugbear to travellers in the Orient. I confess I am still somewhat in the same predicament myself, although I have already been twenty-four hours in Quarantine. But, as a peculiarity of the place is, that one can do nothing, however good a will he has, I propose to set down my experiences each day, hoping that I and my readers may obtain some insight into the nature of Quarantine, before the term of my probation is over.

I left Alexandria on the afternoon of the 14th inst., in company with Mr. Carter Harrison, a fellow-countryman, who had joined me in Cairo, for the tour through Palestine. We had a head wind, and rough sea, and I remained in a torpid state during most of the voyage. There was rain the second night; but, when the clouds cleared away yesterday morning, we were gladdened by the sight of Lebanon, whose summits glittered with streaks of snow. The lower slopes of the mountains were green with fields and forests, and Beyrout, when we ran up to it, seemed buried almost out of sight, in the foliage of its mulberry groves. The town is built along the northern side of a peninsula, which projects about two miles from the main line of the coast, forming a road for vessels. In half an hour after our arrival, several large boats came alongside, and we were told to get our baggage in order and embark for Quarantine. The time necessary to purify a traveller arriving from Egypt from suspicion of the plague, is five days, but the days of arrival and departure are counted, so that the durance amounts to but three full days. The captain of the Osiris mustered the passengers together, and informed them that each one would be obliged to pay six piastres for the transportation of himself and his baggage. Two heavy lighters are now drawn up to the foot of the gangway, but as soon as the first box tumbles into them, the men tumble out. They attach the craft by cables to two smaller boats, in which they sit, to tow the infected loads. We are all sent down together, Jews, Turks, and Christians--a confused pile of men, women, children, and goods. A little boat from the city, in which there are representatives from the two hotels, hovers around us, and cards are thrown to us. The zealous agents wish to supply us immediately with tables, beds, and all other household appliances; but we decline their help until we arrive at the mysterious spot. At last we float off--two lighters full of infected, though respectable, material, towed by oarsmen of most scurvy appearance, but free from every suspicion of taint.

The sea is still rough, the sun is hot, and a fat Jewess becomes sea-sick. An Italian Jew rails at the boatmen ahead, in the Neapolitan patois, for the distance is long, the Quarantine being on the land-side of Beyrout. We see the rows of little yellow houses on the cliff, and with great apparent risk of being swept upon the breakers, are tugged into a small cove, where there is a landing-place. Nobody is there to receive us; the boatmen jump into the water and push the lighters against the stone stairs, while we unload our own baggage. A tin cup filled with sea-water is placed before us, and we each drop six piastres into it--for money, strange as it may seem, is infectious. By this time, the guardianos have had notice of our arrival, and we go up with them to choose our habitations. There are several rows of one-story houses overlooking the sea, each containing two empty rooms, to be had for a hundred piastres; but a square two-story dwelling stands apart from them, and the whole of it may be had for thrice that sum. There are seven Frank prisoners, and we take it for ourselves. But the rooms are bare, the kitchen empty, and we learn the important fact, that Quarantine is durance vile, without even the bread and water. The guardiano says the agents of the hotel are at the gate, and we can order from them whatever we want. Certainly; but at their own price, for we are wholly at their mercy. However, we go down stairs, and the chief officer, who accompanies us, gets into a corner as we pass, and holds a stick before him to keep us off. He is now clean, but if his garments brush against ours, he is lost. The people we meet in the grounds step aside with great respect to let us pass, but if we offer them our hands, no one would dare to touch a finger's tip.

Here is the gate: a double screen of wire, with an interval between, so that contact is impossible. There is a crowd of individuals outside, all anxious to execute commissions. Among them is the agent of the hotel, who proposes to fill our bare rooms with furniture, send us a servant and cook, and charge us the same as if we lodged with him. The bargain is closed at once, and he hurries off to make the arrangements. It is now four o'clock, and the bracing air of the headland gives a terrible appetite to those of us who, like me, have been sea-sick and fasting for forty-eight hours. But there is no food within the Quarantine except a patch of green wheat, and a well in the limestone rock. We two Americans join company with our room-mate, an Alexandrian of Italian parentage, who has come to Beyrout to be married, and make the tour of our territory. There is a path along the cliffs overhanging the sea, with glorious views of Lebanon, up to his snowy top, the pine-forests at his base, and the long cape whereon the city lies at full length, reposing beside the waves. The Mahommedans and Jews, in companies of ten (to save expense), are lodged in the smaller dwellings, where they have already aroused millions of fleas from their state of torpid expectancy. We return, and take a survey of our companions in the pavilion: a French woman, with two ugly and peevish children (one at the breast), in the next room, and three French gentlemen in the other--a merchant, a young man with hair of extraordinary length, and a filateur, or silk-manufacturer, middle-aged and cynical. The first is a gentleman in every sense of the word, the latter endurable, but the young Absalom is my aversion, I am subject to involuntary likings and dislikings, for which I can give no reason, and though the man may be in every way amiable, his presence is very distasteful to me.

We take a pipe of consolation, but it only whets our appetites. We give up our promenade, for exercise is still worse; and at last the sun goes down, and yet no sign of dinner. Our pavilion becomes a Tower of Famine, and the Italian recites Dante. Finally a strange face appears at the door. By Apicius! it is a servant from the hotel, with iron bedsteads, camp-tables, and some large chests, which breathe an odor of the Commissary Department. We go stealthily down to the kitchen, and watch the unpacking. Our dinner is there, sure enough, but alas! it is not yet cooked. Patience is no more; my companion manages to filch a raw onion and a crust of bread, which we share, and roll under our tongues as a sweet morsel, and it gives us strength for another hour. The Greek dragoman and cook, who are sent into Quarantine for our sakes, take compassion on us; the fires are kindled in the cold furnaces; savory steams creep up the stairs; the preparations increase, and finally climax in the rapturous announcement: "Messieurs, dinner is ready." The soup is liquified bliss; the cotelettes d'agneau are cotelettes de bonheur; and as for that broad dish of Syrian larks--Heaven forgive us the regret, that more songs had not been silenced for our sake! The meal is all nectar and ambrosia, and now, filled and contented, we subside into sleep on comfortable couches. So closes the first day of our incarceration.

This morning dawned clear and beautiful. Lebanon, except his snowy crest, was wrapped in the early shadows, but the Mediterranean gleamed like a shield of sapphire, and Beyrout, sculptured against the background of its mulberry groves, was glorified beyond all other cities. The turf around our pavilion fairly blazed with the splendor of the yellow daisies and crimson poppies that stud it. I was satisfied with what I saw, and felt no wish to leave Quarantine to-day. Our Italian friend, however, is more impatient. His betrothed came early to see him, and we were edified by the great alacrity with which he hastened to the grate, to renew his vows at two yards' distance from her. In the meantime, I went down to the Turkish houses, to cultivate the acquaintance of a singular character I met on board the steamer. He is a negro of six feet four, dressed in a long scarlet robe. His name is Mahommed Senoosee, and he is a fakeer, or holy man, from Timbuctoo. He has been two years absent from home, on a pilgrimage to Mecca and Medina, and is now on his way to Jerusalem and Damascus. He has travelled extensively in all parts of Central Africa, from Dar-Fur to Ashantee, and professes to be on good terms with the Sultans of Houssa and Bornou. He has even been in the great kingdom of Waday, which has never been explored by Europeans, and as far south as Iola, the capital of Adamowa. Of the correctness of his narrations I have not the least doubt, as they correspond geographically with all that we know of the interior of Africa. In answer to my question whether a European might safely make the same tour, he replied that there would be no difficulty, provided he was accompanied by a native, and he offered to take me even to Timbuctoo, if I would return with him. He was very curious to obtain information about America, and made notes of all that I told him, in the quaint character used by the Mughrebbins, or Arabs of the West, which has considerable resemblance to the ancient Cufic. He wishes to join company with me for the journey to Jerusalem, and perhaps I shall accept him.

Sunday, April 18.

As Quarantine is a sort of limbo, without the pale of civilized society, we have no church service to-day. We have done the best we could, however, in sending one of the outside dragomen to purchase a Bible, in which we succeeded. He brought us a very handsome copy, printed by the American Bible Society in New York. I tried vainly in Cairo and Alexandria to find a missionary who would supply my heathenish destitution of the Sacred Writings; for I had reached the East through Austria, where they are prohibited, and to travel through Palestine without them, would be like sailing without pilot or compass. It gives a most impressive reality to Solomon's "house of the forest of Lebanon," when you can look up from the page to those very forests and those grand mountains, "excellent with the cedars." Seeing the holy man of Timbuctoo praying with his face towards Mecca, I went down to him, and we conversed for a long time on religious matters. He is tolerably well informed, having read the Books of Moses and the Psalms of David, but, like all Mahommedans, his ideas of religion consist mainly of forms, and its reward is a sensual paradise. The more intelligent of the Moslems give a spiritual interpretation to the nature of the Heaven promised by the Prophet, and I have heard several openly confess their disbelief in the seventy houries and the palaces of pearl and emerald. Shekh Mahommed Senoosee scarcely ever utters a sentence in which is not the word "Allah," and "La illah il' Allah" is repeated at least every five minutes. Those of his class consider that there is a peculiar merit in the repetition of the names and attributes of God. They utterly reject the doctrine of the Trinity, which they believe implies a sort of partnership, or God-firm (to use their own words), and declare that all who accept it are hopelessly damned. To deny Mahomet's prophetship would excite a violent antagonism, and I content myself with making them acknowledge that God is greater than all Prophets or Apostles, and that there is but one God for all the human race. I have never yet encountered that bitter spirit of bigotry which is so frequently ascribed to them; but on the contrary, fully as great a tolerance as they would find exhibited towards them by most of the Christian sects.

This morning a paper was sent to us, on which we were requested to write our names, ages, professions, and places of nativity. We conjectured that we were subjected to the suspicion of political as well as physical taint, but happily this was not the case. I registered myself as a voyageur, the French as negocians and when it came to the woman's turn, Absalom, who is a partisan of female progress, wished to give her the same profession as her husband--a machinist. But she declared that her only profession was that of a "married woman," and she was so inscribed. Her peevish boy rejoiced in the title of "pleuricheur," or "weeper," and the infant as "titeuse," or "sucker." While this was going on, the guardiano of our room came in very mysteriously, and beckoned to my companion, saying that "Mademoiselle was at the gate." But it was the Italian who was wanted, and again, from the little window of our pavilion, we watched his hurried progress over the lawn. No sooner had she departed, than he took his pocket telescope, slowly sweeping the circuit of the bay as she drew nearer and nearer Beyrout. He has succeeded in distinguishing, among the mass of buildings, the top of the house in which she lives, but alas! it is one story too low, and his patient espial has only been rewarded by the sight of some cats promenading on the roof.

I have succeeded in obtaining some further particulars in relation to Quarantine. On the night of our arrival, as we were about getting into our beds, a sudden and horrible gush of brimstone vapor came up stairs, and we all fell to coughing like patients in a pulmonary hospital. The odor increased till we were obliged to open the windows and sit beside them in order to breathe comfortably. This was the preparatory fumigation, in order to remove the ranker seeds of plague, after which the milder symptoms will of themselves vanish in the pure air of the place. Several times a day we are stunned and overwhelmed with the cracked brays of three discordant trumpets, as grating and doleful as the last gasps of a dying donkey. At first I supposed the object of this was to give a greater agitation to the air, and separate and shake down the noxious exhalations we emit; but since I was informed that the soldiers outside would shoot us in case we attempted to escape, I have concluded that the sound is meant to alarm us, and prevent our approaching too near the walls. On inquiring of our guardiano whether the wheat growing within the grounds was subject to Quarantine, he informed me that it did not ecovey infection, and that three old geese, who walked out past the guard with impunity, were free to go and come, as they had never been known to have the plague. Yesterday evening the medical attendant, a Polish physician, came in to inspect us, but he made a very hasty review, looking down on us from the top of a high horse.

Monday, April 19.

Eureka! the whole thing is explained. Talking to day with the guardiano, he happened to mention that he had been three years in Quarantine, keeping watch over infected travellers. "What!" said I, "you have been sick three years." "Oh no," he replied; "I have never been sick at all." "But are not people sick in Quarantine?" "Stafferillah!" he exclaimed; "they are always in better health than the people outside." "What is Quarantine for, then?" I persisted. "What is it for?" he repeated, with a pause of blank amazement at my ignorance, "why, to get money from the travellers!" Indiscreet guardiano! It were better to suppose ourselves under suspicion of the plague, than to have such an explanation of the mystery. Yet, in spite of the unpalatable knowledge, I almost regret that this is our last day in the establishment. The air is so pure and bracing, the views from our windows so magnificent, the colonized branch of the Beyrout Hotel so comfortable, that I am content to enjoy this pleasant idleness--the more pleasant since, being involuntary, it is no weight on the conscience. I look up to the Maronite villages, perched on the slopes of Lebanon, with scarce a wish to climb to them, or turning to the sparkling Mediterranean, view

> "The speronara's sail of snowy hue
>
> Whitening and brightening on that field of blue,"

and have none of that unrest which the sight of a vessel in motion suggests.

To-day my friend from Timbuctoo came up to have another talk. He was curious to know the object of my travels, and as he would not have comprehended the exact truth, I was obliged to convey it to him through the medium of fiction. I informed him that I had been dispatched by the Sultan of my country to obtain information of the countries of Africa; that I wrote in a book accounts of everything I saw, and on my return, would present this book to the Sultan, who would reward me with a high rank--perhaps even that of Grand Vizier. The Orientals deal largely in hyperbole, and scatter numbers and values with the most reckless profusion. The Arabic, like the Hebrew, its sister tongue, and other old original tongues of Man, is a language of roots, and abounds with the boldest metaphors. Now, exaggeration is but the imperfect form of metaphor. The expression is always a splendid amplification of the simple fact. Like skilful archers, in order to hit the mark, they aim above it. When you have once learned his standard of truth, you can readily gauge an Arab's expressions, and regulate your own accordingly. But whenever I have attempted to strike the key-note myself, I generally found that it was below, rather than above, the Oriental pitch.

The Shekh had already informed me that the King of Ashantee, whom he had visited, possessed twenty-four houses full of gold, and that the Sultan of Houssa had seventy thousand horses always standing saddled before his palace, in order that he might take his choice, when he wished to ride out. By this he did not mean that the facts were precisely so, but only that the King was very rich, and the Sultan had a great many horses. In order to give the Shekh an idea of the great wealth and power of the American Nation, I was obliged to adopt the same plan. I told him, therefore, that our country was two years' journey in extent, that the Treasury consisted of four thousand houses filled to the roof with gold, and that two hundred thousand soldiers on horseback kept continual guard around Sultan Fillmore's palace. He received these tremendous statements with the utmost serenity and satisfaction, carefully writing them in his book, together with the name of Sultan Fillmore, whose fame has ere this reached the remote regions of Timbuctoo. The Shekh, moreover, had the desire of visiting England, and wished me to give him a letter to the English Sultan. This rather exceeded my powers, but I wrote a simple certificate explaining who he was, and whence he came, which I sealed with an immense display of wax, and gave him. In return, he wrote his name in my book, in the Mughrebbin character, adding the sentence: "There is no God but God."

This evening the forbidden subject of politics crept into our quiet community, and the result was an explosive contention which drowned even the braying of the agonizing trumpets outside. The gentlemanly Frenchman is a sensible and consistent republican, the old filateur a violent monarchist, while Absalom, as I might have foreseen, is a Red, of the schools of Proudhon and Considerant. The first predicted a Republic in France, the second a Monarchy in America, and the last was in favor of a general and total demolition of all existing systems. Of course, with such elements, anything like a serious discussion was impossible; and, as in most French debates, it ended in a bewildering confusion of cries and gesticulations. In the midst of it, I was struck by the cordiality with which the Monarchist and the Socialist united in their denunciations of England and the English laws. As they sat side by side, pouring out anathemas against "perfide Albion," I could not help exclaiming: "Voilà, comme les extrêmes se rencontrent!" This turned the whole current of their wrath against me, and I was glad to make a hasty retreat.

The physician again visited us to-night, to promise a release to-morrow morning. He looked us all in the faces, to be certain that there were no signs of pestilence, and politely regretted that he could not offer us his hand. The husband of the "married woman" also came, and relieved the other gentlemen from the charge of the "weeper." He was a stout, ruddy Provençal, in a white blouse, and I commiserated him sincerely for having such a disagreeable wife.

To-day, being the last of our imprisonment, we have received many tokens of attention from dragomen, who have sent their papers through the grate to us, to be returned to-morrow after our liberation. They are not very prepossessing specimens of their class, with the exception of Yusef Badra, who brings a recommendation from my friend, Ross Browne. Yusef is a handsome, dashing fellow, with something of the dandy in his dress and air, but he has a fine, clear, sparkling eye, with just enough of the devil in it to make him attractive. I think, however, that, the Greek dragoman, who has been our companion in Quarantine, will carry the day. He is by birth a Boeotian, but now a citizen of Athens, and calls himself François Vitalis. He speaks French, German, and Italian, besides Arabic and Turkish, and as he has been for twelve or fifteen years vibrating between Europe and the East, he must by this time have amassed sufficient experience to answer the needs of rough-and-tumble travellers like ourselves. He has not asked us for the place, which displays so much penetration on his part, that we shall end by offering it to him. Perhaps he is content to rest his claims upon the memory of our first Quarantine dinner. If so, the odors of the cutlets and larks--even of the raw onion, which we remember with tears--shall not plead his cause in vain.

Beyrout (out of Quarantine), *Wednesday, May* 21.

The handsome Greek, Diamanti, one of the proprietors of the "Hotel de Belle Vue," was on hand bright and early yesterday morning, to welcome us out of Quarantine. The gates were thrown wide, and forth we issued between two files of soldiers, rejoicing in our purification. We walked through mulberry orchards to the town, and through its steep and crooked streets to the hotel, which stands beyond, near the extremity of the Cape, or Ras Beyrout. The town is small, but has an active population, and a larger commerce than any other port in Syria. The anchorage, however, is an open road, and in stormy weather it is impossible for a boat to land. There are two picturesque old castles on some rocks near the shore, but they were almost destroyed by the English bombardment in 1841. I noticed two or three granite columns, now used as the lintels of some of the arched ways in the streets, and other fragments of old masonry, the only remains of the ancient Berytus.

Our time, since our release, has been occupied by preparations for the journey to Jerusalem. We have taken François as dragoman, and our mukkairee, or muleteers, are engaged to be in readiness to-morrow morning. I learn that the Druses are in revolt in Djebel Hauaran and parts of the Anti-Lebanon, which will prevent my forming any settled plan for the tour through Palestine and Syria. Up to this time, the country has been considered quite safe, the only robbery this winter having been that of the party of Mr. Degen, of New York, which was plundered near Tiberias. Dr. Robinson left here two weeks ago for Jerusalem, in company with Dr. Eli Smith, of the American Mission at this place.

Chapter II. The Coast of Palestine.

The Pilgrimage Commences--The Muleteers--The Mules--The Donkey--Journey to Sidon--The Foot of Lebanon--Pictures--The Ruins of Tyre--A Wild Morning--The Tyrian Surges--Climbing the Ladder of Tyre--Panorama of the Bay of Acre--The Plain of Esdraelon--Camp in a Garden--Acre--the Shore of the Bay--Haifa--Mount Carmel and its Monastery--A Deserted Coast--The Ruins of Cæsarea--The Scenery of Palestine--We become Robbers--El Haram--Wrecks--the Harbor and Town of Jaffa.

"Along the line of foam, the jewelled chain, The largesse of the ever-giving main."

R. H. Stoddard.

Ramleh, *April* 27, 1852.

We left Beyrout on the morning of the 22d. Our caravan consisted of three horses, three mules, and a donkey, in charge of two men--Dervish, an erect, black-bearded, and most impassive Mussulman, and Mustapha, who is the very picture of patience and good-nature. He was born with a smile on his face, and has never been able to change the expression. They are both masters of their art, and can load a mule with a speed and skill which I would defy any Santa Fé trader to excel. The animals are not less interesting than their masters. Our horses, to be sure, are slow, plodding beasts, with considerable endurance, but little spirit; but the two baggage mules deserve gold medals from the Society for the Promotion of Industry. I can overlook any amount of waywardness in the creatures, in consideration of the steady, persevering energy, the cheerfulness and even enthusiasm with which they perform their duties. They seem to be conscious that they are doing well, and to take a delight in the consciousness. One of them has a band of white shells around his neck, fastened with a tassel and two large blue beads; and you need but look at him to see that he is aware how becoming it is. He thinks it was given to him for good conduct, and is doing his best to merit another. The little donkey is a still more original animal. He is a practical humorist, full of perverse tricks, but all intended for effect, and without a particle of malice. He generally walks behind, running off to one side or the other to crop a mouthful of grass, but no sooner does Dervish attempt to mount him, than he sets off at full gallop, and takes the lead of the caravan. After having performed one of his feats, he turns around with a droll glance at us, as much as to say: "Did you see that?" If we had not been present, most assuredly he would never have done it. I can imagine him, after his return to Beyrout, relating his adventures to a company of fellow-donkeys, who every now and then burst into tremendous brays at some of his irresistible dry sayings.

I persuaded Mr. Harrison to adopt the Oriental costume, which, from five months' wear in Africa, I greatly preferred to the Frank. We therefore rode out of Beyrout as a pair of Syrian Beys, while François, with his belt, sabre, and pistols had much the aspect of a Greek brigand. The road crosses the hill behind the city, between the Forest of Pines and a long tract of red sand-hills next the sea. It was a lovely morning, not too bright and hot, for light, fleecy vapors hung along the sides of Lebanon. Beyond the mulberry orchards, we entered on wild, half-cultivated tracts, covered with a bewildering maze of blossoms. The hill-side and stony shelves of soil overhanging the sea fairly blazed with the brilliant dots of color which were rained upon them. The pink, the broom, the poppy, the speedwell, the lupin, that beautiful variety of the cyclamen, called by the Syrians "deek e-djebel" (cock o' the mountain), and a number of unknown plants dazzled the eye with their profusion, and loaded the air with fragrance as rare as it was unfailing. Here and there, clear, swift rivulets came down from Lebanon, coursing their way between thickets of blooming oleanders. Just before crossing the little river Damoor, François pointed out, on one of the distant heights, the residence of the late Lady Hester Stanhope. During the afternoon we crossed several offshoots of the Lebanon, by paths incredibly steep and stony, and towards evening reached Saïda, the ancient Sidon, where we obtained permission to pitch our tent in a garden. The town is built on a narrow point of land, jutting out from the centre of a bay, or curve in the coast, and contains about five thousand inhabitants. It is a quiet, sleepy sort of a place, and contains nothing of the old Sidon except a few stones and the fragments of a mole, extending into the sea. The fortress in the water, and the Citadel, are remnants of Venitian sway. The clouds gathered after nightfall, and occasionally there was a dash of rain on our tent. But I heard it with the same quiet happiness, as when, in boyhood, sleeping beneath the rafters, I have heard the rain beating all night upon the roof. I breathed the sweet breath of the grasses whereon my carpet was spread, and old Mother Earth, welcoming me back to her bosom, cradled me into calm and refreshing sleep. There is no rest more grateful than that which we take on the turf or the sand, except the rest below it.

We rose in a dark and cloudy morning, and continued our way between fields of barley, completely stained with the bloody hue of the poppy, and meadows turned into golden mosaic by a brilliant yellow daisy. Until noon our road was over a region of alternate meadow land and gentle though stony elevations, making out from Lebanon. We met continually with indications of ancient power and prosperity. The ground was strewn with hewn blocks, and the foundations of buildings remain in many places. Broken sarcophagi lie half-buried in grass, and the gray rocks of the hills are pierced with tombs. The soil, though stony, appeared to be naturally fertile, and the crops of wheat, barley, and lentils were very flourishing. After rounding the promontory which forms the southern boundary of the Gulf of Sidon, we rode for an hour or two over a plain near the sea, and then came down to a valley which ran up among the hills, terminating in a natural amphitheatre. An ancient barrow, or tumulus, nobody knows of whom, stands near the sea. During the day I noticed two charming little pictures. One, a fountain gushing into a broad square basin of masonry, shaded by three branching cypresses. Two Turks sat on its edge, eating their bread and curdled milk, while their horses drank out of the stone trough below. The other, an old Mahommedan, with a green turban and white robe, seated at the foot of a majestic sycamore, over the high bank of a stream that tumbled down its bed of white marble rock to the sea.

The plain back of the narrow, sandy promontory on which the modern Soor is built, is a rich black loam, which a little proper culture would turn into a very garden. It helped me to account for the wealth of ancient Tyre. The approach to the town, along a beach on which the surf broke with a continuous roar, with the wreck of a Greek vessel in the foreground, and a stormy sky behind, was very striking. It was a wild, bleak picture, the white minarets of the town standing out spectrally against the clouds. We rode up the sand-hills, back of the town, and selected a good camping-place among the ruins of Tyre. Near us there was an ancient square building, now used as a cistern, and filled with excellent fresh water. The surf roared tremendously on the rocks, on either hand, and the boom of the more distant breakers came to my ear like the wind in a pine forest. The remains of the ancient sea-wall are still to be traced for the entire circuit of the city, and the heavy surf breaks upon piles of shattered granite columns. Along a sort of mole, protecting an inner harbor on the north side, are great numbers of these columns. I counted fifteen in one group, some of them fine red granite, and some of the marble of Lebanon. The remains of the pharos and the fortresses strengthening the sea-wall, were pointed out by the Syrian who accompanied us as a guide, but his faith was a little stronger than mine. He even showed us the ruins of the jetty built by Alexander, by means of which the ancient city, then insulated by the sea, was taken. The remains of the causeway gradually formed the promontory by which the place is now connected with the main land. These are the principal indications of Tyre above ground, but the guide informed us that the Arabs, in digging among the sand-hills for the stones of the old buildings, which they quarry out and ship to Beyrout, come upon chambers, pillars, arches, and other objects. The Tyrian purple is still furnished by a muscle found upon the coast, but Tyre is now only noted for its tobacco and mill-stones. I saw many of the latter lying in the streets of the town, and an Arab was selling a quantity at auction in the square, as we passed. They are cut out from a species of dark volcanic rock, by the Bedouins of the mountains. There were half a dozen small coasting vessels lying in the road, but the old harbors are entirely destroyed. Isaiah's prophecy is literally fulfilled: "Howl, ye ships of Tarshish; for it is laid waste, so that there is no house, no entering in."

On returning from our ramble we passed the house of the Governor, Daood Agha, who was dispensing justice in regard to a lawsuit then before him. He asked us to stop and take coffee, and received us with much grace and dignity. As we rose to leave, a slave brought me a large bunch of choice flowers from his garden.

We set out from Tyre at an early hour, and rode along the beach around the head of the bay to the Ras-el-Abiad, the ancient Promontorium Album. The morning was wild and cloudy, with gleams of sunshine that flashed out over the dark violet gloom of the sea. The surf was magnificent, rolling up in grand billows, which broke and formed again, till the last of the long, falling fringes of snow slid seething up the sand. Something of ancient power was in their shock and roar, and every great wave that plunged and drew back again, called in its solemn bass: "Where are the ships of Tyre? where are the ships of Tyre?" I looked back on the city, which stood advanced far into the sea, her feet bathed in thunderous spray. By and by the clouds cleared away, the sun came out bold and bright, and our road left the beach for a meadowy plain, crossed by fresh streams, and sown with an inexhaustible wealth of flowers. Through thickets of myrtle and mastic, around which the rue and lavender grew in dense clusters, we reached the foot of the mountain, and began ascending the celebrated Ladder of Tyre. The road is so steep as to resemble a staircase, and climbs along the side of the promontory, hanging over precipices of naked white rock, in some places three hundred feet in height. The mountain is a mass of magnesian limestone, with occasional beds of marble. The surf has worn its foot into hollow caverns, into which the sea rushes with a dull, heavy boom, like distant thunder. The sides are covered with thickets of broom, myrtle, arbutus, ilex, mastic and laurel, overgrown with woodbine, and interspersed with patches of sage, lavender, hyssop, wild thyme, and rue. The whole mountain is a heap of balm; a bundle of sweet spices.

Our horses' hoofs clattered up and down the rounds of the ladder, and we looked our last on Tyre, fading away behind the white hem of the breakers, as we turned the point of the promontory. Another cove of the mountain-coast followed, terminated by the Cape of Nakhura, the northern point of the Bay of Acre. We rode along a stony way between fields of wheat and barley, blotted almost out of sight by showers of scarlet poppies and yellow chrysanthemums. There were frequent ruins: fragments of sarcophagi, foundations of houses, and about half way between the two capes, the mounds of Alexandro-Schœnæ. We stopped at a khan, and breakfasted under a magnificent olive tree, while two boys tended our horses to see that they ate only the edges of the wheat field. Below the house were two large cypresses, and on a little tongue of land the ruins of one of those square towers of the corsairs, which line all this coast. The intense blue of the sea, seen close at hand over a broad field of goldening wheat, formed a dazzling and superb contrast of color. Early in the afternoon we climbed the Ras Nakhura, not so bold and grand, though quite as flowery a steep as the Promontorium Album. We had been jogging half an hour over its uneven summit, when the side suddenly fell away below us, and we saw the whole of the great gulf and plain of Acre, backed by the long ridge of Mount Carmel. Behind the sea, which makes a deep indentation in the line of the coast, extended the plain, bounded on the east, at two leagues' distance, by a range of hills covered with luxuriant olive groves, and still higher, by the distant mountains of Galilee. The fortifications of Acre were visible on a slight promontory near the middle of the Gulf. From our feet the line of foamy surf extended for miles along the red sand-beach, till it finally became like a chalk-mark on the edge of the field of blue.

We rode down the mountain and continued our journey over the plain of Esdraelon--a picture of summer luxuriance and bloom. The waves of wheat and barley rolled away from our path to the distant olive orchards; here the water gushed from a stone fountain and flowed into a turf-girdled pool, around which the Syrian women were washing their garments; there, a garden of orange, lemon, fig, and pomegranate trees in blossom, was a spring of sweet odors, which overflowed the whole land. We rode into some of these forests, for they were no less, and finally pitched our tent in one of them, belonging to the palace of the former Abdallah Pasha, within a mile of Acre. The old Saracen aqueduct, which still conveys water to the town, overhung our tent. For an hour before reaching our destination, we had seen it on the left, crossing the hollows on light stone arches. In one place I counted fifty-eight, and in another one hundred and three of these arches, some of which were fifty feet high. Our camp was a charming place: a nest of deep herbage, under two enormous fig-trees, and surrounded by a balmy grove of orange and citron. It was doubly beautiful when the long line of the aqueduct was lit up by the moon, and the orange trees became mounds of ambrosial darkness.

In the morning we rode to Acre, the fortifications of which have been restored on the land-side. A ponderous double gateway of stone admitted us into the city, through what was once, apparently, the court-yard of a fortress. The streets of the town are narrow, terribly rough, and very dirty, but the bazaars are extensive and well stocked. The principal mosque, whose heavy dome is visible at some distance from the city, is surrounded with a garden, enclosed by a pillared corridor, paved with marble. All the houses of the city are built in the most massive style, of hard gray limestone or marble, and this circumstance alone prevented their complete destruction during the English bombardment in 1841. The marks of the shells are everywhere seen, and the upper parts of the lofty buildings are completely riddled with cannon-balls, some of which remain embedded in the stone. We made a rapid tour of the town on horseback, followed by the curious glances of the people, who were in doubt whether to consider us Turks or Franks. There were a dozen vessels in the harbor, which is considered the best in Syria.

The baggage-mules had gone on, so we galloped after them along the hard beach, around the head of the bay. It was a brilliant morning; a delicious south-eastern breeze came to us over the flowery plain of Esdraelon; the sea on our right shone blue, and purple, and violet-green, and black, as the shadows or sunshine crossed it, and only the long lines of roaring foam, for ever changing in form, did not vary in hue. A fisherman stood on the beach in a statuesque attitude, his handsome bare legs bathed in the frothy swells, a bag of fish hanging from his shoulder, and the large square net, with its sinkers of lead in his right hand, ready for a cast. He had good luck, for the waves brought up plenty of large fish, and cast them at our feet, leaving them to struggle back into the treacherous brine. Between Acre and Haifa we passed six or eight wrecks, mostly of small trading vessels. Some were half buried in sand, some so old and mossy that they were fast rotting away, while a few had been recently hurled there. As we rounded the deep curve of the bay, and approached the line of palm-trees girding the foot of Mount Carmel, Haifa, with its wall and Saracenic town in ruin on the hill above, grew more clear and bright in the sun, while Acre dipped into the blue of the Mediterranean. The town of Haifa, the ancient Caiapha, is small, dirty, and beggarly looking; but it has some commerce, sharing the trade of Acre in the productions of Syria. It was Sunday, and all the Consular flags were flying.

344

It was an unexpected delight to find the American colors in this little Syrian town, flying from one of the tallest poles. The people stared at us as we passed, and I noticed among them many bright Frankish faces, with eyes too clear and gray for Syria. O ye kind brothers of the monastery of Carmel! forgive me if I look to you for an explanation of this phenomenon.

We ascended to Mount Carmel. The path led through a grove of carob trees, from which the beans, known in Germany as St. John's bread, are produced. After this we came into an olive grove at the foot of the mountain, from which long fields of wheat, giving forth a ripe summer smell, flowed down to the shore of the bay. The olive trees were of immense size, and I can well believe, as Fra Carlo informed us, that they were probably planted by the Roman colonists, established there by Titus. The gnarled, veteran boles still send forth vigorous and blossoming boughs. There were all manner of lovely lights and shades chequered over the turf and the winding path we rode. At last we reached the foot of an ascent, steeper than the Ladder of Tyre. As our horses slowly climbed to the Convent of St. Elijah, whence we already saw the French flag floating over the shoulder of the mountain, the view opened grandly to the north and east, revealing the bay and plain of Acre, and the coast as far as Ras Nakhura, from which we first saw Mount Carmel the day previous. The two views are very similar in character, one being the obverse of the other. We reached the Convent--Dayr Mar Elias, as the Arabs call it--at noon, just in time to partake of a bountiful dinner, to which the monks had treated themselves. Fra Carlo, the good Franciscan who receives strangers, showed us the building, and the Grotto of Elijah, which is under the altar of the Convent Church, a small but very handsome structure of Italian marble. The sanctity of the Grotto depends on tradition entirely, as there is no mention in the Bible of Elijah having resided on Carmel, though it was from this mountain that he saw the cloud, "like a man's hand," rising from the sea. The Convent, which is quite new--not yet completed, in fact--is a large, massive building, and has the aspect of a fortress.

As we were to sleep at Tantura, five hours distant, we were obliged to make a short visit, in spite of the invitation of the hospitable Fra Carlo to spend the night there. In the afternoon we passed the ruins of Athlit, a town of the Middle Ages, and the Castel Pellegrino of the Crusaders. Our road now followed the beach, nearly the whole distance to Jaffa, and was in many places, for leagues in extent, a solid layer of white, brown, purple and rosy shells, which cracked and rattled under our horses' feet. Tantura is a poor Arab village, and we had some difficulty in procuring provisions. The people lived in small huts of mud and stones, near the sea. The place had a thievish look, and we deemed it best to be careful in the disposal of our baggage for the night.

In the morning we took the coast again, riding over millions of shells. A line of sandy hills, covered with thickets of myrtle and mastic, shut off the view of the plain and meadows between the sea and the hills of Samaria. After three hours' ride we saw the ruins of ancient Cæsarea, near a small promontory. The road turned away from the sea, and took the wild plain behind, which is completely overgrown with camomile, chrysanthemum and wild shrubs. The ruins of the town are visible at a considerable distance along the coast. The principal remains consist of a massive wall, flanked with pyramidal bastions at regular intervals, and with the traces of gateways, draw-bridges and towers. It was formerly surrounded by a deep moat. Within this space, which may be a quarter of a mile square, are a few fragments of buildings, and toward the sea, some high arches and masses of masonry. The plain around abounds with traces of houses, streets, and court-yards. Cæsarea was one of the Roman colonies, but owed its prosperity principally to Herod. St. Paul passed through it on his way from Macedon to Jerusalem, by the very road we were travelling.

During the day the path struck inland over a vast rolling plain, covered with sage, lavender and other sweet-smelling shrubs, and tenanted by herds of gazelles and flocks of large storks. As we advanced further, the landscape became singularly beautiful. It was a broad, shallow valley, swelling away towards the east into low, rolling hills, far back of which rose the blue line of the mountains--the hill-country of Judea. The soil, where it was ploughed, was the richest vegetable loam. Where it lay fallow it was entirely hidden by a bed of grass and camomile. Here and there great herds of sheep and goats browsed on the herbage. There was a quiet pastoral air about the landscape, a soft serenity in its forms and colors, as if the Hebrew patriarchs still made it their abode. The district is famous for robbers, and we kept our arms in readiness, never suffering the baggage to be out of our sight.

Towards evening, as Mr. H. and myself, with François, were riding in advance of the baggage mules, the former with his gun in his hand, I with a pair of pistols thrust through the folds of my shawl, and François with his long Turkish sabre, we came suddenly upon a lonely Englishman, whose companions were somewhere in the rear. He appeared to be struck with terror on seeing us making towards him, and, turning his horse's head, made an attempt to fly. The animal, however, was restive, and, after a few plunges, refused to move. The traveller gave himself up for lost; his arms dropped by his side; he stared wildly at us, with pale face and eyes opened wide with a look of helpless fright. Restraining with difficulty a shout of laughter, I said to him: "Did you leave Jaffa to-day?" but so completely was his ear the fool of his imagination, that he thought I was speaking Arabic, and made a faint attempt to get out the only word or two of that language which he knew. I then repeated, with as much distinctness as I could command: "Did--you--leave--Jaffa--to-day?" He stammered mechanically, through his chattering teeth, "Y-y-yes!" and we immediately dashed off at a gallop through the bushes. When we last saw him, he was standing as we left him, apparently not yet recovered from the shock.

At the little village of El Haram, where we spent the night, I visited the tomb of Sultan Ali ebn-Aleym, who is now revered as a saint. It is enclosed in a mosque, crowning the top of a hill. I was admitted into the court-yard without hesitation, though, from the porter styling me "Effendi," he probably took me for a Turk. At the entrance to the inner court, I took off my slippers and walked to the tomb of the Sultan--a square heap of white marble, in a small marble enclosure. In one of the niches in the wall, near the tomb, there is a very old iron box, with a slit in the top. The porter informed me that it contained a charm, belonging to Sultan Ali, which was of great use in producing rain in times of drouth.

In the morning we sent our baggage by a short road across the country to this place, and then rode down the beach towards Jaffa. The sun came out bright and hot as we paced along the line of spray, our horses' feet sinking above the fetlocks in pink and purple shells, while the droll sea-crabs scampered away from our path, and the blue gelatinous sea-nettles were tossed before us by the surge. Our view was confined to the sand-hills--sometimes covered with a flood of scarlet poppies--on one hand; and to the blue, surf-fringed sea on the other. The terrible coast was still lined with wrecks, and just before reaching the town, we passed a vessel of some two hundred tons, recently cast ashore, with her strong hull still unbroken. We forded the rapid stream of El Anjeh, which comes down from the Plain of Sharon, the water rising to our saddles. The low promontory in front now broke into towers and white domes, and great masses of heavy walls. The aspect of Jaffa is exceedingly picturesque. It is built on a hill, and the land for many miles around it being low and flat, its topmost houses overlook all the fields of Sharon. The old harbor, protected by a reef of rocks, is on the north side of the town, but is now so sanded up that large vessels cannot enter. A number of small craft were lying close to the shore. The port presented a different scene when the ships of Hiram, King of Tyre, came in with the materials for the Temple of Solomon. There is but one gate on the land side, which is rather strongly fortified. Outside of this there is an open space, which we found filled with venders of oranges and vegetables, camel-men and the like, some vociferating in loud dispute, some given up to silence and smoke, under the shade of the sycamores.

We rode under the heavily arched and towered gateway, and entered the bazaar. The street was crowded, and there was such a confusion of camels, donkeys, and men, that we made our way with difficulty along the only practicable street in the city, to the sea-side, where François pointed out a hole in the wall as the veritable spot where Jonah was cast ashore by the whale. This part of the harbor is the receptacle of all the offal of the town; and I do not wonder that the whale's stomach should have turned on approaching it. The sea-street was filled with merchants and traders, and we were obliged to pick our way between bars of iron, skins of oil, heaps of oranges, and piles of building timber. At last we reached the end, and, as there was no other thoroughfare, returned the same way we went, passed out the gate, and took the road to Ramleh and Jerusalem.

But I hear the voice of François, announcing, "Messieurs, le diner est prêt." We are encamped just beside the pool of Ramleh, and the mongrel children of the town are making a great noise in the meadow below it. Our horses are enjoying their barley; and Mustapha stands at the tent-door tying up his sacks. Dogs are barking and donkeys braying all along the borders of the town, whose filth and dilapidation are happily concealed by the fig and olive gardens which surround it. I have not curiosity enough to visit the Greek and Latin Convents embedded in its foul purlieus, but content myself with gazing from my door upon the blue hills of Palestine, which we must cross to-morrow, on our way to Jerusalem.

Chapter III. From Jaffa to Jerusalem.

The Garden of Jaffa--Breakfast at a Fountain--The Plain of Sharon--The Ruined Mosque of Ramleh--A Judean Landscape--The Streets of Ramleh--Am I in Palestine?--A Heavenly Morning--The Land of Milk and Honey--Entering the Hill-Country--The Pilgrim's Breakfast--The Father of Lies--A Church of the Crusaders--The Agriculture of the Hills--The Valley of Elah--Day-Dreams--The Wilderness--The Approach--We see the Holy City.

--"Through the air sublime,

Over the wilderness and o'er the plain;

Till underneath them fair Jerusalem,

The Holy City, lifted high her towers."

Paradise Regained.

Jerusalem, *Thursday, April* 29, 1852.

Leaving the gate of Jaffa, we rode eastward between delightful gardens of fig, citron, orange, pomegranate and palm. The country for several miles around the city is a complete level--part of the great plain of Sharon--and the gray mass of building crowning the little promontory, is the only landmark seen above the green garden-land, on looking towards the sea. The road was lined with hedges of giant cactus, now in blossom, and shaded occasionally with broad-armed sycamores. The orange trees were in bloom, and at the same time laden down with ripe fruit. The oranges of Jaffa are the finest in Syria, and great numbers of them are sent to Beyrout and other ports further north. The dark foliage of the pomegranate fairly blazed with its heavy scarlet blossoms, and here and there a cluster of roses made good the Scriptural renown of those of Sharon. The road was filled with people, passing to and fro, and several families of Jaffa Jews were having a sort of pic-nic in the choice shady spots.

Ere long we came to a fountain, at a point where two roads met. It was a large square structure of limestone and marble, with a stone trough in front, and a delightful open chamber at the side. The space in front was shaded with immense sycamore trees, to which we tied our horses, and then took our seats in the window above the fountain, where the Greek brought us our breakfast. The water was cool and delicious, as were our Jaffa oranges. It was a charming spot, for as we sat we could look under the boughs of the great trees, and down between the gardens to Jaffa and the Mediterranean. After leaving the gardens, we came upon the great plain of Sharon, on which we could see the husbandmen at work far and near, ploughing and sowing their grain. In some instances, the two operations were made simultaneously, by having a sort of funnel attached to the plough-handle, running into a tube which entered the earth just behind the share. The man held the plough with one hand, while with the other he dropped the requisite quantity of seed through the tube into the furrow. The people are ploughing now for their summer crops, and the wheat and barley which they sowed last winter are already in full head. On other parts of the plain, there were large flocks of sheep and goats, with their attendant shepherds. So ran the rich landscape, broken only by belts of olive trees, to the far hills of Judea.

Riding on over the long, low swells, fragrant with wild thyme and camomile, we saw at last the tower of Ramleh, and down the valley, an hour's ride to the north-east, the minaret of Ludd, the ancient Lydda. Still further, I could see the houses of the village of Sharon, embowered in olives. Ramleh is built along the crest and on the eastern slope of a low hill, and at a distance appears like a stately place, but this impression is immediately dissipated on entering it. West of the town is a large square tower, between eighty and ninety feet in height. We rode up to it through an orchard of ancient olive trees, and over a field of beans. The tower is evidently a minaret, as it is built in the purest Saracenic style, and is surrounded by the ruins of a mosque. I have rarely seen anything more graceful than the ornamental arches of the upper portions. Over the door is a lintel of white marble, with an Arabic inscription. The mosque to which the tower is attached is almost entirely destroyed, and only part of the arches of a corridor around three sides of a court-yard, with the fountain in the centre, still remain. The subterranean cisterns, under the court-yard, amazed me with their extent and magnitude.

They are no less than twenty-four feet deep, and covered by twenty-four vaulted ceilings, each twelve feet square, and resting on massive pillars. The mosque, when entire, must have been one of the finest in Syria.

We clambered over the broken stones cumbering the entrance, and mounted the steps to the very summit. The view reached from Jaffa and the sea to the mountains near Jerusalem, and southward to the plain of Ascalon--a great expanse of grain and grazing land, all blossoming as the rose, and dotted, especially near the mountains, with dark, luxuriant olive-groves. The landscape had something of the green, pastoral beauty of England, except the mountains, which were wholly of Palestine. The shadows of fleecy clouds, drifting slowly from east to west, moved across the landscape, which became every moment softer and fairer in the light of the declining sun.

I did not tarry in Ramleh. The streets are narrow, crooked, and filthy as only an Oriental town can be. The houses have either flat roofs or domes, out of the crevices in which springs a plentiful crop of weeds. Some yellow dogs barked at us as we passed, children in tattered garments stared, and old turbaned heads were raised from the pipe, to guess who the two brown individuals might be, and why they were attended by such a fierce cawass. Passing through the eastern gate, we were gladdened by the sight of our tents, already pitched in the meadow beside the cistern. Dervish had arrived an hour before us, and had everything ready for the sweet lounge of an hour, to which we treat ourselves after a day's ride. I watched the evening fade away over the blue hills before us, and tried to convince myself that I should reach Jerusalem on the morrow. Reason said: "You certainly will!"---but to Faith the Holy City was as far off as ever. Was it possible that I was in Judea? Was this the Holy Land of the Crusades, the soil hallowed by the feet of Christ and his Apostles? I must believe it. Yet it seemed once that if I ever trod that earth, then beneath my feet, there would be thenceforth a consecration in my life, a holy essence, a purer inspiration on the lips, a surer faith in the heart. And because I was not other than I had been, I half doubted whether it was the Palestine of my dreams.

A number of Arab cameleers, who had come with travellers across the Desert from Egypt, were encamped near us. François was suspicious of some of them, and therefore divided the night into three watches, which were kept by himself and our two men. Mustapha was the last, and kept not only himself, but myself, wide awake by his dolorous chants of love and religion. I fell sound asleep at dawn, but was roused before sunrise by François, who wished to start betimes, on account of the rugged road we had to travel. The morning was mild, clear, and balmy, and we were soon packed and in motion. Leaving the baggage to follow, we rode ahead over the fertile fields. The wheat and poppies were glistening with dew, birds sang among the fig-trees, a cool breeze came down from the hollows of the hills, and my blood leaped as nimbly and joyously as a young hart on the mountains of Bether.

Between Ramleh and the hill-country, a distance of about eight miles, is the rolling plain of Arimathea, and this, as well as the greater part of the plain of Sharon, is one of the richest districts in the world. The soil is a dark-brown loam, and, without manure, produces annually superb crops of wheat and barley. We rode for miles through a sea of wheat, waving far and wide over the swells of land. The tobacco in the fields about Ramleh was the most luxuriant I ever saw, and the olive and fig attain a size and lusty strength wholly unknown in Italy. Judea cursed of God! what a misconception, not only of God's mercy and beneficence, but of the actual fact! Give Palestine into Christian hands, and it will again flow with milk and honey. Except some parts of Asia Minor, no portion of the Levant is capable of yielding such a harvest of grain, silk, wool, fruits, oil, and wine. The great disadvantage under which the country labors, is its frequent drouths, but were the soil more generally cultivated, and the old orchards replanted, these would neither be so frequent nor so severe.

We gradually ascended the hills, passing one or two villages, imbedded in groves of olives. In the little valleys, slanting down to the plains, the Arabs were still ploughing and sowing, singing the while an old love-song, with its chorus of "ya, ghazalee! ya, ghazalee!" (oh, gazelle! oh, gazelle!) The valley narrowed, the lowlands behind us spread out broader, and in half an hour more we were threading a narrow pass, between stony hills, overgrown with ilex, myrtle, and dwarf oak. The wild purple rose of Palestine blossomed on all sides, and a fragrant white honeysuckle in some places hung from the rocks. The path was terribly rough, and barely wide enough for two persons on horseback to pass each other. We met a few pilgrims returning from Jerusalem, and a straggling company of armed Turks, who had such a piratical air, that without the solemn asseveration of François that the road was quite safe, I should have felt uneasy about our baggage. Most of the persons we passed were Mussulmen, few of whom gave the customary "Peace be with you!" but once a Syrian Christian saluted me with, "God go with you, O Pilgrim!" For two hours after entering the mountains, there was scarcely a sign of cultivation. The rock was limestone, or marble, lying in horizontal strata, the broken edges of which rose like terraces to the summits. These shelves were so covered with wild shrubs--in some places even with rows of olive trees---that to me they had not the least appearance of that desolation so generally ascribed to them.

In a little dell among the hills there is a small ruined mosque, or chapel (I could not decide which), shaded by a group of magnificent terebinth trees. Several Arabs were resting in its shade, and we hoped to find there the water we were looking for, in order to make breakfast. But it was not to be found, and we climbed nearly to the summit of the first chain of hills, where in a small olive orchard, there was a cistern, filled by the late rains. It belonged to two ragged boys, who brought us an earthen vessel of the water, and then asked, "Shall we bring you milk, O Pilgrims!" I assented, and received a small jug of thick buttermilk, not remarkably clean, but very refreshing. My companion, who had not recovered from his horror at finding that the inhabitants of Ramleh washed themselves in the pool which supplied us and them, refused to touch it. We made but a short rest, for it was now nearly noon, and there were yet many rough miles between us and Jerusalem. We crossed the first chain of mountains, rode a short distance over a stony upland, and then descended into a long cultivated valley, running to the eastward. At the end nearest us appeared the village of Aboo 'l Ghosh (the Father of Lies), which takes its name from a noted Bedouin shekh, who distinguished himself a few years ago by levying contributions on travellers. He obtained a large sum of money in this way, but as he added murder to robbery, and fell upon Turks as well as Christians, he was finally captured, and is now expiating his offences in some mine on the coast of the Black Sea.

Near the bottom of the village there is a large ruined building, now used as a stable by the inhabitants. The interior is divided into a nave and two side-aisles by rows of square pillars, from which spring pointed arches. The door-way is at the side, and is Gothic, with a dash of Saracenic in the ornamental mouldings above it. The large window at the extremity of the nave is remarkable for having round arches, which circumstance, together with the traces of arabesque painted ornaments on the columns, led me to think it might have been a mosque; but Dr. Robinson, who is now here, considers it a Christian church, of the time of the Crusaders. The village of Aboo 'l Ghosh is said to be the site of the birth-place of the Prophet Jeremiah, and I can well imagine it to have been the case. The aspect of the mountain-country to the east and north-east would explain the savage dreariness of his lamentations. The whole valley in which the village stands, as well as another which joins it on the east, is most assiduously cultivated. The stony mountain sides are wrought into terraces, where, in spite of soil which resembles an American turnpike, patches of wheat are growing luxuriantly, and olive trees, centuries old, hold on to the rocks with a clutch as hard and bony as the hand of Death. In the bed of the valley the fig tree thrives, and sometimes the vine and fig grow together, forming the patriarchal arbor of shade familiar to us all. The shoots of the tree are still young and green, but the blossoms of the grape do not yet give forth their goodly savor. I did not hear the voice of the turtle, but a nightingale sang in the briery thickets by the brook side, as we passed along.

Climbing out of this valley, we descended by a stony staircase, as rugged as the Ladder of Tyre, into the Wady Beit-Hanineh. Here were gardens of oranges in blossom, with orchards of quince and apple, overgrown with vines, and the fragrant hawthorn tree, snowy with its bloom. A stone bridge, the only one on the road, crosses the dry bed of a winter stream, and, looking up the glen, I saw the Arab village of Kulonieh, at the entrance of the valley of Elah, glorious with the memories of the shepherd-boy, David. Our road turned off to the right, and commenced ascending a long, dry glen between mountains which grew more sterile the further we went. It was nearly two hours past noon, the sun fiercely hot, and our horses were nigh jaded out with the rough road and our impatient spurring. I began to fancy we could see Jerusalem from the top of the pass, and tried to think of the ancient days of

Judea. But it was in vain. A newer picture shut them out, and banished even the diviner images of Our Saviour and His Disciples. Heathen that I was, I could only think of Godfrey and the Crusaders, toiling up the same path, and the ringing lines of Tasso vibrated constantly in my ear:

> "Ecco apparir Gierusalemm' si vede;
>
> Ecco additar Gierusalemm' si scorge;
>
> Ecco da mille voci unitamente,
>
> Gierusalemme salutar si sente!"

The Palestine of the Bible--the Land of Promise to the Israelites, the land of Miracle and Sacrifice to the Apostles and their followers--still slept in the unattainable distance, under a sky of bluer and more tranquil loveliness than that to whose cloudless vault I looked up. It lay as far and beautiful as it once seemed to the eye of childhood, and the swords of Seraphim kept profane feet from its sacred hills. But these rough rocks around me, these dry, fiery hollows, these thickets of ancient oak and ilex, had heard the trumpets of the Middle Ages, and the clang and clatter of European armor--I could feel and believe that. I entered the ranks; I followed the trumpets and the holy hymns, and waited breathlessly for the moment when every mailed knee should drop in the dust, and every bearded and sunburned cheek be wet with devotional tears.

But when I climbed the last ridge, and looked ahead with a sort of painful suspense, Jerusalem did not appear. We were two thousand feet above the Mediterranean, whose blue we could dimly see far to the west, through notches in the chain of hills. To the north, the mountains were gray, desolate, and awful. Not a shrub or a tree relieved their frightful barrenness. An upland tract, covered with white volcanic rock, lay before us. We met peasants with asses, who looked (to my eyes) as if they had just left Jerusalem. Still forward we urged our horses, and reached a ruined garden, surrounded with hedges of cactus, over which I saw domes and walls in the distance. I drew a long breath and looked at François. He was jogging along without turning his head; he could not have been so indifferent if that was really the city. Presently, we reached another slight rise in the rocky plain. He began to urge his panting horse, and at the same instant we both lashed the spirit into ours, dashed on at a break-neck gallop, round the corner of an old wall on the top of the hill, and lo! the Holy City! Our Greek jerked both pistols from his holsters, and fired them into the air, as we reined up on the steep.

From the descriptions of travellers, I had expected to see in Jerusalem an ordinary modern Turkish town; but that before me, with its walls, fortresses, and domes, was it not still the City of David? I saw the Jerusalem of the New Testament, as I had imagined it. Long lines of walls crowned with a notched parapet and strengthened by towers; a few domes and spires above them; clusters of cypress here and there; this was all that was visible of the city. On either side the hill sloped down to the two deep valleys over which it hangs. On the east, the Mount of Olives, crowned with a chapel and mosque, rose high and steep, but in front, the eye passed directly over the city, to rest far away upon the lofty mountains of Moab, beyond the Dead Sea. The scene was grand in its simplicity. The prominent colors were the purple of those distant mountains, and the hoary gray of the nearer hills. The walls were of the dull yellow of weather-stained marble, and the only trees, the dark cypress and moonlit olive. Now, indeed, for one brief moment, I knew that I was in Palestine; that I saw Mount Olivet and Mount Zion; and--I know not how it was--my sight grew weak, and all objects trembled and wavered in a watery film. Since we arrived, I have looked down upon the city from the Mount of Olives, and up to it from the Valley of Jehosaphat; but I cannot restore the illusion of that first view.

We allowed our horses to walk slowly down the remaining half-mile to the Jaffa gate. An Englishman, with a red silk shawl over his head, was sketching the city, while an Arab held an umbrella over him. Inside the gate we stumbled upon an Italian shop with an Italian sign, and after threading a number of intricate passages under dark archways, and being turned off from one hotel, which was full of travellers, reached another, kept by a converted German Jew, where we found Dr. Robinson and Dr. Ely Smith, who both arrived yesterday. It sounds strange to talk of a hotel in Jerusalem, but the world is progressing, and there are already three. I leave to-morrow for Jericho, the Jordan, and the Dead Sea, and shall have more to say of Jerusalem on my return.

Chapter IV. The Dead Sea and the Jordan River.

Bargaining for a Guard--Departure from Jerusalem--The Hill of Offence--Bethany--The Grotto of Lazarus--The Valley of Fire--Scenery of the Wilderness--The Hills of Engaddi--The shore of the Dead Sea--A Bituminous Bath--Gallop to the Jordan--A watch for Robbers--The Jordan--Baptism--The Plains of Jericho--The Fountain of Elisha--The Mount of Temptation--Return to Jerusalem.

"And the spoiler shall come upon every city, and no city shall escape; the valley also shall perish and the plain shall be destroyed, as the Lord hath spoken."

--Jeremiah, xlviii. 8.

Jerusalem, *May* 1, 1852.

I returned this after noon from an excursion to the Dead Sea, the River Jordan, and the site of Jericho. Owing to the approaching heats, an early visit was deemed desirable, and the shekhs, who have charge of the road, were summoned to meet us on the day after we arrived. There are two of these gentlemen, the Shekh el-Aràb (of the Bedouins), and the Shekh el-Fellaheen (of the peasants, or husbandmen), to whom each traveller is obliged to pay one hundred piastres for an escort. It is, in fact, a sort of compromise, by which the shekhs agree not to rob the traveller, and to protect him against other shekhs. If the road is not actually safe, the Turkish garrison here is a mere farce, but the arrangement is winked at by the Pasha, who, of course, gets his share of the 100,000 piastres which the two scamps yearly levy upon travellers. The shekhs came to our rooms, and after trying to postpone our departure, in order to attach other tourists to the same escort, and thus save a little expense, took half the pay and agreed to be ready the next morning. Unfortunately for my original plan, the Convent of San Saba has been closed within two or three weeks, and no stranger is now admitted. This unusual step was caused by the disorderly conduct of some Frenchmen who visited San Saba. We sent to the Bishop of the Greek Church, asking a simple permission to view the interior of the Convent; but without effect.

We left the city yesterday morning by St. Stephen's Gate, descended to the Valley of Jehosaphat, rode under the stone wall which encloses the supposed Gethsemane, and took a path leading along the Mount of Olives, towards the Hill of Offence, which stands over against the southern end of the city, opposite the mouth of the Vale of Hinnon. Neither of the shekhs made his appearance, but sent in their stead three Arabs, two of whom were mounted and armed with sabres and long guns. Our man, Mustapha, had charge of the baggage-mule, carrying our tent and the provisions for the trip. It was a dull, sultry morning; a dark, leaden haze hung over Jerusalem, and the khamseen, or sirocco-wind, came from the south-west, out of the Arabian Desert. We had again resumed the Oriental costume, but in spite of an ample turban, my face soon began to scorch in the dry heat. From the crest of the Hill of Offence there is a wide view over the heights on both sides of the valley of the Brook Kedron. Their sides are worked into terraces, now green with springing grain, and near the bottom planted with olive and fig trees. The upland ridge or watershed of Palestine is cultivated for a considerable distance around Jerusalem. The soil is light and stony, yet appears to yield a good return for the little labor bestowed upon it.

Crossing the southern flank of Mount Olivet, in half an hour we reached the village of Bethany, hanging on the side of the hill. It is a miserable cluster of Arab huts, with not a building which appears to be more than a century old. The Grotto of Lazarus is here shown, and, of course, we stopped to see it. It belongs to an old Mussulman, who came out of his house with a piece of waxed rope, to light us down. An aperture opens from the roadside into the hill, and there is barely room enough for a person to enter. Descending about twenty steps at a sharp angle, we landed in a small, damp vault, with an opening in the floor, communicating with a short passage below. The vault was undoubtedly excavated for sepulchral purposes, and the bodies were probably deposited (as in many Egyptian tombs) in the pit under it. Our guide, however, pointed to a square mass of masonry in one corner as the tomb of Lazarus, whose body, he informed us, was still walled up there. There was an arch in the side of the vault, once leading to other chambers, but now closed up, and the guide stated that seventy-four Prophets were interred therein. There seems to be no doubt that the present Arab village occupies the site of Bethany; and if it could be proved that this pit existed at the beginning of the Christian Era, and there never had been any other, we might accept it as the tomb of Lazarus. On the crest of a high hill, over against Bethany, is an Arab village on the site of Bethpage.

We descended into the valley of a winter stream, now filled with patches of sparse wheat, just beginning to ripen. The mountains grew more bleak and desolate as we advanced, and as there is a regular descent in the several ranges over which one must pass, the distant hills of the lands of Moab and Ammon were always in sight, rising like a high, blue wall against the sky. The Dead Sea is 4,000 feet below Jerusalem, but the general slope of the intervening district is so regular that from the spires of the city, and the Mount of Olives, one can look down directly upon its waters. This deceived me as to the actual distance, and I could scarcely credit the assertion of our Arab escort, that it would require six hours to reach it. After we had ridden nearly two hours, we left the Jericho road, sending Mustapha and a staunch old Arab direct to our resting-place for the night, in the Valley of the Jordan. The two mounted Bedouins accompanied us across the rugged mountains lying between us and the Dead Sea.

At first, we took the way to the Convent of Mar Saba, following the course of the Brook Kedron down the Wady en-Nar (Valley of Fire). In half an hour more we reached two large tanks, hewn out under the base of a limestone cliff, and nearly filled with rain. The surface was covered with a greenish vegetable scum, and three wild and dirty Arabs of the hills were washing themselves in the principal one. Our Bedouins immediately dismounted and followed their example, and after we had taken some refreshment, we had the satisfaction of filling our water-jug from the same sweet pool. After this, we left the San Saba road, and mounted the height east of the valley. From that point, all signs of cultivation and habitation disappeared. The mountains were grim, bare, and frightfully rugged. The scanty grass, coaxed into life by the winter rains, was already scorched out of all greenness; some bunches of wild sage, gnaphalium, and other hardy aromatic herbs spotted the yellow soil, and in

360

sheltered places the scarlet poppies burned like coals of fire among the rifts of the gray limestone rock. Our track kept along the higher ridges and crests of the hills, between the glens and gorges which sank on either hand to a dizzy depth below, and were so steep as to be almost inaccessible. The region is so scarred, gashed and torn, that no work of man's hand can save it from perpetual desolation. It is a wilderness more hopeless than the Desert. If I were left alone in the midst of it, I should lie down and await death, without thought or hope of rescue.

The character of the day was peculiarly suited to enhance the impression of such scenery. Though there were no clouds, the sun was invisible: as far as we could see, beyond the Jordan, and away southward to the mountains of Moab and the cliffs of Engaddi, the whole country was covered as with the smoke of a furnace; and the furious sirocco, that threatened to topple us down the gulfs yawning on either hand, had no coolness on its wings. The horses were sure-footed, but now and then a gust would come that made them and us strain against it, to avoid being dashed against the rock on one side, or hurled off the brink on the other. The atmosphere was painfully oppressive, and by and by a dogged silence took possession of our party. After passing a lofty peak which François called Djebel Nuttar, the Mountain of Rain, we came to a large Moslem building, situated on a bleak eminence, overlooking part of the valley of the Jordan. This is the tomb called Nebbee Moussa by the Arabs, and believed by them to stand upon the spot where Moses died. We halted at the gate, but no one came to admit us, though my companion thought he saw a man's head at one of the apertures in the wall. Arab tradition here is as much at fault as Christian tradition in many other places. The true Nebo is somewhere in the chain of Pisgah; and though, probably, I saw it, and all see it who go down to the Jordan, yet "no man knoweth its place unto this day."

Beyond Nebbee Moussa, we came out upon the last heights overlooking the Dead Sea, though several miles of low hills remained to be passed. The head of the sea was visible as far as the Ras-el-Feshka on the west; and the hot fountains of Callirhoë on the eastern shore. Farther than this, all was vapor and darkness. The water was a soft, deep purple hue, brightening into blue.

Our road led down what seemed a vast sloping causeway from the mountains, between two ravines, walled by cliffs several hundred feet in height. It gradually flattened into a plain, covered with a white, saline incrustation, and grown with clumps of sour willow, tamarisk, and other shrubs, among which I looked in vain for the osher, or Dead Sea apple. The plants appeared as if smitten with leprosy; but there were some flowers growing almost to the margin of the sea. We reached the shore about 2 P.M. The heat by this time was most severe, and the air so dense as to occasion pains in my ears. The Dead Sea is 1,300 feet below the Mediterranean, and without doubt the lowest part of the earth's surface. I attribute the oppression I felt to this fact and to the sultriness of the day, rather than to any exhalation from the sea itself. François remarked, however, that had the wind--which by this time was veering round to the north-east--blown from the south, we could scarcely have endured it. The sea resembles a great cauldron, sunk between mountains from three to four thousand feet in height; and probably we did not experience more than a tithe of the summer heat.

I proposed a bath, for the sake of experiment, but François endeavored to dissuade us. He had tried it, and nothing could be more disagreeable; we risked getting a fever, and, besides, there were four hours of dangerous travel yet before us. But by this time we were half undressed, and soon were floating on the clear bituminous waves. The beach was fine gravel and shelved gradually down. I kept my turban on my head, and was careful to avoid touching the water with my face. The sea was moderately warm and gratefully soft and soothing to the skin. It was impossible to sink; and even while swimming, the body rose half out of the water. I should think it possible to dive for a short distance, but prefer that some one else would try the experiment. With a log of wood for a pillow, one might sleep as on one of the patent mattresses. The taste of the water is salty and pungent, and stings the tongue like saltpetre. We were obliged to dress in all haste, without even wiping off the detestable liquid; yet I experienced very little of that discomfort which most travellers have remarked. Where the skin had been previously bruised, there was a slight smarting sensation, and my body felt clammy and glutinous, but the bath was rather refreshing than otherwise.

We turned our horses' heads towards the Jordan, and rode on over a dry, barren plain. The two Bedouins at first dashed ahead at full gallop, uttering cries, and whirling their long guns in the air. The dust they raised was blown in our faces, and contained so much salt that my eyes began to smart painfully. Thereupon I followed them at an equal rate of speed, and we left a long cloud of the accursed soil whirling behind us. Presently, however, they fell to the rear, and continued to keep at some distance from us. The reason of this was soon explained. The path turned eastward, and we already saw a line of dusky green winding through the wilderness. This was the Jordan, and the mountains beyond, the home of robber Arabs, were close at hand. Those robbers frequently cross the river and conceal themselves behind the sand-hills on this side. Our brave escort was, therefore, inclined to put us forward as a forlorn-hope, and secure their own retreat in case of an attack. But as we were all well armed, and had never considered their attendance as anything more than a genteel way of buying them off from robbing us, we allowed them to lag as much as they chose. Finally, as we approached the Pilgrims' Ford, one of them took his station at some distance from the river, on the top of a mound, while the other got behind some trees near at hand; in order, as they said, to watch the opposite hills, and alarm us whenever they should see any of the Beni Sukrs, or the Beni Adwams, or the Tyakh, coming down upon us.

The Jordan at this point will not average more than ten yards in breadth. It flows at the bottom of a gully about fifteen feet deep, which traverses the broad valley in a most tortuous course. The water has a white, clayey hue, and is very swift. The changes of the current have formed islands and beds of soil here and there, which are covered with a dense growth of ash, poplar, willow, and tamarisk trees. The banks of the river are bordered with thickets, now overgrown with wild vines, and fragrant with flowering plants. Birds sing continually in the cool, dark coverts of the trees. I found a singular charm in the wild, lonely, luxuriant banks, the tangled undergrowth, and the rapid, brawling course of the sacred stream, as it slipped in sight and out of sight among the trees. It is almost impossible to reach the water at any other point than the Ford of the Pilgrims, the supposed locality of the passage of the Israelites and the baptism of Christ. The plain near it is still blackened by the camp-fires of the ten thousand pilgrims who went down from Jerusalem three weeks ago, to bathe. We tied our horses to the trees, and prepared to follow their example, which was necessary, if only to wash off the iniquitous slime of the Dead Sea. François, in the meantime, filled two tin flasks from the stream and stowed them in the saddle-bags. The current was so swift, that one could not venture far without the risk of being carried away; but I succeeded in obtaining a complete and most refreshing immersion. The taint of Gomorrah was not entirely washed away, but I rode off with as great a sense of relief as if the baptism had been a moral one, as well, and had purified me from sin.

We rode for nearly two hours, in a north-west direction, to the Bedouin village of Rihah, near the site of ancient Jericho. Before reaching it, the gray salt waste vanishes, and the soil is covered with grass and herbs. The barren character of the first region is evidently owing to deposits from the vapors of the Dead Sea, as they are blown over the plain by the south wind. The channels of streams around Jericho are filled with nebbuk trees, the fruit of which is just ripening. It is apparently indigenous, and grows more luxuriantly than on the White Nile. It is a variety of the rhamnus, and is set down by botanists as the Spina Christi, of which the Saviour's mock crown of thorns was made. I see no reason to doubt this, as the twigs are long and pliant, and armed with small, though most cruel, thorns. I had to pay for gathering some of the fruit, with a torn dress and bleeding fingers. The little apples which it bears are slightly acid and excellent for alleviating thirst. I also noticed on the plain a variety of the nightshade with large berries of a golden color. The spring flowers, so plentiful now in all other parts of Palestine, have already disappeared from the Valley of the Jordan.

Rihah is a vile little village of tents and mud-huts, and the only relic of antiquity near it is a square tower, which may possibly be of the time of Herod. There are a few gardens in the place, and a grove of superb fig-trees. We found our tent already pitched beside a rill which issues from the Fountain of Elisha. The evening was very sultry, and the musquitoes gave us no rest. We purchased some milk from an old man who came to the tent, but such was his mistrust of us that he refused to let us keep the earthen vessel containing it until morning. As we had already paid the money to his son, we would not let him take the milk away until he had brought the money back. He then took a dagger from his waist and threw it before us as security, while he carried off the vessel and returned the price. I have frequently seen the same mistrustful spirit exhibited in Egypt. Our two Bedouins, to whom I gave some tobacco in the evening, manifested their gratitude by stealing the remainder of our stock during the night.

This morning we followed the stream to its source, the Fountain of Elisha, so called as being probably that healed by the Prophet. If so, the healing was scarcely complete. The water, which gushes up strong and free at the foot of a rocky mound, is warm and slightly brackish. It spreads into a shallow pool, shaded by a fine sycamore tree. Just below, there are some remains of old walls on both sides, and the stream goes roaring away through a rank jungle of canes fifteen feet in height. The precise site of Jericho, I believe, has not been fixed, but "the city of the palm trees," as it was called, was probably on the plain, near some mounds which rise behind the Fountain. Here there are occasional traces of foundation walls, but so ruined as to give no clue to the date of their erection. Further towards the mountain there are some arches, which appear to be Saracenic. As we ascended again into the hill-country, I observed several traces of cisterns in the bottoms of ravines, which collect the rains. Herod, as is well known, built many such cisterns near Jericho, where he had a palace. On the first crest, to which we climbed, there is part of a Roman tower yet standing. The view, looking back over the valley of Jordan, is magnificent, extending from the Dead Sea to the mountains of Gilead, beyond the country of Ammon. I thought I could trace the point where the River Yabbok comes down from Mizpeh of Gilead to join the Jordan.

The wilderness we now entered was fully as barren, but less rugged than that through which we passed yesterday. The path ascended along the brink of a deep gorge, at the bottom of which a little stream foamed over the rocks. The high, bleak summits towards which we were climbing, are considered by some Biblical geographers to be Mount Quarantana, the scene of Christ's fasting and temptation. After two hours we reached the ruins of a large khan or hostlery, under one of the peaks, which François stated to be the veritable "high mountain" whence the Devil pointed out all the kingdoms of the earth. There is a cave in the rock beside the road, which the superstitious look upon as the orifice out of which his Satanic Majesty issued. We met large numbers of Arab families, with their flocks, descending from the mountains to take up their summer residence near the Jordan. They were all on foot, except the young children and goats, which were stowed together on the backs of donkeys. The men were armed, and appeared to be of the same tribe as our escort, with whom they had a good understanding.

The morning was cold and cloudy, and we hurried on over the hills to a fountain in the valley of the Brook Kedron, where we breakfasted. Before we had reached Bethany a rain came down, and the sky hung dark and lowering over Jerusalem, as we passed the crest of Mount Olivet. It still rains, and the filthy condition of the city exceeds anything I have seen, even in the Orient.

Chapter V. The City of Christ.

Modern Jerusalem--The Site of the City--Mount Zion--Mount Moriah--The Temple--the Valley of Jehosaphat--The Olives of Gethsemane--The Mount of Olives--Moslem Tradition--Panorama from the Summit--The Interior of the City--The Population--Missions and Missionaries--Christianity in Jerusalem--Intolerance--The Jews of Jerusalem--The Face of Christ--The Church of the Holy Sepulchre--The Holy of Holies--The Sacred Localities--Visions of Christ--The Mosque of Omar--The Holy Man of Timbuctoo--Preparations for Departure.

"Cut off thy hair, O Jerusalem, and cast it away, and take up a lamentation in high places; for the Lord hath rejected and forsaken the generation of his wrath."--Jeremiah vii. 29.

"Here pilgrims roam, that strayed so far to seek

In Golgotha him dead, who lives in Heaven."

Milton.

Jerusalem, *Monday, May* 3, 1852.

Since travel is becoming a necessary part of education, and a journey through the East is no longer attended with personal risk, Jerusalem will soon be as familiar a station on the grand tour as Paris or Naples. The task of describing it is already next to superfluous, so thoroughly has the topography of the city been laid down by the surveys of Robinson and the drawings of Roberts. There is little more left for Biblical research. The few places which can be authenticated are now generally accepted, and the many doubtful ones must always be the subjects of speculation and conjecture. There is no new light which can remove the cloud of uncertainties wherein one continually wanders. Yet, even rejecting all these with the most skeptical spirit, there still remains enough to make the place sacred in the eyes of every follower of Christ. The city stands on the ancient site; the Mount of Olives looks down upon it; the foundations of the Temple of Solomon are on Mount

Moriah; the Pool of Siloam has still a cup of water for those who at noontide go down to the Valley of Jehosaphat; the ancient gate yet looketh towards Damascus, and of the Palace of Herod, there is a tower which Time and Turk and Crusader have spared.

Jerusalem is built on the summit ridge of the hill-country of Palestine, just where it begins to slope eastward. Not half a mile from the Jaffa Gate, the waters run towards the Mediterranean. It is about 2,700 feet above the latter, and 4,000 feet above the Dead Sea, to which the descent is much more abrupt. The hill, or rather group of small mounts, on which Jerusalem stands, slants eastward to the brink of the Valley of Jehosaphat, and the Mount of Olives rises opposite, from the sides and summit of which, one sees the entire city spread out like a map before him. The Valley of Hinnon, the bed of which is on a much higher level than that of Jehosaphat, skirts the south-western and southern part of the walls, and drops into the latter valley at the foot of Mount Zion, the most southern of the mounts. The steep slope at the junction of the two valleys is the site of the city of the Jebusites, the most ancient part of Jerusalem. It is now covered with garden-terraces, the present wall crossing from Mount Zion on the south to Mount Moriah on the east. A little glen, anciently called the Tyropeon, divides the mounts, and winds through to the Damascus Gate, on the north, though from the height of the walls and the position of the city, the depression which it causes in the mass of buildings is not very perceptible, except from the latter point, Moriah is the lowest of the mounts, and hangs directly over the Valley of Jehosaphat. Its summit was built up by Solomon so as to form a quadrangular terrace, five hundred by three hundred yards in dimension. The lower courses of the grand wall, composed of huge blocks of gray conglomerate limestone, still remain, and there seems to be no doubt that they are of the time of Solomon. Some of the stones are of enormous size; I noticed several which were fifteen, and one twenty-two feet in length. The upper part of the wall was restored by Sultan Selim, the conqueror of Egypt, and the level of the terrace now supports the great Mosque of Omar, which stands on the very site of the temple. Except these foundation walls, the Damascus Gate and the Tower of Hippicus, there is nothing left of the ancient city. The length of the present wall of circumference is about two miles, but the circuit of Jerusalem, in the time of Herod, was probably double that distance.

The best views of the city are from the Mount of Olives, and the hill north of it, whence Titus directed the siege which resulted in its total destruction. The Crusaders under Godfrey of Bouillon encamped on the same hill. My first walk after reaching here, was to the summit of the Mount of Olives. Not far from the hotel we came upon the Via Dolorosa, up which, according to Catholic tradition, Christ toiled with the cross upon his shoulders. I found it utterly impossible to imagine that I was walking in the same path, and preferred doubting the tradition. An arch is built across the street at the spot where they say he was shown to the populace. (Ecce Homo.) The passage is steep and rough, descending to St. Stephen's Gate by the Governor's Palace, which stands on the site of the house of Pontius Pilate. Here, in the wall forming the northern part of the foundation of the temple, there are some very fine remains of ancient workmanship. From the city wall, the ground descends abruptly to the Valley of Jehosaphat. The Turkish residents have their tombs on the city side, just under the terrace of the mosque, while thousands of Jews find a peculiar beatitude in having themselves interred on the opposite slope of the Mount of Olives, which is in some places quite covered with their crumbling tombstones. The bed of the Brook Kedron is now dry and stony. A sort of chapel, built in the bottom of the valley, is supposed by the Greeks to cover the tomb of the Virgin--a claim which the Latins consider absurd. Near this, at the very foot of the Mount of Olives, the latter sect have lately built a high stone wall around the Garden of Gethsemane, for the purpose, apparently, of protecting the five aged olives. I am ignorant of the grounds wherefore Gethsemane is placed here. Most travellers have given their faith to the spot, but Dr. Robinson, who is more reliable than any amount of mere tradition, does not coincide with them. The trees do not appear as ancient as some of those at the foot of Mount Carmel, which are supposed to date from the Roman colony established by Titus. Moreover, it is well known that at the time of the taking of Jerusalem by that Emperor, all the trees, for many miles around, were destroyed. The olive-trees, therefore, cannot be those under which Christ rested, even supposing this to be the true site of Gethseniane.

The Mount of Olives is a steep and rugged hill, dominating over the city and the surrounding heights. It is still covered with olive orchards, and planted with patches of grain, which do not thrive well on the stony soil. On the summit is a mosque, with a minaret attached, which affords a grand panoramic view. As we reached it, the Chief of the College of Dervishes, in the court of the Mosque of Omar, came out with a number of attendants. He saluted us courteously, which would not have been the case had he been the Superior of the Latin Convent, and we Greek Monks. There were some Turkish ladies in the interior of the mosque, so that we could not gain admittance, and therefore did not see the rock containing the foot-prints of Christ, who, according to Moslem tradition, ascended to heaven from this spot. The Mohammedans, it may not be generally known, accept the history of Christ, except his crucifixion, believing that he passed to heaven without death, another person being crucified in his stead. They call him the Roh-Allah, or Spirit of God, and consider him, after Mahomet, as the holiest of the Prophets.

We ascended to the gallery of the minaret. The city lay opposite, so fairly spread out to our view that almost every house might be separately distinguished. It is a mass of gray buildings, with dome-roofs, and but for the mosques of Omar and El Aksa, with the courts and galleries around them, would be exceedingly tame in appearance. The only other prominent points are the towers of the Holy Sepulchre, the citadel, enclosing Herod's Tower, and the mosque on mount Zion. The Turkish wall, with its sharp angles, its square bastions, and the long, embrasured lines of its parapet, is the most striking feature of the view. Stony hills stretch away from the city on all sides, at present cheered with tracts of springing wheat, but later in the season, brown and desolate. In the south, the convent of St. Elias is visible, and part of the little town of Bethlehem. I passed to the eastern side of the gallery, and looking thence, deep down among the sterile mountains, beheld a long sheet of blue water, its southern extremity vanishing in a hot, sulphury haze. The mountains of Ammon and Moab, which formed the background of my first view of Jerusalem, leaned like a vast wall against the sky, beyond the mysterious sea and the broad valley of the Jordan. The great depression of this valley below the level of the Mediterranean gives it a most remarkable character. It appears even deeper than is actually the case, and resembles an enormous chasm or moat, separating two different regions of the earth. The khamseen was blowing from the south, from out the deserts of Edom, and threw its veil of fiery vapor over the landscape. The muezzin pointed out to me the location of Jericho, of Kerak in Moab, and Es-Salt in the country of Ammon. Ere long the shadow of the minaret denoted noon, and, placing his hands on both sides of his mouth, he cried out, first on the South side, towards Mecca, and then to the West, and North, and East: "God is great: there is no God but God, and Mohammed is His Prophet! Let us prostrate ourselves before Him: and to Him alone be the glory!"

Jerusalem, internally, gives no impression but that of filth, ruin, poverty, and degradation. There are two or three streets in the western or higher portion of the city which are tolerably clean, but all the others, to the very gates of the Holy Sepulchre, are channels of pestilence. The Jewish Quarter, which is the largest, so sickened and disgusted me, that I should rather go the whole round of the city walls than pass through it a second time. The bazaars are poor, compared with those of other Oriental cities of the same size, and the principal trade seems to be in rosaries, both Turkish and Christian, crosses, seals, amulets, and pieces of the Holy Sepulchre. The population, which may possibly reach 20,000, is apparently Jewish, for the most part; at least, I have been principally struck with the Hebrew face, in my walks. The number of Jews has increased considerably within a few years, and there is also quite a number who, having been converted to Protestantism, were brought hither at the expense of English missionary societies for the purpose of forming a Protestant community. Two of the hotels are kept by families of this class. It is estimated that each member of the community has cost the Mission about £4,500: a sum which would have Christianized tenfold the number of English heathen. The Mission, however, is kept up by its patrons, as a sort of religious luxury. The English have lately built a very handsome church within the walls, and the Rev. Dr. Gobat, well known by his missionary labors in Abyssinia, now has the title of Bishop of Jerusalem. A friend of his in Central Africa gave me a letter of introduction for him, and I am quite disappointed in finding him absent. Dr. Barclay, of Virginia, a most worthy man in every respect, is at the head of the American Mission here. There is, besides, what is called the "American Colony," at the village of Artos, near Bethlehem: a little community of religious enthusiasts, whose experiments in cultivation have met with remarkable success, and are much spoken of at present.

Whatever good the various missions here may, in time, accomplish (at present, it does not amount to much), Jerusalem is the last place in the world where an intelligent heathen would be converted to Christianity. Were I cast here, ignorant of any religion, and were I to compare the lives and practices of the different sects as the means of making my choice--in short, to judge of each faith by the conduct of its professors--I should at once turn Mussulman. When you consider that in the Holy Sepulchre there are nineteen chapels, each belonging to a different sect, calling itself Christian, and that a Turkish police is always stationed there to prevent the bloody quarrels which often ensue between them, you may judge how those who call themselves followers of the Prince of Peace practice the pure faith he sought to establish. Between the Greek and Latin churches, especially, there is a deadly feud, and their contentions are a scandal, not only to the few Christians here, but to the Moslems themselves. I believe there is a sort of truce at present, owing to the settlement of some of the disputes--as, for instance, the restoration of the silver star, which the Greeks stole from the shrine of the Nativity, at Bethlehem. The Latins, however, not long since, demolished, vi et armis, a chapel which the Greeks commenced building on Mount Zion. But, if the employment of material weapons has been abandoned for the time, there is none the less a war of words and of sounds still going on. Go into the Holy Sepulchre, when mass is being celebrated, and you can scarcely endure the din. No sooner does the Greek choir begin its shrill chant, than the Latins fly to the assault. They have an organ, and terribly does that organ strain its bellows and labor its pipes to drown the rival singing. You think the Latins will carry the day, when suddenly the cymbals of the Abyssinians strike in with harsh brazen clang, and, for the moment, triumph. Then there are Copts, and Maronites, and Armenians, and I know not how many other sects, who must have their share; and the service that should be a many-toned harmony pervaded by one grand spirit of devotion, becomes a discordant orgie, befitting the rites of Belial.

A long time ago--I do not know the precise number of years--the Sultan granted a firman, in answer to the application of both Jews and Christians, allowing the members of each sect to put to death any person belonging to the other sect, who should be found inside of their churches or synagogues. The firman has never been recalled, though in every place but Jerusalem it remains a dead letter. Here, although the Jews freely permit Christians to enter their synagogue, a Jew who should enter the Holy Sepulchre would be lucky if he escaped with his life. Not long since, an English gentleman, who was taken by the monks for a Jew, was so severely beaten that he was confined to his bed for two months. What worse than scandal, what abomination, that the spot looked upon by so many Christians as the most awfully sacred on earth, should be the scene of such brutish intolerance! I never pass the group of Turkish officers, quietly smoking their long pipes and sipping their coffee within the vestibule of the Church, without a feeling of humiliation. Worse than the money-changers whom Christ scourged out of the Temple, the guardians of this edifice make use of His crucifixion and resurrection as a means of gain. You may buy a piece of the stone covering the Holy Sepulchre, duly certified by the Greek Patriarch of Jerusalem, for about $7. At Bethlehem, which I visited this morning, the Latin monk who showed us the manger, the pit where 12,000 innocents were buried, and other things, had much less to say of the sacredness or authenticity of the place, than of the injustice of allowing the Greeks a share in its possession.

The native Jewish families in Jerusalem, as well as those in other parts of Palestine, present a marked difference to the Jews of Europe and America. They possess the same physical characteristics--the dark, oblong eye, the prominent nose, the strongly-marked cheek and jaw--but in the latter, these traits have become harsh and coarse. Centuries devoted to the lowest and most debasing forms of traffic, with the endurance of persecution and contumely, have greatly changed and vulgarized the appearance of the race. But the Jews of the Holy City still retain a noble beauty, which proved to my mind their descent from the ancient princely houses of Israel The forehead is loftier, the eye larger and more frank in its expression, the nose more delicate in its prominence, and the face a purer oval. I have remarked the same distinction in the countenances of those Jewish families of Europe, whose members have devoted themselves to Art or Literature. Mendelssohn's was a face that might have belonged to the House of David.

On the evening of my arrival in the city, as I set out to walk through the bazaars, I encountered a native Jew, whose face will haunt me for the rest of my life. I was sauntering slowly along, asking myself "Is this Jerusalem?" when, lifting my eyes, they met those of Christ! It was the very face which Raphael has painted--the traditional features of the Saviour, as they are recognised and accepted by all Christendom. The waving brown hair, partly hidden by a Jewish cap, fell clustering about the ears; the face was the most perfect oval, and almost feminine in the purity of its outline; the serene, child-like mouth was shaded with a light moustache, and a silky brown beard clothed the chin; but the eyes--shall I ever look into such orbs again? Large, dark, unfathomable, they beamed with an expression of divine love and divine sorrow, such as I never before saw in human face. The man had just emerged from a dark archway, and the golden glow of the sunset, reflected from a white wall above, fell upon his face. Perhaps it was this transfiguration which made his beauty so unearthly; but, during the moment that I saw him, he was to me a revelation of the Saviour. There are still miracles in the Land of Judah. As the dusk gathered in the deep streets, I could see nothing but the ineffable sweetness and benignity of that countenance, and my friend was not a little astonished, if not shocked, when I said to him, with the earnestness of belief, on my return: "I have just seen Christ."

I made the round of the Holy Sepulchre on Sunday, while the monks were celebrating the festival of the Invention of the Cross, in the chapel of the Empress Helena. As the finding of the cross by the Empress is almost the only authority for the places inclosed within the Holy Sepulchre, I went there inclined to doubt their authenticity, and came away with my doubt vastly strengthened. The building is a confused labyrinth of chapels, choirs, shrines, staircases, and vaults--without any definite plan or any architectural beauty, though very rich in parts and full of picturesque effects. Golden lamps continually burn before the sacred places, and you rarely visit the church without seeing some procession of monks, with crosses, censers, and tapers, threading the shadowy passages, from shrine to shrine It is astonishing how many localities are assembled under one roof. At first, you are shown, the stone on which Christ rested from the burden of the cross; then, the place where the soldiers cast lots for His garments, both of them adjoining the

Sepulchre. After seeing this, you are taken to the Pillar of Flagellation; the stocks; the place of crowning with thorns; the spot where He met His mother; the cave where the Empress Helena found the cross; and, lastly, the summit of Mount Calvary. The Sepulchre is a small marble building in the centre of the church. We removed our shoes at the entrance, and were taken by a Greek monk, first into a sort of ante-chamber, lighted with golden lamps, and having in the centre, inclosed in a case of marble, the stone on which the angel sat. Stooping through a low door, we entered the Sepulchre itself. Forty lamps of gold burn unceasingly above the white marble slab, which, as the monks say, protects the stone whereon the body of Christ was laid. As we again emerged, our guide led us up a flight of steps to a second story, in which stood a shrine, literally blazing with gold. Kneeling on the marble floor, he removed a golden shield, and showed us the hole in the rock of Calvary, where the cross was planted. Close beside it was the fissure produced by the earthquake which followed the Crucifixion. But, to my eyes, aided by the light of the dim wax taper, it was no violent rupture, such as an earthquake would produce, and the rock did not appear to be the same as that of which Jerusalem is built. As we turned to leave, a monk appeared with a bowl of sacred rose-water, which he sprinkled on our hands, bestowing a double portion on a rosary of sandal-wood which I carried But it was a Mohammedan rosary, brought from Mecca, and containing the sacred number of ninety-nine beads.

I have not space here to state all the arguments for and against the localities in the Holy Sepulchre, I came to the conclusion that none of them were authentic, and am glad to have the concurrence of such distinguished authority as Dr. Robinson. So far from this being a matter of regret, I, for one, rejoice that those sacred spots are lost to the world. Christianity does not need them, and they are spared a daily profanation in the name of religion. We know that Christ has walked on the Mount of Olives, and gone down to the Pool of Siloam, and tarried in Bethany; we know that here, within the circuit of our vision, He has suffered agony and death, and that from this little point went out all the light that has made the world greater and happier and better in its later than in its earlier days.

Yet, I must frankly confess, in wandering through this city--revered alike by Christians, Jews and Turks as one of the holiest in the world--I have been reminded of Christ, the Man, rather, than of Christ, the God. In the glory which overhangs Palestine afar off, we imagine emotions which never come, when we tread the soil and walk over the hallowed sites. As I toiled up the Mount of Olives, in the very footsteps of Christ, panting with the heat and the difficult ascent, I found it utterly impossible to conceive that the Deity, in human form, had walked there before me. And even at night, as I walk on the terraced roof, while the moon, "the balmy moon of blessed Israel," restores the Jerusalem of olden days to my imagination, the Saviour who then haunts my thoughts is the Man Jesus, in those moments of trial when He felt the weaknesses of our common humanity; in that agony of struggle in the garden of Gethsemane, in that still more bitter cry of human doubt and human appeal from the cross: "My God, my God, why hast Thou forsaken me!" Yet there is no reproach for this conception of the character of Christ. Better the divinely-inspired Man, the purest and most perfect of His race, the pattern and type of all that is good and holy in Humanity, than the Deity for whose intercession we pray, while we trample His teachings under our feet. It would be well for many Christian sects, did they keep more constantly before their eyes the sublime humanity of Christ. How much bitter intolerance and persecution might be spared the world, if, instead of simply adoring Him as a Divine Mediator, they would strive to walk the ways He trod on earth. But Christianity is still undeveloped, and there is yet no sect which represents its fall and perfect spirit.

It is my misfortune if I give offence by these remarks. I cannot assume emotions I do not feel, and must describe Jerusalem as I found it. Since being here, I have read the accounts of several travellers, and in many cases the devotional rhapsodies--the ecstacies of awe and reverence--in which they indulge, strike me as forced and affected. The pious writers have described what was expected of them, not what they found. It was partly from reading such accounts that my anticipations were raised too high, for the view of the city from the Jaffa road and the panorama from the Mount of Olives are the only things wherein I have been pleasantly disappointed.

By far the most interesting relic left to the city is the foundation wall

376

of Solomon's Temple. The Mosque of Omar, according to the accounts of the Turks, and Mr. Gather wood's examination, rests on immense vaults, which are believed to be the substructions of the Temple itself. Under the dome of the mosque there is a large mass of natural rock, revered by the Moslems as that from which Mahomet mounted the beast Borak when he visited the Seven Heavens, and believed by Mr. Catherwood to have served as part of the foundation of the Holy of Holies. No Christian is allowed to enter the mosque, or even its enclosure, on penalty of death, and even the firman of the Sultan has failed to obtain admission for a Frank. I have been strongly tempted to make the attempt in my Egyptian dress, which happens to resemble that of a mollah or Moslem priest, but the Dervishes in the adjoining college have sharp eyes, and my pronunciation of Arabic would betray me in case I was accosted. I even went so far as to buy a string of the large beads usually carried by a mollah, but unluckily I do not know the Moslem form of prayer, or I might carry out the plan under the guise of religious abstraction. This morning we succeeded in getting a nearer view of the mosque from the roof of the Governor's palace. François, by assuming the character of a Turkish cawass, gained us admission. The roof overlooks the entire enclosure of the Haram, and gives a complete view of the exterior of the mosque and the paved court surrounding it. There is no regularity in the style of the buildings in the enclosure, but the general effect is highly picturesque. The great dome of the mosque is the grandest in all the Orient, but the body of the edifice, made to resemble an octagonal tent, and covered with blue and white tiles, is not high enough to do it justice. The first court is paved with marble, and has four porticoes, each of five light Saracenic arches, opening into the green park, which occupies the rest of the terrace. This park is studded with cypress and fig trees, and dotted all over with the tombs of shekhs. As we were looking down on the spacious area, behold! who should come along but Shekh Mohammed Senoosee, the holy man of Timbuctoo, who had laid off his scarlet robe and donned a green one. I called down to him, whereupon he looked up and recognised us. For this reason I regret our departure from Jerusalem, as I am sure a little persuasion would induce the holy man to accompany me within the mosque.

We leave to-morrow for Damascus, by way of Nazareth and Tiberius.

My original plan was to have gone to Djerash, the ancient Geraza, in the land of Gilead, and thence to Bozrah, in Djebel Hauaran. But Djebel Adjeloun, as the country about Djerash is called, is under a powerful Bedouin shekh, named Abd-el Azeez, and without an escort from him, which involves considerable delay and a fee of $150, it would be impossible to make the journey. We are therefore restricted to the ordinary route, and in case we should meet with any difficulty by the way, Mr. Smith, the American Consul, who is now here, has kindly procured us a firman from the Pasha of Jerusalem. All the travellers here are making preparations to leave, but there are still two parties in the Desert.

Chapter VI. The Hill-Country of Palestine.

Leaving Jerusalem--The Tombs of the Kings--El Bireh--The Hill-Country--First View of Mount Hermon--The Tomb of Joseph--Ebal and Gerizim--The Gardens of Nablous--The Samaritans--The Sacred Book--A Scene in the Synagogue--Mentoi and Telemachus--Ride to Samaria--The Ruins of Sebaste--Scriptural Landscapes--Halt at Genin--The Plain of Esdraelon--Palestine and California--The Hills of Nazareth--Accident--Fra Joachim--The Church of the Virgin--The Shrine of the Annunciation--The Holy Places.

"Blest land of Judea! thrice hallowed of song,

Where the holiest of memories pilgrim-like throng:

In the shade of thy palms, by the shores of thy sea,

On the hills of thy beauty, my heart is with thee!"

J. G. Whittier.

Latin Convent, Nazareth, *Friday May* 7, 1852.

We left Jerusalem by the Jaffa Gate, because within a few months neither travellers nor baggage are allowed to pass the Damascus Gate, on account of smuggling operations having been carried on there. Not far from the city wall there is a superb terebinth tree, now in the full glory of its shining green leaves. It appears to be bathed in a perpetual dew; the rounded masses of foliage sparkle and glitter in the light, and the great spreading boughs flood the turf below with a deluge of delicious shade. A number of persons were reclining on the grass under it, and one of them, a very handsome Christian boy, spoke to us in Italian and English. I scarcely remember a brighter and purer day than that of our departure. The sky was a sheet of spotless blue; every rift and scar of the distant hills was retouched with a firmer pencil, and all the outlines, blurred away by the haze of the previous few days, were restored with wonderful distinctness. The temperature was hot, but not sultry, and the air we breathed was an elixir of immortality.

Through a luxuriant olive grove we reached the Tombs of the Kings, situated in a small valley to the north of the city. Part of the valley, if not the whole of it, has been formed by quarrying away the crags of marble and conglomerate limestone for building the city. Near the edge of the low cliffs overhanging it, there are some illustrations of the ancient mode of cutting stone, which, as well as the custom of excavating tombs in the rock, was evidently borrowed from Egypt. The upper surface of the rocks, was first made smooth, after which the blocks were mapped out and cut apart by grooves chiselled between them. I visited four or five tombs, each of which had a sort of vestibule or open portico in front. The door was low, and the chambers which I entered, small and black, without sculptures of any kind. The tombs bear some resemblance in their general plan to those of Thebes, except that they are without ornaments, either sculptured or painted. There are fragments of sarcophagi in some of them. On the southern side of the valley is a large quarry, evidently worked for marble, as the blocks have been cut out from below, leaving a large overhanging mass, part of which has broken off and fallen down. Some pieces which I picked up were of a very fine white marble, somewhat resembling that of Carrara. The opening of the quarry made a striking picture, the soft pink hue of the weather-stained rock contrasting exquisitely with the vivid green of the vines festooning the entrance.

From the long hill beyond the Tombs, we took our last view of Jerusalem, far beyond whose walls I saw the Church of the Nativity, at Bethlehem. The Jewish synagogue on the top of the mountain called Nebbee Samwil, the highest peak in Palestine, was visible at some distance to the west. Notwithstanding its sanctity, I felt little regret at leaving Jerusalem, and cheerfully took the rough road northward, over the stony hills. There were few habitations in sight, yet the hill-sides were cultivated, wherever it was possible for anything to grow. The wheat was just coming into head, and the people were at work, planting maize. After four hours' ride, we reached El Bireh, a little village on a hill, with the ruins of a convent and a large khan. The place takes its name from a fountain of excellent water, beside which we found our tents already pitched. In the evening, two Englishmen, an ancient Mentor, with a wild young Telemachus in charge, arrived, and camped near us. The night was calm and cool, and the full moon poured a flood of light over the bare and silent hills.

We rose long before sunrise, and rode off in the brilliant morning-- the sky unstained by a speck of vapor. In the valley, beyond El Bireh, the husbandmen were already at their ploughs, and the village boys were on their way to the uncultured parts of the hills, with their flocks of sheep and goats. The valley terminated in a deep gorge, with perpendicular walls of rock on either side. Our road mounted the hill on the eastern side, and followed the brink of the precipice through the pass, where an enchanting landscape opened upon us. The village of Yebrood crowned a hill which rose opposite, and the mountain slopes leaning towards it on all sides were covered with orchards of fig trees; and either rustling with wheat or cleanly ploughed for maize. The soil was a dark brown loam, and very rich. The stones have been laboriously built into terraces; and, even where heavy rocky boulders almost hid the soil, young fig and olive trees were planted in the crevices between them. I have never seen more thorough and patient cultivation. In the crystal of the morning air, the very hills laughed with plenty, and the whole landscape beamed with the signs of gladness on its countenance.

The site of ancient Bethel was not far to the right of our road. Over hills laden with the olive, fig, and vine, we passed to Ain el-Haramiyeh, or the Fountain of the Bobbers. Here there are tombs cut in the rock on both sides of the valley. Over another ridge, we descended to a large, bowl-shaped valley, entirely covered with wheat, and opening eastward towards the Jordan. Thence to Nablous (the Shechem of the Old and Sychar of the New Testament) is four hours through a winding dell of the richest harvest land; On the way, we first caught sight of the snowy top of Mount Hermon, distant at least eighty miles in a straight line. Before reaching Nablous, I stopped to drink at a fountain of clear and sweet water, beside a square pile of masonry, upon which sat two Moslem dervishes. This, we were told, was the Tomb of Joseph, whose body, after having accompanied the Israelites in all their wanderings, was at last deposited near Shechem. There is less reason to doubt this spot than most of the sacred places of Palestine, for the reason that it rests, not on Christian, but on Jewish tradition. The wonderful tenacity with which the Jews cling to every record or memento of their early history, and the fact that from the time of Joseph a portion of them have always lingered near the spot, render it highly probable that the locality of a spot so sacred should have been preserved from generation to generation to the present time. It has been recently proposed to open this tomb, by digging under it from the side. If the body of Joseph was actually deposited here, there are, no doubt, some traces of it remaining. It must have been embalmed, according to the Egyptian custom, and placed in a coffin of the Indian sycamore, the wood of which is so nearly incorruptible, that thirty-five centuries would not suffice for its decomposition. The singular interest of such a discovery would certainly justify the experiment. Not far from the tomb is Jacob's Well, where Christ met the Woman of Samaria. This place is also considered as authentic, for the same reasons. If not wholly convincing to all, there is, at least, so much probability in them that one is freed from that painful coldness and incredulity with which he beholds the sacred shows of Jerusalem.

Leaving the Tomb of Joseph, the road turned to the west, and entered the narrow pass between Mounts Ebal and Gerizim. The former is a steep, barren peak, clothed with terraces of cactus, standing on the northern side of the pass. Mount Gerizim is cultivated nearly to the top, and is truly a mountain of blessing, compared with its neighbor. Through an orchard of grand old olive-trees, we reached Nablous, which presented a charming picture, with its long mass of white, dome-topped stone houses, stretching along the foot of Gerizim through a sea of bowery orchards. The bottom of the valley resembles some old garden run to waste. Abundant streams, poured from the generous heart of the Mount of Blessing, leap and gurgle with pleasant noises through thickets of orange, fig, and pomegranate, through bowers of roses and tangled masses of briars and wild vines. We halted in a grove of olives, and, after our tent was pitched, walked upward through the orchards to the Ras-el-Ain (Promontory of the Fountain), on the side of Mount Gerizim. A multitude of beggars sat at the city gate; and, as they continued to clamor after I had given sufficient alms, I paid them with "Allah deelek!"--(God give it to you!)--the Moslem's reply to such importunity--and they ceased in an instant. This exclamation, it seems, takes away from them the power of demanding a second time.

From under the Ras-el-Ain gushes forth the Fountain of Honey, so called from the sweetness and purity of the water. We drank of it, and I found the taste very agreeable, but my companion declared that it had an unpleasant woolly flavor. When we climbed a little higher, we found that the true source from which the fountain is supplied was above, and that an Arab was washing a flock of sheep in it! We continued our walk along the side of the mountain to the other end of the city, through gardens of almond, apricot, prune, and walnut-trees, bound each to each by great vines, whose heavy arms they seemed barely able to support. The interior of the town is dark and filthy; but it has a long, busy bazaar extending its whole length, and a café, where we procured the best coffee in Syria.

Nablous is noted for the existence of a small remnant of the ancient Samaritans. The stock has gradually dwindled away, and amounts to only forty families, containing little more than a hundred and fifty individuals. They live in a particular quarter of the city, and are easily distinguished from the other inhabitants by the cast of their features. After our guide, a native of Nablous, had pointed out three or four, I had no difficulty in recognising all the others we met. They have long, but not prominent noses, like the Jews; small, oblong eyes, narrow lips, and fair complexions, most of them having brown hair. They appear to be held in considerable obloquy by the Moslems. Our attendant, who was of the low class of Arabs, took the boys we met very unceremoniously by the head, calling out: "Here is another Samaritan!" He then conducted us to their synagogue, to see the celebrated Pentateuch, which is there preserved. We were taken to a small, open court, shaded by an apricot-tree, where the priest, an old man in a green robe and white turban, was seated in meditation. He had a long grey beard, and black eyes, that lighted up with a sudden expression of eager greed when we promised him backsheesh for a sight of the sacred book. He arose and took us into a sort of chapel, followed by a number of Samaritan boys. Kneeling down at a niche in the wall, he produced from behind a wooden case a piece of ragged parchment, written with Hebrew characters. But the guide was familiar with this deception, and rated him so soundly that, after a little hesitation, he laid the fragment away, and produced a large tin cylinder, covered with a piece of green satin embroidered in gold. The boys stooped down and reverently kissed the blazoned cover, before it was removed. The cylinder, sliding open by two rows of hinges, opened at the same time the parchment scroll, which was rolled at both ends. It was, indeed, a very ancient manuscript, and in remarkable preservation. The rents have been carefully repaired and the scroll neatly stitched upon another piece of parchment, covered on the outside with violet satin. The priest informed me that it was written by the son of Aaron; but this does not coincide with the fact that the Samaritan Pentateuch is different from that of the Jews. It is, however, no doubt one of the oldest parchment records in the world, and the Samaritans look upon it with unbounded faith and reverence. The Pentateuch, according to their version, contains their only form of religion. They reject everything else which the Old Testament contains. Three or four days ago was their grand feast of sacrifice, when they made a burnt offering of a lamb, on the top of Mount Gerizim. Within a short time, it is said they have shown some curiosity to become acquainted with the New Testament, and the High Priest sent to Jerusalem to procure Arabic copies.

I asked one of the wild-eyed boys whether he could read the sacred book. "Oh, yes," said the priest, "all these boys can read it;" and the one I addressed immediately pulled a volume from his breast, and commenced reading in fluent Hebrew. It appeared to be a part of their church service, for both the priest and boab, or door-keeper, kept up a running series of responses, and occasionally the whole crowd shouted out some deep-mouthed word in chorus. The old man leaned forward with an expression as fixed and intense as if the text had become incarnate in him, following with his lips the sound of the boy's voice. It was a strange picture of religious enthusiasm, and was of itself sufficient to convince me of the legitimacy of the Samaritan's descent. When I rose to leave I gave him the promised fee, and a smaller one to the boy who read the service. This was the signal for a general attack from the door-keeper and all the boys who were present. They surrounded me with eyes sparkling with the desire of gain, kissed the border of my jacket, stroked my beard coaxingly with their hands, which they then kissed, and, crowding up with a boisterous show of affection, were about to fall on my neck in a heap, after the old Hebrew fashion. The priest, clamorous for more, followed with glowing face, and the whole group had a riotous and bacchanalian character, which I should never have imagined could spring from such a passion as avarice.

On returning to our camp, we found Mentor and Telemachus arrived, but not on such friendly terms as their Greek prototypes. We were kept awake for a long time that night by their high words, and the first sound I heard the next morning came from their tent. Telemachus, I suspect, had found some island of Calypso, and did not relish the cold shock of the plunge into the sea, by which Mentor had forced him away. He insisted on returning to Jerusalem, but as Mentor would not allow him a horse, he had not the courage to try it on foot. After a series of altercations, in which he took a pistol to shoot the dragoman, and applied very profane terms to everybody in the company, his wrath dissolved into tears, and when we left, Mentor had decided to rest a day at Nablous, and let him recover from the effects of the storm.

We rode down the beautiful valley, taking the road to Sebaste (Samaria), while our luggage-mules kept directly over the mountains to Jenin. Our path at first followed the course of the stream, between turfy banks and through luxuriant orchards. The whole country we overlooked was planted with olive-trees, and, except the very summits of the mountains, covered with grain-fields. For two hours our course was north-east, leading over the hills, and now and then dipping into beautiful dells. In one of these a large stream gushes from the earth in a full fountain, at the foot of a great olive-tree. The hill-side above it was a complete mass of foliage, crowned with the white walls of a Syrian village. Descending the valley, which is very deep, we came in sight of Samaria, situated on the summit of an isolated hill. The sanctuary of the ancient Christian church of St. John towers high above the mud walls of the modern village. Riding between olive-orchards and wheat-fields of glorious richness and beauty, we passed the remains of an acqueduct, and ascended the hill The ruins of the church occupy the eastern summit. Part of them have been converted into a mosque, which the Christian foot is not allowed to profane. The church, which is in the Byzantine style, is apparently of the time of the Crusaders. It had originally a central and two side-aisles, covered with groined Gothic vaults. The sanctuary is semi-circular, with a row of small arches, supported by double pillars. The church rests on the foundations of some much more ancient building--probably a temple belonging to the Roman city.

Behind the modern village, the hill terminates in a long, elliptical mound, about one-third of a mile in length. We made the tour of it, and were surprised at finding a large number of columns, each of a single piece of marble. They had once formed a double colonnade, extending from the church to a gate on the western side of the summit. Our native guide said they had been covered with an arch, and constituted a long market or bazaar--a supposition in which he may be correct. From the gate, which is still distinctly marked, we overlooked several deep valleys to the west, and over them all, the blue horizon of the Mediterranean, south of Cæsarea. On the northern side of the hill there are upwards of twenty more pillars standing, besides a number hurled down, and the remains of a quadrangular colonnade, on the side of the hill below. The total number of pillars on the summit cannot be less than one hundred, from twelve to eighteen feet in height. The hill is strewn, even to its base, with large hewn blocks and fragments of sculptured stone. The present name of the city was given to it by Herod, and it must have been at that time a most stately and beautiful place.

We descended to a valley on the east, climbed a long ascent, and after crossing the broad shoulder of a mountain beyond, saw below us a landscape even more magnificent than that of Nablous. It was a great winding valley, its bottom rolling in waves of wheat and barley, while every hill-side, up to the bare rock, was mantled with groves of olive. The very summits which looked into this garden of Israel, were green with fragrant plants--wild thyme and sage, gnaphalium and camomile. Away to the west was the sea, and in the north-west the mountain chain of Carmel. We went down to the gardens and pasture-land, and stopped to rest at the Village of Geba, which hangs on the side of the mountain. A spring of whitish but delicious water gushed out of the soil, in the midst of a fig orchard. The women passed us, going back and forth with tall water-jars on their heads. Some herd-boys brought down a flock of black goats, and they were all given drink in a large wooden bowl. They were beautiful animals, with thick curved horns, white eyes, and ears a foot long. It was a truly Biblical picture in every feature.

Beyond this valley we passed a circular basin, which has no outlet, so that in winter the bottom of it must be a lake. After winding among the hills an hour more, we came out upon the town of Jenin, a Turkish village, with a tall white minaret, at the head of the great plain of Esdraelon. It is supposed to be the ancient Jezreel, where the termagant Jezebel was thrown out of the window. We pitched our tent in a garden near the town, under a beautiful mulberry tree, and, as the place is in very bad repute, engaged a man to keep guard at night. An English family was robbed there two or three weeks ago. Our guard did his duty well, pacing back and forth, and occasionally grounding his musket to keep up his courage by the sound. In the evening, François caught a chameleon, a droll-looking little creature, which changed color in a marvellous manner.

Our road, next day, lay directly across the Plain of Esdraelon, one of the richest districts in the world. It is now a green sea, covered with fields of wheat and barley, or great grazing tracts, on which multitudes of sheep and goats are wandering. In some respects it reminded me of the Valley of San José, and if I were to liken Palestine to any other country I have seen, it would be California. The climate and succession of the seasons are the same, the soil is very similar in quality, and the landscapes present the same general features. Here, in spring, the plains are covered with that deluge of floral bloom, which makes California seem a paradise. Here there are the same picturesque groves, the same rank fields of wild oats clothing the mountain-sides, the same aromatic herbs impregnating the air with balm, and above all, the same blue, cloudless days and dewless nights. While travelling here, I am constantly reminded of our new Syria on the Pacific.

Towards noon, Mount Tabor separated itself from the chain of hills before us, and stood out singly, at the extremity of the plain. We watered our horses at a spring in a swamp, were some women were collected, beating with sticks the rushes they had gathered to make mats. After reaching the mountains on the northern side of the plain, an ascent of an hour and a-half, through a narrow glen, brought us to Nazareth, which is situated in a cul-de-sac, under the highest peaks of the range. As we were passing a rocky part of the road, Mr. Harrison's horse fell with him and severely injured his leg. We were fortunately near our destination, and on reaching the Latin Convent, Fra Joachim, to whose surgical abilities the traveller's book bore witness, took him in charge. Many others besides ourselves have had reason to be thankful for the good offices of the Latin monks in Palestine. I have never met with a class more kind, cordial, and genial. All the convents are bound to take in and entertain all applicants--of whatever creed or nation--for the space of three days.

In the afternoon, Fra Joachim accompanied me to the Church of the Virgin, which is inclosed within the walls of the convent. It is built over the supposed site of the house in which the mother of Christ was living, at the time of the angelic annunciation. Under the high altar, a flight of steps leads down to the shrine of the Virgin, on the threshold of the house, where the Angel Gabriel's foot rested, as he stood, with a lily in his hand, announcing the miraculous conception. The shrine, of white marble and gold, gleaming in the light of golden lamps, stands under a rough arch of the natural rock, from the side of which hangs a heavy fragment of a granite pillar, suspended, as the devout believe, by divine power. Fra Joachim informed me that, when the Moslems attempted to obliterate all tokens of the holy place, this pillar was preserved by a miracle, that the locality might not be lost to the Christians. At the same time, he said, the angels of God carried away the wooden house which stood at the entrance of the grotto; and, after letting it drop in Marseilles, while they rested, picked it up again and set it down in Loretto, where it still remains. As he said this, there was such entire, absolute belief in the good monk's eyes, and such happiness in that belief, that not for ten times the gold on the shrine would I have expressed a doubt of the story. He then bade me kneel, that I might see the spot where the angel stood, and devoutly repeated a paternoster while I contemplated the pure plate of snowy marble, surrounded with vases of fragrant flowers, between which hung cressets of gold, wherein perfumed oils were burning. All the decorations of the place conveyed the idea of transcendent purity and sweetness; and, for the first time in Palestine, I wished for perfect faith in the spot. Behind the shrine, there are two or three chambers in the rock, which served as habitations for the family of the Virgin.

A young Christian Nazarene afterwards conducted me to the House of Joseph, the Carpenter, which is now inclosed in a little chapel. It is merely a fragment of wall, undoubtedly as old as the time of Christ, and I felt willing to consider it a genuine relic. There was an honest roughness about the large stones, inclosing a small room called the carpenter's shop, which I could not find it in my heart to doubt. Besides, in a quiet country town like Nazareth, which has never knows such vicissitudes as Jerusalem, much more dependence can be placed on popular tradition. For the same reason, I looked with reverence on the Table of Christ, also inclosed within a chapel. This is a large, natural rock, about nine feet by twelve, nearly square, and quite flat on the top. It is said that it once served as a table for Christ and his Disciples. The building called the School of Christ, where he went with other children of his age, is now a church of the Syrian Christians, who were performing a doleful mass, in Arabic, at the time of my visit. It is a vaulted apartment, about forty feet long, and only the lower part of the wall is ancient. At each of these places, the Nazarene put into my hand a piece of pasteboard, on which was printed a prayer in Latin, Italian, and Arabic, with the information that whoever visited the place, and made the prayer, would be entitled to seven years' indulgence. I duly read all the prayers, and, accordingly, my conscience ought to be at rest for twenty-one years.

Chapter VII. The Country of Galilee.

Departure from Nazareth--A Christian Guide--Ascent of Mount Tabor--Wallachian Hermits--The Panorama of Tabor--Ride to Tiberias--A Bath in Genesareth--The Flowers of Galilee--The Mount of Beatitude--Magdala--Joseph's Well--Meeting with a Turk--The Fountain of the Salt-Works--The Upper Valley of the Jordan--Summer Scenery--The Rivers of Lebanon--Tell el-Kadi--An Arcadian Region--The Fountains of Banias.

"Beyond are Bethulia's mountains of green,

And the desolate hills of the wild Gadarene;

And I pause on the goat-crags of Tabor to see

The gleam of thy waters, O dark Galilee!"--Whittier.

Banias (Cæsarea Philippi), *May* 10, 1852.

We left Nazareth on the morning of the 8th inst. My companion had done so well under the care of Fra Joachim that he was able to ride, and our journey was not delayed by his accident. The benedictions of the good Franciscans accompanied us as we rode away from the Convent, past the Fountain of the Virgin, and out of the pleasant little valley where the boy Jesus wandered for many peaceful years. The Christian guide we engaged for Mount Tabor had gone ahead, and we did not find him until we had travelled for more than two hours among the hills. As we approached the sacred mountain, we came upon the region of oaks--the first oak I had seen since leaving Europe last autumn. There are three or four varieties, some with evergreen foliage, and in their wild luxuriance and the picturesqueness of their forms and groupings, they resemble those of California. The sea of grass and flowers in which they stood was sprinkled with thick tufts of wild oats--another point of resemblance to the latter country. But here, there is no gold; there, no sacred memories.

The guide was waiting for us beside a spring, among the trees. He was a tall youth of about twenty, with a mild, submissive face, and wore the dark-blue turban, which appears to be the badge of a native Syrian Christian. I found myself involuntarily pitying him for belonging to a despised sect. There is no disguising the fact that one feels much more respect for the Mussulman rulers of the East, than for their oppressed subjects who profess his own faith. The surest way to make a man contemptible is to treat him contemptuously, and the Oriental Christians, who have been despised for centuries, are, with some few exceptions, despicable enough. Now, however, since the East has become a favorite field of travel, and the Frank possesses an equal dignity with the Moslem, the native Christians are beginning to hold up their heads, and the return of self-respect will, in the course of time, make them respectable.

Mount Tabor stands a little in advance of the hill-country, with which it is connected only by a low spur or shoulder, its base being the Plain of Esdraelon. This is probably the reason why it has been fixed upon as the place of the Transfiguration, as it is not mentioned by name in the New Testament. The words are: "an high mountain apart," which some suppose to refer to the position of the mountain, and not to the remoteness of Christ and the three Disciples from men. The sides of the mountain are covered with clumps of oak, hawthorn and other trees, in many places overrun with the white honeysuckle, its fingers dropping with odor of nutmeg and cloves. The ascent, by a steep and winding path, occupied an hour. The summit is nearly level, and resembles some overgrown American field, or "oak opening." The grass is more than knee-deep; the trees grow high and strong, and there are tangled thickets and bowers of vines without end. The eastern and highest end of the mountain is covered with the remains of an old fortress-convent, once a place of great strength, from the thickness of its walls. In a sort of cell formed among the ruins we found two monk-hermits. I addressed them in all languages of which I know a salutation, without effect, but at last made out that they were Wallachians. They were men of thirty-five, with stupid faces, dirty garments, beards run to waste, and fur caps. Their cell was a mere hovel, without furniture, except a horrid caricature of the Virgin and Child, and four books of prayers in the Bulgarian character. One of them walked about knitting a stocking, and paid no attention to us; but the other, after giving us some deliciously cold water, got upon a pile of rubbish, and stood regarding us with open mouth while we took breakfast. So far from this being a cause of annoyance, I felt really glad that our presence had agitated the stagnant waters of his mind.

The day was hazy and sultry, but the panoramic view from Mount Tabor was still very fine. The great Plain of Esdraelon lay below us like a vast mosaic of green and brown--jasper and verd-antique. On the west, Mount Carmel lifted his head above the blue horizon line of the Mediterranean. Turning to the other side, a strip of the Sea of Galilee glimmered deep down among the hills, and the Ghor, or the Valley of the Jordan, stretched like a broad gash through them. Beyond them, the country of Djebel Adjeloun, the ancient Decapolis, which still holds the walls of Gadara and the temples and theatres of Djerash, faded away into vapor, and, still further to the south, the desolate hills of Gilead, the home of Jephthah. Mount Hermon is visible when the atmosphere is clear but we were not able to see it.

From the top of Mount Tabor to Tiberias, on the Sea of Galilee, is a journey of five hours, through a wild country, with but one single miserable village on the road. At first we rode through lonely dells, grown with oak and brilliant with flowers, especially the large purple mallow, and then over broad, treeless tracts of rolling land, but partially cultivated. The heat was very great; I had no thermometer, but should judge the temperature to have been at least 95° in the shade. From the edge of the upland tract, we looked down on the Sea of Galilee--a beautiful sheet of water sunk among the mountains, and more than 300 feet below the level of the Mediterranean. It lay unruffled in the bottom of the basin, reflecting the peaks of the bare red mountains beyond it. Tiberias was at our very feet, a few palm trees alone relieving the nakedness of its dull walls. After taking a welcome drink at the Fountain of Fig-trees, we descended to the town, which has a desolate and forlorn air. Its walls have been partly thrown down by earthquakes, and never repaired. We found our tents already pitched on the bank above the lake, and under one of the tottering towers.

Not a breath of air was stirring; the red hills smouldered in the heat, and the waters of Genesareth at our feet glimmered with an oily smoothness, unbroken by a ripple. We untwisted our turbans, kicked off our baggy trowsers, and speedily releasing ourselves from the barbarous restraints of dress, dipped into the tepid sea and floated lazily out until we could feel the exquisite coldness of the living springs which sent up their jets from the bottom. I was lying on my back, moving my fins just sufficiently to keep afloat, and gazing dreamily through half-closed eyes on the forlorn palms of Tiberias, when a shrill voice hailed me with: "O Howadji, get out of our way!" There, at the old stone gateway below our tent, stood two Galilean damsels, with heavy earthen jars upon their heads. "Go away yourselves, O maidens!" I answered, "if you want us to come out of the water." "But we must fill our pitchers," one of them replied. "Then fill them at once, and be not afraid; or leave them, and we will fill them for you." Thereupon they put the pitchers down, but remained watching us very complacently while we sank the vessels to the bottom of the lake, and let them fill from the colder and purer tide of the springs. In bringing them back through the water to the gate, the one I propelled before me happened to strike against a stone, and its fair owner, on receiving it, immediately pointed to a crack in the side, which she declared I had made, and went off lamenting. After we had resumed our garments, and were enjoying the pipe of indolence and the coffee of contentment, she returned and made such an outcry, that I was fain to purchase peace by the price of a new pitcher. I passed the first hours of-the night in looking out of my tent-door, as I lay, on the stars sparkling in the bosom of Galilee, like the sheen of Assyrian spears, and the glare of the great fires kindled on the opposite shore.

The next day, we travelled northward along the lake, passing through continuous thickets of oleander, fragrant with its heavy pink blossoms. The thistles were more abundant and beautiful than ever. I noticed, in particular, one with a superb globular flower of a bright blue color, which would make a choice ornament for our gardens at home. At the north-western head of the lake, the mountains fall back and leave a large tract of the richest meadow-land, which narrows away into a deep dell, overhung by high mountain headlands, faced with naked cliffs of red rock. The features of the landscape are magnificent. Up the dell, I saw plainly the Mount of Beatitude, beyond which lies the village of Cana of Galilee. In coming up the meadow, we passed a miserable little village of thatched mud huts, almost hidden by the rank weeds which grew around them. A withered old crone sat at one of the doors, sunning herself. "What is the name of this village?" I asked. "It is Mejdel," was her reply. This was the ancient Magdala, the home of that beautiful but sinful Magdalene, whose repentance has made her one of the brightest of the Saints. The crystal waters of the lake here lave a shore of the cleanest pebbles. The path goes winding through oleanders, nebbuks, patches of hollyhock, anise-seed, fennel, and other spicy plants, while, on the west, great fields of barley stand ripe for the cutting. In some places, the Fellahs, men and women, were at work, reaping and binding the sheaves. After crossing this tract, we came to the hill, at the foot of which was a ruined khan, and on the summit, other undistinguishable ruins, supposed by some to be those of Capernaum. The site of that exalted town, however, is still a matter of discussion.

We journeyed on in a most sweltering atmosphere over the ascending hills, the valley of the Upper Jordan lying deep on our right. In a shallow hollow, under one of the highest peaks, there stands a large deserted khan; over a well of very cold; sweet water, called Bir Youssuf by the Arabs. Somewhere near it, according to tradition, is the field where Joseph was sold by his brethren; and the well is, no doubt, looked upon by many as the identical pit into which he was thrown. A stately Turk of Damascus, with four servants behind him, came riding up as we were resting in the gateway of the khan, and, in answer to my question, informed me that the well was so named from Nebbee Youssuf (the Prophet Joseph), and not from Sultan Joseph Saladin. He took us for his countrymen, accosting me first in Turkish, and, even after I had talked with him some time in bad Arabic, asked me whether I had been making a pilgrimage to the tombs of certain holy Moslem saints, in the neighborhood of Jaffa. He joined company with us, however, and shared his pipe with me, as we continued our journey. We rode for two hours more over hills bare of trees, but covered thick with grass and herbs, and finally lost our way. François went ahead, dashing through the fields of barley and lentils, and we reached the path again, as the Waters of Merom came in sight. We then descended into the Valley of the Upper Jordan, and encamped opposite the lake, at Ain el-Mellaha (the Fountain of the Salt-Works), the first source of the sacred river. A stream of water, sufficient to turn half-a-dozen mills, gushes and gurgles up at the foot of the mountain. There are the remains of

394

an ancient dam, by which a large pool was formed for the irrigation of the valley. It still supplies a little Arab mill below the fountain. This is a frontier post, between the jurisdictions of the Pashas of Jerusalem and Damascus, and the mukkairee of the Greek Caloyer, who left us at Tiberias, was obliged to pay a duty of seven and a half piastres on fifteen mats, which he had bought at Jerusalem for one and a half piastres each. The poor man will perhaps make a dozen piastres (about half a dollar) on these mats at Damascus, after carrying them on his mule for more than two hundred miles.

We pitched our tents on the grassy meadow below the mill--a charming spot, with Tell el-Khanzir (the hill of wild boars) just in front, over the Waters of Merom, and the snow-streaked summit of Djebel esh-Shekh--the great Mount Hermon--towering high above the valley. This is the loftiest peak of the Anti-Lebanon, and is 10,000 feet above the sea. The next morning, we rode for three hours before reaching the second spring of the Jordan, at a place which François called Tell el-Kadi, but which did not at all answer with the description given me by Dr. Robinson, at Jerusalem. The upper part of the broad valley, whence the Jordan draws his waters, is flat, moist, and but little cultivated. There are immense herds of sheep, goats, and buffaloes wandering over it. The people are a dark Arab tribe, and live in tents and miserable clay huts. Where the valley begins to slope upward towards the hills, they plant wheat, barley, and lentils. The soil is the fattest brown loam, and the harvests are wonderfully rich. I saw many tracts of wheat, from half a mile to a mile in extent, which would average forty bushels to the acre. Yet the ground is never manured, and the Arab plough scratches up but a few inches of the surface. What a paradise might be made of this country, were it in better hands!

The second spring is not quite so large as Ain el-Mellaha but, like it, pours out a strong stream from a single source The pool was filled with women, washing the heavy fleeces of their sheep, and beating the dirt out of their striped camel's hair abas with long poles. We left it, and entered on a slope of stony ground, forming the head of the valley. The view extended southward, to the mountains closing the northern cove of the Sea of Galilee. It was a grand, rich landscape--so rich that its desolation seems forced and unnatural. High on the summit of a mountain to the west, the ruins of a large

Crusader fortress looked down upon us. The soil, which slowly climbs upward through a long valley between Lebanon and Anti-Lebanon, is cut with deep ravines. The path is very difficult to find; and while we were riding forward at random, looking in all directions for our baggage mules, we started up a beautiful gazelle. At last, about noon, hot, hungry, and thirsty, we reached a swift stream, roaring at the bottom of a deep ravine, through a bed of gorgeous foliage. The odor of the wild grape-blossoms, which came up to us, as we rode along the edge, was overpowering in its sweetness. An old bridge of two arches crossed the stream. There was a pile of rocks against the central pier, and there we sat and took breakfast in the shade of the maples, while the cold green waters foamed at our feet. By all the Naiads and Tritons, what a joy there is in beholding a running stream! The rivers of Lebanon are miracles to me, after my knowledge of the Desert. A company of Arabs, seven in all, were gathered under the bridge; and, from a flute which one of them blew, I judged they were taking a pastoral holiday. We kept our pistols beside us; for we did not like their looks. Before leaving, they told us that the country was full of robbers, and advised us to be on the lookout. We rode more carefully, after this, and kept with our baggage on reaching it, An hour after leaving the bridge, we came to a large circular, or rather annular mound, overgrown with knee-deep grass and clumps of oak-trees. A large stream, of a bright blue color, gushed down the north side, and after half embracing the mound swept off across the meadows to the Waters of Merom. There could be no doubt that this was Tell el-Kadi, the site of Dan, the most northern town of ancient Israel. The mound on which it was built is the crater of an extinct volcano. The Hebrew word Dan signifies "judge," and Tell el-Kadi, in Arabic, is "The Hill of the Judge."

The Anti-Lebanon now rose near us, its northern and western slopes green with trees and grass. The first range, perhaps 5,000 feet in height, shut out the snowy head of Hermon; but still the view was sublime in its large and harmonious outlines. Our road was through a country resembling Arcadia-- the earth hidden by a dense bed of grass and flowers; thickets of blossoming shrubs; old, old oaks, with the most gnarled of trunks, the most picturesque of boughs, and the glossiest of green leaves; olive-trees of amazing antiquity; and, threading and enlivening all, the clear-cold floods of Lebanon. This was the true haunt of Pan, whose altars are now before me, graven on the marble crags of Hermon. Looking on those altars, and on the landscape, lovely as a Grecian dream, I forget that the lament has long been sung:

"Pan, Pan is dead!"

In another hour, we reached this place, the ancient Cæsarea Philippi, now a poor village, embowered in magnificent trees, and washed by glorious waters. There are abundant remains of the old city: fragments of immense walls; broken granite columns; traces of pavements; great blocks of hewn stone; marble pedestals, and the like. In the rock at the foot of the mountain, there are several elegant niches, with Greek inscriptions, besides a large natural grotto. Below them, the water gushes up through the stones, in a hundred streams, forming a flood of considerable size. We have made our camp in an olive grove near the end of the village, beside an immense terebinth tree, which is inclosed in an open court, paved with stone. This is the town-hall of Banias, where the Shekh dispenses justice, and at the same time, the resort of all the idlers of the place. We went up among them, soon after our arrival, and were given seats of honor near the Shekh, who talked with me a long time about America. The people exhibit a very sensible curiosity, desiring to know the extent of our country, the number of inhabitants, the amount of taxation, the price of grain, and other solid information.

The Shekh and the men of the place inform us that the Druses are infesting the road to Damascus. This tribe is in rebellion in Djebel Hauaran, on account of the conscription, and some of them, it appears, have taken refuge in the fastnesses of Hermon, where they are beginning to plunder travellers. While I was talking with the Shekh, a Druse came down from the mountains, and sat for half an hour among the villagers, under the terebinth, and we have just heard that he has gone back the way he came. This fact has given us some anxiety, as he may have been a spy sent down to gather news and, if so, we are almost certain to be waylaid. If we were well armed, we should not fear a dozen, but all our weapons consist of a sword and four pistols. After consulting together, we decided to apply to the Shekh for two armed men, to accompany us. I accordingly went to him again, and exhibited the firman of the Pasha of Jerusalem, which he read, stating that, even without it, he would have felt it his duty to grant our request. This is the graceful way in which the Orientals submit to a peremptory order. He thinks that one man will be sufficient, as we shall probably not meet with any large party.

The day has been, and still is, excessively hot. The atmosphere is sweltering, and all around us, over the thick patches of mallow and wild mustard, the bees are humming with a continuous sultry sound. The Shekh, with a number of lazy villagers, is still seated under the terebinth, in a tent of shade, impervious to the sun. I can hear the rush of the fountains of Banias--the holy springs of Hermon, whence Jordan is born. But what is this? The odor of the velvety weed of Shiraz meets my nostrils; a dark-eyed son of Pan places the narghileh at my feet; and, bubbling more sweetly than the streams of Jordan, the incense most dear to the god dims the crystal censer, and floats from my lips in rhythmic ejaculations. I, too, am in Arcadia!

Chapter VIII. Crossing the Anti-Lebanon.

The Harmless Guard--Cæsarea Philippi--The Valley of the Druses--The Sides of Mount Hermon--An Alarm--Threading a Defile--Distant view of Djebel Hauaran--Another Alarm--Camp at Katana--We Ride into Damascus.

Damascus, *May* 12, 1852.

We rose early, so as to be ready for a long march. The guard came--a mild-looking Arab--without arms; but on our refusing to take him thus, he brought a Turkish musket, terrible to behold, but quite guiltless of any murderous intent. We gave ourselves up to fate, with true Arab-resignation, and began ascending the Anti-Lebanon. Up and up, by stony paths, under the oaks, beside the streams, and between the wheat-fields, we climbed for two hours, and at last reached a comb or dividing ridge, whence we could look into a valley on the other side, or rather inclosed between the main chain and the offshoot named Djebel Heish, which stretches away towards the south-east. About half-way up the ascent, we passed the ruined acropolis of Cæsarea Philippi, crowning the summit of a lower peak. The walls and bastions cover a great extent of ground, and were evidently used as a stronghold in the Middle Ages.

The valley into which we descended lay directly under one of the peaks of Hermon and the rills that watered it were fed from his snow-fields. It was inhabited by Druses, but no men were to be seen, except a few poor husbandmen, ploughing on the mountain-sides. The women, wearing those enormous horns on their heads which distinguish them from the Mohammedan females, were washing at a pool below. We crossed the valley, and slowly ascended the height on the opposite side, taking care to keep with the baggage-mules. Up to this time, we met very few persons; and we forgot the anticipated perils in contemplating the rugged scenery of the Anti-Lebanon. The mountain-sides were brilliant with flowers, and many new and beautiful specimens arrested our attention. The asphodel grew in bunches beside the streams, and the large scarlet anemone outshone even the poppy, whose color here is the quintessence of flame. Five hours after leaving Banias, we reached the highest part of the pass--a dreary volcanic region, covered with fragments of lava. Just at this place, an old Arab met us, and, after scanning us closely, stopped and accosted Dervish. The latter immediately came running ahead, quite excited with the news that the old man had seen a company of about fifty Druses descend from the sides of Mount Hermon, towards the road we were to travel. We immediately ordered the baggage to halt, and Mr. Harrison, François, and myself rode on to reconnoitre. Our guard, the valiant man of Banias, whose teeth already chattered with fear, prudently kept with the baggage. We crossed the ridge and watched the stony mountain-sides for some time; but no spear or glittering gun-barrel could we see. The caravan was then set in motion; and we had not proceeded far before we met a second company of Arabs, who informed us that the road was free.

Leaving the heights, we descended cautiously into a ravine with walls of rough volcanic rock on each side. It was a pass where three men might have stood their ground against a hundred; and we did not feel thoroughly convinced of our safety till we had threaded its many windings and emerged upon a narrow valley. A village called Beit Jenn nestled under the rocks; and below it, a grove of poplar-trees shaded the banks of a rapid stream. We had now fairly crossed the Anti-Lebanon. The dazzling snows of Mount Hermon overhung us on the west; and, from the opening of the valley, we looked across a wild, waste country, to the distant range of Djebel Hauaran, the seat of the present rebellion, and one of the most interesting regions of Syria. I regretted more than ever not being able to reach it. The ruins of Bozrah, Ezra, and other ancient cities, would well repay the arduous character of the journey, while the traveller might succeed in getting some insight into the life and habits of that singular people, the Druses. But now, and perhaps for some time to come, there is no chance of entering the Hauaran.

Towards the middle of the afternoon, we reached a large village, which is usually the end of the first day's journey from Banias. Our men wanted to stop here, but we considered that to halt then would be to increase the risk, and decided to push on to Katana, four hours' journey from Damascus. They yielded with a bad grace; and we jogged on over the stony road, crossing the long hills which form the eastern base of the Anti-Lebanon. Before long, another Arab met us with the news that there was an encampment of Druses on the plain between us and Katana. At this, our guard, who had recovered sufficient spirit to ride a few paces in advance, fell back, and the impassive Dervish became greatly agitated. Where there is an uncertain danger, it is always better to go ahead than to turn back; and we did so. But the guard reined up on the top of the first ridge, trembling as he pointed to a distant hill, and cried out: "Ahò, ahò henàk!" (There they are!) There were, in fact, the shadows of some rocks, which bore a faint resemblance to tents. Before sunset, we reached the last declivity of the mountains, and saw far in the dusky plain, the long green belt of the gardens of Damascus, and here and there the indistinct glimmer of a minaret. Katana, our resting-place for the night, lay below us, buried in orchards of olive and orange. We pitched our tents on the banks of a beautiful stream, enjoyed the pipe of tranquillity, after our long march, and soon forgot the Druses, in a slumber that lasted unbroken till dawn.

In the morning we sent back the man of Banias, left the baggage to take care of itself, and rode on to Damascus, as fast as our tired horses could carry us. The plain, at first barren and stony, became enlivened with vineyards and fields of wheat, as we advanced. Arabs were everywhere at work, ploughing and directing the water-courses. The belt of living green, the bower in which the great city, the Queen of the Orient, hides her beauty, drew nearer and nearer, stretching out a crescent of foliage for miles on either hand, that gradually narrowed and received us into its cool and fragrant heart. We sank into a sea of olive, pomegranate, orange, plum, apricot, walnut, and plane trees, and were lost. The sun sparkled in the rolling surface above; but we swam through the green depths, below his reach, and thus, drifted on through miles of shade, entered the city.

Since our arrival, I find that two other parties of travellers, one of which crossed the Anti-Lebanon on the northern side of Mount Hermon, were obliged to take guards, and saw several Druse spies posted on the heights, as they passed. A Russian gentleman travelling from here to Tiberias, was stopped three times on the road, and only escaped being plundered from the fact of his having a Druse dragoman. The disturbances are more serious than I had anticipated. Four regiments left here yesterday, sent to the aid of a company of cavalry, which is surrounded by the rebels in a valley of Dejebel Hauaran, and unable to get out.

Chapter IX. Pictures of Damascus.

Damascus from the Anti-Lebanon--Entering the City--A Diorama of Bazaars--An Oriental Hotel--Our Chamber--The Bazaars--Pipes and Coffee--The Rivers of Damascus--Palaces of the Jews--Jewish Ladies--A Christian Gentleman--The Sacred Localities--Damascus Blades--The Sword of Haroun Al-Raschid--An Arrival from Palmyra.

"Are not Abana and Pharpar, rivers of Damascus, better than all the waters of Israel?"--2 Kings, v. 12.

Damascus, *Wednesday, May* 19, 1852.

Damascus is considered by many travellers as the best remaining type of an Oriental city. Constantinople is semi-European; Cairo is fast becoming so; but Damascus, away from the highways of commerce, seated alone between the Lebanon and the Syrian Desert, still retains, in its outward aspect and in the character of its inhabitants, all the pride and fancy and fanaticism of the times of the Caliphs. With this judgment, in general terms, I agree; but not to its ascendancy, in every respect, over Cairo. True, when you behold Damascus from the Salahiyeh, the last slope of the Anti-Lebanon, it is the realization of all that you have dreamed of Oriental splendor; the world has no picture more dazzling. It is Beauty carried to the Sublime, as I have felt when overlooking some boundless forest of palms within the tropics. From the hill, whose ridges heave behind you until in the south they rise to the snowy head of Mount Hermon, the great Syrian plain stretches away to the Euphrates, broken at distances of ten and fifteen miles, by two detached mountain chains. In a terrible gorge at your side, the river Barrada, the ancient Pharpar, forces its way to the plain, and its waters, divided into twelve different channels, make all between you and those blue island-hills of the desert, one great garden, the boundaries of which your vision can barely distinguish. Its longest diameter cannot be less than twenty miles. You look down on a world of foliage, and fruit, and blossoms, whose hue, by contrast with the barren mountains and the yellow rim of the desert which incloses it, seems brighter than all other gardens in the world. Through its centre, following the course of the river, lies Damascus; a line of white walls, topped with domes and towers and tall minarets, winding away for miles through the green sea. Nothing less than a city of palaces, whose walls are marble and whose doors are ivory and pearl, could keep up the enchantment of that distant view.

We rode for an hour through the gardens before entering the gate. The fruit-trees, of whatever variety---walnut, olive, apricot, or fig--were the noblest of their kind. Roses and pomegranates in bloom starred the dark foliage, and the scented jasmine overhung the walls. But as we approached the city, the view was obscured by high mud walls on either side of the road, and we only caught glimpses now and then of the fragrant wilderness. The first street we entered was low and mean, the houses of clay. Following this, we came to an uncovered bazaar, with rude shops on either side, protected by mats stretched in front and supported by poles. Here all sorts of common stuns and utensils were sold, and the street was filled with crowds of Fellahs and Desert Arabs. Two large sycamores shaded it, and the Seraglio of the Pasha of Damascus, a plain two-story building, faced the entrance of the main bazaar, which branched off into the city. We turned into this, and after passing through several small bazaars stocked with dried fruits, pipes and pipe-bowls, groceries, and all the primitive wares of the East, reached a large passage, covered with a steep wooden roof, and entirely occupied by venders of silk stuffs. Out of this we passed through another, devoted to saddles and bridles; then another, full of spices, and at last reached the grand bazaar, where all the richest stuffs of Europe and the East were displayed in the shops. We rode slowly along through the cool twilight, crossed here and there by long pencils of white light, falling through apertures in the roof, and illuminating the gay turbans and silk caftans of the lazy merchants. But out of this bazaar, at intervals, opened the grand gate of a khan, giving us a view of its marble court, its fountains, and the dark arches of its storerooms; or the door of a mosque, with its mosaic floor and pillared corridor. The interminable lines of bazaars, with their atmospheres of spice and fruit and fragrant tobacco, the hushed tread of the slippered crowds; the plash of falling fountains and the bubbling of innumerable narghilehs; the picturesque merchants and their customers, no longer in the big trowsers of Egypt, but the long caftans and abas of Syria; the absence of Frank faces and dresses--in all these there was the true spirit of the Orient, and so far, we were charmed with Damascus.

At the hotel in the Soog el-Haràb, or Frank quarter, the illusion was not dissipated. It had once been the house of some rich merchant. The court into which we were ushered is paved with marble, with a great stone basin, surrounded with vases of flowering plants, in the centre. Two large lemon trees shade the entrance, and a vine, climbing to the top of the house, makes a leafy arbor over the flat roof. The walls of the house are painted in horizontal bars of blue, white, orange and white--a gay grotesqueness of style which does not offend the eye under an eastern sun. On the southern side of the court is the liwan, an arrangement for which the houses of Damascus are noted. It is a vaulted apartment, twenty feet high, entirely open towards the court, except a fine pointed arch at the top, decorated with encaustic ornaments of the most brilliant colors. In front, a tesselated pavement of marble leads to the doors of the chambers on each side. Beyond this is a raised floor covered with matting, and along the farther end a divan, whose piled cushions are the most tempting trap ever set to catch a lazy man. Although not naturally indolent, I find it impossible to resist the fascination of this lounge. Leaning back, cross-legged, against the cushions, with the inseparable pipe in one's hand, the view of the court, the water-basin, the flowers and lemon trees, the servants and dragomen going back and forth, or smoking their narghilehs in the shade--all framed in the beautiful arched entrance, is so perfectly Oriental, so true a tableau from the times of good old Haroun Al-Raschid, that one is surprised to find how many hours have slipped away while he has been silently enjoying it.

Opposite the liwan is a large room paved with marble, with a handsome fountain in the centre. It is the finest in the hotel, and now occupied by Lord Dalkeith and his friends. Our own room is on the upper floor, and is so rich in decorations that I have not yet finished the study of them. Along the side, looking down on the court, we have a mosaic floor of white, red, black and yellow marble. Above this is raised a second floor, carpeted and furnished in European style. The walls, for a height of ten feet, are covered with wooden panelling, painted with arabesque devices in the gayest colors, and along the top there is a series of Arabic inscriptions in gold. There are a number of niches or open closets in the walls, whose arched tops are adorned with pendent wooden ornaments, resembling stalactites, and at the corners of the room the heavy gilded and painted cornice drops into similar grotesque incrustations. A space of bare white wall intervenes between this cornice and the ceiling, which is formed of slim poplar logs, laid side by side, and so covered with paint and with scales and stripes and network devices in gold and silver, that one would take them to be clothed with the skins of the magic serpents that guard the Valley of Diamonds. My most satisfactory remembrance of Damascus will be this room.

My walks through the city have been almost wholly confined to the bazaars, which are of immense extent. One can walk for many miles, without going beyond the cover of their peaked wooden roofs, and in all this round will find no two precisely alike. One is devoted entirely to soap; another to tobacco, through which you cough and sneeze your way to the bazaar of spices, and delightedly inhale its perfumed air. Then there is the bazaar of sweetmeats; of vegetables; of red slippers; of shawls; of caftans; of bakers and ovens; of wooden ware; of jewelry---a great stone building, covered with vaulted passages; of Aleppo silks; of Baghdad carpets; of Indian stuffs; of coffee; and so on, through a seemingly endless variety. As I have already remarked, along the line of the bazaars are many khans, the resort of merchants from all parts of Turkey and Persia, and even India. They are large, stately buildings, and some of them have superb gateways of sculptured marble. The interior courts are paved with stone, with fountains in the centre, and many of them are covered with domes resting on massive pillars. The largest has a roof of nine domes, supported by four grand pillars, which inclose a fountain. The mosques, into which no Christian is allowed to enter, are in general inferior to those of Cairo, but their outer courts are always paved with marble, adorned with fountains, and surrounded by light and elegant corridors. The grand mosque is an imposing edifice, and is said to occupy the site of a former Christian church.

Another pleasant feature of the city is its coffee shops, which abound in the bazaars and on the outskirts of the gardens, beside the running streams.

406

Those in the bazaars are spacious rooms with vaulted ceilings, divans running around the four walls, and fountains in the centre. During the afternoon they are nearly always filled with Turks, Armenians and Persians, smoking the narghileh, or water-pipe, which is the universal custom in Damascus. The Persian tobacco, brought here by the caravans from Baghdad, is renowned for this kind of smoking. The most popular coffee-shop is near the citadel, on the banks and over the surface of the Pharpar. It is a rough wooden building, with a roof of straw mats, but the sight and sound of the rushing waters, as they shoot away with arrowy swiftness under your feet, the shade of the trees that line the banks, and the cool breeze that always visits the spot, beguile you into a second pipe ere you are aware. "El mà, wa el khòdra, wa el widj el hassàn--water, verdure and a beautiful face," says an old Arab proverb, "are three things which delight the heart," and the Syrians avow that all three are to be found in Damascus. Not only on the three Sundays of each week, but every day, in the gardens about the city, you may see whole families (and if Jews or Christians, many groups of families) spending the day in the shade, beside the beautiful waters. There are several gardens fitted up purposely for these picnics, with kiosks, fountains and pleasant seats under the trees. You bring your pipes, your provisions and the like with you, but servants are in attendance to furnish fire and water and coffee, for which, on leaving, you give them a small gratuity. Of all the Damascenes I have yet seen, there is not one but declares his city to be the Garden of the World, the Pearl of the Orient, and thanks God and the Prophet for having permitted him to be born and to live in it. But, except the bazaars, the khans and the baths, of which there are several most luxurious establishments, the city itself is neither so rich nor so purely Saracenic in its architecture as Cairo. The streets are narrow and dirty, and the houses, which are never more than two low stories in height, are built of sun-dried bricks, coated with plaster. I miss the solid piles of stone, the elegant doorways, and, above all, the exquisite hanging balconies of carved wood, which meet one in the old streets of Cairo. Damascus is the representative of all that is gay, brilliant, and picturesque, in Oriental life; but for stately magnificence, Cairo, and, I suspect, Baghdad, is its superior.

We visited the other day the houses of some of the richest Jews and Christians. Old Abou-Ibrahim, the Jewish servant of the hotel, accompanied and introduced us. It is customary for travellers to make these visits, and the families, far from being annoyed, are flattered by it. The exteriors of the houses are mean; but after threading a narrow passage, we emerged into a court, rivalling in profusion of ornament and rich contrast of colors one's early idea of the Palace of Aladdin. The floors and fountains are all of marble mosaic; the arches of the liwan glitter with gold, and the walls bewilder the eye with the intricacy of their adornments. In the first house, we were received by the family in a room of precious marbles, with niches in the walls, resembling grottoes of silver stalactites. The cushions of the divan were of the richest silk, and a chandelier of Bohemian crystal hung from the ceiling. Silver narghilehs were brought to us, and coffee was served in heavy silver zerfs. The lady of the house was a rather corpulent lady of about thirty-five, and wore a semi-European robe of embroidered silk and lace, with full trowsers gathered at the ankles, and yellow slippers. Her black hair was braided, and fastened at the end with golden ornaments, and the light scarf twisted around her head blazed with diamonds. The lids of her large eyes were stained with kohl, and her eyebrows were plucked out and shaved away so as to leave only a thin, arched line, as if drawn with a pencil, above each eye. Her daughter, a girl of fifteen, who bore the genuine Hebrew name of Rachel, had even bigger and blacker eyes than her mother; but her forehead was low, her mouth large, and the expression of her face exceedingly stupid. The father of the family was a middle-aged man, with a well-bred air, and talked with an Oriental politeness which was very refreshing. An English lady, who was of our party, said to him, through me, that if she possessed such a house she should be willing to remain in Damascus. "Why does she leave, then?" he immediately answered: "this is her house, and everything that is in it." Speaking of visiting Jerusalem, he asked me whether it was not a more beautiful city than Damascus. "It is not more beautiful," I said, "but it is more holy," an expression which the whole company received with great satisfaction.

The second house we visited was even larger and richer than the first, but had an air of neglect and decay. The slabs of rich marble were loose and broken, about the edges of the fountains; the rich painting of the wood-work was beginning to fade; and the balustrades leading to the upper chambers were broken off in places. We were ushered into a room, the walls and ceilings of which were composed entirely of gilded arabesque frame-work, set with small mirrors. When new, it must have had a gorgeous effect; but the gold is now tarnished, and the glasses dim. The mistress of the house was seated on the cushions, dividing her time between her pipe and her needle-work. She merely made a slight inclination of her head as we entered, and went on with her occupation. Presently her two daughters and an Abyssinian slave appeared, and took their places on the cushions at her feet, the whole forming a charming group, which I regretted some of my artist friends at home could not see. The mistress was so exceedingly dignified, that she bestowed but few words on us. She seemed to resent our admiration of the slave, who was a most graceful creature; yet her jealousy, it afterwards appeared, had reference to her own husband, for we had scarcely left, when a servant followed to inform the English lady that if she was willing to buy the Abyssinian, the mistress would sell her at once for two thousand piastres.

The last visit we paid was to the dwelling of a Maronite, the richest Christian in Damascus. The house resembled those we had already seen, except that, having been recently built, it was in better condition, and exhibited better taste in the ornaments. No one but the lady was allowed to enter the female apartments, the rest of us being entertained by the proprietor, a man of fifty, and without exception the handsomest and most dignified person of that age I have ever seen. He was a king without a throne, and fascinated me completely by the noble elegance of his manner. In any country but the Orient, I should have pronounced him incapable of an unworthy thought: here, he may be exactly the reverse.

Although Damascus is considered the oldest city in the world, the date of its foundation going beyond tradition, there are very few relics of antiquity in or near it. In the bazaar are three large pillars, supporting half the pediment, which are said to have belonged to the Christian Church of St. John, but, if so, that church must have been originally a Roman temple. Part of the Roman walls and one of the city gates remain; and we saw the spot where, according to tradition, Saul was let down from the wall in a basket. There are two localities pointed out as the scene of his conversion, which, from his own account, occurred near the city. I visited a subterranean chapel claimed by the Latin monks to be the cellar of the house of Ananias, in which the Apostle was concealed. The cellar is, undoubtedly, of great antiquity; but as the whole quarter was for many centuries inhabited wholly by Turks, it would be curious to know how the monks ascertained which was the house of Ananias. As for the "street called Straight," it would be difficult at present to find any in Damascus corresponding to that epithet.

The famous Damascus blades, so renowned in the time of the Crusaders, are made here no longer. The art has been lost for three or four centuries. Yet genuine old swords, of the true steel, are occasionally to be found. They are readily distinguished from modern imitations by their clear and silvery ring when struck, and by the finely watered appearance of the blade, produced by its having been first made of woven wire, and then worked over and over again until it attained the requisite temper. A droll Turk, who is the shekh ed-dellàl, or Chief of the Auctioneers, and is nicknamed Abou-Anteeka (the Father of the Antiques), has a large collection of sabres, daggers, pieces of mail, shields, pipes, rings, seals, and other ancient articles. He demands enormous prices, but generally takes about one-third of what he first asks. I have spent several hours in his curiosity shop, bargaining for turquoise rings, carbuncles, Persian amulets, and Circassian daggers. While looking over some old swords the other day, I noticed one of exquisite temper, but with a shorter blade than usual. The point had apparently been snapped off in fight, but owing to the excellence of the sword, or the owner's affection for it, the steel had been carefully shaped into a new point. Abou-Anteeka asked five hundred piastres, and I, who had taken a particular fancy to possess it, offered him two hundred in an indifferent way, and then laid it aside to examine other articles. After his refusal to accept my offer, I said nothing more, and was leaving the shop, when the old fellow called me back, saying: "You have forgotten your sword,"--which I thereupon took at my own price. I have shown it to Mr. Wood, the British Consul, who pronounced it an extremely fine specimen of Damascus steel; and, on reading the inscription enamelled upon the blade, ascertains that it was made in the year of the Hegira, 181, which corresponds to A.D. 798. This was during the Caliphate of Haroun Al-Raschid, and who knows but the sword may have once flashed in the presence of that great and glorious sovereign--nay, been drawn by his own hand! Who knows but that the Milan armor of the Crusaders may have shivered its point, on the field of Askalon! I kiss the veined azure of thy blade, O Sword of Haroun! I hang the crimson cords of thy scabbard upon my shoulder, and thou shalt henceforth clank in silver music at my side, singing to my ear, and mine alone, thy chants of battle, thy rejoicing songs of slaughter!

Yesterday evening, three gentlemen of Lord Dalkeith's party arrived from a trip to Palmyra. The road thither lies through a part of the Syrian Desert belonging to the Aneyzeh tribe, who are now supposed to be in league with the Druses, against the Government. Including this party, only six persons have succeeded in reaching Palmyra within a year, and two of them, Messrs. Noel and Cathcart, were imprisoned four days by the Arabs, and only escaped by the accidental departure of a caravan for Damascus. The present party was obliged to travel almost wholly by night, running the gauntlet of a dozen Arab encampments, and was only allowed a day's stay at Palmyra. They were all disguised as Bedouins, and took nothing with them but the necessary provisions. They made their appearance here last evening, in long, white abas, with the Bedouin keffie bound over their heads, their faces burnt, their eyes inflamed, and their frames feverish with seven days and nights of travel. The shekh who conducted them was not an Aneyzeh, and would have lost his life had they fallen in with any of that tribe.

Chapter X. The Visions of Hasheesh.

"Exulting, trembling, raging, fainting,

Possessed beyond the Muse's painting."

Collins.

During my stay in Damascus, that insatiable curiosity which leads me to prefer the acquisition of all lawful knowledge through the channels of my own personal experience, rather than in less satisfactory and less laborious ways, induced me to make a trial of the celebrated Hasheesh--that remarkable drug which supplies the luxurious Syrian with dreams more alluring and more gorgeous than the Chinese extracts from his darling opium pipe. The use of Hasheesh--which is a preparation of the dried leaves of the cannabis indica--has been familiar to the East for many centuries. During the Crusades, it was frequently used by the Saracen warriors to stimulate them to the work of slaughter, and from the Arabic term of "Hashasheën," or Eaters of Hasheesh, as applied to them, the word "assassin" has been naturally derived. An infusion of the same plant gives to the drink called "bhang," which is in common use throughout India and Malaysia, its peculiar properties. Thus prepared, it is a more fierce and fatal stimulant than the paste of sugar and spices to which the Turk resorts, as the food of his voluptuous evening reveries. While its immediate effects seem to be more potent than those of opium, its habitual use, though attended with ultimate and permanent injury to the system, rarely results in such utter wreck of mind and body as that to which the votaries of the latter drug inevitably condemn themselves.

A previous experience of the effects of hasheesh--which I took once, and in a very mild form, while in Egypt--was so peculiar in its character, that my curiosity, instead of being satisfied, only prompted me the more to throw myself, for once, wholly under its influence. The sensations it then produced were those, physically, of exquisite lightness and airiness--of a wonderfully keen perception of the ludicrous, in the most simple and familiar objects. During the half hour in which it lasted, I was at no time so far under its control, that I could not, with the clearest perception, study the changes through which I passed. I noted, with careful attention, the fine sensations which spread throughout the whole tissue of my nervous fibre, each thrill helping to divest my frame of its earthy and material nature, until my substance appeared to me no grosser than the vapors of the atmosphere, and while sitting in the calm of the Egyptian twilight, I expected to be lifted up and carried away by the first breeze that should ruffle the Nile. While this process was going on, the objects by which I was surrounded assumed a strange and whimsical expression. My pipe, the oars which my boatmen plied, the turban worn by the captain, the water-jars and culinary implements, became in themselves so inexpressibly absurd and comical, that I was provoked into a long fit of laughter. The hallucination died away as gradually as it came, leaving me overcome with a soft and pleasant drowsiness, from which I sank into a deep, refreshing sleep.

My companion and an English gentleman, who, with his wife, was also residing in Antonio's pleasant caravanserai--agreed to join me in the experiment. The dragoman of the latter was deputed to procure a sufficient quantity of the drug. He was a dark Egyptian, speaking only the lingua franca of the East, and asked me, as he took the money and departed on his mission, whether he should get hasheesh "per ridere, a per dormire?" "Oh, per ridere, of course," I answered; "and see that it be strong and fresh." It is customary with the Syrians to take a small portion immediately before the evening meal, as it is thus diffused through the stomach and acts more gradually, as well as more gently, upon the system. As our dinner-hour was at sunset, I proposed taking hasheesh at that time, but my friends, fearing that its operation might be more speedy upon fresh subjects, and thus betray them into some absurdity in the presence of the other travellers, preferred waiting until after the meal. It was then agreed that we should retire to our room, which, as it rose like a tower one story higher than the rest of the building, was in a manner isolated, and would screen us from observation.

We commenced by taking a tea-spoonful each of the mixture which Abdallah had procured. This was about the quantity I had taken in Egypt, and as the effect then had been so slight, I judged that we ran no risk of taking an over-dose. The strength of the drug, however, must have been far greater in this instance, for whereas I could in the former case distinguish no flavor but that of sugar and rose leaves, I now found the taste intensely bitter and repulsive to the palate. We allowed the paste to dissolve slowly on our tongues, and sat some time, quietly waiting the result. But, having been taken upon a full stomach, its operation was hindered, and after the lapse of nearly an hour, we could not detect the least change in our feelings. My friends loudly expressed their conviction of the humbug of hasheesh, but I, unwilling to give up the experiment at this point, proposed that we should take an additional half spoonful, and follow it with a cup of hot tea, which, if there were really any virtue in the preparation, could not fail to call it into action. This was done, though not without some misgivings, as we were all ignorant of the precise quantity which constituted a dose, and the limits within which the drug could be taken with safety. It was now ten o'clock; the streets of Damascus were gradually becoming silent, and the fair city was bathed in the yellow lustre of the Syrian moon. Only in the marble court-yard below us, a few dragomen and mukkairee lingered under the lemon-trees, and beside the fountain in the centre.

I was seated alone, nearly in the middle of the room, talking with my friends, who were lounging upon a sofa placed in a sort of alcove, at the farther end, when the same fine nervous thrill, of which I have spoken, suddenly shot through me. But this time it was accompanied with a burning sensation at the pit of the stomach; and, instead of growing upon me with the gradual pace of healthy slumber, and resolving me, as before, into air, it came with the intensity of a pang, and shot throbbing along the nerves to the extremities of my body. The sense of limitation---of the confinement of our senses within the bounds of our own flesh and blood--instantly fell away. The walls of my frame were burst outward and tumbled into ruin; and, without thinking what form I wore--losing sight even of all idea of form--I felt that I existed throughout a vast extent of space. The blood, pulsed from my heart, sped through uncounted leagues before it reached my extremities; the air drawn into my lungs expanded into seas of limpid ether, and the arch of my skull was broader than the vault of heaven. Within the concave

414

that held my brain, were the fathomless deeps of blue; clouds floated there, and the winds of heaven rolled them together, and there shone the orb of the sun. It was--though I thought not of that at the time--like a revelation of the mystery of omnipresence. It is difficult to describe this sensation, or the rapidity with which it mastered me. In the state of mental exaltation in which I was then plunged, all sensations, as they rose, suggested more or less coherent images. They presented themselves to me in a double form: one physical, and therefore to a certain extent tangible; the other spiritual, and revealing itself in a succession of splendid metaphors. The physical feeling of extended being was accompanied by the image of an exploding meteor, not subsiding into darkness, but continuing to shoot from its centre or nucleus--which corresponded to the burning spot at the pit of my stomach--incessant adumbrations of light that finally lost themselves in the infinity of space. To my mind, even now, this image is still the best illustration of my sensations, as I recall them; but I greatly doubt whether the reader will find it equally clear.

My curiosity was now in a way of being satisfied; the Spirit (demon, shall I not rather say?) of Hasheesh had entire possession of me. I was cast upon the flood of his illusions, and drifted helplessly whithersoever they might choose to bear me. The thrills which ran through my nervous system became more rapid and fierce, accompanied with sensations that steeped my whole being in unutterable rapture. I was encompassed by a sea of light, through which played the pure, harmonious colors that are born of light. While endeavoring, in broken expressions, to describe my feelings to my friends, who sat looking upon me incredulously--not yet having been affected by the drug--I suddenly found myself at the foot of the great Pyramid of Cheops. The tapering courses of yellow limestone gleamed like gold in the sun, and the pile rose so high that it seemed to lean for support upon the blue arch of the sky. I wished to ascend it, and the wish alone placed me immediately upon its apex, lifted thousands of feet above the wheat-fields and palm-groves of Egypt. I cast my eyes downward, and, to my astonishment, saw that it was built, not of limestone, but of huge square plugs of Cavendish tobacco! Words cannot paint the overwhelming sense of the ludicrous which I then experienced. I writhed on my chair in an agony of laughter, which was only relieved by the vision melting away like a dissolving view; till, out of my confusion of indistinct images and fragments of images, another and more wonderful vision arose.

The more vividly I recall the scene which followed, the more carefully I restore its different features, and separate the many threads of sensation which it wove into one gorgeous web, the more I despair of representing its exceeding glory. I was moving over the Desert, not upon the rocking dromedary, but seated in a barque made of mother-of-pearl, and studded with jewels of surpassing lustre. The sand was of grains of gold, and my keel slid through them without jar or sound. The air was radiant with excess of light, though no sun was to be seen. I inhaled the most delicious perfumes; and harmonies, such as Beethoven may have heard in dreams, but never wrote, floated around me. The atmosphere itself was light, odor, music; and each and all sublimated beyond anything the sober senses are capable of receiving. Before me--for a thousand leagues, as it seemed--stretched a vista of rainbows, whose colors gleamed with the splendor of gems--arches of living amethyst, sapphire, emerald, topaz, and ruby. By thousands and tens of thousands, they flew past me, as my dazzling barge sped down the magnificent arcade; yet the vista still stretched as far as ever before me. I revelled in a sensuous elysium, which was perfect, because no sense was left ungratified. But beyond all, my mind was filled with a boundless feeling of triumph. My journey was that of a conqueror--not of a conqueror who subdues his race, either by Love or by Will, for I forgot that Man existed--but one victorious over the grandest as well as the subtlest forces of Nature. The spirits of Light, Color, Odor, Sound, and Motion were my slaves; and, having these, I was master of the universe.

Those who are endowed to any extent with the imaginative faculty, must have at least once in their lives experienced feelings which may give them a clue to the exalted sensuous raptures of my triumphal march. The view of a sublime mountain landscape, the hearing of a grand orchestral symphony, or of a choral upborne by the "full-voiced organ," or even the beauty and luxury of a cloudless summer day, suggests emotions similar in kind, if less intense. They took a warmth and glow from that pure animal joy which degrades not, but spiritualizes and ennobles our material part, and which differs from cold, abstract, intellectual enjoyment, as the flaming diamond of the Orient differs from the icicle of the North. Those finer senses, which occupy a middle ground between our animal and intellectual appetites, were suddenly developed to a pitch beyond what I had ever dreamed, and being thus at one and the same time gratified to the fullest extent of their preternatural capacity, the result was a single harmonious sensation, to describe which human language has no epithet. Mahomet's Paradise, with its palaces of ruby and emerald, its airs of musk and cassia, and its rivers colder than snow and sweeter than honey, would have been a poor and mean terminus for my arcade of rainbows. Yet in the character of this paradise, in the gorgeous fancies of the Arabian Nights, in the glow and luxury of all Oriental poetry, I now recognize more or less of the agency of hasheesh.

The fulness of my rapture expanded the sense of time; and though the whole vision was probably not more than five minutes in passing through my mind, years seemed to have elapsed while I shot under the dazzling myriads of rainbow arches. By and by, the rainbows, the barque of pearl and jewels, and the desert of golden sand, vanished; and, still bathed in light and perfume, I found myself in a land of green and flowery lawns, divided by hills of gently undulating outline. But, although the vegetation was the richest of earth, there were neither streams nor fountains to be seen; and the people who came from the hills, with brilliant garments that shone in the sun, besought me to give them the blessing of water. Their hands were full of branches of the coral honeysuckle, in bloom. These I took; and, breaking off the flowers one by one, set them in the earth. The slender, trumpet-like tubes immediately became shafts of masonry, and sank deep into the earth; the lip of the flower changed into a circular mouth of rose-colored marble, and the people, leaning over its brink, lowered their pitchers to the bottom with cords, and drew them up again, filled to the brim, and dripping with honey.

The most remarkable feature of these illusions was, that at the time when I was most completely under their influence, I knew myself to be seated in the tower of Antonio's hotel in Damascus, knew that I had taken hasheesh, and that the strange, gorgeous and ludicrous fancies which possessed me, were the effect of it. At the very same instant that I looked upon the Valley of the Nile from the pyramid, slid over the Desert, or created my marvellous wells in that beautiful pastoral country, I saw the furniture of my room, its mosaic pavement, the quaint Saracenic niches in the walls, the painted and gilded beams of the ceiling, and the couch in the recess before me, with my two companions watching me. Both sensations were simultaneous, and equally palpable. While I was most given up to the magnificent delusion, I saw its cause and felt its absurdity most clearly. Metaphysicians say that the mind is incapable of performing two operations at the same time, and may attempt to explain this phenomenon by supposing a rapid and incessant vibration of the perceptions between the two states. This explanation, however, is not satisfactory to me; for not more clearly does a skilful musician with the same breath blow two distinct musical notes from a bugle, than I was conscious of two distinct conditions of being in the same moment. Yet, singular as it may seem, neither conflicted with the other. My enjoyment of the visions was complete and absolute, undisturbed by the faintest doubt of their reality, while, in some other chamber of my brain, Reason sat coolly watching them, and heaping the liveliest ridicule on their fantastic features. One set of nerves was thrilled with the bliss of the gods, while another was convulsed with unquenchable laughter at that very bliss. My highest ecstacies could not bear down and silence the weight of my ridicule, which, in its turn, was powerless to prevent me from running into other and more gorgeous absurdities. I was double, not "swan and shadow," but rather, Sphinx-like, human and beast. A true Sphinx, I was a riddle and a mystery to myself.

The drug, which had been retarded in its operation on account of having been taken after a meal, now began to make itself more powerfully felt. The visions were more grotesque than ever, but less agreeable; and there was a painful tension throughout my nervous system--the effect of over-stimulus. I was a mass of transparent jelly, and a confectioner poured me into a twisted mould. I threw my chair aside, and writhed and tortured myself for some time to force my loose substance into the mould. At last, when I had so far succeeded that only one foot remained outside, it was lifted off, and another mould, of still more crooked and intricate shape, substituted. I have no doubt that the contortions through which I went, to accomplish the end of my gelatinous destiny, would have been extremely ludicrous to a spectator, but to me they were painful and disagreeable. The sober half of me went into fits of laughter over them, and through that laughter, my vision shifted into another scene. I had laughed until my eyes overflowed profusely. Every drop that fell, immediately became a large loaf of bread, and tumbled upon the shop-board of a baker in the bazaar at Damascus. The more I laughed, the faster the loaves fell, until such a pile was raised about the baker, that I could hardly see the top of his head. "The man will be suffocated," I cried, "but if he were to die, I cannot stop!"

My perceptions now became more dim and confused. I felt that I was in the grasp of some giant force; and, in the glimmering of my fading reason, grew earnestly alarmed, for the terrible stress under which my frame labored increased every moment. A fierce and furious heat radiated from my stomach throughout my system; my mouth and throat were as dry and hard as if made of brass, and my tongue, it seemed to me, was a bar of rusty iron. I seized a pitcher of water, and drank long and deeply; but I might as well have drunk so much air, for not only did it impart no moisture, but my palate and throat gave me no intelligence of having drunk at all. I stood in the centre of the room, brandishing my arms convulsively, an heaving sighs that seemed to shatter my whole being. "Will no one," I cried in distress, "cast out this devil that has possession of me?" I no longer saw the room nor my friends, but I heard one of them saying, "It must be real; he could not counterfeit such an expression as that. But it don't look much like pleasure." Immediately afterwards there was a scream of the wildest laughter, and my countryman sprang upon the floor, exclaiming, "O, ye gods! I am a locomotive!" This was his ruling hallucination; and, for the space of two or three hours, he continued to pace to and fro with a measured stride, exhaling his breath in violent jets, and when he spoke, dividing his words into syllables, each of which he brought out with a jerk, at the same time turning his hands at his sides, as if they were the cranks of imaginary wheels, The Englishman, as soon as he felt the dose beginning to take effect, prudently retreated to his own room, and what the nature of his visions was, we never learned, for he refused to tell, and, moreover, enjoined the strictest silence on his wife.

By this time it was nearly midnight. I had passed through the Paradise of Hasheesh, and was plunged at once into its fiercest Hell. In my ignorance I had taken what, I have since learned, would have been a sufficient portion for six men, and was now paying a frightful penalty for my curiosity. The excited blood rushed through my frame with a sound like the roaring of mighty waters. It was projected into my eyes until I could no longer see; it beat thickly in my ears, and so throbbed in my heart, that I feared the ribs would give way under its blows. I tore open my vest, placed my hand over the spot, and tried to count the pulsations; but there were two hearts, one beating at the rate of a thousand beats a minute, and the other with a slow, dull motion. My throat, I thought, was filled to the brim with blood, and streams of blood were pouring from my ears. I felt them gushing warm down my cheeks and neck. With a maddened, desperate feeling, I fled from the room, and walked over the flat, terraced roof of the house. My body seemed to shrink and grow rigid as I wrestled with the demon, and my face to become wild, lean and haggard. Some lines which had struck me, years before, in reading Mrs. Browning's "Rhyme of the Duchess May," flashed into my mind:--

> "And the horse, in stark despair, with his front hoofs poised in air,
>
> On the last verge, rears amain;
>
> And he hangs, he rocks between--and his nostrils curdle in--
>
> And he shivers, head and hoof, and the flakes of foam fall off;
>
> And his face grows fierce and thin."

That picture of animal terror and agony was mine. I was the horse, hanging poised on the verge of the giddy tower, the next moment to be borne sheer down to destruction. Involuntarily, I raised my hand to feel the leanness and sharpness of my face. Oh horror! the flesh had fallen from my bones, and it was a skeleton head that I carried on my shoulders! With one bound I sprang to the parapet, and looked down into the silent courtyard, then filled with the shadows thrown into it by the sinking moon. Shall I cast myself down headlong? was the question I proposed to myself; but though the horror of that skeleton delusion was greater than my fear of death, there was an invisible hand at my breast which pushed me away from the brink.

I made my way back to the room, in a state of the keenest suffering.

420

My companion was still a locomotive, rushing to and fro, and jerking out his syllables with the disjointed accent peculiar to a steam-engine. His mouth had turned to brass, like mine, and he raised the pitcher to his lips in the attempt to moisten it, but before he had taken a mouthful, set the pitcher down again with a yell of laughter, crying out: "How can I take water into my boiler, while I am letting off steam?"

But I was now too far gone to feel the absurdity of this, or his other exclamations. I was sinking deeper and deeper into a pit of unutterable agony and despair. For, although I was not conscious of real pain in any part of my body, the cruel tension to which my nerves had been subjected filled me through and through with a sensation of distress which was far more severe than pain itself. In addition to this, the remnant of will with which I struggled against the demon, became gradually weaker, and I felt that I should soon be powerless in his hands. Every effort to preserve my reason was accompanied by a pang of mortal fear, lest what I now experienced was insanity, and would hold mastery over me for ever. The thought of death, which also haunted me, was far less bitter than this dread. I knew that in the struggle which was going on in my frame, I was borne fearfully near the dark gulf, and the thought that, at such a time, both reason and will were leaving my brain, filled me with an agony, the depth and blackness of which I should vainly attempt to portray. I threw myself on my bed, with the excited blood still roaring wildly in my ears, my heart throbbing with a force that seemed to be rapidly wearing away my life, my throat dry as a pot-sherd, and my stiffened tongue cleaving to the roof of my mouth--resisting no longer, but awaiting my fate with the apathy of despair.

My companion was now approaching the same condition, but as the effect of the drug on him had been less violent, so his stage of suffering was more clamorous. He cried out to me that he was dying, implored me to help him, and reproached me vehemently, because I lay there silent, motionless, and apparently careless of his danger. "Why will he disturb me?" I thought; "he thinks he is dying, but what is death to madness? Let him die; a thousand deaths were more easily borne than the pangs I suffer." While I was sufficiently conscious to hear his exclamations, they only provoked my keen anger; but

421

after a time, my senses became clouded, and I sank into a stupor. As near as I can judge, this must have been three o'clock in the morning, rather more than five hours after the hasheesh began to take effect. I lay thus all the following day and night, in a state of gray, blank oblivion, broken only by a single wandering gleam of consciousness. I recollect hearing François' voice. He told me afterwards that I arose, attempted to dress myself, drank two cups of coffee, and then fell back into the same death-like stupor; but of all this, I did not retain the least knowledge. On the morning of the second day, after a sleep of thirty hours, I awoke again to the world, with a system utterly prostrate and unstrung, and a brain clouded with the lingering images of my visions. I knew where I was, and what had happened to me, but all that I saw still remained unreal and shadowy. There was no taste in what I ate, no refreshment in what I drank, and it required a painful effort to comprehend what was said to me and return a coherent answer. Will and Reason had come back, but they still sat unsteadily upon their thrones.

My friend, who was much further advanced in his recovery, accompanied me to the adjoining bath, which I hoped would assist in restoring me. It was with great difficulty that I preserved the outward appearance of consciousness. In spite of myself, a veil now and then fell over my mind, and after wandering for years, as it seemed, in some distant world, I awoke with a shock, to find myself in the steamy halls of the bath, with a brown Syrian polishing my limbs. I suspect that my language must have been rambling and incoherent, and that the menials who had me in charge understood my condition, for as soon as I had stretched myself upon the couch which follows the bath, a glass of very acid sherbet was presented to me, and after drinking it I experienced instant relief. Still the spell was not wholly broken, and for two or three days I continued subject to frequent involuntary fits of absence, which made me insensible, for the time, to all that was passing around me. I walked the streets of Damascus with a strange consciousness that I was in some other place at the same time, and with a constant effort to reunite my divided perceptions.

Previous to the experiment, we had decided on making a bargain with the shekh for the journey to Palmyra. The state, however, in which we now found ourselves, obliged us to relinquish the plan. Perhaps the excitement of a forced march across the desert, and a conflict with the hostile Arabs, which was quite likely to happen, might have assisted us in throwing off the baneful effects of the drug; but all the charm which lay in the name of Palmyra and the romantic interest of the trip, was gone. I was without courage and without energy, and nothing remained for me but to leave Damascus.

Yet, fearful as my rash experiment proved to me, I did not regret having made it. It revealed to me deeps of rapture and of suffering which my natural faculties never could have sounded. It has taught me the majesty of human reason and of human will, even in the weakest, and the awful peril of tampering with that which assails their integrity. I have here faithfully and fully written out my experience, on account of the lesson which it may convey to others. If I have unfortunately failed in my design, and have but awakened that restless curiosity which I have endeavored to forestall, let me beg all who are thereby led to repeat the experiment upon themselves, that they be content to take the portion of hasheesh which is considered sufficient for one man, and not, like me, swallow enough for six.

Chapter XI. A Dissertation on Bathing and Bodies.

"No swan-soft woman, rubbed with lucid oils,

The gift of an enamored god, more fair."

Browning.

We shall not set out from Damascus--we shall not leave the Pearl of the Orient to glimmer through the seas of foliage wherein it lies buried--without consecrating a day to the Bath, that material agent of peace and good-will unto men. We have bathed in the Jordan, like Naaman, and been made clean; let us now see whether Abana and Pharpar, rivers of Damascus, are better than the waters of Israel.

The Bath is the "peculiar institution" of the East. Coffee has become colonized in France and America; the Pipe is a cosmopolite, and his blue, joyous breath congeals under the Arctic Circle, or melts languidly into the soft airs of the Polynesian Isles; but the Bath, that sensuous elysium which cradled the dreams of Plato, and the visions of Zoroaster, and the solemn meditations of Mahomet, is only to be found under an Oriental sky. The naked natives of the Torrid Zone are amphibious; they do not bathe, they live in the water. The European and Anglo-American wash themselves and think they have bathed; they shudder under cold showers and perform laborious antics with coarse towels. As for the Hydropathist, the Genius of the Bath, whose dwelling is in Damascus, would be convulsed with scornful laughter, could he behold that aqueous Diogenes sitting in his tub, or stretched out in his wet wrappings, like a sodden mummy, in a catacomb of blankets and feather beds. As the rose in the East has a rarer perfume than in other lands, so does the Bath bestow a superior purification and impart a more profound enjoyment.

Listen not unto the lamentations of travellers, who complain of the heat, and the steam, and the dislocations of their joints. They belong to the stiff-necked generation, who resist the processes, whereunto the Oriental yields himself body and soul. He who is bathed in Damascus, must be as clay in the hands of a potter. The Syrians marvel how the Franks can walk, so difficult is it to bend their joints. Moreover, they know the difference between him who comes to the Bath out of a mere idle curiosity, and him who has tasted its delight and holds it in due honor. Only the latter is permitted to know all its mysteries. The former is carelessly hurried through the ordinary forms of bathing, and, if any trace of the cockney remain in him, is quite as likely to be disgusted as pleased. Again, there are many second and third-rate baths, whither cheating dragomen conduct their victims, in consideration of a division of spoils with the bath-keeper. Hence it is, that the Bath has received but partial justice at the hands of tourists in the East. If any one doubts this, let him clothe himself with Oriental passiveness and resignation, go to the Hamman el-Khyateën, at Damascus, or the Bath of Mahmoud Pasha, at Constantinople, and demand that he be perfectly bathed.

Come with me, and I will show you the mysteries of the perfect bath. Here is the entrance, a heavy Saracenic arch, opening upon the crowded bazaar. We descend a few steps to the marble pavement of a lofty octagonal hall, lighted by a dome. There is a jet of sparkling water in the centre, falling into a heavy stone basin. A platform about five feet in height runs around the hall, and on this are ranged a number of narrow couches, with their heads to the wall, like the pallets in a hospital ward. The platform is covered with straw matting, and from the wooden gallery which rises above it are suspended towels, with blue and crimson borders. The master of the bath receives us courteously, and conducts us to one of the vacant couches. We kick off our red slippers below, and mount the steps to the platform. Yonder traveller, in Frank dress, who has just entered, goes up with his boots on, and we know, from that fact, what sort of a bath he will get.

As the work of disrobing proceeds, a dark-eyed boy appears with a napkin, which he holds before us, ready to bind it about the waist, as soon as we regain our primitive form. Another attendant throws a napkin over our shoulders and wraps a third around our head, turban-wise. He then thrusts a pair of wooden clogs upon our feet, and, taking us by the arm, steadies our tottering and clattering steps, as we pass through a low door and a warm ante-chamber into the first hall of the bath. The light, falling dimly through a cluster of bull's-eyes in the domed ceiling, shows, first, a silver thread of water, playing in a steamy atmosphere; next, some dark motionless objects, stretched out on a low central platform of marble. The attendant spreads a linen sheet in one of the vacant places, places a pillow at one end, takes off our clogs, deposits us gently on our back, and leaves us. The pavement is warm beneath us, and the first breath we draw gives us a sense of suffocation. But a bit of burning aloe-wood has just been carried through the hall, and the steam is permeated with fragrance. The dark-eyed boy appears with a narghileh, which he places beside us, offering the amber mouth-piece to our submissive lips. The smoke we inhale has an odor of roses; and as the pipe bubbles with our breathing, we feel that the dews of sweat gather heavily upon us. The attendant now reappears, kneels beside us, and gently kneads us with dexterous hands. Although no anatomist, he knows every muscle and sinew whose suppleness gives ease to the body, and so moulds and manipulates them that we lose the rigidity of our mechanism, and become plastic in his hands. He turns us upon our face, repeats the same process upon the back, and leaves us a little longer to lie there passively, glistening in our own dew.

We are aroused from a reverie about nothing by a dark-brown shape, who replaces the clogs, puts his arm around our waist and leads us into an inner hall, with a steaming tank in the centre. Here he slips us off the brink, and we collapse over head and ears in the fiery fluid. Once--twice--we dip into the delicious heat, and then are led into a marble alcove, and seated flat upon the floor. The attendant stands behind us, and we now perceive that his hands are encased in dark hair-gloves. He pounces upon an arm, which he rubs until, like a serpent, we slough the worn-out skin, and resume our infantile smoothness and fairness. No man can be called clean until he has bathed in the East. Let him walk directly from his accustomed bath and self-friction with towels, to the Hammam el-Khateën, and the attendant will exclaim, as he shakes out his hair-gloves: "O Frank! it is a long time since you have bathed." The other arm follows, the back, the breast, the legs, until the work is complete, and we know precisely how a horse feels after he has been curried.

Now the attendant turns two cocks at the back of the alcove, and holding a basin alternately under the cold and hot streams, floods us at first with a fiery dash, that sends a delicious warm shiver through every nerve; then, with milder applications, lessening the temperature of the water by semi-tones, until, from the highest key of heat which we can bear, we glide rapturously down the gamut until we reach the lowest bass of coolness. The skin has by this time attained an exquisite sensibility, and answers to these changes of temperature with thrills of the purest physical pleasure. In fact, the whole frame seems purged of its earthy nature and transformed into something of a finer and more delicate texture.

After a pause, the attendant makes his appearance with a large wooden bowl, a piece of soap, and a bunch of palm-fibres. He squats down beside the bowl, and speedily creates a mass of snowy lather, which grows up to a pyramid and topples over the edge. Seizing us by the crown-tuft of hair upon our shaven head, he plants the foamy bunch of fibres full in our face. The world vanishes; sight, hearing, smell, taste (unless we open our mouth), and breathing, are cut off; we have become nebulous. Although our eyes are shut, we seem to see a blank whiteness; and, feeling nothing but a soft fleeciness, we doubt whether we be not the Olympian cloud which visited Io. But the cloud clears away before strangulation begins, and the velvety mass descends upon the body. Twice we are thus "slushed" from head to foot, and made more slippery than the anointed wrestlers of the Greek games. Then the basin comes again into play, and we glide once more musically through the scale of temperature.

The brown sculptor has now nearly completed his task. The figure of clay which entered the bath is transformed into polished marble. He turns the body from side to side, and lifts the limbs to see whether the workmanship is adequate to his conception. His satisfied gaze proclaims his success. A skilful bath-attendant has a certain aesthetic pleasure in his occupation. The bodies he polishes become to some extent his own workmanship, and he feels responsible for their symmetry or deformity. He experiences a degree of triumph in contemplating a beautiful form, which has grown more airily light and beautiful under his hands. He is a great connoisseur of bodies, and could pick you out the finest specimens with as ready an eye as an artist.

I envy those old Greek bathers, into whose hands were delivered Pericles, and Alcibiades, and the perfect models of Phidias. They had daily before their eyes the highest types of Beauty which the world has ever produced; for of all things that are beautiful, the human body is the crown. Now, since the delusion of artists has been overthrown, and we know that Grecian Art is but the simple reflex of Nature--that the old masterpieces of sculpture were no miraculous embodiments of a beau ideal, but copies of living forms--we must admit that in no other age of the world has the physical Man been so perfectly developed. The nearest approach I have ever seen to the symmetry of ancient sculpture was among the Arab tribes of Ethiopia. Our Saxon race can supply the athlete, but not the Apollo.

Oriental life is too full of repose, and the Ottoman race has become too degenerate through indulgence, to exhibit many striking specimens of physical beauty. The face is generally fine, but the body is apt to be lank, and with imperfect muscular development. The best forms I saw in the baths were those of laborers, who, with a good deal of rugged strength, showed some grace and harmony of proportion. It may be received as a general rule, that the physical development of the European is superior to that of the Oriental, with the exception of the Circassians and Georgians, whose beauty well entitles them to the distinction of giving their name to our race.

So far as female beauty is concerned, the Circassian women have no superiors. They have preserved in their mountain home the purity of the Grecian models, and still display the perfect physical loveliness, whose type has descended to us in the Venus de Medici. The Frank who is addicted to wandering about the streets of Oriental cities can hardly fail to be favored with a sight of the faces of these beauties. More than once it has happened to me, in meeting a veiled lady, sailing along in her balloon-like feridjee, that she has allowed the veil to drop by a skilful accident, as she passed, and startled me with the vision of her beauty, recalling the line of the Persian poet: "Astonishment! is this the dawn of the glorious sun, or is it the full moon?" The Circassian face is a pure oval; the forehead is low and fair, "an excellent thing in woman," and the skin of an ivory whiteness, except the faint pink of the cheeks and the ripe, roseate stain of the lips. The hair is dark, glossy, and luxuriant, exquisitely outlined on the temples; the eyebrows slightly arched, and drawn with a delicate pencil; while lashes like "rays of darkness" shade the large, dark, humid orbs below them. The alabaster of the face, so pure as scarcely to show the blue branching of the veins on the temples, is lighted by those superb eyes--

"Shining eyes, like antique jewels set in Parian statue-stone,"

--whose wells are so dark and deep, that you are cheated into the belief that a glorious soul looks out of them.

Once, by an unforeseen chance, I beheld the Circassian form, in its most perfect development. I was on board an Austrian steamer in the harbor of Smyrna, when the harem of a Turkish pasha came out in a boat to embark for Alexandria. The sea was rather rough, and nearly all the officers of the steamer were ashore. There were six veiled and swaddled women, with a black eunuch as guard, in the boat, which lay tossing for some time at the foot of the gangway ladder, before the frightened passengers could summon courage to step out. At last the youngest of them--a Circassian girl of not more than fifteen or sixteen years of age--ventured upon the ladder, clasping the hand-rail with one hand, while with the other she held together the folds of her cumbrous feridjee. I was standing in the gangway, watching her, when a slight lurch of the steamer caused her to loose her hold of the garment, which, fastened at the neck, was blown back from her shoulders, leaving her body screened but by a single robe of-light, gauzy silk. Through this, the marble whiteness of her skin, the roundness, the glorious symmetry of her form, flashed upon me, as a vision of Aphrodite, seen

"Through leagues of shimmering water, like a star."

It was but a momentary glimpse; yet that moment convinced me that forms of Phidian perfection are still nurtured in the vales of Caucasus.

The necessary disguise of dress hides from us much of the beauty and dignity of Humanity, I have seen men who appeared heroic in the freedom of nakedness, shrink almost into absolute vulgarity, when clothed. The soul not only sits at the windows of the eyes, and hangs upon the gateway of the lips;

she speaks as well in the intricate, yet harmonious lines of the body, and the ever-varying play of the limbs. Look at the torso of Ilioneus, the son of Niobe, and see what an agony of terror and supplication cries out from that headless and limbless trunk! Decapitate Laocoön, and his knotted muscles will still express the same dreadful suffering and resistance. None knew this better than the ancient sculptors; and hence it was that we find many of their statues of distinguished men wholly or partly undraped. Such a view of Art would be considered transcendental now-a-days, when our dress, our costumes, and our modes of speech either ignore the existence of our bodies, or treat them with little of that reverence which is their due.

But, while we have been thinking these thoughts, the attendant has been waiting to give us a final plunge into the seething tank. Again we slide down to the eyes in the fluid heat, which wraps us closely about until we tingle with exquisite hot shiverings. Now comes the graceful boy, with clean, cool, lavendered napkins, which he folds around our waist and wraps softly about the head. The pattens are put upon our feet, and the brown arm steadies us gently through the sweating-room and ante-chamber into the outer hall, where we mount to our couch. We sink gently upon the cool linen, and the boy covers us with a perfumed sheet. Then, kneeling beside the couch, he presses the folds of the sheet around us, that it may absorb the lingering moisture and the limpid perspiration shed by the departing heat. As fast as the linen becomes damp, he replaces it with fresh, pressing the folds about us as tenderly as a mother arranges the drapery of her sleeping babe; for we, though of the stature of a man, are now infantile in our helpless happiness. Then he takes our passive hand and warms its palm by the soft friction of his own; after which, moving to the end of the couch, he lifts our feet upon his lap, and repeats the friction upon their soles, until the blood comes back to the surface of the body with a misty glow, like that which steeps the clouds of a summer afternoon.

We have but one more process to undergo, and the attendant already stands at the head of our couch. This is the course of passive gymnastics, which excites so much alarm and resistance in the ignorant Franks. It is only resistance that is dangerous, completely neutralizing the enjoyment of the

430

process. Give yourself with a blind submission into the arms of the brown Fate, and he will lead you to new chambers of delight. He lifts us to a sitting posture, places himself behind us, and folds his arms around our body, alternately tightening and relaxing his clasp, as if to test the elasticity of the ribs. Then seizing one arm, he draws it across the opposite shoulder, until the joint cracks like a percussion-cap. The shoulder-blades, the elbows, the wrists, and the finger-joints are all made to fire off their muffled volleys; and then, placing one knee between our shoulders, and clasping both hands upon our forehead, he draws our head back until we feel a great snap of the vertebral column. Now he descends to the hip-joints, knees, ankles, and feet, forcing each and all to discharge a salvo de joie. The slight languor left from the bath is gone, and an airy, delicate exhilaration, befitting the winged Mercury, takes its place.

The boy, kneeling, presents us with finjan of foamy coffee, followed by a glass of sherbet cooled with the snows of Lebanon. He presently returns with a narghileh, which we smoke by the effortless inhalation of the lungs. Thus we lie in perfect repose, soothed by the fragrant weed, and idly watching the silent Orientals, who are undressing for the bath or reposing like ourselves. Through the arched entrance, we see a picture of the bazaars: a shadowy painting of merchants seated amid their silks and spices, dotted here and there with golden drops and splashes of sunshine, which have trickled through the roof. The scene paints itself upon our eyes, yet wakes no slightest stir of thought. The brain is a becalmed sea, without a ripple on its shores. Mind and body are drowned in delicious rest; and we no longer remember what we are. We only know that there is an Existence somewhere in the air, and that wherever it is, and whatever it may be, it is happy.

More and more dim grows the picture. The colors fade and blend into each other, and finally merge into a bed of rosy clouds, flooded with the radiance of some unseen sun. Gentlier than "tired eyelids upon tired eyes," sleep lies upon our senses: a half-conscious sleep, wherein we know that we behold light and inhale fragrance. As gently, the clouds dissipate into air, and we are born again into the world. The Bath is at an end. We arise and put on our garments, and walk forth into the sunny streets of Damascus. But as we go homewards, we involuntarily look down to see whether we are really treading upon the earth, wondering, perhaps, that we should be content to do so, when it would be so easy to soar above the house-tops.

Chapter XII. Baalbec and Lebanon.

Departure from Damascus--The Fountains of the Pharpar--Pass of the Anti-Lebanon--Adventure with the Druses--The Range of Lebanon--The Demon of Hasheesh departs--Impressions of Baalbec--The Temple of the Sun--Titanic Masonry--The Ruined Mosque--Camp on Lebanon--Rascality of the Guide--The Summit of Lebanon--The Sacred Cedars--The Christians of Lebanon--An Afternoon in Eden--Rugged Travel--We Reach the Coast--Return to Beyrout.

"Peor and Baälim

Forsake their temples dim."

Milton.

"The cedars wave on Lebanon,

But Judah's statelier maids are gone."

Byron.

Beyrout, *Thursday, May* 27, 1852.

After a stay of eight days in Damascus, we called our men, Dervish and Mustapha, again into requisition, loaded our enthusiastic mules, and mounted our despairing horses. There were two other parties on the way to Baalbec--an English gentleman and lady, and a solitary Englishman, so that our united forces made an imposing caravan. There is always a custom-house examination, not on entering, but on issuing from an Oriental city, but travellers can avoid it by procuring the company of a Consular Janissary as far as the gate. Mr. Wood, the British Consul, lent us one of his officers for the occasion, whom we found waiting, outside of the wall, to receive his private fee for the service. We mounted the long, barren hill west of the plain, and at the summit, near the tomb of a Moslem shekh, turned to take a last long look at the bowery plain, and the minarets of the city, glittering through the blue morning vapor. A few paces further on the rocky road, a different scene presented itself to us. There lay, to the westward, a long stretch of naked yellow mountains, basking in the hot glare of the sun, and through the centre, deep down in the heart of the arid landscape, a winding line of living green showed the course of the Barrada. We followed the river, until the path reached an impassable gorge, which occasioned a detour of two or three hours. We then descended to the bed of the dell, where the vegetation, owing to the radiated heat from the mountains and the fertilizing stimulus of the water below, was even richer than on the plain of Damascus. The trees were plethoric with an overplus of life. The boughs of the mulberries were weighed down with the burden of the leaves; pomegranates were in a violent eruption of blossoms; and the foliage of the fig and poplar was of so deep a hue that it shone black in the sun.

Passing through a gateway of rock, so narrow that we were often obliged to ride in the bed of the stream, we reached a little meadow, beyond which was a small hamlet, almost hidden in the leaves. Here the mountains again approached each other, and from the side of that on the right hand, the main body of the Barrada, or Pharpar, gushed forth in one full stream. The fountain is nearly double the volume of that of the Jordan at Banias, and much more beautiful. The foundations of an ancient building, probably a temple, overhang it, and tall poplars and sycamores cover it with impenetrable shade. From the low aperture, where it bursts into the light, its waters, white with foam, bound away flashing in the chance rays of sunshine, until they are lost to sight in the dense, dark foliage. We sat an hour on the ruined walls, listening to the roar and rush of the flood, and enjoying the shade of the walnuts and sycamores. Soon after leaving, our path crossed a small stream, which comes down to the Barrada from the upper valleys of the Anti-Lebanon, and entered a wild pass, faced with cliffs of perpendicular rock. An old bridge, of one arch, spanned the chasm, out of which we climbed to a tract of high meadow land. In the pass there were some fragments of ancient columns, traces of an aqueduct, and inscriptions on the rocks, among which Mr. H. found the name of Antoninus. The place is not mentioned in any book of travel I have seen, as it is not on the usual road from Damascus to Baalbec.

As we were emerging from the pass, we saw a company of twelve armed

434

men seated in the grass, near the roadside. They were wild-looking characters, and eyed us somewhat sharply as we passed. We greeted them with the usual "salaam aleikoom!" which they did not return. The same evening, as we encamped at the village of Zebdeni, about three hours further up the valley, we were startled by a great noise and outcry, with the firing of pistols. It happened, as we learned on inquiring the cause of all this confusion, that the men we saw in the pass were rebel Druses, who were then lying in wait for the Shekh of Zebdeni, whom, with his son, they had taken captive soon after we passed. The news had by some means been conveyed to the village, and a company of about two hundred persons was then marching out to the rescue. The noise they made was probably to give the Druses intimation of their coming, and thus avoid a fight. I do not believe that any of the mountaineers of Lebanon would willingly take part against the Druses, who, in fact, are not fighting so much against the institution of the conscription law, as its abuse. The law ordains that the conscript shall serve for five years; but since its establishment, as I have been informed, there has not been a single instance of discharge. It amounts, therefore, to lifelong servitude, and there is little wonder that these independent sons of the mountains, as well as the tribes inhabiting the Syrian Desert, should rebel rather than submit.

The next day, we crossed a pass in the Anti-Lebanon beyond Zebdeni, descended a beautiful valley on the western side, under a ridge which was still dotted with patches of snow, and after travelling for some hours over a wide, barren height, the last of the range, saw below us the plain of Baalbec. The grand ridge of Lebanon opposite, crowned with glittering fields of snow, shone out clearly through the pure air, and the hoary head of Hermon, far in the south, lost something of its grandeur by the comparison. Though there is a "divide," or watershed, between Husbeiya, at the foot of Mount Hermon, and Baalbec, whose springs join the Orontes, which flows northward to Antioch, the great natural separation of the two chains continues unbroken to the Gulf of Akaba, in the Red Sea. A little beyond Baalbec, the Anti-Lebanon terminates, sinking into the Syrian plain, while the Lebanon, though its name and general features are lost, about twenty miles further to the north is succeeded by other ranges, which, though broken at intervals, form a regular series, connecting with the Taurus, in Asia Minor.

On leaving Damascus, the Demon of Hasheesh still maintained a partial control over me. I was weak in body and at times confused in my perceptions, wandering away from the scenes about me to some unknown sphere beyond the moon. But the healing balm of my sleep at Zebdeni, and the purity of the morning air among the mountains, completed my cure. As I rode along the valley, with the towering, snow-sprinkled ridge of the Anti-Lebanon on my right, a cloudless heaven above my head, and meads enamelled with the asphodel and scarlet anemone stretching before me, I felt that the last shadow had rolled away from my brain. My mind was now as clear as that sky--my heart as free and joyful as the elastic morning air. The sun never shone so brightly to my eyes; the fair forms of Nature were never penetrated with so perfect a spirit of beauty. I was again master of myself, and the world glowed as if new-created in the light of my joy and gratitude. I thanked God, who had led me out of a darkness more terrible than that of the Valley of the Shadow of Death, and while my feet strayed among the flowery meadows of Lebanon, my heart walked on the Delectable Hills of His Mercy.

By the middle of the afternoon, we reached Baalbec. The distant view of the temple, on descending the last slope of the Anti-Lebanon, is not calculated to raise one's expectations. On the green plain at the foot of the mountain, you see a large square platform of masonry, upon which stand six columns, the body of the temple, and a quantity of ruined walls. As a feature in the landscape, it has a fine effect, but you find yourself pronouncing the speedy judgment, that "Baalbec, without Lebanon, would be rather a poor show." Having come to this conclusion, you ride down the hill with comfortable feelings of indifference. There are a number of quarries on the left hand; you glance at them with an expression which merely says: "Ah! I suppose they got the stones here," and so you saunter on, cross a little stream that flows down from the modern village, pass a mill, return the stare of the quaint Arab miller who comes to the door to see you, and your horse is climbing a difficult path among the broken columns and friezes, before you think it worth while to lift your eyes to the pile above you. Now re-assert your judgment, if you dare! This is Baalbec: what have you to say? Nothing; but you amazedly measure the torsos of great columns which lie piled across one another in magnificent wreck; vast pieces which have dropped from the entablature, beautiful Corinthian capitals, bereft of the last graceful curves of their acanthus leaves, and blocks whose edges are so worn away that they resemble enormous natural boulders left by the Deluge, till at last you look up to the six glorious pillars, towering nigh a hundred feet above your head, and there is a sensation in your brain which would be a shout, if you could give it utterance, of faultless symmetry and majesty, such as no conception of yours and no other creation of art, can surpass.

I know of nothing so beautiful in all remains of ancient Art as these six columns, except the colonnade of the Memnonium, at Thebes, which is of much smaller proportions. From every position, and with all lights of the day or night, they are equally perfect, and carry your eyes continually away from the peristyle of the smaller temple, which is better preserved, and from the exquisite architecture of the outer courts and pavilions. The two temples of Baalbec stand on an artificial platform of masonry, a thousand feet in length, and from fifteen to thirty feet (according to the depression of the soil) in height, The larger one, which is supposed to have been a Pantheon, occupies the whole length of this platform. The entrance was at the north, by a grand flight of steps, now broken away, between two lofty and elegant pavilions which are still nearly entire. Then followed a spacious hexagonal court, and three grand halls, parts of which, with niches for statues, adorned with cornices and pediments of elaborate design, still remain entire to the roof. This magnificent series of chambers was terminated at the southern extremity of the platform by the main temple, which had originally twenty columns on a side, similar to the six now standing.

The Temple of the Sun stands on a smaller and lower platform, which appears to have been subsequently added to the greater one. The cella, or body of the temple, is complete except the roof, and of the colonnade surrounding it, nearly one-half of its pillars are still standing, upholding the frieze, entablature, and cornice, which altogether form probably the most ornate specimen of the Corinthian order of architecture now extant. Only four pillars of the superb portico remain, and the Saracens have nearly ruined these by building a sort of watch-tower upon the architrave. The same unscrupulous race completely shut up the portal of the temple with a blank wall, formed of the fragments they had hurled down, and one is obliged to creep through a narrow hole in order to reach the interior. Here the original doorway faces you--and I know not how to describe the wonderful design of its elaborate sculptured mouldings and cornices. The genius of Greek art seems to have exhausted itself in inventing ornaments, which, while they should heighten the gorgeous effect of the work, must yet harmonize with the grand design of the temple. The enormous keystone over the entrance has slipped down, no doubt from the shock of an earthquake, and hangs within six inches of the bottom of the two blocks which uphold it on either side. When it falls, the whole entablature of the portal will be destroyed. On its lower side is an eagle with outspread wings, and on the side-stones a genius with garlands of flowers, exquisitely sculptured in bas relief. Hidden among the wreaths of vines which adorn the jambs are the laughing heads of fauns. This portal was a continual study to me, every visit revealing new refinements of ornament, which I had not before observed. The interior of the temple, with its rich Corinthian pilasters, its niches for statues, surmounted by pediments of elegant design, and its elaborate cornice, needs little aid of the imagination to restore it to its original perfection. Like that of Dendera, in Egypt, the Temple of the Sun leaves upon the mind an impression of completeness which makes you forget far grander remains.

But the most wonderful thing at Baalbec is the foundation platform upon which the temples stand. Even the colossal fabrics of Ancient Egypt dwindle before this superhuman masonry. The platform itself, 1,000 feet long, and averaging twenty feet in height, suggests a vast mass of stones, but when you come to examine the single blocks of which it is composed, you are crushed with their incredible bulk. On the western side is a row of eleven foundation stones, each of which is thirty-two feet in length, twelve in height, and ten in thickness, forming a wall three hundred and fifty-two feet long! But while you are walking on, thinking of the art which cut and raised these enormous blocks, you turn the southern corner and come upon three stones, the united length of which is one hundred and eighty-seven feet--two of them being sixty-two and the other sixty-three feet in length! There they are, cut with faultless exactness, and so smoothly joined to each other, that you cannot force a cambric needle into the crevice. There is one joint so perfect that it can only be discerned by the minutest search; it is not even so perceptible as the junction of two pieces of paper which have been pasted together. In the quarry, there still lies a finished block, ready for transportation, which is sixty-seven feet in length. The weight of one of these masses has been reckoned at near 9,000 tons, yet they do not form the base of the foundation, but are raised upon other courses, fifteen feet from the ground. It is considered by some antiquarians that they are of a date greatly anterior to that of the temples, and were intended as the basement of a different edifice.

In the village of Baalbec there is a small circular Corinthian temple of very elegant design. It is not more than thirty feet in diameter, and may have been intended as a tomb. A spacious mosque, now roofless and deserted, was constructed almost entirely out of the remains of the temples. Adjoining the court-yard and fountain are five rows of ancient pillars, forty (the sacred number) in all, supporting light Saracenic arches. Some of them are marble, with Corinthian capitals, and eighteen are single shafts of red Egyptian granite. Beside the fountain lies a small broken pillar of porphyry, of a dark violet hue, and of so fine a grain that the stone has the soft rich lustre of velvet. This fragment is the only thing I would carry away if I had the power.

After a day's sojourn, we left Baalbec at noon, and took the road for the Cedars, which lie on the other side of Lebanon, in the direction of Tripoli. Our English fellow-travellers chose the direct road to Beyrout. We crossed the plain in three hours; to the village of Dayr el-Ahmar, and then commenced ascending the lowest slopes of the great range, whose topmost ridge, a dazzling parapet of snow, rose high above us. For several hours, our path led up and down stony ridges, covered with thickets of oak and holly, and with wild cherry, pear, and olive-trees. Just as the sun threw the shadows of the highest Lebanon over us, we came upon a narrow, rocky glen at his very base. Streams that still kept the color and the coolness of the snow-fields from which they oozed, foamed over the stones into the chasm at the bottom. The glen descended into a mountain basin, in which lay the lake of Yemouni, cold and green under the evening shadows. But just opposite us, on a little shelf of soil, there was a rude mill, and a group of superb walnut-trees, overhanging the brink of the largest torrent. We had sent our baggage before us, and the men, with an eye to the picturesque which I should not have suspected in Arabs, had pitched our tents under those trees, where the stream poured its snow-cold beakers beside us, and the tent-door looked down on the plain of Baalbec and across to the Anti-Lebanon. The miller and two or three peasants, who were living in this lonely spot, were Christians.

The next morning we commenced ascending the Lebanon. We had slept just below the snow-line, for the long hollows with which the ridge is cloven were filled up to within a short distance of the glen, out of which we came. The path was very steep, continually ascending, now around the barren shoulder of the mountain, now up some ravine, where the holly and olive still flourished, and the wild rhubarb-plant spread its large, succulent leaves over the soil. We had taken a guide, the day before, at the village of Dayr el-Ahmar, but as the way was plain before us, and he demanded an exorbitant sum, we dismissed him, We had not climbed far, however, before he returned, professing to be content with whatever we might give him, and took us into another road, the first, he said, being impracticable. Up and up we toiled, and the long hollows of snow lay below us, and the wind came cold from the topmost peaks, which began to show near at hand. But now the road, as we had surmised, turned towards that we had first taken, and on reaching the next height we saw the latter at a short distance from us. It was not only a better, but a shorter road, the rascal of a guide having led us out of it in order to give the greater effect to his services. In order to return to it, as was necessary, there were several dangerous snow-fields to be passed. The angle of their descent was so great that a single false step would have hurled our animals, baggage and all, many hundred feet below. The snow was melting, and the crust frozen over the streams below was so thin in places that the animals broke through and sank to their bellies.

It were needless to state the number and character of the anathemas bestowed upon the guide. The impassive Dervish raved; Mustapha stormed; François broke out in a frightful eruption of Greek and Turkish oaths, and the two travellers, though not (as I hope and believe) profanely inclined, could not avoid using a few terse Saxon expressions. When the general indignation had found vent, the men went to work, and by taking each animal separately,

440

succeeded, at imminent hazard, in getting them all over the snow. We then dismissed the guide, who, far from being abashed by the discovery of his trickery, had the impudence to follow us for some time, claiming his pay. A few more steep pulls, over deep beds of snow and patches of barren stone, and at length the summit ridge--a sharp, white wall, shining against the intense black-blue of the zenith--stood before us. We climbed a toilsome zig-zag through the snow, hurried over the stones cumbering the top, and all at once the mountains fell away, ridge below ridge, gashed with tremendous chasms, whose bottoms were lost in blue vapor, till the last heights, crowned with white Maronite convents, hung above the sea, whose misty round bounded the vision. I have seen many grander mountain views, but few so sublimely rugged and broken in their features. The sides of the ridges dropped off in all directions into sheer precipices, and the few villages we could see were built like eagles' nests on the brinks. In a little hollow at our feet was the sacred Forest of Cedars, appearing like a patch of stunted junipers. It is the highest speck of vegetation on Lebanon, and in winter cannot be visited, on account of the snow. The summit on which we stood was about nine thousand feet above the sea, but there were peaks on each side at least a thousand feet higher.

We descended by a very steep path, over occasional beds of snow, and reached the Cedars in an hour and a half. Not until we were within a hundred yards of the trees, and below their level, was I at all impressed with their size and venerable aspect. But, once entered into the heart of the little wood, walking over its miniature hills and valleys, and breathing the pure, balsamic exhalations of the trees, all the disappointment rising to my mind was charmed away in an instant There are about three hundred trees, in all, many of which are of the last century's growth, but at least fifty of them would be considered grand in any forest. The patriarchs are five in number, and are undoubtedly as old as the Christian Era, if not the Age of Solomon. The cypresses in the Garden of Montezuma, at Chapultepec, are even older and grander trees, but they are as entire and shapely as ever, whereas these are gnarled and twisted into wonderful forms by the storms of twenty centuries, and shivered in some places by lightning. The hoary father of them all, nine feet in diameter, stands in the centre of the grove, on a little knoll, and spreads his ponderous arms, each a tree in itself, over the heads of the many generations that have grown up below, as if giving his last benediction before decay. He is scarred less with storm and lightning, than with the knives of travellers, and the marble crags of Lebanon do not more firmly retain their inscriptions than his stony trunk. Dates of the last century are abundant, and I recollect a tablet inscribed: "Souard, 1670," around which the newer wood has grown to the height of three or four inches. The seclusion of the grove, shut in by peaks of barren snow, is complete. Only the voice of the nightingale, singing here by daylight in the solemn shadows, breaks the silence. The Maronite monk, who has charge of a little stone chapel standing in the midst, moves about like a shade, and, not before you are ready to leave, brings his book for you to register your name therein, I was surprised to find how few of the crowd that annually overrun Syria reach the Cedars, which, after Baalbec, are the finest remains of antiquity in the whole country.

After a stay of three hours, we rode on to Eden, whither our men had already gone with the baggage. Our road led along the brink of a tremendous gorge, a thousand feet deep, the bottom of which was only accessible here and there by hazardous foot-paths. On either side, a long shelf of cultivated land sloped down to the top, and the mountain streams, after watering a multitude of orchards and grain-fields, tumbled over the cliffs in long, sparkling cascades, to join the roaring flood below. This is the Christian region of Lebanon, inhabited almost wholly by Maronites, who still retain a portion of their former independence, and are the most thrifty, industrious, honest, and happy people in Syria. Their villages are not concrete masses of picturesque filth, as are those of the Moslems, but are loosely scattered among orchards of mulberry, poplar, and vine, washed by fresh rills, and have an air of comparative neatness and comfort. Each has its two or three chapels, with their little belfries, which toll the hours of prayer. Sad and poetic as is the call from the minaret, it never touched me as when I heard the sweet tongues of those Christian bells, chiming vespers far and near on the sides of Lebanon.

Eden merits its name. It is a mountain paradise, inhabited by people so kind and simple-hearted, that assuredly no vengeful angel will ever drive them out with his flaming sword. It hangs above the gorge, which is here nearly two thousand feet deep, and overlooks a grand wilderness of mountain-piles, crowded on and over each other, from the sea that gleams below, to the topmost heights that keep off the morning sun. The houses are all built of hewn stone, and grouped in clusters under the shade of large walnut-trees. In walking among them, we received kind greetings everywhere, and every one who was seated rose and remained standing as we passed. The women are beautiful, with sprightly, intelligent faces, quite different from the stupid Mahometan females.

The children were charming creatures, and some of the girls of ten or twelve years were lovely as angels. They came timidly to our tent (which the men had pitched as before, under two superb trees, beside a fountain), and offered us roses and branches of fragrant white jasmine. They expected some return, of course, but did not ask it, and the delicate grace with which the offering was made was beyond all pay. It was Sunday, and the men and boys, having nothing better to do, all came to see and talk with us. I shall not soon forget the circle of gay and laughing villagers, in which we sat that evening, while the dark purple shadows gradually filled up the gorges, and broad golden lights poured over the shoulders of the hills. The men had much sport in inducing the smaller boys to come up and salute us. There was one whom they called "the Consul," who eluded them for some time, but was finally caught and placed in the ring before us. "Peace be with you, O Consul," I said, making him a profound inclination, "may your days be propitious! may your shadow be increased!" but I then saw, from the vacant expression on the boy's face, that he was one of those harmless, witless creatures, whom yet one cannot quite call idiots. "He is an unfortunate; he knows nothing; he has no protector but God," said the men, crossing themselves devoutly. The boy took off his cap, crept up and kissed my hand, as I gave him some money, which he no sooner grasped, than he sprang up like a startled gazelle, and was out of sight in an instant.

In descending from Eden to the sea-coast, we were obliged to cross the great gorge of which I spoke. Further down, its sides are less steep, and clothed even to the very bottom with magnificent orchards of mulberry, fig, olive, orange, and pomegranate trees. We were three hours in reaching the opposite side, although the breadth across the top is not more than a mile.

The path was exceedingly perilous; we walked down, leading our horses, and once were obliged to unload our mules to get them past a tree, which would have forced them off the brink of a chasm several hundred feet deep. The view from the bottom was wonderful. We were shut in by steeps of foliage and blossoms from two to three thousand feet high, broken by crags of white marble, and towering almost precipitously to the very clouds. I doubt if Melville saw anything grander in the tropical gorges of Typee. After reaching the other side, we had still a journey of eight hours to the sea, through a wild and broken, yet highly cultivated country.

Beyrout was now thirteen hours distant, but by making a forced march we reached it in a day, travelling along the shore, past the towns of Jebeil, the ancient Byblus, and Joonieh. The hills about Jebeil produce the celebrated tobacco known in Egypt as the Jebelee, or "mountain" tobacco, which is even superior to the Latakiyeh.

Near Beyrout, the mulberry and olive are in the ascendant. The latter tree bears the finest fruit in all the Levant, and might drive all other oils out of the market, if any one had enterprise enough to erect proper manufactories. Instead of this the oil of the country is badly prepared, rancid from the skins in which it is kept, and the wealthy natives import from France and Italy in preference to using it. In the bottoms near the sea, I saw several fields of the taro-plant, the cultivation of which I had supposed was exclusively confined to the Islands of the Pacific. There would be no end to the wealth of Syria were the country in proper hands.

444

Chapter XIII. Pipes and Coffee.

--"the kind nymph to Bacchus born

By Morpheus' daughter, she that seems

Gifted upon her natal morn

By him with fire, by her with dreams--

Nicotia, dearer to the Muse

Than all the grape's bewildering juice." Lowell.

In painting the picture of an Oriental, the pipe and the coffee-cup are indispensable accessories. There is scarce a Turk, or Arab, or Persian-- unless he be a Dervish of peculiar sanctity--but breathes his daily incense to the milder Bacchus of the moderns. The custom has become so thoroughly naturalized in the East, that we are apt to forget its comparatively recent introduction, and to wonder that no mention is made of the pipe in the Arabian Nights. The practice of smoking harmonizes so thoroughly with the character of Oriental life, that it is difficult for us to imagine a time when it never existed. It has become a part of that supreme patience, that wonderful repose, which forms so strong a contrast to the over-active life of the New World--the enjoyment of which no one can taste, to whom the pipe is not familiar. Howl, ye Reformers! but I solemnly declare unto you, that he who travels through the East without smoking, does not know the East.

It is strange that our Continent, where the meaning of Rest is unknown, should have given to the world this great agent of Rest. There is nothing more remarkable in history than the colonization of Tobacco over the whole Earth. Not three centuries have elapsed since knightly Raleigh puffed its fumes into the astonished eyes of Spenser and Shakspeare; and now, find me any corner of the world, from Nova Zembla to the Mountains of the Moon, where the use of the plant is unknown! Tarshish (if India was Tarshish) is less distinguished by its "apes, ivory, and peacocks," than by its hookahs; the valleys of Luzon, beyond Ternate and Tidore, send us more cheroots than spices; the Gardens of Shiraz produce more velvety toombek than roses, and the only fountains which bubble in Samarcand are those of the narghilehs: Lebanon is no longer "excellent with the Cedars," as in the days of Solomon, but most excellent with its fields of Jebelee and Latakiyeh. On the unvisited plains of Central Africa, the table-lands of Tartary, and in the valleys of Japan, the wonderful plant has found a home. The naked negro, "panting at the Line," inhales it under the palms, and the Lapp and Samoyed on the shores of the Frozen Sea.

It is idle for those who object to the use of Tobacco to attribute these phenomena wholly to a perverted taste. The fact that the custom was at once adopted by all the races of men, whatever their geographical position and degree of civilization, proves that there must be a reason for it in the physical constitution of man. Its effect, when habitually used, is slightly narcotic and sedative, not stimulating--or if so, at times, it stimulates only the imagination and the social faculties. It lulls to sleep the combative and destructive propensities, and hence--so far as a material agent may operate--it exercises a humanizing and refining influence. A profound student of Man, whose name is well known to the world, once informed me that he saw in the eagerness with which savage tribes adopt the use of Tobacco, a spontaneous movement of Nature towards Civilization.

I will not pursue these speculations further, for the narghileh (bubbling softly at my elbow, as I write) is the promoter of repose and the begetter of agreeable reverie. As I inhale its cool, fragrant breath, and partly yield myself to the sensation of healthy rest which wraps my limbs as with a velvet mantle, I marvel how the poets and artists and scholars of olden times nursed those dreams which the world calls indolence, but which are the seeds that germinate into great achievements. How did Plato philosophize without the pipe? How did gray Homer, sitting on the temple-steps in the Grecian twilights, drive from his heart the bitterness of beggary and blindness? How did Phidias charm the Cerberus of his animal nature to sleep, while his soul entered the Elysian Fields and beheld the forms of heroes? For, in the higher world of Art, Body and Soul are sworn enemies, and the pipe holds an opiate more potent than all the drowsy syrups of the East, to drug the former into submission. Milton knew this, as he smoked his evening pipe at Chalfont, wandering, the while, among the palms of Paradise.

But it is also our loss, that Tobacco was unknown to the Greeks. They would else have given us, in verse and in marble, another divinity in their glorious Pantheon--a god less drowsy than Morpheus and Somnus, less riotous than Bacchus, less radiant than Apollo, but with something of the spirit of each: a figure, beautiful with youth, every muscle in perfect repose, and the vague expression of dreams in his half-closed eyes. His temple would have been built in a grove of Southern pines, on the borders of a land-locked gulf, sheltered from the surges that buffet without, where service would have been rendered him in the late hours of the afternoon, or in the evening twilight. From his oracular tripod words of wisdom would have been spoken, and the fanes of Delphi and Dodona would have been deserted for his.

Oh, non-smoking friends, who read these lines with pain and incredulity--and you, ladies, who turn pale at the thought of a pipe--let me tell you that you are familiar only with the vulgar form of tobacco, and have never passed between the wind and its gentility. The word conveys no idea to you but that of "long nines," and pig-tail, and cavendish. Forget these for a moment, and look upon this dark-brown cake of dried leaves and blossoms, which exhales an odor of pressed flowers. These are the tender tops of the Jebelee, plucked as the buds begin to expand, and carefully dried in the shade. In order to be used, it is moistened with rose-scented water, and cut to the necessary degree of fineness. The test of true Jebelee is, that it burns with a slow, hidden fire, like tinder, and causes no irritation to the eye when held under it. The smoke, drawn through a long cherry-stick pipe and amber mouth-piece, is pure, cool, and sweet, with an aromatic flavor, which is very pleasant in the mouth. It excites no salivation, and leaves behind it no unpleasant, stale odor.

The narghileh (still bubbling beside me) is an institution known only in the East. It requires a peculiar kind of tobacco, which grows to perfection in the southern provinces of Persia. The smoke, after passing through water (rose-flavored, if you choose), is inhaled through a long, flexible tube directly into the lungs. It occasions not the slightest irritation or oppression, but in a few minutes produces a delicious sense of rest, which is felt even in the finger-ends. The pure physical sensation of rest is one of strength also, and of perfect contentment. Many an impatient thought, many an angry word, have I avoided by a resort to the pipe. Among our aborigines the pipe was the emblem of Peace, and I strongly recommend the Peace Society to print their tracts upon papers of smoking tobacco (Turkish, if possible), and distribute pipes with them.

I know of nothing more refreshing, after the fatigue of a long day's journey, than a well-prepared narghileh. That slight feverish and excitable feeling which is the result of fatigue yields at once to its potency. The blood loses its heat and the pulse its rapidity; the muscles relax, the nerves are soothed into quiet, and the frame passes into a condition similar to sleep, except that the mind is awake and active. By the time one has finished his pipe, he is refreshed for the remainder of the day, and his nightly sleep is sound and healthy. Such are some of the physical effects of the pipe, in Eastern lands. Morally and psychologically, it works still greater transformations; but to describe them now, with the mouth-piece at my lips, would require an active self-consciousness which the habit does not allow.

A servant enters with a steamy cup of coffee, seated in a silver zerf, or cup-holder. His thumb and fore-finger are clasped firmly upon the bottom of the zerf, which I inclose near the top with my own thumb and finger, so that the transfer is accomplished without his hand having touched mine.

After draining the thick brown liquid, which must be done with due deliberation and a pause of satisfaction between each sip, I return the zerf, holding it in the middle, while the attendant places a palm of each hand upon the top and bottom and carries it off without contact. The beverage is made of the berries of Mocha, slightly roasted, pulverized in a mortar, and heated to a foam, without the addition of cream or sugar. Sometimes, however, it is flavored with the extract of roses or violets. When skilfully made, each cup is prepared separately, and the quantity of water and coffee carefully measured.

Coffee is a true child of the East, and its original home was among the hills of Yemen, the Arabia Felix of the ancients. Fortunately for Mussulmen, its use was unknown in the days of Mahomet, or it would probably have fallen under the same prohibition as wine. The word Kahweh (whence café) is an old Arabic term for wine. The discovery of the properties of coffee is attributed to a dervish, who, for some misdemeanor, was carried into the mountains of Yemen by his brethren and there left to perish by starvation. In order to appease the pangs of hunger he gathered the ripe berries from the wild coffee-trees, roasted and ate them. The nourishment they contained, with water from the springs, sustained his life, and after two or three months he returned in good condition to his brethren, who considered his preservation as a miracle, and ever afterwards looked upon him as a pattern of holiness. He taught the use of the miraculous fruit, and the demand for it soon became so great as to render the cultivation of the tree necessary. It was a long time, however, before coffee was introduced into Europe. As late as the beginning of the seventeenth century, Sandys, the quaint old traveller, describes the appearance and taste of the beverage, which he calls "Coffa," and sagely asks: "Why not that black broth which the Lacedemonians used?"

On account of the excellence of the material, and the skilful manner of its preparation, the Coffee of the East is the finest in the world. I have found it so grateful and refreshing a drink, that I can readily pardon the pleasant exaggeration of the Arabic poet, Abd-el Kader Anazari Djezeri Hanbali, the son of Mahomet, who thus celebrates its virtues. After such an exalted eulogy, my own praises would sound dull and tame; and I therefore resume my pipe, commending Abd-el Kader to the reader.

"O Coffee! thou dispellest the cares of the great; thou bringest back those who wander from the paths of knowledge. Coffee is the beverage of the people of God, and the cordial of his servants who thirst for wisdom. When coffee is infused into the bowl, it exhales the odor of musk, and is of the color of ink. The truth is not known except to the wise, who drink it from the foaming coffee-cup. God has deprived fools of coffee, who, with invincible obstinacy, condemn it as injurious.

"Coffee is our gold; and in the place of its libations we are in the enjoyment of the best and noblest society. Coffee is even as innocent a drink as the purest milk, from which it is distinguished only by its color. Tarry with thy coffee in the place of its preparation, and the good God will hover over

449

thee and participate in his feast. There the graces of the saloon, the luxury of life, the society of friends, all furnish a picture of the abode of happiness.

"Every care vanishes when the cup-bearer presents the delicious chalice. It will circulate fleetly through thy veins, and will not rankle there: if thou doubtest this, contemplate the youth and beauty of those who drink it. Grief cannot exist where it grows; sorrow humbles itself in obedience before its powers.

"Coffee is the drink of God's people; in it is health. Let this be the answer to those who doubt its qualities. In it we will drown our adversities, and in its fire consume our sorrows. Whoever has once seen the blissful chalice, will scorn the wine-cup. Glorious drink! thy color is the seal of purity, and reason proclaims it genuine. Drink with confidence, and regard not the prattle of fools, who condemn without foundation."

Chapter XIV. Journey to Antioch and Aleppo.

Change of Plans--Routes to Baghdad--Asia Minor--We sail from Beyrout--Yachting on the Syrian Coast--Tartus and Latakiyeh--The Coasts of Syria--The Bay of Suediah--The Mouth of the Orontes--Landing--The Garden of Syria--Ride to Antioch--The Modern City--The Plains of the Orontes--Remains of the Greek Empire--The Ancient Road--The Plain of Keftin--Approach to Aleppo.

"The chain is loosed, the sails are spread,

The living breath is fresh behind,

As, with dews and sunrise fed,

Comes the laughing morning wind."

Shelley.

Aleppo, *Friday, June* 4, 1852.

A Traveller in the East, who has not unbounded time and an extensive fortune at his disposal, is never certain where and how far he shall go, until his journey is finished. With but a limited portion of both these necessaries, I have so far carried out my original plan with scarcely a variation; but at present I am obliged to make a material change of route. My farthest East is here at Aleppo. At Damascus, I was told by everybody that it was too late in the season to visit either Baghdad or Mosul, and that, on account of the terrible summer heats and the fevers which prevail along the Tigris, it would be imprudent to undertake it. Notwithstanding this, I should probably have gone (being now so thoroughly acclimated that I have nothing to fear from the heat), had I not met with a friend of Col. Rawlinson, the companion of Layard, and the sharer in his discoveries at Nineveh. This gentleman, who met Col. R. not long since in Constantinople, on his way to Baghdad (where he resides as British Consul), informed me that since the departure of Mr. Layard from Mosul, the most interesting excavations have been filled up, in order to preserve the sculptures. Unless one was able to make a new exhumation, he would be by no means repaid for so long and arduous a journey. The ruins of Nineveh are all below the surface of the earth, and the little of them that is now left exposed, is less complete and interesting than the specimens in the British Museum.

There is a route from Damascus to Baghdad, across the Desert, by way of Palmyra, but it is rarely travelled, even by the natives, except when the caravans are sufficiently strong to withstand the attacks of the Bedouins. The traveller is obliged to go in Arab costume, to leave his baggage behind, except a meagre scrip for the journey, and to pay from $300 to $500 for the camels and escort. The more usual route is to come northward to this city, then cross to Mosul and descend the Tigris--a journey of four or five weeks. After weighing all the advantages and disadvantages of undertaking a tour of such length as it would be necessary to make before reaching Constantinople, I decided at Beyrout to give up the fascinating fields of travel in Media, Assyria and Armenia, and take a rather shorter and-perhaps equally interesting route from Aleppo to Constantinople, by way of Tarsus, Konia (Iconium), and the ancient countries of Phrygia, Bithynia, and Mysia. The interior of Asia Minor is even less known to us than the Persian side of Asiatic Turkey, which has of late received more attention from travellers; and, as I shall traverse it in its whole length, from Syria to the Bosphorus, I may find it replete with "green fields and pastures new," which shall repay me for relinquishing the first and more ambitious undertaking. At least, I have so much reason to be grateful for the uninterrupted good health and good luck I have enjoyed during seven months in Africa and the Orient, that I cannot be otherwise than content with the prospect before me.

I left Beyrout on the night of the 28th of May, with Mr. Harrison, who has decided to keep me company as far as Constantinople. François, our classic dragoman, whose great delight is to recite Homer by the sea-side, is retained for the whole tour, as we have found no reason to doubt his honesty or ability. Our first thought was to proceed to Aleppo by land, by way of Homs and Hamah, whence there might be a chance of reaching Palmyra; but as we found an opportunity of engaging an American yacht for the voyage up the coast, it was thought preferable to take her, and save time. She was a neat little craft, called the "American Eagle," brought out by Mr. Smith, our Consul at Beyrout. So, one fine moonlit night, we slowly crept out of the harbor, and after returning a volley of salutes from our friends at Demetri's Hotel, ran into the heart of a thunder-storm, which poured down more rain than all I had seen for eight months before. But our raïs, Assad (the Lion), was worthy of his name, and had two good Christian sailors at his command, so we lay in the cramped little cabin, and heard the floods washing our deck, without fear.

In the morning, we were off Tripoli, which is even more deeply buried than Beyrout in its orange and mulberry groves, and slowly wafted along the bold mountain-coast, in the afternoon reached Tartus, the Ancient Tortosa. A mile from shore is the rocky island of Aradus, entirely covered by a town. There were a dozen vessels lying in the harbor. The remains of a large fortress and ancient mole prove it to have been a place of considerable importance. Tartus is a small old place on the sea-shore--not so large nor so important in appearance as its island-port. The country behind is green and hilly, though but partially cultivated, and rises into Djebel Ansairiyeh, which divides the valley of the Orontes from the sea. It is a lovely coast, especially under the flying lights and shadows of such a breezy day as we had. The wind fell at sunset; but by the next morning, we had passed the tobacco-fields of Latakiyeh, and were in sight of the southern cape of the Bay of Suediah. The mountains forming this cape culminate in a grand conical peak, about 5,000 feet in height, called Djebel Okrab. At ten o'clock, wafted along by a slow wind, we turned the point and entered the Bay of Suediah, formed by the embouchure of the River Orontes. The mountain headland of Akma Dagh, forming the portal of the Gulf of Scanderoon, loomed grandly in front of us across the bay; and far beyond it, we could just distinguish the coast of Karamania, the snow-capped range of Taurus.

The Coasts of Syria might be divided, like those of Guinea, according to the nature of their productions. The northern division is bold and bare, yet flocks of sheep graze on the slopes of its mountains; and the inland plains behind them are covered with orchards of pistachio-trees. Silk is cultivated in the neighborhood of Suediah, but forms only a small portion of the exports. This region may be called the Wool and Pistachio Coast. Southward, from Latakiyeh to Tartus and the northern limit of Lebanon, extends the Tobacco Coast, whose undulating hills are now clothed with the pale-green leaves of the renowned plant. From Tripoli to Tyre, embracing all the western slope of Lebanon, and the deep, rich valleys lying between his knees, the mulberry predominates, and the land is covered with the houses of thatch and matting which shelter the busy worms. This is the Silk Coast. The palmy plains of Jaffa, and beyond, until Syria meets the African sands between Gaza and El-Arish, constitute the Orange Coast. The vine, the olive, and the fig flourish everywhere.

We were all day getting up the bay, and it seemed as if we should never pass Djebel Okrab, whose pointed top rose high above a long belt of fleecy clouds that girdled his waist. At sunset we made the mouth of the Orontes. Our lion of a Captain tried to run into the river, but the channel was very narrow, and when within three hundred yards of the shore the yacht struck. We had all sail set, and had the wind been a little stronger, we should have capsized in an instant. The lion went manfully to work, and by dint of hard poling, shoved us off, and came to anchor in deep water. Not until the danger was past did he open his batteries on the unlucky helmsman, and then the explosion of Arabic oaths was equal to a broadside of twenty-four pounders. We lay all night rocking on the swells, and the next morning, by firing a number of signal guns, brought out a boat, which took us off. We entered the mouth of the Orontes, and sailed nearly a mile between rich wheat meadows before reaching the landing-place of Suediah--two or three uninhabited stone huts, with three or four small Turkish craft, and a health officer. The town lies a mile or two inland, scattered along the hill-side amid gardens so luxuriant as almost to conceal it from view.

This part of the coast is ignorant of travellers, and we were obliged to wait half a day before we could find a sufficient number of horses to take us to Antioch, twenty miles distant. When they came, they were solid farmers' horses, with the rudest gear imaginable. I was obliged to mount astride of a broad pack-saddle, with my legs suspended in coils of rope. Leaving the meadows, we entered a lane of the wildest, richest and loveliest bloom and foliage. Our way was overhung with hedges of pomegranate, myrtle, oleander, and white rose, in blossom, and occasionally with quince, fig, and carob trees, laced together with grape vines in fragrant bloom. Sometimes this wilderness of color and odor met above our heads and made a twilight; then it opened into long, dazzling, sun-bright vistas, where the hues of the oleander, pomegranate and white rose made the eye wink with their gorgeous profusion. The mountains we crossed were covered with thickets of myrtle, mastic, daphne, and arbutus, and all the valleys and sloping meads waved with fig, mulberry, and olive trees. Looking towards the sea, the valley broadened out between mountain ranges whose summits were lost in the clouds. Though the soil was not so rich as in Palestine, the general aspect of the country was much wilder and more luxuriant.

So, by this glorious lane, over the myrtled hills and down into valleys, whose bed was one hue of rose from the blossoming oleanders, we travelled for five hours, crossing the low ranges of hills through which the Orontes forces his way to the sea. At last we reached a height overlooking the valley of the river, and saw in the east, at the foot of the mountain chain, the long lines of barracks built by Ibrahim Pasha for the defence of Antioch. Behind them the ancient wall of the city clomb the mountains, whose crest it followed to the last peak of the chain, From the next hill we saw the city--a large extent of one-story houses with tiled roofs, surrounded with gardens, and half buried in the foliage of sycamores. It extends from the River Orontes, which washes its walls, up the slope of the mountain to the crags of gray rock which overhang it. We crossed the river by a massive old bridge, and entered the town. Riding along the rills of filth which traverse the streets, forming their central avenues, we passed through several lines of bazaars to a large and dreary-looking khan, the keeper of which gave us the best vacant chamber--a narrow place, full of fleas.

Antioch presents not even a shadow of its former splendor. Except the great walls, ten to fifteen miles in circuit, which the Turks have done their best to destroy, every vestige of the old city has disappeared. The houses are all of one story, on account of earthquakes, from which Antioch has suffered more than any other city in the world. At one time, during the Middle Ages, it lost 120,000 inhabitants in one day. Its situation is magnificent, and the modern town, notwithstanding its filth, wears a bright and busy aspect. Situated at the base of a lofty mountain, it overlooks, towards the east, a plain thirty or forty miles in length, producing the most abundant harvests. A great number of the inhabitants are workers in wood and leather, and very thrifty and cheerful people they appear to be.

We remained until the next day at noon, by which time a gray-bearded scamp, the chief of the mukkairees, or muleteers, succeeded in getting us five miserable beasts for the journey to Aleppo. On leaving the city, we travelled along a former street of Antioch, part of the ancient pavement still remaining, and after two miles came to the old wall of circuit, which we passed by a massive gateway, of Roman time. It is now called Bab Boulos, or St. Paul's Gate. Christianity, it will be remembered, was planted in Antioch by Paul and Barnabas, and the Apostle Peter was the first bishop of the city. We now entered the great plain of the Orontes--a level sea, rioting in the wealth of its ripening harvests. The river, lined with luxuriant thickets, meandered through the centre of this glorious picture. We crossed it during the afternoon, and keeping on our eastward course, encamped at night in a meadow near the tents of some wandering Turcomans, who furnished us with butter and milk from their herds.

Leaving the plain the next morning, we travelled due east all day, over long stony ranges of mountains, inclosing only one valley, which bore evidence of great fertility. It was circular, about ten miles in its greater diameter, and bounded on the north by the broad peak of Djebel Saman, or Mount St. Simon. In the morning we passed a ruined castle, standing in a dry, treeless dell, among the hot hills. The muleteers called it the Maiden's Palace, and said that it was built long ago by a powerful Sultan, as a prison for his daughter. For several hours thereafter, our road was lined with remains of buildings, apparently dating from the time of the Greek Empire. There were tombs, temples of massive masonry, though in a bad style of architecture, and long rows of arched chambers, which resembled store-houses. They were all more or less shattered by earthquakes, but in one place I noticed twenty such arches, each of at least twenty feet span. All-the hills, on either hand, as far as we could see, were covered with the remains of buildings. In the plain of St. Simon, I saw two superb pillars, apparently part of a portico, or gateway, and the village of Dana is formed almost entirely of churches and convents, of the Lower Empire. There were but few inscriptions, and these I could not read; but the whole of this region would, no doubt, richly repay an antiquarian research. I am told here that the entire chain of hills, which extends southward for more than a hundred miles, abounds with similar remains, and that, in many places, whole cities stand almost entire, as if recently deserted by their inhabitants.

During the afternoon, we came upon a portion of the ancient road from Antioch to Aleppo, which is still as perfect as when first constructed. It crossed a very stony ridge, and is much the finest specimen of road-making I ever saw, quite putting to shame the Appian and Flaminian Ways at Rome. It is twenty feet wide, and laid with blocks of white marble, from two to four feet square. It was apparently raised upon a more ancient road, which diverges here and there from the line, showing the deeply-cut traces of the Roman chariot-wheels. In the barren depths of the mountains we found every hour cisterns cut in the rock and filled with water left by the winter rains. Many of them, however, are fast drying up, and a month later this will be a desert road.

Towards night we descended from the hills upon the Plain of Keftin, which stretches south-westward from Aleppo, till the mountain-streams which fertilize it are dried up, when it is merged into the Syrian Desert. Its northern edge, along which we travelled, is covered with fields of wheat, cotton, and castor-beans. We stopped all night at a village called Taireb, planted at the foot of a tumulus, older than tradition. The people were in great dread of the Aneyzeh Arabs, who come in from the Desert to destroy their harvests and carry off their cattle. They wanted us to take a guard, but after our experience on the Anti-Lebanon, we felt safer without one.

Yesterday we travelled for seven hours over a wide, rolling country, now waste and barren, but formerly covered with wealth and supporting an abundant population, evidences of which are found in the buildings everywhere scattered over the hills. On and on we toiled in the heat, over this inhospitable wilderness, and though we knew Aleppo must be very near, yet we could see neither sign of cultivation nor inhabitants. Finally, about three o'clock, the top of a line of shattered wall and the points of some minarets issued out of the earth, several miles in front of us, and on climbing a glaring chalky ridge, the renowned city burst at once upon our view. It filled a wide hollow or basin among the white hills, against which its whiter houses and domes glimmered for miles, in the dead, dreary heat of the afternoon, scarcely relieved by the narrow belt of gardens on the nearer side, or the orchards of pistachio trees beyond. In the centre of the city rose a steep, abrupt mound, crowned with the remains of the ancient citadel, and shining minarets shot up, singly or in clusters, around its base. The prevailing hue of the landscape was a whitish-gray, and the long, stately city and long, monotonous hills, gleamed with equal brilliancy under a sky of cloudless and intense blue. This singular monotony of coloring gave a wonderful effect to the view, which is one of the most remarkable in all the Orient.

Chapter XV. Life in Aleppo.

Our Entry into Aleppo--We are conducted to a House--Our Unexpected Welcome--The Mystery Explained--Aleppo--Its Name--Its Situation--The Trade of Aleppo--The Christians--The Revolt of 1850--Present Appearance of the City--Visit to Osman Pasha--The Citadel--View from the Battlements--Society in Aleppo--Etiquette and Costume--Jewish Marriage Festivities--A Christian Marriage Procession--Ride around the Town--Nightingales--The Aleppo Button--A Hospital for Cats--Ferhat Pasha.

Aleppo, *Tuesday, June* 8, 1852.

Our entry into Aleppo was a fitting preliminary to our experiences during the five days we have spent here. After passing a blackamoor, who acted as an advanced guard of the Custom House, at a ragged tent outside of the city, and bribing him with two piastres, we crossed the narrow line of gardens on the western side, and entered the streets. There were many coffee-houses, filled with smokers, nearly all of whom accosted us in Turkish, though Arabic is the prevailing language here. Ignorance made us discourteous, and we slighted every attempt to open a conversation. Out of the narrow streets of the suburbs, we advanced to the bazaars, in order to find a khan where we could obtain lodgings. All the best khans, however, were filled, and we were about to take a very inferior room, when a respectable individual came up to François and said: "The house is ready for the travellers, and I will show you the way." We were a little surprised at this address, but followed him to a neat, quiet and pleasant street near the bazaars, where we were ushered into a spacious court-yard, with a row of apartments opening upon it, and told to make ourselves at home.

The place had evidently been recently inhabited, for the rooms were well furnished, with not only divans, but beds in the Frank style. A lean kitten was scratching at one of the windows, to the great danger of overturning a pair of narghilehs, a tame sea-gull was walking about the court, and two sheep bleated in a stable at the further end. In the kitchen we not only found a variety of utensils, but eggs, salt, pepper, and other condiments. Our guide had left, and the only information we could get, from a dyeing establishment next door, was that the occupants had gone into the country. "Take the good the gods provide thee," is my rule in such cases, and as we were very hungry, we set François to work at preparing dinner. We arranged a divan in the open air, had a table brought out, and by the aid of the bakers in the bazaar, and the stores which the kitchen supplied, soon rejoiced over a very palatable meal. The romantic character of our reception made the dinner a merry one. It was a chapter out of the Arabian Nights, and be he genie or afrite, caliph or merchant of Bassora, into whose hands we had fallen, we resolved to let the adventure take its course. We were just finishing a nondescript pastry which François found at a baker's, and which, for want of a better name, he called méringues à la Khorassan, when there was a loud knock at the street door. We felt at first some little trepidation, but determined to maintain our places, and gravely invite the real master to join us.

It was a female servant, however, who, to our great amazement, made a profound salutation, and seemed delighted to see us. "My master did not expect your Excellencies to-day; he has gone into the gardens, but will soon return. Will your Excellencies take coffee after your dinner?" and coffee was forthwith served. The old woman was unremitting in her attentions; and her son, a boy of eight years, and the most venerable child I ever saw, entertained us with the description of a horse which his master had just bought--a horse which had cost two thousand piastres, and was ninety years old. Well, this Aleppo is an extraordinary place, was my first impression, and the inhabitants are remarkable people; but I waited the master's arrival, as the only means of solving the mystery. About dusk, there was another rap at the door. A lady dressed in white, with an Indian handkerchief bound over her black hair, arrived. "Pray excuse us," said she; "we thought you would not reach here before to-morrow; but my brother will come directly." In fact, the brother did come soon afterwards, and greeted us with a still warmer welcome. "Before leaving the gardens," he said, "I heard of your arrival, and have come in a full gallop the whole way." In order to put an end to this comedy of errors, I declared at once that he was mistaken; nobody in Aleppo could possibly know of our coming, and we were, perhaps, transgressing on his hospitality.

But no: he would not be convinced. He was a dragoman to the English Consulate; his master had told him we would be here the next day, and he must be prepared to receive us. Besides, the janissary of the Consulate had showed us the way to his house. We, therefore, let the matter rest until next morning, when we called on Mr. Very, the Consul, who informed us that the janissary had mistaken us for two gentlemen we had met in Damascus, the travelling companions of Lord Dalkeith. As they had not arrived, he begged us to remain in the quarters which had been prepared for them. We have every reason to be glad of this mistake, as it has made us acquainted with one of the most courteous and hospitable gentlemen in the East.

Aleppo lies so far out of the usual routes of travel, that it is rarely visited by Europeans. One is not, therefore, as in the case of Damascus, prepared beforehand by volumes of description, which preclude all possibility of mistake or surprise. For my part, I only knew that Aleppo had once been the greatest commercial city of the Orient, though its power had long since passed into other hands. But there were certain stately associations lingering around the name, which drew me towards it, and obliged me to include it, at all hazards, in my Asiatic tour. The scanty description of Captains Irby and Mangles, the only one I had read, gave me no distinct idea of its position or appearance; and when, the other day, I first saw it looming grand and gray among the gray hills, more like a vast natural crystallization than the product of human art, I revelled in the novelty of that startling first impression.

The tradition of the city's name is curious, and worth relating. It is called, in Arabic, Haleb el-Shahba--Aleppo, the Gray--which most persons suppose to refer to the prevailing color of the soil. The legend, however, goes much farther. Haleb, which the Venetians and Genoese softened into Aleppo, means literally: "has milked," According to Arab tradition, the patriarch Abraham once lived here: his tent being pitched near the mound now occupied by the citadel. He had a certain gray cow (el-shahba) which was milked every morning for the benefit of the poor. When, therefore, it was proclaimed: "Ibrahim haleb el-shahba" (Abraham has milked the gray cow), all the poor of the tribe came up to receive their share. The repetition of this morning call attached itself to the spot, and became the name of the city which was

461

afterwards founded.

Aleppo is built on the eastern slope of a shallow upland basin, through which flows the little River Koweik. There are low hills to the north and south, between which the country falls into a wide, monotonous plain, extending unbroken to the Euphrates. The city is from eight to ten miles in circuit, and, though not so thickly populated, covers a greater extent of space than Damascus. The population is estimated at 100,000. In the excellence (not the elegance) of its architecture, it surpasses any Oriental city I have yet seen. The houses are all of hewn stone, frequently three and even four stories in height, and built in a most massive and durable style, on account of the frequency of earthquakes. The streets are well paved, clean, with narrow sidewalks, and less tortuous and intricate than the bewildering alleys of Damascus. A large part of the town is occupied with bazaars, attesting the splendor of its former commerce. These establishments are covered with lofty vaults of stone, lighted from the top; and one may walk for miles beneath the spacious roofs. The shops exhibit all the stuffs of the East, especially of Persia and India. There is also an extensive display of European fabrics, as the eastern provinces of Asiatic Turkey, as far as Baghdad, are supplied entirely from Aleppo and Trebizond.

Within ten years--in fact, since the Allied Powers drove Ibrahim Pasha out of Syria--the trade of Aleppo has increased, at the expense of Damascus. The tribes of the Desert, who were held in check during the Egyptian occupancy, are now so unruly that much of the commerce between the latter place and Baghdad goes northward to Mosul, and thence by a safer road to this city. The khans, of which there are a great number, built on a scale according with the former magnificence of Aleppo, are nearly all filled, and Persian, Georgian, and Armenian merchants again make their appearance in the bazaars. The principal manufactures carried on are the making of shoes (which, indeed, is a prominent branch in every Turkish city), and the weaving of silk and golden tissues. Two long bazaars are entirely occupied with shoe-shops, and there is nearly a quarter of a mile of confectionery, embracing more varieties than I ever saw, or imagined possible. I saw yesterday the operation of weaving silk and gold, which is a very slow process. The warp and the body of the woof were of purple silk. The loom only differed from the old hand-looms in general use in having some thirty or forty contrivances for lifting the threads of the warp, so as to form, by variation, certain patterns. The gold threads by which the pattern was worked were contained in twenty small shuttles, thrust by hand under the different parcels of the warp, as they were raised by a boy trained for that purpose, who sat on the top of the loom. The fabric was very brilliant in its appearance, and sells, as the weavers informed me, at 100 piastres per pik--about $7 per yard.

We had letters to Mr. Ford, an American Missionary established here, and Signor di Picciotto, who acts as American Vice-Consul. Both gentlemen have been very cordial in their offers of service, and by their aid we have been enabled to see something of Aleppo life and society. Mr. Ford, who has been here four years, has a pleasant residence at Jedaida, a Christian suburb of the city. His congregation numbers some fifty or sixty proselytes, who are mostly from the schismatic sects of the Armenians. Dr. Smith, who established the mission at Ain-tab (two days' journey north of this), where he died last year, was very successful among these sects, and the congregation there amounts to nine hundred. The Sultan, a year ago, issued a firman, permitting his Christian subjects to erect houses of worship; but, although this was proclaimed in Constantinople and much lauded in Europe as an act of great generosity and tolerance, there has been no official promulgation of it here. So of the aid which the Turkish Government was said to have afforded to its destitute Christian subjects, whose houses were sacked during the fanatical rebellion of 1850. The world praised the Sultan's charity and love of justice, while the sufferers, to this day, lack the first experience of it. But for the spontaneous relief contributed in Europe and among the Christian communities of the Levant, the amount of misery would have been frightful.

To Feridj Pasha, who is at present the commander of the forces here, is mainly due the credit of having put down the rebels with a strong hand. There were but few troops in the city at the time of the outbreak, and as the insurgents, who were composed of the Turkish and Arab population, were in league with the Aneyzehs of the Desert, the least faltering or delay would have led to a universal massacre of the Christians. Fortunately, the troops were divided into two portions, one occupying the barracks on a hill north of the city, and the other, a mere corporal's guard of a dozen men, posted in the citadel. The leaders of the outbreak went to the latter and offered him a large sum of money (the spoils of Christian houses) to give up the fortress. With a loyalty to his duty truly miraculous among the Turks, he ordered his men to fire upon them, and they beat a hasty retreat. The quarter of the insurgents lay precisely between the barracks and the citadel, and by order of Feridj Pasha a cannonade was immediately opened on it from both points. It was not, however, until many houses had been battered down, and a still larger number destroyed by fire, that the rebels were brought to submission. Their allies, the Aneyzehs, appeared on the hill east of Aleppo, to the number of five or six thousand, but a few well-directed cannon-balls told them what they might expect, and they speedily retreated. Two or three hundred Christian families lost nearly all of their property during the sack, and many were left entirely destitute. The house in which Mr. Ford lives was plundered of jewels and furniture to the amount of 400,000 piastres ($20,000). The robbers, it is said, were amazed at the amount of spoil they found. The Government made some feeble efforts to recover it, but the greater part was already sold and scattered through a thousand hands, and the unfortunate Christians have only received about seven per cent. of their loss.

The burnt quarter has since been rebuilt, and I noticed several Christians occupying shops in various parts of it. But many families, who fled at the time, still remain in various parts of Syria, afraid to return to their homes. The Aneyzehs and other Desert tribes have latterly become more daring than ever. Even in the immediate neighborhood of the city, the inhabitants are so fearful of them that all the grain is brought up to the very walls to be threshed. The burying-grounds on both sides are now turned into threshing-floors, and all day long the Turkish peasants drive their heavy sleds around among the tomb-stones.

On the second day after our arrival, we paid a visit to Osman Pasha, Governor of the City and Province of Aleppo. We went in state, accompanied by the Consul, with two janissaries in front, bearing silver maces, and a dragoman behind. The seraï, or palace, is a large, plain wooden building, and a group of soldiers about the door, with a shabby carriage in the court, were the only tokens of its character. We were ushered at once into the presence of the Pasha, who is a man of about seventy years, with a good-humored, though shrewd face. He was quite cordial in his manners, complimenting us on our Turkish costume, and vaunting his skill in physiognomy, which at once revealed to him that we belonged to the highest class of American nobility. In fact, in the firman which he has since sent us, we are mentioned as "nobles." He invited us to pass a day or two with him, saying that he should derive much benefit from our superior knowledge. We replied that such an intercourse could only benefit ourselves, as his greater experience, and the distinguished wisdom which had made his name long since familiar to our ears, precluded the hope of our being of any service to him. After half an hour's stay, during which we were regaled with jewelled pipes, exquisite Mocha coffee, and sherbet breathing of the gardens of Gülistan, we took our leave.

The Pasha sent an officer to show us the citadel. We passed around the moat to the entrance on the western side, consisting of a bridge and double gateway. The fortress, as I have already stated, occupies the crest of an elliptical mound, about one thousand feet by six hundred, and two hundred feet in height. It is entirely encompassed by the city and forms a prominent and picturesque feature in the distant view thereof. Formerly, it was thickly inhabited, and at the time of the great earthquake of 1822, there were three hundred families living within the walls, nearly all of whom perished. The outer walls were very much shattered on that occasion, but the enormous towers and the gateway, the grandest specimen of Saracenic architecture in the East, still remain entire. This gateway, by which we entered, is colossal in its proportions. The outer entrance, through walls ten feet thick, admitted us into a lofty vestibule lined with marble, and containing many ancient inscriptions in mosaic. Over the main portal, which is adorned with sculptured lions' heads, there is a tablet stating that the fortress was built by El Melek el Ashraf (the Holiest of Kings), after which follows: "Prosperity to the True Believers--Death to the Infidels!" A second tablet shows that it was afterwards repaired by Mohammed ebn-Berkook, who, I believe, was one of the Fatimite Caliphs. The shekh of the citadel, who accompanied us, stated the age of the structure at nine hundred years, which, as nearly as I can recollect the Saracenic chronology, is correct. He called our attention to numbers of iron arrow-heads sticking in the solid masonry--the marks of ancient sieges. Before leaving, we were presented with a bundle of arrows from the armory--undoubted relics of Saracen warfare.

The citadel is now a mass of ruins, having been deserted since the earthquake. Grass is growing on the ramparts, and the caper plant, with its white-and-purple blossoms, flourishes among the piles of rubbish. Since the late rebellion, however, a small military barrack has been built, and two companies of soldiers are stationed there, We walked around the walls, which command a magnificent view of the city and the wide plains to the south and east. It well deserves to rank with the panorama of Cairo from the citadel, and that of Damascus from the Anti-Lebanon, in extent, picturesqueness and rich oriental character. Out of the gray ring of the city, which incloses the mound, rise the great white domes and the whiter minarets of its numerous mosques, many of which are grand and imposing structures. The course of the river through the centre of the picture is marked by a belt of the greenest verdure, beyond which, to the west, rises a chain of naked red hills, and still further, fading on the horizon, the blue summit of Mt. St. Simon, and the coast range of Akma Dagh. Eastward, over vast orchards of pistachio trees, the barren plain of the Euphrates fades away to a glimmering, hot horizon. Looking downwards on the heart of the city, I was surprised to see a number of open, grassy tracts, out of which, here and there, small trees were growing. But, perceiving what appeared to be subterranean entrances at various points, I found that these tracts were upon the roofs of the houses and bazaars, verifying what I had frequently heard, that in Aleppo the inhabitants visit their friends in different parts of the city, by passing over the roofs of the houses. Previous to the earthquake of 1822, these vast roof-plains were cultivated as gardens, and presented an extent of airy bowers as large, if not as magnificent, as the renowned Hanging Gardens of ancient Babylon.

Accompanied by Signor di Picciotto, we spent two or three days in visiting the houses of the principal Jewish and Christian families in Aleppo. We found, it is true, no such splendor as in Damascus, but more solid and durable architecture, and a more chastened elegance of taste. The buildings are all of hewn stone, the court-yards paved with marble, and the walls rich with gilding and carved wood. Some of the larger dwellings have small but beautiful gardens attached to them. We were everywhere received with the greatest hospitality, and the visits were considered as a favor rather than an intrusion. Indeed, I was frequently obliged to run the risk of giving offence, by declining the refreshments which were offered us. Each round of visits was a feat of strength, and we were obliged to desist from sheer inability to support more coffee, rose-water, pipes, and aromatic sweetmeats. The character of society in Aleppo is singular; its very life and essence is etiquette. The laws which govern it are more inviolable than those of the Medes and Persians. The question of precedence among the different families is adjusted by the most delicate scale, and rigorously adhered to in the most trifling matters. Even we, humble voyagers as we are, have been obliged to regulate our conduct according to it. After our having visited certain families, certain others would have been deeply mortified had we neglected to call upon them. Formerly, when a traveller arrived here, he was expected to call upon the different Consuls, in the order of their established precedence: the Austrian first, English second, French third, &c. After this, he was obliged to stay at home several days, to give the Consuls an opportunity of returning the visits, which they made in the same order. There was a diplomatic importance about all his movements, and the least violation of etiquette, through ignorance or neglect, was the town talk for days.

This peculiarity in society is evidently a relic of the formal times, when Aleppo was a semi-Venetian city, and the opulent seat of Eastern commerce. Many of the inhabitants are descended from the traders of those times, and they all speak the lingua franca, or Levantine Italian. The women wear a costume partly Turkish and partly European, combining the graces of both; it is, in my eyes, the most beautiful dress in the world. They wear a rich scarf of some dark color on the head, which, on festive occasions, is almost concealed by their jewels, and the heavy scarlet pomegranate blossoms which adorn their dark hair. A Turkish vest and sleeves of embroidered silk, open in front, and a skirt of white or some light color, completes the costume. The Jewesses wear in addition a short Turkish caftan, and full trousers gathered at the ankles. At a ball given by Mr. Very, the English Consul, which we attended, all the Christian beauties of Aleppo were present. There was a fine display of diamonds, many of the ladies wearing several thousand dollars' worth on their heads. The peculiar etiquette of the place was again illustrated on this occasion. The custom is, that the music must be heard for at least one hour before the guests come. The hour appointed was eight, but when we went there, at nine, nobody had arrived. As it was generally supposed that the ball was given on our account, several of the families had servants in the neighborhood to watch our arrival; and, accordingly, we had not been there five minutes before the guests crowded through the door in large numbers. When the first dance (an Arab dance, performed by two ladies at a time) was proposed, the wives of the French and Spanish Consuls were first led, or rather dragged, out. When a lady is asked to dance, she invariably refuses. She is asked a second and a third time; and if the gentleman does not solicit most earnestly, and use some gentle force in getting her upon the floor, she never forgives him.

At one of the Jewish houses which we visited, the wedding festivities of one of the daughters were being celebrated. We were welcomed with great cordiality, and immediately ushered into the room of state, an elegant apartment, overlooking the gardens below the city wall. Half the room was occupied by a raised platform, with a divan of blue silk cushions. Here the ladies reclined, in superb dresses of blue, pink, and gold, while the gentlemen were ranged on the floor below. They all rose at our entrance, and we were conducted to seats among the ladies. Pipes and perfumed drinks were served, and the bridal cake, made of twenty-six different fruits, was presented on a golden salver. Our fair neighbors, some of whom literally blazed with jewels, were strikingly beautiful. Presently the bride appeared at the door, and we all rose and remained standing, as she advanced, supported on each side by the two shebeeniyeh, or bridesmaids. She was about sixteen, slight and graceful in appearance, though not decidedly beautiful, and was attired with the utmost elegance. Her dress was a pale blue silk, heavy with gold embroidery; and over her long dark hair, her neck, bosom, and wrists, played a thousand rainbow gleams from the jewels which covered them. The Jewish musicians, seated at the bottom of the hall, struck up a loud, rejoicing harmony on their violins, guitars, and dulcimers, and the women servants, grouped at the door, uttered in chorus that wild, shrill cry, which accompanies all such festivals in the East. The bride was careful to preserve the decorum expected of her, by speaking no word, nor losing the sad, resigned expression of her countenance. She ascended to the divan, bowed to each of us with a low, reverential inclination, and seated herself on the cushions. The music and dances lasted some time, accompanied by the zughàreet, or cry of the women, which was repeated with double force when we rose to take leave. The whole company waited on us to the street door, and one of the servants, stationed in the court, shouted some long, sing-song phrases after us as we passed out. I could not learn the words, but was told that it was an invocation of prosperity upon us, in return for the honor which our visit had conferred.

In the evening I went to view a Christian marriage procession, which, about midnight, conveyed the bride to the house of the bridegroom. The house, it appeared, was too small to receive all the friends of the family, and I joined a large number of them, who repaired to the terrace of the English Consulate, to greet the procession as it passed. The first persons who appeared were a company of buffoons; after them four janissaries, carrying silver maces; then the male friends, bearing colored lanterns and perfumed torches, raised on gilded poles; then the females, among whom I saw some beautiful Madonna faces in the torchlight; and finally the bride herself, covered from head to foot with a veil of cloth of gold, and urged along by two maidens: for it is the etiquette of such occasions that the bride should resist being taken, and must be forced every step of the way, so that she is frequently three hours in going the distance of a mile. We watched the procession a long time, winding away through the streets--a line of torches, and songs, and incense, and noisy jubilee--under the sweet starlit heaven.

The other evening, Signor di Picciotto mounted us from his fine Arabian stud, and we rode around the city, outside of the suburbs. The sun was low, and a pale yellow lustre touched the clusters of minarets that rose out of the stately masses of buildings, and the bare, chalky hills to the north. After leaving the gardens on the banks of the Koweik, we came upon a dreary waste of ruins, among which the antiquarian finds traces of the ancient Aleppo of the Greeks, the Mongolian conquerors of the Middle Ages, and the Saracens who succeeded them. There are many mosques and tombs, which were once imposing specimens of Saracenic art; but now, split and shivered by wars and earthquakes, are slowly tumbling into utter decay. On the south-eastern side of the city, its chalk foundations have been hollowed into vast, arched caverns, which extend deep into the earth. Pillars have been left at regular intervals, to support the masses above, and their huge, dim labyrinths resemble the crypts of some great cathedral. They are now used as rope-walks, and filled with cheerful workmen.

Our last excursion was to a country-house of Signor di Picciotto, in the Gardens of Babala, about four miles from Aleppo. We set out in the afternoon on our Arabians, with our host's son on a large white donkey of the Baghdad breed. Passing the Turkish cemetery, where we stopped to view the tomb of General Bem, we loosened rein and sped away at full gallop over the hot, white hills. In dashing down a stony rise, the ambitious donkey, who was doing his best to keep up with the horses, fell, hurling Master Picciotto over his head. The boy was bruised a little, but set his teeth together and showed no sign of pain, mounted again, and followed us. The Gardens of Babala are a wilderness of fruit-trees, like those of Damascus. Signor P.'s country-house is buried in a wild grove of apricot, fig, orange, and pomegranate-trees. A large marble tank, in front of the open, arched liwan, supplies it with water. We mounted to the flat roof, and watched the sunset fade from the beautiful landscape. Beyond the bowers of dazzling greenness which surrounded us, stretched the wide, gray hills; the minarets of Aleppo, and the walls of its castled mount shone rosily in the last rays of the sun; an old palace of the Pashas, with the long, low barracks of the soldiery, crowned the top of a hill to the north; dark, spiry cypresses betrayed the place of tombs; and, to the west, beyond the bare red peak of Mount St. Simon, rose the faint blue outline of Giaour Dagh, whose mural chain divides Syria from the plains of Cilicia. As the twilight deepened over the scene, there came a long, melodious cry of passion and of sorrow from the heart of a starry-flowered pomegranate tree in the garden. Other voices answered it from the gardens around, until not one, but fifty nightingales charmed the repose of the hour. They vied with each other in their bursts of passionate music. Each strain soared over the last, or united with others, near and far, in a chorus of the divinest pathos--an expression of sweet, unutterable, unquenchable longing. It was an ecstasy, yet a pain, to listen. "Away!" said Jean Paul to Music: "thou tellest me of that which I have not, and never can have--which I forever seek, and never find!"

But space fails me to describe half the incidents of our stay in Aleppo. There are two things peculiar to the city, however, which I must not omit mentioning. One is the Aleppo Button, a singular ulcer, which attacks every person born in the city, and every stranger who spends more than a month there. It can neither be prevented nor cured, and always lasts for a year. The inhabitants almost invariably have it on the face--either on the cheek, forehead, or tip of the nose--where it often leaves an indelible and disfiguring scar. Strangers, on the contrary, have it on one of the joints; either the elbow, wrist, knee, or ankle. So strictly is its visitation confined to the city proper, that in none of the neighboring villages, nor even in a distant suburb, is it known. Physicians have vainly attempted to prevent it by inoculation, and are at a loss to what cause to ascribe it. We are liable to have it, even after five days' stay; but I hope it will postpone its appearance until after I reach home.

The other remarkable thing here is the Hospital for Cats. This was founded long ago by a rich, cat-loving Mussulman, and is one of the best endowed institutions in the city. An old mosque is appropriated to the purpose, under the charge of several directors; and here sick cats are nursed, homeless cats find shelter, and decrepit cats gratefully purr away their declining years. The whole category embraces several hundreds, and it is quite a sight to behold the court, the corridors, and terraces of the mosque swarming with them. Here, one with a bruised limb is receiving a cataplasm; there, a cataleptic patient is tenderly cared for; and so on, through the long concatenation of feline diseases. Aleppo, moreover, rejoices in a greater number of cats than even Jerusalem. At a rough guess, I should thus state the population of the city: Turks and Arabs, 70,000; Christians of all denominations, 15,000; Jews, 10,000; dogs, 12,000; and cats, 8,000.

Among other persons whom I have met here, is Ferhat Pasha, formerly General Stein, Hungarian Minister of War, and Governor of Transylvania. He accepted Moslemism with Bem and others, and now rejoices in his circumcision and 7,000 piastres a month. He is a fat, companionable sort of man; who, by his own confession, never labored very zealously for the independence of Hungary, being an Austrian by birth. He conversed with me for several hours on the scenes in which he had participated, and attributed the failure of the Hungarians to the want of material means. General Bem, who died here, is spoken of with the utmost respect, both by Turks and Christians. The former have honored him with a large tomb, or mausoleum, covered with a dome.

But I must close, leaving half unsaid. Suffice it to say that no Oriental city has interested me so profoundly as Aleppo, and in none have I received such universal and cordial hospitality. We leave to-morrow for Asia Minor, having engaged men and horses for the whole route to Constantinople.

Chapter XVI. Through the Syrian Gates.

An Inauspicious Departure--The Ruined Church of St. Simon--The Plain of Antioch--A Turcoman Encampment--Climbing Akma Dagh--The Syrian Gates--Scanderoon--An American Captain--Revolt of the Koords--We take a Guard--The Field of Issus--The Robber-Chief, Kutchuk Ali--A Deserted Town--A Land of Gardens.

"Mountains, on whose barren breast

The lab'ring clouds do often rest."

Milton.

In Quarantine (Adana, Asia Minor), *Tuesday, June* 15, 1852.

We left Aleppo on the morning of the 9th, under circumstances not the most promising for the harmony of our journey. We had engaged horses and baggage-mules from the capidji, or chief of the muleteers, and in order to be certain of having animals that would not break down on the way, made a particular selection from a number that were brought us. When about leaving the city, however, we discovered that one of the horses had been changed. Signor di Picciotto, who accompanied us past the Custom-House barriers, immediately dispatched the delinquent muleteer to bring back the true horse, and the latter made a farce of trying to find him, leading the Consul and the capidji (who, I believe, was at the bottom of the cheat) a wild-goose chase over the hills around Aleppo, where of course, the animal was not to be seen. When, at length, we had waited three hours, and had wandered about four miles from the city, we gave up the search, took leave of the Consul and went on with the new horse. Our proper plan would have been to pitch the tent and refuse to move till the matter was settled. The animal, as we discovered during the first day's journey, was hopelessly lame, and we only added to the difficulty by taking him.

We rode westward all day over barren and stony hills, meeting with abundant traces of the power and prosperity of this region during the times of the Greek Emperors. The nevastation wrought by earthquakes has been terrible; there is scarcely a wall or arch standing, which does not bear marks of having been violently shaken. The walls inclosing the fig-orchards near the villages contain many stones with Greek inscriptions, and fragments of cornices. We encamped the first night on the plain at the foot of Mount St. Simon, and not far from the ruins of the celebrated Church of the same name. The building stands in a stony wilderness at the foot of the mountain. It is about a hundred feet long and thirty in height, with two lofty square towers in front. The pavement of the interior is entirely concealed by the masses of pillars, capitals, and hewn blocks that lie heaped upon it. The windows, which are of the tall, narrow, arched form, common in Byzantine Churches, have a common moulding which falls like a mantle over and between them. The general effect of the Church is very fine, though there is much inelegance in the sculptured details. At the extremity is a half-dome of massive stone, over the place of the altar, and just in front of this formerly stood the pedestal whereon, according to tradition, St. Simeon Stylites commenced his pillar-life. I found a recent excavation at the spot, but no pedestal, which has probably been carried off by the Greek monks. Beside the Church stands a large building, with an upper and lower balcony, supported by square stone pillars, around three sides. There is also a paved court-yard, a large cistern cut in the rock and numerous out-buildings, all going to confirm the supposition of its having been a monastery. The main building is three stories high, with pointed gables, and bears a strong resemblance to an American summer hotel, with verandas. Several ancient fig and walnut trees are growing among the ruins, and add to their picturesque appearance.

The next day we crossed a broad chain of hills to the Plain of Antioch, which we reached near its northern extremity. In one of the valleys through which the road lay, we saw a number of hot sulphur springs, some of them of a considerable volume of water. Not far from them was a beautiful fountain of fresh and cold water gushing from the foot of a high rock. Soon after reaching the plain, we crossed the stream of Kara Su, which feeds the Lake of Antioch. This part of the plain is low and swampy, and the streams are literally alive with fish. While passing over the bridge I saw many hundreds, from one to two feet in length. We wandered through the marshy meadows for two or three hours, and towards sunset reached a Turcoman encampment, where the ground was dry enough to pitch our tents. The rude tribe received us hospitably, and sent us milk and cheese in abundance. I visited the tent of the Shekh, who was very courteous, but as he knew no language but Turkish, our conversation was restricted to signs. The tent was of camel's-hair cloth, spacious, and open at the sides. A rug was spread for me, and the Shekh's wife brought me a pipe of tolerable tobacco. The household were seated upon the ground, chatting pleasantly with one another, and apparently not in the least disturbed by my presence. One of the Shekh's sons, who was deaf and dumb, came and sat before me, and described by very expressive signs the character of the road to Scanderoon. He gave me to understand that there were robbers in the mountains, with many grim gestures descriptive of stabbing and firing muskets.

The mosquitoes were so thick during the night that we were obliged to fill the tent with smoke in order to sleep. When morning came, we fancied there would be a relief for us, but it only brought a worse pest, in the shape of swarms of black gnats, similar to those which so tormented me in Nubia. I know of no infliction so terrible as these gnats, which you cannot drive away, and which assail ears, eyes, and nostrils in such quantities that you become mad and desperate in your efforts to eject them. Through glens filled with oleander, we ascended the first slopes of Akma Dagh, the mountain range which divides the Gulf of Scanderoon from the Plain of Antioch. Then, passing a natural terrace, covered with groves of oak, our road took the mountain side, climbing upwards in the shadow of pine and wild olive trees, and between banks of blooming lavender and myrtle. We saw two or three companies of armed guards, stationed by the road-side, for the mountain is infested with robbers, and a caravan had been plundered only three days before. The view, looking backward, took in the whole plain, with the Lake of Antioch glittering in the centre, the valley of the Orontes in the south, and the lofty cone of Djebel-Okrab far to the west. As we approached the summit, violent gusts of wind blew through the pass with such force as almost to overturn our horses. Here the road from Antioch joins that from Aleppo, and both for some distance retain the ancient pavement.

From the western side we saw the sea once more, and went down through the Pylæ Syriæ, or Syrian Gates, as this defile was called by the Romans. It is very narrow and rugged, with an abrupt descent. In an hour from the summit we came upon an aqueduct of a triple row of arches, crossing the gorge. It is still used to carry water to the town of Beilan, which hangs over the mouth of the pass, half a mile below. This is one of the most picturesque spots in Syria. The houses cling to the sides and cluster on the summits of precipitous crags, and every shelf of soil, every crevice where a tree can thrust its roots, upholds a mass of brilliant vegetation. Water is the life of the place. It gushes into the street from exhaustless fountains; it trickles from the terraces in showers of misty drops; it tumbles into the gorge in sparkling streams; and everywhere it nourishes a life as bright and beautiful as its own. The fruit trees are of enormous size, and the crags are curtained with a magnificent drapery of vines. This green gateway opens suddenly upon another, cut through a glittering mass of micaceous rock, whence one looks down on the town and Gulf of Scanderoon, the coast of Karamania beyond, and the distant snows of the Taurus. We descended through groves of pine and oak, and in three hours more reached the shore.

Scanderoon is the most unhealthy place on the Syrian Coast, owing to the malaria from a marsh behind it. The inhabitants are a wretched pallid set, who are visited every year with devastating fevers. The marsh was partly drained some forty years ago by the Turkish government, and a few thousand dollars would be sufficient to remove it entirely, and make the place--which is of some importance as the seaport of Aleppo--healthy and habitable. At present, there are not five hundred inhabitants, and half of these consist of the Turkish garrison and the persons attached to the different Vice-Consulates. The streets are depositories of filth, and pools of stagnant water, on all sides, exhale the most fetid odors. Near the town are the ruins of a castle built by Godfrey of Bouillon. We marched directly down to the sea-shore, and pitched our tent close beside the waves, as the place most free from malaria. There were a dozen vessels at anchor in the road, and one of them proved to be the American bark Columbia, Capt. Taylor. We took a skiff and went on board, where we were cordially welcomed by the mate. In the evening, the captain came to our tent, quite surprised to find two wandering Americans in such a lonely corner of the world. Soon afterwards, with true seamanlike generosity, he returned, bringing a jar of fine Spanish olives and a large bottle of pickles, which he insisted on adding to our supplies. The olives have the choicest Andalusian flavor, and the pickles lose none of their relish from having been put up in New York.

The road from Scanderoon to this place lies mostly along the shore of the gulf, at the foot of Akma Dagh, and is reckoned dangerous on account of the marauding bands of Koords who infest the mountains. These people, like the Druses, have rebelled against the conscription, and will probably hold their ground with equal success, though the Turks talk loudly of invading their strongholds. Two weeks ago, the post was robbed, about ten miles from Scanderoon, and a government vessel, now lying at anchor in the bay, opened a cannonade on the plunderers, before they could be secured. In consequence of the warnings of danger in everybody's mouth, we decided to take an escort, and therefore waited upon the commander of the forces, with the firman of the Pasha of Aleppo. A convoy of two soldiers was at once promised us; and at sunrise, next morning, they took the lead of our caravan.

In order to appear more formidable, in case we should meet with robbers, we put on our Frank pantaloons, which had no other effect than to make the heat more intolerable. But we formed rather a fierce cavalcade, six armed men in all. Our road followed the shore of the bay, having a narrow, uninhabited flat, covered with thickets of myrtle and mastic, between us and the mountains. The two soldiers, more valiant than the guard of Banias, rode in advance, and showed no signs of fear as we approached the suspicious places. The morning was delightfully clear, and the snow-crowned range of Taurus shone through the soft vapors hanging over the gulf. In one place, we skirted the shore for some distance, under a bank twenty feet in height, and so completely mantled with shrubbery, that a small army might have hidden in it. There were gulleys at intervals, opening suddenly on our path, and we looked up them, expecting every moment to see the gleam of a Koordish gun-barrel, or a Turcoman spear, above the tops of the myrtles.

Crossing a promontory which makes out from the mountains, we came upon the renowned plain of Issus, where Darius lost his kingdom to Alexander. On a low cliff overhanging the sea, there are the remains of a single tower of gray stone. The people in Scanderoon call it "Jonah's Pillar," and say that it marks the spot where the Ninevite was cast ashore by the whale. [This makes three places on the Syrian coast where Jonah was vomited forth.] The plain of Issus is from two to three miles long, but not more than half a mile wide, It is traversed by a little river, supposed to be the Pinarus, which comes down through a tremendous cleft in the Akma Dagh. The ground seems too small for the battle-field of such armies as were engaged on the occasion. It is bounded on the north by a low hill, separating it from the plain of Baïas, and it is possible that Alexander may have made choice of this position, leaving the unwieldy forces of Darius to attack him from the plain. His advantage would be greater, on account of the long, narrow form of the ground, which would prevent him from being engaged with more than a small portion of the Persian army, at one time. The plain is now roseate with blooming oleanders, but almost entirely uncultivated. About midway there are the remains of an ancient quay jutting into the sea.

Soon after leaving the field of Issus, we reached the town of Baïas, which is pleasantly situated on the shore, at the mouth of a river whose course through the plain is marked with rows of tall poplar trees. The walls of the town, and the white dome and minaret of its mosque, rose dazzlingly against the dark blue of the sea, and the purple stretch of the mountains of Karamania. A single palm lifted its crest in the foreground. We dismounted for breakfast under the shade of an old bridge which crosses the river. It was a charming spot, the banks above and below being overhung with oleander, white rose, honeysuckle and clematis. The two guardsmen finished the remaining half of our Turcoman cheese, and almost exhausted our supply of bread. I gave one of them a cigar, which he was at a loss how to smoke, until our muleteer showed him.

Baïas was celebrated fifty years ago, as the residence of the robber chief, Kutchuk Ali, who, for a long time, braved the authority of the Porte itself. He was in the habit of levying a yearly tribute on the caravan to Mecca, and the better to enforce his claims, often suspended two or three of his captives at the gates of the town, a day or two before the caravan arrived. Several expeditions were sent against him, but he always succeeded in bribing the commanders, who, on their return to Constantinople, made such representations that Kutchuk Ali, instead of being punished, received one dignity after another, until finally he attained the rank of a Pasha of two tails. This emboldened him to commit enormities too great to be overlooked, and in 1812 Baïas was taken, and the atrocious nest of land-pirates broken up.

I knew that the town had been sacked on this occasion, but was not prepared to find such a complete picture of desolation. The place is surrounded with a substantial wall, with two gateways, on the north and south. A bazaar, covered with a lofty vaulted roof of stone, runs directly through from gate to gate; and there was still a smell of spices in the air, on entering. The massive shops on either hand, with their open doors, invited possession, and might readily be made habitable again. The great iron gates leading from the bazaar into the khans and courts, still swing on their rusty hinges. We rode into the court of the mosque, which is surrounded with a light and elegant corridor, supported by pillars. The grass has as yet but partially invaded the marble pavement, and a stone drinking-trough still stands in the centre. I urged my horse up the steps and into the door of the mosque. It is in the form of a Greek cross, with a dome in the centre, resting on four very elegant pointed arches. There is an elaborately gilded and painted gallery of wood over the entrance, and the pulpit opposite is as well preserved as if the mollah had just left it. Out of the mosque we passed into a second court, and then over a narrow bridge into the fortress. The moat is perfect, and the walls as complete as if just erected. Only the bottom is dry, and now covered with a thicket of wild pomegranate trees. The heavy iron doors of the fortress swung half open, as we entered unchallenged. The interior is almost entire, and some of the cannon still lie buried in the springing grass. The plan of the little town, which appears to have been all built at one time, is most admirable. The walls of circuit, including the fortress, cannot be more than 300 yards square, and yet none of the characteristics of a large Oriental city are omitted.

Leaving Baïas, we travelled northward, over a waste, though fertile plain. The mountains on our right made a grand appearance, with their feet mantled in myrtle, and their tops plumed with pine. They rise from the sea with a long, bold sweep, but each peak falls off in a precipice on the opposite side, as if the chain were the barrier of the world and there was nothing but space beyond. In the afternoon we left the plain for a belt of glorious garden land, made by streams that came down from the mountains. We entered a lane embowered in pomegranate, white rose, clematis, and other flowering vines and shrubs, and overarched by superb plane, lime, and beech trees, chained together with giant grape vines. On either side were fields of ripe wheat and barley, mulberry orchards and groves of fruit trees, under the shade of which the Turkish families sat or slept during the hot hours of the day. Birds sang in the boughs, and the gurgling of water made a cool undertone to their music. Out of fairyland where shall I see again such lovely bowers? We were glad when the soldiers announced that it was necessary to encamp there; as we should find no other habitations for more than twenty miles.

Our tent was pitched under a grand sycamore, beside a swift mountain stream which almost made the circuit of our camp. Beyond the tops of the elm, beech, and fig groves, we saw the picturesque green summits of the lower ranges of Giaour Dagh, in the north-east, while over the southern meadows a golden gleam of sunshine lay upon the Gulf of Scanderoon. The village near us was Chaya, where there is a military station. The guards we had brought from Scanderoon here left us; but the commanding officer advised us to take others on the morrow, as the road was still considered unsafe.

480

Chapter XVII. Adana and Tarsus.

The Black Gate--The Plain of Cilicia--A Koord Village--Missis--Cilician Scenery--Arrival at Adana--Three days in Quarantine--We receive Pratique--A Landscape--The Plain of Tarsus--The River Cydnus--A Vision of Cleopatra--Tarsus and its Environs--The Duniktash--The Moon of Ramazan.

"Paul said, I am a man which am a Jew of Tarsus, a city in Cilicia, a citizen of no mean city."--Acts, xxi. 89.

Khan on Mt. Taurus, *Saturday, June* 19, 1852.

We left our camp at Chaya at dawn, with an escort of three soldiers, which we borrowed from the guard stationed at that place. The path led along the shore, through clumps of myrtle beaten inland by the wind, and rounded as smoothly as if they had been clipped by a gardener's shears. As we approached the head of the gulf, the peaked summits of Giaour Dagh, 10,000 feet in height, appeared in the north-east. The streams we forded swarmed with immense trout. A brown hedgehog ran across our road, but when I touched him with the end of my pipe, rolled himself into an impervious ball of prickles. Soon after turning the head of the gulf, the road swerved off to the west, and entered a narrow pass, between hills covered with thick copse-wood. Here we came upon an ancient gateway of black lava stone, which bears marks of great antiquity It is now called Kara Kapu, the "Black Gate," and some suppose it to have been one of the ancient gates of Cilicia.

Beyond this, our road led over high, grassy hills, without a sign of human habitation, to the ruined khan of Koord Koolak, We dismounted and unloaded our baggage in the spacious stone archway, and drove our beasts into the dark, vaulted halls behind. The building was originally intended for a magazine of supplies, and from the ruined mosque near it, I suspect it was formerly one of the caravan stations for the pilgrims from Constantinople to Mecca. The weather was intensely hot and sultry, and our animals were almost crazy from the attacks of a large yellow gad-fly. After the noonday heat was over we descended to the first Cilician plain, which is bounded on the west by the range of Durdun Dagh. As we had now passed the most dangerous part of the road, we dismissed the three soldiers and took but a single man with us. The entire plain is covered with wild fennel, six to eight feet in height, and literally blazing with its bloomy yellow tops. Riding through it, I could barely look over them, and far and wide, on all sides, spread a golden sea, out of which the long violet hills rose with the liveliest effect. Brown, shining serpents, from four to six feet in length, frequently slid across our path. The plain, which must be sixty miles in circumference, is wholly uncultivated, though no land could possibly be richer.

Out of the region of fennel we passed into one of red and white clover, timothy grass and wild oats. The thistles were so large as to resemble young palm-trees, and the salsify of our gardens grew rank and wild. At length we dipped into the evening shadow of Durdun Dagh, and reached the village of Koord Keui, on his lower slope. As there was no place for our tent on the rank grass of the plain or the steep side of the hill, we took forcible possession of the winnowing-floor, a flat terrace built up under two sycamores, and still covered with the chaff of the last threshing. The Koords took the whole thing as a matter of course, and even brought us a felt carpet to rest upon. They came and seated themselves around us, chatting sociably, while we lay in the tent-door, smoking the pipe of refreshment. The view over the wide golden plain, and the hills beyond, to the distant, snow-tipped peaks of Akma Dagh, was superb, as the shadow of the mountain behind us slowly lengthened over it, blotting out the mellow lights of sunset. There were many fragments of pillars and capitals of white marble built up in the houses, showing that they occupied the site of some ancient village or temple.

The next morning, we crossed Durdun Dagh, and entered the great plain of Cilicia. The range, after we had passed it, presented a grand, bold, broken outline, blue in the morning vapor, and wreathed with shifting belts of cloud. A stately castle, called the Palace of Serpents, on the summit of an isolated peak to the north, stood out clear and high, in the midst of a circle of fog, like a phantom picture of the air. The River Jyhoon, the ancient Pyramus, which rises on the borders of Armenia, sweeps the western base of the mountains. It is a larger stream than the Orontes, with a deep, rapid current, flowing at the bottom of a bed lower than the level of the plain. In three hours, we reached Missis, the ancient Mopsuestia, on the right bank of the river. There are extensive ruins on the left bank, which were probably those of the former city. The soil for some distance around is scattered with broken pillars, capitals, and hewn stones. The ancient bridge still crosses the river, but the central arch having been broken away, is replaced with a wooden platform. The modern town is a forlorn place, and all the glorious plain around it is uncultivated. The view over this plain was magnificent: unbounded towards the sea, but on the north girdled by the sublime range of Taurus, whose great snow-fields gleamed in the sun. In the afternoon, we reached the old bridge over the Jyhoon, at Adana. The eastern bank is occupied with the graves of the former inhabitants, and there are at least fifteen acres of tombstones, as thickly planted as the graves can be dug. The fields of wheat and barley along the river are very rich, and at present the natives are busily occupied in drawing the sheaves on large sleds to the open threshing-floors.

The city is built over a low eminence, and its four tall minarets, with a number of palm-trees rising from the mass of brown brick walls, reminded me of Egypt. At the end of the bridge, we were met by one of the Quarantine officers, who preceded us, taking care that we touched nobody in the streets, to the Quarantine building. This land quarantine, between Syria and Asia Minor, when the former country is free from any epidemic, seems a most absurd thing. We were detained at Adana three days and a half, to be purified, before proceeding further. Lately, the whole town was placed in quarantine for five days, because a Turkish Bey, who lives near Baïas, entered the gates without being noticed, and was found in the bazaars. The Quarantine building was once a palace of the Pashas of Adana, but is now in a half-ruined condition. The rooms are large and airy, and there is a spacious open divan which affords ample shade and a cool breeze throughout the whole day. Fortunately for us, there were only three persons in Quarantine, who occupied a room distant from ours. The Inspector was a very obliging person, and procured us a table and two chairs. The only table to be had in the whole place--a town of 15,000 inhabitants--belonged to an Italian merchant, who kindly gave it for our use. We employed a messenger to purchase provisions in the bazaars; and our days passed quietly in writing, smoking, and gazing indolently from our windows upon the flowery plains beyond the town. Our nights, however, were tormented by small white gnats, which stung us unmercifully. The physician of Quarantine, Dr. Spagnolo, is a Venetian refugee, and formerly editor of La Lega Italiana, a paper published in Venice during the revolution. He informed us that, except the Princess Belgioioso, who passed through Adana on her way to Jerusalem, we were the only travellers he had seen for eleven months.

After three days and four nights of grateful, because involuntary, indolence, Dr. Spagnolo gave us pratique, and we lost no time in getting under weigh again. We were the only occupants of Quarantine; and as we moved out of the portal of the old seraï, at sunrise, no one was guarding it. The Inspector and Mustapha, the messenger, took their back-sheeshes with silent gratitude. The plain on the west side of the town is well cultivated; and as we rode along towards Tarsus, I was charmed with the rich pastoral air of the scenery. It was like one of the midland landscapes of England, bathed in Southern sunshine. The beautiful level, stretching away to the mountains, stood golden with the fields of wheat which the reapers were cutting. It was no longer bare, but dotted with orange groves, clumps of holly, and a number of magnificent terebinth-trees, whose dark, rounded masses of foliage remind one of the Northern oak. Cattle were grazing in the stubble, and horses, almost buried under loads of fresh grass, met us as they passed to the city. The sheaves were drawn to the threshing-floor on sleds, and we could see the husbandmen in the distance treading out and winnowing the grain. Over these bright, busy scenes, rose the lesser heights of the Taurus, and beyond them, mingled in white clouds, the snows of the crowning range.

The road to Tarsus, which is eight hours distant, lies over an unbroken plain. Towards the sea, there are two tumuli, resembling those on the plains east of Antioch. Stone wells, with troughs for watering horses, occur at intervals of three or four miles; but there is little cultivation after leaving the vicinity of Adana. The sun poured down an intense summer heat, and hundreds of large gad-flies, swarming around us, drove the horses wild with their stings. Towards noon, we stopped at a little village for breakfast. We took possession of a shop, which the good-natured merchant offered us, and were about to spread our provisions upon the counter, when the gnats and mosquitoes fairly drove us away. We at once went forward in search of a better place, which gave occasion to our chief mukkairee, Hadji Youssuf, for a violent remonstrance. The terms of the agreement at Aleppo gave the entire control of the journey into our own hands, and the Hadji now sought to violate it. He protested against our travelling more than six hours a day, and conducted himself so insolently, that we threatened to take him before the Pasha of Tarsus. This silenced him for the time; but we hate him so cordially since then, that I foresee we shall have more trouble. In the afternoon, a gust, sweeping along the sides of Taurus, cooled the air and afforded us a little relief.

By three o'clock we reached the River Cydnus, which is bare of trees on its eastern side, but flows between banks covered with grass and shrubs. It is still spanned by the ancient bridge, and the mules now step in the hollow ruts worn long ago by Roman and Byzantine chariot wheels. The stream is not more than thirty yards broad, but has a very full and rapid current of a bluish-white color, from the snows which feed it. I rode down to the brink and drank a cup of the water. It was exceedingly cold, and I do not wonder that a bath in it should have killed the Emperor Barbarossa. From the top of the bridge, there is a lovely view, down the stream, where it washes a fringe of willows and heavy fruit-trees on its western bank, and then winds away through the grassy plain, to the sea. For once, my fancy ran parallel with the inspiration of the scene. I could think of nothing but the galley of Cleopatra slowly stemming the current of the stream, its silken sails filled with the sea-breeze, its gilded oars keeping time to the flutes, whose voluptuous melodies floated far out over the vernal meadows. Tarsus was probably almost hidden then, as now, by its gardens, except just where it touched the river; and the dazzling vision of the Egyptian Queen, as she came up conquering and to conquer, must have been all the more bewildering, from the lovely bowers through which she sailed.

From the bridge an ancient road still leads to the old Byzantine gate of Tarsus. Part of the town is encompassed by a wall, built by the Caliph Haroun Al-Raschid, and there is a ruined fortress, which is attributed to Sultan Bajazet

Small streams, brought from the Cydnus, traverse the environs, and, with such a fertile soil, the luxuriance of the gardens in which the city lies buried is almost incredible. In our rambles in search of a place to pitch the tent, we entered a superb orange-orchard, the foliage of which made a perpetual twilight. Many of the trunks were two feet in diameter. The houses are mostly of one story, and the materials are almost wholly borrowed from the ancient city. Pillars, capitals, fragments of cornices and entablatures abound. I noticed here, as in Adana, a high wooden frame on the top of every house, raised a few steps above the roof, and covered with light muslin, like a portable bathing-house. Here the people put up their beds in the evening, sleep, and come down to the roofs in the morning--an excellent plan for getting better air in these malarious plains and escaping from fleas and mosquitoes. In our search for the Armenian Church, which is said to have been founded by St. Paul ("Saul of Tarsus"), we came upon a mosque, which had been originally a Christian Church, of Greek times.

From the top of a mound, whereupon stand the remains of an ancient circular edifice, we obtained a fine view of the city and plain of Tarsus. A few houses or clusters of houses stood here and there like reefs amid the billowy green, and the minarets--one of them with a nest of young storks on its very summit--rose like the masts of sunken ships. Some palms lifted their tufted heads from the gardens, beyond which the great plain extended from the mountains to the sea. The tumulus near Mersyn, the port of Tarsus, was plainly visible. Two hours from Mersyn are the ruins of Pompeiopolis, the name given by Pompey to the town of Soli, after his conquest of the Cilician pirates. From Soli, on account of the bad Greek spoken by its inhabitants, came the term "solecism." The ruins of Pompeiopolis consist of a theatre, temples, and a number of houses, still in good preservation. The whole coast, as far as Aleya, three hundred miles west of this, is said to abound with ruined cities, and I regret exceedingly that time will not permit me to explore it.

While searching for the antiquities about Tarsus, I accosted a man in a Frank dress, who proved to be the Neapolitan Consul. He told us that the most remarkable relic was the Duniktash (the Round Stone), and procured us a guide. It lies in a garden near the city, and is certainly one of the most remarkable monuments in the East. It consists of a square inclosure of solid masonry, 350 feet long by 150 feet wide, the walls of which are eighteen feet in thickness and twenty feet high. It appears to have been originally a solid mass, without entrance, but a passage has been broken in one place, and in another there is a split or fissure, evidently produced by an earthquake. The material is rough stone, brick and mortar. Inside of the inclosure are two detached square masses of masonry, of equal height, and probably eighty feet on a side, without opening of any kind. One of them has been pierced at the bottom, a steep passage leading to a pit or well, but the sides of the passage thus broken indicate that the whole structure is one solid mass. It is generally supposed that they were intended as tombs: but of whom? There is no sign by which they may be recognized, and, what is more singular, no tradition concerning them.

The day we reached Tarsus was the first of the Turkish fast-month of Ramazan, the inhabitants having seen the new moon the night before. At Adana, where they did not keep such a close look-out, the fast had not commenced. During its continuance, which is from twenty-eight to twenty-nine days, no Mussulman dares eat, drink, or smoke, from an hour before sunrise till half an hour after sunset. The Mohammedan months are lunar, and each month makes the whole round of the seasons, once in thirty-three years. When, therefore, the Ramazan comes in midsummer, as at present, the fulfilment of this fast is a great trial, even to the strongest and most devout. Eighteen hours without meat or drink, and what is still worse to a genuine Turk, without a pipe, is a rigid test of faith. The rich do the best they can to avoid it, by feasting all night and sleeping all day, but the poor, who must perform their daily avocations, as usual, suffer exceedingly. In walking through Tarsus I saw many wretched faces in the bazaars, and the guide who accompanied us had a painfully famished air. Fortunately the Koran expressly permits invalids, children, and travellers to disregard the fast, so that although we eat and drink when we like, we are none the less looked upon as good Mussulmans. About dark a gun is fired and a rocket sent up from the mosque, announcing the termination of the day's fast. The meals are already prepared, the pipes filled, the coffee smokes in the finjans, and the echoes have not died away nor the last sparks of the rocket become extinct, before half the inhabitants are satisfying their hunger, thirst and smoke-lust.

We left Tarsus this morning, and are now encamped among the pines of Mount Taurus. The last flush of sunset is fading from his eternal snows, and I drop my pen to enjoy the silence of twilight in this mountain solitude.

Chapter XVIII. The Pass of Mount Taurus.

We enter the Taurus--Turcomans--Forest Scenery--the Palace of Pan--
Khan Mezarluk--Morning among the Mountains--The Gorge of the Cydnus-
-The Crag of the Fortress--The Cilician Gate--Deserted Forts--A Sublime
Landscape--The Gorge of the Sihoon--The Second Gate--Camp in the Defile-
-Sunrise--Journey up the Sihoon--A Change of Scenery--A Pastoral Valley--
Kolü Kushla--A Deserted Khan--A Guest in Ramazan--Flowers--The Plain of
Karamania--Barren Hills--The Town of Eregli--The Hadji again.

"Lo! where the pass expands

Its stony jaws, the abrupt mountain breaks,

And seems, with its accumulated crags,

To overhang the world." Shelley.

Eregli, in *Karamania, June* 22, 1852.

Striking our tent in the gardens of Tarsus, we again crossed the Cydnus,
and took a northern course across the plain. The long line of Taurus rose
before us, seemingly divided into four successive ranges, the highest of which
was folded in clouds; only the long streaks of snow, filling the ravines, being
visible. The outlines of these ranges were very fine, the waving line of the
summits cut here and there by precipitous gorges--the gateways of rivers that
came down to the plain. In about two hours, we entered the lower hills. They
are barren and stony, with a white, chalky soil; but the valleys were filled
with myrtle, oleander, and lauristinus in bloom, and lavender grew in great
profusion on the hill-sides. The flowers of the oleander gave out a delicate,
almond-like fragrance, and grew in such dense clusters as frequently to hide
the foliage. I amused myself with finding a derivation of the name of this
beautiful plant, which may answer until somebody discovers a better one.
Hero, when the corpse of her lover was cast ashore by the waves, buried him
under an oleander bush, where she was accustomed to sit daily, and lament
over his untimely fate. Now, a foreign horticulturist, happening to pass by

when the shrub was in blossom, was much struck with its beauty, and asked Hero what it was called. But she, absorbed in grief, and thinking only of her lover, clasped her hands, and sighed out: "O Leander! O Leander!" which the horticulturist immediately entered in his note-book as the name of the shrub; and by that name it is known, to the present time.

For two or three hours, the scenery was rather tame, the higher summits being obscured with a thunder-cloud. Towards noon, however, we passed the first chain, and saw, across a strip of rolling land intervening, the grand ramparts of the second, looming dark and large under the clouds. A circular watch-tower of white stone, standing on the summit of a promontory at the mouth of a gorge on our right, flashed out boldly against the storm. We stopped under an oak-tree to take breakfast; but there was no water; and two Turks, who were resting while their horses grazed in the meadow, told us we should find a good spring half a mile further. We ascended a long slope, covered with wheat-fields, where numbers of Turcoman reapers were busy at work, passed their black tents, surrounded with droves of sheep and goats, and reached a rude stone fountain of good water, where two companies of these people had stopped to rest, on their way to the mountains. It was the time of noon prayer, and they went through their devotions with great solemnity. We nestled deep in a bed of myrtles, while we breakfasted; for the sky was clouded, and the wind blew cool and fresh from the region of rain above us. Some of the Turcomans asked us for bread, and were very grateful when we gave it to them.

In the afternoon, we came into a higher and wilder region, where the road led through thickets of wild olive, holly, oak, and lauristinus, with occasional groves of pine. What a joy I felt in hearing, once more, the grand song of my favorite tree! Our way was a woodland road; a storm had passed over the region in the morning; the earth was still fresh and moist, and there was an aromatic smell of leaves in the air. We turned westward into the entrance of a deep valley, over which hung a perpendicular cliff of gray and red rock, fashioned by nature so as to resemble a vast fortress, with windows, portals and projecting bastions. François displayed his knowledge of mythology, by declaring it to be the Palace of Pan. While we were carrying out the idea, by

490

making chambers for the Fauns and Nymphs in the basement story of the precipice, the path wound around the shoulder of the mountain, and the glen spread away before us, branching up into loftier ranges, disclosing through its gateway of cliffs, rising out of the steeps of pine forest, a sublime vista of blue mountain peaks, climbing to the topmost snows. It was a magnificent Alpine landscape, more glowing and rich than Switzerland, yet equalling it in all the loftier characteristics of mountain scenery. Another and greater precipice towered over us on the right, and the black eagles which had made their eyries in its niched and caverned vaults, were wheeling around its crest. A branch of the Cydnus foamed along the bottom of the gorge, and soma Turcoman boys were tending their herds on its banks.

Further up the glen, we found a fountain of delicious water, beside the deserted Khan of Mezarluk, and there encamped for the night. Our tent was pitched on the mountain side, near a fountain of the coolest, clearest and sweetest water I have seen in all the East. There was perfect silence among the mountains, and the place was as lonely as it was sublime. The night was cool and fresh; but I could not sleep until towards morning. When I opened my belated eyes, the tall peaks on the opposite side of the glen were girdled below their waists with the flood of a sparkling sunrise. The sky was pure as crystal, except a soft white fleece that veiled the snowy pinnacles of Taurus, folding and unfolding, rising and sinking, as if to make their beauty still more attractive by the partial concealment. The morning air was almost cold, but so pure and bracing--so aromatic with the healthy breath of the pines--that I took it down in the fullest possible draughts.

We rode up the glen, following the course of the Cydnus, through scenery of the wildest and most romantic character. The bases of the mountains were completely enveloped in forests of pine, but their summits rose in precipitous crags, many hundreds of feet in height, hanging above our very heads. Even after the sun was five hours high, their shadows fell upon us from the opposite side of the glen. Mixed with the pine were occasional oaks, an undergrowth of hawthorn in bloom, and shrubs covered with yellow and white flowers. Over these the wild grape threw its rich festoons, filling the air with exquisite fragrance.

Out of this glen, we passed into another, still narrower and wilder. The road was the old Roman way, and in tolerable condition, though it had evidently not been mended for many centuries. In half an hour, the pass opened, disclosing an enormous peak in front of us, crowned with the ruins of an ancient fortress of considerable extent. The position was almost impregnable, the mountain dropping on one side into a precipice five hundred feet in perpendicular height. Under the cliffs of the loftiest ridge, there was a terrace planted with walnut-trees: a charming little hamlet in the wilderness. Wild sycamore-trees, with white trunks and bright green foliage, shaded the foamy twists of the Cydnus, as it plunged down its difficult bed. The pine thrust its roots into the naked precipices, and from their summits hung out over the great abysses below. I thought of Œnone's

--"tall, dark pines, that fringed the craggy ledge

High over the blue gorge, and all between

The snowy peak and snow-white cataract

Fostered the callow eaglet;"

and certainly she had on Mount Ida no more beautiful trees than these.

We had doubled the Crag of the Fortress, when the pass closed before us, shut in by two immense precipices of sheer, barren rock, more than a thousand feet in height. Vast fragments, fallen from above, choked up the entrance, whence the Cydnus, spouting forth in foam, leaped into the defile. The ancient road was completely destroyed, but traces of it were to be seen on the rocks, ten feet above the present bed of the stream, and on the broken masses which had been hurled below. The path wound with difficulty among these wrecks, and then merged into the stream itself, as we entered the gateway. A violent wind blew in our faces as we rode through the strait, which is not ten yards in breadth, while its walls rise to the region of the clouds. In a few minutes we had traversed it, and stood looking back on the enormous gap. There were several Greek tablets cut in the rock above the old road, but so defaced as to be illegible. This is undoubtedly the principal gate of the Taurus, and the pass through which the armies of Cyrus and Alexander entered Cilicia.

Beyond the gate the mountains retreated, and we climbed up a little dell, past two or three Turcoman houses, to the top of a hill, whence opened a view of the principal range, now close at hand. The mountains in front were clothed with dark cedars to their very tops, and the snow-fields behind them seemed dazzlingly bright and near. Our course for several miles now lay through a more open valley, drained by the upper waters of the Cydnus. On two opposing terraces of the mountain chains are two fortresses, built by Ibraham Pasha, but now wholly deserted. They are large and well-constructed works of stone, and surrounded by ruins of stables, ovens, and the rude houses of the soldiery. Passing between these, we ascended to the shelf dividing the waters of the Cydnus and the Sihoon. From the point where the slope descends to the latter river, there opened before me one of the most glorious landscapes I ever beheld. I stood at the extremity of a long hollow or depression between the two ranges of the Taurus--not a valley, for it was divided by deep cloven chasms, hemmed in by steeps overgrown with cedars. On my right rose a sublime chain, soaring far out of the region of trees, and lifting its peaked summits of gray rock into toe sky. Another chain, nearly as lofty, but not so broken, nor with such large, imposing features, overhung me on the left; and far in front, filling up the magnificent vista--filling up all between the lower steeps, crowned with pine, and the round white clouds hanging on the verge of heaven--were the shining snows of the Taurus. Great God, how shall I describe the grandeur of that view! How draw the wonderful outlines of those mountains! How paint the airy hue of violet-gray, the soft white lights, the thousandfold pencillings of mellow shadow, the height, the depth, the far-reaching vastness of the landscape!

In the middle distance, a great blue gorge passed transversely across the two ranges and the region between. This, as I rightly conjectured, was the bed of the Sihoon. Our road led downward through groves of fragrant cedars, and we travelled thus for two hours before reaching the river. Taking a northward course up his banks, we reached the second of the Pylæ Ciliciæ before sunset. It is on a grander scale than the first gate, though not so startling and violent in its features. The bare walls on either side fall sheer to the water, and the road, crossing the Sihoon by a lofty bridge of a single arch, is cut along the face of the rock. Near the bridge a subterranean stream, almost as large as the river, bursts forth from the solid heart of the mountain. On either side gigantic masses of rock, with here and there a pine to adorn their sterility, tower to the height of 6,000 feet, in some places almost perpendicular from summit to base. They are worn and broken into all fantastic forms. There are pyramids, towers, bastions, minarets, and long, sharp spires, splintered and jagged as the turrets of an iceberg. I have seen higher mountains, but I have never seen any which looked so high as these. We camped on a narrow plot of ground, in the very heart of the tremendous gorge. A soldier, passing along at dusk, told us that a merchant and his servant were murdered in the same place last winter, and advised us to keep watch. But we slept safely all night, while the stars sparkled over the chasm, and slips of misty cloud hung low on the thousand pinnacles of rock.

When I awoke, the gorge lay in deep shadow; but high up on the western mountain, above the enormous black pyramids that arose from the river, the topmost pinnacles of rock sparkled like molten silver, in the full gush of sunrise. The great mountain, blocking up the gorge behind us, was bathed almost to its foot in the rays, and, seen through such a dark vista, was glorified beyond all other mountains of Earth. The air was piercingly cold and keen, and I could scarcely bear the water of the Sihoon on my sun-inflamed face. There was a little spring not far off, from which we obtained sufficient water to drink, the river being too muddy. The spring was but a thread oozing from the soil; but the Hadji collected it in handfuls, which he emptied into his water-skin, and then brought to us.

The morning light gave a still finer effect to the manifold forms of the mountains than that of the afternoon sun. The soft gray hue of the rocks shone clearly against the cloudless sky, fretted all over with the shadows thrown by their innumerable spires and jutting points, and by the natural arches scooped out under the cliffs. After travelling less than an hour, we passed the riven walls of the mighty gateway, and rode again under the shade of pine forests. The height of the mountains now gradually diminished, and their sides, covered with pine and cedar, became less broken and abrupt. The

494

summits, nevertheless, still retained the same rocky spine, shooting up into tall, single towers, or long lines of even parapets Occasionally, through gaps between, we caught glimpses of the snow-fields, dazzlingly high and white.

After travelling eight or nine miles, we emerged from the pass, and left the Sihoon at a place called Chiftlik Khan--a stone building, with a small fort adjoining, wherein fifteen splendid bronze cannon lay neglected on their broken and rotting carriages. As we crossed the stone bridge over the river, a valley opened suddenly on the left, disclosing the whole range of the Taurus, which we now saw on its northern side, a vast stretch of rocky spires, with sparkling snow-fields between, and long ravines filled with snow, extending far down between the dark blue cliffs and the dark green plumage of the cedars.

Immediately after passing the central chain of the Taurus, the character of the scenery changed. The heights were rounded, the rocky strata only appearing on the higher peaks, and the slopes of loose soil were deeply cut and scarred by the rains of ages. Both in appearance, especially in the scattered growth of trees dotted over the dark red soil, and in their formation, these mountains strongly resemble the middle ranges of the Californian Sierra Nevada. We climbed a long, winding glen, until we had attained a considerable height, when the road reached a dividing ridge, giving us a view of a deep valley, beyond which a chain of barren mountains rose to the height of some five thousand feet. As we descended the rocky path, a little caravan of asses and mules clambered up to meet us, along the brinks of steep gulfs. The narrow strip of bottom land along the stream was planted with rye, now in head, and rolling in silvery waves before the wind.

After our noonday halt, we went over the hills to another stream, which came from the north-west. Its valley was broader and greener than that we had left, and the hills inclosing it had soft and undulating outlines. They were bare of trees, but colored a pale green by their thin clothing of grass and herbs. In this valley the season was so late, owing to its height above the sea, that the early spring-flowers were yet in bloom. Poppies flamed among the wheat, and the banks of the stream were brilliant with patches of a creeping plant, with a bright purple blossom. The asphodel grew in great profusion, and an ivy-leaved shrub, covered with flakes of white bloom, made the air faint with its fragrance. Still further up, we came to orchards of walnut and plum trees, and vineyards There were no houses, but the innabitants, who were mostly Turcomans, live in villages during the winter, and in summer pitch their tents on the mountains where they pasture their flocks. Directly over this quiet pastoral, vale towered the Taurus, and I looked at once on its secluded loveliness and on the wintry heights, whose bleak and sublime heads were mantled in clouds. From no point is there a more imposing view of the whole snowy range. Near the head of the valley we passed a large Turcoman encampment, surrounded with herds of sheep and cattle.

We halted for the evening at a place called Kolü-Kushla---an immense fortress-village, resembling Baïas, and like it, wholly deserted. Near it there is a small town of very neat houses, which is also deserted, the inhabitants having gone into the mountains with their flocks. I walked through the fortress, which is a massive building of stone, about 500 feet square, erected by Sultan Murad as a resting-place for the caravans to Mecca. It has two spacious portals, in which the iron doors are still hanging, connected by a vaulted passage, twenty feet high and forty wide, with bazaars on each side. Side gateways open into large courts, surrounded with arched chambers. There is a mosque entire, with its pulpit and galleries, and the gilded crescent still glittering over its dome. Behind it is a bath, containing an entrance hall and half a dozen chambers, in which the water-pipes and stone tanks still remain. With a little alteration, the building would make a capital Phalanstery, where the Fourierites might try their experiment without contact with Society. There is no field for them equal to Asia Minor--a glorious region, abounding in natural wealth, almost depopulated, and containing a great number of Phalansteries ready built.

We succeeded in getting some eggs, fowls, and milk from an old Turcoman who had charge of the village. A man who rode by on a donkey sold us a bag of yaourt (sour milk-curds), which was delicious, notwithstanding the suspicious appearance of the bag. It was made before the cream had been removed, and was very rich and nourishing. The old Turcoman sat down and watched us while we ate, but would not join us, as these wandering tribes are very strict in keeping Ramazan. When we had reached our dessert--a plate of fine cherries--another white-bearded and dignified gentleman visited us. We handed him the cherries, expecting that he would take a few and politely return the dish: but no such thing. He coolly produced his handkerchief, emptied everything into it, and marched off. He also did not venture to eat, although we pointed to the Taurus, on whose upper snows the last gleam of daylight was just melting away.

We arose this morning in a dark, cloudy dawn. There was a heavy black storm hanging low in the west, and another was gathering its forces along the mountains behind us. A cold wind blew down the valley, and long peals of thunder rolled grandly among the gorges of Taurus. An isolated hill, crowned with a shattered crag which bore a striking resemblance to a ruined fortress, stood out black and sharp against the far, misty, sunlit peaks. As far as the springs were yet undried, the land was covered with flowers. In one place I saw a large square plot of the most brilliant crimson hue, burning amid the green wheat-fields, as if some Tyrian mantle had been flung there. The long, harmonious slopes and rounded summits of the hills were covered with drifts of a beautiful purple clover, and a diminutive variety of the achillea, or yarrow, with glowing yellow blossoms. The leaves had a pleasant aromatic odor, and filled the air with their refreshing breath, as they were crushed under the hoofs of our horses.

We had now reached the highest ridge of the hilly country along the northern base of Taurus, and saw, far and wide before us, the great central plain of Karamania. Two isolated mountains, at forty or fifty miles distance, broke the monotony of the desert-like level: Kara Dagh in the west, and the snow-capped summits of Hassan Dagh in the north-east. Beyond the latter, we tried to catch a glimpse of the famous Mons Argseus, at the base of which is Kaisariyeh, the ancient Cæsarea of Cappadocia. This mountain, which is 13,000 feet high, is the loftiest peak of Asia Minor. The clouds hung low on the horizon, and the rains were falling, veiling it from our sight.

Our road, for the remainder of the day, was over barren hills, covered with scanty herbage. The sun shone out intensely hot, and the glare of the white soil was exceedingly painful to my eyes. The locality of Eregli was betrayed, some time before we reached it, by its dark-green belt of fruit trees. It stands in the mouth of a narrow valley which winds down from the Taurus, and is watered by a large rapid stream that finally loses itself in the lakes and morasses of the plain. There had been a heavy black thunder-cloud gathering, and as we reached our camping-ground, under some fine walnut-trees near the stream, a sudden blast of cold wind swept over the town, filling the air with dust. We pitched the tent in all haste, expecting a storm, but the rain finally passed to the northward. We then took a walk through the town, which is a forlorn place. A spacious khan, built apparently for the Mecca pilgrims, is in ruins, but the mosque has an exquisite minaret, eighty feet high, and still bearing traces of the devices, in blue tiles, which once covered it. The shops were mostly closed, and in those which were still open the owners lay at full length on their bellies, their faces gaunt with fasting. They seemed annoyed at our troubling them, even with purchases. One would have thought that some fearful pestilence had fallen upon the town. The cobblers only, who somewhat languidly plied their implements, seemed to retain a little life. The few Jews and Armenians smoked their pipes in a tantalizing manner, in the very faces of the poor Mussulmans. We bought an oka of excellent cherries, which we were cruel enough to taste in the streets, before the hungry eyes of the suffering merchants.

This evening the asses belonging to the place were driven in from pasture--four or five hundred in all; and such a show of curious asinine specimens as I never before beheld. A Dervish, who was with us in Quarantine, at Adana, has just arrived. He had lost his teskeré (passport), and on issuing forth purified, was cast into prison. Finally he found some one who knew him, and procured his release. He had come on foot to this place in five days, suffering many privations, having been forty-eight hours without food. He is bound to Konia, on a pilgrimage to the tomb of Hazret Mevlana, the founder of the sect of dancing Dervishes. We gave him food, in return for which he taught me the formula of his prayers. He tells me I should always pronounce the name of Allah when my horse stumbles, or I see a man in danger of his life, as the word has a saving power. Hadji Youssuf, who has just been begging for an advance of twenty piastres to buy grain for his horses, swore "by the pardon of God" that he would sell the lame horse at Konia and get a better one. We have lost all confidence in the old villain's promises, but the poor beasts shall not suffer for his delinquencies.

Our tent is in a charming spot, and, from without, makes a picture to be remembered. The yellow illumination from within strikes on the under sides of the walnut boughs, while the moonlight silvers them from above. Beyond gardens where the nightingales are singing, the tall minaret of Eregli stands revealed in the vapory glow. The night is too sweet and balmy for sleep, and yet I must close my eyes upon it, for the hot plains of Karamania await us to-morrow.

Chapter XIX. The Plains of Karamania.

The Plains of Karamania--Afternoon Heat--A Well--Volcanic Phenomena--Kara-bounar--A Grand Ruined Khan--Moonlight Picture--A Landscape of the Plains-Mirages--A Short Interview--The Village of Ismil---Third Day on the Plains--Approach to Konia.

"A weary waste, expanding to the skies."--Goldsmith.

Konia, Capital of Karamania, *Friday, June* 25, 1854.

François awoke us at the break of day, at Eregli, as we had a journey of twelve hours before us. Passing through the town, we traversed a narrow belt of garden and orchard land, and entered the great plain of Karamania. Our road led at first northward towards a range called Karadja Dagh, and then skirted its base westward. After three hours' travel we passed a village of neat, whitewashed houses, which were entirely deserted, all the inhabitants having gone off to the mountains. There were some herds scattered over the plain, near the village. As the day wore on, the wind, which had been chill in the morning, ceased, and the air became hot and sultry. The glare from the white soil was so painful that I was obliged to close my eyes, and so ran a continual risk of falling asleep and tumbling from my horse. Thus, drowsy and half unconscious of my whereabouts, I rode on in the heat and arid silence of the plain until noon, when we reached a well. It was a shaft, sunk about thirty feet deep, with a long, sloping gallery slanting off to the surface. The well was nearly dry, but by descending the gallery we obtained a sufficient supply of cold, pure water. We breakfasted in the shaded doorway, sharing our provisions with a Turcoman boy, who was accompanying his father to Eregli with a load of salt.

Our road now crossed a long, barren pass, between two parts of Karadja Dagh. Near the northern side there was a salt lake of one hundred yards in diameter, sunk in a deep natural basin. The water was intensely saline. On the other side of the road, and a quarter of a mile distant, is an extinct volcano, the crater of which, near two hundred feet deep, is a salt lake, with a trachytic cone three hundred feet high rising from the centre. From the slope of the mountain we overlooked another and somewhat deeper plain, extending to the north and west. It was bounded by broken peaks, all of which betrayed a volcanic origin. Far before us we saw the tower on the hill of Kara-bounar, our resting-place for the night. The road thither was over a barren plain, cheered here and there by patches of a cushion-like plant, which was covered with pink blossoms. Mr. Harrison scared up some coveys of the frankolin, a large bird resembling the pheasant, and enriched our larder with a dozen starlings.

Kara-bounar is built on the slope of a mound, at the foot of which stands a spacious mosque, visible far over the plain. It has a dome, and two tall, pencil-like towers, similar to those of the Citadel-mosque of Cairo. Near it are the remains of a magnificent khan-fortress, said to have been built by the eunuch of one of the former Sultans. As there was no water in the wells outside of the town, we entered the khan and pitched the tent in its grass-grown court. Six square pillars of hewn stone made an aisle to our door, and the lofty, roofless walls of the court, 100 by 150 feet, inclosed us. Another court, of similar size, communicated with it by a broad portal, and the remains of baths and bazaars lay beyond. A handsome stone fountain, with two streams of running water, stood in front of the khan. We were royally lodged, but almost starved in our splendor, as only two or three Turcomans remained out of two thousand (who had gone off with their herds to the mountains), and they were unable to furnish us with provisions. But for our frankolins and starlings we should have gone fasting.

The mosque was a beautiful structure of white limestone, and the galleries of its minarets were adorned with rich arabesque ornaments. While the muezzin was crying his sunset-call to prayer, I entered the portico and looked into the interior, which was so bare as to appear incomplete. As we sat in our palace-court, after dinner, the moon arose, lighting up the niches in the walls, the clusters of windows in the immense eastern gable, and the rows of massive columns. The large dimensions of the building gave it a truly grand effect, and but for the whine of a distant jackal I could have believed that we were sitting in the aisles of a roofless Gothic cathedral, in the heart of Europe. François was somewhat fearful of thieves, but the peace and repose of the place we've so perfect that I would not allow any such apprehensions to disturb me. In two minutes after I touched my bed I was insensible, and I did not move a limb until sunrise.

Beyond Kara-bounar, there is a low, barren ridge, climbing which, we overlooked an immense plain, uncultivated, apparently unfertile, and without a sign of life as far as the eye could reach. Kara Dagh, in the south, lifted nearer us its cluster of dark summits; to the north, the long ridge of Üsedjik Dagh (the Pigmy Mountain) stretched like a cape into the plain; Hassan Dagh; wrapped in a soft white cloud, receded behind us, and the snows of Taurus seemed almost as distant as when we first beheld them from the Syrian Gates. We rode for four hours over the dead level, the only objects that met our eyes being an occasional herd of camels in the distance. About noon, we reached a well, similar to that of the previous day, but of recent construction. A long, steep gallery led down to the water, which was very cold, but had a villainous taste of lime, salt, and sulphur.

After an hour's halt, we started again. The sun was intensely hot, and for hours we jogged on over the dead level, the bare white soil blinding our eyes with its glare. The distant hills were lifted above the horizon by a mirage. Long sheets of blue water were spread along their bases, islanding the isolated peaks, and turning into ships and boats the black specks of camels far away. But the phenomena were by no means on so grand a scale as I had seen in the Nubian Desert. On the south-western horizon, we discerned the summits of the Karaman range of Taurus, covered with snow. In the middle of the afternoon, we saw a solitary tent upon the plain, from which an individual advanced to meet us. As he drew nearer, we noticed that he wore white Frank pantaloons, similar to the Turkish soldiery, with a jacket of brown cloth, and a heavy sabre. When he was within convenient speaking distance, he cried out: "Stop! why are you running away from me?" "What do you call running away?" rejoined François; "we are going on our journey." "Where do you come from?" he then asked. "From there," said François, pointing behind us "Where are you going?" "There!" and the provoking Greek simply pointed forwards. "You have neither faith nor religion!" said the man, indignantly; then, turning upon his heel, he strode back across the plain.

502

About four o'clock, we saw a long line of objects rising before us, but so distorted by the mirage that it was impossible to know what they were. After a while, however, we decided that they were houses interspersed with trees; but the trees proved to be stacks of hay and lentils, heaped on the flat roofs. This was Ismil, our halting-place. The houses were miserable mud huts; but the village was large, and, unlike most of those we have seen this side of Taurus, inhabited. The people are Turcomans, and their possessions appear to be almost entirely in their herds. Immense numbers of sheep and goats were pasturing on the plain. There were several wells in the place, provided with buckets attached to long swing-poles; the water was very cold, but brackish. Our tent was pitched on the plain, on a hard, gravelly strip of soil. A crowd of wild-haired Turcoman boys gathered in front, to stare at us, and the shepherds quarrelled at the wells, as to which should take his turn at watering his flocks. In the evening a handsome old Turk visited us, and, finding that we were bound to Constantinople, requested François to take a letter to his son, who was settled there.

François aroused us this morning before the dawn, as we had a journey of thirty-five miles before us. He was in a bad humor; for a man, whom he had requested to keep watch over his tent, while he went into the village, had stolen a fork and spoon. The old Turk, who had returned as soon as we were stirring, went out to hunt the thief, but did not succeed in finding him. The inhabitants of the village were up long before sunrise, and driving away in their wooden-wheeled carts to the meadows where they cut grass. The old Turk accompanied us some distance, in order to show us a nearer way, avoiding a marshy spot. Our road lay over a vast plain, seemingly boundless, for the lofty mountain-ranges that surrounded it on all sides were so distant and cloud-like, and so lifted from the horizon by the deceptive mirage, that the eye did not recognize their connection with it. The wind blew strongly from the north-west, and was so cold that I dismounted and walked ahead for two or three hours.

Before noon, we passed two villages of mud huts, partly inhabited, and with some wheat-fields around them. We breakfasted at another well, which furnished us with a drink that tasted like iced sea-water. Thence we rode forth again into the heat, for the wind had fallen by this time, and the sun shone out with great force. There was ever the same dead level, and we rode directly towards the mountains, which, to my eyes, seemed nearly as distant as ever. At last, there was a dark glimmer through the mirage, at their base, and a half-hour's ride showed it to be a line of trees. In another hour, we could distinguish a minaret or two, and finally, walls and the stately domes of mosques. This was Konia, the ancient Iconium, one of the most renowned cities of Asia Minor.

Chapter XX. Scenes in Konia.

Kpproach to Konia---Tomb of Hazret Mevlana--Lodgings in a Khan--An American Luxury--A Night-Scene in Ramazan--Prayers in the Mosque--Remains of the Ancient City--View from the Mosque--The Interior--A Leaning Minaret--The Diverting History of the Muleteers.

"But they shook off the dust on their feet, and came unto Iconium."--Acts, xiii. 51.

Konia (Ancient Iconium), *June* 27, 1852.

The view of Konia from the plain is not striking until one has approached within a mile of the suburbs, when the group of mosques, with their heavy central domes lifted on clusters of smaller ones, and their tall, light, glittering minarets, rising above the foliage of the gardens, against the background of airy hills, has a very pleasing effect. We approached through a long line of dirty suburbs, which looked still more forlorn on account of the Ramazan. Some Turkish officials, in shabby Frank dresses, followed us to satisfy their curiosity by talking with our Katurjees, or muleteers. Outside the city walls, we passed some very large barracks for cavalry, built by Ibrahim Pasha. On the plain north-east of the city, the battle between him and the forces of the Sultan, resulting in the defeat of the latter, was fought.

We next came upon two magnificent mosques, built of white limestone, with a multitude of leaden domes and lofty minarets, adorned with galleries rich in arabesque ornaments. Attached to one of them is the tomb, of Hazret Mevlana, the founder of the sect of Mevlevi Dervishes, which is reputed one of the most sacred places in the East. The tomb is surmounted by a dome, upon which stands a tall cylindrical tower, reeded, with channels between each projection, and terminating in a long, tapering cone. This tower is made of glazed tiles, of the most brilliant sea-blue color, and sparkles in the sun like a vast pillar of icy spar in some Polar grotto. It is a most striking and fantastic object, surrounded by a cluster of minarets and several cypress-trees, amid which it seems placed as the central ornament and crown of the group.

The aspect of the city was so filthy and uninviting that we preferred pitching our tent; but it was impossible to find a place without going back upon the plain; so we turned into the bazaar, and asked the way to a khan. There was a tolerable crowd in the street, although many of the shops were shut. The first khan we visited was too filthy to enter; but the second, though most unpromising in appearance, turned out to be better than it looked. The oda-bashi (master of the rooms) thoroughly swept and sprinkled the narrow little chamber he gave us, laid clean mats upon the floor, and, when our carpets and beds were placed within, its walls of mud looked somewhat comfortable. Its single window, with an iron grating in lieu of glass, looked upon an oblong court, on the second story, surrounded by the rooms of Armenian merchants. The main court (the gate of which is always closed at sunset) is two stories in height, with a rough wooden balcony running around it, and a well of muddy water in the centre.

The oda-bashi lent us a Turkish table and supplied us with dinner from his own kitchen; kibabs, stewed beans, and cucumber salad. Mr. H. and I, forgetting the Ramazan, went out to hunt for an iced sherbet; but all the coffee-shops were closed until sunset. The people stared at our Egyptian costumes, and a fellow in official dress demanded my teskeré. Soon after we returned, François appeared with a splendid lump of ice in a basin and some lemons. The ice, so the khangee said, is taken from a lake among the mountains, which in winter freezes to the thickness of a foot. Behind the lake is a natural cavern, which the people fill with ice, and then close up. At this season they take it out, day by day, and bring it down to the city. It is very pure and thick, and justifies the Turkish proverb in regard to Konia, which is celebrated for three excellent things: "dooz, booz, küz"--salt, ice, and girls.

Soon after sunset, a cannon announced the close of the fast. We waited an hour or two longer, to allow the people time to eat, and then sallied out into the streets. Every minaret in the city blazed with a crown of lighted lamps around its upper gallery, while the long shafts below, and the tapering cones above, topped with brazen crescents, shone fair in the moonlight. It was a strange, brilliant spectacle. In the square before the principal mosque we found a crowd of persons frolicking around the fountain, in the light of a

506

number of torches on poles planted in the ground. Mats were spread on the stones, and rows of Turks of all classes sat thereon, smoking their pipes. Large earthen water-jars stood here and there, and the people drank so often and so long that they seemed determined to provide against the morrow. The boys were having their amusement in wrestling, shouting and firing off squibs, which they threw into the crowd. We kicked off our slippers, sat down among the Turks, smoked a narghileh, drank a cup of coffee and an iced sherbet of raisin juice, and so enjoyed the Ramazan as well as the best of them.

Numbers of True Believers were drinking and washing themselves at the picturesque fountain, and just as we rose to depart, the voice of a boy-muezzin, on one of the tallest minarets, sent down a musical call to prayer. Immediately the boys left off their sports and started on a run for the great mosque, and the grave, gray-bearded Turks got up from the mats, shoved on their slippers, and marched after them. We followed, getting a glimpse of the illuminated interior of the building, as we passed; but the oda-bashi conducted us still further, to a smaller though more beautiful mosque, surrounded with a garden-court. It was a truly magical picture. We entered the gate, and passed on by a marble pavement, under trees and arbors of vines that almost shut out the moonlight, to a paved space, in the centre whereof was a beautiful fountain, in the purest Saracenic style. Its heavy, projecting cornices and tall pyramidal roof rested on a circle of elegant arches, surrounding a marble structure, whence the water gushed forth in a dozen sparkling streams. On three sides it was inclosed by the moonlit trees and arbors; on the fourth by the outer corridor of the mosque, the door of entrance being exactly opposite.

Large numbers of persons were washing their hands and feet at the fountain, after which they entered and knelt on the floor. We stood unobserved in the corridor, and looked in on the splendidly illuminated interior and the crowd at prayer, all bending their bodies to the earth at regular intervals and murmuring the name of Allah. They resembled a plain, of reeds bending before the gusts of wind which precede a storm. When all had entered and were united in solemn prayer, we returned, passing the grand mosque. I stole up to the door, lifted the heavy carpet that hung before it, and looked in. There was a Mevlevi Dervish standing in the entrance, but his eyes were lifted in heavenly abstraction, and he did not see me. The interior was brilliantly lit by white and colored lamps, suspended from the walls and the great central dome. It was an imposing structure, simple in form, yet grand from its dimensions. The floor was covered with kneeling figures, and a deep voice, coming from the other end of the mosque, was uttering pious phrases in a kind of chant. I satisfied my curiosity quickly, and we then returned to the khan.

Yesterday afternoon I made a more thorough examination of the city. Passing through the bazaars, I reached the Serai, or Pasha's Palace, which stands on the site of that of the Sultans of Iconium. It is a long, wooden building, with no pretensions to architectural beauty. Near it there is a large and ancient mosque, with a minaret of singular elegance. It is about 120 feet high, with two hanging galleries; the whole built of blue and red bricks, the latter projecting so as to form quaint patterns or designs. Several ancient buildings near this mosque are surmounted with pyramidal towers, resembling Pagodas of India. Following the long, crooked lanes between mud buildings, we passed these curious structures and reached the ancient wall of the city. In one of the streets lay a marble lion, badly executed, and apparently of the time of the Lower Empire. In the wall were inserted many similar figures, with fragments of friezes and cornices. This is the work of the Seljook Kings, who, in building the wall, took great pains to exhibit the fragments of the ancient city. The number of altars they have preserved is quite remarkable. On the square towers are sunken tablets, containing long Arabic inscriptions.

The high walls of a ruined building in the southern part of the city attracted us, and on going thither we found it to be an ancient mosque, standing on an eminence formed apparently of the debris of other buildings. Part of the wall was also ancient, and in some places showed the marks of an earthquake. A long flight of steps led up to the door of the mosque, and as we ascended we were rewarded by the most charming view of the city and the grand plain. Konia lay at our feet--a wide, straggling array of low mud dwellings, dotted all over with patches of garden verdure, while its three superb mosques, with the many smaller tombs and places of worship, appeared like buildings left from some former and more magnificent capital. Outside of this circle ran a belt of garden land, adorned with groves and

508

long lines of fruit trees; still further, the plain, a sea of faded green, flecked with the softest cloud-shadows, and beyond all, the beautiful outlines and dreamy tints of the different mountain chains. It was in every respect a lovely landscape, and the city is unworthy such surroundings. The sky, which in this region is of a pale, soft, delicious blue, was dotted with scattered fleeces of white clouds, and there was an exquisite play of light and shade over the hills.

There were half a dozen men and boys about the door, amusing themselves with bursting percussion caps on the stone. They addressed us as "hadji!" (pilgrims), begging for more caps. I told them I was not a Turk, but an Arab, which they believed at once, and requested me to enter the mosque. The interior had a remarkably fine effect. It was a maze of arches, supported by columns of polished black marble, forty in number. In form it was nearly square, and covered with a flat, wooden roof. The floor was covered with a carpet, whereon several persons were lying at full length, while an old man, seated in one of the most remote corners, was reading in a loud, solemn voice. It is a peculiar structure, which I should be glad to examine more in detail.

Not far from this eminence is a remarkable leaning minaret, more than a hundred feet in height, while in diameter it cannot be more than fifteen feet. In design it is light and elegant, and the effect is not injured by its deviation from the perpendicular, which I should judge to be about six feet. From the mosque we walked over the mounds of old Iconium to the eastern wall, passing another mosque, wholly in ruin, but which must have once been more splendid than any now standing. The portal is the richest specimen of Saracenic sculpture I have ever seen: a very labyrinth of intricate ornaments. The artist must have seen the great portal of the Temple of the Sun at Baalbec. The minarets have tumbled down, the roof has fallen in, but the walls are still covered with white and blue tiles, of the finest workmanship, resembling a mosaic of ivory and lapis lazuli. Some of the chambers seem to be inhabited, for two old men with white beards lay in the shade, and were not a little startled by our sudden appearance.

We returned to the great mosque, which we had visited on the evening of our arrival, and listened for some time to the voice of a mollah who was preaching an afternoon sermon to a small and hungry congregation. We then entered the court before the tomb of Hazret Mevlana. It was apparently forbidden ground to Christians, but as the Dervishes did not seem to suspect us we walked about boldly, and were about to enter, when an indiscretion of my companion frustrated our plans. Forgetting his assumed character, he went to the fountain and drank, although it was no later than the asser, or afternoon prayer. The Dervishes were shocked and scandalized by this violation of the fast, in the very court-yard of their holiest mosque, and we judged it best to retire by degrees. We sent this morning to request an interview with the Pasha, but he had gone to pass the day in a country palace, about three hours distant. It is a still, hot, bright afternoon, and the silence of the famished populace disposes us to repose. Our view is bounded by the mud walls of the khan, and I already long for the freedom of the great Karamanian Plain. Here, in the heart of Asia Minor, all life seems to stagnate. There is sleep everywhere, and I feel that a wide barrier separates me from the living world.

We have been detained here a whole day, through a chain of accidents, all resulting from the rascality of our muleteers on leaving Aleppo. The lame horse they palmed upon us was unable to go further, so we obliged them to buy another animal, which they succeeded in getting for 350 piastres. We advanced the money, although they were still in our debt, hoping to work our way through with the new horse, and thus avoid the risk of loss or delay. But this morning at sunrise Hadji Youssuf comes with a woeful face to say that the new horse has been stolen in the night, and we, who are ready to start, must sit down and wait till he is recovered. I suspected another trick, but when, after the lapse of three hours, François found the hadji sitting on the ground, weeping, and Achmet beating his breast, it seemed probable that the story was true. All search for the horse being vain, François went with them to the shekh of the horses, who promised, in case it should hereafter be found, to place it in the general pen, where they would be sure to get it on their return. The man who sold them the horse offered them another for the lame one and 150 piastres, and there was no other alternative but to accept it. But we must advance the 150 piastres, and so, in mid-journey, we have already paid them to the end, with the risk of their horses breaking down, or they, horses and all, absconding from us. But the knavish varlets are hardly bold enough for such a climax of villany.

Chapter XXI. The Heart of Asia Minor.

Scenery of the Hills--Ladik, the Ancient Laodicea--The Plague of Gad-Flies--Camp at Ilgün--A Natural Warm Bath--The Gad-Flies Again--A Summer Landscape--Ak-Sheher--The Base of Sultan Dagh--The Fountain of Midas--A Drowsy Journey--The Town of Bolawadün.

"By the forests, lakes, and fountains,

Though the many-folded mountains." Shelley.

Bolawadün, *July* 1, 1852.

Our men brought all the beasts into the court-yard of the khan at Konia, the evening before our departure, so that no more were stolen during the night. The oda-bashi, indefatigable to the last in his attention to us, not only helped load the mules, but accompanied us some distance on our way. All the merchants in the khan collected in the gallery to see us start, and we made our exit in some state. The morning was clear, fresh, and delightful. Turning away from the city walls, we soon emerged from the lines of fruit-trees and interminable fields of tomb-stones, and came out upon the great bare plain of Karamania. A ride of three hours brought us to a long, sloping hill, which gave us a view of the whole plain, and its circuit of mountains. A dark line in the distance marked the gardens of Konia. On the right, near the centre of the plain, the lake, now contracted to very narrow limits, glimmered in the sun. Notwithstanding the waste and unfertile appearance of the country, the soft, sweet sky that hangs over it, the pure, transparent air, the grand sweep of the plain, and the varied forms of the different mountain chains that encompass it, make our journey an inspiring one. A descent of the hills soon shut out the view; and the rest of the day's journey lay among them, skirting the eastern base of Allah Dagh.

The country improved in character, as we advanced. The bottoms of the dry glens were covered with wheat, and shrubbery began to make its appearance on the mountain-sides In the afternoon, we crossed a watershed, dividing Karamania from the great central plain of Asia Minor, and descended to a village called Ladik, occupying the site of the ancient Laodicea, at the foot of Allah Dagh. The plain upon which we came was greener and more flourishing than that we had left. Trees were scattered here and there in clumps, and the grassy wastes, stretching beyond the grain-fields, were dotted with herds of cattle. Emir Dagh stood in the north-west, blue and distant, while, towards the north and north-east, the plain extended to the horizon--a horizon fifty miles distant--without a break. In that direction lay the great salt lake of Yüzler, and the strings of camels we met on the road, laden with salt, were returning from it. Ladik is surrounded with poppy-fields, brilliant with white and purple blossoms. When the petals have fallen, the natives go carefully over the whole field and make incisions in every stalk, whence the opium exudes.

We pitched our tent under a large walnut tree, which we found standing in a deserted inclosure. The graveyard of the village is studded with relics of the ancient town. There are pillars, cornices, entablatures, jambs, altars, mullions and sculptured tablets, all of white marble, and many of them in an excellent state of preservation. They appear to date from the early time of the Lower Empire, and the cross has not yet been effaced from some which serve as head-stones for the True Believers. I was particularly struck with the abundance of altars, some of which contained entire and legible inscriptions. In the town there is the same abundance of ruins. The lid of a sarcophagus, formed of a single block of marble, now serves as a water-trough, and the fountain is constructed of ancient tablets. The town stands on a mound which appears to be composed entirely of the debris of the former place, and near the summit there are many holes which the inhabitants have dug in their search for rings, seals and other relics.

The next day we made a journey of nine hours over a hilly country lying between the ranges of Allah Dagh and Emir Dagh. There were wells of excellent water along the road, at intervals of an hour or two. The day was excessively hot and sultry during the noon hours, and the flies were so bad as to give great inconvenience to our horses. The animal I bestrode kicked so incessantly that I could scarcely keep my seat. His belly was swollen and covered with clotted blood, from their bites. The hadji's mule began to show symptoms of illness, and we had great difficulty in keeping it on its legs. Mr. Harrison bled it in the mouth, as a last resource, and during the afternoon it partly recovered.

An hour before sunset we reached Ilgün, a town on the plain, at the foot of one of the spurs of Emir Dagh. To the west of it there is a lake of considerable size, which receives the streams that flow through the town and water its fertile gardens. We passed through the town and pitched our tent upon a beautiful grassy meadow. Our customary pipe of refreshment was never more heartily enjoyed than at this place. Behind us was a barren hill, at the foot of which was a natural hot bath, wherein a number of women and children were amusing themselves. The afternoon heat had passed away, the air was calm, sweet, and tempered with the freshness of coming evening, and the long shadows of the hills, creeping over the meadows, had almost reached the town. Beyond the line of sycamore, poplar and fig-trees that shaded the gardens of Ilgün, rose the distant chain of Allah Dagh, and in the pale-blue sky, not far above it, the dim face of the gibbous moon showed like the ghost of a planet. Our horses were feeding on the green meadow; an old Turk sat beside us, silent with fasting, and there was no sound but the shouts of the children in the bath. Such hours as these, after a day's journey made in the drowsy heat of an Eastern summer, are indescribably grateful.

After the women had retired from the bath, we were allowed to enter. The interior consisted of a single chamber, thirty feet high, vaulted and almost dark. In the centre was a large basin of hot water, filled by four streams which poured into it. A ledge ran around the sides, and niches in the wall supplied places for our clothes. The bath-keeper furnished us with towels, and we undressed and plunged in. The water was agreeably warm (about 90°), had a sweet taste, and a very slight sulphury smell. The vaulted hall redoubled the slightest noise, and a shaven Turk, who kept us company, sang in his delight, that he might hear the echo of his own voice. When we went back to the tent we found our visitor lying on the ground, trying to stay his hunger. It was rather too bad in us to light our pipes, make a sherbet and drink and smoke in his face, while we joked him about the Ramazan; and he at last got up and walked off, the picture of distress.

We made an early start the next morning, and rode on briskly over the rolling, grassy hills. A beautiful lake, with an island in it, lay at the foot of Emir Dagh. After two hours we reached a guard-house, where our teskerés were demanded, and the lazy guardsman invited us in to take coffee, that he might establish a right to the backsheesh which he could not demand. He had seen us afar off, and the coffee was smoking in the finjans when we arrived. The sun was already terribly hot, and the large, green gad-flies came in such quantities that I seemed to be riding in the midst of a swarm of bees. My horse suffered very much, and struck out his hind feet so violently, in his endeavors to get rid of them, that he racked every joint in my body. They were not content with sucking his blood, but settling on the small segment of my calf, exposed between the big Tartar boot and the flowing trowsers, bit through my stockings with fierce bills. I killed hundreds of them, to no purpose, and at last, to relieve my horse, tied a bunch of hawthorn to a string, by which I swung it under his belly and against the inner side of his flanks. In this way I gave him some relief--a service which he acknowledged by a grateful motion of his head.

As we descended towards Ak-Sheher the country became exceedingly rich and luxuriant. The range of Sultan Dagh (the Mountain of the Sultan) rose on our left, its sides covered with a thick screen of shrubbery, and its highest peak dotted with patches of snow; opposite, the lower range of Emir Dagh (the Mountain of the Prince) lay blue and bare in the sun shine. The base of Sultan Dagh was girdled with groves of fruit-trees, stretching out in long lines on the plain, with fields of ripening wheat between. In the distance the large lake of Ak-Sheher glittered in the sun. Towards the north-west, the plain stretched away for fifty miles before reaching the hills. It is evidently on a much lower level than the plain of Konia; the heat was not only greater, but the season was further advanced. Wheat was nearly ready for cutting, and the poppy-fields where, the day previous, the men were making their first incisions for opium, here had yielded their harvest and were fast ripening their seed. Ak-Sheher is beautifully situated at the entrance of a deep gorge in the mountains. It is so buried in its embowered gardens that little, except the mosque, is seen as you approach it. It is a large place, and boasts a fine mosque, but contains nothing worth seeing. The bazaar, after that of Konia, was the largest we had seen since leaving Tarsus. The greater part of the shopkeepers lay at full length, dozing, sleeping, or staying their appetites till the sunset gun. We found some superb cherries, and plenty of snow, which is brought down from the mountain. The natives were very friendly and good-humored, but seemed surprised at Mr. Harrison tasting the cherries, although I told them we were upon a journey. Our tent was pitched under a splendid walnut tree, outside of the town. The green mountain rose between us and the fading sunset, and the yellow moon was hanging in the east, as we took our dinner at the tent-door. Turks were riding homewards on donkeys, with loads of grass which they had been cutting in the meadows. The gun was fired, and the shouts of the children announced the close of the day's fast, while the sweet, melancholy voice of a boy muezzin called us to sunset prayer, from the minaret.

Leaving Ak-Sheher this morning, we rode along the base of Sultan Dagh. The plain which we overlooked was magnificent. The wilderness of shrubbery which fringed the slopes of the mountain gave place to great orchards and gardens, interspersed with fields of grain, which extended far out on the plain, to the wild thickets and wastes of reeds surrounding the lake. The sides of Sultan Dagh were terraced and cultivated wherever it was practicable, and I saw some fields of wheat high up on the mountain. There were many, people in the road or laboring in the fields; and during the forenoon we passed several large villages. The country is more thickly inhabited, and has a more thrifty and prosperous air than any part of Asia Minor which I have seen. The people are better clad, have more open, honest, cheerful and intelligent faces, and exhibit a genuine courtesy and good-will in their demeanor towards us. I never felt more perfectly secure, or more certain of being among people whom I could trust.

We passed under the summit of Sultan Dagh, which shone out so clear and distinct in the morning sun, that I could scarcely realize its actual height above the plain. From a tremendous gorge, cleft between the two higher peaks, issued a large stream, which, divided into a hundred channels, fertilizes a wide extent of plain. About two hours from Ak-Sheher we passed a splendid fountain of crystal water, gushing up beside the road. I believe it is the same called by some travellers the Fountain of Midas, but am ignorant wherefore the name is given it. We rode for several hours through a succession of grand, rich landscapes. A smaller lake succeeded to that of Ak-Sheher, Emir Dagh rose higher in the pale-blue sky, and Sultan Dagh showed other peaks, broken and striped with snow; but around us were the same glorious orchards and gardens, the same golden-green wheat and rustling phalanxes of poppies--armies of vegetable Round-heads, beside the bristling and bearded Cavaliers. The sun was intensely hot during the afternoon, as we crossed the plain, and I became so drowsed that it required an agony of exertion to keep from tumbling off my horse. We here left the great post-road to Constantinople, and took a less frequented track. The plain gradually became a meadow, covered with shrub cypress, flags, reeds, and wild water-plants. There were vast wastes of luxuriant grass, whereon thousands of black buffaloes were feeding. A stone causeway, containing many elegant fragments of ancient sculpture, extended across this part of the plain, but we took a summer path beside it, through beds of iris in bloom--a fragile snowy blossom, with a lip of the clearest golden hue. The causeway led to a bare salt plain, beyond which we came to the town of Bolawadün, and terminated our day's journey of forty miles.

Bolawadün is a collection of mud houses, about a mile long, situated on an eminence at the western base of Emir Dagh. I went into the bazaar, which was a small place, and not very well supplied, though, as it was near sunset, there was quite a crowd of people, and the bakers were shovelling out their fresh bread at a brisk rate. Every one took me for a good Egyptian Mohammedan, and I was jostled right and left among the turbans, in a manner that certainly would not have happened me had I not also worn one. Mr. H., who had fallen behind the caravan, came up after we had encamped, and might have wandered a long time without finding us, but for the good-natured efforts of the inhabitants to set him aright. This evening he knocked over a hedgehog, mistaking it for a cat. The poor creature was severely hurt, and its sobs of distress, precisely like those of a little child, were to painful to hear, that we were obliged to have it removed from the vicinity of the tent

516

Chapter XXII. The Forests of Phrygia.

The Frontier of Phrygia--Ancient Quarries and Tombs--We Enter the Pine Forests--A Guard-House--Encampments of the Turcomans--Pastoral Scenery--A Summer Village--The Valley of the Tombs--Rock Sepulchres of the Phrygian Kings--The Titan's Camp--The Valley of Kümbeh--A Land of Flowers--Turcoman Hospitality--The Exiled Effendis--The Old Turcoman--A Glimpse of Arcadia--A Landscape--Interested Friendship--The Valley of the Pursek--Arrival at Kiutahya.

"And round us all the thicket rang To many a flute of Arcady." Tennyson.

Kiutahya, *July* 5, 1852.

We had now passed through the ancient provinces of Cilicia, Cappadocia, and Lycaonia, and reached the confines of Phrygia--a rude mountain region, which was never wholly penetrated by the light of Grecian civilization. It is still comparatively a wilderness, pierced but by a single high-road, and almost unvisited by travellers, yet inclosing in its depths many curious relics of antiquity. Leaving Bolawadün in the morning, we ascended a long, treeless mountain-slope, and in three or four hours reached the dividing ridge---the watershed of Asia Minor, dividing the affluents of the Mediterranean and the central lakes from the streams that flow to the Black Sea. Looking back, Sultan Dagh, along whose base we had travelled the previous day, lay high and blue in the background, streaked with shining snow, and far away behind it arose a still higher peak, hoary with the lingering winter. We descended into a grassy plain, shut in by a range of broken mountains, covered to their summits with dark-green shrubbery, through which the strata of marble rock gleamed like patches of snow. The hills in front were scarred with old quarries, once worked for the celebrated Phrygian marble. There was neither a habitation nor a human being to be seen, and the landscape had a singularly wild, lonely, and picturesque air.

Turning westward, we crossed a high rolling tract, and entered a valley entirely covered with dwarf oaks and cedars. In spite of the dusty road, the heat, and the multitude of gad-flies, the journey presented an agreeable contrast to the great plains over which we had been travelling for many days. The opposite side of the glen was crowned with a tall crest of shattered rock, in which were many old Phrygian tombs. They were mostly simple chambers, with square apertures. There were traces of many more, the rock having been blown up or quarried down--the tombs, instead of protecting it, only furnishing one facility the more for destruction. After an hour's rest at a fountain, we threaded the windings of the glen to a lower plain, quite shut in by the hills, whose ribs of marble showed through the forests of oak, holly, cedar, and pine, which dotted them. We were now fully entered into the hill-country, and our road passed over heights and through hollows covered with picturesque clumps of foliage. It resembled some of the wild western downs of America, and, but for the Phrygian tombs, whose doorways stared at us from every rock, seemed as little familiar with the presence of Man.

Hadji Youssuf, in stopping to arrange some of the baggage, lost his hold of his mule, and in spite of every effort to secure her, the provoking beast kept her liberty for the rest of the day. In vain did we head her off, chase her, coax her, set traps for her: she was too cunning to be taken in, and marched along at her ease, running into every field of grain, stopping to crop the choicest bunches of grass, or walking demurely in the caravan, allowing the hadji to come within arm's length before she kicked up her heels and dashed away again. We had a long chase through the clumps of oak and holly, but all to no purpose. The great green gad-flies swarmed around us, biting myself as well as my horse. Hecatombs, crushed by my whip, dropped dead in the dust, but the ranks were immediately filled from some invisible reserve. The soil was no longer bare, but entirely covered with grass and flowers. In one of the valleys I saw a large patch of the crimson larkspur, so thick as to resemble a pool of blood. While crossing a long, hot hill, we came upon a little arbor of stones, covered with pine branches. It inclosed an ancient sarcophagus of marble, nearly filled with water. Beside it stood a square cup, with a handle, rudely hewn out of a piece of pine wood. This was a charitable provision for travellers, and constantly supplied by the Turcomans who lived in the vicinity.

The last two hours of our journey that day were through a glorious forest

518

of pines. The road lay in a winding glen, green and grassy, and covered to the summits on both sides with beautiful pine trees, intermixed with cedar. The air had the true northern aroma, and was more grateful than wine. Every turn of the glen disclosed a charming woodland view. It was a wild valley of the northern hills, filled with the burning lustre of a summer sun, and canopied by the brilliant blue of a summer sky. There were signs of the woodman's axe, and the charred embers of forest camp-fires. I thought of the lovely cañadas in the pine forests behind Monterey, and could really have imagined myself there. Towards evening we reached a solitary guard-house, on the edge of the forest. The glen here opened a little, and a stone fountain of delicious water furnished all that we wanted for a camping-place. The house was inhabited by three soldiers; sturdy, good-humored fellows, who immediately spread a mat in the shade for us and made us some excellent coffee. A Turcoman encampment in the neighborhood supplied us with milk and eggs.

The guardsmen were good Mussulmans, and took us for the same. One of them asked me to let him know when the sun was down, and I prolonged his fast until it was quite dark, when I gave him permission to eat. They all had tolerable stallions for their service, and seemed to live pleasantly enough, in their wild way. The fat, stumpy corporal, with his enormously broad pantaloons and automaton legs, went down to the fountain with his musket, and after taking a rest and sighting full five minutes, fired at a dove without hitting it. He afterwards joined us in a social pipe, and we sat on a carpet at the door of the guard-house, watching the splendid moonrise through the pine boughs. When the pipes had burned out I went to bed, and slept a long, sweet sleep until dawn.

We knew that the tombs of the Phrygian Kings could not be far off, and, on making inquiries of the corporal, found that he knew the place. It was not four hours distant, by a by-road and as it would be impossible to reach it without a guide, he would give us one of his men, in consideration of a fee of twenty piastres. The difficulty was evident, in a hilly, wooded country like this, traversed by a labyrinth of valleys and ravines, and so we accepted the soldier. As we were about leaving, an old Turcoman, whose beard was dyed a bright red, came up, saying that he knew Mr. H. was a physician, and could cure him of his deafness. The morning air was sweet with the breath of cedar and pine, and we rode on through the woods and over the open turfy glades, in high spirits. We were in the heart of a mountainous country, clothed with evergreen forests, except some open upland tracts, which showed a thick green turf, dotted all over with park-like clumps, and single great trees. The pines were noble trunks, often sixty to eighty feet high, and with boughs disposed in all possible picturesqueness of form. The cedar frequently showed a solid white bole, three feet in diameter.

We took a winding footpath, often a mere track, striking across the hills in a northern direction. Everywhere we met the Turks of the plain, who are now encamped in the mountains, to tend their flocks through the summer months. Herds of sheep and goats were scattered over the green pasture-slopes, and the idle herd-boys basked in the morning sun, playing lively airs on a reed flute, resembling the Arabic zumarra. Here and there was a woodman, busy at a recently felled tree, and we met several of the creaking carts of the country, hauling logs. All that we saw had a pleasant rural air, a smack of primitive and unsophisticated life. From the higher ridges over which we passed, we could see, far to the east and west, other ranges of pine-covered mountains, and in the distance the cloudy lines of loftier chains. The trunks of the pines were nearly all charred, and many of the smaller trees dead, from the fires which, later in the year, rage in these forests.

After four hours of varied and most inspiring travel, we reached a district covered for the most part with oak woods--a more open though still mountainous region. There was a summer village of Turks scattered over the nearest slope--probably fifty houses in all, almost perfect counterparts of Western log-cabins. They were built of pine logs, laid crosswise, and covered with rough boards. These, as we were told, were the dwellings of the people who inhabit the village of Khosref Pasha Khan during the winter. Great numbers of sheep and goats were browsing over the hills or lying around the doors of the houses. The latter were beautiful creatures, with heavy, curved horns, and long, white, silky hair, that entirely hid their eyes. We stopped at a house for water, which the man brought out in a little cask. He at first proposed giving us yaourt, and his wife suggested kaïmak (sweet curds), which we agreed to take, but it proved to be only boiled milk.

Leaving the village, we took a path leading westward, mounted a long hill, and again entered the pine forests. Before long, we came to a well-built country-house, somewhat resembling a Swiss cottage. It was two stories high, and there was an upper balcony, with cushioned divans, overlooking a thriving garden-patch and some fruit-trees. Three or four men were weeding in the garden, and the owner came up and welcomed us. A fountain of ice-cold water gushed into a stone trough at the door, making a tempting spot for our breakfast, but we were bent on reaching the tombs. There were convenient out-houses for fowls, sheep, and cattle. The herds were out, grazing along the edges of the forest, and we heard the shrill, joyous melodies of the flutes blown by the herd-boys.

We now reached a ridge, whence we looked down through the forest upon a long valley, nearly half a mile wide, and bordered on the opposite side by ranges of broken sandstone crags. This was the place we sought--the Valley of the Phrygian Tombs. Already we could distinguish the hewn faces of the rocks, and the dark apertures to the chambers within. The bottom of the valley was a bed of glorious grass, blazoned with flowers, and redolent of all vernal smells. Several peasants, finding it too hot to mow, had thrown their scythes along the swarths, and were lying in the shade of an oak. We rode over the new-cut hay, up the opposite side, and dismounted at the face of the crags. As we approached them, the number of chambers hewn in the rock, the doors and niches now open to the day, surmounted by shattered spires and turrets, gave the whole mass the appearance of a grand fortress in ruins. The crags, which are of a very soft, reddish-gray sandstone, rise a hundred and fifty feet from their base, and their summits are worn by the weather into the most remarkable forms.

The principal monument is a broad, projecting cliff, one side of which has been cut so as to resemble the façade of a temple. The sculptured part is about sixty feet high by sixty in breadth, and represents a solid wall with two pilasters at the ends, upholding an architrave and pediment, which is surmounted by two large volutes. The whole face of the wall is covered with ornaments resembling panel-work, not in regular squares, but a labyrinth of intricate designs. In the centre, at the bottom, is a shallow square recess, surrounded by an elegant, though plain moulding, but there is no appearance of an entrance to the sepulchral chamber, which may be hidden in the heart of the rock. There is an inscription in Greek running up one side, but it is of a later date than the work itself. On one of the tombs there is an inscription: "To King Midas." These relics are supposed to date from the period of the Gordian Dynasty, about seven centuries before Christ.

A little in front of a headland, formed by the summit walls of two meeting valleys, rises a mass of rocks one hundred feet high, cut into sepulchral chambers, story above story, with the traces of steps between them, leading to others still higher. The whole rock, which may be a hundred and fifty feet long by fifty feet broad, has been scooped out, leaving but narrow partitions to separate the chambers of the dead. These chambers are all plain, but some are of very elegant proportions, with arched or pyramidal roofs, and arched recesses at the sides, containing sarcophagi hewn in the solid stone. There are also many niches for cinerary urns. The principal tomb had a portico, supported by columns, but the front is now entirely hurled down, and only the elegant panelling and stone joists of the ceiling remain. The entire hill was a succession of tombs. There is not a rock which does not bear traces of them. I might have counted several hundred within a stone's throw. The position of these curious remains in a lonely valley, shut in on all sides by dark, pine-covered mountains---two of which are crowned with a natural acropolis of rock, resembling a fortress--increases the interest with which they inspire the beholder. The valley on the western side, with its bed of ripe wheat in the bottom, its tall walls, towers, and pinnacles of rock, and its distant vista of mountain and forest, is the most picturesque in Phrygia.

The Turcoman reapers, who came up to see us and talk with us, said that there were the remains of walls on the summit of the principal acropolis opposite us, and that, further up the valley, there was a chamber with two columns in front. Mr. Harrison and I saddled and rode off, passing along a wall of fantastic rock-turrets, at the base of which was a natural column, about ten feet high, and five in diameter, almost perfectly round, and upholding an immense rock, shaped like a cocked hat. In crossing the meadow we saw a Turk sitting in the sun beside a spring, and busily engaged in knitting a stocking. After a ride of two miles we found the chamber, hewn like the façade of a temple in an isolated rock, overlooking two valleys of wild meadow-land. The pediment and cornice were simple and beautiful, but the columns had been broken away. The chambers were perfectly plain, but the panel-work on the ceiling of the portico was entire.

After passing three hours in examining these tombs, we took the track which our guide pointed out as the road to Kiutahya. We rode two hours through the forest, and came out upon a wooded height, overlooking a grand, open valley, rich in grain-fields and pasture land. While I was contemplating this lovely view, the road turned a corner of the ridge, and lo! before me there appeared (as I thought), above the tops of the pines, high up on the mountain side, a line of enormous tents. Those snow-white cones, uprearing their sharp spires, and spreading out their broad bases--what could they be but an encampment of monster tents? Yet no; they were pinnacles of white rock--perfect cones, from thirty to one hundred feet in height, twelve in all, and ranged side by side along the edge of the cliff, with the precision of a military camp. They were snow-white, perfectly smooth and full, and their bases touched. What made the spectacle more singular, there was no other appearance of the same rock on the mountain. All around them was the dark-green of the pines, out of which they rose like drifted horns of unbroken snow. I named this singular phenomenon--which seems to have escaped the notice of travellers--The Titan's Camp.

In another hour we reached a fountain near the village of Kümbeh, and pitched our tents for the night. The village, which is half a mile in length, is built upon a singular crag, which shoots up abruptly from the centre of the valley, rising at one extremity to a height of more than a hundred feet. It was entirely deserted, the inhabitants having all gone off to the mountains with their herds. The solitary muezzin, who cried the mughreb at the close of the fast, and lighted the lamps on his minaret, went through with his work in most unclerical haste, now that there was no one to notice him. We sent Achmet, the katurgee, to the mountain camp of the villagers, to procure a supply of fowls and barley. We rose very early yesterday morning, shivering in the cold air of the mountains, and just as the sun, bursting through the pines, looked down the little hollow where our tents were pitched, set the caravan in motion. The ride down the valley was charming. The land was naturally rich and highly cultivated, which made its desertion the more singular. Leagues of wheat, rye and poppies spread around us, left for the summer warmth to do its silent work. The dew sparkled on the fields as we rode through them, and the splendor of the flowers in blossom was equal to that of the plains of Palestine. There were purple, white and scarlet poppies; the rich crimson larkspur; the red anemone; the golden daisy; the pink convolvulus; and a host of smaller blooms, so intensely bright and dazzling in their hues, that the meadows were richer than a pavement of precious jewels. To look towards the sun, over a field of scarlet poppies, was like looking on a bed of live coals; the light, striking through the petals, made them burn as with an inward fire. Out of this wilderness of gorgeous color, rose the tall spires of a larger plant, covered with great yellow flowers, while here and there the snowy blossoms of a clump of hawthorn sweetened the morning air.

A short distance beyond Kümbeh, we passed another group of ancient tombs, one of which was of curious design. An isolated rock, thirty feet in height by twenty in diameter, was cut so as to resemble a triangular tower, with the apex bevelled. A chamber, containing a sarcophagus, was hewn out of the interior. The entrance was ornamented with double columns in bas-relief, and a pediment. There was another arched chamber, cut directly through the base of the triangle, with a niche on each side, hollowed out at the bottom so as to form a sarcophagus.

Leaving these, the last of the Phrygian tombs, we struck across the valley and ascended a high range of hills, covered with pine, to an upland, wooded region. Here we found a summer village of log cabins, scattered over a grassy slope. The people regarded us with some curiosity, and the women hastily concealed their faces. Mr. H. rode up to a large new house, and peeped in between the logs. There were several women inside, who started up in great confusion and threw over their heads whatever article was most convenient. An old man, with a long white beard, neatly dressed in a green jacket and shawl turban, came out and welcomed us. I asked for kaïmak, which he promised, and immediately brought out a carpet and spread it on the ground. Then followed a large basin of kaïmak, with wooden spoons, three loaves of bread, and a plate of cheese. We seated ourselves on the carpet, and delved in with the spoons, while the old man retired lest his appetite should be provoked. The milk was excellent, nor were the bread and cheese to be despised.

While we were eating, the Khowagee, or schoolmaster of the community, a genteel little man in a round white turban, came op to inquire of François who we were. "That effendi in the blue dress," said he, "is the Bey, is he not?" "Yes," said F. "And the other, with the striped shirt and white turban, is a writer?" [Here he was not far wrong.] "But how is it that the effendis do not speak Turkish?" he persisted. "Because," said François, "their fathers were exiled by Sultan Mahmoud when they were small children. They have grown up in Aleppo like Arabs, and have not yet learned Turkish; but God grant that the Sultan may not turn his face away from them, and that they may regain the rank their fathers once had in Stamboul." "God grant it!" replied the Khowagee, greatly interested in the story. By this time we had eaten our full share of the kaïmak, which was finished by François and the katurgees. The old man now came up, mounted on a dun mare, stating that he was bound for Kiutahya, and was delighted with the prospect of travelling in such good company, I gave one of his young children some money, as the kaïmak was tendered out of pure hospitality, and so we rode off.

Our new companion was armed to the teeth, having a long gun with a heavy wooden stock and nondescript lock, and a sword of excellent metal. It was, in fact, a weapon of the old Greek empire, and the cross was still enamelled in gold at the root of the blade, in spite of all his efforts to scratch it out. He was something of a fakeer, having made a pilgrimage to Mecca and Jerusalem. He was very inquisitive, plying François with questions about the government. The latter answered that we were not connected with the government, but the old fellow shrewdly hinted that he knew better--we were persons of rank, travelling incognito. He was very attentive to us, offering us water at every fountain, although he believed us to be good Mussulmans. We found him of some service as a guide, shortening our road by taking by-paths through the woods.

For several hours we traversed a beautifully wooded region of hills. Graceful clumps of pine shaded the grassy knolls, where the sheep and silky-haired goats were basking at rest, and the air was filled with a warm, summer smell, blown from the banks of golden broom. Now and then, from the thickets of laurel and arbutus, a shrill shepherd's reed piped some joyous woodland melody. Was it a Faun, astray among the hills? Green dells, open to the sunshine, and beautiful as dreams of Arcady, divided the groves of pine. The sky overhead was pure and cloudless, clasping the landscape with its belt of peace and silence. Oh, that delightful region, haunted by all the bright spirits of the immortal Grecian Song! Chased away from the rest of the earth, here they have found a home--here secret altars remain to them from the times that are departed!

Out of these woods, we passed into a lonely plain, inclosed by piny hills that brightened in the thin, pure ether. In the distance were some shepherds' tents, and musical goat-bells tinkled along the edges of the woods. From the crest of a lofty ridge beyond this plain, we looked back over the wild solitudes wherein we had been travelling for two days--long ranges of dark hills, fading away behind each other, with a perspective that hinted of the hidden gulfs between. From the western slope, a still more extensive prospect opened before us. Over ridges covered with forests of oak and pine, we saw the valley of the Pursek, the ancient Thymbrius, stretching far away to the misty line of Keshish Dagh, The mountains behind Kintahya loomed up high and grand, making a fine feature in the middle distance. We caught but fleeting glimpses of the view through the trees; and then, plunging into the forest again, descended to a cultivated slope, whereon there was a little village, now deserted. The graveyard beside it was shaded with large cedar-trees, and near it there was a fountain of excellent water. "Here," said the old man, "you can wash and pray, and then rest awhile under the trees." François excused us by saying that, while on a journey, we always bathed before praying; but, not to slight his faith entirely, I washed my hands and face before sitting down to our scanty breakfast of bread and water.

Our path now led down through long, winding glens, over grown with oaks, from which the wild yellow honeysuckles fell in a shower of blossoms.

526

As we drew near the valley, the old man began to hint that his presence had been of great service to us, and deserved recompense. "God knows," said he to François, "in what corner of the mountains you might now be, if I had not accompanied you." "Oh," replied François, "there are always plenty of people among the woods, who would have been equally as kind as yourself in showing us the way." He then spoke of the robbers in the neighborhood, and pointed out some graves by the road-side, as those of persons who had been murdered. "But," he added, "everybody in these parts knows me, and whoever is in company with me is always safe." The Greek assured him that we always depended on ourselves for our safety. Defeated on these tacks, he boldly affirmed that his services were worthy of payment. "But," said François "you told us at the village that you had business in Kiutahya, and would be glad to join us for the sake of having company on the road." "Well, then," rejoined the old fellow, making a last effort, "I leave the matter to your politeness." "Certainly," replied the imperturbable dragoman, "we could not be so impolite as to offer money to a man of your wealth and station; we could not insult you by giving you alms." The old Turcoman thereupon gave a shrug and a grunt, made a sullen good-by salutation, and left us.

It was nearly six o'clock when we reached the Pursek. There was no sign of the city, but we could barely discern an old fortress on the lofty cliff which commands the town. A long stone bridge crossed the river, which here separates into half a dozen channels. The waters are swift and clear, and wind away in devious mazes through the broad green meadows. We hurried on, thinking we saw minarets in the distance, but they proved to be poplars. The sun sank lower and lower, and finally went down before there was any token of our being in the vicinity of the city. Soon, however, a line of tiled roofs appeared along the slope of a hill on our left, and turning its base, we saw the city before us, filling the mouth of a deep valley or gorge, which opened from the mountains.

But the horses are saddled, and François tells me it is time to put up my pen. We are off, over the mountains, to the Greek city of Œzani, in the valley of the Rhyndacus.

Chapter XXIII. Kiutahya and the Ruins of Œzani.

Entrance into Kiutahya--The New Khan--An Unpleasant Discovery--Kiutahya--The Citadel--Panorama from the Walls--The Gorge of the Mountains--Camp in a Meadow--The Valley of the Rhyndacus--Chavdür--The Ruins of Œzani--The Acropolis and Temple--The Theatre and Stadium--Ride down the Valley--Camp at Daghje Köi

"There is a temple in ruin stands,

Fashioned by long-forgotten hands;

Two or three columns and many a stone,

Marble and granite, with grass o'ergrown!

Out upon Time! it will leave no more

Of the things to come than the things before!"

Daghje Köi, on the Rhyndacus, *July* 6, 1852.

On entering Kiutahya, we passed the barracks, which were the residence of Kossuth and his companions in exile. Beyond them, we came to a broad street, down which flowed the vilest stream of filth of which even a Turkish city could ever boast. The houses on either side were two stories high, the upper part of wood, with hanging balconies, over which shot the eaves of the tiled roofs. The welcome cannon had just sounded, announcing the close of the day's fast. The coffee-shops were already crowded with lean and hungry customers, the pipes were filled and lighted, and the coffee smoked in the finjans. In half a minute such whiffs arose on all sides as it would have cheered the heart of a genuine smoker to behold. Out of these cheerful places we passed into other streets which were entirely deserted, the inhabitants being at dinner. It had a weird, uncomfortable effect to ride through streets where the clatter of our horses' hoofs was the only sound of life. At last we reached the entrance to a bazaar, and near it a khan--a new khan, very neatly built, and with a spare room so much better than we expected, that we congratulated ourselves heartily. We unpacked in a hurry, and François ran off to the bazaar, from which he speedily returned with some roast kid, cucumbers, and cherries. We lighted two lamps, I borrowed the oda-bashi's narghileh, and François, learning that it was our national anniversary, procured us a flask of Greek wine, that we might do it honor. The beverage, however, resembled a mixture of vinegar and sealing-wax, and we contented ourselves with drinking patriotic toasts, in two finjans of excellent coffee. But in the midst of our enjoyment, happening to cast my eye on the walls, I saw a sight that turned all our honey into gall. Scores on scores--nay, hundreds on hundreds--of enormous bed-bugs swarmed on the plaster, and were already descending to our beds and baggage. To sleep there was impossible, but we succeeded in getting possession of one of the outside balconies, where we made our beds, after searching them thoroughly.

In the evening a merchant, who spoke a little Arabic, came up to me and asked: "Is not your Excellency's friend the hakim pasha" (chief physician). I did not venture to assent, but replied: "No; he is a sowakh" This was beyond his comprehension, and he went away with the impression that Mr. H. was much greater than a hakim pasha. I slept soundly on my out-doors bed, but was awakened towards morning by two tremendous claps of thunder, echoing in the gorge, and the rattling of rain on the roof of the khan.

I spent two or three hours next morning in taking a survey of Kiutahya. The town is much larger than I had supposed: I should judge it to contain from fifty to sixty thousand inhabitants. The situation is remarkable, and gives a picturesque effect to the place when seen from above, which makes one forget its internal filth. It is built in the mouth of a gorge, and around the bases of the hills on either side. The lofty mountains which rise behind it supply it with perpetual springs of pure water. At every dozen steps you come upon a fountain, and every large street has a brook in the centre. The houses are all two and many of them three stories high, with hanging balconies, which remind me much of Switzerland. The bazaars are very extensive, covering all the base of the hill on which stands the ancient citadel. The goods displayed were mostly European cotton fabrics, quincaillerie, boots and slippers, pipe-sticks and silks. In the parts devoted to the produce of the country, I saw very fine cherries, cucumbers and lettuce, and bundles of magnificent clover, three to four feet high.

We climbed a steep path to the citadel, which covers the summit of an abrupt, isolated hill, connected by a shoulder with the great range. The walls are nearly a mile in circuit, consisting almost wholly of immense circular buttresses, placed so near each other that they almost touch. The connecting walls are broken down on the northern side, so that from below the buttresses have the appearance of enormous shattered columns. They are built of rough stones, with regular layers of flat, burnt bricks. On the highest part of the hill stands the fortress, or stronghold, a place which must have been almost impregnable before the invention of cannon. The structure probably dates from the ninth or tenth century, but is built on the foundations of more ancient edifices. The old Greek city of Cotyaeum (whence Kiutahya) probably stood upon this hill. Within the citadel is an upper town, containing about a hundred houses, the residence, apparently of poor families.

From the circuit of the walls, on every side, there are grand views over the plain, the city, and the gorges of the mountains behind. The valley of the Pursek, freshened by the last night's shower, spread out a sheet of vivid green, to the pine-covered mountains which bounded it on all sides. Around the city it was adorned with groves and gardens, and, in the direction of Brousa, white roads went winding away to other gardens and villages in the distance. The mountains of Phrygia, through which we had passed, were the loftiest in the circle that inclosed the valley. The city at our feet presented a thick array of red-tiled roofs, out of which rose here and there the taper shaft of a minaret, or the dome of a mosque or bath. From the southern side of the citadel, we looked down into the gorge which supplies Kiutahya with water--a wild, desert landscape of white crags and shattered peaks of gray rock, hanging over a narrow winding bed of the greenest foliage.

Instead of taking the direct road to Brousa, we decided to make a detour of two days, in order to visit the ruins of the old Greek city of Œzani, which are thirty-six miles south of Kiutahya. Leaving at noon, we ascended the gorge behind the city, by delightfully embowered paths, at first under the eaves of superb walnut-trees, and then through wild thickets of willow, hazel, privet, and other shrubs, tangled together with the odorous white honeysuckle. Near the city, the mountain-sides were bare white masses of gypsum and other rock, in many places with the purest chrome-yellow hue; but as we advanced they were clothed to the summit with copsewood. The streams that foamed down these perennial heights were led into buried channels, to come to light again in sparkling fountains, pouring into ever-full stone basins. The day was cool and cloudy, and the heavy shadows which hung on the great sides of the mountain gateway, heightened, by contrast, the glory of the sunlit plain seen through them.

After passing the summit ridge, probably 5,000 feet above the sea, we came upon a wooded, hilly region, stretching away in long misty lines to Murad Dagh, whose head was spotted with snow. There were patches of wheat and rye in the hollows, and the bells of distant herds tinkled occasionally among the trees. There was no village on the road, and we were on the way to one which we saw in the distance, when we came upon a meadow of good grass, with a small stream running through it. Here we encamped, sending Achmet, the katurgee, to the village for milk and eggs. The ewes had just been milked for the suppers of their owners, but they went over the flock again, stripping their udders, which greatly improved the quality of the milk. The night was so cold that I could scarcely sleep during the morning hours. There was a chill, heavy dew on the meadow; but when François awoke me at sunrise, the sky was splendidly clear and pure, and the early beams had a little warmth in them. Our coffee, before starting, made with sheep's milk, was the richest I ever drank.

After riding for two hours across broad, wild ridges, covered with cedar, we reached a height overlooking the valley of the Rhyndacus, or rather the plain whence he draws his sources--a circular level, ten or twelve miles in diameter, and contracting towards the west into a narrow dell, through which his waters find outlet; several villages, each embowered in gardens, were scattered along the bases of the hills that inclose it. We took the wrong road, but were set aright by a herdsman, and after threading a lane between thriving grain-fields, were cheered by the sight of the Temple of Œzani, lifted on its acropolis above the orchards of Chavdür, and standing out sharp and clear against the purple of the hills.

Our approach to the city was marked by the blocks of sculptured marble that lined the way: elegant mouldings, cornices, and entablatures, thrown together with common stone to make walls between the fields. The village is built on both sides of the Rhyndacus; it is an ordinary Turkish hamlet, with tiled roofs and chimneys, and exhibits very few of the remains of the old city in its composition. This, I suspect, is owing to the great size of the hewn blocks, especially of the pillars, cornices, and entablatures, nearly all of which are from twelve to fifteen feet long. It is from the size and number of these scattered blocks, rather than from the buildings which still partially exist, that one obtains an idea of the size and splendor of the ancient Œzani. The place is filled with fragments, especially of columns, of which there are several hundred, nearly all finely fluted. The Rhyndacus is still spanned by an ancient bridge of three arches, and both banks are lined with piers of hewn stone. Tall poplars and massy walnuts of the richest green shade the clear waters, and there are many picturesque combinations of foliage and ruin--death and life--which would charm a painter's eye. Near the bridge we stopped to examine a pile of immense fragments which have been thrown together by the Turks--pillars, cornices, altars, pieces of a frieze, with bulls' heads bound together by hanging garlands, and a large square block, with a legible tablet. It resembled an altar in form, and, from the word "Artemidoron" appeared to have belonged to some temple to Diana.

Passing through the village we came to a grand artificial platform on its western side, called the Acropolis. It is of solid masonry, five hundred feet square, and averaging ten feet in height. On the eastern side it is supported on rude though massive arches, resembling Etruscan workmanship. On the top and around the edges of this platform lie great numbers of fluted columns, and immense fragments of cornice and architrave. In the centre, on a foundation platform about eight feet high, stands a beautiful Ionic temple, one hundred feet in length. On approaching, it appeared nearly perfect, except the roof, and so many of the columns remain standing that its ruined condition scarcely injures the effect. There are seventeen columns on the side and eight at the end, Ionic in style, fluted, and fifty feet in height.

About half the cella remains, with an elegant frieze and cornice along the top, and a series of tablets, set in panels of ornamental sculpture, running along the sides. The front of the cella includes a small open peristyle, with two composite Corinthian columns at the entrance, making, with those of the outer colonnade, eighteen columns standing. The tablets contain Greek inscriptions, perfectly legible, where the stone has not been shattered. Under the temple there are large vaults, which we found filled up with young kids, who had gone in there to escape the heat of the sun. The portico was occupied by sheep, which at first refused to make room for us, and gave strong olfactory evidence of their partiality for the temple as a resting-place.

On the side of a hill, about three hundred yards to the north, are the remains of a theatre. Crossing some patches of barley and lentils, we entered a stadium, forming an extension of the theatre---that is, it took the same breadth and direction, so that the two might be considered as one grand work, more than one thousand feet long by nearly four hundred wide. The walls of the stadium are hurled down, except an entrance of five arches of massive masonry, on the western side. We rode up the artificial valley, between high, grassy hills, completely covered with what at a distance resembled loose boards, but which were actually the long marble seats of the stadium. Urging our horses over piles of loose blocks, we reached the base of the theatre, climbed the fragments that cumber the main entrance, and looked on the spacious arena and galleries within. Although greatly ruined, the materials of the whole structure remain, and might be put together again. It is a grand wreck; the colossal fragments which have tumbled from the arched proscenium fill the arena, and the rows of seats, though broken and disjointed, still retain their original order. It is somewhat more than a semicircle, the radius being about one hundred and eighty feet. The original height was upwards of fifty feet, and there were fifty rows of seats in all, each row capable of seating two hundred persons, so that the number of spectators who could be accommodated was eight thousand.

The fragments cumbering the arena were enormous, and highly interesting from their character. There were rich blocks of cornice, ten feet long; fluted and reeded pillars; great arcs of heavily-carved sculpture, which appeared to have served as architraves from pillar to pillar, along the face of the proscenium, where there was every trace of having been a colonnade; and other blocks sculptured with figures of animals in alto-relievo. There were generally two figures on each block, and among those which could be recognized were the dog and the lion. Doors opened from the proscenium into the retiring-rooms of the actors, under which were the vaults where the beasts were kept. A young fox or jackal started from his siesta as we entered the theatre, and took refuge under the loose blocks. Looking backwards through the stadium from the seats of the theatre, we had a lovely view of the temple, standing out clear and bright in the midst of the summer plain, with the snow-streaked summits of Murad Dagh in the distance. It was a picture which I shall long remember. The desolation of the magnificent ruins was made all the more impressive by the silent, solitary air of the region around them.

Leaving Chavdür in the afternoon, we struck northward, down the valley of the Rhyndacus, over tracts of rolling land, interspersed with groves of cedar and pine. There were so many branch roads and crossings that we could not fail to go wrong; and after two or three hours found ourselves in the midst of a forest, on the broad top of a mountain, without any road at all. There were some herdsmen tending their flocks near at hand, but they could give us no satisfactory direction. We thereupon, took our own course, and soon brought up on the brink of a precipice, overhanging a deep valley. Away to the eastward we caught a glimpse of the Rhyndacus, and the wooden minaret of a little village on his banks. Following the edge of the precipice, we came at last to a glen, down which ran a rough footpath that finally conducted us, by a long road through the forests, to the village of Daghje Köi, where we are now encamped.

The place seems to be devoted to the making of flints, and the streets are filled with piles of the chipped fragments. Our tent is pitched on the bank of the river, in a barren meadow. The people tell us that the whole region round about has just been visited by a plague of grasshoppers, which have destroyed their crops. Our beasts have wandered off to the hills, in search for grass, and the disconsolate Hadji is hunting them. Achmet, the katurgee,

534

lies near the fire, sick; Mr. Harrison complains of fever, and François moves about languidly, with a dismal countenance. So here we are in the solitudes of Bithynia, but there is no God but God, and that which is destined comes to pass.

Chapter XXIV. The Mysian Olympus.

Journey Down the Valley--The Plague of Grasshoppers--A Defile--The Town of Taushanlü--The Camp of Famine--We leave the Rhyndacus--The Base of Olympus--Primeval Forests--The Guard-House--Scenery of the Summit--Forests of Beech--Saw-Mills--Descent of the Mountain--The View of Olympus--Morning--The Land of Harvest--Aineghiöl--A Showery Ride--The Plain of Brousa--The Structure of Olympus--We reach Brousa--The Tent is Furled.

"I looked yet farther and higher, and saw in the heavens a silvery cloud that stood fast, and still against the breeze; * * * * and so it was as a sign and a testimony--almost as a call from the neglected gods, that I now saw and acknowledged the snowy crown of the Mysian Olympus!" Kinglake.

Brousa, *July* 9, 1852.

From Daghje Küi, there were two roads to Taushanlü, but the people informed us that the one which led across the mountains was difficult to find, and almost impracticable. We therefore took the river road, which we found picturesque in the highest degree. The narrow dell of the Rhyndacus wound through a labyrinth of mountains, sometimes turning at sharp angles between craggy buttresses, covered with forests, and sometimes broadening out into a sweep of valley, where the villagers were working in companies among the grain and poppy fields. The banks of the stream were lined with oak, willow and sycamore, and forests of pine, descending from the mountains, frequently overhung the road. We met numbers of peasants, going to and from the fields, and once a company of some twenty women, who, on seeing us, clustered together like a flock of frightened sheep, and threw their mantles over their heads. They had curiosity enough, however, to peep at us as we went by, and I made them a salutation, which they returned, and then burst into a chorus of hearty laughter. All this region was ravaged by a plague of grasshoppers. The earth was black with them in many places, and our horses ploughed up a living spray, as they drove forward through the meadows. Every spear of grass was destroyed, and the wheat and rye fields were terribly cut up. We passed a large crag where myriads of starlings had built their nests, and every starling had a grasshopper in his mouth.

We crossed the river, in order to pass a narrow defile, by which it forces its way through the rocky heights of Dumanidj Dagh. Soon after passing the ridge, a broad and beautiful valley expanded before us. It was about ten miles in breadth, nearly level, and surrounded by picturesque ranges of wooded mountains. It was well cultivated, principally in rye and poppies, and more thickly populated than almost any part of Europe. The tinned tops of the minarets of Taushanlü shone over the top of a hill in front, and there was a large town nearly opposite, on the other bank of the Rhyndacus, and seven small villages scattered about in various directions. Most of the latter, however, were merely the winter habitations of the herdsmen, who are now living in tents on the mountain tops. All over the valley, the peasants were at work in the harvest-fields, cutting and binding grain, gathering opium from the poppies, or weeding the young tobacco. In the south, over the rim of the hills that shut in this pastoral solitude, rose the long blue summits of Urus Dagh. We rode into Taushanlü, which is a long town, filling up a hollow between two stony hills. The houses are all of stone, two stories high, with tiled roofs and chimneys, so that, but for the clapboarded and shingled minarets, it would answer for a North-German village.

The streets were nearly deserted, and even in the bazaars, which are of some extent, we found but few persons. Those few, however, showed a laudable curiosity with regard to us, clustering about us whenever we stopped, and staring at us with provoking pertinacity. We had some difficulty in procuring information concerning the road, the directions being so contradictory that we were as much in the dark as ever. We lost half an hour in wandering among the hills; and, after travelling four hours over piny uplands, without finding the village of Kara Köi, encamped on a dry plain, on the western bank of the river. There was not a spear of grass for the beasts, everything being eaten up by the grasshoppers, and there were no Turcomans near who could supply us with food. So we dined on hard bread and black coffee, and our forlorn beasts walked languidly about, cropping the dry stalks of weeds and the juiceless roots of the dead grass.

We crossed the river next morning, and took a road following its course, and shaded with willows and sycamores. The lofty, wooded ranges of the Mysian Olympus lay before us, and our day's work was to pass them. After passing the village of Kara Köi, we left the valley of the Rhyndacus, and commenced ascending one of the long, projecting spurs thrust out from the main chain of Olympus. At first we rode through thickets of scrubby cedar, but soon came to magnificent pine forests, that grew taller and sturdier the higher we clomb. A superb mountain landscape opened behind us. The valleys sank deeper and deeper, and at last disappeared behind the great ridges that heaved themselves out of the wilderness of smaller hills. All these ridges were covered with forests; and as we looked backwards out of the tremendous gulf up the sides of which we were climbing, the scenery was wholly wild and uncultivated. Our path hung on the imminent side of a chasm so steep that one slip might have been destruction to both horse and rider. Far below us, at the bottom of the chasm, roared an invisible torrent. The opposite side, vapory from its depth, rose like an immense wall against Heaven. The pines were even grander than those in the woods of Phrygia. Here they grew taller and more dense, hanging their cloudy boughs over the giddy depths, and clutching with desperate roots to the almost perpendicular sides of the gorges. In many places they were the primeval forests of Olympus, and the Hamadryads were not yet frightened from their haunts.

Thus, slowly toiling up through the sublime wilderness, breathing the cold, pure air of those lofty regions, we came at last to a little stream, slowly trickling down the bed of the gorge. It was shaded, not by the pine, but by the Northern beech, with its white trunk and close, confidential boughs, made for the talks of lovers and the meditations of poets. Here we stopped to breakfast, but there was nothing for the poor beasts to eat, and they waited for us droopingly, with their heads thrust together. While we sat there three camels descended to the stream, and after them a guard with a long gun. He was a well-made man, with a brown face, keen, black eye, and piratical air, and would have made a good hero of modern romance. Higher up we came to a guard house, on a little cleared space, surrounded by beech forests. It

538

was a rough stone hut, with a white flag planted on a pole before it, and a miniature water-wheel, running a miniature saw at a most destructive rate, beside the door.

Continuing our way, we entered on a region such as I had no idea could be found in Asia. The mountains, from the bottoms of the gorges to their topmost summits, were covered with the most superb forests of beech I ever saw--masses of impenetrable foliage, of the most brilliant green, touched here and there by the darker top of a pine. Our road was through a deep, dark shade, and on either side, up and down, we saw but a cool, shadowy solitude, sprinkled with dots of emerald light, and redolent with the odor of damp earth, moss, and dead leaves. It was a forest, the counterpart of which could only be found in America--such primeval magnitude of growth, such wild luxuriance, such complete solitude and silence! Through the shafts of the pines we had caught glorious glimpses of the blue mountain world below us; but now the beech folded us in its arms, and whispered in our ears the legends of our Northern home. There, on the ridges of the Mysian Olympus, sacred to the bright gods of Grecian song, I found the inspiration of our darker and colder clime and age. "O gloriosi spiriti degli boschi!"

I could scarcely contain myself, from surprise and joy. François failed to find French adjectives sufficient for his admiration, and even our cheating katurgees were touched by the spirit of the scene. On either side, whenever a glimpse could be had through the boughs, we looked upon leaning walls of trees, whose tall, rounded tops basked in the sunshine, while their bases were wrapped in the shadows cast by themselves. Thus, folded over each other like scales, or feathers on a falcon's wing, they clad the mountain. The trees were taller, and had a darker and more glossy leaf than the American beech. By and by patches of blue shone between the boughs before us, a sign that the summit was near, and before one o'clock we stood upon the narrow ridge forming the crest of the mountain. Here, although we were between five and six thousand feet above the sea, the woods of beech were a hundred feet in height, and shut out all view. On the northern side the forest scenery is even grander than on the southern. The beeches are magnificent trees, straight as an arrow, and from a hundred to a hundred and fifty feet in height. Only now and then could we get any view beyond the shadowy depths sinking below us, and then it was only to see similar mountain ranges, buried in foliage, and rolling far behind each other into the distance. Twice, in the depth of the gorge, we saw a saw-mill, turned by the snow-cold torrents. Piles of pine and beechen boards were heaped around them, and the sawyers were busily plying their lonely business. The axe of the woodman echoed but rarely through the gulfs, though many large trees lay felled by the roadside. The rock, which occasionally cropped out of the soil, was white marble, and there was a shining precipice of it, three hundred feet high, on the opposite side of the gorge.

After four hours of steady descent, during the last hour of which we passed into a forest entirely of oaks, we reached the first terrace at the base of the mountain. Here, as I was riding in advance of the caravan, I met a company of Turkish officers, who saluted me with an inclination of the most profound reverence. I replied with due Oriental gravity, which seemed to justify their respect, for when they met François, who is everywhere looked upon as a Turkish janissary, they asked: "Is not your master a Shekh el-Islàm?" "You are right: he is," answered the unscrupulous Greek. A Shekh el-Islàm is a sort of high-priest, corresponding in dignity to a Cardinal in the Roman Catholic Church. It is rather singular that I am generally taken for a Secretary of some kind, or a Moslem priest, while my companion, who, by this time, has assumed the Oriental expression, is supposed to be either medical or military.

We had no sooner left the forests and entered the copsewood which followed, than the blue bulk, of Olympus suddenly appeared in the west, towering far into the sky. It is a magnificent mountain, with a broad though broken summit, streaked with snow. Before us, stretching away almost to his base, lay a grand mountain slope, covered with orchards and golden harvest-fields. Through lanes of hawthorn and chestnut trees in blossom, which were overgrown with snowy clematis and made a shady roof above our heads, we reached the little village of Orta Köi, and encamped in a grove of pear-trees. There was grass for our beasts, who were on the brink of starvation, and fowls and cucumbers for ourselves, who had been limited to bread and coffee for two days. But as one necessity was restored, another disappeared. We had smoked the last of our delicious Aleppo tobacco, and that which the villagers gave us was of very inferior quality. Nevertheless, the pipe which we smoked with them in the twilight, beside the marble fountain, promoted that peace of mind which is the sweetest preparative of slumber.

François was determined to finish our journey to-day. He had a presentiment that we should reach Brousa, although I expected nothing of the kind. He called us long before the lovely pastoral valley in which we lay had a suspicion of the sun, but just in time to see the first rays strike the high head of Olympus. The long lines of snow blushed with an opaline radiance against the dark-blue of the morning sky, and all the forests and fields below lay still, and cool, and dewy, lapped in dreams yet unrecalled by the fading moon. I bathed my face in the cold well that perpetually poured over its full brim, drank the coffee which François had already prepared, sprang into the saddle, and began the last day of our long pilgrimage. The tent was folded, alas! for the last time; and now farewell to the freedom of our wandering life! Shall I ever feel it again?

The dew glistened on the chestnuts and the walnuts, on the wild grape-vines and wild roses, that shaded our road, as we followed the course of an Olympian stream through a charming dell, into the great plain below. Everywhere the same bountiful soil, the same superb orchards, the same ripe fields of wheat and barley, and silver rye. The peasants were at work, men and women, cutting the grain with rude scythes, binding it into sheaves, and stacking it in the fields. As we rode over the plain, the boys came running out to us with handfuls of grain, saluting us from afar, bidding us welcome as pilgrims, wishing us as many years of prosperity as there were kernels in their sheaves, and kissing the hands that gave them the harvest-toll. The whole landscape had an air of plenty, peace, and contentment. The people all greeted us cordially; and once a Mevlevi Dervish and a stately Turk, riding in company, saluted me so respectfully, stopping to speak with me, that I quite regretted being obliged to assume an air of dignified reserve, and ride away from them.

Ere long, we saw the two white minarets of Aineghiöl, above the line of orchards in front of us, and, in three hours after starting, reached the place. It is a small town, not particularly clean, but with brisk-looking bazaars. In one of the houses, I saw half-a-dozen pairs of superb antlers, the spoils of Olympian stags. The bazaar is covered with a trellised roof, overgrown with grape-vines, which hang enormous bunches of young grapes over the shop-boards. We were cheered by the news that Brousa was only eight hours distant, and I now began to hope that we might reach it. We jogged on as fast as we could urge our weary horses, passed another belt of orchard land, paid more harvest-tolls to the reapers, and commenced ascending a chain of low hills which divides the plain of Aineghiöl from that of Brousa.

At a fountain called the "mid-day konnàk" we met some travellers coming from Brousa, who informed us that we could get there by the time of asser prayer. Rounding the north-eastern base of Olympus, we now saw before us the long headland which forms his south-western extremity. A storm was arising from the sea of Marmora, and heavy white clouds settled on the topmost summits of the mountain. The wind began to blow fresh and cool, and when we had reached a height overlooking the deep valley, in the bottom of which lies the picturesque village of Ak-su, there were long showery lines coming up from the sea, and a filmy sheet of gray rain descended between us and Olympus, throwing his vast bulk far into the background. At Ak-su, the first shower met us, pouring so fast and thick that we were obliged to put on our capotes, and halt under a walnut-tree for shelter. But it soon passed over, laying the dust, for the time, and making the air sweet and cool.

We pushed forward over heights covered with young forests of oak, which are protected by the government, in order that they may furnish ship-timber. On the right, we looked down into magnificent valleys, opening towards the west into the plain of Brousa; but when, in the middle of the afternoon, we reached the last height, and saw the great plain itself, the climax was attained. It was the crown of all that we had yet seen. This superb plain or valley, thirty miles long, by five in breadth, spread away to the westward, between the mighty mass of Olympus on the one side, and a range of lofty mountains on the other, the sides of which presented a charming mixture of forest and cultivated land. Olympus, covered with woods of beech and oak, towered to the clouds that concealed his snowy head; and far in advance, under the last cape he threw out towards the sea, the hundred minarets of Brousa stretched in a white and glittering line, like the masts of a navy, whose hulls were buried in the leafy sea. No words can describe the beauty of the valley, the blending of the richest cultivation with the wildest natural luxuriance. Here were gardens and orchards; there groves of superb chestnut-trees in blossom; here, fields of golden grain or green pasture-land; there, Arcadian thickets overgrown with clematis and wild rose; here, lofty poplars growing beside the streams; there, spiry cypresses looking down from the slopes: and all blended in one whole, so rich, so grand, so gorgeous, that I scarcely breathed when it first burst upon me.

And now we descended to its level, and rode westward along the base of Olympus, grandest of Asian mountains. This after-storm view, although his head was shrouded, was sublime. His base is a vast sloping terrace, leagues in length, resembling the nights of steps by which the ancient temples were approached. From this foundation rise four mighty pyramids, two thousand feet in height, and completely mantled with forests. They are very nearly regular in their form and size, and are flanked to the east and west by headlands, or abutments, the slopes of which are longer and more gradual, as if to strengthen the great structure. Piled upon the four pyramids are others nearly as large, above whose green pinnacles appear still other and higher ones, bare and bleak, and clustering thickly together, to uphold the great central dome of snow. Between the bases of the lowest, the streams which drain the gorges of the mountain issue forth, cutting their way through the foundation terrace, and widening their beds downwards to the plain, like the throats of bugles, where, in winter rains, they pour forth the hoarse, grand monotone of their Olympian music. These broad beds are now dry and stony tracts, dotted all over with clumps of dwarfed sycamores and threaded by the summer streams, shrunken in bulk, but still swift, cold, and clear as ever.

We reached the city before night, and François is glad to find his presentiment fulfilled. We have safely passed through the untravelled heart of Asia Minor, and are now almost in sight of Europe. The camp-fire is extinguished; the tent is furled. We are no longer happy nomads,

543

masquerading in Moslem garb. We shall soon become prosaic Christians, and meekly hold out our wrists for the handcuffs of Civilization. Ah, prate as we will of the progress of the race, we are but forging additional fetters, unless we preserve that healthy physical development, those pure pleasures of mere animal existence, which are now only to be found among our semi-barbaric brethren. Our progress is nervous, when it should be muscular.

Chapter XXV. Brousa and the Sea of Marmora.

The City of Brousa--Return to Civilization--Storm--The Kalputcha Hammam--A Hot Bath--A Foretaste of Paradise--The Streets and Bazaars of Brousa--The Mosque--The Tombs of the Ottoman Sultans--Disappearance of the Katurgees--We start for Moudania--The Sea of Marmora--Moudania--Passport Difficulties--A Greek Caïque--Breakfast with the Fishermen--A Torrid Voyage--The Princes' Islands--Prinkipo--Distant View of Constantinople--We enter the Golden Horn.

"And we glode fast o'er a pellucid plain

Of waters, azure with the noontide ray.

Ethereal mountains shone around--a fane

Stood in the midst, beyond green isles which lay

On the blue, sunny deep, resplendent far away."

Shelley.

Constantinople, *Monday, July* 12, 1852.

Before entering Brousa, we passed the whole length of the town, which is built on the side of Olympus, and on three bluffs or spurs which project from it. The situation is more picturesque than that of Damascus, and from the remarkable number of its white domes and minarets, shooting upward from the groves of chestnut, walnut, and cypress-trees, the city is even more beautiful. There are large mosques on all the most prominent points, and, near the centre of the city, the ruins of an ancient castle, built upon a crag. The place, as we rode along, presented a shifting diorama of delightful views. The hotel is at the extreme western end of the city, not far from its celebrated hot baths. It is a new building, in European style, and being built high on the slope, commands one of the most glorious prospects I ever enjoyed from windows made with hands. What a comfort it was to go up stairs into a clean, bright, cheerful room; to drop at full length on a broad divan; to eat a Christian meal; to smoke a narghileh of the softest Persian tobacco; and finally, most exquisite of all luxuries, to creep between cool, clean sheets, on a curtained bed, and find it impossible to sleep on account of the delicious novelty of the sensation!

At night, another storm came up from the Sea of Marmora. Tremendous peals of thunder echoed in the gorges of Olympus and sharp, broad flashes of lightning gave us blinding glimpses of the glorious plain below. The rain fell in heavy showers, but our tent-life was just closed, and we sat securely at our windows and enjoyed the sublime scene.

The sun, rising over the distant mountains of Isnik, shone full in my face, awaking me to a morning view of the valley, which, freshened by the night's thunder-storm, shone wonderfully bright and clear. After coffee, we went to see the baths, which are on the side of the mountain, a mile from the hotel. The finest one, called the Kalputcha Hammam, is at the base of the hill. The entrance hall is very large, and covered by two lofty domes. In the centre is a large marble urn-shaped fountain, pouring out an abundant flood of cold water. Out of this, we passed into an immense rotunda, filled with steam and traversed by long pencils of light, falling from holes in the roof. A small but very beautiful marble fountain cast up a jet of cold water in the centre. Beyond this was still another hall, of the same size, but with a circular basin, twenty-five feet in diameter, in the centre. The floor was marble mosaic, and the basin was lined with brilliantly-colored tiles. It was kept constantly full by the natural hot streams of the mountain. There were a number of persons in the pool, but the atmosphere was so hot that we did not long disturb them by our curiosity.

We then ascended to the Armenian bath, which is the neatest of all, but it was given up to the women, and we were therefore obliged to go to a Turkish one adjoining. The room into which we were taken was so hot that a violent perspiration immediately broke out all over my body, and by the time the dellèks were ready to rasp me, I was as limp as a wet towel, and as plastic as a piece of putty. The man who took me was sweated away almost to nothing; his very bones appeared to have become soft and pliable. The water was slightly sulphureous, and the pailfuls which he dashed over my

546

head were so hot that they produced the effect of a chill--a violent nervous shudder. The temperature of the springs is 180° Fahrenheit, and I suppose the tank into which he afterwards plunged me must have been nearly up to the mark. When, at last, I was laid on the couch, my body was so parboiled that I perspired at all pores for full an hour--a feeling too warm and unpleasant at first, but presently merging into a mood which was wholly rapturous and heavenly. I was like a soft white cloud, that rests all of a summer afternoon on the peak of a distant mountain. I felt the couch on which I lay no more than the cloud might feel the cliffs on which it lingers so airily. I saw nothing but peaceful, glorious sights; spaces of clear blue sky; stretches of quiet lawns; lovely valleys threaded by the gentlest of streams; azure lakes, unruffled by a breath; calms far out on mid-ocean, and Alpine peaks bathed in the flush of an autumnal sunset. My mind retraced all our journey from Aleppo, and there was a halo over every spot I had visited. I dwelt with rapture on the piny hills of Phrygia, on the gorges of Taurus, on the beechen solitudes of Olympus. Would to heaven that I might describe those scenes as I then felt them! All was revealed to me: the heart of Nature lay bare, and I read the meaning and knew the inspiration of her every mood. Then, as my frame grew cooler, and the fragrant clouds of the narghileh, which had helped my dreams, diminished, I was like that same summer cloud, when it feels a gentle breeze and is lifted above the hills, floating along independent of Earth, but for its shadow.

Brousa is a very long, straggling place, extending for three or four miles along the side of the mountain, but presenting a very picturesque appearance from every point. The houses are nearly all three stories high, built of wood and unburnt bricks, and each story projects over the other, after the manner of German towns of the Middle Ages. They have not the hanging balconies which I have found so quaint and pleasing in Kiutahya. But, especially in the Greek quarter, many of them are plastered and painted of some bright color, which gives a gay, cheerful appearance to the streets. Besides, Brousa is the cleanest Turkish town I have seen. The mountain streams traverse most of the streets, and every heavy rain washes them out thoroughly. The whole city has a brisk, active air, and the workmen appear both more skilful and more industrious than in the other parts of Asia Minor. I noticed a great

547

many workers in copper, iron, and wood, and an extensive manufactory of shoes and saddles. Brousa, however, is principally noted for its silks, which are produced in this valley, and others to the South and East. The manufactories are near the city. I looked over some of the fabrics in the bazaars, but found them nearly all imitations of European stuffs, woven in mixed silk and cotton, and even more costly than the silks of Damascus.

We passed the whole length of the bazaars, and then, turning up one of the side streets on our right, crossed a deep ravine by a high stone bridge. Above and below us there were other bridges, under which a stream flowed down from the mountains. Thence we ascended the height, whereon stands the largest and one of the oldest mosques in Brousa. The position is remarkably fine, commanding a view of nearly the whole city and the plain below it. We entered the court-yard boldly, François taking the precaution to speak to me only in Arabic, as there was a Turk within. Mr. H. went to the fountain, washed his hands and face, but did not dare to swallow a drop, putting on a most dolorous expression of countenance, as if perishing with thirst. The mosque was a plain, square building, with a large dome and two minarets. The door was a rich and curious specimen of the stalactitic style, so frequent in Saracenic buildings. We peeped into the windows, and, although the mosque, which does not appear to be in common use, was darkened, saw enough to show that the interior was quite plain.

Just above this edifice stands a large octagonal tomb, surmounted by a dome, and richly adorned with arabesque cornices and coatings of green and blue tiles. It stood in a small garden inclosure, and there was a sort of porter's lodge at the entrance. As we approached, an old gray-bearded man in a green turban came out, and, on François requesting entrance for us, took a key and conducted us to the building. He had not the slightest idea of our being Christians. We took off our slippers before touching the lintel of the door, as the place was particularly holy. Then, throwing open the door, the old man lingered a few moments after we entered, so as not to disturb our prayers--a mark of great respect. We advanced to the edge of the parapet, turned our faces towards Mecca, and imitated the usual Mohammedan prayer on entering a mosque, by holding both arms outspread for a few moments, then bringing the hands together and bowing the face upon them. This done, we leisurely examined the building, and the old man was ready enough to satisfy our curiosity. It was a rich and elegant structure, lighted from the dome. The walls were lined with brilliant tiles, and had an elaborate cornice, with Arabic inscriptions in gold. The floor was covered with a carpet, whereon stood eight or ten ancient coffins, surrounding a larger one which occupied a raised platform in the centre. They were all of wood, heavily carved, and many of them entirely covered with gilded inscriptions. These, according to the old man, were the coffins of the Ottoman Sultans, who had reigned at Brousa previous to the taking of Constantinople, with some members of their families. There were four Sultans, among whom were Mahomet I., and a certain Achmet. Orchan, the founder of the Ottoman dynasty, is buried somewhere in Brousa, and the great central coffin may have been his. François and I talked entirely in Arabic, and the old man asked: "Who are these Hadjis?" whereupon F. immediately answered: "They are Effendis from Baghdad."

We had intended making the ascent of Olympus, but the summit was too thickly covered with clouds. On the morning of the second day, therefore, we determined to take up the line of march for Constantinople. The last scene of our strange, eventful history with the katurgees had just transpired, by their deserting us, being two hundred piastres in our debt. They left their khan on the afternoon after our arrival, ostensibly for the purpose of taking their beasts out to pasture, and were never heard of more. We let them go, thankful that they had not played the trick sooner. We engaged fresh horses for Moudania, on the Sea of Marmora, and dispatched François in advance, to procure a caïque for Constantinople, while we waited to have our passports signed. But after waiting an hour, as there was no appearance of the precious documents, we started the baggage also, under the charge of a surroudjee, and remained alone. Another hour passed by, and yet another, and the Bey was still occupied in sleeping off his hunger. Mr. Harrison, in desperation, went to the office, and after some delay, received the passports with a visè, but not, as we afterwards discovered, the necessary one.

It was four o'clock by the time we left Brousa. Our horses were stiff, clumsy pack-beasts; but, by dint of whips and the sharp shovel-stirrups, we forced them into a trot and made them keep it. The road was well travelled, and by asking everybody we met: "Bou yôl Moudania yedermi?" ("Is this the way to Moudania?"), we had no difficulty in finding it. The plain in many places is marshy, and traversed by several streams. A low range of hills stretches across, and nearly closes it, the united waters finding their outlet by a narrow valley to the north. From the top of the hill we had a grand view, looking back over the plain, with the long line of Brousa's minarets glittering through the interminable groves at the foot of the mountain Olympus now showed a superb outline; the clouds hung about his shoulders, but his snowy head was bare. Before us lay a broad, rich valley, extending in front to the mountains of Moudania. The country was well cultivated, with large farming establishments here and there.

The sun was setting as we reached the summit ridge, where stood a little guard-house. As we rode over the crest, Olympus disappeared, and the Sea of Marmora lay before us, spreading out from the Gulf of Moudania, which was deep and blue among the hills, to an open line against the sunset. Beyond that misty line lay Europe, which I had not seen for nearly nine months, and the gulf below me was the bound of my tent and saddle life. But one hour more, old horse! Have patience with my Ethiopian thong, and the sharp corners of my Turkish stirrups: but one hour more, and I promise never to molest you again! Our path was downward, and I marvel that the poor brute did not sometimes tumble headlong with me. He had been too long used to the pack, however, and his habits were as settled as a Turk's. We passed a beautiful village in a valley on the right, and came into olive groves and vineyards, as the dusk was creeping on. It was a lovely country of orchards and gardens, with fountains spouting by the wayside, and country houses perched on the steeps. In another hour, we reached the sea-shore. It was now nearly dark, but we could see the tower of Moudania some distance to the west.

Still in a continual trot, we rode on; and as we drew near, Mr. H. fired his gun to announce our approach. At the entrance of the town, we found the sourrudjee waiting to conduct us. We clattered through the rough streets for what seemed an endless length of time. The Ramazan gun had just fired,

550

the minarets were illuminated, and the coffee-houses were filled with people. Finally, François, who had been almost in despair at our non-appearance, hailed us with the welcome news that he had engaged a caïque, and that our baggage was already embarked. We only needed the visès of the authorities, in order to leave. He took our teskerés to get them, and we went upon the balcony of a coffee-house overhanging the sea, and smoked a narghileh.

But here there was another history. The teskerés had not been properly visèd at Brousa, and the Governor at first decided to send us back. Taking François, however, for a Turk, and finding that we had regularly passed quarantine, he signed them after a delay of an hour and a half, and we left the shore, weary, impatient, and wolfish with twelve hours' fasting. A cup of Brousan beer and a piece of bread brought us into a better mood, and I, who began to feel sick from the rolling of the caïque, lay down on my bed, which was spread at the bottom, and found a kind of uneasy sleep. The sail was hoisted at first, to get us across the mouth of the Gulf, but soon the Greeks took to their oars. They were silent, however, and though I only slept by fits, the night wore away rapidly. As the dawn was deepening, we ran into a little bight in the northern side of a promontory, where a picturesque Greek village stood at the foot of the mountains. The houses were of wood, with balconies overgrown with grape-vines, and there was a fountain of cold, excellent water on the very beach. Some Greek boatmen were smoking in the portico of a café on shore, and two fishermen, who had been out before dawn to catch sardines, were emptying their nets of the spoil. Our men kindled a fire on the sand, and roasted us a dish of the fish. Some of the last night's hunger remained, and the meal had enough of that seasoning to be delicious.

After giving our men an hour's rest, we set off for the Princes' Islands, which now appeared to the north, over the glassy plain of the sea. The Gulf of Iskmid, or Nicomedia, opened away to the east, between two mountain headlands. The morning was intensely hot and sultry, and but for the protection of an umbrella, we should have suffered greatly. There was a fiery blue vapor on the sea, and a thunder-cloud hid the shores of Thrace. Now and then came a light puff of wind, whereupon the men would ship the little mast, and crowd on an enormous quantity of sail. So, sailing and rowing, we neared the islands with the storm, but it advanced slowly enough to allow a sight of the mosques of St. Sophia and Sultan Achmed, gleaming far and white, like icebergs astray on a torrid sea. Another cloud was pouring its rain over the Asian shore, and we made haste to get to the landing at Prinkipo before it could reach us. From the south, the group of islands is not remarkable for beauty. Only four of them--Prinkipo, Chalki, Prote, and Antigone--are inhabited, the other five being merely barren rocks.

There is an ancient convent on the summit of Prinkipo, where the Empress Irene--the contemporary of Charlemagne--is buried. The town is on the northern side of the island, and consists mostly of the summer residences of Greek and Armenian merchants. Many of these are large and stately houses, surrounded with handsome gardens. The streets are shaded with sycamores, and the number of coffee-houses shows that the place is much frequented on festal days. A company of drunken Greeks were singing in violation of all metre and harmony--a discord the more remarkable, since nothing could be more affectionate than their conduct towards each other. Nearly everybody was in Frank costume, and our Oriental habits, especially the red Tartar boots, attracted much observation. I began to feel awkward and absurd, and longed to show myself a Christian once more.

Leaving Prinkipo, we made for Constantinople, whose long array of marble domes and gilded spires gleamed like a far mirage over the waveless sea. It was too faint and distant and dazzling to be substantial. It was like one of those imaginary cities which we build in a cloud fused in the light of the setting sun. But as we neared the point of Chalcedon, running along the Asian shore, those airy piles gathered form and substance. The pinnacles of the Seraglio shot up from the midst of cypress groves; fantastic kiosks lined the shore; the minarets of St. Sophia and Sultan Achmed rose more clearly against the sky; and a fleet of steamers and men-of-war, gay with flags, marked the entrance of the Golden Horn. We passed the little bay where St. Chrysostom was buried, the point of Chalcedon, and now, looking up the renowned Bosphorus, saw the Maiden's Tower, opposite Scutari. An enormous pile, the barracks of the Anatolian soldiery, hangs over the high bank, and, as we row abreast of it, a fresh breeze comes up from the Sea of Marmora. The prow of the caïque is turned across the stream, the sail is set, and we glide rapidly and noiselessly over the Bosphorus and into the Golden Horn, between the banks of the Frank and Moslem--Pera and Stamboul. Where on the earth shall we find a panorama more magnificent?

The air was filled with the shouts and noises of the great Oriental metropolis; the water was alive with caïques and little steamers; and all the world of work and trade, which had grown almost to be a fable, welcomed us back to its restless heart. We threaded our rather perilous way over the populous waves, and landed in a throng of Custom-House officers and porters, on the wharf at Galata.

Chapter XXVI. The Night of Predestination.

Constantinople in Ramazan--The Origin of the Fast--Nightly Illuminations--The Night of Predestination--The Golden Horn at Night--Illumination of the Shores--The Cannon of Constantinople--A Fiery Panorama--The Sultan's Caïque--Close of the Celebration--A Turkish Mob--The Dancing Dervishes.

"Skies full of splendid moons and shooting stars,

And spouting exhalations, diamond fires." Keats.

Constantinople, *Wednesday, July* 14, 1862.

Constantinople, during the month of Ramazan, presents a very different aspect from Constantinople at other times. The city, it is true, is much more stern and serious during the day; there is none of that gay, careless life of the Orient which you see in Smyrna, Cairo, and Damascus; but when once the sunset gun has fired, and the painful fast is at an end, the picture changes as if by magic. In all the outward symbols of their religion, the Mussulmans show their joy at being relieved from what they consider a sacred duty. During the day, it is quite a science to keep the appetite dormant, and the people not only abstain from eating and drinking, but as much as possible from the sight of food. In the bazaars, you see the famished merchants either sitting, propped back against their cushions, with the shawl about their stomachs, tightened so as to prevent the void under it from being so sensibly felt, or lying at full length in the vain attempt to sleep. It is whispered here that many of the Turks will both eat and smoke, when there is no chance of detection, but no one would dare infringe the fast in public. Most of the mechanics and porters are Armenians, and the boatmen are Greeks.

I have endeavored to ascertain the origin of this fast month. The Syrian Christians say that it is a mere imitation of an incident which happened to Mahomet. The Prophet, having lost his camels, went day after day seeking them in the Desert, taking no nourishment from the time of his departure in the morning until his return at sunset. After having sought them thus daily, for the period of one entire moon, he found them, and in token of joy, gave a three days' feast to the tribe, now imitated in the festival of Bairam, which lasts for three days after the close of Ramazan. This reason, however, seems too trifling for such a rigid fast, and the Turkish tradition, that the Koran was sent down from heaven during this month, offers a more probable explanation. During the fast, the Mussulmans, as is quite natural, are much more fanatical than at other times. They are obliged to attend prayers at the mosque every night, or to have a mollah read the Koran to them at their own houses. All the prominent features of their religion are kept constantly before their eyes, and their natural aversion to the Giaour, or Infidel, is increased tenfold. I have heard of several recent instances in which strangers have been exposed to insults and indignities.

At dusk the minarets are illuminated; a peal of cannon from the Arsenal, echoed by others from the forts along the Bosphorus, relieves the suffering followers of the Prophet, and after an hour of silence, during which they are all at home, feasting, the streets are filled with noisy crowds, and every coffee-shop is thronged. Every night there are illuminations along the water, which, added to the crowns of light sparkling on the hundred minarets and domes, give a magical effect to the night view of the city. Towards midnight there is again a season of comparative quiet, most of the inhabitants having retired to rest; but, about two hours afterwards a watchman comes along with a big drum, which he beats lustily before the doors of the Faithful, in order to arouse them in time to eat again before the daylight-gun, which announces the commencement of another day's fast.

Last night was the holiest night of Islam, being the twenty-fifth of the fast. It is called the Leilet-el-Kadr, or Night of the Predestination, the anniversary of that on which the Koran was miraculously communicated to the Prophet. On this night the Sultan, accompanied by his whole suite, attends service at the mosque, and on his return to the Seraglio, the Sultana Valide, or Sultana-Mother, presents him with a virgin from one of the noble families of Constantinople. Formerly, St. Sophia was the theatre of this celebration, but this year the Sultan chose the Mosque of Tophaneh, which stands on the shore--probably as being nearer to his imperial palace at Beshiktashe, on the Bosphorus. I consider myself fortunate in having reached Constantinople in season to witness this ceremony, and the illumination of the Golden Horn, which accompanies it.

After sunset the mosques crowning the hills of Stamboul, the mosque of Tophaneh, on this side of the water, and the Turkish men-of-war and steamers afloat at the mouth of the Golden Horn, began to blaze with more than their usual brilliance. The outlines of the minarets and domes were drawn in light on the deepening gloom, and the masts and yards of the vessel were hung with colored lanterns. From the battery in front of the mosque and arsenal of Tophaneh a blaze of intense light streamed out over the water, illuminating the gliding forms of a thousand caïques, and the dark hulls of the vessels lying at anchor. The water is the best place from which to view the illumination, and a party of us descended to the landing-place. The streets of Tophaneh were crowded with swarms of Turks, Greeks and Armenians. The square around the fountain was brilliantly lighted, and venders of sherbet and kaïmak were ranged along the sidewalks. In the neighborhood of the mosque the crowd was so dense that we could with difficulty make our way through. All the open space next the water was filled up with the clumsy arabas, or carriages of the Turks, in which sat the wives of the Pashas and other dignitaries.

We took a caïque, and were soon pulled out into the midst of a multitude of other caïques, swarming all over the surface of the Golden Horn. The view from this point was strange, fantastic, yet inconceivably gorgeous. In front, three or four large Turkish frigates lay in the Bosphorus, their hulls and spars outlined in fire against the dark hills and distant twinkling lights of Asia. Looking to the west, the shores of the Golden Horn were equally traced by the multitude of lamps that covered them, and on either side, the hills on which the city is built rose from the water--masses of dark buildings, dotted all over with shafts and domes of the most brilliant light. The gateway on Seraglio Point was illuminated, as well as the quay in front of the mosque of Tophaneh, all the cannons of the battery being covered with lamps. The commonest objects shared in the splendor, even a large lever used for hoisting goods being hung with lanterns from top to bottom. The mosque was a mass of light, and between the tall minarets flanking it, burned the inscription, in Arabic characters, "Long life to you, O our Sovereign!"

The discharge of a cannon announced the Sultan's departure from his palace, and immediately the guns on the frigates and the batteries on both shores took up the salute, till the grand echoes, filling the hollow throat of the Golden Horn, crashed from side to side, striking the hills of Scutari and the point of Chalcedon, and finally dying away among the summits of the Princes' Islands, out on the Sea of Marmora. The hulls of the frigates were now lighted up with intense chemical fires, and an abundance of rockets were spouted from their decks. A large Drummond light on Seraglio Point, and another at the Battery of Tophaneh, poured their rival streams across the Golden Horn, revealing the thousands of caïques jostling each other from shore to shore, and the endless variety of gay costumes with which they were filled. The smoke of the cannon hanging in the air, increased the effect of this illumination, and became a screen of auroral brightness, through which the superb spectacle loomed with large and unreal features. It was a picture of air--a phantasmagoric spectacle, built of luminous vapor and meteoric fires, and hanging in the dark round of space. In spite of ourselves, we became eager and excited, half fearing that the whole pageant would dissolve the next moment, and leave no trace behind.

Meanwhile, the cannon thundered from a dozen batteries, and the rockets burst into glittering rain over our heads. Grander discharges I never heard; the earth shook and trembled under the mighty bursts of sound, and the reverberation which rattled along the hill of Galata, broken by the scattered buildings into innumerable fragments of sound, resembled the crash of a thousand falling houses. The distant echoes from Asia and the islands in the sea filled up the pauses between the nearer peals, and we seemed to be in the midst of some great naval engagement. But now the caïque of the Sultan is discerned, approaching from the Bosphorus. A signal is given, and a sunrise of intense rosy and golden radiance suddenly lights up the long arsenal and stately mosque of Tophaneh, plays over the tall buildings on the hill of Pera, and falls with a fainter lustre on the Genoese watch-tower that overlooks Galata. It is impossible to describe the effect of this magical illumination. The mosque, with its taper minarets, its airy galleries, and its great central dome, is built of compact, transparent flame, and in the shifting of the red and yellow fires, seems to flicker and waver in the air. It is as lofty, and gorgeous, and unsubstantial as the cloudy palace in Cole's picture of "Youth." The long white front of the arsenal is fused in crimson heat, and burns against the dark as if it were one mass of living coal. And over all hangs the luminous canopy of smoke, redoubling its lustre on the waters of the Golden Horn, and mingling with the phosphorescent gleams that play around the oars of the caïques.

A long barge, propelled by sixteen oars, glides around the dark corner of Tophaneh, and shoots into the clear, brilliant space in front of the mosque. It is not lighted, and passes with great swiftness towards the brilliant landing-place. There are several persons seated under a canopy in the stern, and we are trying to decide which is the Sultan, when a second boat, driven by twenty-four oarsmen, comes in sight. The men rise up at each stroke, and the long, sharp craft flies over the surface of the water, rather than forces its way through it. A gilded crown surmounts the long, curved prow, and a light though superb canopy covers the stern. Under this, we catch a glimpse of the Sultan and Grand Vizier, as they appear for an instant like black silhouettes against the burst of light on shore.

After the Sultan had entered the mosque, the fires diminished and the cannon ceased, though the illuminated masts, minarets and gateways still threw a brilliant gleam over the scene. After more than an hour spent in devotion, he again entered his caïque and sped away to greet his new wife, amid a fresh discharge from the frigates and the batteries on both shores, and a new dawn of auroral splendor. We made haste to reach the landing-place, in order to avoid the crowd of caïques; but, although we were among the first, we came near being precipitated into the water, in the struggle to get ashore. The market-place at Tophaneh was so crowded that nothing but main force brought us through, and some of our party had their pockets picked. A number of Turkish soldiers and police-men were mixed up in the melee, and they were not sparing of blows when they came in contact with a Giaour. In making my way through, I found that a collision with one of the soldiers was inevitable, but I managed to plump against him with such force as to take the breath out of his body, and was out of his reach before he had recovered himself. I saw several Turkish women striking right and left in their endeavors to escape, and place their hands against the faces of those who opposed them, pushing them aside. This crowd was contrived by thieves, for the purpose of plunder, and, from what I have since learned, must have been very successful.

I visited to-day the College of the Mevlevi Dervishes at Pera, and witnessed their peculiar ceremonies. They assemble in a large hall, where they take their seats in a semi-circle, facing the shekh. After going through several times with the usual Moslem prayer, they move in slow march around the room, while a choir in the gallery chants Arabic phrases in a manner very similar to the mass in Catholic churches. I could distinguish the sentences "God is great," "Praise be to God," and other similar ejaculations. The chant was accompanied with a drum and flute, and had not lasted long before the Dervishes set themselves in a rotary motion, spinning slowly around the shekh, who stood in the centre. They stretched both arms out, dropped their heads on one side, and glided around with a steady, regular motion, their long white gowns spread out and floating on the air. Their steps were very similar to those of the modern waltz, which, it is possible, may have been derived from the dance of the Mevlevis. Baron Von Hammer finds in this ceremony an imitation of the dance of the spheres, in the ancient Samothracian Mysteries; but I see no reason to go so far back for its origin. The dance lasted for about twenty minutes, and the Dervishes appeared very much exhausted at the close, as they are obliged to observe the fast very strictly.

Chapter XXVII. The Solemnities of Bairam.

The Appearance of the New Moon--The Festival of Bairam--The Interior of the Seraglio--The Pomp of the Sultan's Court--Rescind Pasha--The Sultan's Dwarf--Arabian Stallions--The Imperial Guard--Appearance of the Sultan--The Inner Court--Return of the Procession--The Sultan on his Throne--The Homage of the Pashas--An Oriental Picture--Kissing the Scarf--The Shekh el-Islàm--The Descendant of the Caliphs--Bairam Commences.

Constantinople, *Monday, July* 19, 1852.

Saturday was the last day of the fast-month of Ramazan, and yesterday the celebration of the solemn festival of Bairam took place. The moon changed on Friday morning at 11 o'clock, but as the Turks have no faith in astronomy, and do not believe the moon has actually changed until they see it, all good Mussulmen were obliged to fast an additional day. Had Saturday been cloudy, and the new moon invisible, I am not sure but the fast would have been still further prolonged. A good look-out was kept, however, and about four o'clock on Saturday afternoon some sharp eyes saw the young crescent above the sun. There is a hill near Gemlik, on the Gulf of Moudania, about fifty miles from here, whence the Turks believe the new moon can be first seen. The families who live on this hill are exempted from taxation, in consideration of their keeping a watch for the moon, at the close of Ramazan. A series of signals, from hill to hill, is in readiness, and the news is transmitted to Constantinople in a very short time Then, when the muezzin proclaims the asser, or prayer two hours before sunset, he proclaims also the close of Ramazan. All the batteries fire a salute, and the big guns along the water announce the joyful news to all parts of the city. The forts on the Bosphorus take up the tale, and both shores, from the Black Sea to the Propontis, shake with the burden of their rejoicing. At night the mosques are illuminated for the last time, for it is only during Ramazan that they are lighted, or open for night service.

After Ramazan, comes the festival of Bairam, which lasts three days, and is a season of unbounded rejoicing. The bazaars are closed, no Turk does any work, but all, clothed in their best dresses, or in an entire new suit if they can afford it, pass the time in feasting, in paying visits, or in making excursions to the shores of the Bosphorus, or other favorite spots around Constantinople. The festival is inaugurated by a solemn state ceremony, at the Seraglio and the mosque of Sultan Achmed, whither the Sultan goes in procession, accompanied by all the officers of the Government. This is the last remaining pageant which has been spared to the Ottoman monarchs by the rigorous reforming measures of Sultan Mahmoud, and shorn as it is of much of its former splendor, it probably surpasses in brilliant effect any spectacle which any other European Court can present. The ceremonies which take place inside of the Seraglio were, until within three or four years, prohibited to Frank eyes, and travellers were obliged to content themselves with a view of the procession, as it passed to the mosque. Through the kindness of Mr. Brown, of the American Embassy, I was enabled to witness the entire solemnity, in all its details.

As the procession leaves the Seraglio at sunrise, we rose with the first streak of dawn, descended to Tophaneh, and crossed to Seraglio Point, where the cavass of the Embassy was in waiting for us. He conducted us through the guards, into the garden of the Seraglio, and up the hill to the Palace. The Capudan Pasha, or Lord High Admiral, had just arrived in a splendid caïque, and pranced up the hill before us on a magnificent stallion, whose trappings blazed with jewels and gold lace. The rich uniforms of the different officers of the army and marine glittered far and near under the dense shadows of the cypress trees, and down the dark alleys where the morning twilight had not penetrated. We were ushered into the great outer court-yard of the Seraglio, leading to the Sublime Porte. A double row of marines, in scarlet jackets and white trowsers, extended from one gate to the other, and a very excellent brass band played "Suoni la tromba" with much spirit. The groups of Pashas and other officers of high rank, with their attendants, gave the scene a brilliant character of festivity. The costumes, except those of the secretaries and servants, were after the European model, but covered with a lavish profusion of gold lace. The horses were all of the choicest Eastern breeds, and the broad housings of their saddles of blue, green, purple, and crimson cloth, were enriched with gold lace, rubies, emeralds and turquoises.

The cavass took us into a chamber near the gate, and commanding a view of the whole court. There we found Mr. Brown and his lady, with several officers from the U.S. steamer San Jacinto. At this moment the sun, appearing above the hill of Bulgaria, behind Scutari, threw his earliest rays upon the gilded pinnacles of the Seraglio. The commotion in the long court-yard below increased. The marines were formed into exact line, the horses of the officers clattered on the rough pavement as they dashed about to expedite the arrangements, the crowd pressed closer to the line of the procession, and in five minutes the grand pageant was set in motion. As the first Pasha made his appearance under the dark archway of the interior gate, the band struck up the Marseillaise (which is a favorite air among the Turks), and the soldiers presented arms. The court-yard was near two hundred yards long, and the line of Pashas, each surrounded with the officers of his staff, made a most dazzling show. The lowest in rank came first. I cannot recollect the precise order, nor the names of all of them, which, in fact, are of little consequence, while power and place are such uncertain matters in Turkey.

Each Pasha wore the red fez on his head, a frock-coat of blue cloth, the breast of which was entirely covered with gold lace, while a broad band of the same decorated the skirts, and white pantaloons. One of the Ministers, Mehemet Ali Pasha, the brother-in-law of the Sultan, was formerly a cooper's apprentice, but taken, when a boy, by the late Sultan Mahmoud, to be a playmate for his son, on account of his extraordinary beauty. Rescind Pasha, the Grand Vizier, is a man of about sixty years of age. He is frequently called Giaour, or Infidel, by the Turks, on account of his liberal policy, which has made him many enemies. The expression of his face denotes intelligence, but lacks the energy necessary to accomplish great reforms. His son, a boy of about seventeen, already possesses the rank of Pasha, and is affianced to the Sultan's daughter, a child of ten, or twelve years old. He is a fat, handsome youth, with a sprightly face, and acted his part in the ceremonies with a nonchalance which made him appear graceful beside his stiff, dignified elders.

After the Pashas came the entire household of the Sultan, including even his eunuchs, cooks, and constables. The Kislar Aga, or Chief Eunuch, a tall African in resplendent costume, is one of the most important personages connected with the Court. The Sultan's favorite dwarf, a little man about forty years old and three feet high, bestrode his horse with as consequential an air as any of them. A few years ago, this man took a notion to marry, and applied to the Sultan for a wife. The latter gave him permission to go into his harem and take the one whom he could kiss. The dwarf, like all short men, was ambitious to have a long wife. While the Sultan's five hundred women, who knew the terms according to which the dwarf was permitted to choose, were laughing at the amorous mannikin, he went up to one of the tallest and handsomest of them, and struck her a sudden blow on the stomach. She collapsed with the pain, and before she could recover he caught her by the neck and gave her the dreaded kiss. The Sultan kept his word, and the tall beauty is now the mother of the dwarfs children.

The procession grows more brilliant as it advances, and the profound inclination made by the soldiers at the further end of the court, announces the approach of the Sultan himself. First come three led horses, of the noblest Arabian blood--glorious creatures, worthy to represent

"The horse that guide the golden eye of heaven,

And snort the morning from their nostrils,

Making their fiery gait above the glades."

Their eyes were more keen and lustrous than the diamonds which studded their head-stalls, and the wealth of emeralds, rubies, and sapphires that gleamed on their trappings would have bought the possessions of a German Prince. After them came the Sultan's body-guard, a company of tall, strong men, in crimson tunics and white trousers, with lofty plumes of peacock feathers in their hats. Some of them carried crests of green feathers, fastened upon long staves. These superb horses and showy guards are the only relics of that barbaric pomp which characterized all State processions during the time of the Janissaries. In the centre of a hollow square of plume-bearing guards rode Abdul-Medjid himself, on a snow-white steed. Every one bowed profoundly as he passed along, but he neither looked to the right or left, nor made the slightest acknowledgment of the salutations. Turkish etiquette exacts the most rigid indifference on the part of the Sovereign, who, on all public occasions, never makes a greeting. Formerly, before the change of costume, the Sultan's turbans were carried before him in the processions, and the servants who bore them inclined them to one side and the other, in answer to the salutations of the crowd.

Sultan Abdul-Medjid is a man of about thirty, though he looks older. He has a mild, amiable, weak face, dark eyes, a prominent nose, and short, dark brown mustaches and beard. His face is thin, and wrinkles are already making their appearance about the corners of his mouth and eyes. But for a certain vacancy of expression, he would be called a handsome man. He sits on his horse with much ease and grace, though there is a slight stoop in his shoulders. His legs are crooked, owing to which cause he appears awkward when on his feet, though he wears a long cloak to conceal the deformity. Sensual indulgence has weakened a constitution not naturally strong, and increased that mildness which has now become a defect in his character. He is not stern enough to be just, and his subjects are less fortunate under his easy rule than under the rod of his savage father, Mahmoud. He was dressed in a style of the utmost richness and elegance. He wore a red Turkish fez, with an immense rosette of brilliants, and a long, floating plume of bird-of-paradise feathers. The diamond in the centre of the rosette is of unusual size; it was picked up some years ago in the Hippodrome, and probably belonged to the treasury of the Greek Emperors. The breast and collar of his coat were one mass of diamonds, and sparkled in the early sun with a thousand rainbow gleams. His mantle of dark-blue cloth hung to his knees, concealing the deformity of his legs. He wore white pantaloons, white kid gloves, and patent leather boots, thrust into his golden stirrups.

A few officers of the Imperial household followed behind the Sultan, and the procession then terminated. Including the soldiers, it contained from two to three thousand persons. The marines lined the way to the mosque of Sultan Achmed, and a great crowd of spectators filled up the streets and the square of the Hippodrome. Coffee was served to us, after which we were all conducted into the inner court of the Seraglio, to await the return of the cortège. This court is not more than half the size of the outer one, but is shaded with large sycamores, embellished with fountains, and surrounded with light and elegant galleries, in pure Saracenic style. The picture which it presented was therefore far richer and more characteristic of the Orient than the outer court, where the architecture is almost wholly after Italian models. The portals at either end rested on slender pillars, over which projected broad eaves, decorated with elaborate carved and gilded work, and above all rose a dome, surmounted by the Crescent. On the right, the tall chimneys of the Imperial kitchens towered above the walls. The sycamores threw their broad, cool shadows over the court, and groups of servants, in gala dresses, loitered about the corridors.

After waiting nearly half an hour, the sound of music and the appearance of the Sultan's body-guard proclaimed the return of the procession. It came in reversed order, headed by the Sultan, after whom followed the Grand Vizier and other Ministers of the Imperial Council, and the Pashas, each surrounded by his staff of officers. The Sultan dismounted at the entrance to the Seraglio, and disappeared through the door. He was absent for more than half an hour, during which time he received the congratulations of his family, his wives, and the principal personages of his household, all of whom came to kiss his feet. Meanwhile, the Pashas ranged themselves in a semicircle around the arched and gilded portico. The servants of the Seraglio brought out a large Persian carpet, which they spread on the marble pavement. The throne, a large square seat, richly carved and covered with gilding, was placed in the centre, and a dazzling piece of cloth-of-gold thrown over the back of it. When the Sultan re-appeared, he took his seat thereon, placing his feet on a small footstool. The ceremony of kissing his feet now commenced. The first who had this honor was the Chief of the Emirs, an old man in a green robe, embroidered with pearls. He advanced to the throne, knelt, kissed the Sultan's patent-leather boot, and retired backward from the presence.

The Ministers and Pashas followed in single file, and, after they had made the salutation, took their stations on the right hand of the throne. Most of them were fat, and their glittering frock-coats were buttoned so tightly that they seemed ready to burst. It required a great effort for them to rise from their knees. During all this time, the band was playing operatic airs, and

565

as each Pasha knelt, a marshal, or master of ceremonies, with a silver wand, gave the signal to the Imperial Guard, who shouted at the top of their voices: "Prosperity to our Sovereign! May he live a thousand years!" This part of the ceremony was really grand and imposing. All the adjuncts were in keeping: the portico, wrought in rich arabesque designs; the swelling domes and sunlit crescents above; the sycamores and cypresses shading the court; the red tunics and peacock plumes of the guard; the monarch himself, radiant with jewels, as he sat in his chair of gold--all these features combined to form a stately picture of the lost Orient, and for the time Abdul-Medjid seemed the true representative of Caliph Haroun Al-Raschid.

After the Pashas had finished, the inferior officers of the Army, Navy, and Civil Service followed, to the number of at least a thousand. They were not considered worthy to touch the Sultan's person, but kissed his golden scarf, which was held out to them by a Pasha, who stood on the left of the throne. The Grand Vizier had his place on the right, and the Chief of the Eunuchs stood behind him. The kissing of the scarf occupied an hour. The Sultan sat quietly during all this time, his face expressing a total indifference to all that was going on. The most skilful physiognomist could not have found in it the shadow of an expression. If this was the etiquette prescribed for him, he certainly acted it with marvellous skill and success.

The long line of officers at length came to an end, and I fancied that the solemnities were now over; but after a pause appeared the Shekh el-Islàm, or High Priest of the Mahometan religion. His authority in religious matters transcends that of the Sultan, and is final and irrevocable. He was a very venerable man, of perhaps seventy-five years of age, and his tottering steps were supported by two mollahs. He was dressed in a long green robe, embroidered with gold and pearls, over which his white beard flowed below his waist. In his turban of white cambric was twisted a scarf of cloth-of-gold. He kissed the border of the Sultan's mantle, which salutation was also made by a long line of the chief priests of the mosques of Constantinople, who followed him. These priests were dressed in long robes of white, green, blue, and violet, many of them with collars of pearls and golden scarfs wound about their turbans, the rich fringes falling on their shoulders. They were grave, stately men, with long gray beards, and the wisdom of age and study in their deep-set eyes.

Among the last who came was the most important personage of all. This was the Governor of Mecca (as I believe he is called), the nearest descendant of the Prophet, and the successor to the Caliphate, in case the family of Othman becomes extinct. Sultan Mahmoud, on his accession to the throne, was the last descendant of Orchan, the founder of the Ottoman Dynasty, the throne being inherited only by the male heirs. He left two sons, who are both living, Abdul-Medjid having departed from the practice of his predecessors, each of whom slew his brothers, in order to make his own sovereignty secure. He has one son, Muzad, who is about ten years old, so that there are now three males of the family of Orchan. In case of their death, the Governor of Mecca would become Caliph, and the sovereignty would be established in his family. He is a swarthy Arab, of about fifty, with a bold, fierce face. He wore a superb dress of green, the sacred color, and was followed by his two sons, young men of twenty and twenty-two. As he advanced to the throne, and was about to kneel and kiss the Sultan's robe, the latter prevented him, and asked politely after his health--the highest mark of respect in his power to show. The old Arab's face gleamed with such a sudden gush of pride and satisfaction, that no flash of lightning could have illumined it more vividly.

The sacred writers, or transcribers of the Koran, closed the procession, after which the Sultan rose and entered the Seraglio. The crowd slowly dispersed, and in a few minutes the grand reports of the cannon on Seraglio Point announced the departure of the Sultan for his palace on the Bosphorus. The festival of Bairam was now fairly inaugurated, and all Stamboul was given up to festivity. There was no Turk so poor that he did not in some sort share in the rejoicing. Our Fourth could scarcely show more flags, let off more big guns or send forth greater crowds of excursionists than this Moslem holiday.

Chapter XXVIII. The Mosques of Constantinople.

Sojourn at Constantinople--Semi-European Character of the City--The Mosque--Procuring a Firman--The Seraglio--The Library--The Ancient Throne-Room--Admittance to St. Sophia--Magnificence of the Interior--The Marvellous Dome--The Mosque of Sultan Achmed--The Sulemanye--Great Conflagrations--Political Meaning of the Fires--Turkish Progress--Decay of the Ottoman Power.

"Is that indeed Sophia's far-famed dome,

Where first the Faith was led in triumph home,

Like some high bride, with banner and bright sign,

And melody, and flowers?" Audrey de Vere.

Constantinople, *Tuesday, August* 8, 1852.

The length of my stay in Constantinople has enabled me to visit many interesting spots in its vicinity, as well as to familiarize myself with the peculiar features of the great capital. I have seen the beautiful Bosphorus from steamers and caïques; ridden up the valley of Buyukdere, and through the chestnut woods of Belgrade; bathed in the Black Sea, under the lee of the Symplegades, where the marble altar to Apollo still invites an oblation from passing mariners; walked over the flowery meadows beside the "Heavenly Waters of Asia;" galloped around the ivy-grown walls where Dandolo and Mahomet II. conquered, and the last of the Palæologi fell; and dreamed away many an afternoon-hour under the funereal cypresses of Pera, and beside the Delphian tripod in the Hippodrome. The historic interest of these spots is familiar to all, nor; with one exception, have their natural beauties been exaggerated by travellers. This exception is the village of Belgrade, over which Mary Montague went into raptures, and set the fashion for tourists ever since. I must confess to having been wofully disappointed. The village is a miserable cluster of rickety houses, on an open piece of barren land, surrounded by the forests, or rather thickets, which keep alive the springs that supply

Constantinople with water. We reached there with appetites sharpened by our morning's ride, expecting to find at least a vender of kibabs (bits of fried meat) in so renowned a place; but the only things to be had were raw salt mackerel, and bread which belonged to the primitive geological formation.

The general features of Constantinople and the Bosphorus are so well known, that I am spared the dangerous task of painting scenes which have been colored by abler pencils. Von Hammer, Lamartine, Willis, Miss Pardoe, Albert Smith, and thou, most inimitable Thackeray! have made Pera and Scutari, the Bazaars and Baths, the Seraglio and the Golden Horn, as familiar to our ears as Cornhill and Wall street. Besides, Constantinople is not the true Orient, which is to be found rather in Cairo, in Aleppo, and brightest and most vital, in Damascus. Here, we tread European soil; the Franks are fast crowding out the followers of the Prophet, and Stamboul itself, were its mosques and Seraglio removed, would differ little in outward appearance from a third-rate Italian town. The Sultan lives in a palace with a Grecian portico; the pointed Saracenic arch, the arabesque sculptures, the latticed balconies, give place to clumsy imitations of Palladio, and every fire that sweeps away a recollection of the palmy times of Ottoman rule, sweeps it away forever.

But the Mosque--that blossom of Oriental architecture, with its crowning domes, like the inverted bells of the lotus, and its reed-like minarets, its fountains and marble courts--can only perish with the faith it typifies. I, for one, rejoice that, so long as the religion of Islam exists (and yet, may its time be short!), no Christian model can shape its houses of worship. The minaret must still lift its airy tower for the muezzin; the dome must rise like a gilded heaven above the prayers of the Faithful, with its starry lamps and emblazoned phrases; the fountain must continue to pour its waters of purification. A reformation of the Moslem faith is impossible. When it begins to give way, the whole fabric must fall. Its ceremonies, as well as its creed, rest entirely on the recognition of Mahomet as the Prophet of God. However the Turks may change in other respects, in all that concerns their religion they must continue the same.

Until within a few years, a visit to the mosques, especially the more sacred ones of St. Sophia and Sultan Achmed, was attended with much difficulty.

Miss Pardoe, according to her own account, risked her life in order to see the interior of St. Sophia, which she effected in the disguise of a Turkish Effendi. I accomplished the same thing, a few days since, but without recourse to any such romantic expedient. Mr. Brown, the interpreter of the Legation, procured a firman from the Grand Vizier, on behalf of the officers of the San Jacinto, and kindly invited me, with several other American and English travellers, to join the party. During the month of Ramazan, no firmans are given, and as at this time there are few travellers in Constantinople, we should otherwise have been subjected to a heavy expense. The cost of a firman, including backsheesh to the priests and doorkeepers, is 700 piastres (about $33).

We crossed the Golden Horn in caïques, and first visited the gardens and palaces on Seraglio Point. The Sultan at present resides in his summer palace of Beshiktashe, on the Bosphorus, and only occupies the Serai Bornou, as it is called, during the winter months. The Seraglio covers the extremity of the promontory on which Constantinople is built, and is nearly three miles in circuit. The scattered buildings erected by different Sultans form in themselves a small city, whose domes and pointed turrets rise from amid groves of cypress and pine. The sea-wall is lined with kiosks, from whose cushioned windows there are the loveliest views of the European and Asian shores. The newer portion of the palace, where the Sultan now receives the ambassadors of foreign nations, shows the influence of European taste in its plan and decorations. It is by no means remarkable for splendor, and suffers by contrast with many of the private houses in Damascus and Aleppo. The building is of wood, the walls ornamented with detestable frescoes by modern Greek artists, and except a small but splendid collection of arms, and some wonderful specimens of Arabic chirography, there is nothing to interest the visitor.

In ascending to the ancient Seraglio, which was founded by Mahomet II., on the site of the palace of the Palæologi, we passed the Column of Theodosius, a plain Corinthian shaft, about fifty feet high. The Seraglio is now occupied entirely by the servants and guards, and the greater part of it shows a neglect amounting almost to dilapidation. The Saracenic corridors surrounding its courts are supported by pillars of marble, granite, and porphyry, the spoils of the Christian capital. We were allowed to walk about at leisure, and inspect the different compartments, except the library, which unfortunately was locked. This library was for a long time supposed to contain many lost treasures of ancient literature--among other things, the missing books of Livy--but the recent researches of Logothetos, the Prince of Samos, prove that there is little of value, among its manuscripts. Before the door hangs a wooden globe, which is supposed to be efficacious in neutralizing the influence of the Evil Eye. There are many ancient altars and fragments of pillars scattered about the courts, and the Turks have even commenced making a collection of antiquities, which, with the exception of two immense sarcophagi of red porphyry, contains nothing of value. They show, however, one of the brazen heads of the Delphian tripod in the Hippodrome, which, they say, Mahomet the Conqueror struck off with a single blow of his sword, on entering Constantinople.

The most interesting portion of the Seraglio is the ancient throne-room, now no longer used, but still guarded by a company of white eunuchs. The throne is an immense, heavy bedstead, the posts of which are thickly incrusted with rubies, turquoises, emeralds, and sapphires. There is a funnel-shaped chimney-piece in the room, a master-work of Benevenuto Cellini. There, half a century ago, the foreign ambassadors were presented, after having been bathed, fed, and clothed with a rich mantle in the outer apartments. They were ushered into the imperial presence, supported by a Turkish official on either side, in order that they might show no signs of breaking down under the load of awe and reverence they were supposed to feel. In the outer Court, adjoining the Sublime Porte, is the Chapel of the Empress Irene, now converted into an armory, which, for its size, is the most tasteful and picturesque collection of weapons I have ever seen. It is especially rich in Saracenic armor, and contains many superb casques of inlaid gold. In a large glass case in the chancel, one sees the keys of some thirty or forty cities, with the date of their capture. It is not likely that another will ever be added to the list.

We now passed out through the Sublime Porte, and directed our steps to the famous Aya Sophia--the temple dedicated by Justinian to the Divine Wisdom. The repairs made to the outer walls by the Turks, and the addition of the four minarets, have entirely changed the character of the building, without injuring its effect. As a Christian Church, it must have been less imposing than in its present form. A priest met us at the entrance, and after reading the firman with a very discontented face, informed us that we could not enter until the mid-day prayers were concluded. After taking off our shoes, however, we were allowed to ascend to the galleries, whence we looked down on the bowing worshippers. Here the majesty of the renowned edifice, despoiled as it now is, bursts at once upon the eye. The wonderful flat dome, glittering with its golden mosaics, and the sacred phrase from the Koran: "God is the Light of the Heavens and the Earth," swims in the air, one hundred and eighty feet above the marble pavement. On the eastern and western sides, it rests on two half domes; which again rise from or rest upon a group of three small half-domes, so that the entire roof of the mosque, unsupported by a pillar, seems to have been dropped from above on the walls, rather than to have been built up from them. Around the edifice run an upper and a lower gallery, which alone preserve the peculiarities of the Byzantine style. These galleries are supported by the most precious columns which ancient art could afford: among them eight shafts of green marble, from the Temple of Diana, at Ephesus; eight of porphyry, from the Temple of the Sun, at Baalbek; besides Egyptian granite from the shrines of Isis and Osiris, and Pentelican marble from the sanctuary of Pallas Athena. Almost the whole of the interior has been covered with gilding, but time has softened its brilliancy, and the rich, subdued gleam of the walls is in perfect harmony with the varied coloring of the ancient marbles.

Under the dome, four Christian seraphim, executed in mosaic, have been allowed to remain, but the names of the four archangels of the Moslem faith are inscribed underneath. The bronze doors are still the same, the Turks having taken great pains to obliterate the crosses with which they were adorned. Around the centre of the dome, as on that of Sultan Achmed, may be read, in golden letters, and in all the intricacy of Arabic penmanship, the beautiful verse:--"God is the Light of the Heavens and the Earth. His wisdom is a light on the wall, in which burns a lamp covered with glass. The glass shines like a star, the lamp is lit with the oil of a blessed tree. No Eastern, no Western oil, it shines for whoever wills." After the prayers were over, and we had descended to the floor of the mosque, I spent the rest of my time under the dome, fascinated by its marvellous lightness and beauty. The worshippers present looked at us with curiosity, but without ill-will; and before we left, one of the priests came slyly with some fragments of the ancient gilded mosaic, which, he was heathen enough to sell, and we to buy.

From St. Sophia we went to Sultan Achmed, which faces the Hippodrome, and is one of the stateliest piles of Constantinople. It is avowedly an imitation of St. Sophia, and the Turks consider it a more wonderful work, because the dome is seven feet higher. It has six minarets, exceeding in this respect all the mosques of Asia. The dome rests on four immense pillars, the bulk of which quite oppresses the light galleries running around the walls. This, and the uniform white color of the interior, impairs the effect which its bold style and imposing dimensions would otherwise produce. The outside view, with the group of domes swelling grandly above the rows of broad-armed sycamores, is much more satisfactory. In the tomb of Sultan Achmed, in one corner of the court, we saw his coffin, turban, sword, and jewelled harness. I had just been reading old Sandys' account of his visit to Constantinople, in 1610, during this Sultan's reign, and could only think of him as Sandys represents him, in the title-page to his book, as a fat man, with bloated cheeks, in a long gown and big turban, and the words underneath:-- "Achmed, sive Tyrannus."

The other noted mosques of Constantinople are the Yeni Djami, or Mosque of the Sultana Valide, on the shore of the Golden Horn, at the end of the bridge to Galata; that of Sultan Bajazet; of Mahomet II., the Conqueror, and of his son, Suleyman the Magnificent, whose superb mosque well deserves this title. I regret exceedingly that our time did not allow us to view the interior, for outwardly it not only surpasses St. Sophia, and all other mosques in the city, but is undoubtedly one of the purest specimens of Oriental architecture extant. It stands on a broad terrace, on one of the seven hills of Stamboul, and its exquisitely proportioned domes and minarets shine as if crystalized in the blue of the air. It is a type of Oriental, as the Parthenon is of Grecian, and the Cologne Cathedral of Gothic art. As I saw it the other night, lit by the flames of a conflagration, standing out red and clear against the darkness, I felt inclined to place it on a level with either of those renowned structures. It is a product of the rich fancy of the East, splendidly ornate, and not without a high degree of symmetry--yet here the symmetry is that of ornament alone, and not the pure, absolute proportion of forms, which we find in Grecian Art. It requires a certain degree of enthusiasm--nay, a slight inebriation of the imaginative faculties--in order to feel the sentiment of this Oriental Architecture. If I rightly express all that it says to me, I touch the verge of rapsody. The East, in almost all its aspects, is so essentially poetic, that a true picture of it must be poetic in spirit, if not in form.

Constantinople has been terribly ravaged by fires, no less than fifteen having occurred during the past two weeks. Almost every night the sky has been reddened by burning houses, and the minarets of the seven hills lighted with an illumination brighter than that of the Bairam. All the space from the Hippodrome to the Sea of Marmora has been swept away; the lard, honey, and oil magazines on the Golden Horn, with the bazaars adjoining; several large blocks on the hill of Galata, with the College of the Dancing Dervishes; a part of Scutari, and the College of the Howling Dervishes, all have disappeared; and to-day, the ruins of 3,700 houses, which were destroyed last night, stand smoking in the Greek quarter, behind the aqueduct of Valens. The entire amount of buildings consumed in these two weeks is estimated at between five and six thousand! The fire on the hill of Galata threatened to destroy a great part of the suburb of Pera. It came, sweeping over the brow of the hill, towards my hotel, turning the tall cypresses in the burial ground into shafts of angry flame, and eating away the crackling dwellings of hordes of hapless Turks. I was in bed; from a sudden attack of fever, but seeing the other guests packing up their effects and preparing to leave, I was obliged to do the same; and this, in my weak state, brought on such a perspiration that the ailment left me, The officers of the United States steamer San Jacinto, and the French frigate Charlemagne, came to the rescue with their men and fire-engines, and the flames were finally quelled. The proceedings of the Americans, who cut holes in the roofs and played through them upon the fires within, were watched by the Turks with stupid amazement. "Máshallah!" said a fat Bimbashi, as he stood sweltering in the heat; "The Franks are a wonderful people."

To those initiated into the mysteries of Turkish politics, these fires are

574

more than accidental; they have a most weighty significance. They indicate either a general discontent with the existing state of affairs, or else a powerful plot against the Sultan and his Ministry. Setting fire to houses is, in fact, the Turkish method of holding an "indignation meeting," and from the rate with which they are increasing, the political crisis must be near at hand. The Sultan, with his usual kindness of heart, has sent large quantities of tents and other supplies to the guiltless sufferers; but no amount of kindness can soften the rancor of these Turkish intrigues. Reschid Pasha, the present Grand Vizier, and the leader of the party of Progress, is the person against whom this storm of opposition is now gathering.

In spite of all efforts, the Ottoman Power is rapidly wasting away. The life of the Orient is nerveless and effete; the native strength of the race has died out, and all attempts to resuscitate it by the adoption of European institutions produce mere galvanic spasms, which leave it more exhausted than before. The rosy-colored accounts we have had of Turkish Progress are for the most part mere delusions. The Sultan is a well-meaning but weak man, and tyrannical through his very weakness. Had he strength enough to break through the meshes of falsehood and venality which are woven so close about him, he might accomplish some solid good. But Turkish rule, from his ministers down to the lowest cadi, is a monstrous system of deceit and corruption. These people have not the most remote conception of the true aims of government; they only seek to enrich themselves and their parasites, at the expense of the people and the national treasury. When we add to this the conscript system, which is draining the provinces of their best Moslem subjects, to the advantage of the Christians and Jews, and the blindness of the Revenue Laws, which impose on domestic manufactures double the duty levied on foreign products, it will easily be foreseen that the next half-century, or less, will completely drain the Turkish Empire of its last lingering energies.

Already, in effect, Turkey exists only through the jealousy of the European nations. The treaty of Unkiar-iskelessi, in 1833, threw her into the hands of Russia, although the influence of England has of late years reigned almost exclusively in her councils. These are the two powers who are lowering at each other with sleepless eyes, in the Dardanelles and the Bosphorus. The people, and most probably the government, is strongly preposessed in favor of the English; but the Russian Bear has a heavy paw, and when he puts it into the scale, all other weights kick the beam. It will be a long and wary struggle, and no man can prophecy the result. The Turks are a people easy to govern, were even the imperfect laws, now in existence, fairly administered. They would thrive and improve under a better state of things; but I cannot avoid the conviction that the regeneration of the East will never be effected at their hands.

Chapter XXIX. Farewell to the Orient--Malta.

Embarcation--Farewell to the Orient--Leaving Constantinople--A Wreck--The Dardanelles--Homeric Scenery--Smyrna Revisited--The Grecian Isles--Voyage to Malta--Detention--La Valetta--The Maltese--The Climate--A Boat for Sicily.

"Farewell, ye mountains,

By glory crowned

Ye sacred fountains

Of Gods renowned;

Ye woods and highlands,

Where heroes dwell;

Ye seas and islands,

Farewell! Farewell!"

Frithiof's Saga.

In The Dardanelles, *Saturday, August* 7, 1852.

At last, behold me fairly embarked for Christian Europe, to which I bade adieu in October last, eager for the unknown wonders of the Orient. Since then, nearly ten months have passed away, and those wonders are now familiar as every-day experiences. I set out, determined to be satisfied with no slight taste of Eastern life, but to drain to the bottom its beaker of mingled sunshine and sleep. All this has been accomplished; and if I have not wandered so far, nor enriched myself with such varied knowledge of the relics of ancient history, as I might have purposed or wished, I have at least learned to know the Turk and the Arab, been soothed by the patience inspired by their fatalism, and warmed by the gorgeous gleams of fancy that animate their poetry and religion. These ten months of my life form an episode which seems to belong to a separate existence. Just refined enough to be poetic, and just barbaric enough to be freed from all conventional fetters, it is as grateful to brain and soul, as an Eastern bath to the body. While I look forward, not without pleasure, to the luxuries and conveniences of Europe, I relinquish with a sigh the refreshing indolence of Asia.

We have passed between the Castles of the two Continents, guarding the mouth of the Dardanelles, and are now entering the Grecian Sea. To-morrow, we shall touch, for a few hours, at Smyrna, and then turn westward, on the track of Ulysses and St. Paul. Farewell, then, perhaps forever, to the bright Orient! Farewell to the gay gardens, the spicy bazaars, to the plash of fountains and the gleam of golden-tipped minarets! Farewell to the perfect morn's, the balmy twilights, the still heat of the blue noons, the splendor of moon and stars! Farewell to the glare of the white crags, the tawny wastes of dead sand, the valleys of oleander, the hills of myrtle and spices! Farewell to the bath, agent of purity and peace, and parent of delicious dreams--to the shebook, whose fragrant fumes are breathed from the lips of patience and contentment--to the narghileh, crowned with that blessed plant which grows in the gardens of Shiraz, while a fountain more delightful than those of Samarcand bubbles in its crystal bosom I Farewell to the red cap and slippers, to the big turban, the flowing trousers, and the gaudy shawl--to squatting on broad divans, to sipping black coffee in acorn cups, to grave faces and salaam aleikooms, and to aching of the lips and forehead! Farewell to the evening meal in the tent door, to the couch on the friendly earth, to the yells of the muleteers, to the deliberate marches of the plodding horse, and the endless rocking of the dromedary that knoweth his master! Farewell, finally, to annoyance without anger, delay without vexation, indolence without ennui, endurance without fatigue, appetite without intemperance, enjoyment without pall!

La Valetta, Malta, Saturday, August 14, 1852.

My last view of Stamboul was that of the mosques of St. Sophia and Sultan Achmed, shining faintly in the moonlight, as we steamed down the Sea of Marmora. The Caire left at nine o'clock, freighted with the news of Reschid Pasha's deposition, and there were no signs of conflagration in all the long miles of the city that lay behind us. So we speculated no more on the exciting topics of the day, but went below and took a vapor bath in our berths; for I need not assure you that the nights on the Mediterranean at this season are anything but chilly. And here I must note the fact, that the French steamers, while dearer than the Austrian, are more cramped in their accommodations, and filled with a set of most uncivil servants. The table is good, and this is the only thing to be commended. In all other respects, I prefer the Lloyd vessels.

Early next morning, we passed the promontory of Cyzicus, and the Island of Marmora, the marble quarries of which give name to the sea. As we were approaching the entrance to the Dardanelles, we noticed an Austrian brig drifting in the current, the whiff of her flag indicating distress. Her rudder was entirely gone, and she was floating helplessly towards the Thracian coast. A boat was immediately lowered and a hawser carried to her bows, by which we towed her a short distance; but our steam engine did not like this drudgery, and snapped the rope repeatedly, so that at last we were obliged to leave her to her fate. The lift we gave, however, had its effect, and by dexterous maneuvering with the sails, the captain brought her safely into the harbor of Gallipoli, where she dropped anchor beside us.

Beyond Gallipoli, the Dardanelles contract, and the opposing continents rise into lofty and barren hills. In point of natural beauty, this strait is greatly inferior to the Bosphorus. It lacks the streams and wooded valleys which open upon the latter. The country is but partially cultivated, except around the town of Dardanelles, near the mouth of the strait. The site of the bridge of Xerxes is easily recognized, the conformation of the different shores seconding the decision of antiquarians. Here, too, are Sestos and Abydos, of passionate and poetic memory. But as the sun dipped towards the sea, we passed out of the narrow gateway. On our left lay the plain of Troy, backed by the blue range of Mount Ida. The tamulus of Patroclus crowned a low bluff looking on the sea. On the right appeared the long, irregular island of Imbros, and the peaks of misty Samothrace over and beyond it. Tenedos was before us. The red flush of sunset tinged the grand Homeric landscape, and lingered and lingered on the summit of Ida, as if loth to depart. I paced the deck until long after it was too dark to distinguish it any more.

The next morning we dropped anchor in the harbor of Smyrna, where we remained five hours. I engaged a donkey, and rode out to the Caravan Bridge, where the Greek driver and I smoked narghilehs and drank coffee in the shade of the acacias. I contrasted my impressions with those of my first visit to Smyrna last October--my first glimpse of Oriental ground. Then, every dog barked at me, and all the horde of human creatures who prey upon innocent travellers ran at my heels, but now, with my brown face and Turkish aspect of grave indifference, I was suffered to pass as quietly as my donkey-driver himself. Nor did the latter, nor the ready cafidji, who filled our pipes on the banks of the Meles, attempt to overcharge me--a sure sign that the Orient had left its seal on my face. Returning through the city, the same mishap befel me which travellers usually experience on their first arrival. My donkey, while dashing at full speed through a crowd of Smyrniotes in their Sunday dresses, slipped up in a little pool of black mud, and came down with a crash. I flew over his head and alighted firmly on my feet, but the spruce young Greeks, whose snowy fustanelles were terribly bespattered, came off much worse. The donkey shied back, levelled his ears and twisted his head on one side, awaiting a beating, but his bleeding legs saved him.

We left at two o'clock, touched at Scio in the evening, and the next morning at sunrise lay-to in the harbor of Syra. The Piræus was only twelve hours distant; but after my visitation of fever in Constantinople, I feared to encounter the pestilential summer heats of Athens. Besides, I had reasons for hastening with all speed to Italy and Germany. At ten o'clock we weighed anchor again and steered southwards, between the groups of the Cyclades, under a cloudless sky and over a sea of the brightest blue. The days were endurable under the canvas awning of our quarter-deck, but the nights in our berths were sweat-baths, which left us so limp and exhausted that we were almost fit to vanish, like ghosts, at daybreak.

Our last glimpse of the Morea--Cape Matapan--faded away in the moonlight, and for two days we travelled westward over the burning sea. On the evening of the 11th, the long, low outline of Malta rose gradually against the last flush of sunset, and in two hours thereafter, we came to anchor in Quarantine Harbor. The quarantine for travellers returning from the East, which formerly varied from fourteen to twenty-one days, is now reduced to one day for those arriving from Greece or Turkey, and three days for those from Egypt and Syria. In our case, it was reduced to sixteen hours, by an official courtesy. I had intended proceeding directly to Naples; but by the contemptible trickery of the agents of the French steamers--a long history, which it is unnecessary to recapitulate--am left here to wait ten days for another steamer. It is enough to say that there are six other travellers at the same hotel, some coming from Constantinople, and some from Alexandria, in the same predicament. Because a single ticket to Naples costs some thirty or forty francs less than by dividing the trip into two parts, the agents in those cities refuse to give tickets further than Malta to those who are not keen enough to see through the deception. I made every effort to obtain a second ticket in time to leave by the branch steamer for Italy, but in vain.

La Valetta is, to my eyes, the most beautiful small city in the world. It is a jewel of a place; not a street but is full of picturesque effects, and all the look-outs, which you catch at every turn, let your eyes rest either upon one of the beautiful harbors on each side, or the distant horizon of the sea. The streets are so clean that you might eat your dinner off the pavement; the white balconies and cornices of the houses, all cleanly cut in the soft Maltese stone, stand out in intense relief against the sky, and from the manifold reflections and counter reflections, the shadows (where there are any) become a sort of milder light. The steep sides of the promontory, on which the city is built, are turned into staircases, and it is an inexhaustible pastime to watch the groups, composed of all nations who inhabit the shores of the Mediterranean, ascending and descending. The Auberges of the old Knights, the Palace of the Grand Master, the Church of St. John, and other relics of past time, but more especially the fortifications, invest the place with a romantic interest, and I suspect that, after Venice and Granada, there are few cities where the Middle Ages have left more impressive traces of their history.

The Maltese are contented, and appear to thrive under the English administration. They are a peculiar people, reminding me of the Arab even more than the Italian, while a certain rudeness in their build and motions suggests their Punic ancestry. Their language is a curious compound of Arabic and Italian, the former being the basis. I find that I can understand more than half that is said, the Arabic terminations being applied to Italian words. I believe it has never been successfully reduced to writing, and the restoration of pure Arabic has been proposed, with much reason, as preferable to an attempt to improve or refine it. Italian is the language used in the courts of justice and polite society, and is spoken here with much more purity than either in Naples or Sicily.

The heat has been so great since I landed that I have not ventured outside of the city, except last evening to an amateur theatre, got up by the non-commissioned officers and privates in the garrison. The performances were quite tolerable, except a love-sick young damsel who spoke with a rough masculine voice, and made long strides across the stage when she rushed into her lover's arms. I am at a loss to account for the exhausting character of the heat. The thermometer shows 90° by day, and 80° to 85° by night--a much lower temperature than I have found quite comfortable in Africa and Syria. In the Desert 100° in the shade is rather bracing than otherwise; here, 90° renders all exercise, more severe than smoking a pipe, impossible. Even in a state of complete inertia, a shirt-collar will fall starchless in five minutes.

Rather than waste eight more days in this glimmering half-existence, I have taken passage in a Maltese speronara, which sails this evening for Catania, in Sicily, where the grand festival of St. Agatha, which takes place once in a hundred years, will be celebrated next week. The trip promises a new experience, and I shall get a taste, slight though it be, of the golden Trinacria of the ancients. Perhaps, after all, this delay which so vexes me (bear in mind, I am no longer in the Orient!) may be meant solely for my good. At least, Mr. Winthrop, our Consul here, who has been exceedingly kind and courteous to me, thinks it a rare good fortune that I shall see the Catanian festa.

Chapter XXX. The Festival of St. Agatha.

Departure from Malta--The Speronara--Our Fellow-Passengers--The First Night on Board--Sicily--Scarcity of Provisions--Beating in the Calabrian Channel--The Fourth Morning--The Gulf of Catania--A Sicilian Landscape--The Anchorage--The Suspected List--The Streets of Catania--Biography of St. Agatha--The Illuminations--The Procession of the Veil--The Biscari Palace--The Antiquities of Catania--The Convent of St. Nicola.

"The morn is full of holiday, loud bells

With rival clamors ring from every spire;

Cunningly-stationed music dies and swells

In echoing places; when the winds respire,

Light flags stream out like gauzy tongues of fire."--Keats.

Catania, Sicily, *Friday, August* 20, 1852.

I went on board the speronara in the harbor of La Valetta at the appointed hour (5 P.M.), and found the remaining sixteen passengers already embarked. The captain made his appearance an hour later, with our bill of health and passports, and as the sun went down behind the brown hills of the island, we passed the wave-worn rocks of the promontory, dividing the two harbors, and slowly moved off towards Sicily.

The Maltese speronara resembles the ancient Roman galley more than any modern craft. It has the same high, curved poop and stern, the same short masts and broad, square sails. The hull is too broad for speed, but this adds to the security of the vessel in a gale. With a fair wind, it rarely makes more than eight knots an hour, and in a calm, the sailors (if not too lazy) propel it forward with six long oars. The hull is painted in a fanciful style, generally blue, red, green and white, with bright red masts. The bulwarks are low, and the deck of such a convexity that it is quite impossible to walk it in a heavy sea. Such was the vessel to which I found myself consigned. It was not more than fifty feet long, and of less capacity than a Nile dahabiyeh. There was a sort of deck cabin, or crib, with two berths, but most of the passengers slept in the hold. For a passage to Catania I was obliged to pay forty francs, the owner swearing that this was the regular price; but, as I afterwards discovered, the Maltese only paid thirty-six francs for the whole trip. However, the Captain tried to make up the money's worth in civilities, and was incessant in his attentions to "your Lordships," as he styled myself and my companion, Cæsar di Cagnola, a young Milanese.

The Maltese were tailors and clerks, who were taking a holiday trip to witness the great festival of St. Agatha. With two exceptions, they were a wild and senseless, though good-natured set, and in spite of sea-sickness, which exercised them terribly for the first two days, kept up a constant jabber in their bastard Arabic from morning till night. As is usual in such a company, one of them was obliged to serve as a butt for the rest, and "Maestro Paolo," as they termed him, wore such a profoundly serious face all the while, from his sea-sickness, that the fun never came to an end. As they were going to a religious festival, some of them had brought their breviaries along with them; but I am obliged to testify that, after the first day, prayers were totally forgotten. The sailors, however, wore linen bags, printed with a figure of the Madonna, around their necks.

The sea was rather rough, but Cæsar and I fortified our stomachs with a bottle of English ale, and as it was dark by this time, sought our resting-places for the night. As we had paid double, places were assured us in the coop on deck, but beds were not included in the bargain. The Maltese, who had brought mattresses and spread a large Phalansteriau bed in the hold, fared much better. I took one of my carpet bags for a pillow and lay down on the planks, where I succeeded in getting a little sleep between the groans of the helpless land-lubbers. We had the ponente, or west-wind, all night, but the speronara moved sluggishly, and in the morning it changed to the greco-levante, or north-east. No land was in sight; but towards noon, the sky became clearer, and we saw the southern coast of Sicily--a bold mountain-shore, looming phantom-like in the distance. Cape Passaro was to the east, and the rest of the day was spent in beating up to it. At sunset, we were near enough to see the villages and olive-groves of the beautiful shore, and, far behind the nearer mountains, ninety miles distant, the solitary cone of Etna.

The second night passed like the first, except that our bruised limbs were rather more sensitive to the texture of the planks. We crawled out of our coop at dawn, expecting to behold Catania in the distance; but there was Cape Passaro still staring us in the face. The Maltese were patient, and we did not complain, though Cæsar and I began to make nice calculations as to the probable duration of our two cold fowls and three loaves of bread. The promontory of Syracuse was barely visible forty miles ahead; but the wind was against us, and so another day passed in beating up the eastern coast. At dusk, we overtook another speronara which had left Malta two hours before us, and this was quite a triumph to our captain, All the oars were shipped, the sailors and some of the more courageous passengers took hold, and we shot ahead, scudding rapidly along the dark shores, to the sound of the wild Maltese songs. At length, the promontory was gained, and the restless current, rolling down from Scylla and Charybdis, tossed our little bark from wave to wave with a recklessness that would have made any one nervous but an old sailor like myself.

"To-morrow morning," said the Captain, "we shall sail into Catania;" but after a third night on the planks, which were now a little softer, we rose to find ourselves abreast of Syracuse, with Etna as distant as ever. The wind was light, and what little we made by tacking was swept away by the current, so that, after wasting the whole forenoon, we kept a straight course across the mouth of the channel, and at sunset saw the Calabrian Mountains. This move only lost us more ground, as it happened. Cæsar and I mournfully and silently consumed our last fragment of beef, with the remaining dry crusts of bread, and then sat down doggedly to smoke and see whether the captain would discover our situation. But no; while we were supplied, the whole vessel was at our Lordships' command, and now that we were destitute, he took care to make no rash offers. Cæsar, at last, with an imperial dignity becoming his name, commanded dinner. It came, and the pork and maccaroni, moistened with red Sicilian wine, gave us patience for another day.

The fourth morning dawned, and--Great Neptune be praised!--we were actually within the Gulf of Catania. Etna loomed up in all his sublime bulk, unobscured by cloud or mist, while a slender jet of smoke, rising from his crater, was slowly curling its wreaths in the clear air, as if happy to receive the first beam of the sun. The towers of Syracuse, which had mocked us all the preceding day, were no longer visible; the land-locked little port of Augusta lay behind us; and, as the wind continued favorable, ere long we saw a faint white mark at the foot of the mountain. This was Catania. The shores of the bay were enlivened with olive-groves and the gleam of the villages, while here and there a single palm dreamed of its brothers across the sea. Etna, of course, had the monarch's place in the landscape, but even his large, magnificent outlines could not usurp all my feeling. The purple peaks to the westward and farther inland, had a beauty of their own, and in the gentle curves with which they leaned towards each other, there was a promise of the flowery meadows of Enna. The smooth blue water was speckled with fishing-boats. We hailed one, inquiring when the festa was to commence; but, mistaking our question, they answered: "Anchovies." Thereupon, a waggish Maltese informed them that Maestro Paolo thanked them heartily. All the other boats were hailed in the name of Maestro Paolo, who, having recovered from his sea-sickness, took his bantering good-humoredly.

Catania presented a lovely picture, as we drew near the harbor. Planted at the very foot of Etna, it has a background such as neither Naples nor Genoa can boast. The hills next the sea are covered with gardens and orchards, sprinkled with little villages and the country palaces of the nobles--a rich, cultured landscape, which gradually merges into the forests of oak and chestnut that girdle the waist of the great volcano. But all the wealth of southern vegetation cannot hide the footsteps of that Ruin, which from time to time visits the soil. Half-way up, the mountain-side is dotted with cones of ashes and cinders, some covered with the scanty shrubbery which centuries have called forth, some barren and recent; while two dark, winding streams of sterile lava descend to the very shore, where they stand congealed in ragged needles and pyramids. Part of one of these black floods has swept the town, and, tumbling into the sea, walls one side of the port.

We glided slowly past the mole, and dropped anchor a few yards from the shore. There was a sort of open promenade planted with trees, in front of us, surrounded with high white houses, above which rose the dome of the Cathedral and the spires of other churches. The magnificent palace of Prince Biscari was on our right, and at its foot the Customs and Revenue offices. Every roof, portico, and window was lined with lamps, a triumphal arch spanned the street before the palace, and the landing-place at the offices was festooned with crimson and white drapery, spangled with gold. While we were waiting permission to land, a scene presented itself which recalled the pagan days of Sicily to my mind. A procession came in sight from under the trees, and passed along the shore. In the centre was borne a stately shrine, hung with garlands, and containing an image of St. Agatha. The sound of flutes and cymbals accompanied it, and a band of children, bearing orange and palm branches, danced riotously before. Had the image been Pan instead of St. Agatha, the ceremonies would have been quite as appropriate.

The speronara's boat at last took us to the gorgeous landing place, where we were carefully counted by a fat Sicilian official, and declared free from quarantine. We were then called into the Passport Office where the Maltese underwent a searching examination. One of the officers sat with the Black Book, or list of suspected persons of all nations, open before him, and looked for each name as it was called out. Another scanned the faces of the frightened tailors, as if comparing them with certain revolutionary visages in his mind. Terrible was the keen, detective glance of his eye, and it went straight through the poor Maltese, who vanished with great rapidity when they were declared free to enter the city. At last, they all passed the ordeal, but Cæsar and I remained, looking in at the door. "There are still these two Frenchmen," said the captain. "I am no Frenchman," I protested; "I am an American." "And I," said Cæsar, "am an Austrian subject." Thereupon we received a polite invitation to enter; the terrible glance softened into a benign, respectful smile; he of the Black Book ran lightly over the C's and T's, and said, with a courteous inclination: "There is nothing against the signori." I felt quite relieved by this; for, in the Mediterranean, one is never safe from spies, and no person is too insignificant to escape the ban, if once suspected.

Calabria was filled to overflowing with strangers from all parts of the Two

Sicilies, and we had some difficulty in finding very bad and dear lodgings. It was the first day of the festa, and the streets were filled with peasants, the men in black velvet jackets and breeches, with stockings, and long white cotton caps hanging on the shoulders, and the women with gay silk shawls on their heads, after the manner of the Mexican reboza. In all the public squares, the market scene in Masaniello was acted to the life. The Sicilian dialect is harsh and barbarous, and the original Italian is so disguised by the admixture of Arabic, Spanish, French, and Greek words, that even my imperial friend, who was a born Italian, had great difficulty in understanding the people.

I purchased a guide to the festa, which, among other things, contained a biography of St. Agatha. It is a beautiful specimen of pious writing, and I regret that I have not space to translate the whole of it. Agatha was a beautiful Catanian virgin, who secretly embraced Christianity during the reign of Nero. Catania was then governed by a prætor named Quintianus, who, becoming enamored of Agatha, used the most brutal means to compel her to submit to his desires, but without effect. At last, driven to the cruelest extremes, he cut off her breasts, and threw her into prison. But at midnight, St. Peter, accompanied by an angel, appeared to her, restored the maimed parts, and left her more beautiful than ever. Quintianus then ordered a furnace to be heated, and cast her therein. A terrible earthquake shook the city; the sun was eclipsed; the sea rolled backwards, and left its bottom dry; the prætor's palace fell in ruins, and he, pursued by the vengeance of the populace, fled till he reached the river Simeto, where he was drowned in attempting to cross. "The thunders of the vengeance of God," says the biography, "struck him down into the profoundest Hell." This was in the year 252.

The body was carried to Constantinople in 1040, "although the Catanians wept incessantly at their loss;" but in 1126, two French knights, named Gilisbert and Goselin, were moved by angelic influences to restore it to its native town, which they accomplished, "and the eyes of the Catanians again burned with joy." The miracles effected by the saint are numberless, and her power is especially efficacious in preventing earthquakes and eruptions of Mount Etna. Nevertheless, Catania has suffered more from these causes than any other town in Sicily. But I would that all saints had as good a claim to

588

canonization as St. Agatha. The honors of such a festival as this are not out of place, when paid to such youth, beauty, and "heavenly chastity," as she typifies.

The guide, which I have already consulted, gives a full account of the festa, in advance, with a description of Catania. The author says: "If thy heart is not inspired by gazing on this lovely city, it is a fatal sign--thou wert not born to feel the sweet impulses of the Beautiful!" Then, in announcing the illuminations and pyrotechnic displays, he exclaims: "Oh, the amazing spectacle! Oh, how happy art thou, that thou beholdest it! I What pyramids of lamps! What myriads of rockets! What wonderful temples of flame! The Mountain himself is astonished at such a display." And truly, except the illumination of the Golden Horn on the Night of Predestination, I have seen nothing equal to the spectacle presented by Catania, during the past three nights. The city, which has been built up from her ruins more stately than ever, was in a blaze of light--all her domes, towers, and the long lines of her beautiful palaces revealed in the varying red and golden flames of a hundred thousand lamps and torches. Pyramids of fire, transparencies, and illuminated triumphal arches filled the four principal streets, and the fountain in the Cathedral square gleamed like a jet of molten silver, spinning up from one of the pores of Etna. At ten o'clock, a gorgeous display of fireworks closed the day's festivities, but the lamps remained burning nearly all night.

On the second night, the grand Procession of the Veil took place. I witnessed this imposing spectacle from the balcony of Prince Gessina's palace. Long lines of waxen torches led the way, followed by a military band, and then a company of the highest prelates, in their most brilliant costumes, surrounding the Bishop, who walked under a canopy of silk and gold, bearing the miraculous veil of St. Agatha. I was blessed with a distant view of it, but could see no traces of the rosy hue left upon it by the flames of the Saint's martyrdom. Behind the priests came the Intendente of Sicily, Gen. Filangieri, the same who, three years ago, gave up Catania to sack and slaughter. He was followed by the Senate of the City, who have just had the cringing cowardice to offer him a ball on next Sunday night. If ever a man deserved the vengeance of an outraged people, it is this Filangieri, who was first a Liberal, when the cause promised success, and then made himself the scourge of the vilest of kings. As he passed me last night in his carriage of State, while the music pealed in rich rejoicing strains, that solemn chant with which the monks break upon the revellers, in "Lucrezia Borgia," came into my mind:

"La gioja del profani

'E un fumo passagier'--"

[the rejoicing of the profane is a transitory mist.] I heard, under the din of all these festivities, the voice of that Retribution which even now lies in wait, and will not long be delayed.

To-night Signor Scavo, the American Vice-Consul, took me to the palace of Prince Biscari, overlooking the harbor, in order to behold the grand display of fireworks from the end of the mole. The showers of rockets and colored stars, and the temples of blue and silver fire, were repeated in the dark, quiet bosom of the sea, producing the most dazzling and startling effects. There was a large number of the Catanese nobility present, and among them a Marchesa Gioveni, the descendant of the bloody house of Anjou. Prince Biscari is a benign, courtly old man, and greatly esteemed here. His son is at present in exile, on account of the part he took in the late revolution. During the sack of the city under Filangieri, the palace was plundered of property to the amount of ten thousand dollars. The museum of Greek and Roman antiquities attached to it, and which the house of Biscari has been collecting for many years, is probably the finest in Sicily. The state apartments were thrown open this evening, and when I left, an hour ago, the greater portion of the guests were going through mazy quadrilles on the mosaic pavements.

Among the antiquities of Catania which I have visited, are the Amphitheatre, capable of holding 15,000 persons, the old Greek Theatre, the same in which Alcibiades made his noted harangue to the Catanians, the Odeon, and the ancient Baths. The theatre, which is in tolerable preservation, is built of lava, like many of the modern edifices in the city. The Baths proved to me, what I had supposed, that the Oriental Bath of the present day is identical with that of the Ancients. Why so admirable an institution has never been introduced into Europe (except in the Bains Chinois of Paris) is more than I can tell. From the pavement of these baths, which is nearly twenty feet below the surface of the earth, the lava of later eruptions has burst up, in places, in hard black jets. The most wonderful token of that flood which whelmed Catania two hundred years ago, is to be seen at the Grand Benedictine Convent of San Nicola, in the upper part of the city. Here the stream of lava divides itself just before the Convent, and flows past on both sides, leaving the building and gardens untouched. The marble courts, the fountains, the splendid galleries, and the gardens of richest southern bloom and fragrance, stand like an epicurean island in the midst of the terrible stony waves, whose edges bristle with the thorny aloe and cactus. The monks of San Nicola are all chosen from the Sicilian nobility, and live a comfortable life of luxury and vice. Each one has his own carriage, horses, and servants, and each his private chambers outside of the convent walls and his kept concubines. These facts are known and acknowledged by the Catanians, to whom they are a lasting scandal.

It is past midnight, and I must close. Cæsar started this afternoon, alone, for the ascent of Etna. I would have accompanied him, but my only chance of reaching Messina in time for the next steamer to Naples is the diligence which leaves here to-morrow. The mountain has been covered with clouds for the last two days, and I have had no view at all comparable to that of the morning of my arrival. To-morrow the grand procession of the Body of St. Agatha takes place, but I am quite satisfied with three days of processions and horse races, and three nights of illuminations.

I leave in the morning, with a Sicilian passport, my own availing me nothing, after landing.

Chapter XXXI. The Eruption of Mount Etna.

The Mountain Threatens--The Signs Increase--We Leave Catania--Gardens Among the Lava--Etna Labors--Aci Reale--The Groans of Etna--The Eruption--Gigantic Tree of Smoke--Formation of the New Crater--We Lose Sight of the Mountain--Arrival at Messina--Etna is Obscured--Departure.

-------"the shattered side

Of thundering Ætna, whose combustible

And fuel'd entrails thence conceiving fire,

Sublimed with mineral fury, aid the winds,

And leave a singed bottom." Milton.

Messina, Sicily, *Monday, August* 23, 1852.

The noises of the festival had not ceased when I closed my letter at midnight, on Friday last. I slept soundly through the night, but was awakened before sunrise by my Sicilian landlord. "O, Excellenza! have you heard the Mountain? He is going to break out again; may the holy Santa Agatha protect us!" It is rather ill-timed on the part of the Mountain, was my involuntary first thought, that he should choose for a new eruption precisely the centennial festival of the only Saint who is supposed to have any power over him. It shows a disregard of female influence not at all suited to the present day, and I scarcely believe that he seriously means it. Next came along the jabbering landlady: "I don't like his looks. It was just so the last time. Come, Excellenza, you can see him from the back terrace." The sun was not yet risen, but the east was bright with his coming, and there was not a cloud in the sky. All the features of Etna were sharply sculptured in the clear air. From the topmost cone, a thick stream of white smoke was slowly puffed out at short intervals, and rolled lazily down the eastern side. It had a heavy, languid character, and I should have thought nothing of the appearance but for the alarm of my hosts. It was like the slow fire of Earth's incense, burning on that grand mountain altar.

I hurried off to the Post Office, to await the arrival of the diligence from Palermo. The office is in the Strada Etnea, the main street of Catania, which runs straight through the city, from the sea to the base of the mountain, whose peak closes the long vista. The diligence was an hour later than usual, and I passed the time in watching the smoke which continued to increase in volume, and was mingled, from time to time, with jets of inky blackness. The postilion said he had seen fires and heard loud noises during the night. According to his account, the disturbances commenced about midnight. I could not but envy my friend Cæsar, who was probably at that moment on the summit, looking down into the seething fires of the crater.

At last, we rolled out of Catania. There were in the diligence, besides myself, two men and a woman, Sicilians of the secondary class. The road followed the shore, over rugged tracts of lava, the different epochs of which could be distinctly traced in the character of the vegetation. The last great flow (of 1679) stood piled in long ridges of terrible sterility, barely allowing the aloe and cactus to take root in the hollows between. The older deposits were sufficiently decomposed to nourish the olive and vine; but even here, the orchards were studded with pyramids of the harder fragments, which are laboriously collected by the husbandmen. In the few favored spots which have been untouched for so many ages that a tolerable depth of soil has accumulated, the vegetation has all the richness and brilliancy of tropical lands. The palm, orange, and pomegranate thrive luxuriantly, and the vines almost break under their heavy clusters. The villages are frequent and well built, and the hills are studded, far and near, with the villas of rich proprietors, mostly buildings of one story, with verandahs extending their whole length. Looking up towards Etna, whose base the road encircles, the views are gloriously rich and beautiful. On the other hand is the blue Mediterranean and the irregular outline of the shore, here and there sending forth promontories of lava, cooled by the waves into the most fantastic forms.

We had sot proceeded far before a new sign called my attention to the mountain. Not only was there a perceptible jar or vibration in the earth, but a dull, groaning sound, like the muttering of distant thunder, began to be heard. The smoke increased in volume, and, as we advanced further to the eastward, and much nearer to the great cone, I perceived that it consisted of two jets, issuing from different mouths. A broad stream of very dense white smoke still flowed over the lip of the topmost crater and down the eastern side. As its breadth did not vary, and the edges were distinctly defined, it was no doubt the sulphureous vapor rising from a river of molten lava. Perhaps a thousand yards below, a much stronger column of mingled black and white smoke gushed up, in regular beats or pants, from a depression in the mountain side, between two small, extinct cones. All this part of Etna was scarred with deep chasms, and in the bottoms of those nearest the opening, I could see the red gleam of fire. The air was perfectly still, and as yet there was no cloud in the sky.

When we stopped to change horses at the town of Aci Reale, I first felt the violence of the tremor and the awful sternness of the sound. The smoke by this time seemed to be gathering on the side towards Catania, and hung in a dark mass about half-way down the mountain. Groups of the villagers were gathered in the streets which looked upwards to Etna, and discussing the chances of an eruption. "Ah," said an old peasant, "the Mountain knows how to make himself respected. When he talks, everybody listens." The sound was the most awful that ever met my ears. It was a hard, painful moan, now and then fluttering like a suppressed sob, and had, at the same time, an expression of threatening and of agony. It did not come from Etna alone. It had no fixed location; it pervaded all space. It was in the air, in the depths of the sea, in the earth under my feet--everywhere, in fact; and as it continued to increase in violence, I experienced a sensation of positive pain. The people looked anxious and alarmed, although they said it was a good thing for all Sicily; that last year they had been in constant fear from earthquakes, and that an eruption invariably left the island quiet for several years. It is true that, during the past year, parts of Sicily and Calabria have been visited with severe shocks, occasioning much damage to property. A merchant of this city informed me yesterday that his whole family had slept for two months in the vaults of his warehouse, fearing that their residence might be shaken down in the night.

As we rode along from Aci Reale to Taormina, all the rattling of the diligence over the rough road could not drown the awful noise. There was a strong smell of sulphur in the air, and the thick pants of smoke from the lower crater continued to increase in strength. The sun was fierce and hot, and the edges of the sulphureous clouds shone with a dazzling whiteness. A mounted soldier overtook us, and rode beside the diligence, talking with the postillion. He had been up to the mountain, and was taking his report to the Governor of the district. The heat of the day and the continued tremor of the air lulled me into a sort of doze, when I was suddenly aroused by a cry from the soldier and the stopping of the diligence. At the same time, there was a terrific peal of sound, followed by a jar which must have shaken the whole island. We looked up to Etna, which was fortunately in full view before us. An immense mass of snow-white smoke had burst up from the crater and was rising perpendicularly into the air, its rounded volumes rapidly whirling one over the other, yet urged with such impetus that they only rolled outwards after they had ascended to an immense height. It might have been one minute or five--for I was so entranced by this wonderful spectacle that I lost the sense of time--but it seemed instantaneous (so rapid and violent were the effects of the explosion), when there stood in the air, based on the summit of the mountain, a mass of smoke four or five miles high, and shaped precisely like the Italian pine tree.

Words cannot paint the grandeur of this mighty tree. Its trunk of columned smoke, one side of which was silvered by the sun, while the other, in shadow, was lurid with red flame, rose for more than a mile before it sent out its cloudy boughs. Then parting into a thousand streams, each of which again threw out its branching tufts of smoke, rolling and waving in the air, it stood in intense relief against the dark blue of the sky. Its rounded masses of foliage were dazzlingly white on one side, while, in the shadowy depths of the branches, there was a constant play of brown, yellow, and crimson tints, revealing the central shaft of fire. It was like the tree celebrated in the Scandinavian sagas, as seen by the mother of Harold Hardrada--that tree, whose roots pierced through the earth, whose trunk was of the color of blood, and whose branches filled the uttermost corners of the heavens.

This outburst seemed to have relieved the mountain, for the tremors were now less violent, though the terrible noise still droned in the air, and earth, and sea. And now, from the base of the tree, three white streams slowly crept into as many separate chasms, against the walls of which played the flickering glow of the burning lava. The column of smoke and flame was still hurled upwards, and the tree, after standing about ten minutes--a new and awful revelation of the active forces of Nature--gradually rose and spread, lost its form, and, slowly moved by a light wind (the first that disturbed the dead calm of the day), bent over to the eastward. We resumed our course. The vast belt of smoke at last arched over the strait, here about twenty miles wide, and sank towards the distant Calabrian shore. As we drove under it, for some miles of our way, the sun was totally obscured, and the sky presented the singular spectacle of two hemispheres of clear blue, with a broad belt of darkness drawn between them. There was a hot, sulphureous vapor in the air, and showers of white ashes fell, from time to time. We were distant about twelve miles, in a straight line, from the crater; but the air was so clear, even under the shadow of the smoke, that I could distinctly trace the downward movement of the rivers of lava.

This was the eruption, at last, to which all the phenomena of the morning had been only preparatory. For the first time in ten years the depths of Etna had been stirred, and I thanked God for my detention at Malta, and the singular hazard of travel which had brought me here, to his very base, to witness a scene, the impression of which I shall never lose, to my dying day. Although the eruption may continue and the mountain pour forth fiercer fires and broader tides of lava, I cannot but think that the first upheaval, which lets out the long-imprisoned forces, will not be equalled in grandeur by any later spectacle. After passing Taormina, our road led us under the hills of the coast, and although I occasionally caught glimpses of Etna, and saw the reflection of fires from the lava which was filling up his savage ravines, the smoke at last encircled his waist, and he was then shut out of sight by the intervening mountains. We lost a bolt in a deep valley opening on the sea, and during our stoppage I could still hear the groans of the Mountain, though farther off and less painful to the ear. As evening came on, the beautiful hills of Calabria, with white towns and villages on their sides, gleamed in the purple light of the setting sun. We drove around headland after headland, till the strait opened, and we looked over the harbor of Messina to Capo Faro, and the distant islands of the Tyrrhene Sea.

I leave this afternoon for Naples and Leghorn. I have lost already so much time between Constantinople and this place, that I cannot give up ten days more to Etna. Besides, I am so thoroughly satisfied with what I have seen, that I fear no second view of the eruption could equal it. Etna cannot be seen from here, nor from a nearer point than a mountain six or eight miles distant. I tried last evening to get a horse and ride out to it, in order to see the appearance of the eruption by night; but every horse, mule and donkey in the place was engaged, except a miserable lame mule, for which five dollars was demanded. However, the night happened to be cloudy so that I could have seen nothing.

My passport is finally en règle. It has cost the labors of myself and an able-bodied valet-de-place since yesterday morning, and the expenditure of five dollars and a half, to accomplish this great work. I have just been righteously abusing the Neapolitan Government to a native merchant whom, from his name, I took to be a Frenchman, but as I am off in an hour or two, hope to escape arrest. Perdition to all Tyranny!

Chapter XXXII. Gibraltar.

Unwritten Links of Travel--Departure from Southampton--The Bay of Biscay--Cintra--Trafalgar--Gibraltar at Midnight--Landing--Search for a Palm-Tree--A Brilliant Morning--The Convexity of the Earth--Sun-Worship--The Rock.

------"to the north-west, Cape St. Vincent died away,

Sunset ran, a burning blood-red, blushing into Cadiz Bay.

In the dimmest north-east distance dawned Gibraltar, grand and gray."

Browning.

Gibraltar, *Saturday, November* 6, 1852.

I leave unrecorded the links of travel which connected Messina and Gibraltar. They were over the well-trodden fields of Europe, where little ground is left that is not familiar. In leaving Sicily I lost the Saracenic trail, which I had been following through the East, and first find it again here, on the rock of Calpe, whose name, Djebel el-Tarik (the Mountain of Tarik), still speaks of the fiery race whose rule extended from the unknown ocean of the West to "Ganges and Hydaspes, Indian streams." In Malta and Sicily, I saw their decaying watch-towers, and recognized their sign-manual in the deep, guttural, masculine words and expressions which they have left behind them. I now design following their footsteps through the beautiful Belàd-el-Andaluz, which, to the eye of the Melek Abd-er-rahmàn, was only less lovely than the plains of Damascus.

While in Constantinople, I received letters which opened to me wider and richer fields of travel than I had already traversed. I saw a possibility of exploring the far Indian realms, the shores of farthest Cathay and the famed Zipango of Marco Polo. Before entering on this new sphere of experiences, however, it was necessary for me to visit Italy, Germany, and England. I sailed from Messina to Leghorn, and travelled thence, by way of Florence, Venice, and the Tyrol, to Munich. After three happy weeks at Gotha, and among the valleys of she Thüringian Forest, I went to London, where business and the preparation for my new journeys detained me two or three weeks longer. Although the comforts of European civilization were pleasant, as a change, after the wild life of the Orient, the autumnal rains of England soon made me homesick for the sunshine I had left. The weather was cold, dark, and dreary, and the oppressive, sticky atmosphere of the bituminous metropolis weighed upon me like a nightmare. Heartily tired of looking at a sun that could show nothing brighter than a red copper disk, and of breathing an air that peppered my face with particles of soot, I left on the 28th of October. It was one of the dismalest days of autumn; the meadows of Berkshire were flooded with broad, muddy streams, and the woods on the hills of Hampshire looked brown and sodden, as if slowly rotting away. I reached Southampton at dusk, but there the sky was neither warmer nor clearer, so I spent the evening over a coal fire, all impatience for the bright beloved South, towards which my face was turned once more.

The Madras left on the next day, at 2 P.M., in the midst of a cheerless rain, which half blotted out the pleasant shores of Southampton Water, and the Isle of Wight. The Madras was a singularly appropriate vessel for one bound on such a journey as mine. The surgeon was Dr. Mungo Park, and one of my room-mates was Mr. R. Crusoe. It was a Friday, which boded no good for the voyage; but then my journey commenced with my leaving London the day previous, and Thursday is a lucky day among the Arabs. I caught a watery view of the gray cliffs of the Needles, when dinner was announced, but many were those (and I among them) who commenced that meal, and did not stay to finish it.

Is there any piece of water more unreasonably, distressingly, disgustingly rough and perverse than the British Channel? Yes: there is one, and but one--the Bay of Biscay. And as the latter succeeds the former, without a pause between, and the head-winds never ceased, and the rain continually poured, I leave you to draw the climax of my misery. Four days and four nights in a berth, lying on your back, now dozing dull hour after hour, now making faint endeavors to eat, or reading the feeblest novel ever written, because the mind cannot digest stronger aliment--can there be a greater contrast to the wide-awake life, the fiery inspiration, of the Orient? My blood became so sluggish and my mind so cloudy and befogged, that I despaired of ever thinking clearly or feeling vividly again. "The winds are rude" in Biscay, Byron says. They are, indeed: very rude. They must have been raised in some most disorderly quarter of the globe. They pitched the waves right over our bulwarks, and now and then dashed a bucketful of water down the cabin skylight, swamping the ladies' cabin, and setting scores of bandboxes afloat. Not that there was the least actual danger; but Mrs. ---- would not be persuaded that we were not on the brink of destruction, and wrote to friends at home a voluminous account of her feelings. There was an Irishman on board, bound to Italy, with his sister. It was his first tour, and when asked why he did not go direct, through France, he replied, with brotherly concern, that he was anxious his sister should see the Bay of Biscay.

This youth's perceptions were of such an emerald hue, that a lot of wicked Englishmen had their own fun out of him. The other day, he was trying to shave, to the great danger of slicing off his nose, as the vessel was rolling fearfully. "Why don't you have the ship headed to the wind?" said one of the Englishmen, who heard his complaints; "she will then lie steady, and you can shave beautifully." Thereupon the Irishman sent one of the stewards upon deck with a polite message to the captain, begging him to put the vessel about for five minutes.

Towards noon of the fifth day, we saw the dark, rugged mountains that guard the north-western corner of the Spanish Peninsula. We passed the Bay of Corunna, and rounding the bold headland of Finisterre, left the Biscayan billows behind us. But the sea was still rough and the sky clouded, although the next morning the mildness of the air showed the change in our latitude. About noon that day, we made the Burlings, a cluster of rocks forty miles north of Lisbon, and just before sunset, a transient lifting of the clouds revealed the Rock of Cintra, at the mouth of the Tagus. The tall, perpendicular cliffs, and the mountain slopes behind, covered with gardens, orchards, and scattered villas and hamlets, made a grand though dim picture, which was soon hidden from our view.

On the 4th, we were nearly all day crossing the mouth of the Bay of Cadiz, and only at sunset saw Cape Trafalgar afar off, glimmering through the reddish haze. I remained on deck, as there were patches of starlight in the sky. After passing the light-house at Tarifa, the Spanish shore continued to be visible. In another hour, there was a dim, cloudy outline high above the horizon, on our right. This was the Lesser Atlas, in Morocco. And now, right ahead, distinctly visible, though fifteen miles distant, lay a colossal lion, with his head on his outstretched paws, looking towards Africa. If I had been brought to the spot blindfolded, I should have known what it was. The resemblance is certainly very striking, and the light-house on Europa Point seemed to be a lamp held in his paws. The lights of the city and fortifications rose one by one, glittering along the base, and at midnight we dropped anchor before them on the western side.

I landed yesterday morning. The mists, which had followed me from England, had collected behind the Rock, and the sun, still hidden by its huge bulk, shone upwards through them, making a luminous background, against which the lofty walls and jagged ramparts of this tremendous natural fortification were clearly defined. I announced my name, and the length of time I designed remaining, at a little office on the quay, and was then allowed to pass into the city. A number of familiar white turbans met me on entering, and I could not resist the temptation of cordially saluting the owners in their own language. The town is long and narrow, lying steeply against the Rock. The houses are white, yellow and pink, as in Spanish towns, but the streets are clean and well paved. There is a square, about the size of an ordinary building-lot, where a sort of market of dry goods and small articles is held The "Club-House Hotel" occupies one side of it; and, as I look out of my window upon it, I see the topmost cliffs of the Rock above me, threatening to topple down from a height of 1,500 feet.

My first walk in Gibraltar was in search of a palm-tree. After threading the whole length of the town, I found two small ones in a garden, in the bottom of the old moat. The sun was shining, and his rays seemed to fall with double warmth on their feathery crests. Three brown Spaniards, bare-armed, were drawing water with a pole and bucket, and filling the little channels which conveyed it to the distant vegetables. The sea glittered blue below; an Indian fig-tree shaded me; but, on the rock behind, an aloe lifted its blossoming stem, some twenty feet high, into the sunshine. To describe what a weight was lifted from my heart would seem foolish to those who do not know on what little things the whole tone of our spirits sometimes depends.

But if an even balance was restored yesterday, the opposite scale kicked the beam this morning. Not a speck of vapor blurred the spotless crystal of the sky, as I walked along the hanging paths of the Alameda. The sea was dazzling ultra-marine, with a purple lustre; every crag and notch of the mountains across the bay, every shade of brown or gray, or the green of grassy patches, was drawn and tinted with a pencil so exquisitely delicate as almost to destroy the perspective. The white houses of Algeciras, five miles off, appeared close at hand: a little toy-town, backed by miniature hills. Apes' Hill, the ancient Abyla, in Africa, advanced to meet Calpe, its opposing pillar, and Atlas swept away to the east ward, its blue becoming paler and paler, till the powers of vision finally failed. From the top of the southern point of the Rock, I saw the mountain-shore of Spain, as far as Malaga, and the snowy top of one of the Sierra Nevada. Looking eastward to the horizon line of the Mediterranean, my sight extended so far, in the wonderful clearness of the air, that the convexity of the earth's surface was plainly to be seen. The sea, instead of being a plane, was slightly convex, and the sky, instead of resting upon it at the horizon, curved down beyond it, as the upper side of a horn curves over the lower, when one looks into the mouth. There is none of the many aspects of Nature more grand than this, which is so rarely seen, that I believe the only person who has ever described it is Humboldt, who saw it, looking from the Silla de Caraccas over the Caribbean Sea. It gives you the impression of standing on the edge of the earth, and looking off into space. From the mast-head, the ocean appears either flat or slightly concave, and æronauts declare that this apparent concavity becomes more marked, the higher they ascend. It is only at those rare periods when the air is so miraculously clear as to produce the effect of no air--rendering impossible the slightest optical illusion--that our eyes can see things as they really are. So pure was the atmosphere to-day, that, at meridian, the moon, although a thin sickle, three days distant from the sun, shone perfectly white and clear.

As I loitered in the Alameda, between thick hedges of ever-blooming geraniums, clumps of heliotrope three feet high, and luxuriant masses of ivy, around whose warm flowers the bees clustered and hummed, I could only think of the voyage as a hideous dream. The fog and gloom had been in my own eyes and in my own brain, and now the blessed sun, shining full in my face, awoke me. I am a worshipper of the Sun. I took off my hat to him, as I stood there, in a wilderness of white, crimson, and purple flowers, and let him blaze away in my face for a quarter of an hour. And as I walked home with my back to him, I often turned my face from side to side that I might feel his touch on my cheek. How a man can live, who is sentenced to a year's imprisonment, is more than I can understand.

But all this (you will say) gives you no picture of Gibraltar. The Rock is so familiar to all the world, in prints and descriptions, that I find nothing new to say of it, except that it is by no means so barren a rock as the island of Malta, being clothed, in many places, with beautiful groves and the greenest turf; besides, I have not yet seen the rock-galleries, having taken passage for Cadiz this afternoon. When I return--as I hope to do in twenty days, after visiting Seville and Granada--I shall procure permission to view all the fortifications, and likewise to ascend to the summit.

Chapter XXXIII. Cadiz And Seville.

Voyage to Cadiz--Landing--The City--Its Streets--The Women of Cadiz--Embarkation for Seville--Scenery of the Guadalquivir--Custom House Examination--The Guide--The Streets of Seville--The Giralda--The Cathedral of Seville--The Alcazar-Moorish Architecture--Pilate's House--Morning View from the Giralda--Old Wine--Murillos--My Last Evening in Seville.

"The walls of Cadiz front the shore,

And shimmer o'er the sea."

R. H. Stoddard.

"Beautiful Seville!

Of which I've dreamed, until I saw its towers

In every cloud that hid the setting sun."

George H. Boker.

Seville, *November* 10, 1852.

I left Gibraltar on the evening of the 6th, in the steamer Iberia. The passage to Cadiz was made in nine hours, and we came to anchor in the harbor before day-break. It was a cheerful picture that the rising sun presented to us. The long white front of the city, facing the East, glowed with a bright rosy lustre, on a ground of the clearest blue. The tongue of land on which Cadiz stands is low, but the houses are lifted by the heavy sea-wall which encompasses them. The main-land consists of a range of low but graceful hills, while in the south-east the mountains of Ronda rise at some distance. I went immediately on shore, where my carpet-bag was seized upon by a boy, with the rich brown complexion of one Murillo's beggars, who trudged off with it to the gate. After some little detention there, I was conducted to a long, deserted, barn-like building, where I waited half an hour before the proper officer came. When the latter had taken his private toll of my contraband cigars, the brown imp conducted me to Blanco's English Hotel, a neat and comfortable house on the Alameda.

Cadiz is soon seen. Notwithstanding its venerable age of three thousand years--having been founded by Hercules, who figures on its coat-of-arms--it is purely a commercial city, and has neither antiquities, nor historic associations that interest any but Englishmen. It is compactly built, and covers a smaller space than accords with my ideas of its former splendor. I first walked around the sea-ramparts, enjoying the glorious look-off over the blue waters. The city is almost insulated, the triple line of fortifications on the land side being of but trifling length. A rocky ledge stretches out into the sea from the northern point, and at its extremity rises the massive light-house tower, 170 feet high. The walls toward the sea were covered with companies of idle anglers, fishing with cane rods of enormous length. On the open, waste spaces between the bastions, boys had spread their limed cords to catch singing birds, with chirping decoys placed here and there in wicker cages. Numbers of boatmen and peasants, in their brown jackets, studded with tags and bugles, and those round black caps which resemble smashed bandboxes, loitered about the walls or lounged on the grass in the sun.

Except along the Alameda, which fronts the bay, the exterior of the city has an aspect of neglect and desertion. The interior, however, atones for this in the gay and lively air of its streets, which, though narrow, are regular and charmingly clean. The small plazas are neatness itself, and one is too content with this to ask for striking architectural effects. The houses are tall and stately, of the most dazzling whiteness, and though you could point out no one as a pattern of style, the general effect is chaste and harmonious. In fact, there are two or three streets which you would almost pronounce faultless. The numbers of hanging balconies and of court-yards paved with marble and surrounded with elegant corridors, show the influence of Moorish taste. There is not a mean-looking house to be seen, and I have no doubt that Cadiz is the best built city of its size in the world. It lies, white as new-fallen snow, like a cluster of ivory palaces, between sea and sky. Blue and silver are its colors, and, as everybody knows, there can be no more charming contrast.

I visited both the old and new cathedrals, neither of which is particularly interesting. The latter is unfinished, and might have been a fine edifice had the labor and money expended on its construction been directed by taste. The interior, rich as it is in marbles and sculpture, has a heavy, confused effect. The pillars dividing the nave from the side-aisles are enormous composite masses, each one consisting of six Corinthian columns, stuck around and against a central shaft. More satisfactory to me was the Opera-House, which I visited in the evening, and where the dazzling array of dark-eyed Gaditanas put a stop to architectural criticism. The women of Cadiz are noted for their beauty and their graceful gait. Some of them are very beautiful, it is true; but beauty is not the rule among them. Their gait, however, is the most graceful possible, because it is perfectly free and natural. The commonest serving-maid who walks the streets of Cadiz would put to shame a whole score of our mincing and wriggling belles.

Honest old Blanco prepared me a cup of chocolate by sunrise next morning, and accompanied me down to the quay, to embark for Seville. A furious wind was blowing from the south-east, and the large green waves raced and chased one another incessantly over the surface of the bay. I took a heavy craft, which the boatmen pushed along under cover of the pier, until they reached the end, when the sail was dropped in the face of the wind, and away we shot into the watery tumult. The boat rocked and bounced over the agitated surface, running with one gunwale on the waves, and sheets of briny spray broke over me. I felt considerably relieved when I reached the deck of the steamer, but it was then diversion enough to watch those who followed. The crowd of boats pitching tumultuously around the steamer, jostling against each other, their hulls gleaming with wet, as they rose on the beryl-colored waves, striped with long, curded lines of wind-blown foam, would have made a fine subject for the pencil of Achenbach.

At last we pushed off, with a crowd of passengers fore and aft, and a pyramid of luggage piled around the smoke-pipe. There was a party of four Englishmen on board, and, on making their acquaintance, I found one of them to be a friend to some of my friends--Sir John Potter, the progressive ex-Mayor of Manchester. The wind being astern, we ran rapidly along the coast, and in two hours entered the mouth of the Guadalquivir. [This name comes from the Arabic wadi el-kebeer--literally, the Great Valley.] The shores are a dead flat. The right bank is a dreary forest of stunted pines, abounding with deer and other game; on the left is the dilapidated town of San Lucar, whence Magellan set sail on his first voyage around the world. A mile further is Bonanza, the port of Xeres, where we touched and took on board a fresh lot of passengers. Thenceforth, for four hours, the scenery of the Guadalquivir had a most distressing sameness. The banks were as flat as a board, with here and there a straggling growth of marshy thickets. Now and then we passed a herdsman's hut, but there were no human beings to be seen, except the peasants who tended the large flocks of sheep and cattle. A sort of breakfast was served in the cabin, but so great was the number of guests that I had much difficulty in getting anything to eat. The waiters were models of calmness and deliberation.

As we approached Seville, some low hills appeared on the left, near the river. Dazzling white villages were planted at their foot, and all the slopes were covered with olive orchards, while the banks of the stream were bordered with silvery birch trees. This gave the landscape, in spite of the African warmth and brightness of the day, a gray and almost wintry aspect. Soon the graceful Giralda, or famous Tower of Seville, arose in the distance; but, from the windings of the river, we were half an hour in reaching the landing-place. One sees nothing of the far-famed beauty of Seville, on approaching it. The boat stops below the Alameda, where the passengers are received by Custom-House officers, who, in my case, did not verify the stories told of them in Cadiz. I gave my carpet-bag to a boy, who conducted me along the hot and dusty banks to the bridge over the Guadalquivir, where he turned into the city. On passing the gate, two loafer-like guards stopped my baggage, notwithstanding it had already been examined. "What!" said I, "do you examine twice on entering Seville?" "Yes," answered one; "twice, and even three times;" but added in a lower tone, "it depends entirely on yourself." With that he slipped behind me, and let one hand fall beside my pocket. The transfer of a small coin was dexterously made, and I passed on without further stoppage to the Fonda de Madrid.

Sir John Potter engaged Antonio Bailli, the noted guide of Seville, who professes to have been the cicerone of all distinguished travellers, from Lord Byron and Washington Irving down to Owen Jones, and I readily accepted his invitation to join the party. Bailli is recommended by Ford as "fat and good-humored" Fat he certainly is, and very good-humored when speaking of himself, but he has been rather spoiled by popularity, and is much too profuse in his critical remarks on art and architecture. Nevertheless, as my stay in Seville is limited, I have derived no slight advantage from his services.

On the first morning I took an early stroll through the streets. The houses are glaringly white, like those of Cadiz, but are smaller and have not the same stately exteriors. The windows are protected by iron gratings, of florid patterns, and, as many of these are painted green, the general effect is pleasing. Almost every door opens upon a patio, or courtyard, paved with black and white marble and adorned with flowers and fountains. Many of these remain from the time of the Moors, and are still surrounded by the delicate arches and brilliant tile-work of that period. The populace in the streets are entirely Spanish--the jaunty majo in his queer black cap, sash, and embroidered jacket, and the nut-brown, dark-eyed damsel, swimming along in her mantilla, and armed with the irresistible fan.

We went first to the Cathedral, built on the site of the great mosque of Abou Youssuf Yakoub. The tall Giralda beckoned to us over the tops of the intervening buildings, and finally a turn in the street brought us to the ancient Moorish gateway on the northern side. This is an admirable specimen of the horse-shoe arch, and is covered with elaborate tracery. It originally opened into the court, or hàram, of the mosque, which still remains, and is shaded by a grove of orange trees. The Giralda, to my eye, is a more perfect tower than the Campanile of Florence, or that of San Marco, at Venice, which is evidently an idea borrowed from it. The Moorish structure, with a base of fifty feet square, rises to the height of two hundred and fifty feet. It is of a light pink color, and the sides, which are broken here and there by exquisitely proportioned double Saracenic arches, are covered from top to bottom with arabesque tracery, cut in strong relief. Upon this tower, a Spanish architect has placed a tapering spire, one hundred feet high, which fortunately harmonizes with the general design, and gives the crowning grace to the work.

608

The Cathedral of Seville may rank as one of the grandest Gothic piles in Europe. The nave lacks but five feet of being as high as that of St. Peter's, while the length and breadth of the edifice are on a commensurate scale. The ninety-three windows of stained glass fill the interior with a soft and richly-tinted light, mellower and more gentle than the sombre twilight of the Gothic Cathedrals of Europe. The wealth lavished on the smaller chapels and shrines is prodigious, and the high altar, inclosed within a gilded railing fifty feet high, is probably the most enormous mass of wood-carving in existence. The Cathedral, in fact, is encumbered with its riches. While they bewilder you as monuments of human labor and patience, they detract from the grand simplicity of the building. The great nave, on each side of the transept, is quite blocked up, so that the choir and magnificent royal chapel behind it have almost the effect of detached edifices.

We returned again this morning, remaining two hours, and succeeded in making a thorough survey, including a number of trashy pictures and barbarously rich shrines. Murillo's "Guardian Angel" and the "Vision of St. Antonio" are the only gems. The treasury contains a number of sacred vessels of silver, gold and jewels--among other things, the keys of Moorish Seville, a cross made of the first gold brought from the New-World by Columbus, and another from that robbed in Mexico by Cortez. The Cathedral won my admiration more and more. The placing of the numerous windows, and their rich coloring, produce the most glorious effects of light in the lofty aisles, and one is constantly finding new vistas, new combinations of pillar, arch and shrine. The building is in itself a treasury of the grandest Gothic pictures.

From the Cathedral we went to the Alcazar (El-Kasr), or Palace of the Moorish Kings. We entered by a long passage, with round arches on either side, resting on twin pillars, placed at right angles to the line of the arch, as one sees both in Saracenic and Byzantine structures. Finally, old Bailli brought us into a dull, deserted court-yard, where we were surprised by the sight of an entire Moorish façade, with its pointed arches, its projecting roof, its rich sculptured ornaments and its illuminations of red, blue, green and gold. It has been lately restored, and now rivals in freshness and brilliancy any of the rich houses of Damascus. A doorway, entirely too low and mean for the splendor of the walls above it, admitted us into the first court. On each side of the passage are the rooms of the guard and the Moorish nobles. Within, all is pure Saracenic, and absolutely perfect in its grace and richness. It is the realization of an Oriental dream; it is the poetry and luxury of the East in tangible forms. Where so much depends on the proportion and harmony of the different parts--on those correspondences, the union of which creates that nameless soul of the work, which cannot be expressed in words--it is useless to describe details. From first to last--the chambers of state; the fringed arches; the open tracery, light and frail as the frost-stars crystallized on a window-pane; the courts, fit to be vestibules to Paradise; the audience-hall, with its wondrous sculptures, its columns and pavement of marble, and its gilded dome; the garden, gorgeous with its palm, banana, and orange-trees--all were in perfect keeping, all jewels of equal lustre, forming a diadem which still lends a royal dignity to the phantom of Moorish power.

We then passed into the gardens laid out by the Spanish monarchs--trim, mathematical designs, in box and myrtle, with concealed fountains springing up everywhere unawares in the midst of the paven walks; yet still made beautiful by the roses and jessamines that hung in rank clusters over the marble balustrades, and by the clumps of tall orange trees, bending to earth under the weight of their fruitage. We afterward visited Pilate's House, as it is called--a fine Spanish-Moresco palace, now belonging to the Duke of Medina Coeli. It is very rich and elegant, but stands in the same relation to the Alcazar as a good copy does to the original picture. The grand staircase, nevertheless, is a marvel of tile work, unlike anything else in Seville, and exhibits a genius in the invention of elaborate ornamental patterns, which is truly wonderful. A number of workmen were busy in restoring the palace, to fit it for the residence of the young Duke. The Moorish sculptures are reproduced in plaster, which, at least, has a better effect than the fatal whitewash under which the original tints of the Alcazar are hidden. In the courts stand a number of Roman busts--Spanish antiquities, and therefore not of great merit--singularly out of place in niches surrounded by Arabic devices and sentences from the Koran.

This morning, I climbed the Giralda. The sun had just risen, and the clay was fresh and crystal-clear. A little door in the Cathedral, near the foot of the tower, stood open, and I entered. A rather slovenly Sevillaña had just completed her toilet, but two children were still in undress. However, she opened a door in the tower, and I went up without hindrance. The ascent is by easy ramps, and I walked four hundred yards, or nearly a quarter of a mile, before reaching the top of the Moorish part. The panoramic view was superb. To the east and west, the Great Valley made a level line on a far-distant horizon. There were ranges of hills in the north and south, and those rising near the city, clothed in a gray mantle of olive-trees, were picturesquely crowned with villages. The Guadalquivir, winding in the most sinuous mazes, had no longer a turbid hue; he reflected the blue morning sky, and gleamed brightly between his borders of birch and willow. Seville sparkled white and fair under my feet, her painted towers and tiled domes rising thickly out of the mass of buildings. The level sun threw shadows into the numberless courts, permitting the mixture of Spanish and Moorish architecture to be plainly discerned, even at that height. A thin golden vapor softened the features of the landscape, towards the sun, while, on the opposite side, every object stood out in the sharpest and clearest outlines.

On our way to the Muséo, Bailli took us to the house of a friend of his, in order that we might taste real Manzanilla wine. This is a pale, straw-colored vintage, produced in the valley of the Guadalquivir. It is flavored with camomile blossoms, and is said to be a fine tonic for weak stomachs. The master then produced a dark-red wine, which he declared to be thirty years old. It was almost a syrup in consistence, and tasted more of sarsaparilla than grapes. None of us relished it, except Bailli, who was so inspired by the draught, that he sang us two Moorish songs and an Andalusian catch, full of fun and drollery.

The Muséo contains a great amount of bad pictures, but it also contains twenty-three of Murillo's works, many of them of his best period. To those who have only seen his tender, spiritual "Conceptions" and "Assumptions," his "Vision of St. Francis" in this gallery reveals a mastery of the higher walks of his art, which they would not have anticipated. But it is in his "Cherubs" and his "Infant Christs" that he excels. No one ever painted infantile grace and beauty with so true a pencil. There is but one Velasquez in the collection,

611

and the only thing that interested me, in two halls filled with rubbish, was a "Conception" by Murillo's mulatto pupil, said by some to have been his slave. Although an imitation of the great master, it is a picture of much sweetness and beauty. There is no other work of the artist in existence, and this, as the only production of the kind by a painter of mixed African blood, ought to belong to the Republic of Liberia.

Among the other guests at the Fonda de Madrid is Mr. Thomas Hobhouse, brother of Byron's friend. We had a pleasant party in the Court this evening, listening to blind Pépé, who sang to his guitar a medley of merry Andalusian refrains. Singing made the old man courageous, and, at the close, he gave us the radical song of Spain, which is now strictly prohibited. The air is charming, but too gay; one would sooner dance than fight to its measures. It does not bring the hand to the sword, like the glorious Marseillaise.

Adios, beautiful Seville!

Chapter XXXIV. Journey in a Spanish Diligence.

Spanish Diligence Lines--Leaving Seville--An Unlucky Start--Alcalà of the Bakers--Dinner at Carmona--A Dehesa--The Mayoral and his Team--Ecija--Night Journey--Cordova--The Cathedral-Mosque--Moorish Architecture--The Sierra Morena--A Rainy Journey--A Chapter of Accidents--Baylen--The Fascination of Spain--Jaen--The Vega of Granada.

Granada, *November* 14, 1852.

It is an enviable sensation to feel for the first time that you are in Granada. No amount of travelling can weaken the romantic interest which clings about this storied place, or take away aught from the freshness of that emotion with which you first behold it, I sit almost at the foot of the Alhambra, whose walls I can see from my window, quite satisfied for to-day with being here. It has been raining since I arrived, the thunder is crashing overhead, and the mountains are covered with clouds, so I am kept in-doors, with the luxury of knowing that all the wonders of the place are within my reach. And now let me beguile the dull weather by giving you a sketch of my journey from Seville hither.

There are three lines of stages from Seville to Madrid, and their competition has reduced the fare to $12, which, for a ride of 350 miles, is remarkably cheap. The trip is usually made in three days and a half. A branch line from Baylen--nearly half-way--strikes southward to Granada, and as there is no competition on this part of the road, I was charged $15 for a through seat in the coupé. On account of the lateness of the season, and the limited time at my command, this was preferable to taking horses and riding across the country from Seville to Cordova. Accordingly, at an early hour on Thursday morning last, furnished with a travelling ticket inscribed: "Don Valtar de Talor" (myself!), I took leave of my English friends at the Fonda de Madrid, got into an immense, lumbering yellow vehicle, drawn by ten mules, and started, trusting to my good luck and bad Spanish to get safely through. The commencement, however, was unpropitious, and very often a stumble at starting makes the whole journey limp. The near mule in the foremost span was a horse, ridden by our postillion, and nothing could prevent that horse from darting into all sorts of streets and alleys where we had no desire to go. As all mules have implicit faith in horses, of course the rest of the animals followed. We were half an hour in getting out of Seville, and when at last we reached the open road and dashed off at full gallop, one of the mules in the traces fell and was dragged in the dust some twenty or thirty yards before we could stop. My companions in the coupé were a young Spanish officer and his pretty Andalusian bride, who was making her first journey from home, and after these mishaps was in a state of constant fear and anxiety.

The first stage across the valley of the Guadalquivir took us to the town of Alcalà, which lies in the lap of the hills above the beautiful little river Guadaira. It is a picturesque spot; the naked cliffs overhanging the stream have the rich, red hue of cinnabar, and the trees and shrubbery in the meadows, and on the hill-sides are ready grouped to the artist's hand. The town is called Alcalà de los Panadores (of the Bakers) from its hundreds of flour mills and bake-ovens, which supply Seville with those white, fine, delicious twists, of which Spain may be justly proud. They should have been sent to the Exhibition last year, with the Toledo blades and the wooden mosaics. We left the place and its mealy-headed population, and turned eastward into wide, rolling tracts, scattered here and there with gnarled olive trees. The soil was loose and sandy, and hedges of aloes lined the road. The country is thinly populated, and very little of it under cultivation.

About noon we reached Carmona, which was founded by the Romans, as, indeed, were nearly all the towns of Southern Spain. It occupies the crest and northern slope of a high hill, whereon the ancient Moorish castle still stands. The Alcazar, or palace, and the Moorish walls also remain, though in a very ruinous condition. Here we stopped to dinner, for the "Nueva Peninsular," in which I was embarked, has its hotels all along the route, like that of Zurutuza, in Mexico. We were conducted into a small room adjoining the stables, and adorned with colored prints illustrating the history of Don John of Austria. The table-cloths, plates and other appendages were of very ordinary quality, but indisputably clean; we seated ourselves, and presently the dinner appeared. First, a vermicelli pilaff, which I found palatable, then the national olla, a dish of enormous yellow peas, sprinkled with bits of bacon and flavored with oil; then three successive courses of chicken, boiled, stewed and roasted, but in every case done to rags, and without a particle of the original flavor. This was the usual style of our meals on the road, whether breakfast, dinner or supper, except that kid was sometimes substituted for fowl, and that the oil employed, being more or less rancid, gave different flavors to the dishes, A course of melons, grapes or pomegranates wound up the repast, the price of which varied from ten to twelve reals--a real being about a half-dime. In Seville, at the Fonda de Madrid, the cooking is really excellent; but further in the interior, judging from what I have heard, it is even worse than I have described.

Continuing our journey, we passed around the southern brow of the hill, under the Moorish battlements. Here a superb view opened to the south and east over the wide Vega of Carmona, as far as the mountain chain which separates it from the plain of Granada. The city has for a coat of arms a silver star in an azure field, with the pompous motto: "As Lucifer shines in the morning, so shines Carmona in Andalusia." If it shines at all, it is because it is a city set upon a hill; for that is the only splendor I could find about the place. The Vega of Carmona is partially cultivated, and now wears a sombre brown hue, from its tracts of ploughed land.

Cultivation soon ceased, however, and we entered on a dehesa, a boundless plain of waste land, covered with thickets of palmettos. Flocks of goats and sheep, guarded by shepherds in brown cloaks, wandered here and there, and except their huts and an isolated house, with its group of palm-trees, there was no sign of habitation. The road was a deep, red sand, and our mules toiled along slowly and painfully, urged by the incessant cries of the mayoral, or conductor, and his mozo. As the mayoral's whip could only reach the second span, the business of the latter was to jump down every ten minutes, run ahead and belabor the flanks of the foremost mules, uttering at the same time a series of sharp howls, which seemed to strike the poor beasts with quite as much severity as his whip. I defy even a Spanish ear to distinguish the import of these cries, and the great wonder was how they could all come out of one small throat. When it came to a hard pull, they cracked and exploded like volleys of musketry, and flew like hail-stones about the ears of the machos (he-mules). The postillion, having only the care of the foremost span, is a silent man, but he has contracted a habit of sleeping in the saddle, which I mention for the benefit of timid travellers, as it adds to the interest of a journey by night.

The clouds which had been gathering all day, now settled down upon the plain, and night came on with a dull rain. At eight o'clock we reached the City of Ecija, where we had two hours' halt and supper. It was so dark and rainy that I saw nothing, not even the classic Xenil, the river of Granada, which flows through the city on its way to the Guadalquivir, The night wore slowly away, and while the mozo drowsed on his post, I caught snatches of sleep between his cries. As the landscape began to grow distinct in the gray, cloudy dawn, we saw before us Cordova, with the dark range of the Sierra Morena rising behind it. This city, once the glory of Moorish Spain, the capital of the great Abd-er-Rahman, containing, when in its prime, a million of inhabitants, is now a melancholy wreck. It has not a shadow of the art, science, and taste which then distinguished it, and the only interest it now possesses is from these associations, and the despoiled remnant of its renowned Mosque.

We crossed the Guadalquivir on a fine bridge built on Roman foundations, and drove slowly down the one long, rough, crooked street. The diligence stops for an hour, to allow passengers to breakfast, but my first thought was for the Cathedral-mosque, la Mezquita, as it is still called. "It is closed," said the ragged crowd that congregated about us; "you cannot get in until eight o'clock." But I remembered that a silver key will open anything in Spain, and taking a mozo as a guide we hurried off as fast as the rough pavements would permit. We had to retrace the whole length of the city, but on reaching the Cathedral, found it open. The exterior is low, and quite plain, though of great extent. A Moorish gateway admitted me into the original court-yard, or hàram, of the mosque, which is planted with orange trees and contains the fountain, for the ablutions of Moslem worshippers, in the centre. The area of the Mosque proper, exclusive of the court-yard, is about

616

400 by 350 feet. It was built on the plan of the great Mosque of Damascus, about the end of the eighth century. The materials--including twelve hundred columns of marble, jasper and porphyry, from the ruins of Carthage, and the temples of Asia Minor---belonged to a Christian basilica, of the Gothic domination, which was built upon the foundations of a Roman temple of Janus; so that the three great creeds of the world have here at different times had their seat. The Moors considered this mosque as second in holiness to the Kaaba of Mecca, and made pilgrimages to it from all parts of Moslem Spain and Barbary. Even now, although shorn of much of its glory, it surpasses any Oriental mosque into which I have penetrated, except St. Sophia, which is a Christian edifice.

All the nineteen original entrances--beautiful horse-shoe arches--are closed, except the central one. I entered by a low door, in one corner of the corridor. A wilderness of columns connected by double arches (one springing above the other, with an opening between), spread their dusky aisles before me in the morning twilight. The eight hundred and fifty shafts of this marble forest formed labyrinths and mazes, which at that early hour appeared boundless, for their long vistas disappeared in the shadows. Lamps were burning before distant shrines, and a few worshippers were kneeling silently here and there. The sound of my own footsteps, as I wandered through the ranks of pillars, was all that I heard. In the centre of the wood (for such it seemed) rises the choir, a gaudy and tasteless excrescence added by the Christians. Even Charles V., who laid a merciless hand on the Alhambra, reproved the Bishop of Cordova for this barbarous and unnecessary disfigurement.

The sacristan lighted lamps in order to show me the Moorish chapels. Nothing but the precious materials of which these exquisite structures are composed could have saved them from the holy hands of the Inquisition, which intentionally destroyed all the Roman antiquities of Cordova. Here the fringed arches, the lace-like filigrees, the wreathed inscriptions, and the domes of pendent stalactites which enchant you in the Alcazar of Seville, are repeated, not in stucco, but in purest marble, while the entrance to the "holy of holies" is probably the most glorious piece of mosaic in the world. The pavement of the interior is deeply worn by the knees of the Moslem pilgrims, who compassed it seven times, kneeling, as they now do in the Kaaba, at Mecca. The sides are embroidered with sentences from the Koran, in Cufic characters, and the roof is in the form of a fluted shell, of a single piece of pure white marble, fifteen feet in diameter. The roof of the vestibule is a wonderful piece of workmanship, formed of pointed arches, wreathed and twined through each other, like basket-work. No people ever wrought poetry into stone so perfectly as the Saracens. In looking on these precious relics of an elegant and refined race, I cannot help feeling a strong regret that their kingdom ever passed into other hands.

Leaving Cordova, our road followed the Guadalquivir, along the foot of the Sierra Morena, which rose dark and stern, a barrier to the central table-lands of La Mancha. At Alcolea, we crossed the river on a noble bridge of black marble, out of all keeping with the miserable road. It rained incessantly, and the scenery through which we passed had a wild and gloomy character. The only tree to be seen was the olive, which covered the hills far and near, the profusion of its fruit showing the natural richness of the soil. This part of the road is sometimes infested with robbers, and once, when I saw two individuals waiting for us in a lonely defile, with gun-barrels thrust out from under their black cloaks, I anticipated a recurrence of a former unpleasant experience. But they proved to be members of the guardia civil, and therefore our protectors.

The ruts and quagmires, made by the rain, retarded our progress, and it was dark when we reached Andujar, fourteen leagues from Cordova. To Baylen, where I was to quit the diligence, and take another coming down from Madrid to Granada, was four leagues further. We journeyed on in the dark, in a pouring rain, up and down hill for some hours, when all at once the cries of the mozo ceased, and the diligence came to a dead stop. There was some talk between our conductors, and then the mayoral opened the door and invited us to get out. The postillion had fallen asleep, and the mules had taken us into a wrong road. An attempt was made to turn the diligence, but failed, leaving it standing plump against a high bank of mud. We stood, meanwhile, shivering in the cold and wet, and the fair Andalusian shed abundance of tears. Fortunately, Baylen was close at hand, and, after some delay, two men came with lanterns and escorted us to the posada, or inn, where we arrived at midnight. The diligence from Madrid, which was due six hours before, had not made its appearance, and we passed the rest of the night in a cold room, fasting, for the meal was only to be served when the other passengers came. At day-break, finally, a single dish of oily meat was vouchsafed to us, and, as it was now certain that some accident had happened, the passengers to Madrid requested the Administrador to send them on in an extra conveyance. This he refused, and they began to talk about getting up a pronunciamento, when a messenger arrived with the news that the diligence had broken down at midnight, about two leagues off. Tools were thereupon dispatched, nine hours after the accident happened, and we might hope to be released from our imprisonment in four or five more.

Baylen is a wretched place, celebrated for having the first palm-tree which those see who come from Madrid, and for the victory gained by Castaños over the French forces under Dupont, which occasioned the flight of Joseph Buonaparte from Madrid, and the temporary liberation of Spain from the French yoke. Castaños, who received the title of Duke de Baylen, and is compared by the Spaniards to Wellington, died about three months ago. The battle-field I passed in the night; the palm-tree I found, but it is now a mere stump, the leaves having been stripped off to protect the houses of the inhabitants from lightning. Our posada had one of them hung at the window. At last, the diligence came, and at three P.M., when I ought to have been in sight of Granada, I left the forlorn walls of Baylen. My fellow-passengers were a young sprig of the Spanish nobility and three chubby-faced nuns.

The rest of the journey that afternoon was through a wide, hilly region, entirely bare of trees and habitations, and but partially cultivated. There was something sublime in its very nakedness and loneliness, and I felt attracted to it as I do towards the Desert. In fact, although I have seen little fine scenery since leaving Seville, have had the worst of weather, and no very pleasant travelling experiences, the country has exercised a fascination over me, which I do not quite understand. I find myself constantly on the point of making a vow to return again. Much to my regret, night set in before we reached Jaen, the capital of the Moorish kingdom of that name. We halted for a short time in the large plaza of the town, where the dash of fountains mingled with the sound of the rain, and the black, jagged outline of a mountain overhanging the place was visible through the storm.

All night we journeyed on through the mountains, sometimes splashing through swollen streams, sometimes coming almost to a halt in beds of deep mud. When this morning dawned, we were ascending through wild, stony hills, overgrown with shrubbery, and the driver said we were six leagues from Granada. Still on, through a lonely country, with now and then a large venta, or country inn, by the road-side, and about nine o'clock, as the sky became more clear, I saw in front of us, high up under the clouds, the snow-fields of the Sierra Nevada. An hour afterwards we were riding between gardens, vineyards, and olive orchards, with the magnificent Vega of Granada stretching far away on the right, and the Vermilion Towers of the Alhambra crowning the heights before us.

Chapter XXXV. Granada And The Alhambra.

Mateo Ximenez, the Younger--The Cathedral of Granada--A Monkish Miracle--Catholic Shrines--Military Cherubs--The Royal Chapel--The Tombs of Ferdinand and Isabella--Chapel of San Juan de Dios--The Albaycin--View of the Vega--The Generalife--The Alhambra--Torra de la Vela--The Walls and Towers--A Visit to Old Mateo--The Court of the Fish-pond--The Halls of the Alhambra--Character of the Architecture--Hall of the Abencerrages--Hall of the Two Sisters--The Moorish Dynasty in Spain.

"Who has not in Granada been,

Verily, he has nothing seen."

Andalusian Proverb.

Granada, *Wednesday, Nov.* 17, 1852.

Immediately on reaching here, I was set upon by an old gentleman who wanted to act as guide, but the mozo of the hotel put into my hand a card inscribed "Don Mateo Ximenez, Guide to the celebrated Washington Irving," and I dismissed the other applicant. The next morning, as the mozo brought me my chocolate, he said; "Señor, el chico is waiting for you." The "little one" turned out to be the son of old Mateo, "honest Mateo," who still lives up in the Alhambra, but is now rather too old to continue his business, except on great occasions. I accepted the young Mateo, who spoke with the greatest enthusiasm of Mr. Irving, avowing that the whole family was devoted to him, in life and death. It was still raining furiously, and the golden Darro, which roars in front of the hotel, was a swollen brown flood. I don't wonder that he sometimes threatens, as the old couplet says, to burst up the Zacatin, and bear it down to his bride, the Xenil.

Towards noon, the clouds broke away a little, and we sallied out. Passing through the gate and square of Vivarrambla (may not this name come from the Arabic bob er-raml, the "gate of the sand?"), we soon reached the Cathedral. This massive structure, which makes a good feature in the distant view of

Granada, is not at all imposing, near at hand. The interior is a mixture of Gothic and Roman, glaring with whitewash, and broken, like that of Seville, by a wooden choir and two grand organs, blocking up the nave. Some of the side chapels, nevertheless, are splendid masses of carving and gilding. In one of them, there are two full-length portraits of Ferdinand and Isabella, supposed to be by Alonzo Cano. The Cathedral contains some other good pictures by the same master, but all its former treasures were carried off by the French.

We next went to the Picture Gallery, which is in the Franciscan Convent. There are two small Murillos, much damaged, some tolerable Alonzo Canos, a few common-place pictures by Juan de Sevilla, and a hundred or more by authors whose names I did not inquire, for a more hideous collection of trash never met my eye. One of them represents a miracle performed by two saints, who cut off the diseased leg of a sick white man, and replace it by the sound leg of a dead negro, whose body is seen lying beside the bed. Judging from the ghastly face of the patient, the operation is rather painful, though the story goes that the black leg grew fast, and the man recovered. The picture at least illustrates the absence of "prejudice of color" among the Saints.

We went into the adjoining Church of Santo Domingo, which has several very rich shrines of marble and gold. A sort of priestly sacristan opened the Church of the Madonna del Rosario---a glittering mixture of marble, gold, and looking-glasses, which has rather a rich effect. The beautiful yellow and red veined marbles are from the Sierra Nevada. The sacred Madonna--a big doll with staring eyes and pink cheeks--has a dress of silver, shaped like an extinguisher, and encrusted with rubies and other precious stones. The utter absence of taste in most Catholic shrines is an extraordinary thing. It seems remarkable that a Church which has produced so many glorious artists should so constantly and grossly violate the simplest rules of art. The only shrine which I have seen, which was in keeping with the object adored, is that of the Virgin, at Nazareth, where there is neither picture nor image, but only vases of fragrant flowers, and perfumed oil in golden lamps, burning before a tablet of spotless marble.

Among the decorations of the chapel, there are a host of cherubs frescoed on the ceiling, and one of them is represented in the act of firing off a blunderbuss. "Is it true that the angels carry blunderbusses?" I asked the priest. He shrugged his shoulders with a sort of half-smile, and said nothing. In the Cathedral, on the plinths of the columns in the outer aisles, are several notices to the effect that "whoever speaks to women, either in the nave or the aisles, thereby puts himself in danger of excommunication." I could not help laughing, as I read this monkish and yet most unmonk-like statute. "Oh," said Mateo, "all that was in the despotic times; it is not so now."

A deluge of rain put a stop to my sight-seeing until the next morning, when I set out with Mateo to visit the Royal Chapel. A murder had been committed in the night, near the entrance of the Zacatin, and the paving-stones were still red with the blood of the victim. A funcion of some sort was going on in the Chapel, and we went into the sacristy to wait. The priests and choristers were there, changing their robes; they saluted me good-humoredly, though there was an expression in their faces that plainly said: "a heretic!" When the service was concluded, I went into the chapel and examined the high altar, with its rude wood-carvings, representing the surrender of Granada. The portraits of Ferdinand and Isabella, Cardinal Ximenez, Gonzalvo of Cordova, and King Boabdil, are very curious. Another tablet represents the baptism of the conquered Moors.

In the centre of the chapel stand the monuments erected to Ferdinand and Isabella, and their successors Philip L, and Maria, by Charles V. They are tall catafalques of white marble, superbly sculptured, with the full length effigies of the monarchs upon them. The figures are admirable; that of Isabella, especially, though the features are settled in the repose of death, expresses all the grand and noble traits which belonged to her character. The sacristan removed the matting from a part of the floor, disclosing an iron grating underneath, A damp, mouldly smell, significant of death and decay, came up through the opening. He lighted two long waxen tapers, lifted the grating, and I followed him down the narrow steps into the vault where lie the coffins of the Catholic Sovereigns. They were brought here from the Alhambra, in 1525. The leaden sarcophagi, containing the bodies of Ferdinand and Isabella, lie, side by side, on stone slabs; and as I stood between the two, resting a

623

hand on each, the sacristan placed the tapers in apertures in the stone, at the head and foot. They sleep, as they wished, in their beloved Granada, and no profane hand has ever disturbed the repose of their ashes.

After visiting the Church of San Jeronimo, founded by Gonzalvo of Cordova, I went to the adjoining Church and Hospital of San Juan de Dios. A fat priest, washing his hands in the sacristy, sent a boy to show me the Chapel of San Juan, and the relics. The remains of the Saint rest in a silver chest, standing in the centre of a richly-adorned chapel. Among the relics is a thorn from the crown of Christ, which, as any botanist may see, must have grown on a different plant from the other thorn they show at Seville; and neither kind is found in Palestine. The true spina christi, the nebbuk, has very small thorns; but nothing could be more cruel, as I found when riding through patches of it near Jericho. The boy also showed me a tooth of San Lorenzo, a crooked brown bicuspis, from which I should infer that the saint was rather an ill-favored man. The gilded chapel of San Juan is in singular contrast with one of the garments which he wore when living--a cowl of plaited reeds, looking like an old fish basket--which is kept in a glass case. His portrait is also to be seen--a mild and beautiful face, truly that of one who went about doing good. He was a sort of Spanish John Howard, and deserved canonization, if anybody ever did.

I ascended the street of the Darro to the Albaycin, which we entered by one of the ancient gates. This suburb is still surrounded by the original fortifications, and undermined by the capacious cisterns of the Moors. It looks down on Granada; and from the crumbling parapets there are superb views over the city, the Vega, and its inclosing mountains. The Alhambra rose opposite, against the dark-red and purple background of the Sierra Nevada, and a canopy of heavy rain-clouds rested on all the heights. A fitful gleam of sunshine now and then broke through and wandered over the plain, touching up white towers and olive groves and reaches of the winding Xenil, with a brilliancy which suggested the splendor of the whole picture, if once thus restored to its proper light. I could see Santa Fé in the distance, toward Loxa; nearer, and more eastward, the Sierra de Elvira, of a deep violet color, with the woods of the Soto de Roma, the Duke of Wellington's estate, at its base; and beyond it the Mountain of Parapanda, the weather-guage of Granada, still covered with clouds. There is an old Granadian proverb which says:--"When Parapanda wears his bonnet, it will rain whether God wills it or no." From the chapel of San Miguel, above the Albaycin, there is a very striking view of the deep gorge of the Darro, at one's feet, with the gardens and white walls of the Generalife rising beyond, and the Silla del Moro and the Mountain of the Sun towering above it. The long, irregular lines of the Alhambra, with the huge red towers rising here and there, reminded me somewhat of a distant view of Karnak; and, like Karnak, the Alhambra is picturesque from whatever point it is viewed.

We descended through wastes of cactus to the Darro, in whose turbid stream a group of men were washing for gold. I watched one of them, as he twirled his bowl in precisely the California style, but got nothing for his pains. Mateo says that they often make a dollar a day, each. Passing under the Tower of Comares and along the battlements of the Alhambra, we climbed up to the Generalife. This charming villa is still in good preservation, though its exquisite filigree and scroll-work have been greatly injured by whitewash. The elegant colonnades surround gardens rich in roses, myrtles and cypresses, and the fountains that lulled the Moorish Kings in their summer idleness still pour their fertilizing streams. In one of the rooms is a small and bad portrait gallery, containing a supposed portrait of Boabdil. It is a mild, amiable face, but wholly lacks strength of character.

To-day I devoted to the Alhambra. The storm, which, as the people say, has not been equalled for several years, showed no signs of breaking up, and in the midst of a driving shower I ascended to the Vermilion Towers, which are supposed to be of Phoenician origin. They stand on the extremity of a long, narrow ledge, which stretches out like an arm from the hill of the Alhambra. The paséo lies between, and is shaded by beautiful elms, which the Moors planted.

I entered the Alhambra by the Gate of Justice, which is a fine specimen of Moorish architecture, though of common red brick and mortar. It is singular what a grace the horse-shoe arch gives to the most heavy and lumbering mass of masonry. The round arches of the Christian edifices of Granada seem tame and inelegant, in comparison. Over the arch of the vestibule of this gate is the colossal hand, and over the inner entrance the key, celebrated in the tales of Washington Irving and the superstitions of the people. I first ascended the Torre de la Vela, where the Christian flag was first planted on the 2d of January, 1492. The view of the Vega and City of Granada was even grander than from the Albaycin. Parapanda was still bonneted in clouds, but patches of blue sky began to open above the mountains of Loxa. A little boy accompanied us, to see that I did not pull the bell, the sound of which would call together all the troops in the city. While we stood there, the funeral procession of the man murdered two nights before came up the street of Gomerez, and passed around the hill under the Vermilion Towers.

I made the circuit of the walls before entering the Palace. In the Place of the Cisterns, I stopped to take a drink of the cool water of the Darro, which is brought thither by subterranean channels from the hills. Then, passing the ostentatious pile commenced by Charles V., but which was never finished, and never will be, nor ought to be, we walked along the southern ramparts to the Tower of the Seven Floors, amid the ruins of winch I discerned the top of the arch by which the unfortunate Boabdil quitted Granada, and which was thenceforth closed for ever. In the Tower of the Infantas, a number of workmen were busy restoring the interior, which has been cruelly damaged. The brilliant azulejo, or tile-work, the delicate arches and filigree sculpture of the walls, still attest its former elegance, and give some color to the tradition that it was the residence of the Moorish Princesses.

As we passed through the little village which still exists among the ruins of the fortress, Mateo invited me to step in and see his father, the genuine "honest Mateo," immortalized in the "Tales of the Alhambra." The old man has taken up the trade of silk-weaving, and had a number of gay-colored ribbons on his loom. He is more than sixty years old and now quite gray-headed, but has the same simple manners, the same honest face that attracted his temporary master. He spoke with great enthusiasm of Mr. Irving, and brought out from a place of safety the "Alhambra" and the "Chronicles of the Conquest," which he has carefully preserved. He then produced an Andalusian sash, the work of his own hands, which he insisted on binding around my waist, to see how it would look. I must next take off my coat and hat, and put on his Sunday jacket and jaunty sombrero. "Por Dios!" he exclaimed: "que buen mozo! Senor, you are a legitimate Andalusian!" After this, of course, I could do no less than buy the sash. "You must show it to Washington Irving," said he, "and tell him it was made by Mateo's own hands;" which I promised. I must then go into the kitchen, and eat a pomegranate from his garden--a glorious pomegranate, with kernels of crimson, and so full of blood that you could not touch them but it trickled through your fingers. El Marques, a sprightly dog, and a great slate-colored cat, took possession of my legs, and begged for a share of every mouthful I took, while old Mateo sat beside me, rejoicing in the flavor of a Gibraltar cigar which I gave him. But my time was precious, and so I let the "Son of the Alhambra" go back to his loom, and set out for the Palace of the Moorish Kings.

This palace is so hidden behind the ambitious shell of that of Charles V. that I was at a loss where it could be. I thought I had compassed the hill, and yet had seen no indications of the renowned magnificence of the Alhambra. But a little door in a blank wall ushered me into a true Moorish realm, the Court of the Fishpond, or of the Myrtles, as it is sometimes called. Here I saw again the slender pillars, the fringed and embroidered arches, and the perforated, lace-like tracery of the fairy corridors. Here, hedges of roses and myrtles still bloomed around the ancient tank, wherein hundreds of gold-fish disported. The noises of the hill do not penetrate here, and the solitary porter who admitted me went back to his post, and suffered me to wander at will through the enchanted halls.

I passed out of this court by an opposite door, and saw, through the vistas of marble pillars and the wonderful fret-work which seems a thing of air rather than of earth, the Fountain of the Lions. Thence I entered in succession the Hall of the Abencerrages, the Hall of the Two Sisters, the apartments of the Sultanas, the Mosque, and the Hall of the Ambassadors. These places--all that is left of the renowned palace--are now well kept, and carefully guarded. Restorations are going on, here and there, and the place is scrupulously watched, that no foreign Vandal, may further injure what the native Goths have done their best to destroy. The rubbish has been cleared away; the rents in the walls have been filled up, and, for the first time since it passed into Spanish hands, there seems a hope that the Alhambra will be allowed to stand. What has been already destroyed we can only partially conjecture; but no one sees what remains without completing the picture in his own imagination, and placing it among the most perfect and marvellous creations of human genius.

Nothing can exceed the richness of invention which, in this series of halls, corridors, and courts, never repeats the same ornaments, but, from the simplest primitive forms and colors, produces a thousand combinations, not one of which is in discord with the grand design. It is useless to attempt a detailed description of this architecture; and it is so unlike anything else in the world, that, like Karnak and Baalbec, those only know the Alhambra who see it. When you can weave stone, and hang your halls with marble tapestry, you may rival it. It is nothing to me that these ornaments are stucco; to sculpture them in marble is only the work of the hands. Their great excellence is in the design, which, like all great things, suggests even more than it gives. If I could create all that the Court of Lions suggested to me for its completion, it would fulfil the dream of King Sheddad, and surpass the palaces of the Moslem Paradise.

The pavilions of the Court of Lions, and the halls which open into it, on either side, approach the nearest to their original perfection. The floors are marble, the wainscoting of painted tiles, the walls of embroidery, still gleaming with the softened lustre of their original tints, and the lofty conical domes seem to be huge sparry crystalizations, hung with dropping stalactites, rather than any work of the human hand. Each of these domes is composed of five thousand separate pieces, and the pendent prismatic blocks, colored and gilded, gradually resolve themselves, as you gaze, into the most intricate and elegant designs. But you must study long ere you have won all the secret of their beauty. To comprehend them, one should spend a whole day, lying on his back, under each one. Mateo spread his cloak for me in the fountain in the Hall of the Abencerrages, over the blood-stains made by the decapitation of those gallant chiefs, and I lay half an hour looking upward: and this is what I made out of the dome. From its central pinnacle hung the chalice of a flower with feathery petals, like the "crape myrtle" of our Southern States Outside of this, branched downward the eight rays of a large star, whose points touched the base of the dome; yet the star was itself composed of flowers, while between its rays and around its points fell a shower of blossoms, shells, and sparry drops. From the base of the dome hung a gorgeous pattern of lace, with a fringe of bugles, projecting into eight points so as to form a star of drapery, hanging from the points of the flowery star in the dome. The spaces between the angles were filled with masses of stalactites, dropping one below the other, till they tapered into the plain square sides of the hall.

In the Hall of the Two Sisters, I lay likewise for a considerable time, resolving its misty glories into shape. The dome was still more suggestive of flowers. The highest and central piece was a deep trumpet-flower, whose mouth was cleft into eight petals. It hung in the centre of a superb lotus-cup, the leaves of which were exquisitely veined and chased. Still further below swung a mass of mimosa blossoms, intermixed with pods and lance-like leaves, and around the base of the dome opened the bells of sixteen gorgeous tulips. These pictures may not be very intelligible, but I know not how else to paint the effect of this fairy architecture.

In Granada, as in Seville and Cordova, one's sympathies are wholly with the Moors. The few mutilated traces which still remain of their power, taste, and refinement, surpass any of the monuments erected by the race which conquered them. The Moorish Dynasty in Spain was truly, as Irving observes, a splendid exotic, doomed never to take a lasting root in the soil It was choked to death by the native weeds; and, in place of lands richly cultivated and teeming with plenty, we now have barren and-almost depopulated wastes-- in place of education, industry, and the cultivation of the arts and sciences, an enslaved, ignorant and degenerate race. Andalusia would be far more prosperous at this day, had she remained in Moslem hands. True, she would not have received that Faith which is yet destined to be the redemption of the world, but the doctrines of Mahomet are more acceptable to God, and more beneficial to Man than those of that Inquisition, which, in Spain alone, has shed ten times as much Christian blood as all the Moslem races together for the last six centuries. It is not from a mere romantic interest that I lament

629

the fate of Boabdil, and the extinction of his dynasty. Had he been a king worthy to reign in those wonderful halls, he never would have left them. Had he perished there, fighting to the last, he would have been freed from forty years of weary exile and an obscure death. Well did Charles V. observe, when speaking of him: "Better a tomb in the Alhambra than a palace in the Alpujanas!"

Chapter XXXVI. The Bridle-Roads of Andalusia.

Change of Weather--Napoleon and his Horses--Departure from Granada--My Guide, José Garcia--His Domestic Troubles--The Tragedy of the Umbrella--The Vow against Aguardiente--Crossing the Vega--The Sierra Nevada--The Baths of Alhama--"Woe is Me, Alhama!"--The Valley of the River Vélez--Vélez Malaga--The Coast Road--The Fisherman and his Donkey--Malaga--Summer Scenery--The Story of Don Pedro, without Fear and without Care--The Field of Monda--A Lonely Venta.

Venta de Villalon, *November* 20, 1852.

The clouds broke away before I had been two hours in the Alhambra, and the sunshine fell broad and warm into its courts. They must be roofed with blue sky, in order to give the full impression of their brightness and beauty. Mateo procured me a bottle of vino rancio, and we drank it together in the Court of Lions. Six hours had passed away before I knew it, and I reluctantly prepared to leave. The clouds by this time had disappeared; the Vega slept in brilliant sunshine, and the peaks of the Sierra Nevada shone white and cold against the sky.

On reaching the hotel, I found a little man, nicknamed Napoleon, awaiting me. He was desirous to furnish me with horses, and, having a prophetic knowledge of the weather, promised me a bright sky as far as Gibraltar. "I furnish all the señors," said he; "they know me, and never complain of me or my horses;" but, by way of security, on making the bargain, I threatened to put up a card in the hotel at Gibraltar, warning all travellers against him, in case I was not satisfied. My contract was for two horses and a guide, who were to be ready at sunrise the next morning. Napoleon was as good as his word; and before I had finished an early cup of chocolate, there was a little black Andalusian stallion awaiting me. The alforjas, or saddle-bags, of the guide were strengthened by a stock of cold provisions, the leathern bota hanging beside it was filled with ripe Granada wine; and now behold me ambling over the Vega, accoutred in a gay Andalusian jacket, a sash woven by Mateo

Ximenes, and one of those bandboxy sombreros, which I at first thought so ungainly, but now consider quite picturesque and elegant.

My guide, a short but sinewy and well-knit son of the mountains, named José Garcia, set off at a canter down the banks of the Darro. "Don't ride so fast!" cried Napoleon, who watched our setting out, from the door of the fonda; but José was already out of hearing. This guide is a companion to my liking. Although he is only twenty-seven, he has been for a number of years a correo, or mail-rider, and a guide for travelling parties. His olive complexion is made still darker by exposure to the sun and wind, and his coal-black eyes shine with Southern heat and fire. He has one of those rare mouths which are born with a broad smile in each corner, and which seem to laugh even in the midst of grief. We had not been two hours together, before I knew his history from beginning to end. He had already been married eight years, and his only trouble was a debt of twenty-four dollars, which the illness of his wife had caused him. This money was owing to the pawnbroker, who kept his best clothes in pledge until he could pay it. "Señor," said he, "if I had ten million dollars, I would rather give them all away than have a sick wife." He had a brother in Puerto Principe, Cuba, who sent over money enough to pay the rent of the house, but he found that children were a great expense. "It is most astonishing," he said, "how much children can eat. From morning till night, the bread is never out of their mouths."

José has recently been travelling with some Spaniards, one of whom made him pay two dollars for an umbrella which was lost on the road. This umbrella is a thorn in his side. At every venta where we stop, the story is repeated, and he is not sparing of his maledictions. The ghost of that umbrella is continually raised, and it will be a long time before he can shut it. "One reason why I like to travel with foreign Señors," said he to me, "is, that when I lose anything, they never make me pay for it." "For all that," I answered, "take care you don't lose my umbrella: it cost three dollars." Since then, nothing can exceed José's attention to that article. He is at his wit's end how to secure it best. It appears sometimes before, sometimes behind him, lashed to the saddle with innumerable cords; now he sticks it into the alforja, now carries it in his hand, and I verily believe that he sleeps with it in his arms. Every evening, as he tells his story to the muleteers, around the kitchen fire, he always winds up by triumphantly appealing to me with: "Well, Señor, have I lost your umbrella yet?"

Our bargain is that I shall feed him on the way, and as we travel in the primitive style of the country, we always sit down together to the same dish. To his supervision, the olla is often indebted for an additional flavor, and no "thorough-bred" gentleman could behave at table with more ease and propriety. He is as moderate as a Bedouin in his wants, and never touches the burning aguardiente which the muleteers are accustomed to drink. I asked him the reason of this. "I drink wine. Senor," he replied, "because that, you know, is like meat and bread; but I have made a vow never to drink aguardiente again. Two of us got drunk on it, four or five years ago, in Granada, and we quarrelled. My comrade drew his knife and stabbed me here, in the left shoulder. I was furious and cut him across the breast. We both went to the hospital--I for three months and he for six--and he died in a few days after getting out. It cost my poor father many a thousand reals; and when I was able to go to work, I vowed before the Virgin that I would never touch aguardiente again."

For the first league, our road lay over the rich Vega of Granada, but gradually became wilder and more waste. Passing the long, desert ridge, known as the "Last Sigh of the Moor," we struck across a region of low hills. The road was very deep, from the recent rains, and studded, at short intervals, by rude crosses, erected to persons who had been murdered. José took a grim delight in giving me the history of each. Beyond the village of Lamala, which lies with its salt-pans in a basin of the hills, we ascended the mountain ridge which forms the southern boundary of the Vega. Granada, nearly twenty miles distant, was still visible. The Alhambra was dwindled to a speck, and I took my last view of it and the magnificent landscape which lies spread out before it. The Sierra Nevada, rising to the height of 13,000 feet above the sea, was perfectly free from clouds, and the whole range was visible at one glance. All its chasms were filled with snow, and for nearly half-way down its sides there was not a speck of any other color. Its summits were almost wholly devoid of shadow, and their notched and jagged outlines rested flatly against the sky, like ivory inlaid on a table of lapis-lazuli.

From these waste hills, we descended into the valley of Cacia, whose poplar-fringed river had been so swollen by the rains that the correo from Malaga had only succeeded in passing it that morning. We forded it without accident, and, crossing a loftier and bleaker range, came down into the valley of the Marchan. High on a cliff over the stream stood Alhama, my resting-place for the night. The natural warm baths, on account of which this spot was so beloved by the Moors, are still resorted to in the summer. They lie in the bosom of a deep and rugged gorge, half a mile further down the river. The town occupies the crest of a narrow promontory, bounded, on all sides but one, by tremendous precipices. It is one of the most picturesque spots imaginable, and reminded me--to continue the comparison between Syria and Andalusia, which I find so striking--of the gorge of the Barrada, near Damascus. Alhama is now a poor, insignificant town, only visited by artists and muleteers. The population wear long brown cloaks and slouched hats, like the natives of La Mancha.

I found tolerable quarters in a house on the plaza, and took the remaining hour of daylight to view the town. The people looked at me with curiosity, and some boys, walking on the edge of the tajo, or precipice, threw over stones that I might see how deep it was. The rock, in some places, quite overhung the bed of the Marchan, which half-girdles its base. The close scrutiny to which I was subjected by the crowd in the plaza called to mind all I had heard of Spanish spies and robbers. At the venta, I was well treated, but received such an exorbitant bill in the morning that I was ready to exclaim, with King Boabdil, "Woe is me, Alhama!" On comparing notes with José, I found that he had been obliged to pay, in addition, for what he received--a discovery which so exasperated that worthy that he folded his hands, bowed his head, made three kisses in the air, and cried out: "I swear before the Virgin that I will never again take a traveller to that inn."

We left Alhama an hour before daybreak, for we had a rough journey of more than forty miles before us. The bridle-path was barely visible in the darkness, but we continued ascending to a height of probably 5,000 feet above the sea, and thus met the sunrise half-way. Crossing the llano of Ace faraya, we reached a tremendous natural portal in the mountains, from whence, as from a door, we looked down on all the country lying between us and the sea. The valley of the River Vélez, winding among the hills, pointed out the course of our road. On the left towered over us the barren Sierra Tejeda, an isolated group of peaks, about 8,000 feet in height. For miles, the road was a rocky ladder, which we scrambled down on foot, leading our horses. The vegetation gradually became of a warmer and more luxuriant cast; the southern slopes were planted with the vine that produces the famous Malaga raisins, and the orange groves in the sunny depths of the valleys were as yellow as autumnal beeches, with their enormous loads of fruit. As the bells of Vélez Malaga were ringing noon, we emerged from the mountains, near the mouth of the river, and rode into the town to breakfast.

We halted at a queer old inn, more like a Turkish khan than a Christian hostlery. It was kept by a fat landlady, who made us an olla of kid and garlic, which, with some coarse bread and the red Malaga wine, soon took off the sharp edge of our mountain appetites. While I was washing my hands at a well in the court-yard, the mozo noticed the pilgrim-seal of Jerusalem, which is stamped indelibly on my left arm. His admiration and reverence were so great that he called the fat landlady, who, on learning that it had been made in Jerusalem, and that I had visited the Holy Sepulchre, summoned her children to see it. "Here, my children!" she said; "cross yourselves, kneel down, and kiss this holy seal; for, as long as you live, you may never see the like of it again." Thus I, a Protestant heretic, became a Catholic shrine. The children knelt and kissed my arm with touching simplicity; and the seal will henceforth be more sacred to me than ever.

The remaining twenty miles or more of the road to Malaga follow the line of the coast, passing headlands crowned by the atalayas, or watch-towers, of the Moors. It is a new road, and practicable for carriages, so that, for Spain, it may be considered an important achievement. The late rains have, however, already undermined it in a number of places. Here, as among the mountains, we met crowds of muleteers, all of whom greeted me with: "Vaya usted con Dios, caballero!"--("May you go with God, cavalier!") By this time, all my forgotten Spanish had come back again, and a little experience of the simple ways of the people made me quite at home among them. In almost every instance, I was treated precisely as a Spaniard would have been, and less annoyed by the curiosity of the natives than I have been in Germany, and even America.

We were still two leagues from Malaga, at sunset, The fishermen along the coast were hauling in their nets, and we soon began to overtake companies of them, carrying their fish to the city on donkeys. One stout, strapping fellow, with flesh as hard and yellow as a sturgeon's, was seated sideways on a very small donkey, between two immense panniers of fish, As he trotted before us, shouting, and slapping the flanks of the sturdy little beast, José and I began to laugh, whereupon the fellow broke out into the following monologue, addressed to the donkey: "Who laughs at this burrico? Who says he's not fine gold from head to foot? What is it that he can't do? If there was a mountain ever so high, he would gallop over it. If there was a river ever so deep, he would swim through it If he could but speak, I might send him to market alone with the fish, and not a chavo of the money would he spend on the way home. Who says he can't go as far as that limping horse? Arrrre, burrico! punate--ar-r-r-r-e-e!"

We reached Malaga, at last, our horses sorely fagged. At the Fonda de la Alameda, a new and very elegant hotel, I found a bath and a good dinner, both welcome things to a tired traveller. The winter of Malaga is like spring in other lands and on that account it is much visited by invalids, especially English. It is a lively commercial town of about 80,000 inhabitants, and, if the present scheme of railroad communication with Madrid is carried out, must continue to increase in size and importance. A number of manufacturing establishments have lately been started, and in this department it bids fair to rival Barcelona. The harbor is small, but good, and the country around rich in all the productions of temperate and even tropical climates. The city contains little to interest the tourist. I visited the Cathedral, an immense unfinished mass, without a particle of architectural taste outwardly, though the interior has a fine effect from its large dimensions.

At noon to-day we were again in the saddle, and took the road to the Baths of Caratraca. The tall factory chimneys of Malaga, vomiting forth

636

streams of black smoke, marred the serenity of the sky; but the distant view of the city is very fine. The broad Vega, watered by the Guadaljorce, is rich and well cultivated, and now rejoices in the verdure of spring. The meadows are clothed with fresh grass, butter-cups and daisies are in blossom, and larks sing in the olive-trees. Now and then, we passed a casa del campo, with its front half buried in orange-trees, over which towered two or three sentinel palms. After two leagues of this delightful travel, the country became more hilly, and the groups of mountains which inclosed us assumed the most picturesque and enchanting forms. The soft haze in which the distant peaks were bathed, the lovely violet shadows filling up their chasms and gorges, and the fresh meadows, vineyards, and olive groves below, made the landscape one of the most beautiful I have seen in Spain.

As we were trotting along through the palmetto thickets, José asked me if I should not like to hear an Andalusian story. "Nothing would please me better," I replied. "Ride close beside me, then," said he, "that you may understand every word of it." I complied, and he gave me the following, just as I repeat it: "There was once a very rich man, who had thousands of cattle in the Sierra Nevada, and hundreds of houses in the city. Well: this man put a plate, with his name on it, on the door of the great house in which he lived, and the name was this: Don Pedro, without Fear and without Care. Now, when the King was making his paséo, he happened to ride by this house in his carriage, and saw the plate on the door. 'Read me the name on that plate!' said he to his officer. Then the officer read the name: Don Pedro, without Fear and without Care. 'I will see whether Don Pedro is without Fear and without Care,' said the King. The next day came a messenger to the house, and, when he saw Don Pedro, said he to him; 'Don Pedro, without Fear and without Care, the King wants you!' 'What does the King want with me?' said Don Pedro. 'He sends you four questions which you must answer within four days, or he will have you shot; and the questions are:--How can the Sierra Nevada be cleared of snow? How can the sea be made smaller? How many arrobas does the moon weigh? And: How many leagues from here to the Land of Heavenly Glory?' Then Don Pedro without Fear and without Care began to sweat from fright, and knew not what he should do. He called some of his arrieros and loaded twenty mules with money, and went up into the Sierra

Nevada, where his herdsmen tended his flocks; for, as I said, he had many thousand cattle. 'God keep you, my master!' said the chief herdsman, who was young, and buen mozo, and had as good a head as ever was set on two shoulders. 'Anda, hombre! said Don Pedro, 'I am a dead man;' and so he told the herdsman all that the King had said. 'Oh, is that all?' said the knowing mozo. 'I can get you out of the scrape. Let me go and answer the questions in your name, my master!' 'Ah, you fool! what can you do?' said Don Pedro without Fear and without Care, throwing himself upon the earth, and ready to die.

"But, nevertheless, the herdsman dressed himself up as a caballero, went down to the city, and, on the fourth day, presented himself at the King's palace. 'What do you want?' said the officers. 'I am Don Pedro without Fear and without Care, come to answer the questions which the King sent to me.' 'Well,' said the King, when he was brought before him, 'let me hear your answers, or I will have you shot this day.' 'Your Majesty,' said the herdsman, 'I think I can do it. If you were to set a million of children to playing among the snow of the Sierra Nevada, they would soon clear it all away; and if you were to dig a ditch as wide and as deep as all Spain, you would make the sea that much smaller,' 'But,' said the King, 'that makes only two questions; there are two more yet,' 'I think I can answer those, also,' said the herdsman: 'the moon contains four quarters, and therefore weighs only one arroba; and as for the last question, it is not even a single league to the Land of Heavenly Glory--for, if your Majesty were to die after breakfast, you would get there before you had an appetite for dinner,' 'Well done! said the King; and he then made him Count, and Marquez, and I don't know how many other titles. In the meantime, Don Pedro without Fear and without Care had died of his fright; and, as he left no family, the herdsman took possession of all his estates, and, until the day of his death, was called Don Pedro without Fear and without Care."

I write, sitting by the grated window of this lonely inn, looking out on the meadows of the Guadaljorce. The chain of mountains which rises to the west of Malaga is purpled by the light of the setting sun, and the houses and Castle of Carlama hang on its side, in full view. Further to the right, I see the smoke of Monda, where one of the greatest battles of antiquity was fought--that which overthrew the sons of Pompey, and gave the Roman Empire to Cæsar. The mozo of the venta is busy, preparing my kid and rice, and José is at his elbow, gently suggesting ingredients which may give the dish a richer flavor. The landscape is softened by the hush of coming evening; a few birds are still twittering among the bushes, and the half-moon grows whiter and clearer in mid-heaven. The people about me are humble, but appear honest and peaceful, and nothing indicates that I am in the wild Serrania de Ronda, the country of robbers, contrabandistas, and assassins.

Chapter XXXVII. The Mountains of Ronda.

Orange Valleys--Climbing the Mountains--José's Hospitality--El Burgo--The Gate of the Wind--The Cliff and Cascades of Ronda--The Mountain Region--Traces of the Moors--Haunts of Robbers--A Stormy Ride--The Inn at Gaucin--Bad News--A Boyish Auxiliary--Descent from the Mountains--The Ford of the Guadiaro--Our Fears Relieved--The Cork Woods--Ride from San Roque to Gibraltar--Parting with José--Travelling in Spain--Conclusion.

Gibraltar, *Thursday, November* 25, 1852.

I passed an uncomfortable night at the Venta de Villalon, lying upon a bag stuffed with equal quantities of wool and fleas. Starting before dawn, we followed a path which led into the mountains, where herdsmen and boys were taking out their sheep and goats to pasture; then it descended into the valley of a stream, bordered with rich bottom-lands. I never saw the orange in a more flourishing state. We passed several orchards of trees thirty feet high, and every bough and twig so completely laden with fruit, that the foliage was hardly to be seen.

At the Venta del Vicario, we found a number of soldiers just setting out for Ronda. They appeared to be escorting a convoy of goods, for there were twenty or thirty laden mules gathered at the door. We now ascended a most difficult and stony path, winding through bleak wastes of gray rock, till we reached a lofty pass in the mountain range. The wind swept through the narrow gateway with a force that almost unhorsed us. From the other side, a sublime but most desolate landscape opened to my view. Opposite, at ten miles' distance, rose a lofty ridge of naked rock, overhung with clouds. The country between was a chaotic jumble of stony hills, separated by deep chasms, with just a green patch here and there, to show that it was not entirely forsaken by man. Nevertheless as we descended into it, we found valleys with vineyards and olive groves, which were invisible from above. As we were both getting hungry, José stopped at a ventorillo and ordered two cups of wine, for which he insisted on paying. "If I had as many horses as my master, Napoleon," said he, "I would regale the Señors whenever I travelled with them. I would have puros, and sweetmeats, with plenty of Malaga or Valdepeñas in the bota, and they should never complain of their fare." Part of our road was studded with gray cork-trees, at a distance hardly to be distinguished from olives, and José dismounted to gather the mast, which was as sweet and palatable as chestnuts, with very little of the bitter quercine flavor. At eleven o'clock, we reached El Burgo, so called, probably, from its ancient Moorish fortress. It is a poor, starved village, built on a barren hill, over a stream which is still spanned by a lofty Moorish bridge of a single arch.

The remaining three leagues to Ronda were exceedingly rough and difficult. Climbing a barren ascent of nearly a league in length, we reached the Puerto del Viento, or Gate of the Wind, through which drove such a current that we were obliged to dismount; and even then it required all my strength to move against it. The peaks around, far and near, faced with precipitous cliffs, wore the most savage and forbidding aspect: in fact, this region is almost a counterpart of the wilderness lying between Jerusalem and the Dead Sea, Very soon, we touched the skirt of a cloud, and were enveloped in masses of chill, whirling vapor, through which we travelled for three or four miles to a similar gate on the western side of the chain. Descending again, we emerged into a clearer atmosphere, and saw below us a wide extent of mountain country, but of a more fertile and cheerful character. Olive orchards and wheat-fields now appeared; and, at four o'clock, we rode into the streets of Ronda.

No town can surpass this in the grandeur and picturesqueness of its position. It is built on the edge of a broad shelf of the mountains, which falls away in a sheer precipice of from six to eight hundred feet in height, and, from the windows of many of the houses you can look down the dizzy abyss. This shelf, again, is divided in the centre by a tremendous chasm, three hundred feet wide, and from four to six hundred feet in depth, in the bed of which roars the Guadalvin, boiling in foaming whirlpools or leaping in sparkling cascades, till it reaches the valley below. The town lies on both sides of the chasm, which is spanned by a stone bridge of a single arch, with abutments nearly four hundred feet in height. The view of this wonderful cleft, either from above or below, is one of the finest of its kind in the world.

Honda is as far superior to Tivoli, as Tivoli is to a Dutch village, on the dead levels of Holland. The panorama which it commands is on the grandest scale. The valley below is a garden of fruit and vines; bold yet cultivated hills succeed, and in the distance rise the lofty summits of another chain of the Serrania de Honda. Were these sublime cliffs, these charming cascades of the Guadalvin, and this daring bridge, in Italy instead of in Spain, they would be sketched and painted every day in the year; but I have yet to know where a good picture of Ronda may be found.

In the bottom of the chasm are a number of corn-mills as old as the time of the Moors. The water, gushing out from the arches of one, drives the wheel of that below, so that a single race supplies them all. I descended by a very steep zig-zag path nearly to the bottom. On a little point or promontory overhanging the black depths, there is a Moorish gateway still standing. The sunset threw a lovely glow over the brown cliffs and the airy town above; but they were far grander when the cascades glittered in the moonlight, and the gulf out of which they leap was lost in profound shadow. The window of my bed-room hung over the chasm.

Honda was wrapped in fog, when José awoke me on the morning of the 22d. As we had but about twenty-four miles to ride that day, we did not leave until sunrise. We rode across the bridge, through the old town and down the hill, passing the triple lines of the Moorish walls by the original gateways. The road, stony and rugged beyond measure, now took to the mountains. From the opposite height, there was a fine view of the town, perched like an eagle's nest on the verge of its tremendous cliffs; but a curtain of rain soon fell before it, and the dense dark clouds settled around us, and filled up the gorges on either hand. Hour after hour, we toiled along the slippery paths, scaling the high ridges by rocky ladders, up which our horses climbed with the greatest difficulty. The scenery, whenever I could obtain a misty glimpse of it, was sublime. Lofty mountain ridges rose on either hand; bleak jagged summits of naked rock pierced the clouds, and the deep chasms which separated them sank far below us, dark and indistinct through the rain. Sometimes I caught sight of a little hamlet, hanging on some almost inaccessible ledge, the home of the lawless, semi-Moorish mountaineers who inhabit this wild region. The faces of those we met exhibited marked traces of their Moslem ancestry, especially in the almond-shaped eye and the dusky olive complexion. Their dialect retains many Oriental forms of expression, and I was not a little surprised at finding the Arabic "eiwa" (yes) in general use, instead of the Spanish "si."

About eleven o'clock, we reached the rude village of Atajate, where we procured a very good breakfast of kid, eggs, and white Ronda wine. The wind and rain increased, but I had no time to lose, as every hour swelled the mountain floods and made the journey more difficult. This district is in the worst repute of any in Spain; it is a very nest of robbers and contrabandistas. At the venta in Atajate, they urged us to take a guard, but my valiant José declared that he had never taken one, and yet was never robbed; so I trusted to his good luck. The weather, however, was our best protection. In such a driving rain, we could bid defiance to the flint locks of their escopettes, if, indeed, any could be found, so fond of their trade, as to ply it in a storm

"Wherein the cub-drawn bear would crouch,

The lion and the belly-pinched wolf

Keep their furs dry."

Nevertheless, I noticed that each of the few convoys of laden mules which we met, had one or more of the guardia cicia accompanying it. Besides these, the only persons abroad were some wild-looking individuals, armed to the teeth, and muffled in long cloaks, towards whom, as they passed, José would give his head a slight toss, and whisper to me: "more contrabandistas."

We were soon in a condition to defy the weather. The rain beat furiously in our faces, especially when threading the wind-blown passes between the higher peaks. I raised my umbrella as a defence, but the first blast snapped it in twain. The mountain-sides were veined with rills, roaring downward into the hollows, and smaller rills soon began to trickle down my own sides. During the last part of our way, the path was notched along precipitous steeps, where the storm was so thick that we could see nothing either above or below. It was like riding along the outer edge of the world, When once you are thoroughly wet, it is a great satisfaction to know that you can be no wetter; and so José and I went forward in the best possible humor, finding so much diversion in our plight that the dreary leagues were considerably shortened.

At the venta of Gaucin, where we stopped, the people received us kindly. The house consisted of one room--stable, kitchen, and dining-room all in one. There was a small apartment in a windy loft, where a bed (much too short) was prepared for me. A fire of dry heather was made in the wide fireplace, and the ruddy flames, with a change of clothing and a draught of the amber vintage of Estepona, soon thawed out the chill of the journey. But I received news which caused me a great deal of anxiety. The River Guadiaro was so high that nobody could cross, and two forlorn muleteers had been waiting eight days at the inn, for the waters to subside. Augmented by the rain which had fallen, and which seemed to increase as night came on, how could I hope to cross it on the morrow? In two days, the India steamer would be at Gibraltar; my passage was already taken, and I must be there. The matter was discussed for some time; it was pronounced impossible to travel by the usual road, but the landlord knew a path among the hills which led to a ferry on the Guadiaro, where there was a boat, and from thence we could make our way to San Roque, which is in sight of Gibraltar. He demanded rather a large fee for accompanying me, but there was nothing else to be done. José and I sat down in great tribulation to our accustomed olla, but neither of us could do justice to it, and the greater part gladdened the landlord's two boys--beautiful little imps, with faces like Murillo's cherubs.

Nevertheless, I passed rather a merry evening, chatting with some of the villagers over a brazier of coals; and one of the aforesaid boys, who, although only eight years old, already performed the duties of mozo, lighted me to my loft. When he had put down the lamp, he tried' the door, and asked me: "Have you the key?" "No," said I, "I don't want one; I am not afraid." "But," he rejoined, "perhaps you may get afraid in the night; and if you do, strike on this part of the wall (suiting the action to the word)--I sleep on that side." I willingly promised to call him to my aid, if I should get alarmed. I slept but little, for the wind was howling around the tiles over my head, and I was busy with plans for constructing rafts and swimming currents with a rope around my waist. Finally, I found a little oblivion, but it seemed that I had scarcely closed my eyes, when José pushed open the door. "Thanks be to God, senor!" said he, "it begins to dawn, and the sky is clear: we shall certainly get to Gibraltar to-day."

The landlord was ready, so we took some bread and a basket of olives, and set out at once. Leaving Gaucin, we commenced descending the mountain staircase by which the Serrania of Ronda is scaled, on the side towards Gibraltar. "The road," says Mr. Ford, "seems made by the Evil One in a hanging garden of Eden." After four miles of frightfully rugged descent, we reached an orange grove on the banks of the Xenar, and then took a wild path leading along the hills on the right of the stream. We overtook a few muleteers, who were tempted out by the fine weather, and before long the correo, or mail-rider from Ronda to San Roque, joined us. After eight miles more of toilsome travel we reached the valley of the Guadiaro. The river was not more than twenty yards wide, flowing with a deep, strong current, between high banks. Two ropes were stretched across, and a large, clumsy boat was moored to the shore. We called to the ferrymen, but they hesitated, saying that nobody had yet been able to cross. However, we all got in, with our horses, and two of the men, with much reluctance, drew us over. The current was very powerful, although the river had fallen a little during the night, but we reached the opposite bank without accident.

We had still another river, the Guargante, to pass, but we were cheered by some peasants whom we met, with the news that the ferry-boat had resumed operations. After this current lay behind us, and there was now nothing but firm land all the way to Gibraltar, José declared with much earnestness that he was quite as glad, for my sake, as if somebody had given him a million of dollars. Our horses, too, seemed to feel that something had been achieved, and showed such a fresh spirit that we loosened the reins and let them gallop to their hearts' content over the green meadows. The mountains were now behind us, and the Moorish castle of Gaucin crested a peak blue with the distance. Over hills covered with broom and heather in blossom, and through hollows grown with oleander, arbutus and the mastic shrub, we rode to the cork-wood forests of San Roque, the sporting-ground of Gibraltar officers.

The barking of dogs, the cracking of whips, and now and then a distant halloo, announced that a hunt was in progress, and soon we came upon a company of thirty or forty horsemen, in caps, white gloves and top-boots, scattered along the crest of a hill. I had no desire to stop and witness the sport, for the Mediterranean now lay before me, and the huge gray mass of "The Rock" loomed in the distance.

At San Roque, which occupies the summit of a conical hill, about half-way between Gibraltar and Algeciras, the landlord left us, and immediately started on his return. Having now exchanged the rugged bridle-paths of Ronda for a smooth carriage-road, José and I dashed on at full gallop, to the end of our journey. We were both bespattered with mud from head to foot, and our jackets and sombreros had lost something of their spruce air. We met a great many ruddy, cleanly-shaven Englishmen, who reined up on one side to let us pass, with a look of wonder at our Andalusian impudence. Nothing diverted José more than to see one of these Englishmen rising in his stirrups, as he went by on a trot. "Look, look, Señor!" he exclaimed; "did you ever see the like?" and then broke into a fresh explosion of laughter. Passing the Spanish Lines, which stretch across the neck of the sandy little peninsula, connecting Gibraltar with the main land, we rode under the terrible batteries which snarl at Spain from this side of the Rock. Row after row of enormous guns bristle the walls, or look out from the galleries hewn in the sides of inaccessible cliffs An artificial moat is cut along the base of the Rock, and a simple bridge-road leads into the fortress and town. After giving up my passport I was allowed to enter, José having already obtained a permit from the Spanish authorities.

I clattered up the long street of the town to the Club House, where I found a company of English friends. In the evening, José made his appearance, to settle our accounts and take his leave of me. While scrambling down the rocky stair-way of Gaucin, José had said to me: "Look you, Señor, I am very fond of English beer, and if I get you to Gibraltar to day you must give me a glass of it." When, therefore, he came in the evening, his eyes sparkled at the sight of a bottle of Alsop's Ale, and a handful of good Gibraltar cigars. "Ah, Señor," said he, after our books were squared, and he had pocketed his gratification, "I am sorry we are going to part; for we are good friends, are we not, Señor?" "Yes, José," said I; "if I ever come to Granada again, I shall take no other guide than José Garcia; and I will have you for a longer journey than this. We shall go over all Spain together, mi amigo!" "May God grant it!" responded José, crossing himself; "and now, Señor, I must go. I shall travel back to Granada, muy triste, Señor, muy triste" The faithful fellows eyes were full of tears, and, as he lifted my hand twice to his lips, some warm drops fell upon it. God bless his honest heart; wherever he goes!

And now a word as to travelling in Spain, which is not attended with half the difficulties and annoyances I had been led to expect. My experience, of course, is limited to the provinces of Andalusia, but my route included some of the roughest roads and most dangerous robber-districts in the Peninsula. The people with whom I came in contact were invariably friendly and obliging, and I was dealt with much more honestly than I should have been in Italy. With every disposition to serve you, there is nothing like servility among the Spaniards. The native dignity which characterizes their demeanor prepossesses me very strongly in their favor. There is but one dialect of courtesy, and the muleteers and common peasants address each other with the same grave respect as the Dons and Grandees. My friend José was a model of good-breeding.

I had little trouble either with passport-officers or custom-houses. My passport, in fact, was never once demanded, although I took the precaution to have it viséd in all the large cities. In Seville and Malaga, it was signed by the American Consuls, without the usual fee of two dollars--almost the only instances which have come under my observation. The regulations of the American Consular System, which gives the Consuls no salary, but permits them, instead, to get their pay out of travellers, is a disgrace to our government. It amounts, in effect, to a direct tax on travel, and falls heavily on the hundreds of young men of limited means, who annually visit Europe for the purpose of completing their education. Every American citizen who travels in Italy pays a passport tax of ten dollars. In all the ports of the Mediterranean, there is an American Vice-Consul, who does not even get the postage paid on his dispatches, and to whom the advent of a traveller is of course a welcome sight. Misled by a false notion of economy, our government is fast becoming proverbial for its meanness. If those of our own citizens who represent us abroad only worked as they are paid, and if the foreigners who act as Vice-Consuls without pay did not derive some petty trading advantages from their position, we should be almost without protection.

With my departure from Spain closes the record of my journey in the Lands of the Saracen; for, although I afterwards beheld more perfect types of Saracenic Art on the banks of the Jumna and the Ganges, they grew up under the great Empire of the descendants of Tamerlane, and were the creations of artists foreign to the soil. It would, no doubt, be interesting to contrast the remains of Oriental civilization and refinement, as they still exist at the extreme eastern and western limits of the Moslem sway, and to show how that Art, which had its birth in the capitals of the Caliphs--Damascus and Baghdad--attained its most perfect development in Spain and India; but my visit to the latter country connects itself naturally with my voyage to China, Loo-Choo, and Japan, forming a separate and distinct field of travel.

On the 27th of November, the Overland Mail Steamer arrived at Gibraltar, and I embarked in her for Alexandria, entering upon another year of even more varied, strange, and adventurous experiences, than that which had closed. I am almost afraid to ask those patient readers, who have accompanied me thus far, to travel with me through another volume; but next to the pleasure of seeing the world, comes the pleasure of telling of it, and I must needs finish my story.

WHO WAS SHE?

WHO WAS SHE?

From "The Atlantic Monthly" for September, 1874

Come, now, there may as well be an end of this! Every time I meet your eyes squarely, I detect the question just slipping out of them. If you had spoken it, or even boldly looked it; if you had shown in your motions the least sign of a fussy or fidgety concern on my account; if this were not the evening of my birthday, and you the only friend who remembered it; if confession were not good for the soul, though harder than sin to some people, of whom I am one—well, if all reasons were not at this instant converged into a focus, and burning me rather violently, in that region where the seat of emotion is supposed to lie, I should keep my trouble to myself.

Yes, I have fifty times had it on my mind to tell you the whole story. But who can be certain that his best friend will not smile—or, what is worse, cherish a kind of charitable pity ever afterward—when the external forms of a very serious kind of passion seem trivial, fantastic, foolish? And the worst of all is that the heroic part which I imagined I was playing proves to have been almost the reverse. The only comfort which I can find in my humiliation is that I am capable of feeling it. There isn't a bit of a paradox in this, as you will see; but I only mention it, now, to prepare you for, maybe, a little morbid sensitiveness of my moral nerves.

The documents are all in this portfolio under my elbow. I had just read them again completely through when you were announced. You may examine them as you like afterward: for the present, fill your glass, take another Cabana, and keep silent until my "ghastly tale" has reached its most lamentable conclusion.

The beginning of it was at Wampsocket Springs, three years ago last summer. I suppose most unmarried men who have reached, or passed, the age of thirty—and I was then thirty-three—experience a milder return of their adolescent warmth, a kind of fainter second spring, since the first has not fulfilled its promise. Of course, I wasn't clearly conscious of this at the time:

who is? But I had had my youthful passion and my tragic disappointment, as you know: I had looked far enough into what Thackeray used to call the cryptic mysteries to save me from the Scylla of dissipation, and yet preserved enough of natural nature to keep me out of the Pharisaic Charybdis. My devotion to my legal studies had already brought me a mild distinction; the paternal legacy was a good nest-egg for the incubation of wealth—in short, I was a fair, respectable "party," desirable to the humbler mammas, and not to be despised by the haughty exclusives.

The fashionable hotel at the Springs holds three hundred, and it was packed. I had meant to lounge there for a fortnight and then finish my holidays at Long Branch; but eighty, at least, out of the three hundred were young and moved lightly in muslin. With my years and experience I felt so safe that to walk, talk, or dance with them became simply a luxury, such as I had never—at least so freely—possessed before. My name and standing, known to some families, were agreeably exaggerated to the others, and I enjoyed that supreme satisfaction which a man always feels when he discovers, or imagines, that he is popular in society. There is a kind of premonitory apology implied in my saying this, I am aware. You must remember that I am culprit, and culprit's counsel, at the same time.

You have never been at Wampsocket? Well, the hills sweep around in a crescent, on the northern side, and four or five radiating glens, descending from them, unite just above the village. The central one, leading to a waterfall (called "Minne-hehe" by the irreverent young people, because there is so little of it), is the fashionable drive and promenade; but the second ravine on the left, steep, crooked, and cumbered with bowlders which have tumbled from somewhere and lodged in the most extraordinary groupings, became my favorite walk of a morning. There was a footpath in it, well-trodden at first, but gradually fading out as it became more like a ladder than a path, and I soon discovered that no other city feet than mine were likely to scale a certain rough slope which seemed the end of the ravine. With the aid of the tough laurel-stems I climbed to the top, passed through a cleft as narrow as a doorway, and presently found myself in a little upper dell, as wild and sweet and strange as one of the pictures that haunts us on the brink of sleep.

There was a pond—no, rather a bowl—of water in the centre; hardly twenty yards across, yet the sky in it was so pure and far down that the circle of rocks and summer foliage inclosing it seemed like a little planetary ring, floating off alone through space. I can't explain the charm of the spot, nor the selfishness which instantly suggested that I should keep the discovery to myself. Ten years earlier I should have looked around for some fair spirit to be my "minister," but now—

One forenoon—I think it was the third or fourth time I had visited the place—I was startled to find the dent of a heel in the earth, half-way up the slope. There had been rain during the night and the earth was still moist and soft. It was the mark of a woman's boot, only to be distinguished from that of a walking-stick by its semicircular form. A little higher, I found the outline of a foot, not so small as to awake an ecstasy, but with a suggestion of lightness, elasticity, and grace. If hands were thrust through holes in a board-fence, and nothing of the attached bodies seen, I can easily imagine that some would attract and others repel us: with footprints the impression is weaker, of course, but we cannot escape it. I am not sure whether I wanted to find the unknown wearer of the boot within my precious personal solitude: I was afraid I should see her, while passing through the rocky crevice, and yet was disappointed when I found no one.

But on the flat, warm rock overhanging the tarn—my special throne—lay some withering wild-flowers and a book! I looked up and down, right and left: there was not the slightest sign of another human life than mine. Then I lay down for a quarter of an hour, and listened: there were only the noises of bird and squirrel, as before. At last, I took up the book, the flat breadth of which suggested only sketches. There were, indeed, some tolerable studies of rocks and trees on the first pages; a few not very striking caricatures, which seemed to have been commenced as portraits, but recalled no faces I knew; then a number of fragmentary notes, written in pencil. I found no name, from first to last; only, under the sketches, a monogram so complicated and laborious that the initials could hardly be discovered unless one already knew them.

The writing was a woman's, but it had surely taken its character from certain features of her own: it was clear, firm, individual. It had nothing of that air of general debility which usually marks the manuscript of young ladies, yet its firmness was far removed from the stiff, conventional slope which all Englishwomen seem to acquire in youth and retain through life, I don't see how any man in my situation could have helped reading a few lines—if only for the sake of restoring lost property. But I was drawn on and on, and finished by reading all: thence, since no further harm could be done, I reread, pondering over certain passages until they stayed with me. Here they are, as I set them down, that evening, on the back of a legal blank:

> "It makes a great deal of difference whether we wear social forms as bracelets or handcuffs."

> "Can we not still be wholly our independent selves, even while doing, in the main, as others do? I know two who are so; but they are married."

> "The men who admire these bold, dashing young girls treat them like weaker copies of themselves. And yet they boast of what they call 'experience'!"

> "I wonder if any one felt the exquisite beauty of the noon as I did to-day? A faint appreciation of sunsets and storms is taught us in youth, and kept alive by novels and flirtations; but the broad, imperial splendor of this summer noon!—and myself standing alone in it—yes, utterly alone!" "The men I seek must exist: where are they? How make an acquaintance, when one obsequiously bows himself away, as I advance? The fault is surely not all on my side."

There was much more, intimate enough to inspire me with a keen interest in the writer, yet not sufficiently so to make my perusal a painful indiscretion. I yielded to the impulse of the moment, took out my pencil, and wrote a dozen lines on one of the blank pages. They ran something in this wise:

"IGNOTUS IGNOTÆ!—You have bestowed without intending it,

and I have taken without your knowledge. Do not regret the

accident which has enriched another. This concealed idyl of

the hills was mine, as I supposed, but I acknowledge your

equal right to it. Shall we share the possession, or will

you banish me?"

There was a frank advance, tempered by a proper caution, I fancied, in the words I wrote. It was evident that she was unmarried, but outside of that certainty there lay a vast range of possibilities, some of them alarming enough. However, if any nearer acquaintance should arise out of the incident, the next step must be taken by her. Was I one of the men she sought? I almost imagined so—certainly hoped so.

I laid the book on the rock, as I had found it, bestowed another keen scrutiny on the lonely landscape, and then descended the ravine. That evening, I went early to the ladies' parlor, chatted more than usual with the various damsels whom I knew, and watched with a new interest those whom I knew not. My mind, involuntarily, had already created a picture of the unknown. She might be twenty-five, I thought; a reflective habit of mind would hardly be developed before that age. Tall and stately, of course; distinctly proud in her bearing, and somewhat reserved in her manners. Why she should have large dark eyes, with long dark lashes, I could not tell; but so I seemed to see her. Quite forgetting that I was (or had meant to be) Ignotus, I found myself staring rather significantly at one or the other of the young ladies, in whom I discovered some slight general resemblance to the imaginary character. My fancies, I must confess, played strange pranks with me. They had been kept in a coop so many years that now, when I suddenly turned them loose, their rickety attempts at flight quite bewildered me.

No! there was no use in expecting a sudden discovery. I went to the glen betimes, next morning: the book was gone and so were the faded flowers, but some of the latter were scattered over the top of another rock, a few yards from mine. Ha! this means that I am not to withdraw, I said to myself: she makes room for me! But how to surprise her?—for by this time I was fully resolved to make her acquaintance, even though she might turn out to be forty, scraggy, and sandy-haired.

I knew no other way so likely as that of visiting the glen at all times of the day. I even went so far as to write a line of greeting, with a regret that our visits had not yet coincided, and laid it under a stone on the top of her rock. The note disappeared, but there was no answer in its place. Then I suddenly remembered her fondness for the noon hours, at which time she was "utterly alone." The hotel table d'hôte was at one o'clock: her family, doubtless, dined later, in their own rooms. Why, this gave me, at least, her place in society! The question of age, to be sure, remained unsettled; but all else was safe.

The next day I took a late and large breakfast, and sacrificed my dinner. Before noon the guests had all straggled back to the hotel from glen and grove and lane, so bright and hot was the sunshine. Indeed, I could hardly have supported the reverberation of heat from the sides of the ravine but for a fixed belief that I should be successful. While crossing the narrow meadow upon which it opened, I caught a glimpse of something white among the thickets higher up. A moment later it had vanished, and I quickened my pace, feeling the beginning of an absurd nervous excitement in my limbs. At the next turn, there it was again! but only for another moment. I paused, exulting, and wiped my drenched forehead. "She cannot escape me!" I murmured between the deep draughts of cooler air I inhaled in the shadow of a rock.

A few hundred steps more brought me to the foot of the steep ascent, where I had counted on overtaking her. I was too late for that, but the dry, baked soil had surely been crumbled and dislodged, here and there, by a rapid foot. I followed, in reckless haste, snatching at the laurel branches right and left, and paying little heed to my footing. About, one-third of the way up I slipped, fell, caught a bush which snapped at the root, slid, whirled over, and before I fairly knew what had happened, I was lying doubled up at the bottom of the slope.

I rose, made two steps forward, and then sat down with a groan of pain; my left ankle was badly sprained, in addition to various minor scratches and bruises. There was a revulsion of feeling, of course—instant, complete, and hideous. I fairly hated the Unknown. "Fool that I was!" I exclaimed, in the theatrical manner, dashing the palm of my hand softly against my brow: "lured to this by the fair traitress! But, no!—not fair: she shows the artfulness of faded, desperate spinsterhood; she is all compact of enamel, 'liquid bloom of youth' and hair dye!"

There was a fierce comfort in this thought, but it couldn't help me out of the scrape. I dared not sit still, lest a sunstroke should be added, and there was no resource but to hop or crawl down the rugged path, in the hope of finding a forked sapling from which I could extemporize a crutch. With endless pain and trouble I reached a thicket, and was feebly working on a branch with my pen-knife, when the sound of a heavy footstep surprised me.

A brown harvest-hand, in straw hat and shirtsleeves, presently appeared. He grinned when he saw me, and the thick snub of his nose would have seemed like a sneer at any other time.

"Are you the gentleman that got hurt?" he asked. "Is it pretty tolerable bad?"

"Who said I was hurt?" I cried, in astonishment.

"One of your town-women from the hotel—I reckon she was. I was binding oats, in the field over the ridge; but I haven't lost no time in comin' here."

While I was stupidly staring at this announcement, he whipped out a big clasp-knife, and in a few minutes fashioned me a practicable crutch. Then, taking me by the other arm, he set me in motion toward the village.

Grateful as I was for the man's help, he aggravated me by his ignorance.

When I asked if he knew the lady, he answered: "It's more'n likely you know her better," But where did she come from? Down from the hill, he guessed, but it might ha' been up the road. How did she look? was she old or young? what was the color of her eyes? of her hair? There, now, I was too much for him. When a woman kept one o' them speckled veils over her face, turned her head away, and held her parasol between, how were you to know her from Adam? I declare to you, I couldn't arrive at one positive particular. Even when he affirmed that she was tall, he added, the next instant: "Now I come to think on it, she stepped mighty quick; so I guess she must ha' been short."

By the time we reached the hotel, I was in a state of fever; opiates and lotions had their will of me for the rest of the day. I was glad to escape the worry of questions, and the conventional sympathy expressed in inflections of the voice which are meant to soothe, and only exasperate. The next morning, as I lay upon my sofa, restful, patient, and properly cheerful, the waiter entered with a bouquet of wild flowers.

"Who sent them?" I asked.

"I found them outside your door, sir. Maybe there's a card; yes, here's a bit o' paper."

I opened the twisted slip he handed me, and read: "From your dell—and mine." I took the flowers; among them were two or three rare and beautiful varieties which I had only found in that one spot. Fool, again! I noiselessly kissed, while pretending to smell them, had them placed on a stand within reach, and fell into a state of quiet and agreeable contemplation.

Tell me, yourself, whether any male human being is ever too old for sentiment, provided that it strikes him at the right time and in the right way! What did that bunch of wild flowers betoken? Knowledge, first; then, sympathy; and finally, encouragement, at least. Of course she had seen my accident, from above; of course she had sent the harvest laborer to aid me home. It was quite natural she should imagine some special, romantic interest in the lonely dell, on my part, and the gift took additional value from her conjecture.

Four days afterward, there was a hop in the large dining-room of the hotel. Early in the morning, a fresh bouquet had been left at my door. I was tired of my enforced idleness, eager to discover the fair unknown (she was again fair, to my fancy!), and I determined to go down, believing that a cane and a crimson velvet slipper on the left foot would provoke a glance of sympathy from certain eyes, and thus enable me to detect them.

The fact was, the sympathy was much too general and effusive. Everybody, it seemed, came to me with kindly greetings; seats were vacated at my approach, even fat Mrs. Huxter insisting on my taking her warm place, at the head of the room. But Bob Leroy—you know him—as gallant a gentleman as ever lived, put me down at the right point, and kept me there. He only meant to divert me, yet gave me the only place where I could quietly inspect all the younger ladies, as dance or supper brought them near.

One of the dances was an old-fashioned cotillon, and one of the figures, the "coquette," brought every one, in turn, before me. I received a pleasant word or two from those whom I knew, and a long, kind, silent glance from Miss May Danvers. Where had been my eyes? She was tall, stately, twenty-five, had large dark eyes, and long dark lashes! Again the changes of the dance brought her near me; I threw (or strove to throw) unutterable meanings into my eyes, and cast them upon hers. She seemed startled, looked suddenly away, looked back to me, and—blushed. I knew her for what is called "a nice girl"— that is, tolerably frank, gently feminine, and not dangerously intelligent. Was it possible that I had overlooked so much character and intellect?

As the cotillon closed, she was again in my neighborhood, and her partner led her in my direction. I was rising painfully from my chair, when Bob Leroy pushed me down again, whisked another seat from somewhere, planted it at my side, and there she was!

She knew who was her neighbor, I plainly saw; but instead of turning toward me, she began to fan herself in a nervous way and to fidget with the buttons of her gloves. I grew impatient.

"Miss Danvers!" I said, at last.

"Oh!" was all her answer, as she looked at me for a moment.

"Where are your thoughts?" I asked.

Then she turned, with wide, astonished eyes, coloring softly up to the roots of her hair. My heart gave a sudden leap.

"How can you tell, if I can not?" she asked.

"May I guess?"

She made a slight inclination of the head, saying nothing. I was then quite sure.

"The second ravine to the left of the main drive?"

This time she actually started; her color became deeper, and a leaf of the ivory fan snapped between her fingers.

"Let there be no more a secret!" I exclaimed. "Your flowers have brought me your messages; I knew I should find you—"

Full of certainty, I was speaking in a low, impassioned voice. She cut me short by rising from her seat; I felt that she was both angry and alarmed. Fisher, of Philadelphia, jostling right and left in his haste, made his way toward her. She fairly snatched his arm, clung to it with a warmth I had never seen expressed in a ballroom, and began to whisper in his ear. It was not five minutes before he came to me, alone, with a very stern face, bent down, and said:

"If you have discovered our secret, you will keep silent. You are certainly a gentleman."

I bowed, coldly and savagely. There was a draught from the open window; my ankle became suddenly weary and painful, and I went to bed. Can you believe that I didn't guess, immediately, what it all meant? In a vague way, I fancied that I had been premature in my attempt to drop our mutual incognito, and that Fisher, a rival lover, was jealous of me. This was rather flattering than otherwise; but when I limped down to the ladies' parlor, the next day, no Miss Danvers was to be seen. I did not venture to ask for her; it might seem importunate, and a woman of so much hidden capacity was evidently not to be wooed in the ordinary way.

So another night passed by; and then, with the morning, came a letter which made me feel, at the same instant, like a fool and a hero. It had been dropped in the Wampsocket post-office, was legibly addressed to me and delivered with some other letters which had arrived by the night mail. Here it is; listen:

"*Noto Ignota!*—*Haste is not a gift of the gods, and you have been impatient, with the usual result. I was almost prepared for this, and thus am not wholly disappointed. In a day or two more you will discover your mistake, which, so far as I can learn, has done no particular harm. If you wish to find me, there is only one way to seek me; should I tell you what it is, I should run the risk of losing you—that is, I should preclude the manifestation of a certain quality which I hope to find in the man who may—or—, rather, must—be my friend. This sounds enigmatical, yet you have read enough of my nature, as written in those random notes in my sketch-book, to guess, at least, how much I require. Only this let me add: mere guessing is useless.*

"*Being unknown, I can write freely. If you find me, I shall be justified; if not, I shall hardly need to blush, even to myself, over a futile experiment.*

"*It is possible for me to learn enough of your life, henceforth, to direct my relation toward you. This may be the end; if so, I shall know it soon. I shall also know*

whether you continue to seek me. Trusting in your honor as a

man, I must ask you to trust in mine, as a woman."

I did discover my mistake, as the Unknown promised. There had been a secret betrothal between Fisher and Miss Danvers, and, singularly enough, the momentous question and answer had been given in the very ravine leading to my upper dell! The two meant to keep the matter to themselves; but therein, it seems, I thwarted them; there was a little opposition on the part of their respective families, but all was amicably settled before I left Wampsocket.

The letter made a very deep impression upon me. What was the one way to find her? What could it be but the triumph that follows ambitious toil—the manifestation of all my best qualities as a man? Be she old or young, plain or beautiful, I reflected, hers is surely a nature worth knowing, and its candid intelligence conceals no hazards for me. I have sought her rashly, blundered, betrayed that I set her lower, in my thoughts, than her actual self: let me now adopt the opposite course, seek her openly no longer, go back to my tasks, and, following my own aims vigorously and cheerfully, restore that respect which she seemed to be on the point of losing. For, consciously or not, she had communicated to me a doubt, implied in the very expression of her own strength and pride. She had meant to address me as an equal, yet, despite herself, took a stand a little above that which she accorded to me.

I came back to New York earlier than usual, worked steadily at my profession and with increasing success, and began to accept opportunities (which I had previously declined) of making myself personally known to the great, impressible, fickle, tyrannical public. One or two of my speeches in the hall of the Cooper Institute, on various occasions—as you may perhaps remember—gave me a good headway with the party, and were the chief cause of my nomination for the State office which I still hold. (There, on the table, lies a resignation, written to-day, but not yet signed. We'll talk of it afterward.) Several months passed by, and no further letter reached me. I gave up much of my time to society, moved familiarly in more than one province of the kingdom here, and vastly extended my acquaintance, especially among the women; but not one of them betrayed the mysterious something or other—really I can't explain precisely what it was!—which I was looking for. In fact, the more I endeavored quietly to study the sex, the more confused I became.

At last, I was subjected to the usual onslaught from the strong-minded. A small but formidable committee entered my office one morning and demanded a categorical declaration of my principles. What my views on the subject were, I knew very well; they were clear and decided; and yet, I hesitated to declare them! It wasn't a temptation of Saint Anthony—that is, turned the other way—and the belligerent attitude of the dames did not alarm me in the least; but she! What was her position? How could I best please her? It flashed upon my mind, while Mrs. ——— was making her formal speech that I had taken no step for months without a vague, secret reference to her. So I strove to be courteous, friendly, and agreeably noncommittal; begged for further documents, and promised to reply by letter in a few days.

I was hardly surprised to find the well-known hand on the envelope of a letter shortly afterward. I held it for a minute in my palm, with an absurd hope that I might sympathetically feel its character before breaking the seal. Then I read it with a great sense of relief.

"I have never assumed to guide a man, except toward the full

exercise of his powers. It is not opinion in action, but

opinion in a state of idleness or indifference, which repels

me. I am deeply glad that you have gained so much since you

left the country. If, in shaping your course, you have

thought of me, I will frankly say that, to that extent,

you have drawn nearer. Am I mistaken in conjecturing that

you wish to know my relation to the movement concerning

which you were recently interrogated? In this, as in other

instances which may come, I must beg you to consider me only as a spectator. The more my own views may seem likely to

sway your action, the less I shall be inclined to declare

them. If you find this cold or unwomanly, remember that it

is not easy!"

Yes! I felt that I had certainly drawn much nearer to her. And from this time on, her imaginary face and form became other than they were. She was twenty-eight—three years older; a very little above the middle height, but not tall; serene, rather than stately, in her movements; with a calm, almost grave face, relieved by the sweetness of the full, firm lips; and finally eyes of pure, limpid gray, such as we fancy-belonged to the Venus of Milo. I found her thus much more attractive than with the dark eyes and lashes—but she did not make her appearance in the circles which I frequented.

Another year slipped away. As an official personage, my importance increased, but I was careful not to exaggerate it to myself. Many have wondered (perhaps you among the rest) at my success, seeing that I possess no remarkable abilities. If I have any secret, it is simply this—doing faithfully, with all my might, whatever I undertake. Nine-tenths of our politicians become inflated and careless, after the first few years, and are easily forgotten when they once lose place.

I am a little surprised now that I had so much patience with the Unknown. I was too important, at least, to be played with; too mature to be! subjected to a longer test; too earnest, as I had proved, to be doubted, or thrown aside without a further explanation.

Growing tired, at last, of silent waiting, I bethought me of advertising. A carefully written "Personal," in which Ignotus informed Ignota of the necessity of his communicating with her, appeared simultaneously in the "Tribune," "Herald," "World," and "Times." I renewed the advertisement as the time expired without an answer, and I think it was about the end of the third week before one came, through the post, as before.

Ah, yes! I had forgotten. See! my advertisement is pasted on the note, as a heading or motto for the manuscript lines. I don't know why the printed slip should give me a particular feeling of humiliation as I look at it, but such is the fact. What she wrote is all I need read to you:

"I could not, at first, be certain that this was meant for

me. If I were to explain to you why I have not written for

so long a time, I might give you one of the few clews which

I insist on keeping in my own hands. In your public

capacity, you have been (so far as a woman may judge)

upright, independent, wholly manly in your relations with

other men I learn nothing of you that is not honorables

toward women you are kind, chivalrous, no doubt, overflowing

with the usual social refinements, but—Here, again, I

run hard upon the absolute necessity of silence. The way to

me, if you care to traverse it, is so simple, so very simple!

Yet, after what I have written, I can not even wave my

hand in the direction of it, without certain self-contempt.

When I feel free to tell you, we shall draw apart and remain

unknown forever.

"You desire to write? I do not prohibit it. I have

heretofore made no arrangement for hearing from you, in

turn, because I could not discover that any advantage would

accrue from it. But it seems only fair, I confess, and you

dare not think me capricious. So, three days hence, at six

o'clock in the evening, a trusty messenger of mine will call at your door. If you have anything to give her for me, the

act of giving it must be the sign of a compact on your part

that you will allow her to leave immediately, unquestioned

and unfollowed."

You look puzzled, I see: you don't catch the real drift of her words? Well, that's a melancholy encouragement. Neither did I, at the time: it was plain that I had disappointed her in some way, and my intercourse with or manner toward women had something to do with it. In vain I ran over as much of my later social life as I could recall. There had been no special attention, nothing to mislead a susceptible heart; on the other side, certainly no rudeness, no want of "chivalrous" (she used the word!) respect and attention. What, in the name of all the gods, was the matter?

In spite of all my efforts to grow clearer, I was obliged to write my letter in a rather muddled state of mind. I had so much to say! sixteen folio pages, I was sure, would only suffice for an introduction to the case; yet, when the creamy vellum lay before me and the moist pen drew my fingers toward it, I sat stock dumb for half an hour. I wrote, finally, in a half-desperate mood, without regard to coherency or logic. Here's a rough draft of a part of the letter, and a single passage from it will be enough:

I can conceive of no simpler way to you than the knowledge

of your name and address. I have drawn airy images of you,

but they do not become incarnate, and I am not sure that I

should recognize you in the brief moment of passing. Your

nature is not of those which are instantly legible. As an

abstract power, it has wrought in my life and it continually

moves my heart with desires which are unsatisfactory because

so vague and ignorant. Let me offer you, personally, my

gratitude, my earnest friendship: you would laugh if I were now to offer more.

Stay! here is another fragment, more reckless in tone:

"I want to find the woman whom I can love—who can love me.

But this is a masquerade where the features are hidden, the

voice disguised, even the hands grotesquely gloved. Come! I

will venture more than I ever thought was possible to me.

You shall know my deepest nature as I myself seem to know

it. Then, give me the commonest chance of learning yours,

through an intercourse which shall leave both free, should

we not feel the closing of the inevitable bond!"

After I had written that, the pages filled rapidly. When the appointed hour arrived, a bulky epistle, in a strong linen envelope, sealed with five wax seals, was waiting on my table. Precisely at six there was an announcement: the door opened, and a little outside, in the shadow, I saw an old woman, in a threadbare dress of rusty black.

"Come in!" I said.

"The letter!" answered a husky voice. She stretched out a bony hand, without moving a step.

"It is for a lady—very important business," said I, taking up the letter; "are you sure that there is no mistake?"

She drew her hand under the shawl, turned without a word, and moved toward the hall door.

"Stop!" I cried: "I beg a thousand pardons! Take it—take it! You are the right messenger!"

She clutched it, and was instantly gone.

Several days passed, and I gradually became so nervous and uneasy that

I was on the point of inserting another "Personal" in the daily papers, when the answer arrived. It was brief and mysterious; you shall hear the whole of it:

> "I thank you. Your letter is a sacred confidence which I
>
> pray you never to regret. Your nature is sound and good. You
>
> ask no more than is reasonable, and I have no real right to
>
> refuse. In the one respect which I have hinted, I may have
>
> been unskilful or too narrowly cautious: I must have the
>
> certainty of this. Therefore, as a generous favor, give me
>
> six months more! At the end of that time I will write to you
>
> again. Have patience with these brief lines: another word
>
> might be a word too much."

You notice the change in her tone? The letter gave me the strongest impression of a new, warm, almost anxious interest on her part. My fancies, as first at Wampsocket, began to play all sorts of singular pranks: sometimes she was rich and of an old family, sometimes moderately poor and obscure, but always the same calm, reposeful face and clear gray eyes. I ceased looking for her in society, quite sure that I should not find her, and nursed a wild expectation of suddenly meeting her, face to face, in the most unlikely places and under startling circumstances. However, the end of it all was patience—patience for six months.

There's not much more to tell; but this last letter is hard for me to read. It came punctually, to a day. I knew it would, and at the last I began to dread the time, as if a heavy note were falling due, and I had no funds to meet it. My head was in a whirl when I broke the seal. The fact in it stared at me blankly, at once, but it was a long time before the words and sentences became intelligible.

> "The stipulated time has come, and our hidden romance is at
>
> an end. Had I taken this resolution a year ago, it would

have saved me many vain hopes, and you, perhaps, a little
uncertainty. Forgive me, first, if you can, and then hear
the explanation!

"You wished for a personal interview: you have had, not
one, but many. We have met, in society, talked face to
face, discussed the weather, the opera, toilettes, Queechy,
Aurora Floyd, Long Branch, and Newport, and exchanged a
weary amount of fashionable gossip; and you never guessed
that I was governed by any deeper interest! I have purposely
uttered ridiculous platitudes, and you were as smilingly
courteous as if you enjoyed them: I have let fall remarks
whose hollowness and selfishness could not have escaped you,
and have waited in vain for a word of sharp, honest, manly
reproof. Your manner to me was unexceptionable, as it was to
all other women: but there lies the source of my
disappointment, of—yes—of my sorrow!

"You appreciate, I can not doubt, the qualities in woman
which men value in one another—culture, independence of
thought, a high and earnest apprehension of life; but you
know not how to seek them. It is not true that a mature and
unperverted woman is flattered by receiving only the general
obsequiousness which most men give to the whole sex. In the
man who contradicts and strives with her, she discovers a

671

truer interest, a nobler respect. The empty-headed, spindle-

shanked youths who dance admirably, understand something of

billiards, much less of horses, and still less of

navigation, soon grow inexpressibly wearisome to us; but the

men who adopt their social courtesy, never seeking to

arouse, uplift, instruct us, are a bitter disappointment.

"What would have been the end, had you really found me?

Certainly a sincere, satisfying friendship. No mysterious

magnetic force has drawn you to me or held you near me, nor

has my experiment inspired me with an interest which can not

be given up without a personal pang. I am grieved, for the

sake of all men and all women. Yet, understand me! I mean no

slightest reproach. I esteem and honor you for what you

are. Farewell!"

There! Nothing could be kinder in tone, nothing more humiliating in substance, I was sore and offended for a few days; but I soon began to see, and ever more and more clearly, that she was wholly right. I was sure, also, that any further attempt to correspond with her would be vain. It all comes of taking society just as we find it, and supposing that conventional courtesy is the only safe ground on which men and women can meet.

The fact is—there's no use in hiding it from myself (and I see, by your face, that the letter cuts into your own conscience)—she is a free, courageous, independent character, and—I am not. But who was she?

672

About Author

Bayard Taylor (January 11, 1825 – December 19, 1878) was an American poet, literary critic, translator, travel author, and diplomat.

Life and work

Taylor was born on January 11, 1825, in Kennett Square in Chester County, Pennsylvania. He was the fourth son, the first to survive to maturity, of the Quaker couple, Joseph and Rebecca (née Way) Taylor. His father was a wealthy farmer. Bayard received his early instruction in an academy at West Chester, Pennsylvania, and later at nearby Unionville. At the age of seventeen, he was apprenticed to a printer in West Chester. The influential critic and editor Rufus Wilmot Griswold encouraged him to write poetry. The volume that resulted, Ximena, or the Battle of the Sierra Morena, and other Poems, was published in 1844 and dedicated to Griswold.

Using the money from his poetry and an advance for travel articles, he visited parts of England, France, Germany and Italy, making largely pedestrian tours for almost two years. He sent accounts of his travels to the Tribune, The Saturday Evening Post, and Gazette of the United States.

In 1846, a collection of his articles was published in two volumes as Views Afoot, or Europe seen with Knapsack and Staff. That publication resulted in an invitation to serve as an editorial assistant for Graham's Magazine for a few months in 1848. That same year, Horace Greeley, editor of the New York Tribune, hired Taylor and sent him to California to report on the gold rush. He returned by way of Mexico and published another two-volume collection of travel essays, El Dorado; or, Adventures in the Path of Empire (1850). Within two weeks of release, the books sold 10,000 copies in the U.S. and 30,000 in Great Britain.

In 1849 Taylor married Mary Agnew, who died of tuberculosis the next year. That same year, Taylor won a popular competition sponsored by P. T. Barnum to write an ode for the "Swedish Nightingale", singer Jenny Lind. His poem "Greetings to America" was set to music by Julius Benedict and performed by the singer at numerous concerts on her tour of the United States.

In 1851 he traveled to Egypt, where he followed the Nile River as far as 12° 30' N. He also traveled in Palestine and Mediterranean countries, writing poetry based on his experiences. Toward the end of 1852, he sailed from England to Calcutta, and then to China, where he joined the expedition of Commodore Matthew Calbraith Perry to Japan. The results of these journeys were published as A Journey to Central Africa; or, Life and Landscapes from Egypt to the Negro Kingdoms of the White Nile (1854); The Lands of the Saracen; or, Pictures of Palestine, Asia Minor, Sicily and Spain (1854); and A Visit to India, China and Japan in the Year 1853 (1855).

He returned to the U.S. on December 20, 1853, and undertook a successful public lecturer tour that extended from Maine to Wisconsin. After two years, he went to northern Europe to study Swedish life, language and literature. The trip inspired his long narrative poem Lars. His series of articles Swedish Letters to the Tribune were republished as Northern Travel: Summer and Winter Pictures (1857).

In Berlin in 1856, Taylor met the great German scientist Alexander von Humboldt, hoping to interview him for the New York Tribune. Humboldt was welcoming, and inquired whether they should speak English or German. Taylor planned to go to central Asia, where Humboldt had traveled in 1829. Taylor informed Humboldt of Washington Irving's death; Humboldt had met him in Paris. Taylor saw Humboldt again in 1857 at Potsdam.

In October 1857, he married Maria Hansen, the daughter of the Danish/German astronomer Peter Hansen. The couple spent the following winter in Greece. In 1859 Taylor returned to the American West and lectured at San Francisco.

In 1862, he was appointed to the U.S. diplomatic service as secretary of legation at St. Petersburg, and acting minister to Russia for a time during 1862-3 after the resignation of Ambassador Simon Cameron.

He published his first novel Hannah Thurston in 1863. The newspaper

The New York Times first praised him for "break new ground with such assured success". A second much longer appreciation in the same newspaper was thoroughly negative, describing "one pointless, aimless situation leading to another of the same stamp, and so on in maddening succession". It concluded: "The platitudes and puerilities which might otherwise only raise a smile, when confronted with such pompous pretensions, excite the contempt of every man who has in him the feeblest instincts of common honesty in literature." It proved successful enough for his publisher to announce another novel from him the next year.

In 1864 Taylor and his wife Maria returned to the U.S. In 1866, Taylor traveled to Colorado and made a large loop through the northern mountains on horseback with a group that included William Byers, editor of the newspaper Rocky Mountain News. His letters describing this adventure were later compiled and published as Colorado: A Summer Trip.

His late novel, Joseph and His Friend: A Story of Pennsylvania (1870), first serialized in the magazine The Atlantic, was described as a story of young man in rural Pennsylvania and "the troubles which arise from the want of a broader education and higher culture". It is believed to be based on the poets Fitz-Greene Halleck and Joseph Rodman Drake, and since the late 20th-century has been called America's first gay novel. Taylor spoke at the dedication of a monument to Halleck in his native town, Guilford, Connecticut. He said that in establishing this monument to an American poet "we symbolize the intellectual growth of the American people.... The life of the poet who sleeps here represents the long period of transition between the appearance of American poetry and the creation of an appreciative and sympathetic audience for it."

Taylor imitated and parodied the writings of various poets in Diversions of the Echo Club (London, 1873; Boston, 1876).In 1874 Taylor traveled to Iceland to report for the Tribune on the one thousandth anniversary of the first European settlement there.

During March 1878, the U.S. Senate confirmed his appointment as United States Minister to Prussia. Mark Twain, who traveled to Europe on the same ship, was envious of Taylor's command of German.

Taylor's travel writings were widely quoted by congressmen seeking to defend racial discrimination. Richard Townshend quoted passages from Taylor such as "the Chinese are morally, the most debased people on the face of the earth" and "A Chinese city is the greatest of all abominations."

A few months after arriving in Berlin, Taylor died there on December 19, 1878. His body was returned to the U.S. and buried in Kennett Square, Pennsylvania. The New York Times published his obituary on its front page, referring to him as "a great traveler, both on land and paper". Shortly after his death, Henry Wadsworth Longfellow wrote a memorial poem in Taylor's memory, at the urging of Oliver Wendell Holmes, Sr.

Legacy and honors

Cedarcroft, Taylor's home from 1859 to 1874, which he built near Kennett Square, is preserved as a National Historic Landmark.

The Bayard Taylor School was added to the National Register of Historic Places in 1988.

The Bayard Taylor Memorial Library is in Kennett Square.

Evaluations

Though he wanted to be known most as a poet, Taylor was mostly recognized as a travel writer during his lifetime. Modern critics have generally accepted him as technically skilled in verse, but lacking imagination and, ultimately, consider his work as a conventional example of 19th-century sentimentalism.

His translation of Faust, however, was recognized for its scholarly skill and remained in print through 1969. According to the 1920 edition of Encyclopedia Americana:

> It is by his translation of Faust, one of the finest attempts of the kind in any literature, that Taylor is generally known; yet as an original poet he stands well up in the second rank of Americans. His Poems of the Orient and his Pennsylvania ballads comprise his best work. His verse is finished and sonorous, but at times over-rhetorical.

According to the 1911 edition of Encyclopædia Britannica:

Taylor's most ambitious productions in poetry—- his Masque of the Gods (Boston, 1872), Prince Deukalion; a lyrical drama (Boston, 1878), The Picture of St John (Boston, 1866), Lars; a Pastoral of Norway (Boston, 1873), and The Prophet; a tragedy (Boston, 1874)— are marred by a ceaseless effort to overstrain his power. But he will be remembered by his poetic and excellent translation of Goethe's Faust (2 vols, Boston, 1870-71) in the original metres.

Taylor felt, in all truth, the torment and the ecstasy of verse; but, as a critical friend has written of him, his nature was so ardent, so full-blooded, that slight and common sensations intoxicated him, and he estimated their effect, and his power to transmit it to others, beyond the true value. He had, from the earliest period at which he began to compose, a distinct lyrical faculty: so keen indeed was his ear that he became too insistently haunted by the music of others, pre-eminently of Tennyson. But he had often a true and fine note of his own. His best short poems are The Metempsychosis of the Pine and the well-known Bedouin love-song.

In his critical essays Bayard Taylor had himself in no inconsiderable degree what he wrote of as that pure poetic insight which is the vital spirit of criticism. The most valuable of these prose dissertations are the Studies in German Literature (New York, 1879).

In Appletons' Cyclopædia of American Biography of 1889, Edmund Clarence Stedman gives the following critique:

His poetry is striking for qualities that appeal to the ear and eye, finished, sonorous in diction and rhythm, at times too rhetorical, but rich in sound, color, and metrical effects. His early models were Byron and Shelley, and his more ambitious lyrics and dramas exhibit the latter's peculiar, often vague, spirituality. Lars, somewhat after the manner of Tennyson, is his longest and most attractive narrative poem. Prince Deukalion was designed for a masterpiece; its blank verse and choric interludes are noble in spirit and mould. Some of Taylor's songs, oriental idyls, and the true and tender Pennsylvanian ballads, have passed into lasting favor, and show the native quality of his poetic gift. His fame rests securely upon his unequalled rendering of Faust in the original metres, of which the first and second parts appeared in 1870 and 1871. His commentary upon Part II for the first time interpreted the motive and allegory of that unique structure. (source: wikipedia)

NOTABLE WORKS

Ximena, or the Battle of the Sierra Morena, and other Poems (1844)

Views Afoot, or Europe seen with Knapsack and Staff (1846)

Rhymes of Travel: Ballads and Poems (1849)

El Dorado; or, Adventures in the Path of Empire (1850)

Romances, Lyrics, and Songs (1852)

Journey to Central Africa; or, Life and Landscapes from Egypt to the Negro Kingdoms of the White Nile, A (1854)

Lands of the Saracen; or, Pictures of Palestine, Asia Minor, Sicily and Spain, The (1854)

A visit to India, China, and Japan in the year 1853 (1855)

Lands of the Saracen; or, Pictures of Palestine, Asia Minor, Sicily and Spain, The (1855)

Poems of the Orient (Boston: Ticknor and Fields, 1855)

Poems of Home and Travel (1856)

Cyclopedia of Modern Travel (1856)

Northern Travel: Summer and Winter Pictures (1857)

View A-Foot, or Europe Seen with Knapsack and Staff (1859)

Life, Travels And Books Of Alexander Von Humboldt, The (1859)

At Home and Abroad, First Series: A Sketch-book of Life, Scenery, and Men (1859)

Cyclopaedia of Modern Travel Vol I (1861)

Prose Writings: India, China, and Japan (1862)

Travels in Greece and Russia, with an Excursion to Crete (1859)

Poet's Journal (1863)

Hanna Thurston (1863)

John Godfrey's Fortunes Related by Himself: A story of American Life (1864)

"Cruise On Lake Ladoga, A" (1864)

"The Poems of Bayard Taylor" (1865)

John Godrey's Fortunes Related By Himself - A story of American Life (1865)

The Story of Kennett (1866)

Visit To The Balearic Islands, Complete in Two Parts, A (1867)

Picture of St. John, The (1867)

Colorado: A Summer Trip (1867)

"Little Land Of Appenzell, The" (1867)

"Island of Maddalena with a Distant View of Caprera, The" (1868)

"Land Of Paoli, The" (1868)

"Catalonian Bridle-Roads" (1868)

"Kyffhauser And Its Legend, The" (1868)

By-Ways Of Europe (1869)

Joseph and His Friend: A Story of Pennsylvania (1870)

Ballad of Abraham Lincoln, The (1870)

"Sights In And Around Yedo" (1871)

Northern Travel (1871)

Japan in Our Day (1872)

Masque of the Gods, The (1872)

"Heart Of Arabia, The" (1872)

Travels in South Africa (1872)

At Home and Abroad: A Sketch-Book of Life, Scenery and Men (1872)

Diversions of the Echo Club (1873)

Lars: A Pastoral of Norway (1873)

Wonders of the Yellowstone - The Illustrated Library of Travel, Exploration and Adventure (with James Richardson) (1873)

Northern Travel: Summer and Winter Pictures - Sweden, Denmark and Lapland (1873).

Lake Regions of Central Africa (1873)

Prophet: A Tragedy, The. (1874)

Home Pastorals Ballads & Lyrics (1875)

Egypt And Iceland In The Year 1874 (1875)

Boys of Other Countries: Stories for American Boys (1876)

Echo Club and Other Literary Diversions (1876)

Picturesque Europe Part Thirty-Six (1877)

National Ode: The Memorial Freedom Poem, The (1877)

Bismarck: His Authentic Biography (1877)

"Assyrian Night-Song" (August 1877)

Prince Deukalion (1878)

Picturesque Europe (1878)

Studies in German Literature (1879)

Faust: A Tragedy translated in the Original Metres (1890)

Travels in Arabia (1892).

A school history of Germany (1882).

EDITIONS

Collected editions of his Poetical Works and his Dramatic Works were published at Boston in 1888; his Life and Letters (Boston, 2 vols., 1884) were edited by his wife and Horace Scudder.

Marie Hansen Taylor translated into German Bayard's Greece (Leipzig, 1858), Hannah Thurston (Hamburg, 1863), Story of Kennett (Gotha, 1868), Tales of Home (Berlin, 1879), Studies in German Literature (Leipzig, 1880), and notes to Faust, both parts (Leipzig, 1881). After her husband's death, she edited, with notes, his Dramatic Works (1880), and in the same year his Poems in a "Household Edition", and brought together his Critical Essays and Literary Notes. In 1885 she prepared a school edition of Lars, with notes and a sketch of its author's life.